JUL   2002

SOCIAL AND PSYCHOLOGICAL ASPECTS OF DISABILITY

SOCIAL AND PSYCHOLOGICAL ASPECTS OF DISABILITY

A Handbook for Practitioners

Edited by

Joseph Stubbins, Ph.D.

Professor of Rehabilitation Counseling
California State University, Los Angeles

University Park Press
Baltimore · London · Tokyo

UNIVERSITY PARK PRESS
International Publishers in Science, Medicine, and Education
233 East Redwood Street
Baltimore, Maryland 21202

Copyright © 1977 by University Park Press
Typeset by The Composing Room of Michigan, Inc.

Manufactured in the United States of America by Universal Lithographers,
Inc., and The Maple Press Company.

Second printing, December 1978

Library of Congress Cataloging in Publication Data
Main entry under title:

Social and psychological aspects of disability.

1. Handicapped—Addresses, essays, lectures.
2. Rehabilitation—Addresses, essays, lectures.
I. Stubbins, Joseph. [DNLM: 1. Handicapped—Collected
works. 2. Rehabilitation—Collected works. HD7255
s678]
HV3000.S7   362.4   77-4136
ISBN 0-8391-1119-3

Contents

Part III
PSYCHOLOGICAL ASPECTS OF DISABILITY

Part IV
NORMALIZATION OF DISABLED PERSONS

Preface

Physicians, nurses, psychologists, social workers, counselors, physical therapists, occupational therapists, speech therapists—each understands disability from the point of view of his or her professional training. It is, therefore, easy to overlook the fact that there is a common core of knowledge that all rehabilitation professionals can be expected to master. This book identifies the common core concerned with the social and psychological aspects of disability.

While the fine division of labor in the helping professions has produced better trained specialists, it has tended to lessen the communication among them. Each specialty has its own professional association and journals and shares a trend for friendships to form within rather than across specialties. Hence good ideas originating in one setting or in one profession take a long time to permeate among all who should know them. The Social and Rehabilitation Service of the Department of Health, Education, and Welfare has shown its concern for the dissemination of rehabilitation ideas by funding conferences on research and demonstration projects dealing with the communication of findings.

The fractionation based on disciplines and professions extends to categories of disability. The blind, the deaf, the spinal cord injured, and dozens of other categories of disability have independent organizations to advance their interests and to promote public education and legislative and community support. There is relatively little that takes place in the public arena on behalf of *the disabled-in-general,* such as the campaign against architectural barriers.

Still other barriers to knowledge dissemination are the status differences within an organization. These serve useful functions in ensuring that everyone in a given facility does what he or she is competent to do and inhibits meddling in the tasks of others. But status differences can be counter-productive when personnel are kept in ignorance to ensure task orientation. Everyone working in rehabilitation facilities should understand the problems of disabled persons to the limit of their abilities.

The common core in social and psychological aspects of disability presented here is intended to bridge the communication gap among professionals, among types of disabilities, and among professionals of different status levels. This book speaks especially to first-line professionals, the ones with daily contacts with disabled persons. These professionals have little time to scour the many journals in which useful generic knowledge is buried.

This book is limited to articles with clear implications for practice with disabled persons. Since there is already a voluminous literature on counseling, articles of this type were avoided unless they contained information peculiar to disabled persons. Articles with implications for at least a broad band of disabilities were favored. Rehabilitation reports of primarily methodological and theoretical interest were by-passed. In summary, outstanding articles were chosen that were broadly related to disability, that were written in nontechnical language, and that dealt with empirical issues of interest to first-line professionals. Many years of working closely with psychosocial workers in the field of rehabilitation gave this editor a sense of what was readable and useful to them.

The articles selected provide an over-view of the current thinking on the sociology and psychology of disability. The selection was guided by pragmatic and eclectic aims. These aims are evident in the range of types of articles: clinical, empirical, philosophic, theoretical, and experimental. Each article had to meet the criteria of having useful ideas for professional workers and expressing them clearly and without the necessity of decoding complex research methods.

The book is organized around four themes. Part I, *The Lived World of Disabled Persons*, contrasts the viewpoints and concerns of disabled persons and the professionals who serve them. Part II, *Sociological Aspects of Disability*, deals with problems of disability generated at the social level. Part III, *Psychological Aspects of Disability*, deals with a wide range of problems that can be conceptualized and dealt with on an individual basis. Part IV takes up the problem of mainstreaming disabled persons and treating them the same as nondisabled persons except as specifically dictated by their dysfunctions, hence the title, *Normalization of Disabled Persons*.

Each of the four parts leads off with an essay. Here, the rationale for the arrangement of the articles and this editor's views on critical professional issues in disability are given. The professionally trained reader would find it convenient to follow the sequence of the book. However, those unfamiliar with psychology and sociology or those in the pre-service phase of their careers would find it more useful to read the articles first and then to return to the introductory essays. The latter presume some knowledge of disability which the beginning professional can acquire by going to the articles directly.

I am indebted to the many authors and publishers who consented to the inclusion of their articles in this book. Individual acknowledgments are made in the text. The arduous task of locating the hundreds of publications from which a final selection was made and of assisting in their evaluation was the work of June Houle. Her dedication and professional judgment are inseparable aspects of the final product.

SOCIAL AND PSYCHOLOGICAL ASPECTS OF DISABILITY

Part I

THE LIVED WORLD
OF DISABLED PERSONS

Editorial
Introduction

Joseph Stubbins

I cannot conceive of myself as nothing but a bit of the world, a mere object of biological, psychological or sociological investigation. I cannot shut myself up within the realm of science. All my knowledge of the world, even my scientific knowledge, is gained from my own particular point of view, or from some experience of the world without which the symbols of science would be meaningless. The whole universe of science is built upon the world as directly experienced, and if we want to subject science itself to rigorous scrutiny and arrive at a precise assessment of its meaning and scope, we must begin by reawakening the basic experience of the world of which science is the second order expression.[1]

Maurice Merleau-Ponty, Phenomenology of Perception

The articles of Part I were selected to bring into focus the different perspectives of professional helper and patient. The essential difference is that *they are not in the same world* and their needs and interests are quite different. This conclusion is, on the one hand, amazingly simple and self-evident; and on the other, it has required a long, painful evolution of the social sciences to uncover it. We can say that the subject of this essay is the significance of this "discovery."

DISABILITY AND THE SOCIAL SCIENCES

Professionals understand disability from the point of view of natural science, and many of them would wonder about the relevance of the series of autobiographical accounts presented in this part of the book. It is indicative of the enormous influence of natural science that the relevance of autobiography and accounts of personal experiences with disability need to be justified. Natural science became a pervasive influence that literally transformed the nature of reality.

Enormous advances in the physical and biological sciences during the 19th and 20th centuries transformed the western world. Physics, chemistry, and biology ushered in great benefits for mankind. The methods of natural science brought progress in conquering infectious disease, generating low-cost energies in quantities undreamed of until recently, and generally brought about the progress that everyone welcomed. Of course, there were still unsolved problems on the agenda, like poverty, urban sprawl, the despoliation of the natural environment, and the social alienation of disabled persons. But these had to await their turn for scientific solutions. Mental patients piled up in our state hospitals while

---

[1] Quoted with permission of Humanities Press.

scientists sought the biological basis of schizophrenia. Since a "solution" was probably just around the corner, why worry about the inhuman conditions of the emotionally disturbed in hospitals. Soon, perhaps a vaccine would be discovered that would wipe out mental illness just as small pox and poliomyelitis were! So secure was everyone in this belief that it took some crusading social psychologists and psychiatrists to tell us that in the meantime the state mental hospitals had become snake pits. How was it that we did not see the obvious? Natural science had become a fundamentalist religion with its own definitions of reality, its own blind spots and myths. When something was wrong, it called for more research, a stricter objectivity, and a more determined collection of the building blocks of knowledge. "Science" informed us that the phantom limb, depression following trauma, and the hostility of the physically handicapped were psychopathologies that could be treated like any other disease. An individually oriented psychology blithely ignored the social context of behavior and the existential experiences of patients.

From the perspective of the present, we can begin to appreciate the errors of those who studied human behavior and society by natural science methods, namely the errors of social scientists. The relation between the researcher and natural objects is quite different from that between the social scientist and his human subjects. The objects of natural science cannot adopt an attitude toward the researchers subjecting them to certain interventions, whereas human subjects can and do. The uniformities or laws sought are also different. The benefits of the Salk vaccine are not influenced by the social and psychological characteristics of subjects. A given *regularity*, or *law*, in natural science has a certain invariance independent of human concerns. On the other hand, the discoveries of social scientists are not laws in this sense at all, but rather interpretations of existing human relations which, in turn, were man-made. There can be an incongruence between the interests of social scientists and subjects, an issue which is less relevant in the field of natural science. It does not make sense to speak of the interests of oxygen and hydrogen and water; but when human subjects are studied, the methods of research and outcomes frequently are of great concern to them.

Social scientists have not been particularly conscious of the incongruence in interests between subject and investigator. For instance, disability is still viewed primarily by professionals as an individual problem to be overcome by the just-right attitude and motivation of the disabled person himself. However, disabled persons usually view their condition in terms of prejudice. Thus, what an amputee said almost 30 years ago is still true, "You can't write an article about it. It can be said in one sentence—There is no acceptance" (Ladieu, Adler, and Dembo, 1948). So, to this disabled person, disability is a social problem, and much less a matter of rearranging his inner psyche. Social scientists and the practitioners in this field have hardly begun to study the issue of why some problems are researched endlessly, others a little, and still others not at all. I intend to touch on this problem below.

The disarray in the social sciences is a fundamental questioning rather than a passing factionalism. It seemed appropriate, therefore, to begin Part I, not with an autobiographical article that might be dismissed as the voice of a disgruntled patient but with one that poses questions about the usefulness of scientific psychological knowledge in rehabilitation. That article raises to a proper level of importance the different perspectives held by patient or client and researcher or practitioner. In "The Utilization of Psychological Knowledge," Tamara Dembo, the distinguished rehabilitation psychologist, pleads with us to study the different ground on which patient and professional stand. Certainly, she would not abandon scientific psychology; she would put it in its proper place.

SCIENTIFIC AND EXPERIENTIAL PERSPECTIVES

Rehabilitation practitioners have had to contend with the mind-boggling influence of the natural sciences that fed information to the psycho-social workers in this field. They may have dutifully read the journals in their fields, grappled with statistics, and pondered the findings of research reports. But somehow, little of all this added to their capacity to influence the present status of the disabled person. For fear of being considered ignorant, they rarely voiced this disappointment with what they were taught and with what they read at present. They were caught up in a status system that not only placed the practicing psycho-social worker far below the researcher but robbed him or her of intellectual integrity.

The spirit of science directed the investigator to focus on observable behavior rather than experience. While this was admirably suited to the requirements of studying natural phenomena, it was only one perspective on the world and led to certain knowledge and away from others. Thus, it was common for rehabilitation researchers to write monographs on stroke, paraplegia, blindness, and so on without a single insight based on an interpersonal encounter with a patient. They were only interested in their "behavior" and only in certain types of behavior, e.g., whether the patient cooperated with the physical therapist, how he performed on physical and psychological tests, and other performances that could be *measured*.

The professional tended to view the disabled person as a reactive agent. The fundamental procedure of psychological testing and of therapeutic interventions usually operated on such an assumption. Technical methods of helping were rooted in mechanistic views of human behavior. However, the over-arching concerns of the disabled person regarding his reduced life space and his depreciation, in brief, the intentional and purposive aspects of behavior, were marginally attended to. But even the scientific professional proceeded with *his* own intentions. It so happened that acquiring professional respectability and the good opinion of his superiors coincided with *his* deeper personal needs.

If the researchers' and practitioners' approach to the disabled may be tainted by their personal needs, are we justified in describing it as "objective"? Looked at more closely, "objective" is a particular approach or perspective that presumes to generate dependable knowledge. Yet, always, this particular perspective—the diagnostic, the professional, the scientific—is grounded on a human subjective *value* that makes some sense of the researchers' or practitioners' activities. Thus, the state-federal programs of vocational rehabilitation assume that it is an appropriate use of public funds to ready a disabled person for employment but not otherwise. If the "objective" findings that result from the preliminary evaluation of the candidate for rehabilitation are to make sense, they must be viewed in the light of the legal mandate of the vocational rehabilitation agency. However, the objectivity with which this inquiry into the disabled person's assets proceeds does not require the counselor to evaluate the justness of making *employability* a worthy criterion. We wish to direct our readers' attention to examine the objective and scientific findings as viewed by the writers of Part I, who themselves were disabled, and to note the differences between their concerns and those who authored the articles of Part II and Part III.

The psychological, sociological, legal, and economic perspectives are each circumscribed. Each of these perspectives tells us both more and less than the experiential. More, because the disabled person necessarily has the limited horizon of the sufferer and lacks the detachment and knowledge that may contribute to the evaluation of rehabilitation techniques. Less, because the "objectivity" of each of the disciplines we mentioned arises from detachment rather than involvement, from not being-in-the-situation, and from the biases inherent in a specific scientific approach. Paradoxically, the foregoing limitations hardly signify objectivity, because not any one of these perspectives is able to reconstitute the lived experience of any disabled person. The common sense notion of objectivity is the biased and reductionistic view dictated by the current status of a particular discipline. Thus, to view the patient as an *object* is to disregard the most distinguishing features of the human being: his consciousness and his intentionality. The objectivity of the professional, therefore, already alienates the patient, for one's relations to objects are quite different from one's relations to colleagues, friends, or even one's enemies. The objective stance robs the professional of much understanding that lies beyond the convenience of the concepts and conclusions potentially available within a professional discipline; that is, it robs the professional of his common sense and his creative prospects of original ways of conceptualizing the patient's problems.

PRIORITIES OF DISABLED PERSONS AND THEIR HELPERS

What is significant, bears examination, and is tangential is very much a function of the professional's home base, whether it be that of physician, psychologist, social worker, or physical therapist. By virtue of professional training, each is concerned with a particular segment of human welfare and each reaches for certain target behaviors. During the crisis and early phases of disability, there is a congruence of interests between disabled and helpers in the common defense against life-threatening dangers. Also, in helping the disabled person make the best of physical limitations, patient and helper can usually see eye to eye. But as the disabled person and professional helper move toward the realities of the social and occupational world, the more their perspectives digress. Often disabled persons go through a long period of frustration that amounts to reconquering childhood problems all over again and anger at the way they are regarded by non-disabled persons. Fundamentally, they know that a critical aspect of successful adjustment to disability is coming to terms with being a pariah in the larger community. On this subject, there is little honest dialogue between professionals and patients. There is no evidence that professional helpers are any less biased in their personal lives than others in the community. There is rarely anyone around to help disabled persons frame the problem of their devaluation as a social one. Personal depreciation resulting from disability belongs, so to speak, in a no-man's land located between the disciplines and professions of the rehabilitation team.

Autobiographical accounts of disabled persons provide an overview of the priorities of concern. Architectural barriers and access to public transportation are mentioned much more frequently by the disabled than by professionals. The disabled are painfully aware of being declassed, of being patronized, of losing their friends, of the difficulties of making new friends, of being considered helpless and stupid, of being stereotyped, and of the boredom of institutional life. One author wrote of the disabled as having to become accustomed to "a lifestyle of fear, frustration, failure, and even despair" (Race, 1972). How does this compare with the concerns of practitioners and researchers?

Practitioners and researchers have their priorities, too. Rehabilitation counselors are expected to attain a certain quota of "successful" rehabilitations. In the state-federal programs, this would mean that the client has remained in a job for several months or was placed in a rehabilitation workshop. Since there are generally many more clients than can be given adequate services, it would be natural for counselors to sift through the pool and select those who are good prospects for successful closure, ignoring other reasons for priorities, for example, the severity of disability. So rampant was this practice that it required an amendment of the Vocational Rehabilitation Act and new federal directives to counteract it. At this point, it is almost redundant to state that, to the rehabilitation counselor, the disabled person is not only a suffering person as described in the preceding paragraphs but also an important statistic vital to maintaining his job and being able to do so with a reasonable amount of effort.

Similarly, in sociological and psychological research, investigators are, to a degree, captives of their discipline. It tells them what to study and how to study it. But we shall take up this critique in Parts II and III, which deal with sociological and psychological aspects of disability. But too often the topics researched are far from the realities of disabilities as actually experienced.

To take on the frame of reference of the suffering patient must be threatening to the professional; there must be a protective shield to enable the practitioner to go about his business in a reasonably efficient way. A psychologist who went through a five-day period of being admitted and treated as a "patient" in a comprehensive rehabilitation center discovered that the experience of simulating a patient was considerably more emotionally arousing than he had anticipated (French, McDowell, and Keith, 1972). Even for an experienced psychologist, this uncomplicated sojourn into the life of disability and its social feedback was a most revealing lesson. We might discover that the wall between patient and professional had better be permeable; in this way, some congruence of interest and goals is more likely to be discovered.

EXPERIENTIAL VIEW OF DISABILITY

When the articles of Part I are scanned for a common denominator, we find the writers telling us of suffering, of the search for hope, of wanting to participate in more open ways with professional personnel, and of having a sense of estrangement from those who had been friends. The disabled seem to be telling us that a substantial part of their problems are the nondisabled's lack of understanding, evasions, and rejection. Now, such problems have been researched as we shall note when we get to the part of the book on the social aspects of disability. Obviously, the implications of studying the *attitudes of citizens* toward the mentally ill, alcoholics, and physically disabled are quite different from studying the performance of a stroke patient on the Bender Gestalt, the Rorschach, or asking him to draw a picture of a house and a tree. The stroke patient being put through these psychological hurdles is apt to feel even more frustrated when these are over because he would view the psychologist as Nero fiddling while Rome burned. I think we have made the point that the patient's priorities are often different from those of the personnel. The patient is not as out of it as he seems; just a short while ago he was a respected citizen; now, he is treated as a child.

A theme that runs through autobiographical accounts of the transition from wholeness to disability is the acquisition of an inferior status. In the introductions to Part II and Part III, we shall return to this subject and attempt some hypotheses concerning why sociology and psychology have largely escaped this important concern of disabled persons. At this point, we are suggesting that few psycho-social workers view as their own the agenda of priorities of disabled persons. I have not heard disabled persons call for more researchers, psychologists, and social workers; but they *are* participating more in legal and political processes as remedies.

Most psycho-social workers condemn the "medical model" for inhibiting an adult participation of patients in their own rehabilitation. Yet, for professionals, it is less crucial an issue than for disabled persons. The lessons of the experiential viewpoint, however, are not limited to a better understanding of the disabled. Every paid helper can also learn about himself or herself by an in-depth analysis of what is self-serving for himself and his professional group. Such an analysis might reveal that disabled persons have to contend with the same contradictions as the poor and the powerless everywhere: what they are experiencing and what they are led to believe they are experiencing just do not jibe.

Patients' versions of their hospital and rehabilitation experience account for a minute fraction of the published literature on disability. One might say that disabled persons have generally a poor and meagre press. They are victims of a social science elitism that makes the dullest academic exercise on disability more publishable than an account of the pressing needs of handicapped persons.

The authors of the autobiographies of Part I have voiced many insights. They help to remind professionals that rehabilitation is a distinctively human enterprise to which scientific approaches must be subordinated. I hope that I have not created the impression that the interests of disabled persons and the interests of professionals are irreconcilable. On the contrary, they could have a symbiotic relation. Disabled persons may reflect that we are all victims to one degree or another of ideologies, paymasters, and social systems; and professional rehabilitation workers are far from free agents.

As we shall note in Part II, the professional worker carries out a distinct role whose prerogatives and responsibilities differ from those of a disabled person in treatment. On the one hand, these role differences help to generate the complaints of this essay: the objectification of the patient, the inattention to his priorities, and so on. But, on the other hand, they are essential to the long-term development of rehabilitation services. The fact that the professional helper can see beyond the immediate demands of the disabled person and separate himself or herself with emotional distance is an important aspect of the helping role. Of course, the rehabilitation worker must be a good listener; but this listening is largely subordinated to the service of getting the disabled person to do what he or she must to live happily and productively in spite of physical limitations. The primary experience of the suffering patient is not necessarily a proper guide to beneficial action; he might be depressed, have lost hope and a sense of direction. Disabled persons are subject to all the self-defeating behavior that the non-disabled are prone to. They may be unrealistic, alienate the ones whose love they want, and opt for a life of dependency and exploitation. However, pointing up the existential discontinuity between patient and helper can bring a fresh point of view to bear on the problem of the disabled. In Part I, we are concerned with what the professional can discover by listening to the disabled person directly, not as an investigator, psychologist, or other professional, but as a fellow human being. As Part I is but one of the major sections of this book, it should be clear that we do *not* subscribe to psychological *Populism* or the simplistic notion that understanding and helping the disabled person are nothing more than empathetic listening and that patient and professional come together with equal resources. There *are* significant functions for professional psychology and sociology, subjects which will be taken up in the remaining parts.

It was my purpose in this essay and the remaining articles to de-mystify sociology's and psychology's contribution to the understanding of disability. In doing so, I have tried to avoid establishing another mystique, that of the phenomenological method. It was not my intention to raise the personal perspective of the disabled person to a new religion to challenge existing ones in rehabilitation. But, it could serve as a gyroscope for researchers and helpers to keep them on a humanistic course.

REFERENCES

French, D. J., McDowell, R. E., and Keith, R. A. 1972. Participant observation as a patient in a rehabilitation hospital. Rehab. Psych. 19(2):89–95.

Ladieu, G., Adler, D. L., and Dembo, T. 1948. Studies in adjustment to visible injuries: social acceptance of the injured. J. Soc. Issues 4(4):55–61.

Merleau-Ponty, M. 1962. Phenomenology of Perception. Translated by Colin Smith. Humanities Press, New York.

Race, W. 1972. The disabled speak. Intern. Rehab. Rev. 23(2):6–9.

Section 1

UNDERSTANDING DISABILITY VERSUS BEING DISABLED

1 The Utilization of Psychological Knowledge in Rehabilitation

Tamara Dembo

Handicapped people, representatives of different professions, and laymen all believe that psychological problems are involved in rehabilitation. Expectations are widespread that psychology offers solutions to such problems. Yet, in actuality, scientific psychological knowledge is rarely usable in rehabilitation. The failure to apply such knowledge is frequently ascribed to the difficulty of putting theoretical knowledge into practice, to matching concepts to concrete contents and specific cases. The major issue of this article is that the difficulty lies not in "translation" but elsewhere.

THE ACTUALITY

Before we can use research findings in everyday life, we will have to do more than direct ourselves to methods of applying abstract knowledge to concrete situations—we will also have to place considerable effort into acquiring relevant knowledge. Though such knowledge is available in psychology to some extent, psychologists disregard whole aspects of concern relevant to everyday life and frequently reject them on the grounds that they are "not scientific," that is, they cannot be studied objectively.

In raising the question of the relevance of our scientific knowledge to life problems, we must first consider whether the word *problem* means the same in science as in everyday life. Actually it does not. In science *problem* means a content worthy of investigation; in everyday life *problem* means trouble needing alleviation. Both kinds of problems are worthy of concern but on very different grounds: the scientific *problem* on the grounds of theoretical importance, the life *problem* as entailing human suffering to be overcome. The scientific problem evolved from theoretical considerations might be of little pertinence to the everyday problems of people, and vice versa. But *problem* is not the only term with different meanings in scientific psychology and life. Even *to be concerned* has different meanings. The scientist concerns himself with a scientifically interesting or valuable problem; in life to be concerned means being worried about and trying to overcome a problem. Also, solving a problem means something

This article is adapted from the author's Division 22 Presidential Address at the American Psychological Association Convention, held in Washington, D.C., in September 1969.

Reprinted from Welfare in Review, 1970, 8(4):1–7.

different in both cases: in the first—placing within a theoretical framework, in the second—finding a remedy.

I strongly believe that to arrive at knowledge relevant to life, instead of selecting scientific topics for their theoretical importance, we must deal theoretically with problems of concern to people in everyday life. If life problems do not fit existing psychological theories—too bad for the existing theories—a new theory will have to be developed. At the very inception of research, in selecting a problem, the merger needed between the scientific quest and life problems has to take place. The use of scientific knowledge requires the introduction of life problems at the very start of psychological investigations.

The necessary connection of scientific work with life is not fulfilled by an appropriate initial choice of a problem—it requires a permanent liaison between the scientific endeavor and life, an interrelating of the two throughout the investigation. It is necessary to consider how the investigation should be approached, which data should be taken into account, how they should be analyzed, how to arrive at novel conceptualizations, and what kind of principles and conclusions should be drawn.

To have a psychology permitting application, a psychology able to alleviate everyday problems, basic scientific beliefs, assumptions, and evaluations will have to be reconsidered. Only then will psychology become more useful.

Among the most severe changes needed is that of introducing two viewpoints instead of one concerning investigation. Traditionally, psychology investigates matters from the standpoint of the investigator, deals with what he considers important and what he selects. Rehabilitation psychologists need to add to the investigator's view the view of the subject, that is, the client or sufferer. Traditional psychologists do not deny that the subject-sufferer's view may be different from their own, but they do not think that in selecting and dealing with the problem of investigation the sufferer's view is important and should be taken into account. Those psychologists who believe that *theory* is their only guide in selecting and dealing with problems and that *behavioral observations* are the only method of acquiring valid data expect the subject to "be seen but not heard." They believe that the governance of the investigation is the matter of the investigator alone and should be left to him. The person whose problem is investigated should not take part in the investigation—he is just a subject, not a coworker.

However, in everyday life a very appropriate question is asked: Whose problem should be alleviated, the investigator's or the sufferer's? Who really knows how it hurts, when it hurts more, or when it starts to hurt less? Of course, it could be argued that theories are the realm of the learned man. But to know how it feels, a man does not have to be learned. In its vivid fullness, directly and in an unadulterated way, hurting is accessible to observation as an experience only to the sufferer. His view of what brings up suffering and lessens it is important, and his view might be different from that of the best outside observer.

In suggesting that the choice of a problem for investigation should be based on its importance in everyday life and not on its pertinence to preconceived theoretical development, I am not only suggesting that the unilateral reign of the goddess of science, Theory, be terminated but also that the investigator be asked to give up his position as the only determiner of scientific procedures. This will not be easy for some. But where the alleviation of suffering is intended, differences in the views of the investigator and the sufferer have to be studied. The investigator and the sufferer together have to perform these tasks: determine the problem for investigation; investigate it; judge whether attempts at alleviation have been successful; and, most important, insure that the sufferer's view has been taken into account by the investigator in his choice of methods and procedures. The need for this basic change will become clearer as we go further.

THE DIFFERENCES IN VIEWS

Of course, it is not enough to point out that the views and judgments of the investigator and the sufferer differ. The differences must be specified. This I will attempt to do.

First of all, the sufferer and the observer differ in the way they are *connected* with the problem: one is afflicted with the problem, the other perceives the problem as that of another person, that is, from the outside. In other words, the sufferer is in direct contact with the problem, wrapped up in it. It is what he experiences; it is *his* problem. The investigator-observer, however, perceives the problem from a distance, that is, he can reach it only indirectly through another person's reaction to the problem. The direct connection of the sufferer with the problem means that his psychological makeup, or personality, and his situation will influence his perception of the problem and his way of dealing with it. In the case of the observer, in addition to determinants expressed in the reaction of the sufferer, his personal views and his situation will determine his view of, his dealing with, and his judgments concerning the sufferer's matters. Expressed conceptually, the observer is the outsider to the person observed and to his suffering. The sufferer, enwrapped in his problem, is the insider. This description is in quasi-spatial psychological terms; it defines the psychological *position* of the sufferer and observer in regard to suffering.

The position of the insider and the outsider is of importance not only in rehabilitation psychology but also in psychology as a whole. Generally, in the social-relations space, the particular position of the carrier of a problem, or of the observer of the carrier, is an essential determinant of their views. It is to be taken into account in a great number of interpersonal relations such as those of the observer and the observed, the investigator and the investigated (whether investigated scientifically or otherwise), the interrogator and the interrogated, the examiner and the examined (for example, when a student is examined by a teacher or a patient by a physician).

It is the difference in the distance from a problem that produces *discrepancies* in viewing the problem. As a concrete example, take the attitudes of the insider and the outsider as to the urgency of relieving pain. The sufferer wants to be helped and helped *now*. He is hardly interested in the profits that may accrue to the next generation, if a choice between helping him or helping humanity has to be made. The investigator thinks of benefiting humanity. The sacrifice of "only one person" is made easier through his distance from the person's suffering. Also, the views of "facts" are different: the sufferer will see the slightest change as an indication of progress, the professional person will see it within the entire process of rehabilitation as a minor change.

TWO PSYCHOLOGIES

Neither the sufferer nor the observer is correct or right in his opinions, recommendations, and observations. Only by introducing superordinate principles stemming from a set of values (those of a particular person or a professional code) can we judge who is right or wrong. When such principles are lacking, we can only say this: whether you believe you are correct in your statements depends on your position and, therefore, which viewpoint presents itself to you.

In taking seriously the viewpoint not only of the observer but also of the sufferer, one comes to the radical conclusion that there are two psychologies: namely, the psychology of the observer and the psychology of the sufferer. Faced by the two, we have to take a stand whether to deal with one or with both. This demand leads to another question: Under what conditions in everyday life or in science will we, and perhaps should we, lean in our views, decisions, and conclusions—toward the psychology of the observer or that of the sufferer, or can we (and how can we) take both into account?

Arguments for the special importance of one or the other viewpoint are many. The sufferer can argue his case thus: he is the person who needs help and he cannot wait until remote, theoretical problems are solved; being closest to the problem—he knows it best; and he has to judge what is helpful to him. The researcher could argue for his viewpoint this way: the observer is objective, not emotional, and, therefore, closer to the truth of the matter; he is concerned with stating facts and checks the certainty of his statements; as a trained person he has more knowledge; he knows more cases and their outcome; and it is he who can help when the sufferer does not know how to help himself. These are only a few of the general reasons; there are many more that might prompt us to take sides. Both viewpoints should at least be considered where the application of research is in question.

Some scientists argue that the sufferer does not need to participate in scientific investigations because the observer is able to "look with the eyes" of the sufferer. The importance of trying to see with the eyes of the other cannot be stressed enough: in trying to do so we frequently come closer to the view of the sufferer. However, a sharp distinction has to be made between the views of a person rising from his own position and the view he takes when attempting to see with the eyes of another. In trying to take the standpoint of the other, he cannot actually get into the other's position; and when he tries to look with the eyes of the other, he only imagines how the other perceives and evaluates matters. It is very important that the correspondence between the view of the observer taking the standpoint of the sufferer and the actual view of the sufferer *can* be checked. A simple and valid method is to ask the sufferer whether and in what way his views are correctly perceived by the outsider.

Traditional psychology is the one-sided psychology of a particular kind of observer, namely, an aloof, objective observer. The traditional psychologist, strictly behavioristically and observationally inclined, considers no other psychology but his to be scientifically legitimate. The scientific psychologist is ready to accuse his experimental subject of having a biased view, and he tends to reject the subject's statements as egocentric and emotional. Further, he believes that he himself is not emotional and evaluative in his choice of problems, selection of data, and method of dealing with problems. He believes he investigates

what really exists, that he gets to the facts. In actuality, he sees things from a given angle, that of an objective observer whose observations are stripped of everyday connotations by his aloofness.

When the traditional scientist deals with values, he tries to treat them as facts and asserts that his own values do not influence his research. In actuality he feels and evaluates. His propensities are not filtered out from his research through the "factual approach," because being aloof is also an emotional state and he cannot escape evaluating. The investigator evaluates when he chooses what he believes is important to investigate and when he selects methods and procedures. His evaluation shows up clearly in his belief that he is a better investigator than the sufferer and other subjects. It shows up also in his disregard for their opinions, in his treating them as inarticulate objects. As long as the scientific psychologist decides on what should and should not be done, as long as he judges the importance of matters, he evaluates. The "oughts" of traditional research—choice of the problem because of its theoretical importance, demand for objectivity in the performance of the research, the emphasis on dealing with reliable and most probable occurrences, and the like, all accepted as "oughts" by the scientific psychologist—are values guiding psychologists in what they do. Thus, what the aloof scientific psychologist does is not less value-directed and emotional than what is done by the "emotional" and "value-directed" sufferer: only the character of the feelings and values of the insider are different from those of the outsider.

INCLUSIVENESS OF UNITS

That a difference exists between the feelings and values of the investigator and those of the sufferer should not just be accepted as fact: the differences must be taken into consideration in research. I will discuss one specific difference in the structure of the cognitive field of the investigator and sufferer: the difference in units encompassed by people in viewing matters from different distances.

All of us sometimes perceive a single thing, at other times a unit subsuming several units. The same holds for our thoughts; sometimes we think of a single object, at others of a unit subsuming a number of units. Sometimes we think of a tree, sometimes of a forest. This observation is not new, nor does it seem to be of special interest. However, systematic conditions accounting for differences in units encompassed by the investigator or sufferer lead, in rehabilitation, to serious consequences worthy of attention.

An examination of how the sufferer and investigator think shows that the sufferer thinks in less inclusive units than the scientifically trained professional observer. The statement holds for units of population and units of time, as well as for conceptual units. The sufferer tends to think about one sufferer, whether himself or another person; the scientific observer more easily thinks about handicapped people in general. Also, the sufferer

wants help with an immediate problem, the observer is concerned with the future. Conceptually, the observer thinks more abstractly than the sufferer: when the mother of a retarded or severely handicapped child asks the specialist whether her child will improve, she means will he be able to sit up, but the specialist thinks the mother asks whether the child will reach normalcy.

The difference in units encompassed by the scientific observer and by the sufferer leads to serious misunderstandings. The kind of misconceptions and misunderstandings due to difference in units encompassed should be studied. The knowledge gained should then be taught to prospective professional persons.

The examples of different units encompassed are familiar. Two things, however, are novel about these units. First, the differences in the inclusiveness of units encompassed are not just a matter of individual differences among people or situations. These differences are related to the positions of the insider and the outsider. Second, the units that encompass a number of units in comparison with the single unit are frequently global, that is less detailed, and may appear superficial in comparison with the single unit.

As to the first point, we know that when the distance from an object perceived increases, a greater number of objects in the surrounding area enter the field of vision. So also in thinking, the inclusiveness of the unit encompassed depends on the distance of the person from the subject matter. The distance here, however, is not a geographic but an emotional distance that characterizes the insider as closer and the outsider as farther away from the subject matter. As in the case of visual perception, a person when close to a house can perceive only that house but going father away can perceive a row of houses—so also a sufferer close to his problems is likely to think of himself; but a distant observer, even when facing a single handicapped person, is concerned with the whole group of handicapped people to which he believe the single sufferer belongs.

As to the second point, again let us consider a visual example. Houses running in a line, more or less, make up a street. Within the notion of street, the individuality of houses disappears. Similarly, the distant investigator deals with an abstract notion, that of a handicapped group, and leaves out the characteristics of individual persons. An outside investigator, thinking globally of abnormality, cannot understand a mother's carefully selecting a dress for her severely crippled child. Because of the global notion of normalcy, the professional person tends to conclude that it is not worth money and effort to improve the treatment of a profoundly retarded child. Of course the outside observer can focus on a single person and the insider can think about all handicapped persons, but these thoughts are not natural to them: the feeling of being the affected person or the detached observer brings about only an inclination toward thinking about particular units.

The subsumption of units, a psychological aspect of the world we live in, and the effect of the subsumption of units, aspects little taken into account in psychology, are of great importance in life. Teaching the professional person to understand the differences between his views and those of the sufferer should lead to better understanding of the sufferer.

In using knowledge in the field of rehabilitation it is important who decides what kind of knowledge is valuable, that is, who investigates and who teaches. Usually the investigator and the teacher are outsiders, and the knowledge they gather or teach is primarily that of the outsider. The outsider is inclined to teach about large units, that is, about what seems to hold for most cases, and will value the knowledge arrived at from a large number of groups. This helps make him *quantitatively inclined* and interested in what happens in most cases and what has a greater chance of occurring in a new group of cases, though not necessarily in a particular case. The result of such training will make the practitioner use standard prescriptions (standards arrived at from knowledge about groups of cases and frequently not fitting the single case). Directed during his training toward the value of large units, he will measure his success by the *number* of cases he could help. Because he counts success by the number of cases, he will divide handicapped people into promising and hopeless cases. He will lean toward spending his time, whether in an institution or in a community, with groups of less severely handicapped persons and will give up treatment and reduce to the bare minimum the care of "custodial" or "hopeless" cases.

Teaching involving the view of the handicapped persons would be quite different. Handicapped people would not divide cases easily into those worth or not worth the effort. Every handicapped person, even with a relatively minor handicap, knows that he is considered "not normal" by some "nonhandicapped" people (that is, in regard to normalcy, is considered a hopeless case) and thus is cautious in classifying handicapped people as hopeful or hopeless, as worthy or unworthy of care. Even the relatively mildly handicapped person knows of many situations in which his abilities were underestimated, and therefore he was not given opportunities to do things. Some outsiders think quadraplegic persons are so severely handicapped they would not encourage them to become college teachers and, therefore, would not support their admission for study or recommend them for jobs. Also, outsiders think a person with an IQ of 20 is unable to profit from training in the activities of daily living. However, many handicapped persons believe that some quadraplegics and some persons with low IQ's can "make it." And they are right, as they know—it has been proved possible.

It is the handicapped person who will prompt the investigator to work at the frontiers of knowledge, where hopes rather than realistic expectations govern. He is ready to expect things to happen against realistic odds. In a situation in which the need for a desired occurrence is of paramount importance, he not only wishes it to happen, he also believes that it will happen and is ready to work against great odds. The sufferer gives up following the dictum of probability (that is, expecting the most probable to happen) and exchanges it for the dictum of the possible, expecting the exceptional outcome. Until now the scientific investigator in psychology has been concerned with the most probable outcome, making his estimates and predictions on the basis of the outcome in most cases. Because of the concern of the sufferer with the possible, the investigator will have to shift the emphasis to consideration of a range of possible outcomes, including the rarest. This necessarily will lead him away from high evaluation of the probability of occurrences to new views concerning quantification in psychology.

The stress to be placed on the participation of the handicapped person in selecting problems for research and methodological questions such as determining the range of possible occurrences, including the hardly possible outcome rather than the most probable, may lead some psychologists to this facetious question: Is there anything left for the psychologist to do? The answer: as important as it is to have handicapped people involved in research and its application, there is plenty for psychologists to do in rehabilitation. The viewpoint of the nonhandicapped partners in the relationship must be determined, if only because they possess the keys to the institutions in which many handicapped people are locked, because nonhandicapped people set up and administer the policies that determine the rights and benefits of handicapped people, because some of the nonhandicapped people are the medical and other professional people who can help the deprived and disabled, and because they are the neighbors, strangers, and coworkers whom handicapped persons meet. Professional people who are not handicapped have to be understood in interrelation with handicapped people. And if the handicapped person has something to contribute toward understanding his psychological ways of dealing with matters, so has the person not handicapped much to contribute to the understanding of how to deal with handicapped people. Last but not least, it is in the domain of the psychologist to puzzle over the relation between theories and facts in his own particular way.

LACK OF ENVIRONMENTAL OPPORTUNITIES

Possibility does not only designate a concept complementary to probability—it is also a synonym for opportunity. This is the case when we say "the possibility (or opportunity) was given to him to do what he wanted." Providing opportunity refers to the arrangement of environmental conditions. Perhaps for too long some psychologists in rehabilitation, when investigating and trying to use findings, have concentrated on the problems of a person's abilities without paying enough attention to environmental conditions, especially as set and kept by people. However, problems are frequently due to lack of environmental opportunities

and, further, in a great number of cases their provision and also their lack are social-psychological in origin. Thus the outsider, being oblivious of the needs of the man in the wheelchair, unintentionally sets up architectural barriers. When his attention is drawn to the barriers, he can let them stay or remove them, that is, provide or not provide opportunities to the handicapped person.

Frustration as a situation in which attainment of the goal is made impossible is a worked and perhaps overworked topic in psychology. Considerable attention has been paid to the effects of deprivation. But the reverse—detection of opportunities, providing opportunities, and determining their effect—is hardly studied. Yet many frustrating situations would be eliminated if people would not deprive others of opportunities. Much of rehabilitation psychology, therefore, should consist in discovering and providing opportunities. Psychologists should be taught to survey social and physical environmental settings in regard to opportunities and to examine professional contacts, care, and treatment under this aspect. Any care given to the disabled should include checking whether needed opportunities have been given to the handicapped person as seen by the outsider and by the insider. Investigation of environmental conditions and use of knowledge are closely linked.

"Is the checking of the entrance to and exit from buildings a psychological problem?" Yes: blindness to hindrances and the provision of opportunities are psychological issues that require the psychologist's attention. For example, a prison, or any institution with residents behind locked doors, is characterized by restriction of freedom of movement and communication and by lack of opportunities to do things. More specifically: in an institution for the retarded, in a building for the profoundly retarded, the incidence of incontinence was very high. Afraid that the residents would stuff the toilets with objects and would be burned using the hot water, the staff kept the doors to the bathrooms locked and did not have time to open them frequently. What could the residents do but be incontinent? The psychological consequence was that they appeared more profoundly retarded than they actually were because they lacked the opportunity to remain clean.

To find solutions for such problems is not difficult intellectually and answers could be found by asking the insider, but professional workers require a lot of training and a lot of wisdom to change the conditions in such a building, that is, to provide opportunities to the residents for decent living. It is one of the most urgent tasks of rehabilitation psychologists and other professional workers not only to prepare residents in institutions for living in the community but also to provide opportunity for dignified living for those who have to remain in institutions. Detecting lack of opportunities and providing the opportunities is a part of proper custodial care. With the help of diverse social-psychological means the bare, restricting environment should be changed to one that presents needed opportunities.

THE PRINCIPAL POINTS

The points I have been trying to make are briefly these:

The use of knowledge in rehabilitation psychology is not primarily a question of application but requires the acquisition of relevant knowledge. Relevant knowledge involves taking for scientific investigation problems considered to be problems in everyday life.

The use of research requires reevaluation of current scientific psychological approaches and methods. New theoretical views have been discussed.

The unilateral view of the investigator as the one and only person to select problems for investigation and to investigate them is subject to challenge. Two views, that of the observer and that of the sufferer, have to be taken into account. In understanding both views, that of the handicapped person and that of the professional, we can arrive at utilizable knowledge.

The need for coordinating two psychologies is necessary because of the different positions occupied by the professional worker and the sufferer. The difference in position, characterized by the distance from the problem, leads the insider and outsider to encompass different rehabilitation units.

The outsider is usually concerned with

more inclusive units—with abstract knowledge and theories rather than with the needs of an individual case, with large groups, with final outcome, with abstract standards. He is removed from the problems of the individual sufferer, who feels he needs help here and now and seeks and welcomes signs of even the slightest improvement. Principles permitting the resolution of conflicts resulting from contrary feelings and evaluations of matters by the outsider and sufferer have to be developed and taught, if better use of knowledge is to take place.

Although at present most psychologists are guided by the statistically most probable outcome, which they deem to be the realistic way of solving problems, the sufferer emphasizes the importance of the desirable but exceptional outcome and the necessity of dealing not only with promising cases but also with the whole range of cases, including those with hardly a chance of alleviation.

The concept of opportunities needs to be used. The concern with and provision of opportunities are very important in considering care in institutions both for those who will leave them and for those who are expected to be under lifelong care. The meaning of "custodial care" has to change.

Throughout, gaining and using knowledge require the common effort of the sufferer and the professional worker.

What I have presented is one way of thinking about how rehabilitation psychology can increase the use of its knowledge. There are different ways of attempting it, and all of them should be considered. I am not an eclectic but would welcome theoretical approaches by different investigators from different viewpoints. My own views are an outgrowth of the Field Theoretical Gestalt approach, known also as Topological Psychology, to which I adhere.

2 On Posing as Mental Patients:

Reminiscences and Recommendations

Arnold R. Goldman,
Ronald H. Bohr, and
Thomas A. Steinberg

Two investigators posed as mental patients on contrasting wards of a large metropolitan state mental hospital. It was found that fear of betrayal by significant others and intense boredom were highly salient individual responses to hospitalization. From the perspective of a patient, the psychiatric ward consists of two sharply distinct worlds: the realm of patients and psychiatric aides and the realm of all other staff members. Out of necessity, aides and patients have developed a system of social exchange which appears to have significant influence on ward functioning, patient socialization, and resistance by aides to therapeutic innovation.

This paper is based on the firsthand experiences of two investigators who served as disguised observers in a large metropolitan state hospital. The second author, a social psychologist, posed as an acute depressed patient on an admissions ward for one week; the third author, a clinical research psychologist, lived the role of a long-term psychotic for 51 hours on a continued-treatment ward for chronic patients. Throughout the entire period of their observations, both investigators were fully believed to be mental patients; indeed, neither ward personnel nor patients were ever aware of the investigators' identities. This report represents the combined views of the observers and of the senior author who conceived and organized the project.

PURPOSE AND RATIONALE

Despite their responsibility for the care and treatment of the mentally ill, mental health professionals seem to lack an existential awareness of what it means to be a hospitalized patient. The present investigators believed that enacting the patient role, and being reacted to by others as mentally ill, could provide such an awareness. As has been discussed more fully elsewhere (Goldman & Bohr, 1968), enacting a given role can provide differ-

A version of part of this paper was presented at the annual meeting of the Society for the Study of Social Problems, Boston, August 1968.

Thanks are extended to Richard Sanders, Daniel Blain, Franklyn R. Clarke, Anthony Dunfield, Jane Perrine, and Louis H. Muzekari for their valuable assistance in conducting the project described in this paper.

ent information from what can be gained either by direct observation or even by engaging in conventional role-playing. Moreover, despite the serious ethical questions which have been raised about disguised observation (Caudill, 1958; Erikson, 1967), this technique has been used in the past to enhance mental health workers' understanding of the realities of patienthood (Caudill, Redlich, Gilmore, & Brody, 1952; Deane, 1961; Ishiyama, Batman, & Hewitt, 1967).

In brief, it was thought that disguised observation of the patient role could be of considerable value in the training of mental health professionals on the staff of the hospital under study. Because there were so many apparent risks to committing observers into a hospital as patients, however, the present project was designed as an exploratory study. Hence, the hospitalization of the two psychologists would serve to determine the risks, feasibility, and utility of posing as a patient in a state hospital. If disguised observation did show potential heuristic value, it was intended that students in various hospital traineeship programs (e.g., psychiatric aides, resident physicians, psychologists) would even-tually undergo the procedure as an adjunct to their formal training.

A second reason for the present project arose from the intention of the new administration of the hospital under study to seek out and eliminate antitherapeutic ward practices. Because ward personnel might themselves be "too close" to the situation or "too defensive" to identify practices inimical to patient care, the disguised observers were charged with the responsibility of providing recommendations for ward improvement.[1]

SETTING

At the time of the investigation, the institution studied embodied a great many of the undesirable features of a large public mental hospital. The facility, which was designed originally for 3,000 patients, housed a population of about 6,000; the degree of understaffing had long reached emergency levels, with the complement of professional personnel in some services falling 90% below acceptable staff requirements. Moreover, the hospital's discharge ratio was distressingly low, with the result that over 80% of the population

---

[1] While the results reported in this paper suggest the applied and theoretical value of this endeavor, it is unfortunate that few of the original goals have been achieved. It has not proved possible to train numbers of hospital workers by having them adopt the patient role. However, the perspective gained in the present project has influenced subsequent training efforts. For example, trainees in social interaction therapy have recently received part of their instruction by serving in the role of assistants to psychiatric aides for short periods of time, performing typical aide duties, and discussing their responses to the experience with one another and with the aides with whom they worked (Bohr, 1969; Bohr & Offenberg, 1969). Furthermore, although some specific changes in ward procedures have been instituted since this project (e.g., changes in hour of waking up patients, new methods for distributing tobacco, candy, and magazines on various wards), the general lack of innovation bears witness to the difficulty of reforming institutional care.

had been in residence over two years (Steinberg, Goldman, & Sanders, 1968). Finally, like many state institutions, it evolved over the years into two virtually distinct hospitals: a very small but dynamic rehabilitation facility for schizophrenic patients in remission, and a very large but quiescent custodial hospital for organics and hard-core, refractory chronic psychotics (Sanders, Smith, & Weinman, 1967). In order to sample both types of facilities, as well as to test the administrative problems of "planting" observers, one author was "admitted" directly from the community into the admissions ward and the other was transferred from the rehabilitation unit to a chronic "back ward."

The male admissions ward entered by one observer housed approximately 60 patients and was located in a building constructed in 1950 which has remained in fair condition. The ward was comprised of seven nine-bed dormitory rooms and two dayrooms—one appealing and one not. The latter dayroom, which was referred to by some patients as the "dungeon" or "alley," contained only hard, stiff-backed chairs; the principal diversion in this barren room was an old television set. Ordinarily, the "dungeon" was the assignment for brand-new admissions as well as for patients judged "unable to leave the ward unescorted." The other dayroom was reserved for use by the "better" patients and was rather attractively furnished with drapes, comfortable chairs, books, games, and a large-screen television set.

The 80-bed "back ward" for chronic patients was located on a large, dilapidated (insect- and rodent-infested) and subsequently condemned building. As might be expected, physical conditions on the ward approached the ignominious. The ward housed primarily "good chronics" who were allowed to leave the ward unaccompanied.

THE EXPERIENCE OF HOSPITALIZATION

For both observers the hospitalization experience aroused two painfully insistent feelings: agitated boredom and, quite unexpectedly, the fear of betrayal.

Betrayal

Immediately upon admission and throughout the course of their hospitalization, both researchers experienced a fear that they had been betrayed by their colleagues. Each was remarkably concerned about whether he would be left in the hospital indefinitely, only to be forgotten by friends and relatives. One observer in particular was so alarmed by the prospect that by the end of the week he had planned an escape route. Although no one connected with this project had anticipated the arousal of this feeling, it was interesting to find it foremost in the minds of laymen. Indeed, up to the present, the question invariably asked of the observers by staff, by journalists, and by lay audiences is usually along the lines of, "Weren't you afraid they'd leave you in there?" That a fear of betrayal may be a common apprehension under such circumstances is further suggested in the findings of Ishiyama, who reports that, among the psychiatric attendants who experienced only one-half hour in a seclusion room, many became extremely anxious over the possibility of their being forgotten and left in the room (Ishiyama & Hewitt, 1966).

If a fear of betrayal can readily be evoked in "normals," it is likely that similar apprehensions and suspicions are aroused in mentally ill persons upon their initiation into a mental hospital. Certainly, many patients, as Goffman (1961, pp. 131–146) indicates, have just cause for "feeling betrayed," especially after having been told that they were "going for a ride in the country" or given some other subterfuge to get them into the hospital.

Since one obvious reaction to involuntary confinement is escape, certain flight responses might well be expected, particularly during the very first stages of a patient's hospitalization. In this context, it is useful to recall one observer's tentative escape plan and relate it to the results of a 36-month cohort study of escapes from the hospital under study. The investigation indicated that escape is an early occurring phenomenon, with more than half of all escapes having occurred between the first and eighth week following admission (Goldman & Offenberg, 1969).

Although fear of betrayal has long been a central theme in the autobiographical accounts of mental patienthood (e.g., Beers, 1956), hospital personnel have been sensitive neither to its occurrence nor to its possible consequences. The personal experiences of the two observers suggest that many of the suspicions harbored by patients may be situationally induced and, therefore, not always classically paranoid reactions. Perhaps the impersonalization as well as the ambiguity of hospital admission procedures—at least as they would appear to new patients—might be dealt with directly by clinicians and administrators. Indeed, much symptomatic behavior, including fear of betrayal, could be allayed or even precluded by better orientation procedures for new admissions and by clear structuring of the patients' initial hospital experiences.

Agitated Boredom

An immediate and overwhelming reaction in both observers to hospital life was boredom. More important, and contrary to the views of many of the hospital staff, mental patients themselves were not at all oblivious to the barrenness and emptiness of their physical surroundings.

Many patients with whom the observers interacted were painfully bored and sought something meaningful to occupy their time. As a consequence, at least for the observers themselves, relatively minor events quickly began to take on disproportionate significance. For example, a different dessert at dinnertime became the "event of the day," and success in obtaining change for a quarter became an accomplishment to be remembered. Closely related to this psychological magnification of minor events was a subjective change in the observers' time perspectives. Thus, once minor events were subjectively transformed into major occasions, they assumed the status of chronological landmarks, and it was by these landmarks that the observers and other patients marked the passage of hospital time. As one articulate patient on the admissions ward reported,

> Little things become very important around here. You don't use the days of the week to tell time, but you say, "Oh, that was the day we waited in the hall for the floor to dry after breakfast instead of going right into the dayroom." Or "That was the day we had ice cream." You start to think just about what happens in here, and any change in the routine becomes tremendously important.

It was noteworthy to find on both wards studied, and presumably throughout the hospital, that patients did not have easy access to newspapers or calendars. While it was the hospital's policy to deliver one newspaper daily to every ward, these periodicals were seldom if ever available to the majority of patients. The primary medium for current events was television, but television programs of an informational nature were generally vetoed by the patients in favor of the popular, bland situation comedies and variety shows. In the opinion of the observers, the impoverished environment of the ward fostered in patients an apathy toward the world outside.

In light of the scarcity of information available in the custodial psychiatric ward, it seems unrealistic to measure a mental patient's progress, degree of pathology, or readiness for release by his awareness of the date, of the names of various governmental leaders, or of other topical items of information.

THE EXCHANGE SYSTEM: A CONSEQUENCE OF DEPRIVATION

From the perspective of the patient, the hospital ward was divided into two distinct social worlds. On the one hand, there was the remote realm of nurses, mental health professionals, and all those persons on the other side of the locked ward door who wore shirts, ties, and were present weekdays from 8:30 A.M. to 4:30 P.M. On the other hand, there was the immediate domain of patients and attendants. In this domain there existed between patients and attendants an elaborate informal system of exchange (see Homans, 1961). This system existed, in part, because the parties involved had something of value to offer one another. An examination of the existing roles of attendants and patients makes abundantly clear the necessity of an exchange and reveals the tradable commodities each group possessed.

Since the size of the attendant staff was insufficient to allow them to fulfill all of their responsibilities (i.e., patient care *and* ward maintenance), attendants were in great need of assistance. And the patients met this need. Indeed, it has been often asserted (e.g., Bartlett, 1967) that most state hospitals could not operate without patient labor. However, what could attendants, low-echelon workers with little formal authority, offer to patients in return?

Mental patients, who are characteristically restricted to such a degree that they are extremely dependent on others for even the most minor amenities of life, could "win back" some of these apparently minor rights by assisting attendants. Since attendants had at their disposal few resources for rewarding patients, the abridgment of many rights served a utilitarian purpose. The attendants could trade small privileges (e.g., extra food, cigarettes, coffee, permission to carry matches, and violation of other hospital rules) for patient cooperation. Therefore, because of the nature of these two interacting social roles (i.e., mental patient and hospital attendant), there was established a basis for a system of mutual rewards.

This exchange was viewed as "just," and both parties felt that patients should be rewarded for assisting aides in their work. Failure to reward patients for cooperation was generally viewed as a violation of ward mores— even when this failure resulted from an attendant's strict adherence to hospital rules. To cite just one example, it was usual for "helpful" patients to be permitted to use the more desirable "front" dayroom despite the fact that some of them did not have ground privileges (i.e., permission to leave the ward unattended). Indeed, as one helpful patient without ground privileges explained when he was sent to the back dayroom, "It isn't fair—you work but they send you back here to the dungeon."

In the hierarchy of the hospital, attendants are the intermediaries between patients and other staff members. To enhance their own position, aides reinterpreted the actions of upper-echelon medical personnel in terms of the exchange system. Thus, decisions by professionals which were intended to have therapeutic utility were eventually communicated to patients by their attendants as rewards for cooperation. Typically, patients were given the distinct impression that it was the attendants themselves who were responsible for granting these rewards. For example, while physicians prescribed ground privileges for therapeutic reasons, attendants always passed them on to patients as a reward for cooperation in ward maintenance, with the implication that continued cooperation was expected if the patient wanted to keep his ground privileges.

This system of exchange may also play an indirect role in the process by which new patients are transformed into chronic ones. Part of the socialization of the new patient seems to involve his accepting a new image of himself, that of a mentally ill person who must be totally dependent upon others for even the most minor gratuities. The second author's initial introductions to the exchange system were most humbling. In one instance, a number of patients were being given dimes for having helped an attendant mop a floor. The observer had just arrived on the scene and was told by the attendant, "I'll buy you some coffee too when you've helped us clean up this utility room." At another time, the observer helped another attendant mop a floor and was told, "Go get something to eat—you helped us." The strong sense of humiliation experienced by the observer did not seem to be a reaction limited to middle class professionals; even working class patients, comparing this compensation with wages in industry, realized its inadequacy. It is of interest to note that within the course of just one week, however, these meager rewards came to be expected as payoffs for services rendered.

On the custodial ward, as far as the third author could see, there was no explicit exchange system; ward life seemed to go on automatically. With virtually no cues from attendants, patients would leave the building at the proper time to go to their assigned jobs, carry out routine ward chores, or assist the staff during special events in a seemingly spontaneous manner.

Some events occurred, however, which raised the question as to whether the absence of overt exchange behavior was more apparent than real. While patients were not positively reinforced for compliance on the custodial ward, uncooperative behavior was met with negative reinforcement. Any patient disrupting the harmony of ward life would quickly receive negative sanctions. Indeed, one attendant was observed telling a recalcitrant patient, "You know this floor is for patients who work—if you don't, we'll have to move you up to the third floor." Such proscriptions on the custodial ward, in contrast to direct positive reinforcements on the admission ward, suggest the possibility that the mode of reinforcement—positive or negative—is not the same for the novice and for the veteran patient, or possibly not the same for the acute and the chronic. In other words, one might speculate that new patients are initiated into the hospital system through the distribution of positive rewards and, once having been incorporated into the system, these patients are controlled by the threatened loss of such rewards.

While the nature of the differences between the admissions ward and other settings remains equivocal, interviews with various personnel throughout the hospital suggested that exchange between patients and attendants was widespread. For example, it was reported that aides often gave ground privileges to "deserving" patients without the approval of ward physicians, and withdrew ground privileges without the approval of ward physicians if they felt a patient was not working to capacity. Also, on various wards, state-issued tobacco and cigarette paper, the privilege of watching television in the evening, and coffee were employed as rewards. At one staff meeting, it was reported, an attendant complained that, because he could not obtain state coffee to "reward good patients," he had had to purchase coffee himself.

IMPLICATIONS

Knowledge of the hospital system of exchange seems to be of value in understanding several aspects of the behavior of patients and staff in psychiatric facilities. Parenthetically, it is of considerable interest to note that, long before the advent of behavior therapy, psychiatric attendants had evolved their own form of "token economy" by which to mold patient behavior.

In terms of staff behavior, the

present analysis suggests the possibility that severe restriction of patient behavior has an important latent function, in addition to the manifest one of "protecting patients from themselves and others." In effect, restriction provides lower echelon staff members with the means by which patient behavior can be rewarded. Seen from this perspective, the many ward restrictions placed upon patients become more comprehensible.

In contrast with interpretations of attendant behavior which stress the role of class-linked individual characteristics (e.g., educational background, beliefs about mental illness) as determinants of "antitherapeutic" job performance, the present paper emphasizes the possible significance of other variables. Notably, it seems quite possible that the organizational structure of the attendant role and the realities of his job (i.e., understaffing, responsibilities for both patient care and building maintenance) give him a vested interest in restricting the self-determination of patients. Viewing past investigations of mental health ideology (e.g., Cohen & Struening, 1962; Gilbert & Levinson, 1956), it is conceivable that custodial, "authoritarian" beliefs may be influenced in some measure by hospital structure and functioning—not only by the typical personality and social class characteristics of attendants. Certainly, just as the hospital as a social system elicits certain behaviors in patients, it can also elicit certain behaviors in staff members. These considerations raise the possibility that attendant attitudes may be changed through job restructuring, as well as through traditional educational attempts. Indeed,

some research (see Colarelli & Siegel, 1966) indicates that psychiatric attendants do adopt considerably more therapeutic attitudes and behaviors when given greater autonomy of job performance and more authority in making decisions about patient treatment.

CONCLUSION

It is hoped that this account of the experiences of two trained observers posing as mental patients in a large state hospital has raised some significant questions about the effects of the institutional environment upon the behavior of mental patients. Specifically, reflecting the interests of both the clinical and social psychologists involved in this project, the issues focused on here suggest the intimate relationship between individual behavior and the immediate social environment. The experiences reported here hint at the relationship which exists between the reaction of the mental patient to boredom, poverty, and loss of status and responsibility, on the one hand, and the characteristics of hospitals which elicit these reactions, on the other. Enhanced awareness of this relationship may suggest experimental reforms aimed at correcting the environmental conditions which elicit "chronic" behavior in psychiatric patients.

REFERENCES

Bartlett, F. L. Present-day requirements for state hospitals joining the community. New England Journal of Medicine, 1967, 267, 90—94.

Beers, C. W. A mind that found itself. Garden City, N.Y.: Doubleday, 1956.

Bohr, R. H. Instruction in organizational psychology: A "survival kit" for new workers in a state hospital. American Psychologist, 1969, 24, 765—766.

Bohr, R. H., & Offenberg, R. M. A factor analytic study of job perceptions in a state psychiatric hospital. Psychological Reports, 1969, 24, 899—902.

Caudill, W. The psychiatric hospital as a small society. Cambridge: Harvard University Press, 1958.

Caudill, W., Redlich, F. C., Gilmore, H. R., & Brody, E. B. Social structure and interaction processes on a psychiatric ward. American Journal of Orthopsychiatry, 1952, 22, 314—334.

Cohen, J., & Struening, E. L. Opinions about mental health in the personnel of two large mental hospitals. Journal of Abnormal and Social Psychology, 1962, 64, 349—360.

Colarelli, N. J., & Siegel, S. M. Ward H: An adventure in innovation. New York: Van Nostrand, 1966.

Deane, W. N. The reactions of a nonpatient to a stay on a mental hospital ward. Psychiatry, 1961, 24, 61—68.

Erikson, K. T. A comment on disguised observation in sociology. Social Problems, 1967, 14, 366—372.

Gilbert, D. C., & Levinson, D. J. Ideology, personality, and institutional policy in the mental hospital. Journal of Abnormal and Social Psychology, 1956, 53, 263—271.

Goffman, E., Asylums. Garden City, N.Y.: Doubleday, 1961.

Goldman, A. R., & Bohr, R. H. Methods of observation: Implications for research and training. Paper presented at the meeting of the Pennsylvania Sociological Society, Villanova University, October 1968.

Goldman, A. R., & Offenberg, R. M. Escape from the mental hospital: A cohort analysis. Unpublished manuscript, Philadelphia State Hospital, 1969.

Homans, G. C. Social behavior: Its elementary forms. New York: Harcourt, Brace & World, 1961.

Ishiyama, T., Batman, R., & Hewitt, E. Let's be patients. American Journal of Nursing, 1967, 67, 569—571.

Ishiyama, T., & Hewitt, E. B. Seclusion: A lesson for aides. Journal of Psychiatric Nursing, 1966, 4, 563—570.

Sanders, R., Smith, R. S., & Weinman, B. S. Chronic psychoses and recovery. San Francisco: Jossey-Bass, 1967.

Steinberg, T. A., Goldman, A. R., & Sanders, R. Demographic factors associated with release from Philadelphia State Hospital: A preliminary report. Pennsylvania Psychiatric Quarterly, 1968, 8, 38—47.

Section 2
ON BEING DISABLED

3 Listen: The Patient

Eric Hodgins

Long years ago, in my Boston student days, the way home led past a down-slope from Beacon Hill that gave onto Tremont Street. It was too narrow for wheeled traffic, so it was ideal for a curbstone evangelist who preached to a sidewalk crowd there every evening except Sunday. I used to listen to him occasionally; when after a while I gave up it was because, although he was an accomplished outdoor orator, I could never seem to get tuned in on his subject. I know it was religion only because of a truly spectacular happening one autumn evening in 1919.

On that evening, just before I came along, someone in the crowd had heckled the old boy, and he was in a fury. His usual voice was a good 40-watt bellow without distortion, but now he was shouting. His gray hair was rumpled, his eyes were blazing, and his face was crimson with anger. I have spent the intervening forty-six years trying to imagine what his heckler could have said. I am still stumped. All I can give is the evangelist's final challenge. This was a stopper, all right, in the form of the question to his heckler: "What the hell do *you* know about the Holy Ghost?"

I fully expect to provoke some similar inquiry from one or more members of the Maricopa County Medical Society before this session is over, because I have no official papers to entitle me to be on this platform at all. But before I came it was agreed that if my presence here was to be of value, that value did not lie in my objectivity but, to the direct contrary, in my subjectivity. I was the patient, and thanks in part to you (collectively) I still am. We are talking about stroke, and stroke survival.

Let me approach the brain by way of the groin—a fairly direct route. My own physician in New York is a man I hadn't known at the time of my cere-brovascular accident in 1960, but heartily wish I had. A few months ago I went to him because I had a slight, soft, painless swelling in my left groin. Dr. T. laid his hands on my belly in various ways, asking me to cough, and the like. After the last cough he said, "What do *you* think this is?" I told him I thought it was an inguinal hernia. He said, "That's what I think, too." So I said, "Why in the world did you ask me?" "Oh," he said, "I always ask my patients what they think they've brought me—and it's amazing how helpful it is even when they guess wrong." Then he quoted for me an early nineteenth-century medical sage

Remarks presented at the Maricopa County Medical Society Health Forum, Phoenix, Arizona, October 19, 1965.

Reprinted with permission from the New England Journal of Medicine, 1966, 274: 657–661.

37

who died at the age of forty-five, but not before he had invented the stethoscope seven years earlier. This was René Théophile Hyacinthe Laënnec, who used to exhort his students: "Listen! Listen to your patient! He is giving you the diagnosis." This revolutionary sentiment must now be almost a hundred and fifty years old, for its author died in 1826. It now seems safe for a general field tryout. (I realize there are physicians—psychiatrists—who do very little except listen to their patients, but I am not speaking tonight, so far as I know, to the analytically oriented.)

A year ago (October, 1964) I had the privilege of attending and speaking at the National Stroke Congress, in Chicago. Banquet night was a considerable success, for Dr. Frank Krusen presided and Dr. Morris Fishbein spoke, and both these ornaments to articulate medicine were in high good form. At conclusion, the audience of many hundreds began to take its noisy and disordered departure from the hotel ballroom. It is the noise I want to emphasize, for in the midst of it, a lady I had never seen before bore down on me and said, "Good evening, I am Mrs. So-and-So in physical therapy at the Such-and-Such Hospital in Florida, and your cane needs a new tip."

I found this—I still find it—absolutely delightful. A few weeks before, I myself had noticed that my cane had begun going *click* instead of *thump*, but I hadn't done anything about it. That a trained ear could first separate out the sound of one cane from all the other sounds in that room, and then assess the appropriateness of the sound—this is what I found so delightful. And I am not telling this small story tonight without a purpose. The men and women of the medical and other health professions have spent blood, tears, and dollars in training and retraining their powers of observation. My suggestion this evening is that they share with the patient—particularly the stroke patient—more, much more, of what they so acutely observe. There is no universal patient, of course, and there is no universal doctor either, and stroke is not an entity, so what I am saying is appropriately imprecise and just what one would expect from a layman—except that it's universally agreed that the stroke patient is in need of all the honest reassurance he can get. And confidence in the doctor and his staff is powerful reassurance. But how is the confidence first established and then copperriveted?

I don't know who first used the expression "an interesting invalid," and neither does *Bartlett's Familiar Quotations*, but he was not a physician, I feel sure, and probably not an invalid, either. In literature and the drama, there seem to be two stereotypes for invalids: the Christlike and the querulous. You knew that the former existed for the purpose of dying in the last act or chapter; the latter usually existed to keep on harassing everybody until someone, hitherto in perfect health, suddenly kicked the bucket, being unable to stand any more guff from Grandma.

Not to strain too hard with these archetypes, I think there would be general agreement that the stroke patient is apt to resemble the latter more than the former. But a legitimate question arises, Could any of the querulous outbursts of the stroke patient, or his deep descents into gloom, be *caused* by the kind and quality of medical care he gets? If you ask me, the answer to this shining question is "Yes."

It seems to me that many persons in medicine today continue to foster and cherish mystery for mystery's sake. I am thinking of the prescriptions still written illegibly in pig-Latin. I am thinking of the enigmatic smile after the blood-pressure readings, and the utter silence after the retinal blood vessels are examined. I am thinking of the nurse's stolid mask after the removal of the thermometer from wherever it was. Your own minds will supply other examples more quickly and completely than I could cite them.

These are procedures and conventions for the convenience and protection of doctors; their effect and *perhaps* their intent is to diminish the patient. Doubtless, many patients must be diminished to be made manageable or even tolerable, but diminishing the stroke patient is risky business, for he has already been diminished by Act of God and in addition to his neurologic symptoms, he is full of fear—raw, elemental fear—not necessarily of death but of incapacity or destitution. From whom is he going to draw the courage without which he will not truly recover? Not from a silent practitioner; not from a stuffy practitioner; not from a practitioner, whether doctor, therapist or nurse, who is aloof. He will draw courage as he perceives human understanding un-derlying the professional technics of those into whose care he has been given.

My memory gets driven back here, with some force, to a quotation from Harvard's great professor of biochemistry, Lawrence Henderson, when he was generalizing about conditions essential to success in various endeavors. As I remember, one sentence ran, "Hard, unremitting work *at the locus of the problem*; for the physician, at the bedside, not in the library."

Professor Henderson was no man to disparage books, a library or study in it: he was one of the most scholarly men of his times. I think we know what he *was* disparaging: he was disparaging remoteness, whether physical or of the spirit. When a patient exhibits remoteness he gets charted for it—or perhaps he gets transferred to the psychiatric wing. But whose criticism of the remote physician or nurse will find its way onto their charts? Granted, no doctor can enter fully into his patient's problems and sufferings, for then he has no reserves of his own on which to live and function. But there is such a thing as warmth, which can be radiated and which doesn't cost much to put forth. The lady from Florida who told me about my cane was a radiator, and like the best radiators, may not fully know she is one—any more than she knows I love her but don't know her name or address.

There are certain persons in our society who incessantly hear complaints, excuses, evasions, rationalizations and just plain self-serving lies—and are permitting the boredom of it to kill them. I am thinking of motor-cycle cops, police-court magistrates, hotel clerks, call girls, customs officers, credit managers, department-store detectives, headwaiters and cash-iers. From these, the wooden face and the fishy eye are perhaps inevitable. Doctors, therapists and nurses, too, hear the same stories over and over again, but they cannot join the head-waiter or the call girl in their boredom with life. In fact, I think they have sworn their oaths that they never will.

It is true, I have never faced a parade of the ill. I *have* faced a parade of the well, and that is tough enough. Twenty years ago, when I was a vice-president of Time Incoporated, Mr. Henry Luce, of Phoenix and New York, gave me the task of searching for new, high editorial talent after the war had completely disordered our ranks. Although I had a few assistants who acted as screens, the ultimate in-terviews were up to me. It was then that I learned how successions of peo-ple, all with the same thing on their minds, presented a pattern; given the same stimulus they gave back the same clichés, the same jokes, the same anxi-eties, the same everything. It could be a narcotic, this repetition. But I was charged to look for *differences*, not *similarities*, and it was this, of course, that saved me. It's what saves most doctors and nurses, I feel sure. But it doesn't save quite all of them.

I think the stroke patient (I limit myself to him because that is my top-ic) is entitled to the same understand-ing compassion as the person who has survived a hard airplane crash. I think he is less likely to get it. The drama of his plight is mostly internal: little meets the eye—no gross injury, no compound fracture, no massive blood loss. But both patients are shocked. Into the bargain, the stroke patient is also deeply enigmatic: in the beginning there is much doubt about what he is going to "do." If he is not going to die he will soon get a lot of examination and neurologic testing. Indeed, it is possible that everyone is going to look so hard at his eyegrounds, watch his reflexes so carefully and test his gnos-tic sensibilities so often that he him-self, the person, the personality, the individual, may become neglected.

Yet there he remains, existing and pleading. The communication diffi-culties between him and those who want to help him may be considerable. If he is conscious but aphasic the diffi-culties become tremendous, and much more frustrating to everybody than if he were in a coma. Even if he is not aphasic but has lost his proprioceptive sense on the affected side he will be at a loss for words with which to describe this. (I have been trying for five and a half years and have not yet come up with anything that satisfied even my-self.) Plenty of physicians in practice have broken a bone, come down with a hot appendix, passed a kidney stone, endured a hangover or experienced an-ginal pain, but the physician whose proprioceptive sense has been knocked out on one side is probably not still in active medical practice. Thus, I think it amazing that doctors can understand a condition that no patient can ade-quately describe—that is painless but quite disturbing, and into which they themselves cannot enter. It is not surprising, however, that with the best of intentions the doctor-to-patient quotient of understanding, when the patient has had a stroke, is considerably less than 100 per cent—or that the doctor who has just given a remarkable demonstration of his hard-bought second-hand knowledge will then make a remark or issue an order showing that he has instantaneously forgotten it. The patient, however, does not forget. The occupational therapist is much less likely to forget, for this is one of the specific areas of her training; she lives with this sort of thing every day. Not every doctor does.

One of the truly remarkable occupational-therapy heads in the country, Miss Cecilia Sattely, expressed to me a month or so ago her concern in the problem of the patient who raised no questions to health personnel about things that obviously troubled him. Miss Sattely, as chief of the Occupational Therapy Section at the Kingsbridge Veterans Administration Hospital in the Bronx, New York, must deal with a good many severely disabled patients. She asked me how, as a patient, I could account for this problem of silence. I did not and do not know, but answering for myself I listed these few possibilities:

Expectation of no answer at all.
Expectation of worse than no answer at all.
Expectation of double-talk, evasion or condescension.
Expectation of bringing forth unwanted examples of sweet, suffering patience.

All these answers boil down to one, I suppose: loss of hope, or loss of confidence in hospital or medical personnel. Either way, it isn't good. I remind you that I am being subjective: I shall have to leave to you the extent to which my own peculiarities account for these answers versus how much is due to a situation inherent in medical routines or in hospitals, and correctable. I am not suggesting that patients should be given free access to their charts, and obviously, *some* patients cannot be told *some* things. I am suggesting that too much mystery can breed more fears than too much candor. Of course, if reassurance cannot honestly be given, silence, or its idiot brother, double-talk, may be the only recourses. But they are last recourses. For the patient is part of the treatment. Sometimes, the treatment gains less from the physician's knowledge than it gains from his attention to the things that are of importance to the patient, even when the doctor's and the patient's scale of importances is quite different.

In stroke there are two basic sets of assumptions which *could* govern treatment. One set proceeds from what the patient perceives, or thinks he perceives; the other comes from what the doctor knows, or thinks he knows. These are two very different sets of things. Before the doctors among you tell me that this is so with every illness, let me say only that there is *something* in what the patient says, no matter what it is, so "Listen! Listen to the patient!" A rigid doctor intensifies a rigid patient. And almost everyone who has been in a hospital has seen examples—perhaps not in his own case—where the relations between patient and health personnel have become adversary proceedings.

Curiously enough, there is no article on stroke in that bible for practitioners, the Cecil and Loeb *Textbook of Medicine*. Under the big, major section heading, "Diffuse and Focal Diseases of the Brain," there are articles on cerebral hemorrhage and cerebral thrombosis, along with a great many other disorders. But aphasia or hemiplegia, the two most serious and frequent residuals from stroke, are treated many pages previously, under the section heading, "Diseases of the Nervous System." How about "Arteriosclerosis," a condition likely to be antecedent to stroke? Turn back again, this time to "Diseases of the Cardiovascular System," for that's where that is parked. But "Atherosclerosis," again an antecedent, turns up under the section "Diseases of Metabolism." A certain logic is discernible here, all right, but it is an indexer's logic, and it does chop up the stroke patient, present or potential, into rather small pieces.

Obviously, the later the patient can have his stroke, the better, in every sense of the phrase. The steady advance of physical medicine and rehabilitation and its effects on the post-stroke patient can be wonderful to contemplate, if he is brought to it early enough. But before the physiatrist can get to the stroke patient, he must be called in. Who calls him and when? This is a vital question, not yet satisfactorily answered by medicine-at-large, or in the country-at-large. It is precisely at this point, so my own hopes run, that the Report of the President's Commission on Heart Disease, Cancer and Stroke will have one of its best overall effects. The distinguished head of the distinguished commission was, as you know, Dr. Michael DeBakey, of Houston. If I had to boil the essence of his commission's report down to one short sentence it would be "The concerns of all of us are the concerns of all of us." Like Laënnec's plea to listen to the patient, this is a revolutionary utterance and will thus not find an immediate welcome everywhere. But in the long run I think it will win.

Meanwhile, I have my own private doubts about the degree to which some physicians, those not themselves engaged in physical medicine and rehabilitation, are aware of the subtleties that separate functioning from nonfunctioning. For example, I go for an annual physical checkup to the medical department of the corporation that used to employ me, and the doctor, having banged a few of my tendons with his hammer, says, "That left side seems pretty good. Squeeze my two fingers as hard as you can with your left hand."

Over the recent years this has come to be an invitation I accept with constantly mounting enthusiasm; I can squeeze quite hard with my "weak" left hand. So I mash his fingers good and proper, whereupon he returns good for evil by saying "Fine. You can use your typewriter again?" When I say, "No," he looks puzzled as well as hurt. But my ability to crush his fingers in my left fist has nothing to do with my ability to typewrite, which has vanished. Many subtle things are involved here, which the squeeze-and-ouch test tells no one anything about. Let me list a few:

The loss of proprioceptive sense on the left side means that the eye must watch, and help control, what the left hand is doing; it has no time to watch anything else. That upsets one applecart.

Loss of normal tactile sensation in the left hand's fingers robs the hand of its knowledge of accomplishment. There goes another applecart.

Although the hand has good power and *almost* complete freedom of motion the small muscles of its fingers are disobedient; thus, it cannot perform skilled acts (Applecart No. 3).

These are the primary applecarts. There are secondaries. For example, when the left hand stumbles the right hand becomes confused—much as one actor can become confused when another actor forgets his lines, although the first actor knows his part without flaw.

A residual of a cerebrovascular accident occurring in the brain's "dominant" hemisphere (with me the right, since I was born a southpaw) is a certain amount of speech and spelling difficulty. My spelling troubles mysteriously involve the letters *r* and *n*, and words with doubled letters, more than any others. When such words flash across the mind screen, a fuse is likely to blow somewhere in the motor circuits. The mind involved in writing something must then abandon its thought processes (if that's what they were) and give up its selection systems for clothing thoughts in words. Now you must open the syntax switch, unplug the grammar jacks and go fussing around with a flashlight to find out what went wrong in the brain-to-fingertips diagram.

I am using figurative language here because I don't know enough to use the literal. A process like using the typewriter takes place at a sort of fluid gallop. When the fluid flow is disturbed or when something breaks the rhythm of the gallop, *everything* goes to pieces. A moment ago things were clear, or reasonably so. Now they are confused. And in confusion I will leave this very deep subject, saying only that an equation between the muscular ability to squeeze and the psychoneuromuscular ability to get a set of words down on paper by pecking at keys with symbols on them simply doesn't exist, even if the words convey no thought deeper than "Now is the time for all good men to come to the aid of the party."

Yet, all in all, the possibilities that today lie in rehabilitation are tremendous: in the prevention of deformity; in improving range of motion; and in coming to hard grips with the activities of daily living. I know that some stroke patients cannot be rehabilitated. But on the other hand, some can be, when to the outward eye very little seems left to rehabilitate. When you have rehabilitated a wage-earner you have helped save a family. When you have rehabilitated a housewife you have helped save a family. And when you have saved a family you have helped protect your community wherever it is.

For *all* illness is communicable; not just the infectious or contagious diseases that are "reportable" to boards of health. All illness is communicable; today we stand only on the verge of recognizing this, and laymen must help the health professions in spreading these tidings.

It still takes too long to find the right things. For example, it took me five years to find that gem of a book, *Home Nursing and Medical Care*, by Dr. I. J. Rossman and Miss Doris Schwartz, R.N. Dr. Rossman is chief of professional services, Home Care Department, the Montefiore Hospital, New York City; Miss Schwartz is associate professor of public-health nursing at Cornell University—New York Hospital School of Nursing. Their book is a Dolphin Reference Book (paperback) and costs $1.45—if you can find it. It's worth ten times that, being written with wonderful, simple clarity and arranged by someone who knows how books are *used*.

There always arises, for the recovering stroke patient, the business of the tremendous trifle. I should have used a cane as soon as I was up and about again after my own stroke. I didn't have the brains to. Nor did any doctor ever advise it. (I had no foot drop, but I was tottery.) So I had to fall and crack my hip, thus bringing me into immediate contact with an orthopedic surgeon. After the accident *he* told me to use a cane, and the crack in my greater trochanter has thus been my individual contribution toward the multidisciplinary approach to stroke.

But there are even lesser things. When one hand is adrift and disobedient to your will, and its palm is insensate, making change and handling coins becomes a difficult act. This detail is too small for a physician's attention. But, in our capitalist society, one must go on making change or perish.

And where is one most likely to be called on to make change in a hurry? In a taxicab, of course, where even the art of breathing has now been rendered uncomfortable by the implacable designers in Detroit. It was a devoted nurse who solved this change-making problem for me: "Every night before you go to bed empty out your pockets and put all the pennies into that beer mug." She gestured toward a sentimental stein that has never held an ounce of brew. "Then," she explained, "you'll have fewer coins in your pocket and no confusion next day between dimes and pennies." Yes, of course I could have thought of that myself; so could a lot of other people. The point is, they didn't.

I did as I was told—I'm the ideal patient, really—and lo and behold another problem was reduced to manageable size. Moreover, there was a payoff. In my life, and in the present Great Society, the beer mug accumulates $5 worth of pennies every three months. My daughter takes these to the bank, at regular intervals, to relieve the coin shortage—and, of course, keeps the change. Everyone profits, just as Adam Smith said they would.

But there are some things a hemiparetic must learn for himself. Why do I never, in the privacy of my own apartment, go about barefoot or in my stockinged feet? Is it because I am afraid I may step on a tack? No! I have never stepped on a tack in my life, and I am convinced I never shall. The danger comes from above. When your muscular responses are laterally uneven, you are constantly fumbling things and dropping them—particularly things so light and impalpable that you get no neurogenic feedback from their weight on your affected side. Have you ever dropped a light, impalpable letter-opener, point down, on your unprotected big toe? It is a dagger through the heart—all the more so because you get no sensory warning that Brutus is about to lunge. You did not feel the dagger slip; thus, the toe took no evasive action.

Those who *really* specialize in dealing with the aftermaths of stroke or who have studied and systematized ADL—those activities of daily living—on behalf of patients with other disabilities deserve a special kind of medal. I pray they may get it. They seldom appear cast as heroes or heroines. But slowly, and gained from experience largely, they accumulate the kind of wisdom that is also the property of airline pilots, locomotive engineers or the masters of ships at sea and all those people, similarly marked, who know that although things are forever the same, they are also forever different, and that nothing can be so routine that it cannot be suddenly punctured by danger.

The medical arts have by now, today, such substantial and dramatic new accomplishments to show that I think the time has at last come when they can afford to drop the last remnants of the medieval mystery to which they still needed to cling when this century was younger. What I should like to say to today's physicians is: "Show your gifts, gentlemen; the patient needs to see them." The stroke patient asks, not to be told that "everything's going to be all right"—if it isn't—but to be told, honestly, and with proper knowledge and authority, how much there is that can help him and how new some of these things are.

The stroke patient would like a miracle, of course. In telling him he cannot have a miracle it is becoming less and less necessary to take hope away from him. I am thinking of the delicate ear of the therapist from Florida; how she could use it to pick one person out of a crowd of a thousand, and then tell him that his cane needed a new tip. *That* is therapy; it is medicine, it is healing, it is hope. It comes modestly packaged, and makes no great claims—indeed, perhaps none at all. But it can do a stroke patient more good than a *National Formulary* filled with pig-Latin from top to bottom for a thousand pages. It says to him in plain language, "Have confidence: I know what I'm doing."

4 Staff Expectations for Disabled Persons:
Helpful or Harmful

Nancy Kerr

Becoming disabled and finding oneself in a wheelchair alters a person's life situation not only with respect to what he can or cannot do physically— which is often the major focus of rehabilitation personnel—but also with respect to social interactions with others. Of particular importance are the places, activities, and relationships that the disabled person is restricted to or barred from entering.

The newly disabled person *knows*, phenomenologically, that he is the same person that he was before the injury to his body occurred. Yet, he is so frequently and persistently placed in inferior status positions by his professional "helpers" that, in time, he is coerced into wondering if he has become a different kind of person. The whole illness and disability experience places him in such new psychological situations where his customary behavior may stimulate responses so radically different from what he is accustomed to that he may often consciously or unconsciously question who he is, what roles are appropriate for him, and what he can expect to be able to do.

The earliest and possibly the critical answers to such identity and role questions come from the hospital or rehabilitation center's personnel in the everyday situations during treatment. In this paper, six pairs of situations drawn from personal experience suggest the implicit questions asked by patients and the subtle, often nonverbal, answers given by hospital and rehabilitation center staff members.

The first situation in each pair illustrates an answer that may lead a paraplegic patient to learn that the problem of adjustment to disability involves more than learning to get around on wheels: It makes explicit the probability that he may have to adjust to being a second-class citizen faced not only with physical obstacles but also with social devaluation. It teaches him that as society views him, he is no longer a responsible, employable adult but psychologically and sociologically a child. The answer given in the second situation in each pair of examples shows how a similar situation was handled in a way that told the patient that he was still a respectable and responsible human being.

This paper was adapted from one presented at the American Psychological Association, Washington, D.C., September 1969.

SITUATION I

Patient: Who am I?

Staff I: You Are a Second-Class Citizen The submissive and devaluating aspects of the *role* of patient are so frequently accepted by both patient and staff that some curious phenomena become apparent only when a person in a wheelchair enters a medical institution as a professional. On countless occasions, I have been wheeling along in treatment settings in various parts of the country, attending to my business as a teacher, researcher, or clinical psychologist when an attendant or nurse would hustle alongside and challengingly or sarcastically say, "Hey, where do you think you're going?" or sometimes, "You're not supposed to be out here—go to your room." On one occasion, solely on the basis of my occupancy of a wheelchair, a nurse tried physically to put me to bed! More than once my wheelchair has been hijacked by an attendant who, without comment, wheeled me to the dining room of his institution.

Although I have no objection to consuming a free meal, in general, following one of the "You can't come in here" comments or, "You must go there" actions, I tactfully explain my business. Invariably, the response is, "Oh, I'm sorry, I thought you were a patient!" There is immediate recognition by the staff member that his behavior toward me was inappropriate. But there does not seem to be the slightest trace of awareness that the same ordering, grabbing, and shoving would be inappropriate even if I were a patient.

One is reminded of the unwritten rules of the army: "If it moves, salute it; if it's on the ground, pick it up; if it's a lineup, join it." The unwritten rule of perhaps too many rehabilitation personnel often seems to be "If *it's* in a wheelchair, *it* must be a patient—push *it* somewhere else."

Staff II: You Are a Human Being In good rehabilitation centers, alternative kinds of behavior can be found among institutional personnel. I remember one attendant in particular who was named as "outstandingly helpful" by every person I interviewed in a study on the meaning of help. Each day when the rest of the staff rushed out of the physical therapy room for a coffee break while leaving me stranded on a floor mat to rest, this gentleman would return to bring me a cup of hot coffee and a portion of whatever goodies were in the dining room. In general, when he had taken a person somewhere, he never failed to wait a moment to ask if there was anything else he could do. He always approached patients from the front where he could be seen (rather than suddenly grabbing their wheelchairs from behind); and he asked, for example, if one was ready to go to dinner. He was the person who would stand by and give moral support when a frightened patient was supposed to be transferring into bed independently. (Few people realize that the space between a wheelchair and a bed can look as deep and forbidding as the Grand Canyon!) He was one of those rare people who had the sensitivity to handle hundreds of situations, big and little, in ways that were truly helpful from the patients' standpoint.

There was another attendant in the same institution who was liked by patients almost as well because he practiced the kinds of behavior just described, although his actions appeared to be somewhat less skillful and natural. When I asked him where he had learned to be so considerate, he replied that he had had a course for psychiatric attendants at Michael Reese Hospital in Chicago. When he came to a rehabilitation center, he was surprised to learn that disabled persons like to be treated as *people* just as psychotics do. His approach, however, was pragmatic rather than empathic. He had learned that if he told a patient he was going to be five minutes late, if he asked whether the patient was ready to go, if he chatted about the weather or the topics of the day, then, he found, the patients didn't gripe so much about matters over which he had no control and his job was much easier.

Apparently some people are naturally therapeutic in their relationships with patients, others can be educated to behave nicely and therapeutically even if it doesn't come naturally.

SITUATION II

Patient: How Hard Is It Going to Be to Get Around in a Wheelchair? Can I Really Be Independent?

Staff I: It Is Going to Be Very Difficult Indeed   I have a special problem with elevators. If I try to enter one of the elevators for "regular people," usually I am told that I must go to the patient's elevators somewhere in the rear since regular elevators are for regular people and not for wheelchairs or wheelchair people. (Comments, in this situation, about "the patient as nigger" are not appreciated.) After finding the patient elevator, two potential problems remain: (a) If some observant soul discovers that I am not wearing pajamas or a hospital robe, I may not be allowed in *that* elevator either; (b) some hospitals have a role that all patients in transit must be accompanied at all times by an attendant.

Staff II: You Are a Responsible Person Who Is Quite Capable of Getting Around on Your Own   On the brighter side, some treatment centers have a system that allows mobile patients to go almost anywhere in or out of the institution if they leave a note at the nurses' station specifying where they can be found if needed and when they will return. In institutions using this system, usually, the patients are responsible also for getting themselves to appointments and therapies on time.

SITUATION III

Patient: Can a Disabled Person Really Go Out and Earn a Living?

Staff I: Probably Not   One of the finest and most prestigious rehabilitation centers in the country has excellent ramps and bathroom facilities in all patient areas. The room used for professional meetings, however, can be reached only by a long stairway: There is no elevator. While the patients back on the wards are being told that they can enter or re-enter the world of work, apparently no one ever expected that someone in a wheelchair might attend a professional meeting on rehabilitation. If rehabilitation centers contain impassable architectural barriers, how realistic is it to expect that other settings will be accessible?

Staff II: Sure. See for Yourself Another well-known rehabilitation center[1] employs disabled persons for responsible positions in the organization without discrimination. At one time the bookkeeper, head receptionist, head nurse, building manager, a physician, and many others did their jobs efficiently from wheelchairs. Some of them had extensive arm involvement as well as paraplegia, and some used breathing aids. However, there were no cosmetic criteria. All that was asked was that the person should do his job well. Equally important, there was no physical space in the entire center that was inaccessible by wheelchair. Of course, not every person with a disability can or should work in a rehabilitation center. But the high visibility of *some* workers with serious physical disabilities holding responsible positions, and functioning well in them, had striking effects on both patients and staff. No amount of reassuring verbalization alone could have yielded the same result. The whole story that employ-ment was possible for the disabled was believable in that setting. And no one dared make impertinent remarks to a person occupying a wheelchair—he might turn out to be one's boss!

SITUATION IV

Patient: Do I Have Any Control Over My Own Fate, or Am I Just a Body Being Run Through the Repair Shop?

Staff I: Just Put Yourself in Our Hands. We Know What's Best for You Frank Shontz reported on interesting research at APA a year or two ago in which he demonstrated that at the staff meeting where the patient supposedly participated in his own rehabilitation planning, the "team" did almost all the talking. The few remarks made by the patient were generally confined to "Yes, sir."

When patients inquire about why some therapeutic procedure is being employed, it is not uncommon for them to be told: "It's good for you," or "Doctor's orders."

It is quite possible that patients would be more cooperative and work harder in physical therapy, for example, if they had a very clear idea of what the exercises were intended to accomplish, if they knew *why* the pain should be endured, and if their agreement was solicited in advance. Does any wheelchair-loving paraplegic ever forget the battle over whether or not he was entitled to refuse to learn brace-walking?

---

[1] A well deserved pat on the back to William Spencer, M.D. and his staff at the Texas Institute for Rehabilitation and Research.

Perhaps the most common way of telling the patient that he is a machine in the shop for repair is the habit some staffers have of communicating with the attendant pushing the wheelchair instead of with the patient himself. The patient thus finds himself sandwiched between two white coats with one asking the other, "Now, where does she go?"

Staff II: You Are an Active Member of Your Rehabilitation Team I had a physical therapist who, while working within the framework of the medical prescription, let me make every decision possible concerning therapy. To be sure, the initial options were small, like which exercises we'd work on first, or which chair I'd learn to transfer into next. Later I was encouraged to make more crucial decisions such as whether it was more important to me—with my plans and obligations—to be a resident patient or a day patient.

SITUATION V

Patient: Because I Am Dependent and Must Ask for Help, Am I an Inferior or Bad Person?

Staff I: You Sure Are I can think of no single experience more humiliating than having an attendant complain about what a nuisance it is to have to turn you over in bed or give you a glass of water. And yet, the pecking order of most hospitals is such that the only safe way for an attendant to gripe about being overworked is to unleash his hostility on the patient.

Staff II: We're Here to Help

There are true professionals in every occupation, i.e., people who do their jobs well and graciously even when they don't feel like it. The image they present is that they are pleased to be of service.

For three months following the onset of polio, I had been in intense pain that was relieved temporarily only by being repositioned. I had done battle with a nurse throughout each night about how often I could be turned over. Upon arriving at another hospital, I asked the attendant the first night what the schedule was for turning patients. She seemed surprised and said, "There's no schedule. Whenever you feel uncomfortable, just press this button and I'll be in. That's what I'm here for."

I said, "But, ma'am—I'm *always* uncomfortable!"

"That's okay. We'll move you every five minutes if necessary." She fixed me up with the nine pillows I needed in those days. The next morning, when I awoke from my first night's sleep in three months, I discovered that the other 20 patients for whom she cared had had similar experiences.

SITUATION VI

Patient: Sometimes I Worry That Being Disabled is the Same As Being a Child

Staff I: Right! Probably no one has ever survived extensive rehabilitation without undergoing one or more of the parties put on by some well-intentioned community group. On such occasions, appropriate patient behavior consists of smiling while someone places a party hat on your head, saying "thank-you" for the lollypop or other goody that traditionally is handed out, and applauding with some enthusiasm when the little darlings from Kook City's School of Elocution, Singing, and Dancing sing "Kookaberra." The consequences of declining to attend such an affair may range from mild reprimands for being uncooperative to a referral to the psychiatrist on suspicion of "situational depression."

Staff II: You Are an Adult Who Happens to Be in a Wheelchair Probably one good rule of thumb for any recreational therapist might be to ask whether a proposed party is something she herself would like to attend or if she would throw such a party for her own adult friends. In some degree, a seriously ill person may tend to become more egocentric in thought and childish in behavior, but these are transient responses to stress that should be extinguished.

There are many aspects of a patient's medical regimen in which it might be unrealistic to allow him complete freedom of choice. Other regions of the rehabilitation center, such as the recreational activities for example, are not so circumscribed. The staff has the option of strengthening childish behavior by placing patients in childish situations or they can use recreational activities, from the very beginning, to create situations that encourage mature freedom of choice, relearning or maintenance of "taking responsibility," and strengthening of the process of decision making.

DISCUSSION

Common questions asked by patients, consciously or unconsciously, have been outlined together with some positive and negative answers they receive from the behavior of the treatment staff in everyday situations. There are many more such questions often unverbalized or unperceived but which, nevertheless, may have marked effects on the rehabilitation process. Unfortunately, there is little objective evidence.

Although there have been a number of excellent, descriptive reports of the mental hospital milieu by psychologists and sociologists who have entered such institutions posing as patients, there appear to be no similar participant studies of the social-psychological environment of hospitals or rehabilitation centers. Such studies are needed. Both formal research studies to provide "hard data" and informal participation to increase the understanding of staff would be valuable. The latter could be accomplished easily by any person working with the disabled simply by borrowing a wheelchair and moving into a center for a day, a week, or a month.

The following are obvious possibilities for needed research:
1. What is the nature of staff-patient interactions? In the light of our ignorance, descriptive and counting studies are of first importance, but ultimately such work must lead to the specification of the conditions under which such interactions can become more positive and growth-inducing.
2. What is the social structure of the

general hospital or the rehabilitation center? What are the realistic barriers that impede or frustrate patients' psychological progress? Considerable and instructive work along this line had been done for the mental hospital and the mentally ill. Similar studies of the physically ill and the disabled are desirable.

3. On a more limited basis, what can be done within one small aspect of an institution's structure to describe and modify the roles that patients play? In particular, attention might be paid to the restrictions on personal freedom, freedom to choose and select, and the reduced responsibility for one's own fate that seem inevitably to come with living in an institution. What can be done to increase the decision-making powers of the patient? Equally important are studies of patients who have accepted the patient role too well. Under what conditions can staff facilitate their relearning of the mature and responsible adult role?

4. The chronic problem patient who is perceived as too demanding and too dependent is an example of a specific research problem that can be studied independently of institutional structure. Often we jump to the conclusion that such a person has unmet dependence needs stemming from childhood experiences. That may be so. Systematic observation of the social-psychological situation, however, may suggest equally tenable explanations. For example, the patient may fear injury if he attempts new tasks or fear being left alone unaided in situations with which he cannot cope if he ever starts doing things for himself. Some-

times these fears actually may be reasonable; sometimes not. Under such beliefs, however, it is reasonable for the person to play it safe and to insist that someone else take responsibility.

Similarly, a patient may fear the loss of social contact. If the only way a patient obtains attention and social contact is to ask for something, it is predictable that patients will do a lot of asking.

Finally, the level of hostility between patients and staff may be an important variable. If patients and attendants are fighting, the demand "you are going to do this for me—or else" is one way for a patient to sustain his self-esteem, even if it is an unhealthy and less desirable way than some others.

It may be reasonable to start looking for unmet dependence needs only if it is certain that (a) the patient has reason to know that he will succeed in a task that is requested of him; (b) he is not afraid; (c) he is assured of social contact and appropriate attention even if he does take care of himself; and (d) he is not "mad" at anyone. No doubt there are some patients who demand that others do for them what they are well able to do for themselves. Even here, however, the problem is not how to classify them but how to create a therapeutic environment that will help resolve infantile problems.

In summary, the expectations of staff are helpful if they help the patient to gain or regain maturity and self-esteem. They hinder if they impede the patient's progress. *Help*, as Tamara Dembo has said, is whatever the person perceives as help. Such a definition is good to remember because it constantly leads us back to the patient with the simple question: "What can I do to help?" Lee Meyerson has described the ideal helper as being like the blockers on a football team who run interference, clear the paths, create the opportunities, and make it as easy as possible for the patient to take the ball and run with it. That, perhaps, is our major task as rehabilitation workers. It is the patient's ball game, and by our appropriate or inappropriate expectations and behavior, we can help or we can hinder.

5 The Language Disorders:

A Personal and Professional Account of Aphasia

McKenzie Buck

In light of professional contacts with stricken patients during my post-stroke years, it has become evident that my personal experiences are markedly similar to the majority of those expressed by other patients and their family groups. It is important to stress that patients with similar degrees of recovery are those who were fortunate in having family members demonstrate positive warmth, affection, and acceptance as a result of continuous professional guidance.

Unfortunately far too many immediate families, as well as professional personnel, seem to concentrate on isolated behavioral and physical problems. If we are to provide maximum assistance, the patient must be viewed as a total human being. Sole concentration upon the deviated aspects of the illness is bound to have a negative effect upon well members of the family for they, too, may demonstrate obvious behavioral changes that can be detrimental to the patient's adjustment.

A stroke is actually a family illness and assistance should be readily available for the entire household.

The side effects of brain damage may markedly deter the recovery process. When there is a history of neurological trauma, such as a stroke, epilepsy is apt to develop. This is not a shameful disorder and is a condition that has nothing to do with insanity or heredity. Physicians now know that approximately 8 out of every 10 persons who have seizures can lead relatively normal lives. We in the behavioral areas must do our utmost to recognize symptoms that may reveal one of the many types of seizure patterns and thus assist physicians in their diagnostic procedures.

Epileptic attacks are most assuredly frightening for both the patient and his family. I can speak of this with firsthand information. Shortly after my first stroke in 1957, I experienced a severe convulsion. It was not until this extreme attack occurred that a *Jacksonian* type of epilepsy was recognized. Since this time, medication has controlled the severity and frequency of such episodes. This kind of attack is similar to the *Grand-Mal* seizure in that there may be a total loss of consciousness. However, immediately after the stroke, I was one of the vast number of stricken patients who

Reprinted from the Journal of Rehabilitation, 1963, (6):37–38.

did not experience a complete loss of consciousness; consequently, it was extremely difficult to diagnose without an accurate observational report from my own family group.

Without a competent degree of language recovery to assist in my description of sensations, it was impossible for laymen to understand periods of extreme irritability and increased aphasic type disruptions. One of the major psychological avenues of relief and adjustment was highly dependent upon my ventilating feelings of fear and depression that were so easily stimulated by the approach of the epileptic attacks.

Such attacks, far too often, are simply interpreted as patterns of functional obnoxious behavior, and often result in a patient's being dropped from therapeutic programs prior to interprofessional consultations.

As one may readily understand, the lessening or complete removal of such attacks may greatly contribute to emotional and intellectual improvements in such patients. The family must maintain close contact with their attending physician, thus assisting him in the acquisition of information that may be pertinent to thorough medical treatment.

We as professionals are obligated to provide careful family instruction to assist in lessening the fears that may exist in the minds of those within the household. Such a procedure is far more important to patient recovery than any retraining techniques recommended in our literature. As may be well recognized, *your* best learning situations were those in which you experienced the least amount of depressing threats.

It is important to be continually aware of the fact that the patient may have an extreme inability to quickly recall both current and past events. The stricken patient can suffer drastic emotional disturbances all too suddenly when we do not have a thorough understanding of this behavior. If he is subjected to a continuous sequence of unreasonable demands, he has no choice but to voluntarily remain silent and completely withdraw from any social situation. When this occurs, the depressive psychological overlay may stimulate extreme suicidal plans and/or actual attempts.

If we can only recognize our own limitations in trying to follow a highly technical discussion of some topic such as atomic energy, we may gain some insight into the conversational problems being experienced by the stricken patient. For example, in reading the newspaper we "normals" seek articles that have a personal appeal. These bits of information usually have a vocabulary that is easily understood, resulting in an appropriate interpretation of the content. We tend to ignore articles utilizing a lengthy technical vocabulary.

This type of behavior is actually no different from that of a patient who has even more difficulty with memory spans and language interpretations. We must be extremely cautious, when speaking with stroke patients, to utilize a simple vocabulary combined with a frequent referral to the topic being discussed.

An example of the extreme limitations in memory may be demonstrated by a discussion of my own deviations immediately following the stroke. For a matter of several months, it was not uncommon for me to eat a large breakfast at 8 a.m., then by 9 a.m. be wondering why I had not had breakfast. During this hour my internal body pressure from the food intake had often completely disappeared. Aside from the basic necessities of survival—combined with an attempt to acquire a pleasurable experience—there was little else to occupy my mind.

My insightful wife would calmly discuss the fact that I had eaten breakfast and, for the most part, I would have an immediate recall when I was *quietly* reminded of the event.

However, behavior of this type is not as readily understood by personnel outside of the family; we, as professional persons, must keep in mind that the patient usually has an immediate recall of events if they are noted in a kind and easy manner by those within the situation. This kind of behavior is usually not pursued merely to attract attention, for it is most often a result of an extremely short memory span and self-disgust.

When the patient begins to initiate obvious symptoms of insight, it is necessary that we remember he is bound to have some internal disgust concerning his failure in recalling current activities. He is condemning himself enough without suffering an increase of frustration resulting from negative comments by family and clinical personnel. You may assuredly contribute to the alleviation of deep and morbid depression through the quiet acceptance of repeated behavior for, as time progresses, the patient will likely acquire further insight to assist himself in maintaining improved emotional stability.

At this point, it must be strongly emphasized that there is an unfortunate degree of professional failure concerning careful intellectual evaluations. Intelligence tests frequently reveal variations in different types of thought processes. For the most part, the normal individual will acquire scores that are relatively equal in the various portions of the test such as problem solving, vocabulary, arithmetic, etc. This is not necessarily true of the brain damaged patient, however, for he may reveal a high problem solving score in contrast to a very low vocabulary score. In other words, there is not an over-all reduction of scores on all types of tests in the intellectual evaluation.

Prior to any clinical retraining, every attempt should be made to at least estimate the patient's current intellectual ability. If, for example, he has a score in the 60's—such as I experienced initially—extreme care must be taken to avoid an unrealistically high degree of professional expectation. Far too often, this particular means of evaluation is overlooked and retesting is completely absent.

The patient should have repeated intellectual evaluations at least every four to six weeks. In this manner, our clinical procedures may be far more realistic, both in terms of family insights and patient abilities. Forced retraining may destroy even reasonable expectations when the patient is continually confronted with demoralizing results which, in turn, amplify stronger desires for complete withdrawal from society. Again it must be stressed that we are obligated to maintain consistent and lengthy family contact to assist us in the maintenance of appropriate training procedures.

Family and professional personnel must keep in mind that the patient is basically starting over again and it is absolutely essential that we demonstrate as much insight and kindness in this instance as we do with the very young child who is acquiring initial language and social development.

We rarely push, over-pressure, or over-anticipate rapid vocabulary development within the child. A youngster acquires his language through kind, patient, and nondirect stimulation over a period of several years. Perhaps with this in mind, we should re-examine our professional approach to the language problem of the stricken patient.

From a personal standpoint, I found no assistance from direct vocabulary and language drills. The majority of my successes were almost wholly dependent upon my psychological security and the deletion of unrealistic pressures concerning word by word expression in conversations. It was not until the word and language drills were withdrawn entirely that I began to experience a significant degree of reasonable expression. Professionally, we need to examine our own language behavior in order that we may understand the problems involved with the aphasic disorder.

Some persons reading this article may have had very disturbing experiences in classes dealing with public address. Initially at least the greatest difficulties in formulating speeches were concerned with an over-attention to language formation and expression. This resulted in grossly uninteresting presentations combined with emotional traumas that disturbed reasonable communication, leaving the student in a complete state of exhaustion upon the completion of the exercise.

As time progresses, however, such persons may acquire an ability to pay less attention to the sequence of verbal expression, thus returning to a more normal conversational manner. Consequently, a predominance of the efforts can be concentrated upon thought processes of interest to the speaker and contagious to those within the audience. Unfortunately, certain individuals are unable to eventually delete their attention to verbal expressions and, as a result, the message continues to be lost to both the speaker and his listener.

If this occurs among those who have no apparent neurological damage, does it not seem reasonable that a stricken patient should also have markedly similar anxieties? It is important to stress that such a patient is already over-concerned without having negative reactions from those within the immediate environment and clinical settings.

It was not until I found it possible to ignore the "big ears" of those about me that I began to demonstrate progress in free expression. Language exercises were useless despite the word drills in booklets, pictures, etc. The recovery process was really no different than the initial vocabulary enlarge-ment experienced as a youngster. The less I concentrated upon individual words, the more meaningful my ex-pression became, resulting in fewer fears and thus lessening feelings of in-adequacy.

I still have unpredictable periods of difficulty concerning the recall of proper names. Fatigue appears to have no bearing upon the disorder and, quite frankly, I have no explanation for the causation of the apparent neurological short circuits. It is quite evident that I shall be unsuccessful, for the most part, in attempting to explain the problem. My emotional adjust-ments are far more secure if I simply skip any explanation and proceed as though I feel as normal as those about me. This, as you may well understand, was not an easy attitude to develop and it requires an abundance of self-discipline.

Other patients, with a similar his-tory, have expressed identical reac-tions to their experiences with word drills, picture games, and over-stimula-tion. Also, the families of other pa-tients who progressed satisfactorily simply accepted each individual as a *person* who may respond appropri-ately with extensive patience, cour-tesy, and time. In view of the preced-ing, it seems apparent that we need to carefully re-examine our clinical proce-dures.

In summary, the major considera-tions in personal and language adjust-ment of the stricken patient involve far more than language drills in isola-tion. First of all, careful medical care must be established. Unless the family members have enough information to assist in motivating them to be ex-tremely conscientious, the medical fol-low-up may be deterred due to their lack of careful cooperation.

As far as any language retraining is concerned, same will be of little value until the overlying psychological dis-ruptions are well-controlled. Undue pressures in solving unrealistic lan-guage drills may markedly interfere with both psychological and physical adjustments.

This point is stressed to empha-size the fact that most brain damaged patients have unpredictable periods of extreme neurological and physical fa-tigue. With fatigue comes discourage-ment, and any learning process of ab-stract materials may well lead to chronic states of depressive with-drawal.

Careful family guidance should continually be available, for it is the family who can do most to assist in language retraining. Unless they have a thorough understanding of the total picture, they, too, may join the pa-tient in attempting to escape from the situation.

6 A Quadriplegic Young Man Looks at Treatment

Twelve years ago I was out with the boys for an evening of fun that included beer drinking and riding around in a car. I was later told that we had hit an oak tree dead center. All I can remember is that one minute I was walking around a closed gas station, and the next thing I knew I was waking up in a hospital room, with my dad looking down at me and saying "Don't try and move because you're paralyzed and you can't." By that time the doctors had given me pain killers, and I was not too alert. But I still tried to move. Finding that my father was right, I went back to sleep thinking to myself, "Well, it won't last long." For the next week or two I remembered little. But four incidents or periods of awareness do stand out in my mind related to the initial adjustment. The first was the sound of a drill and many voices. They were drilling holes in my head for traction, but I remember I didn't ask *what* they were doing or *why* they were doing it. I not only had complete confidence they knew what they were doing, I had no choice or say in the matter. My first adjustment concerned *being dependent* on those people who knew and were capable of dealing with all the details of my injury. As time passed I gained faith and

hope that I was going to walk again, and it was this faith and hope that helped me make the initial adjustment despite the extreme frustration of being so helpless. If at this time a doctor or nurse had told me that I was never going to walk again, I might have given up altogether or just made everyone's life, including mine, miserable. *It is for this reason that I firmly believe that a patient in this early stage should not be told anything that will take away any hope he may have.*

HE SUFFERED FROM GUILT

The second incident deals with the boy who was driving the car. I had not seen him since the day he checked out of the hospital. This lead to the realization that what happened to me did not affect just me. It affected everyone who was close to me. He suffered guilt, even though I never blamed him for what happened. A friend of the family left my hospital room, went into a linen closet and fainted. I knew that it was my responsibility to set people at ease—friends, family members, and strangers.

This can be a very strained process especially if people come in groups.

Reprinted from the Journal of Rehabilitation, 1974, 49(6):22–25.

There were times during these early months that I would pretend I was asleep so visitors would not come in, especially people I did not know well. But it is important that an injured person not get so caught up with his troubles that he forgets the people around him. This early realization will be a big factor in his ultimate adjustment.

FACIAL EXPRESSIONS SPEAK

The third experience was the awareness of the faces I saw in the waiting room as I was being taken to surgery. I can still see the expressions I saw that night, and later, on the faces of people who came to visit me. At that time I could not really understand why I saw expressions of pity, sadness, confusion, and inquisitiveness. My attitude was one of hope and faith.

Still, I find some people (now as then) that see me as a person—maybe with a problem, but just a person. This takes a lot of pressure off me, especially when meeting someone for the first time. Whatever people's reactions are to a disabled individual, there has to be a two-way adjustment. Learning how to deal with people who appear uncomfortable is very important for the disabled person. But the learning period is slow in the beginning stages.

ANGER AT THE WORLD CONTROLLED

The fourth experience that I can link to adjustment was the helpless feeling.

In most cases of cervical injury, there is total paralysis for many weeks, depending on how high the lesion and how extensive the damage. During these weeks of total paralysis, you can do nothing for yourself. For me, those first weeks were spent lying in traction on a stryker frame staring at the ceiling for four hours, then at the floor for four hours, turned every four hours night and day. Someone had to feed me, bathe me, brush my teeth, help my bowels move, even scratch my nose. I was totally dependent on other people to do everything for me. It is hard to move from complete independence to complete reliance. However, it is an adjustment you must make or frustration will eat at you until anger at the whole world turns to depression. You can develop an "I don't care" attitude or even a "death wish." When a person gives up at this point, his road to recovery will be that much longer and harder. This is why I emphasized earlier the importance of hope. Nothing or no one should be allowed to take it away or destroy it. Call it denial—and a counselor would—but it is an important defensive weapon for the newly injured individual. At this point an injured person is so disoriented and confused that hope and faith or denial is one of the most important psychological attitudes he or she can have.

A DIFFERENT HOSPITAL CONCEPT

When I was told about the rehabilitation center—in my case Kaiser Rehabilitation Center—I could hardly wait to get there to begin working. I told myself, "I'm helpless now, but just wait until I get there; these things will change. All I need is exercise to build myself back up." I already had leg movement, even if it was involuntary. This attitude carried over into my transfer from the general hospital to the rehabilitation center.

By the time my transfer was complete, I did have partial movement in my arms and hands, and my expectations were high. When I entered the rehabilitation center, I soon became aware that it was not like an ordinary hospital. I had entered a whole new world.

Everyone at one time or another has either been in a general hospital, as a patient, or as a visitor. When you think of a hospital you associate it with quietness, people lying in bed, and soft-spoken nurses present. Few people think or hear about rehabilitation centers—let alone visit them. When I became a patient in one I was in a kind of shock because I did not know what to expect. I had to reorient myself to the whole rehabilitation hospital concept which was so different from my earlier idea of "hospital."

patient, a patient they were trained to deal with, and they were not pampering anyone. Sometimes it made be feel like something they wanted to study instead of a person who needed help. However, when I talked with a doctor on a one-to-one basis, I found he understood my situation.

The other patients and the atmosphere go together because it was the patients who made up the atmosphere, at least the majority of it. For the first time I saw disabilities to which I had previously never given any thought. I also saw people who had the same injury that I did, which, in a strange way made me feel better. I no longer felt like I was the only one going through this. What really got to me at first were the screams and blank stares from those totally incapable of adjusting.

The second major adjustment was the therapy and all it entailed. When one begins therapy it suddenly brings him into full view of himself, where he is, where he is headed, and what point he wants to try and reach. It is the first few weeks and in particular the first day that contains the most frustrating and in some ways most embarrassing experiences yet faced.

HARD OR INSENSITIVE?

First, I had to become accustomed to the staff, the patients, and the whole atmosphere of the center. I had to understand what seemed to be a hard or insensitive attitude on the part of the nurses and orderlies. I was no longer a special case. I was just another

NURSES HELP ME

The first day went something like this. The hospital routine began early with breakfast. Next came the bed bath, toothbrushing and a shave, which a student nurse had to do for me. I had been told that I would be seeing the gym, but when they told me that I would be fully dressed, it came as a surprise. Soon I had two student nurses, with the help of an orderly, stuffing me into my clothes. When they had finished, there I was, a 145-pound body stuck into clothes that were two sizes too big, clothes that I had only worn a few months before when I weighed 195 pounds. The next thing I knew I was being lifted by two orderlies into a wheelchair. All of a sudden things began going dark, and I knew I was going to pass out, but before I could say anything it was too late. When my eyes focused, I could smell flowers and see a hand waving something in front of my face. I found myself looking up at a lot of worried faces, someone had tipped my chair back so the blood could get back to my head. Then the sweet flower smell turned into ammonia. I said something, and someone said, "He's all right." Soon I was on my way for my first look at the gym.

A FRIENDLY PHYSICAL THERAPIST

When the attendant pushed me closer, I could hear noises, some familiar and some very strange. I was pushed through the door, and there was the gym. My first reaction was that it looked like a zoo! Still in a daze, I was wheeled over to a floor pulley. A physical therapist walked over, introduced himself and welcomed me, which made me a little more comfortable. As I was looking around in amazement, the therapist strapped me to a pulley

and said, "Try that." When I pulled it, it felt like I was pulling 50 pounds, but when I looked down I was just barely budging five pounds. I knew I was weak, but I wasn't quite ready for that. All I could think was that I had a long way to go. Deep down, frustration was beginning, but at the same time my hope was stronger than before.

Then I made the mistake of turning my head to see what was going on behind me. As I turned I came face-to-face with myself in a full length mirror, and for the first time I saw what I really looked like. The best description I can give is an advertisement for a care package—skinny, mussy hair, and oversized clothes.

When the end of that first day came I was totally frustrated and very tired, so tired that I didn't care if I had to be fed. The day had shown me that I had a long way to go and would need a lot of help in doing it. It was then that the *reality* of my situation caught up with me. The first few weeks in a rehabilitation center is a trying time for the newly disabled. Some lose all motivation, and some even begin to contemplate suicide because they see the problems they face as insurmountable. It is quite hard to face the fact that you are going to have to learn to do things all over again—things once taken for granted.

MAKING "OUTSIDE" A REALITY

As time passes, a person progresses in physical strength and independence, but progress, especially for the quadriplegic, is slow. There are times when you can only gauge your progress by the comments of visiting family and friends who have not seen you for awhile. When visitors do come, little time is spent on what is happening within the center, conversation is usually centered around outside activities. Although like most patients, I felt secure in the rehabilitation center, talking about what was happening outside seemed to be a way to escape for a time. Engaging in this type of interaction can also become a necessity. It sets everyone at ease and relaxes what sometimes can be an awkward atmosphere. As I mentioned earlier, putting people at ease is an adjustment a disabled person must make because meeting people is a continuous process unless you withdraw from society completely.

It was about a month and a half into my five-month stay at the rehabilitation center when I began thinking about the future. I was getting stronger and more independent in some areas of personal care. I could now, with time, push myself back to the ward from the gym. I did not want to be a burden to anyone, so I vowed that I would not let them send me home until I could do as much as possible for myself. That included transferring myself to and from my wheelchair.

Two events caused me to think about my future. One was when I was given my own wheelchair. It struck me when they brought it that this chair is part of me—also how many ways is it

going to limit me. Deep down I still had hope of walking again, but still I knew I must adjust to my situation.

PROBE GENERATES HOSTILITY

The second event was a visit to the social worker. She not only probed into my family life but also began to question me about what I would like to do occupationally. I was not ready for this. Of all the problems I had facing me at that time, my future job was the least of my worries.

I immediately became hostile toward her. I felt she didn't understand and was pushing me into something I did not feel was important. Our visits stopped. Dealing with the future is something that should be approached slowly in the initial sessions.

It was at this point that my doctor hit me with "this is it; you are paralyzed, and you have to *accept* it." I struck back with "I may adjust to it, but I will never accept it." This was the first time this had been said to me in the eight months since my accident. I thank God that, at least in my own case, it was not said earlier because I don't know what my reaction would have been. A person will in his own time and way come to terms with what has happened and adjust to it. It is something that cannot be forced.

To summarize this area of adjustment, I must emphasize the importance I place on the rehabilitation center in relation to the spinal cord injured person. It is here that some of his most important adjustments to himself and to his limitations are made, allowing him to cope successfully on the outside.

AMBIVALENCE TOWARD HOME

I did not really want to go home because I felt secure in the center. I was surrounded by people who were in the same situation or even worse than myself which, in a strange way, made me feel better. Also, when I needed something done there were those there who were paid just for that purpose. This eliminated any guilt feelings that I had about being a burden.

I feel that I was fortunate to be able to adjust to home and family life in stages. There are many who have either progressed physically as far as they can, or for personal or financial reasons, must make a complete break from the center. Many who voluntarily or involuntarily make this break find it difficult adjusting to the outside world. Some have been known to do something to themselves to be readmitted, and a few have taken their lives. As for myself, I knew that I would be dependent on my family. I was fortunate, however. I had a family more than willing to take on this responsibility. I have seen and heard of a few parents who had to be forced into coming and taking their son or daughter home. There have also been cases where parents have had to assume this responsibility because the husband or wife of a patient just couldn't face it. These are usually unstable marriages to begin with, and the end result is divorce. Except for parents, you really cannot blame these people because as I mentioned earlier, the injured person is not the only one traumatically affected by the injury.

Once I was home, some of the pessimism that I had built up in my mind was removed. But much of what I expected came true, not regarding my family but with the barriers I would encounter. There were architectural barriers which I had not even considered. *Home* is a house that for the most part is not suitable or adapted for a wheelchair. One evening eight months earlier, I left a beautiful and comfortable home in the country, and when I returned it was full of obstacles. There were narrow hallways with sharp corners, narrow bathroom doors, carpets that made pushing the chair difficult, sinks that were either too high or difficult to get to, a few steps, and outside, rough ground except on the patio. Once again, I felt frustrated and helpless. But like others, I had to adjust to these barriers because they were obstacles I would continue to face. I could no longer use my car unless someone lifted me in and would drive. It became a big production for me to leave the house. Now I could only sit and look and think back on things that used to be, or regret that I had put off things I wanted to do. I was forced to find different ways to spend my time and keep myself busy at anything that would take my mind off the past. Still my mind would at times wander into the past or a make-believe present.

Time became an important factor

to family activities. Everyone's schedule revolved around me in many ways. Since I was still pretty helpless, things that once took me a few minutes to accomplish now took much longer, even with help. A simple task such as getting up in the morning became a family project; three people accomplished in an hour what at one time took me no more than 30 minutes. To this day I still find myself not allowing enough time. I guess, it's a way of fighting my disability even though I continue to lose.

OFF TO COLLEGE

My basic personality had been that of an introvert, especially around large groups of people. This added to my self-consciousness about being in a wheelchair. To put it simply, I did not want to go out into the public again. All my arguments and objections were to no avail. On the opening day of school, I was practically thrown into the car, and I was off to school—a junior college. I remember that all the way down there I wished that it all would have ended the night of the accident.

My resocialization baptism was very sudden. In all my classes I had to sit in the front of the room so everyone saw me as they walked in or as they sat in their seats. There was nothing I could do except try to ignore the other students, which was impossible. I soon found myself staring back at those who were staring at me. It was a simple matter of "sink or swim." I

guess I decided that I had gone too far to sink, so I swam. This can be a point in some people's lives where sinking, to them, is preferable.

Resocialization—getting back into society—is a big step. Those who do make it step forward. Those who don't simply dig a hole for themselves, and this can become a lonely and depressing place. I was again fortunate that I had people around me who would not let me isolate myself.

SURVIVE WE MUST

The biggest problem in making the adjustment in resocialization is that there is a big conflict between what you now are—disabled—and how society is structured. I have been told by a few people that during this adjustment period I tried so hard to look and act normal. In some ways I still do; I don't deny it. Society demands that people act and be "normal," not deviate. At the same time, I was constantly reminded that I was not "normal," through interpersonal relationships, architectural barriers, and vocational goals.

In the vocational field, this "normal" structure is particularly true. When a disabled individual starts school or training, his future occupation is by and large not dictated by what he would like to do or even by his intellectual capacity. It is dictated by what he is physically capable of doing.

This conflict between the real self and society should not force anyone into isolation. It should make the individual take an honest look at himself and his potentials, and then develop these to the fullest of his capabilities.

This is just one more of the major adjustments a spinal cord injured individual, along with other disabled people who are involved with society, must make. For some, it takes longer than others; for some it is more painful, but to survive they must be made.

Part II

SOCIOLOGICAL ASPECTS OF DISABILITY

Editorial
Introduction

Joseph Stubbins

A recurrent theme of the articles of Part I was the disruption in social relations suffered by disabled persons. Our aim in Part II is a continuation of this subject but from the perspective of sociology. Sociology, being the study of groups and society, assumes that the behavior of persons can best be understood in terms of the dynamics of society and aims to bring to light the "laws" governing behavior in groups. Sociologists study such subjects as poverty, race relations, population growth, bureaucracy, and political behavior. The best known of the great sociologists was Karl Marx. He and his adherents tried to account for phenomena such as the above in terms of property relationships or the economic system. Poverty, for instance, could be explained by the way capitalism operated.

The sociological perspective makes a definite contribution to the understanding of disability because the course of a disabled person's life or his career subsequent to injury cannot be explained by referring to individual behavior alone. The person with a newly acquired visible handicap soon discovers that his or her encounters with others are quite different from what they were formerly. The disabled person finds his friendship, love and sex, family, employment, and civic responsibilities all disrupted. A critical meaning of disability is lost unless it is seen as a social phenomenon. Each of the articles in Part II views disability in that light. It should be noted, however, that not all the authors are professional sociologists and some may even be surprised to find their writing classified as sociological.

The sociology of disability includes Sections 3, 4, 5, and 6. Section 3, on "Social Interaction," comprises articles that deal with social relations between the disabled and non-disabled, appropriate behavior for the disabled and the expectations of the non-disabled (roles). Section 4, "Treatment Environments," consists of a series of articles about professionals, management of patients, and environmental conditions that influence the rehabilitation of disabled persons. The articles in Section 5, "Social Controls," were grouped here because they deal with aspects of the disabled role that relate to the regulating functions of society. The final section of Part II, "Social Theory," consists of articles that theorize about why the disabled are victims of prejudice.

Whether it was a matter of analyzing disability, understanding it, or treating it, each article dealt with the subject at the social level. More specifically, it meant that disability was viewed from its relation to the family, community groups, professional helpers, organizations such as hospitals, agencies, and businesses, the welfare system, and the government.

Below, we take up each of the four sections on the sociology of disability to examine their themes more carefully.

SOCIAL INTERACTION

Each of the six articles of Section 3 deals with a somewhat different aspect of the impact of disability on social relations. Major attention is directed to the *disabled role*. The disabled role constitutes a new set of relations between the newly disabled person and others. It embraces a flexible constellation of "done ways" for the disabled person with emphasis on meeting the expectations of the non-disabled. The types of behaviors appropriate to this role involved accepting a decreased social status, having a certain attitude toward one's physical limitations, and glossing over the discomfitures that others experience in the presence of the disabled person. Much of this role behavior is touchingly illustrated in the Davis article.

Davis deals with initial encounters between visibly disabled and normal persons and interprets them in terms of social dynamics. Thus, Davis sees the underlying problem of the disabled person as resulting from the attribution of deviance to him, how to escape from it, and normalize the relationship. His mode of explanation is classically sociological. The Malone article describes the changed role relationships in the family resulting from disability. Chaiklin and Warfield make the point that the way the disabled person manages his devaluation has implications for successful rehabilitation. Skipper examines the impact of disability on husband-wife relations. Cogswell feels that after the paraplegic leaves the hospital he must master a fundamentally new set of social relations which she refers to as "resocialization." Nigro mentions for consideration the sexual needs of the disabled, a subject that was not discussed at all until recently.

The problems of disabled persons are viewed in these articles as a function of the social world. The paraplegic would prefer to maintain his friendships but finds that he cannot. Disabled persons find themselves caught up in a system of expectations that is as predictable and almost as regularized as that of patient, doctor, or teacher. For instance, they are expected to accomodate to their exclusion from many physical settings with good humor. An amputee who protests aloud about a meeting being held in a location inaccessible to him is presumed to be behaving in bad taste. If the disabled husband and father can no longer work, he is usually expected to gracefully give up the influence and authority he had with other members of the family. On the other hand, the injured person experiences a continuity in his identity and subjectivity and from this arises the difficulty of learning the altered expectations that others have of him. These altered expectations extend far beyond the brute facts of his changed physical relation to the world into that ambiguous world of people.

Several of the writers in this section allude to the social ambiguity in which disabled persons find themselves. Everyone finds himself frequently in such ill-defined situations. One makes overtures to a potential friend, engages in casual conversation at a cocktail party, and attempts a deeper intimacy with one of the opposite sex; these are examples of social situations of ambiguity. Often in such situations, one's own self-worth hangs in the balance. Anyone who has worked with disabled persons knows that the occasions of ambiguity are greatly increased. On the part of non-disabled persons, there is the fear of disclosing dread and uncanny feelings; on the part of disabled persons, the need to pretend that he or she does not observe these feelings and to avoid being the object of pity. We have here a complex social situation totally enmeshed in uncertainty— overlaid on the normal ambiguities of ordinary life.

In the long run, the disabled person learns to play his part with some skill, learns to avoid situations that tend to degrade him, and comes to terms with his new status realistically. His role behavior becomes crystallized, unless he is one of those exceptional persons that succeeds in breaking out of the usual constraints of the disabled role.

TREATMENT ENVIRONMENTS

For Section 4 we selected six articles that present critical analyses of settings in which disabled persons are treated. The lengthy article by Morgan, Hohmann, and Davis is a model of survey research in its presentation of a wide range of factors affecting the treatment of spinal cord injured persons. The authors and all those cooperating in this survey are to be congratulated for their candor and willingness to face up to public scrutiny. Virtually all parts of this survey have implications for disabled persons in general. The Schlesinger and Gellman articles deal with the hierarchy of authority in rehabilitation settings and their impact on the patients. Kutner outlines some of the iatrogenic effects associated with the bureaucratic structure of large hospitals which he calls "anti-therapy." Katz presents an alternative to the medical model of the organization of treatment through his analysis of self-help groups and their therapeutic results. Finally, Bitter reminds us that there are disabled persons requiring services in rural areas, and almost all discussions of psycho-social services assume an urban environment. Though the delivery systems Bitter discusses were improvised for the rural environment, some of them could be considered for urban areas as well.

These articles have something more in common than discussing treatment environments. In one way or another, they cite the "medical model" as problematic. This authoritative system of patient management does not mobilize the intelligence of staff persons, fails to engage patients themselves as creative participants in their rehabilitation, and provides meagre feedback by which to monitor failures in patient programs.

In ordinary practice, a patient's physician typically admits him or her to the hospital and directs the course of diagnosis and treatment. As hospitals became larger and the practice of medicine more technologically sophisticated, encroachments on the physician's authority were made. But basically, the physician remained in charge of his patients and retained final authority over them. The team treatment concept of comprehensive rehabilitation centers required the subordination of a single physician's opinion to the larger vision of rehabilitation that the center attempted to implement. The team concept, though much discussed, largely remained on the drawing boards. Among the reasons for this were the following. Physicians tended to avoid sending their patients where they would "lose" them because, at least in some comprehensive centers, the patient once admitted belonged to the rehabilitation center. Medical practices that needed modification in the light of social and psychological considerations did not occur in settings where medical authority was rigid. With some exceptions, comprehensive rehabilitation centers failed to attract the best psycho-social workers, who preferred settings that gave them more latitude and scope for professional initiative.

It would be an over-simplification, however, to believe that the problem of the medical model is a struggle for power among the various disciplines in a rehabilitation facility. There are real conceptual differences on how best to promote the adjustment of disabled persons. The writers of these articles would move toward an ecological or psycho-ecological model. The science of physical restoration of patients is at a more advanced stage than that concerned with their psychological well-being. This might be one reason why those responsible for physical restoration tend to drift into social and psychological realms, even though there are others better qualified. There are now well trained specialists capable of applying techniques of group and individual counseling to mobilize patients to assume maximum responsibility for their progress. Behavioral techniques of counseling have been adapted to institutional settings with patients defining their objectives and moving in a gradual way to their achievement. Model facilities have moved toward closer articulation with the resources of the community by having community advisory groups, encouraging volunteers, and employing para-professionals. Finally, a psycho-ecological model would employ objective evaluation of alternative modes for the management and treatment of rehabilitation patients.

The many issues raised in this section constitute an agenda of needed research for the improvement of treatment settings. The most critical aspects of optimizing treatment environments does not merely involve the assessment of ideas and practices and the allocation of needed monies but also reflect stubborn political and psychological questions of human relations.

SOCIAL CONTROLS

Section 5 comprises a group of articles dealing with the social status and dependency of disabled persons in relation to the structures of the larger society. There are defined roles for disabled persons both within treatment facilities and in the ordinary world of social relations. In a manner of speaking, the things that happen to disabled persons are made more understandable by interpreting them in terms of well-entrenched social customs, particularly those dealing with the enforcement of social rules.

Yamamoto, for instance, claims that attitudes toward disabled persons are more comprehensible when viewed in the light of society's larger function in defining deviancy. Although there appears to be no similarity between the physically disabled and homosexuals and criminals, Yamamoto would find the common bond in the social need for group norms and the need to preserve stability in society. English's empirical study is intended to reveal "the anatomy of prejudice" toward physically disabled persons. Many of his findings are productive for theorizing and discovery, e.g., that females have more accepting attitudes toward disabled persons than do males. Ludwig and Adams are concerned with client role characteristics such as submissiveness and compliance to hospital authority; they found that the submissive patients were more likely to complete the recommended treatment which, they remind us, is not necessarily the same as successful rehabilitation. Starkey's discussion of Parson's sick-role theory was more interesting than the data and findings of her empirical study. The notion of *sick role* brings into relief the fact that one cannot declare oneself sick and be legitimately so regarded; only certain designated persons may confer this status. Those who insist on assuming the sick role without proper legitimation or in spite of its denial are variously referred to as malingerers, hypochondriacs, or hysterics.

The notion that there are social mechanisms for keeping disabled persons at a low status or for preventing their social acceptance sounds preposterous. Similarly, it is difficult to believe that patients are kept in a submissive role for the convenience of physicians and their helpers and that the most self-sufficient persons resist rehabilitation authority. In short, it is difficult to credit the possibility that society's need for control through conformity causes major difficulties for physically disabled persons. The credibility of this theory is further thrown into doubt by the fact that government agencies spend great sums of money on behalf of disabled persons. Who, then, are the enforcers that stigmatize disabled persons?

The low status of patients in institutions has a plausible explanation. To some degree, rehabilitation services are organized to protect the interests of the professionals involved. It is certainly easier to manage a rehabilitation center in which patients are habituated to follow all prescriptions than one in which patients' cooperation is earned and skillfully exploited to foster their maximum independence. But, in the world outside the rehabilitation facility, how to explain the omnipresent discrimination against disabled persons? The lack of a theory about this phenomenon is like knowing that a terrible crime has been committed in sight of a large crowd without a criminal being identified; and yet not having an explanation for such an unusual event.

This difficulty is made manageable by postulating the existence of a *social system* before the individual actors appear on the scene, a system that spells out the parts that the actors are to play. The social system controls the actors the way a playwright controls the emotions of theatre-goers (Goffman, 1974). One theatre-goer might laugh when all the other patrons are weeping. But to do so, this highly deviant patron would have to be in a different frame, perhaps thinking about dramatic techniques or recognizing some of the actors as his personal friends who had spent many hours memorizing their lines.

Our feelings and attitudes toward disabled persons are given to us by history and custom just as the playwright gives us the emotions we experience in the theatre. But in the real world, there is no well-marked exit to inform us that we have passed from the unreal to the real. The social system provides us with ready-made meanings based on its need for coherence, conformity, stability, division of labor, and differentiated roles—all of which transcend the individuals making up that system.

We shall return to the matter of social control in the next section of Part II under the subject of social theory. We can conclude this section with the following observation. Because there are apparently no "bad guys" responsible for the plight of disabled persons, we must continue to look for explanations deep in the fabric of society.

SOCIAL THEORY

The five articles of Section 6 all relate the problems of disabled persons to some structural dimension of society. These explanations result in the transformation of disability problems into pervasive social ones. Each article will be capsuled to highlight this theme.

Sussman sees similarities between the poor, the aged, and the disabled, all of whom are socially defined and by extension "needed" by society. Prejudice against disabled persons is seen by Safilios-Rothschild as a pervasive phenomenon found in all societies and warns against any simplistic notions of counteracting it. On the same subject, Anthony considers society as the patient in need of treatment to cure it of distorted views of disabled persons. Even rehabilitation workers themselves and their rehabilitation agencies are capable of prejudiced attitudes. In this vein, disability prejudice is viewed by Hammond as similar to ethnocentrism. The last article in this section by Worthington reports a simple but creative piece of research that illustrates the spatial distance that separates disabled and non-disabled persons. One might think of the spatial dimension of social relations as paralleling the more abstract concept of social distance.

Each article tries to explain prejudice in the dispassionate manner of theory and science. These articles are preliminary attempts at social theories. The causes of the disvalued status of disabled persons must be sought at the social level.

Even Worthington's pragmatic study has its theoretical side in its support of Goffman's "spoiled identity" (Goffman, 1963).

The basic mechanism of prejudice, then, is a function of conformity. In smaller and less developed societies, the means by which conformity are achieved are transparent. In our complex pluralistic society, it is achieved through the distractions of institutionalized sports and media entertainment, an emphasis on dramatic news events, and the reporting of social unrest in a manner to distort its significance. Leaders who succeed in becoming effective in mobilizing discontent and threatening conformity are often appropriated by being given high salaried jobs, are defused by presenting their activities as media entertainment, or are harassed. The reality of power and economic influence is obscured by the myth of social mobility, namely that in our kind of society the really able persons, including disabled persons, can get ahead and join the successful.

There is a strain toward conformity in every society and each has its myths and other devices to obscure all but the official versions of social reality. From the viewpoint of the scientific study of society, it is first necessary to understand the phenomenon of conformity and later decide how much of it is necessary for social survival. The rationale for discrimination against the ex-offender is clear; that against the mentally ill somewhat less clear; and that against the physically disabled, least of all. Criminals threaten our life and property. The mentally ill are usually unable to work; they refuse to observe the most elementary social customs; they reveal aspects of our mental life that the culture taboos; they remind the normal how close to the abyss they are.

Conformity is a vital defensive need of society. The social norms by which we live become highly habitual; note, for instance, the speed with which so many adopt the apparel dictates of designers and fashion setters. It may be said that there is a *surplus of conformity* that spreads over into manners, customs, and modes of behaving that is beyond that needed for social cohesion and a rational interdependent existence. Visibly disabled persons are victimized by this surplus conformity.

The mass media exploit beautiful bodies, physical agility, and aphoristic and humorous conversation. The tragic dimensions of life are under-represented. When they do appear, they are cleaned up and divested of pain and grief. Death may be an occasion for joy and relief. The consequence is a misrepresentation of life but especially the degradation of the lived lives of the vast majority. Few can measure up to the standards of studied casualness and grace displayed in the media. Ordinary persons must appear like bumpkins and the disabled as freaks.

Though advances have been made in bringing disabled persons into public view on streets and public places, similar gains have not occurred in the media and employment. When handicapped persons are presented to public view, it is in a dramatic situation designed to stir pathos rather than in normalized roles.

To what extent are these prejudiced practices an adaptation to existing public attitudes and to what extent do they actively induce negative public attitudes? Probably, they are a little of both. If I am right, then the surplus conformity is both an integral part of our industrial-social system and is aided and abetted by those persons responsible for policy decisions.

In directing attention to the social and societal problematics of disability, a bleaker picture of the actual lives of disabled persons may have emerged than that suggested by first-hand contact. Sociologists are less concerned with the consciousness of individuals than they are with social phenomena and processes. This perspective has its peculiar strength and weakness. As we remarked in the introduction to Part I, disabled persons have their own agenda of preoccupations; and it can be said now that few of them want to make a career of the social problem of their devaluation. The vast majority want to get on with the business of living. Many handicapped persons are goaded into lives of extraordinary fulfillment and achievement. Most come to some kind of philosophic peace and life purpose which place their handicap in the background. To recognize this, however, does not invalidate the sociological perspective nor the many serious questions it raises about the place of disabled persons in our society.

REFERENCES

Goffman, E. Stigma. 1963. Prentice-Hall, Englewood Cliffs, N.J.
Goffman, E. 1974. Frame Analysis. Harper & Row, New York.

Section 3

SOCIAL INTERACTION

7 Deviance Disavowal:

The Management of Strained Interaction by the Visibly Handicapped

Fred Davis

A recurring issue in social relations is the refusal of those who are viewed as deviant[1] to concur in the verdict. Or, if in some sense it can be said that they do concur, they usually place a very different interpretation on the fact or allegation than do their judges. In our society this is especially true of deviance which results from ascription (e.g., the Negro) as against that which partakes to some significant degree of election (e.g., the homosexual). And, while it may be conjectured that ultimately neither the Negro nor the homosexual would be cast in a deviant role were it not for society's devaluation of these attributes in the first place, barring such a hypothetical contingency it remains the more persuasive argument in a democracy to be able to claim that the social injury from which one suffers was in no way self-inflicted.

In these pages I wish to discuss another kind of non self-inflicted social injury, the visible physical handicap. My aim though is not to survey and describe the many hardships of the visibly handicapped,[2] but to analyze certain facets of their coping behavior as it relates to the generalized imputations of deviance

Reprinted from Social Problems, 1961, 9(2):121–132. The Society for the Study of Social Problems.

The study from which this paper derives was supported by a grant from the Association for the Aid of Crippled Children. I am indebted to Stephen A. Richardson and David Klein of the Association for their help and advice. I also wish to thank Frances C. Macgregor, Cornell Medical Center, New York, for having so generously made available to me case materials from her research files on persons with facial disfigurements. See Frances C. Macgregor et al., Facial Deformities and Plastic Surgery: A Psychosocial Study, Springfield, Ill.: Charles C. Thomas, 1953.

[1] Following Lemert, as used here the term deviant (or deviance) refers 1) to a person's deviation from prevalent or valued norms, 2) to which the community-at-large reacts negatively or punitively, 3) so as to then lead the person to define his situation largely in terms of this reaction. All three conditions must be fulfilled for it to be said that deviance exists (secondary deviation, in Lemert's definition). In this sense the Negro, the career woman, the criminal, the Communist, the physically handicapped, the mentally ill, the homosexual, to mention but a few, are all deviants, albeit in different ways and with markedly different consequences for their life careers. Edwin M. Lemert, Social Pathology, New York: McGraw-Hill, 1951. 75–77.

[2] Comprehensive and excellent reviews are to be found in R. G. Barker et al., Adjustment to Physical Handicap and Illness: A Survey of the Social Psychology of Physique and Disability, New York: Soc. Sci. Res. Council, 1953, Bulletin 55, 2nd ed. and Beatrice A. Wright, Physical Disability, A Psychological Approach, New York: Harper, 1960.

they elicit from society, imputations which many of them feel it necessary to resist and reject.

There are, of course, many areas in which such imputations bear heavily upon them: employment, friendship, courtship, sex, travel, recreation, residence, education. But the area I treat here is enmeshed to some extent in all of these without being as categorically specific as any. I refer to situations of sociability, and more specifically to that genre of everyday intercourse which has the characteristics of being: 1) face-to-face, 2) prolonged enough to permit more than a fleeting glimpse or exchange, but not so prolonged that close familiarity immediately ensues, 3) intimate to the extent that the parties must pay more than perfunctory attention to one another, but not so intimate that the customary social graces can be dispensed with, and 4) ritualized to the extent that all know in general what to expect, but not so ritualized as to preclude spontaneity and the slightly novel turn of events. A party or other social affair, a business introduction, getting to know a person at work, meeting neighbors,

dealing with a salesman, conversing with a fellow passenger, staying at a resort hotel—these are but a few of the everyday social situations which fall within this portion of the spectrum of sociability, a range of involvement which can also be thought of as the zone of first impressions.

In interviews I conducted with a small number of very articulate and socially skilled informants who were visibly handicapped[3] I inquired into their handling of the imputation that they were not "normal, like everyone else." This imputation usually expresses itself in a pronounced stickiness of interactional flow and in the embarrassment of the normal by which he conveys the all too obvious message that he is having difficulty in relating to the handicapped person[4] as he would to "just an ordinary man or woman." Frequently he will make *faux pas*, slips of the tongue, revealing gestures and inadvertent remarks which overtly betray this attitude and place the handicapped person in an even more delicate situation.[5] The triggering of such a chain of interpersonal incidents is more likely with

---

[3] Six were orthopedically handicapped, three blind and two facially disfigured. Additional detailed biographical and clinical materials were secured on one blind and four facially disfigured persons, making for a total of sixteen records.

[4] Throughout this paper, whether or not the term 'handicap' or 'handicapped' is joined by the qualifier 'visible,' it should be read in this way. Unfortunately, it will not be possible to discuss here that which sociologically distinguishes the situation of the visibly handicapped from that of persons whose physical handicaps are not visible or readily apparent, and how both differ from what is termed the 'sick role.' These are though important distinctions whose analysis might illuminate key questions in the study of deviance.

[5] In the sections that follow the discussion draws heavily on the framework of dramaturgic analysis developed by Erving Goffman. See especially his "Alienation from Interaction," Human Relations, 10 (1957), 47–60; "Embarrassment and Social Organization," American Journal of Sociology, 62 (November, 1956), 264–71; Presentation of Self in Everyday Life, New York: Doubleday and Co., Inc., 1959.

new persons than with those with whom the handicapped have well-established and continuing relations. Hence, the focus here on more or less sociable occasions, it being these in which interactional discomfort is felt most acutely and coping behavior is brought into relief most sharply.

Because the visibly handicapped do not comprise a distinct minority group or subculture, the imputations of generalized deviance that they elicit from many normals are more nearly genuine interactional emergents than conventionalized sequelae to inter-group stereotyping as, for example, might obtain between a Negro and white. A sociable encounter between a visibly handicapped person and a normal is usually more subject to ambiguity and experimentation in role postures than would be the case were the parties perceived by each other primarily in terms of member group characteristics. The visibly handi-capped person must with each new acquaintance explore the *possibilities* of a relationship. As a rule there is no ready-made symbolic shorthand (e.g., "a Southerner can't treat a Negro as a social equal," "the Irish are anti-Semitic," "working class people think intellectuals are effeminate") for anti-cipating the quality and degree of ac-ceptance to be accorded him. The exchange must be struck before its dangers and potentialities can be seen and before appropriate corrective maneuvers can be fed into the inter-action.[6]

THE HANDICAP AS THREAT TO SOCIABLE INTERACTION

Before discussing how the visibly handicapped cope with difficult inter-action, it is appropriate to first con-sider the general nature of the threat posed to the interactional situation *per se* as a result of their being perceived routinely (if not necessarily according to some prevalent stereotype) as "dif-ferent," "odd," "estranged from the common run of humanity," etc.; in short, other than normal. (Achieving ease and naturalness of interaction with normals serves naturally as an im-portant index to the handicapped person of the extent to which his pre-ferred definition of self—i.e., that of someone who is merely different physically but not socially deviant—has been accepted. Symbolically, as long as the interaction remains stiff, strained or otherwise mired in inhibi-tion, he has good reason to believe that he is in effect being denied the status of social normalcy he aspires to or regards as his due.) The threat posed by the handicap to sociability is, at minimum, fourfold: its tendency to become an exclusive focal point of the interaction, its potential for inun-dating expressive boundaries, its dis-cordance with other attributes of the person and, finally, its ambiguity as a predicator of joint activity. These are not discrete entities in themselves as much as varying contextual emergents which, depending on the particular situation, serve singly or in combina-

---

[6] Cf. Anselm Strauss, Mirrors and Masks, Glencoe, Ill.: Free Press, 1959, 31–43.

tion to strain the framework of normative rules and assumptions in which sociability develops. Let us briefly consider each in turn.

A Focal Point of Interaction

The rules of sociable interaction stipulate a certain generality and diffuseness in the attentions that parties are expected to direct to each other. Even if only superficially, one is expected to remain oriented to the whole person and to avoid the expression of a precipitous or fixed concern with any single attribute of his, however noteworthy or laudable it may be.[7] When meeting someone with a visible handicap, a number of perceptual and interpretative responses occur which make adherence to this rule tenuous for many. First, there is the matter of visibility as such. By definition, the visibly handicapped person cannot control his appearance sufficiently so that its striking particularity will not call a certain amount of concentrated attention to itself.[8] Second, the normal, while having his attention so narrowly channeled, is immediately constrained by the requirements of sociability to act as if he were oriented to the totality of the other rather than to that which is uppermost in his awareness, i.e., the handicap. Although the art of sociability may be said to thrive on a certain playful discrepancy between felt and expressed interests, it is perhaps equally true that when these are too discrepant strain and tension begin to undermine the interaction. (Conversely, when not discrepant enough, flatness and boredom frequently ensue.)[9] Whether the handicap is overtly and tactlessly responded to as such or, as is more commonly the case, no explicit reference is made to it, the underlying condition of heightened, narrowed, awareness causes the interaction to be articulated too exclusively in terms of it. This, as my informants described it, is usually accompanied by one or more of the familiar signs of discomfort and stickiness: the guarded references, the common everyday words suddenly made taboo, the fixed stare elsewhere, the artificial levity, the compulsive loquaciousness, the awkward solemnity.[10]

Second-order interactional elaborations of the underlying impedance are also not uncommon. Thus, for example, the normal may take great pains to disguise his awareness, an exertion that is usually so effortful and

---

[7] Kurt H. Wolff, ed., The Sociology of Georg Simmel, Glencoe, Ill.: Free Press, 1950. 45–46.

[8] Cf. R. K. White, B. A. Wright and T. Dembo, "Studies in Adjustment to Visible Injuries," Journal of Abnormal and Social Psychology, 43 (1948), 13–28.

[9] In a forthcoming paper, "Fun in Games: An Analysis of the Dynamics of Social Interaction," Goffman discusses the relationship between spontaneous involvement in interaction and the manner in which "external attributes"—those which in a formal sense are not situationally relevant—are permitted to penetrate the situation's boundaries.

[10] Cf. Goffman on "other-consciousness" as a type of faulty interaction. "Alienation from Interaction," op. cit.

transparent that the handicapped person is then enjoined to disguise his awareness of the normal's disguise. In turn, the normal sensing the disguise erected in response to his disguise . . . and so forth. But unlike the infinitely multiplying reflections of an object located between opposing mirrors, this process cannot sustain itself for long without the pretense of unawareness collapsing, as witness the following report by a young woman:

I get suspicious when somebody says, "Let's go for a uh, ah [imitates confused and halting speech] push with me down the hall," or something like that. This to me is suspicious because it means that they're aware, really aware, that there's a wheelchair here, and that this is probably uppermost with them. . . . A lot of people in trying to show you that they don't care that you're in a chair will do crazy things. Oh, there's one person I know who constantly kicks my chair, as if to say "I don't care that you're in a wheelchair. I don't even know that it's there." But that is just an indication that he *really* knows it's there.

Inundating Potential

The expressive requirements of sociability are such that rather strict limits obtain with respect to the types and amount of emotional display that are deemed appropriate. Even such fitting expressions as gaiety and laughter can, we know, reach excess and lessen satisfaction with the occasion. For many normals, the problem of sustaining sociable relations with someone who is visibly handicapped is not

wholly that of the discrepancy of the inner feeling evoked, e.g., pity, fear, repugnance, avoidance. As with much else in sociability, a mere discrepancy of the actor's inner state with the social expectation need not result in a disturbance of interaction. In this instance it is specifically the marked dissonance of such emotions with those outward expressions deemed *most* salient for the occasion (e.g., pleasure, identification, warm interest) that seems to result frequently in an inundation and enfeeblement of the expressive controls of the individual. With some persons, the felt intrusion of this kind of situationally inappropriate emotion is so swift and overwhelming as to approximate a state of shock, leaving them expressively naked, so to speak. A pointed incident is told by a young blind girl:

One night when I was going to visit a friend two of the people from my office put me into a taxi. I could tell that at first the taxi driver didn't know I was blind because for a while there he was quite a conversationalist. Then he asked me what these sticks were for [a collapsible cane]. I told him it was a cane, and then he got so different . . . He didn't talk about the same things that he did at first. Before this happened he joked and said, "Oh, you're a very quiet person. I don't like quiet people, they think too much." And he probably wouldn't have said that to me had he known I was blind because he'd be afraid of hurting my feelings. He didn't say anything like that afterwards.

The visibly handicapped are of course aware of this potential for inundating the expressive boundaries of situations and many take precautions to minimize such occurrences as much as possible. Thus, an interior decorator with a facial deformity would when admitted to a client's house by the maid station himself whenever he could so that the client's entrance would find him in a distantly direct line of vision from her. This, he stated, gave the client an opportunity to compose herself, as she might not be able to were she to come upon him at short range.

Contradiction of Attributes

Even when the inundating potential is well contained by the parties and the normal proves fully capable of responding in a more differentiated fashion to the variety of attributes presented by the handicapped person (e.g., his occupational identity, clothes, speech, intelligence, interests, etc.), there is frequently felt to be an unsettling discordance between these and the handicap. Sociable interaction is made more difficult as a result because many normals can only resolve the seeming incongruence by assimilating or subsuming (often in a patronizing or condescending way) the other attributes to that of the handicap, a phenomenon which in analogous connections has been well described by Hughes.[11] Thus, one informant, a strikingly attractive girl, reports that she frequently elicits from new acquaintances the comment, "How strange that someone so pretty should be in a wheelchair." Another informant, a professional worker for a government agency, tells of the fashionable female client who after having inquired on how long the informant had been in her job remarked, "How nice that you have something to do." Because the art of sociability deigns this kind of reductionism of the person, expressions of this type, even when much less blatant, almost invariably cast a pall on the interaction and embarrass the recovery of smooth social posture. The general threat inherent in the perceived discordance of personal attributes is given pointed expression by still another informant, a paraplegic of upper middle class background who comments on the attitude of many persons in his class:

> Now, where this affects them, where this brace and a crutch would affect them, is if they are going someplace or if they are doing something, they feel that, first, you would call attention and, second—you wouldn't believe this but it's true; I'll use the cruelest words I can—no cripple could possibly be in their social stratum.

Ambiguous Predicator

Finally, to the extent to which sociability is furthered by the free and spontaneous initiation of joint activity (e.g., dancing, games, going out to eat; in short, "doing things") there is frequently considerable ambiguity as regards the ability of the handicapped person to so participate and as regards the propriety of efforts which seek to

---

[11] Everett C. Hughes, Men and Their Work, Glencoe, Ill.: Free Press, 1958, 102–06.

ascertain whether he wants to. For the normal who has had limited experience with the handicapped it is by no means always clear whether, for example, a blind person can be included in a theater party or a crippled person in a bowling game. Even if not able to engage in the projected activity as such, will he want to come along mainly for the sake of company? How may his preferences be gauged without, on the one hand, appearing to "make a thing" out of the proposal or, on the other, conveying the impression that his needs and limitations are not being sufficiently considered? Should he refuse, is it genuine or is he merely offering his hosts a polite, though half-hearted, out? And, for each enigma thus posed for the normal, a counter-enigma is posed for the handicapped person. Do they really want him? Are they merely being polite? In spite of the open invitation, will his acceptance and presence lessen somehow their enjoyment of the activity? It is easy to see how a profusion of anticipatory ambiguities of this kind can strain the operative assumptions underlying sociable relations.

PROCESS OF DEVIANCE DISAVOWAL AND NORMALIZATION

The above features then, may be said to comprise the threat that a visible handicap poses to the framework of rules and assumptions that guide sociability. We may now ask how socially adept handicapped persons cope with it so as to either keep it at bay, dissipate it or lessen its impact upon the interaction. In answering this question we will not consider those broad personality adjustments of the person (e.g., aggression, denial, compensation, dissociation, etc.) which at a level once removed, so to speak, can be thought of as adaptive or maladaptive for, among other things, sociability. Nor, at the other extreme, is it possible in the allotted space to review the tremendous variety of specific approaches, ploys and stratagems that the visibly handicapped employ in social situations. Instead, the analysis will attempt to delineate in transactional terms the stages through which a sociable relationship with a normal typically passes, assuming, of course, that the confrontation takes place and that both parties possess sufficient social skill to sustain a more than momentary engagement.

For present purposes we shall designate these stages as: 1) fictional acceptance, 2) the facilitation of reciprocal role-taking around a normalized projection of self and 3) the institutionalization in the relationship of a definition of self that is normal in its moral dimension, however qualified it may be with respect to its situational contexts. As we shall indicate, the unfolding of these stages comprises what may be thought of as a process of deviance disavowal or normalization,[12] depending on

_____

[12] As used here the term 'normalization' denotes a process whereby the alter for whatever reason comes to view as normal and morally acceptable that which initially strikes him as

whether one views the process from the vantage point of the "deviant" actor or his alters.[13]

Fictional Acceptance

In Western society the overture phases of a sociable encounter are to a pronounced degree regulated by highly elastic fictions of equality and normalcy. In meeting those with whom we are neither close nor familiar, manners dictate that we refrain from remarking on or otherwise reacting too obviously to those aspects of their persons which in the privacy of our thoughts betoken important differences between ourselves. In America at least, these fictions tend to encompass sometimes marked divergencies in social status as well as a great variety of expressive styles; and, it is perhaps the extreme flexibility of such fictions in our culture rather than, as is mistakenly assumed by many foreign observers, their absence that accounts for the seeming lack of punctiliousness in American manners. The point is nicely illustrated in the following news item:

NUDE TAKES A STROLL IN MIAMI

MIAMI, Fla., Nov. 13 (UPI)—A shapely brunette slowed traffic to a snail's pace here yesterday with a 20-minute nude stroll through downtown Miami. . . .

"The first thing I knew something was wrong," said Biscayne Bay bridgetender E. E. Currey, who was working at his post about one block away, "was when I saw traffic was going unusually slow."

Currey said he looked out and called police. They told him to stop the woman, he said.

Currey said he walked out of his little bridge house, approached the woman nervously, and asked, "Say, girl, are you lost?"

"Yes," she replied. "I'm looking for my hotel."

Currey offered help and asked, "Say, did you lose your clothes?"

"No," he said the woman replied, "Why?"

Currey said that he had to step away for a moment to raise the bridge for a ship and the woman walked away. . . .[14]

Unlike earlier societies and some present day ones in which a visible handicap automatically relegates the person to a caste-like, inferior, status like that of mendicant, clown or

odd, unnatural, "crazy," deviant, etc., irrespective of whether his perception was in the first instance reasonable, accurate or justifiable. Cf. Charlotte G. Schwartz, "Perspectives on Deviance—Wives' Definitions of their Husbands' Mental Illness," Psychiatry, 20 (August, 1957), 275—91.

[13] Because of the paper's focus on the visibly handicapped person, in what follows his interactional work is highlighted to the relative glossing over of that of the normal. Actually, the work of normalization calls for perhaps as much empathic expenditure as that of deviance disavowal and is, obviously, fully as essential for repairing the interactional breach occasioned by the encounter.

[14] San Francisco Chronicle, November 14, 1960.

thief—or more rarely to an elevated one like that of oracle or healer—in our society the visibly handicapped are customarily accorded, save by children,[15] the surface acceptance that democratic manners guarantee to nearly all. But, as regards sociability, this proves a mixed blessing for many. Although the polite fictions do afford certain entrée rights, as fictions they can too easily come to serve as substitutes for "the real thing" in the minds of their perpetrators. The interaction is kept starved at a bare subsistence level of sociability. As with the poor relation at the wedding party, so the reception given the handicapped person in many social situations: sufficient that he is here, he should not expect to dance with the bride.

At this stage of the encounter, the interactional problem confronting the visibly handicapped person is the delicate one of not permitting his identity to be circumscribed by the fiction while at the same time playing along

with it and showing appropriate regard for its social legitimacy. For, as transparent and confining as the fiction is, it frequently is the only basis upon which the contact can develop into something more genuinely sociable. In those instances in which the normal fails or refuses to render even so small a gesture toward normalizing the situation, there exists almost no basis for the handicapped person to successfully disavow his deviance.[16] The following occurrence related by a young female informant is an apt, if somewhat extreme, illustration:

> I was visiting my girl friend's house and I was sitting in the lobby waiting for her when this woman comes out of her apartment and starts asking me questions. She just walked right up. I didn't know her from Adam, I never saw her before in my life. "Gee, what do you have? How long have you been that way? Oh gee, that's terrible." And so I answered her questions, but I got very annoyed and wanted

---

[15] The blunt questions and stares of small children are typically of the 'Emperor's Clothes' variety. "Mister, why is your face like that?" "Lady, what are you riding around in that for? Can't you walk?" Nearly all of my informants spoke of how unnerving such incidents were for them, particularly when other adults were present. None the less, some claimed to value the child's forthrightness a good deal more than they did the genteel hypocrisy of many adults.

[16] On the other side of the coin there are of course some handicapped persons who are equally given to undermining sociable relations by intentionally flaunting the handicap so that the fiction becomes extremely difficult to sustain. An equivalent of the "bad nigger" type described by Strong, such persons were (as in Strong's study) regarded with a mixture of admiration and censure by a number of my informants. Admiration, because the cruel stripping away of pretenses and forcing of issues was thought morally refreshing, especially since, as the informants themselves recognized, many normals refuse to grant anything more than fictional acceptance while at the same time imagining themselves ennobled for having made the small sacrifice. Censure, because of the conviction that such behavior could hardly improve matters in the long run and would make acceptance even more difficult for other handicapped persons who later came into contact with a normal who had received such treatment. Cf. Samuel M. Strong, "Negro-White Relations as Reflected in Social Types," American Journal of Sociology, 52 (July, 1946), p. 24.

to say, "Lady, mind your own business."

"Breaking Through" — Facilitating Normalized Role-Taking

In moving beyond fictional acceptance what takes place essentially is a re-definitional process in which the handicapped person projects images, attitudes and concepts of self which encourage the normal to identify with him (i.e., "take his role") in terms other than those associated with imputations of deviance.[17] Coincidentally, in broadening the area of minor verbal involvements, this also functions to drain away some of the stifling burden of unspoken awareness that, as we have seen, so taxes ease of interaction. The normal is cued into a larger repertoire of appropriate responses, and even when making what he, perhaps mistakenly, regards as an inappropriate response (for example, catching himself in the use of such a word as cripple or blind) the handicapped person can by his response relieve him of his embarrassment. One young informant insightfully termed the process "breaking through":

> The first reaction a normal individual or good-legger has is, "Oh gee, there's a fellow in a wheelchair," or "there's a fellow with a brace." And they don't say, "Oh gee, there is so-and-so, he's handsome" or "he's intelligent," or "he's a boor," or what have you. And then as the relationship develops they don't see the handicap. It doesn't exist any more. And that's the point that you as a handicapped individual become sensitive to. You know after talking with someone for awhile when they don't see the handicap any more. That's when you've broken through.

What this process signifies from a social psychological standpoint is that as the handicapped person expands the interactional nexus he simultaneously disavows the deviancy latent in his status; concurrently, to the degree to which the normal is led to reciprocally assume the redefining (and perhaps unanticipated) self-attitudes proffered by the handicapped person, he comes to normalize (i.e., view as more like himself) those aspects of the other which at first connoted deviance for him. (Sometimes, as we shall see, the normal's normalizing is so complete that it is unwittingly applied to situations in which the handicapped person cannot possibly function "normally" due to sheer physical limitations.) These dynamics might also be termed a process of identification. The term is immaterial, except that in "identifying" or "taking the role of the other" much more is implicated sociologically than a mere subjective congruence of responses. The fashioning of shared perspectives also implies a progressively more binding legitimation of the altered self-representations enacted in the encounter; that is, having once normalized his perception of the handi-

---

[17] George H. Mead, Mind, Self and Society, Chicago: University of Chicago Press, 1934. See also the discussion on interaction in Strauss, *op. cit.*, 44–88.

capped person, it becomes increasingly more compromising—self-discrediting, as it were—for the normal to revert to treating him as a deviant again.

The ways in which the visibly handicapped person can go about disavowing deviance are, as we have stated, many and varied. These range from relatively straightforward conversational offerings in which he alludes in passing to his involvement in a normal round of activities, to such forms of indirection as interjecting taboo or privatized references by way of letting the normal know that he does not take offense at the latter's uneasiness or regard it as a fixed obstacle toward achieving rapport. In the above quote, for example, the informant speaks of "good-leggers," an in-group term from his rehabilitation hospital days, which along with "dirty normals" he sometimes uses with new acquaintances "because it has a humorous connotation ... and lots of times it puts people at their ease."[18]

Still other approaches to disavowing deviance and bridging fictional acceptance include: an especially attentive and sympathetic stance with respect to topics introduced by the normal, showing oneself to be a comic, wit or other kind of gifted participant, and, for some, utilizing the normalization potential inherent in being seen in the company of a highly presentable normal companion.[19] These, and others too numerous to mention, are not of course invariably or equally successful in all cases; neither are such resources equally available to all handicapped persons, nor are the handicapped equally adept at exploiting them. As a class of corrective strategies however, they have the common aim of overcoming the interactional barrier that lies between narrow fictional acceptance and more spontaneous forms of relatedness.

Inextricably tied in with the matter of approach are considerations of setting, activity and social category of participants, certain constellations of which are generally regarded as favorable for successful deviance disavowal and normalization while others are thought unfavorable. Again, the ruling contingencies appear to be the extent to which the situation is seen as containing elements in it which: 1) contextually reduce the threat posed by the visible handicap to the rules and assumptions of the particular sociable occasion, and 2) afford the handicapped person opportunities for "breaking through" beyond fictional acceptance.

The relevance of one or both of these is apparent in the following social situations and settings about

---

[18] Parallel instances can easily be cited from minority group relations as, for example, when a Jew in conversation with a non-Jew might introduce a Yiddish phrase by way of suggesting that the other's covert identification of him as a Jew need not inhibit the interaction unduly. In some situations this serves as a subtle means of declaring, "O.K., I know what's bothering you. Now that I've said it, let's forget about it and move on to something else."

[19] Alan G. Gowman, "Blindness and the Role of the Companion," Social Problems, 4 (July, 1956).

which my informants expressed considerable agreement as regards their preferences, aversions and inner reactions. To begin with, mention might again be made of the interactional rule violations frequently experienced at the hands of small children. Many of the informants were quite open in stating that a small child at a social occasion caused them much uneasiness and cramped their style because they were concerned with how, with other adults present, they would handle some barefaced question from the child. Another category of persons with whom many claimed to have difficulty is the elderly. Here the problem was felt to be the tendency of old people to indulge in patronizing sympathy, an attitude which peculiarly resists re-definition because of the fulsome virtue it attributes to itself. In another context several of the informants laid great stress on the importance of maintaining a calm exterior whenever the physical setting unavoidably exposed them to considerable bodily awkwardness. (At the same time, of course, they spoke of the wisdom of avoiding, whenever possible, such occasions altogether.) Their attitude was that to expressively reflect gracelessness and a loss of control would result in further interactional obstacles toward assimilating the handicapped person to a normal status.

> It makes me uncomfortable to watch anyone struggling, so I try to do what I must as inconspicuously as possible. In new situations or in strange places, even though I may be very anxious, I will maintain a deadly calm. For example, if people have to lift the chair and I'm scared that they are going to do it wrong, I remain perfectly calm and am very direct in the instructions I give.

As a final example, there is the unanimity with which the informants expressed a strong preference for the small, as against the large or semi-public social gathering. Not only do they believe that, as one handicapped person among the non-handicapped, they stand out more at large social gatherings, but also that in the anonymity which numbers further there resides a heightened structural tendency for normals to practice avoidance relations with them. The easy assumption on such occasions is that "some other good soul" will take responsibility for socializing with the handicapped person. Even in the case of the handicapped person who is forward and quite prepared to take the initiative in talking to others, the organization and ecology of the large social gathering is usually such as to frustrate his attempts to achieve a natural, non-deviant, place for himself in the group. As one young man, a paraplegic, explained:

> The large social gathering presents a special problem. It's a matter of repetition. When you're in a very large group of people whom you don't know, you don't have an opportunity of talking to three, four or five at a time. Maybe you'll talk to one or two usually. After you've gone through a whole basic breakdown in making a relationship with one—after all, it's only a cocktail party—to do it again, and

again, and again, it's wearing and it's no good. You don't get the opportunity to really develop something.

Institutionalization of the Normalized Relationship

In "breaking through" many of the handicapped are confronted by a delicate paradox, particularly in those of their relationships which continue beyond the immediate occasion. Having disavowed deviance and induced the other to respond to him as he would to a normal, the problem then becomes one of sustaining the normalized definition in the face of the many small amendments and qualifications that must frequently be made to it. The person confined to a wheelchair, for example, must brief a new acquaintance on what to do and how to help when they come to stairs, doorways, vehicle entrances, etc. Further briefings and rehearsals may be required for social obstructions as well: for example, how to act in an encounter with—to cite some typical situations at random—an overly helpful person, a waitress who communicates to the handicapped person only through his companion, a person who stares in morbid fascination.[20]

Generally, such amendments and special considerations are as much as possible underplayed in the early stages of the relationship because, as in the case of much minority group protest, the fundamental demand of the handicapped is that they first be granted an irreducibly equal and normal status, it being only then regarded as fitting and safe to admit to certain incidental incapacities, limitations, and needs. At some point however, the latter must be broached if the relationship to the normal is to endure in viable form. But to integrate effectively a major claim to "normalcy" with numerous minor waivers of the same claim is a tricky feat and one which exposes the relationship to the many situational and psychic hazards of apparent duplicity: the tension of transferring the special arrangements and understandings worked out between the two to situations and settings in which everyone else is "behaving normally"; the sometimes lurking suspicion of the one that it is only guilt or pity that cements the relationship, of the other that the infirmity is being used exploitatively, and of on-lookers that there is something "neurotic" and "unhealthy" about it all.[21]

From my informants' descriptions it appears that this third, "normal, but . . ." stage of the relationship, if it

---

[20] Ibid.

[21] The rhetoric of race relations reflects almost identical rationalizations and "insights" which are meant among other things to serve as cautions for would-be transgressors. "Personally I have nothing against Negroes [the handicapped], but it would be bad for my reputation if I were seen socializing with them." "She acts nice now, but with the first argument she'll call you a dirty Jew [good-for-nothing cripple]." "Regardless of how sympathetic you are toward Negroes [the disabled], the way society feels about them you'd have to be a masochist to marry one."

endures, is institutionalized mainly in either one of two ways. In the first, the normal normalizes his perceptions to such an extent as to suppress his effective awareness of many of the areas in which the handicapped person's behavior unavoidably deviates from the normal standard. In this connection several of the informants complained that a recurring problem they have with close friends is that the latter frequently overlook the fact of the handicap and the restrictions it imposes on them. The friends thoughtlessly make arrangements and involve them in activities in which they, the handicapped, cannot participate conveniently or comfortably.

The other major direction in which the relationship is sometimes institutionalized is for the normal to surrender some of his normalcy by joining the handicapped person in a marginal, half-alienated, half-tolerant, outsider's orientation to "the Philistine world of normals."[22] Gowman [23] nicely describes the tenor and style of this relationship and its possibilities for sharply disabusing normals of their stereotyped approaches to the handicapped. *Épater le bourgeois* behavior is often prominently associated with it, as is a certain strictly in-group license to lampoon and mock the handicap in a way which would be regarded as highly offensive were it to come from

an uninitiated normal. Thus, a blind girl relates how a sighted friend sometimes chides her by calling her "a silly blink." A paraplegic tells of the old friend who tries to revive his flagging spirits by telling him not to act "like a helpless cripple." Unlike that based on over-normalization, the peculiar strength of this relationship is perhaps its very capacity to give expressive scope to the negative reality of the larger world of which it is inescapably a part while simultaneously removing itself from a primary identification with it.

IMPLICATIONS

Two, more general, implications seem worth drawing from this analysis.[24]

First, in studies which trace the process wherein an actor who deviates comes to be increasingly defined as a deviant (e.g., the pre-mental patient, the pre-alcoholic, the pre-juvenile delinquent), unusual prominence is given to the normalizing behavior of those close to him (spouse, parents, friends, etc.). The picture that emerges is one of these persons assuming nearly the whole burden—by rationalizing, denying and overlooking his offensive acts—of attempting to re-establish a socially acceptable relationship with him. He is depicted typically as com-

---

[22] Students of race relations will recognize in this a phenomenon closely akin to "inverse passing" as when a white becomes closely identified with Negroes and passes into a Negro subculture.

[23] Gowman, *op. cit.*

[24] I am indebted to Sheldon Messinger for his valuable comments in these connections.

pulsively wedded to his deviance and incapable of or uninterested in making restitutive efforts of his own. Finally, following some critical act of his, normalization fails *in toto* and community agencies are called in to relieve the primary group of its unmanageable burden.

There is much about this picture that is doubtlessly true and consonant with the ascertainable facts as we later come to learn of them from family, friends, police, courts and social agencies. We may question, however, whether it is a wholly balanced picture and whether, given the situational biases of these informational sources, all of the relevant facts have had an equal chance to surface. The perspective developed here suggests that it may be useful to consider whether, and to what extent, the deviator himself is not also engaged, albeit ineffectively, in somehow trying to sustain a normal definition of his person. Were research to indicate that such is the case, we might then ask what it is about his reparative efforts and the situations in which they occur that, as contrasted with the subjects of this study, so often lead to failure and an exacerbation of the troublesome behavior. (We probably will never know, except inferentially by gross extrapolation, of the possibly many cases in which some such interactive process succeeds in favorably resolving the deviating behavior.) In other words, as against the simplistic model of a com-

pulsive deviant and a futile normalizer we would propose one in which it is postulated that both are likely to become engaged in making corrective interactional efforts toward healing the breach. And, when such efforts fail, as they frequently do, it is as important in accounting for the failure to weigh the interactional dynamics and situational contexts of these efforts as it is the nature of the deviant acts and the actor.

Second, we would note that the interactional problems of the visibly handicapped are not so dissimilar from those which all of us confront, if only now and then and to a lesser degree. We too on occasion find ourselves in situations in which some uncamouflageable attribute of ours jars the activity and the expectations of our company. We too, if we wish to sustain—and, as is typically the case, our company wishes us to sustain—a fitting and valued representation of ourselves, will tacitly begin to explore with them ways of redressing, insulating and separating the discrepant attribute from ourselves.[25] Our predicament though is much less charged with awareness, more easily set to rights, than that of the visibly handicapped person and his company. But it is precisely this exaggeration of a common interactional predicament that affords us an added insight into the prerequisites and unwitting assumptions of sociable behavior in general. Put differently, it can be said that our

---

[25] Goffman, "Embarrassment and Social Organization," *op. cit.*

understanding of a mechanism is often crude and incomplete until it breaks down and we try to repair it. Breakdown and repair of interaction are what many of the visibly handicapped experience constantly in their lives. In studying this with them we are also studying much about ourselves of which we were heretofore unaware.

8 Expressed Attitudes of Families of Aphasics

Russell L. Malone

The importance of the place of the family on the aphasia rehabilitation team cannot be overemphasized. Turnblom and Myers (1952) stressed the importance of the family in "setting the atmosphere and determining the motivation for rehabilitation." Biorn-Hansen (1957) found that the nature of the relationship between the person with aphasia and his family exerted a considerable influence on the patient's progress. And Wepman (1951) pointed out that most often the major responsibility of aphasia rehabilitation rested upon the family and friends.

In view of the recognition of the important role the family will play in rehabilitation, it is interesting to note that the literature is almost barren of information on how the family is affected by aphasia. This information is of value clinically because the speech pathologist who is familiar with problems the family may experience is in a position to help them to avoid those situations which can be avoided, to change those situations which can be changed, and to accept those which cannot be altered. I, therefore, investigated reported changes in families following the onset of aphasia in one family member.

I held interviews with 25 persons representing the families of 20 persons with aphasia. The group consisted of 12 wives, four husbands, three daughters, two sons, two sisters, one niece, and one nephew. Eleven of the 20 families had children living at home at the time of the onset of aphasia. The aphasic conditions with which they had come in contact ranged from relatively minor problems to severe expressive-receptive problems. Five of the aphasic patients discussed were female, 15 were male. The socioeconomic status of the groups ranged from lower-middle to high-middle according to the Index of Status Characteristics (Warner, Meeker, and Eells, 1949).

All 25 interviews, with the exception of two, were held in the absence of the patient. In the two instances where the patient was included, it was felt that because of the extent of his recovery, he would be an asset rather than a hindrance to the discussion. All interviews were taped for the sake of accuracy. To obtain spontaneity, a routine set of questions was avoided and instead a list of broad categories of inquiry was employed.

PROBLEMS REPORTED BY FAMILY MEMBERS

Role Change

One of the most frequently reported problems was that of role change. This

Reprinted from the Journal of Speech and Hearing Disorders, 1969, 34:146–151.

change, reported by all spouses, is especially traumatic if the patient is the sole support of the family. If the husband is stricken, it is usually necessary for the wife to assume the traditionally male role of supporting the family. With this responsibility usually come certain other duties, such as making decisions on financial matters, exerting increased authority in the home, and having the "last word" on most subjects. Frequently the wife will react to these changes in one of two ways: (1) she will resent or fear the new responsibilities, or (2) she will enjoy her new authority and be reluctant to surrender it. Either reaction can create an obstacle to recovery for the patient.

The wife of Case I feared the responsibilities. She said that she had never had financial worries, but now she had to handle all financial dealings and it "terrified" her.

In contrast, the wife of Case H, whose husband had made excellent strides toward language recovery, reported that only recently had she been giving up some decision making to her husband. She recognized that he could probably handle more responsibilities "if I would let him."

The role change for the healthy husband can be equally extensive. Although he does not have to make the sudden change from a sheltered life to competing in the business world, he must assume many new responsibilities.

The husband of Case A said that after he closed his office for the night, he had to hurry home to do the household chores. On weekends he did the grocery shopping.

The husband of Case G, who had a top position in industry, explained that his responsibilities at home were more exhausting than those at work. He listed the household chores he must do each evening and added to that a list of his morning duties. Besides the housework, he had to walk his wife each morning for five or 10 minutes to prevent swelling in her weakened right leg and foot.

One of the more frequently reported effects of this role change is the new way in which the nonaphasic spouse sees his or her marriage partner. The wife of Case P said that she thought of him "not as a husband, but as a boarder." The husband of Case A reported that he now thought of his wife as a daughter. The wives of Case D and Case N regarded their husbands as "convalescent" children.

In every instance the families stated that in most cases the family as a closely knit unit no longer existed. They no longer enjoyed the same things; they no longer discussed their problems with one another.

Irritability

Upon examining their own personalities, 13 family members admitted to being irritable more often and to a greater degree than was true before their relative became aphasic. "I've heard it said," commented the wife of Case D, "that the aphasic person is different than he was before. I'm not sure, but I do know that I've changed." She stated that she had learned to control her irritation, but "sometimes I think if I could just lash out, it would help."

The daughter of Case J indicated similar feelings when she said that she sometimes felt like "screaming at her—slapping her—but I remain silent."

Irritability is an especially disturbing characteristic when it creates, as it frequently does, guilt feelings. Mr. A said that his daughter often would get upset with her mother's nagging, but then she would be very ashamed for not being more understanding.

Guilt Feelings

Feelings of guilt were reported by 17 relatives interviewed. Turnblom and Myers (1952) reported that guilt was manifested by the family in different ways: a feeling (1) that they were responsible for the patient's problems, (2) that the aphasia was a punishment for wrongs done, or (3) that they were not doing all they should be doing for their relative.

The wife of Case I disclosed guilt feelings of the third type when she said, "I just couldn't take it anymore. I had to put my husband in a home. I know he'd be happier at home, but I'm not equal to it." To help quiet these feelings, she visited her husband daily, "even though the nurses tell me that it upsets him when I come so often. I don't care. Visiting is the only thing that I can do and I'm going to do it."

Altered Social Life

The families of 18 patients reported that their own social lives had been changed in many ways. Nearly all families reported that their friends gradually stopped coming to visit. One wife felt that their friends received little satisfaction from their frustrated attempts to communicate with her husband; another felt that her friends were afraid of her husband; another reported that her husband would insult their friends and order them out of the house. Many of the families admitted, however, that it was they and not their friends who were responsible for the estrangement. Many of the families had been ashamed and embarrassed by the conduct of their relative with aphasia and had discouraged visits by their friends. One wife, after months of loneliness, said that perhaps she should have explained her husband's difficulty rather than trying to hide him from family and friends.

The wife of Case D reported that she refused to attend athletic events with her husband any more because he embarrassed her. She stated that he became very angry with the umpire and accosted him with more than customary ferocity. She found that even going to church with her husband would be disrupting. "He swears when he disagrees with the minister."

The husband of Case G reported that he had no social life anymore. "I can't even take time for a drink with the boys after work without feeling guilty."

Financial Problems

The many problems which the family of the person with aphasia must face are aggravated by financial complications. Fifteen families stated concerns related to finances. Not only are expenses sharply increased, but in many instances income is suddenly reduced.

The wife of Case K, a mother of five school-aged children, found that she had to depend on "my church, family, and friends for all my money." Some of her friends took up collections and her church took care of her household and hospital bills.

The husband of Case A reported that, for a period of time immediately following his wife's attack, he hired two full-time people, a housekeeper and a companion. To this he added the expense of the medical doctor and the speech pathologist. He stated that his financial worries were aggravated by his wife's insistence on "things we can't afford any longer."

The husband of Case G reported that he had spent $2800 the previous year for medical expenses in addition to paying the salary of a full-time person to stay with his wife during the day.

Job Neglect

Because of time and thought devoted to their wives after they became aphasic, the husbands of Case A and Case G reported that they had neglected their jobs. Mr. G said that he no longer spent the time on the job that he knew he should. Since he was in a position where he could leave the office at various times during the day, he frequently did so. "It's good for the wife, but not for the job."

Mr. A said that he found it hard to keep his mind on his work after his wife became aphasic. He stated that his business had suffered considerably during the first couple of years, "just when I needed money the most."

Mr. A also pointed out that his inability to entertain at home or accept social invitations had been a business handicap. The public relations which his job demanded had been seriously impaired.

Health Problems

Seven families reported health problems related to the condition of the relative with aphasia. The wife of Case I reported that her rest had been disturbed each night. Her husband was incontinent and, although she padded the bed, he would want to get up each night.

The wife of Case E stated that the three weeks that her husband spent at home between hospitals were almost unbearable. "I got no sleep because I was constantly watching over him."

The wife of Case O said that she had been under a doctor's care for four months. Her doctor stated that her problem was caused, she said, by the "strain of my husband's sickness."

Mental health as well as physical health can be impaired. The daughter of Case I said that she felt that her mother (the nonaphasic parent) should visit a psychiatrist in order to "help her out of her sedentary life, an existence loaded with guilt feelings."

Oversolicitousness and Rejection

The husband of Case G said that he had to send his wife away frequently or else he would not be able to bear the responsibility of caring for her. He stated that an arrangement would have to be worked out whereby each of his three daughters would care for her four months a year, otherwise, with the effect his wife's illness was having on him, the children would eventually be "stuck with both of us all the time."

Family attitudes of oversolicitousness or rejection, reported by 18 relatives, may stem from what Turnblom and Myers (1952) referred to as a feeling of "anxiety and uncertainty" by the families "in the family-patient relationship." There was evidence that the family members, not quite certain how to act or react to their relative with aphasia, either gave excessive attention to the patient or pretended that there was no change, attempting to ignore or avoid the very real problems which had to be met. Mrs. O, for example, anxiously awaited the day when her 82-year-old husband, with severe receptive-expressive aphasia, would be cured so that "we can move back to our house again."

Effect on Children

Children in the family of a person with aphasia present a special problem. The children reported many of the same experiences related by other family members, but because of their youth these problems can have more far-reaching effects.

The husband of Case A believed that his daughter's social life had been seriously impaired because of the lack of interest and attention paid to developing her social graces. "For practical purposes she hasn't had a mother since she was 11 years old." The daughter, in a separate interview, said, "After Mother became aphasic, I didn't have a

mother or a father. His time was so taken up with Mother that he didn't have much left for me." The son of Case A said that he left home shortly after his mother became aphasic; "I never did spend much time at home again."

CLINICAL IMPLICATIONS

Expressed attitudes of families of patients with aphasia strongly suggest the need for speech pathologists to recognize the necessity of providing a counseling program for the significant family members. The family cannot function as positive members of "the rehabilitation team" until they have been educated to the many and varied problems associated with aphasia and given some help in coping with these problems. The disruption, which may begin with the language and personality disorder within the patient, creates severe problems for the family which in turn aggravate the condition of the patient.

This self-perpetuating circle of events must be broken if the most progress is to be obtained in rehabilitation. The speech pathologist can achieve this by working with both the patient and his family.

A counseling program for families should be instituted as soon as possible after the onset of aphasia. Problems such as those resulting from oversolicitousness and social withdrawal may be avoided through early counseling. Problems which have already developed, such as those associated with feelings of guilt or rejection, may be reduced; and problems related to changes which cannot be altered, such as role change, may be more easily accepted.

Relatives who are able to cope with the problems which aphasia presents for them will be best able to help the patient to cope with his. The family can, with the help of the speech pathologist, make a positive contribution toward the recovery from aphasia.

ACKNOWLEDGMENT

This report is based in part on an M.S. thesis submitted to the University of Utah under the direction of Wallace A. Goates.

REFERENCES

Biorn-Hansen, Vera, Social and emotional aspects of aphasia. J. Speech Hearing Dis., 22, 53–59 (1957).

Turnblom, M., and Myers, J. S., Group discussion programs with the families of aphasic patients. J. Speech Hearing Dis., 17, 393–396 (1952).

Warner, W. L., Meeker, M., and Eells, K. Social Class in America. Chicago: Science Research Associates (1949).

Wepman, J. M., Recovery from Aphasia. New York: Ronald Press Company (1951).

9 Stigma Management and Amputee Rehabilitation

Harris Chaiklin and
Martha Warfield

In the United States about two-thirds of the disabled receive at least some physical therapy; only 18 percent complete their rehabilitation (18). Treatment that is not provided, is incomplete, or has failed creates a cosmic human deficit. While the physical and psychological components in rehabilitation have been thoroughly plumbed, physicians have been slow to consider other treatment agents. It was not until the 1960's that social factors began to be seriously entertained (21).

The study reported here explores the way amputees handle the interpersonal tensions instigated through their handicap. An interactional focus was chosen in order to move beyond static social variables to the process through which the practitioner can integrate social factors in therapeutic procedure (5). In the words of Elledge, the social worker:

> must be able to define the social situation of the patient in such a way as to help the other members of the team see the life situation of the patient in all its social reality .... [The psychosocial evaluation] individualizes the meaning of the illness or handicap to that particular patient and his family (7, p. 415).

Goffman's stigma concept sums up important social realities that the disabled faces. Stigma describes "the situation of the individual who is disqualified from full social acceptance" (12, Preface). Where the stigmatizing attribute is manifest, as amputation is, one is faced with managing tensions generated by the discrepancy between what is expected (a whole "normal" other person) and what he actually is (a "cripple"). The way one copes with these interactions is called *stigma management*. Management strategies range from trying to "pass" for normal to limiting associations to fellow outcasts.

The stigmatized status and social marginality of the physically handicapped have long been recognized (1). A slowly developing literature substantiates the hypothesis that the stigmatized feelings of people who deviate from expected and accepted normals affect their behavior in significant ways (3, 4, 6, 8, 10, 23).

In spite of the growing awareness of the importance of interpersonal factors in the treatment of the handicapped, the most recent literature reviews indicate stigma continues to be neglected by social workers and other team members. Freidson suggests that the reluctance of rehabilitation professionals to recognize and deal with

Reprinted from Rehabilitation Literature, 1973, 34(6):162–166.

stigma is a real failing of the profession. He states that for the very reason that agencies do not concede stigma, they are too prone to ignore the fact that it does exist socially in the community and so deny the consequences ... for the individual's community life" (11, p. 96). Siller, too, stresses the importance of the psychological components of rehabilitation and flatly states, "We are grossly negligent in discharging persons without adequate orientation as to reality problems generated by interaction with family and the community" (20, p. 296).

Studies that have used social variables in attempting to predict rehabilitation success have focused on static factors, e.g., age, sex, and self-concept, rather than the dynamics that result during interaction (2, 14, 15, 16, 20). Fishman has suggested that what is needed is to work with three sets of variables: 1) the experiences and reality problems with which the amputee must cope; 2) the variety of behavioral and emotional responses with which the person reacts to these experiences; and 3) identifying the dynamic processes that relate objective experiences and behavioral and emotional responses (9). That is the strategy of this study.

The general argument developed from the literature review is that the way a person sees himself affects his ability to carry through a rehabilitation course. If being stigmatized by others affects behavior, this should affect progress in rehabilitation. What would intervene in this progress are ways of handling the stigmatization so

that its effects are neutralized. Accordingly, this project's working hypothesis is: There is a relationship between modes of stigma management and progress toward rehabilitation goals.

THE SAMPLE

To test this proposition required a study group with the degree of disability controlled. The outpatient Prosthetic Clinic of the department of physical medicine and rehabilitation of the University of Maryland Hospital provided such a setting. After permission was secured from the physical therapist, all lower extremity amputees being treated at the Clinic during February, March, and April, 1970, were requested to participate in the study. Criteria for inclusion were: 1) to have been evaluated and accepted for prosthetic rehabilitation; 2) to be fitted with a first prosthesis rather than a replacement; 3) to have attended the clinic regularly for one prior month to allow time for progress to be evaluated; and 4) to be over age 18. Of the 26 patients who met these criteria, 24 participated. (The dropouts were one person with major additional physical impairment and one who refused, who came regularly to the clinic but who interacted with no one.)

Except for the limits imposed by selection criteria, the study group is representative of the general prosthetic population in public hospital clinics. In Table 1 descriptive characteristics are presented. An important paren-

Table 1. Description of prosthetic sample

Sex	Percent
Male	58
Female	42
Age	
50+	83
−50	17
Race	
Negro	63
White	37
Marital status	
Married	75
Other	25
Social class Hollingshead ISP	
IV	38
V	62
Source of support	
Welfare	38
Social Security	8
Pension	22
Family	27
Self-supporting	5
Reason for amputation	
Diabetes	67
Circulatory disorder	17
Accident	16
Treatment initiated	
3 months prior	54
3−6 months prior	34
6 months plus prior	12
Vocational rehabilitation client	
Yes	75
No	25

N = 24.

thetical implication of these data is that they duplicate the analysis Schon made of services to the blind (19). The amputee population is changing from young victims of accidents who can be returned to the labor force to older people whose general physical condition precludes effective work participation. The available services do not match the needs of the population they are intended to serve.

DATA COLLECTION

Stigma management was divided into the categories of *perception* and *interaction*. Perception of stigma was obtained by using eight items from the New York University Prosthetic Devices Study (17, p. 46–49). Each item has five alternatives ranging from "always" to "never." Scores could range from 8, perception of stigma, to 40, denial of stigma. For data analysis, scores were split at 25.

The interactional component was obtained from an open-ended questionnaire modeled on the one used by Feinblatt (8). Patients were asked to complete statements like: "When a child stares at me I. . . ." The 18 items in the questionnaire were scored in terms of: 1) positive interaction; 2) negative interaction; 3) lack of interaction. Each response was scored independently by at least two people; agreement was achieved on first scoring on over 98 percent of the responses. If 60 percent of the responses fell into one of these categories, that was defined as the modal response.

As we will illustrate in the final part of the paper, this scoring procedure subsumes a rich variety of responses. Patients responded to questions in terms of feelings, attitudes, or behavior; they described situations that actually occurred or those that they imagined; they focused on the physical, social, or emotional aspects of their disability; and they reported on their own reactions or the actual or anticipated reactions of others.

Rehabilitation movement was evaluated by the physical therapist in terms of physical progress, prognosis, motivation, attitude, and patient satisfaction. Ratings were summed on a four-point scale ranging from excellent to poor.

Patients and staff were very cooperative in collection of data. Indeed, an important finding is that the majority of the patients were glad to have the chance to discuss feelings about amputation. As one of them said, "It was a pleasure for you to ask me questions like this."

FINDINGS

In Table 2 there is a modest relationship between perception of stigma and

Table 2. Perception of stigma and progress in rehabilitation

	Perception	
Progress	Low	High
Excellent	3	7
Less than excellent[a]	8	6
N = 24	11	13

[a]Since 10 patients were rated excellent and 11 good for purposes of this analysis the 3 less than satisfactory progress ratings were grouped with the good.

Table 3. Mode of interaction and progress in rehabilitation

	Mode of interaction		
Progress	Positive	None	Variable
Excellent	6	1	3
Less than excellent	10	3	1
N =	16	4	4

progress in rehabilitation. Those who tended to deny stigma made less adequate progress in their treatment.

In Table 3 there is a modest relationship between mode of interaction and progress in rehabilitation. Those who responded with positive interaction or no interaction to stigma-identifying situations are less likely to make excellent progress in rehabilitation than those with a variable response. Table 3 does not contain a negative interaction category; of the 504 responses to the stigma interaction questionnaire, only 9 responded with negative interaction. Almost all the negative-response people were in the variable category.

We interpret Tables 2 and 3 to mean that extreme denial of stigma hinders the rehabilitation process. In Table 2 denial is directly reflected. In Table 3 it is inferred because several people in the positive interaction category gave flat, stereotyped "goody-goody" answers to questions.

The conclusion about denial, though tentative, is supported by other work. Feinblatt found that mothers of emotionally disturbed children who accepted their stigmatized role functioned more adequately (8). Kaplan, Boyd, and Bloom have noted that mentally ill people who do not accept a patient role tend not to accept treatment. They say of people in this position that

> If they are to achieve maximum therapeutic benefits from their experience, they must resolve this conflict in a way that permits acceptance of the fact of their patienthood while minimizing the stress occasioned by the perceived disparagement of their status (13, p. 122).

This is a critical issue facing any person in a stigmatized status. Organizations of ex-mental patients, prisoners, alcoholics, the disabled, and other socially leprous categories always exact a price for the strength that comes from group participation. More needs to be known about both the long- and short-run effects of accepting a deviant status. It seems probable that immediate advantages in facilitating social reintegration and treatment are lost if one's social status continues to depend on identification with a warped role.

Aside from the limitation of a small pilot study sample, three factors combine to suggest why our attained differences were not larger and further statistical analysis was not practical. The first of these is that, by limiting the sample to those effectively involved in treatment, there was a loading at the good progress end of the scale. The second was that the clinic, in contrast to other hospital clinics, provided excellent continuity of care. Each patient was treated by the same physical therapist and physician throughout. Since each patient came

to the clinic two or three times a week and stayed several hours there was much interaction between staff and other patients. While this allowed for much exchange of information, it may also have contributed to stereotyping interaction responses and created a response set. At the time of this study no social worker was on the team; rehabilitation professionals focused on the physical and technical aspects of the prosthesis and not on the interpersonal pressures associated with life in the community.

Third, and most important, there was a complex interaction between sex, race, stigma management, and progress in rehabilitation. For example, in Table 4, Negro men who use a positive mode of interaction are making excellent progress but Negro women and white men who use the same mode are making unsatisfactory progress. While there are many speculations that can be made about these data, they are not profitable. At the very least, age would have to be included as another factor. Even though

Table 4. Sex, race, mode of interaction, and progress in rehabilitation

Sex and race	Positive		None		Variable	
	E[a]	E−[b]	E	E−	E	E−
Negro male	4	−	−	1	2	−
Negro female	1	7	−	−	−	−
White male	1	3	1	1	−	1
White female	−	−	−	1	1	−
N =	6	10	1	3	3	1

[a]Excellent.
[b]Less than excellent.

our study group is homogeneous in regard to physical disability there was so much variance in the social factors that further analysis was shortstopped.

On the basis of responses to the interaction questionaire, we can present some illustrations providing clinical support for the role actual and anticipated denial responses played in rehabiliation treatment.

With people in general and with strangers, the amputee responds positively in those situations in which he is physically present and can really participate. This includes circumstances of "being with," "being comfortable with," "talking with," and "being helped." Where he is "stared at" or labeled "cripple," the amputee tends to avoid interaction or to be negative. Eight out of the nine negative responses were on staring and labeling items.

It would appear that the most difficult situations are those where the person feels he is an object to be gawked at or is related to as a stereotype. There is too much social difference to make initiating interaction easy and too much of a sense of powerlessness to do anything about the resulting frustration. The item that elicited the most negative responses was one dealing explicitly with labeling: "If I were in a crowd and heard someone say 'cripple' I would . . ."

> I'd just tell them 'Well, I couldn't help it.' (Said in an angry tone of voice.)

> Well, I'd like to know what he's talking about saying I'm crippled! I know I'm crippled! (Also angrily.)

> Get mad!

> I blew my stack one day with a cab driver. He said people with crutches and wheelchairs should stay home. I can't tell you what I said to him!

The negative responses contributed to making a person's interactions "variable." While their numbers are small, these people made excellent progress (Table 3). This item also generated many no-interaction answers that were denying or rationalizing. Typical responses included:

> I'd feel sorry for them.

> Don't know. I never heard no one make remarks about cripples. People don't usually.

> Do nothing. I wouldn't feel so bad about it. I'd just be crippled.

> Well, that's what I am, crippled, and I'm satisfied with that.

It was our impression that while many of the patients had experienced these reactions they had not had much practice in thinking through how to handle them. These people tended to be in the less-than-excellent progress category.

Where the amputees were asked to evaluate the attitude of others toward them or to evaluate changes in relationships with others, they tended to mix positive interaction and no interaction in their responses. While almost all the patients wanted to be with other people they were not really sure about how others "really" felt about them. For example, typical responses to the item "When people know you are an amputee, they . . ."

> Will talk. I guess . . . to me.

I haven't found anything like that. No one has said anything like that.

Well they don't. I don't know what they think. The average one tries to help you.

Some of them look like they feel sorry for you.

The group was about evenly split between feelings closer and farther away from friends since becoming an amputee. The chief reason for declining social participation seemed to be isolation caused by the physical disability. For example:

I'm not around them like I used to be. Most are working and on Sunday be down drinking. I just be sitting around the house.

I have trouble getting around. I don't see them as often.

I haven't seen my old friends. One is all I've seen since I had my leg off. I just stay home. I never go out.

I guess . . . I can't do anything. I don't participate.

These people tended to make less than excellent progress. Those who felt closer to their friends tended to identify social and interpersonal reasons for this:

I never thought about it . . . closer. . . . They always call me up and take me places.

Seems like they help you more than when you had both of them.

They think they can be of service to you without imposing on your hospitality. Someone's always watching to give me a hand.

I guess they feel sorry for me.

These people made excellent progress. The Stigma Interaction Questionnaire provides rich illustrations of the way amputees handle persons and situations where they must confront the reality of their amputation. It was found, for instance, that children create a special problem and are responded to differently and that health professionals are not seen as having time to discuss feelings about amputation. All this adds up to the fact that making an adjustment to amputation is a complex process that requires developing new patterns of interaction.

CONCLUSION

While the limitations of a pilot study precluded definitive support for linking stigma management to rehabilitation progress, the findings do warrant suggesting further study of the dynamic processes that link the amputee's experiences and reality problems to treatment procedures. Amputee behavior in social situations is not random but follows predictable patterns that vary with the people involved and the situation. Stigma and stigma management provide conceptual tools that make intelligible the behavior of the amputee as he relates to others.

Rehabilitation professionals should discuss stigma as part of their practice. The rehabilitation social worker should help the patient deal with his feelings and work out effective methods of stigma management. This is especially important at the beginning of treatment, when other members of the family are included as part of the psychosocial evaluation. The social worker must correctly interpret the patient's feelings and reality needs to the rest of the team and to his family. Without this the patient has to bear the entire burden of adjusting to his difference. Consideration of stigma management is one factor that can increase the rate of successfully completing rehabilitation treatment. Amputation and other forms of disability are an interpersonal as well as a personal process.

ACKNOWLEDGMENTS

For their support and cooperation thanks are due to Katharine Kemp, M.D., the Prosthetic Clinic director, and Jean Dockhorn, ACSW, the director of social services at the University of Maryland Hospital.

LIST OF REFERENCES

1. Barker, Roger G. The Social Psychology of Physical Disability. J. Social Issues. Fall, 1948. 4:4:28–38.
2. Barker, Roger G., Wright, Beatrice A., Meyerson, Lee, and Gonick, Mollie R. Adjustment to Physical Handicap and Illness: A Survey of the Social Psychology of Physique and Disability. New York: Social Science Research Council, 1953 (Bull. 55).
3. Birenbaum, Arnold. On Managing a Courtesy Stigma. J. Health and Social Behavior. Sept., 1970. 11:3:196–206.
4. Cahnman, Werner J. The Stigma of Obesity. Sociolog. Quart. Summer, 1968. 9:283–299.
5. Chaiklin, Harris. Social System, Personality System, and Practice

Theory, p. 1–14, in: National Conference on Social Welfare. Social Work Practice, 1969. New York: Columbia Univ. Pr., 1969.
6. Dembo, Tamara, Levitan, Gloria L., and Wright, Beatrice A. Adjustment to Misfortune—A Problem of Social Psychological Rehabilitation. Artificial Limbs. Autumn, 1956. 3:2:4–62.
7. Elledge, Caroline H. Medical Social Worker, Ch. 19, p. 414–426, in: Pattison, Harry A., ed. The Handicapped and Their Rehabilitation. Springfield, Ill.: Charles C Thomas, 1957.
8. Feinblatt, Marjorie W. Stigma Management Strategies of Mothers of Emotionally Disturbed Children. Unpublished Master's project, School of Social Work, University of Maryland, 1965.
9. Fishman, Sidney. Amputation, p. 1–50, in: Garrett, James F., and Levine, Edna S., eds. Psychological Practice with the Physically Disabled. New York: Columbia Univ. Pr., 1962.
10. Freeman, Howard E., and Simmons, Ozzie G. Feelings of Stigma Among Relatives of Former Mental Patients. Social Problems. Spring, 1961. 8:4:312–321.
11. Freidson, Eliot. Disability as Social Deviance, Ch. 4, p. 71–99, in Sussman, Marvin B., ed. Sociology and Rehabilitation. Chicago: American Sociological Association (1966).
12. Goffman, Erving. Stigma: Notes on the Management of Spoiled Identity. Englewood Cliffs, N.J.: Prentice-Hall, 1963.
13. Kaplan, Howard B., Boyd, Ina, and Bloom, Samuel W. Patient Culture and the Evaluation of Self. Psychiatry. May, 1964. 27:2:116–126. (Reprinted in: Rubington, Earl, and Weinberg, Martin S., eds. Deviance: The Interactionist Perspective. New York: Macmillan Co., 1968.)

14. Litman, Theodor J. Self-Conception and Physical Rehabilitation, Ch. 29, p. 550–574, in: Rose, Arnold M., ed. Human Behavior and Social Processes: An Interaction Approach. Boston: Houghton Mifflin, 1962.

15. Ludwig, Edward G., and Adams, Shirley Davidson. Patient Cooperation in a Rehabilitation Center: Assumption of the Client Role. J. Health and Social Behavior. Dec., 1968. 9:4:328–336.

16. MacGuffie, Robert A., and others. Self-Concept and Ideal-Self in Assessing the Rehabilitation Applicant. J. Counsel. Psychol. Mar., 1969. 16: 2(Pt.1):157–161.

17. Peizer, Edward. Studies of the Upper-Extremity Amputee. 1. Design and Scope. Artificial Limbs. Spring, 1958, 5:1:4–56.

18. Rusk, Howard A. The Re-entry Problem: Enabling the Disabled. Washington, D.C.: U.S. Social and Rehabilitation Service, 1970. (pamphlet)

19. Schon, Donald A. The Blindness System. Public Interest. Winter, 1970. 18:25–38.

20. Siller, Jerome. Psychological Situation of the Disabled with Spinal Cord Injuries. Rehab. Lit. Oct., 1969. 30:10:290–296.

21. Usdane, William M. Technology Transfer. In: O'Toole, Richard, ed. The Organization, Management, and Tactics of Social Research. Cambridge, Mass.: Schenkman Publ. Co., 1971.

22. Wright, Beatrice A. Physical Disability—A Psychological Approach. New York: Harper, 1960.

23. Yarrow, Marion Radke, Clausen, John A., and Robbins, Paul R. The Social Meaning of Mental Illness. J. Social Issues. 1955. 11:4:33–48.

10 Physical Disability Among Married Women:
Problems in the Husband-Wife Relationship

James K. Skipper, Jr.,
Stephen L. Fink, and
Phyllis N. Hallenbeck

It has been argued that the wife's role is central in the structure of the family, that its impairment will strain the entire family system. This paper examines the effect of the wife's long-term disability on the marital relationship. It focuses on husbands' and wives' need satisfaction and marital satisfaction as each attempts to adapt to problems generated by the wife's impairment. The goal of our research was to develop a broader understanding of the effects which a major disability may have on a wife's need and marriage satisfaction, and on those of her husband.

The study consisted of a series of interviews with 36 disabled women between the ages of 21 and 60, and with their husbands. To be included in the sample, the women's disability must have occurred after marriage, and interfered with the active pursuit of homemaking activities; the women lived at home with their husbands; and they were willing and physically able to be interviewed. The sample included completely disabled women,

bed-ridden and unable to move, as well as those with less severe impairments, such as inability to manage stairs. Ten of the families were Negro and 26 white. As defined by the Hollingshead Index of Social Position, 21 of the 36 families fell at the lower end of the Index in classes IV and V, seven in class III, and eight in classes I and II.

Three basic measures were used in the study: a Perception of Needs Interview Schedule; a Marital Satisfaction Interview Schedule; and a Mobility Dimension Scale. The Perception of Needs Schedule was based on Maslow's theory (1954) that human needs may be classified on five levels: physiological, safety, love and belongingness, esteem, and self-actualization, in that order of precedence. Five items for each of the five need levels were adapted for use with the disabled women.

The Marital Satisfaction Schedule consisted of 26 items concerning seven previously identified, important components of marital satisfaction: companionship, social status, power,

Reprinted from the Journal of Rehabilitation, 1968, 34:16–19.

This investigation was supported in part by grant RD-1584 from the Rehabilitation Services Administration of HEW. The authors wish to express their appreciation to Olive K. Banister, executive director of the Vocational Guidance and Rehabilitation Services in Cleveland, for her assistance throughout the project.

understanding, affection, marital esteem, and sex.

The Mobility Dimension Scale was based on one devised by Christopherson (1963) but revised to take into account impairment of the upper extremities. Evaluation of the degree of impaired mobility was made either by the attending physician or a physical therapist. From this evaluation a total mobility score was devised for each of the disabled women.

Total need satisfaction scores and marital satisfaction scores were compiled for both wives *and* husbands. In addition, subtotals were compiled for all respondents on each of the five need levels, and each of the seven components of marital satisfaction.

PHYSICAL MOBILITY AND NEED SATISFACTION

One of the major goals of the study was to explore the relationship between the physical mobility of the disabled woman and the satisfaction of her everyday needs and the needs of her spouse. The correlation between the total need satisfaction and mobility of the disabled women was low and not significant. This indicates that greater mobility does not automatically result in greater need satisfaction even though in many cases the tendency may be in that direction. The finding is consistent with Christopherson's observations (1960) about the role effectiveness of disabled homemakers:

> ... The woman's reaction ... and her effectiveness in the role of

homemaker seemed to bear little relation to the relative seriousness of her case. Indeed, some of the physically most limited homemakers seemed to have the best organized and smoothly operating households. (p. 112)

When the five need levels were examined separately, only safety need satisfaction correlated with physical mobility at a statistically significant level. This finding suggests that the greater the physical mobility of the disabled woman, the greater will be her safety need satisfaction.

Closer inspection of the raw data indicated that most of the extremely low scores for satisfaction of safety needs were polio patients, dependent upon respiratory apparatus and other people for satisfaction of safety needs. For example, one woman stressed her dependence on mechanical breathing equipment and her fear of a power failure or other breakdown.

Low scores were also attained by women who could not get up to answer their doors and felt unsafe because the door was customarily kept open or unlocked for accessibility of friends and family.

We know that disabled women with very low physical mobility become almost completely dependent upon others for their personal protection and safety. It is logical to expect that this is a source of concern and distress for them, especially when they are left alone for any length of time.

The same relationship does not hold true for mobility and physiological need satisfaction. Evidently dependence at this level does not cause as much concern as it does at the safety level. This may indicate that in the eyes of the very disabled woman, safety needs require greater attention than physiological needs.

The correlation between the husband's need satisfaction and his disabled wife's physical mobility was actually very low. This was also true of each of the five individual need levels, none of them approaching a statistically significant level. This evidence indicates that there is no simple connection between the wife's level of functional mobility and the satisfaction of basic needs of the non-disabled husband. And even though it was not at a statistically significant level, the highest correlation was with safety and satisfaction, as it was in the case of the disabled wife. An examination of the raw data indicated the men who had the lowest safety need satisfaction scores were married to the least mobile women. Several of the husbands expressed dissatisfaction with their wives' medical care (one of the safety items). Although the few cases were not enough to produce more than a trend in the data, they do point to the husband's concern about the wife's situation as it affects his own sense of safety.

PHYSICAL MOBILITY AND MARRIAGE SATISFACTION

The data revealed that little could be predicted about the disabled women's marriage satisfaction from knowledge of their physical mobility. Total marriage satisfaction and all sub-areas showed very low correlations. This

finding is in line with Nagi and Clark's conclusion (1962) in a study of 806 severely disabled post-polio patients: degree of disability was not related to changes in marital status.

The fact that mobility did not correlate strongly with *either* index of satisfaction (need or marriage) is important. This reveals how difficult it is to establish simple connections between physical and psychological variables. One might argue that greater disability should lead to greater frustration of needs and greater strain on the marital relationship. But, with the exception of safety needs, this was not the case. An alternative argument might place the relationship within the context of a role-model. We know that two people can relate more easily with each other when their respective roles are clearly defined. When a wife becomes disabled, both she and her husband will sooner or later have to redefine and reevaluate their relationship. During the period of adjustment there is apt to be a high degree of role strain and role conflict. This may be greater for the partially disabled than for the totally disabled, since the former is likely to experience more ambiguity. A woman with an arthritic condition may, along with her husband, struggle a great deal more to redefine what may be considered normal everyday activities for her, than a woman who is confined to a bed.

We can therefore hypothesize two counter-forces acting upon the disabled individual and affecting the degree of need or marital satisfaction experienced: One force is the physical impairment itself, which blocks off habitual ways of satisfying needs, particularly safety needs. The other force (which runs counter to the first) is the change in the person's role expectations, which may be more ambiguous with little disability and clearer with severe disability.

As in the case of the women's marriage satisfaction, the women's physical mobility did not correlate highly with the husbands' total marriage satisfaction. However, when the seven sub-areas were examined separately, it was discovered that one of them, companionship satisfaction, did correlate significantly with the women's physical mobility.

This finding deserves careful consideration. Evidently the woman's companionship satisfaction is not dependent on her level of physical mobility and can be met in spite of great physical restrictions and limitations. However, this does not seem to be the case with the husbands. *The less the disabled woman's physical mobility, the less her husband's companionship satisfaction.*

Closer inspection of the original interviews uncovered a possible explanation for these correlations. Some of the husbands with severely disabled wives spend more time at home in companionship activities than they did prior to the disability. Although this appears to provide satisfying companionship for the wives, it does not for the husbands. They tend to miss the companionship of their wives in activities they previously enjoyed outside the home, such as visiting friends, seeing movies, etc.

MARRIAGE SATISFACTION AND NEED SATISFACTION

The correlation between the husbands' need satisfaction and marriage satisfaction was very high. All sub-category correlations (physiological, safety, love and belongingness, esteem, and self-actualization) were also high and at a significant level. This finding is not surprising. It reflects the close interrelationship between needs and marriage. Personal need gratification is likely to occur within the context of a marriage relationship. The correlation between the women's need satisfaction and marriage satisfaction was also high. In addition, all sub-category correlations were high and at a significant level, with the exception of physiological need satisfaction.

In order to explore more thoroughly this one low correlation, the five components of the physiological need level (pain, body processes, sleep, eating, and sex) were analyzed separately. None of the items showed a strong relationship with marriage satisfaction except sex. The correlation between satisfaction with sex and general marriage satisfaction was at a significant level. This suggests that the greater the disabled woman's sexual satisfaction, the greater will be her marriage satisfaction.

As Comarr (1962) and Guttman (1964) have noted, the physical condition of disabled persons has little to do with marital sexual role. In our sample of 36, only one woman was not participating in sexual activities because of the disability.

In all probability, from the point

of view of the women in our sample, the sex item is misclassified in Maslow's physiological category. It bears the same positive relationship to marriage satisfaction as the total categories of safety, love, esteem, and self-actualization. It is our interpretation that most women, including those in our sample, think of sex in broader terms than strictly physiological ones.

The correlation between wives' and husbands' need satisfaction was low and non-significant. Analysis of subcategories revealed a strong association only with love and belongingness needs. These results are readily explainable. Of all the need categories, love and belongingness tap the most direct relationship between wife and husband. In a sample of marriages which have survived the stresses of crippling diseases or injuries, we could be reasonably certain that some bond of love has been maintained and that each partner is directly dependent upon the other for satisfaction of love needs.

The absence of strong associations for the higher needs suggests that the source of satisfaction may be largely *outside* the husband-wife relationship. It may also reflect the possibility that except for the satisfaction of love needs, each spouse carves out a different way of life in order to meet needs, and that one spouse's satisfaction of these needs bears no significant relationship to the other's satisfaction.

The correlation between wives' and husbands' total marriage satisfaction was not significant. Thus, we cannot predict much about one marriage partner's satisfaction by a knowledge of the other's. In spite of the low total marriage satisfaction correlation when each of the sub-categories was examined separately, only companionship and sex were not at a significant level. We have already commented on the different meanings which sex gratification and companionship satisfaction have for the disabled women and their husbands in relation to their individual total marriage satisfaction. All of the significant correlations, marital esteem, affection, understanding, and social status, are consistent with the findings that there is a strong association between the wives' and husbands' love and belongingness satisfaction.

We now have an enriched picture of some of the most important aspects of the marital relationship. The significance of marital esteem tells us that mutual satisfaction is built not only upon the love aspects of the relationship, but also upon the mutual respect or esteem the partners hold for one another. Further, we can see the importance of mutuality in the satisfaction related to affection and understanding as well as to one's sense of influence or power in the relationship.

The social status sub-category consisted of three items for the men: satisfaction with self as provider, pride in job and money earned (compared with other people he knows), and satisfaction with conduct within the family (if any family member behaves in a shameful way). For the women, it consisted of satisfaction with *husband* as provider, satisfaction with *his* job and money earned, and satisfaction with conduct within the family. The significant correlation between husbands and wives reflects the degree to which they share these satisfactions. As one woman put it, "I'm happy if he's happy—he's the one who works there." Although four of our wives were helping to earn some minimal additional money, all were dependent on the husband's income, and most agreed with their spouses' evaluation as to its adequacy.

IMPLICATIONS FOR PROFESSIONAL PRACTICE

Historically in rehabilitation, disabilities have been categorized and treated as separate entities based almost entirely on their medical etiology. Separate programs are instituted for each type of disability—multiple sclerosis, poliomyelitis, muscular dystrophy, cerebral palsy, etc. However, in considering a physical disability from other than a medical treatment viewpoint, other factors are likely to be of equal importance. The type of onset (sudden or gradual), and the progressive or static nature of the condition may have much more impact on the individual than the fact of the etiology.

Furthermore, the nature and extent of the impairment may be much the same for several different etiologies. The problems of a bed-ridden arthritic are apt to be much more similar to those of a bed-ridden polio or spinal injury case than they are to another arthritic who is up and around.

There has also been an historical tendency to treat disease categories as stereotypes, and to search for the "TB personality" and so on. This approach tends to obliterate social and psychological patterns which transcend medical categories. We suspect that for most individuals there is an orderly pattern of emotional adjustment to severe disability (Shontz, 1962; Hallenbeck, 1964). An understanding of these social and psychological patterns would seem essential if rehabilitation professionals are to provide the best possible service to their clients. Several of the patterns found in this study may be useful in rehabilitation counseling.

First, the counselor or therapist should not make the mistake of thinking that the more severe the difficulty, the more problems of need gratification the patient will have. We postulate that *more* problems in daily living may be anticipated for disabled women who have a great deal of physical mobility than for those who have little mobility. It would be an error to assume that the completely paralyzed woman will automatically have more marriage and family problems than a less disabled woman. Greater mobility may cause greater role ambiguity. Neither the disabled woman nor her family knows exactly what she can do and what she can't do, or how close to her former self she is.

Adaptation may take time and cannot be rushed. Some trial and error, flexibility, and reality testing are necessary in these circumstances. Clear statements of medical facts may help a family in this struggle, and counseling with all members, including children, is necessary.

Second, as Fink, Fantz, and Zinker (1962) have argued, all five need levels are likely to be present at once. Rehabilitation procedures should not attempt to focus exclusively on any one set of needs to the total exclusion of the others. It should also be recognized that the physical condition of a disabled woman is *not* a very useful predictor of what she may report her important needs to be. Our subjects were not preoccupied with their physical condition to the exclusion of the higher needs of esteem and self-actualization. Some individuals showed an inverse relationship between physical condition (paralysis, pain, bladder problems, etc.) and physiological need satisfaction. This is exemplified in the words of the husband of a double leg amputee: "Seems like the more she suffers, the less she complains."

Others, whose mobility dimension score was high (indicating less severe loss), had low physiological need satisfaction, and complained bitterly that they didn't sleep well, that their meals didn't satisfy them, that their body processes "weren't working right," and that they were in constant pain.

For some individuals, coping with the hardships of a disability may become a challenge and an achievement-generating situation. The coping itself may be an esteem-producing and self-actualizing activity. The constant complaining by less-disabled women may be not only an expression of their unhappiness, but of their role ambiguity.

Third, the disability may have a different psychological meaning for the disabled woman than for the members of her family, and the different meanings are not always adequately communicated. A disabled woman may not know that her failure to perform household tasks is resented by her daughter, who now has to do them, or that her husband has a need to take her outside the home. A husband may believe that because his wife cannot go out alone, she needs no spending money of her own. Wives often feel very differently about the matter. Problem-solving may be accelerated when partners are able to recognize and verbalize their attitudes and desires. The professional person may be able to aid the family in this endeavor.

Finally, we cannot emphasize too much that the disability affects the social relationships of other members of the family group as well as those of the disabled woman herself. A change in her role precipitates changes in the roles of other family members. The disabled woman does not live in isolation, but as a socially and psychologically active member of a family group.

Just as Marra and Novis (1959) and Christopherson (1963) have urged vocational counselors to consider disabled men as having important family ties which greatly affect their rehabilitation, so we must urge all medical and professional rehabilitation personnel to consider disabled married women in the same way. McPhee, Griffiths, and Magleby (1963) and Litman (1964) have stressed the importance of family solidarity and family encouragement of the disabled as a positive factor in rehabilitation. The growing realization among rehabilitation personnel of the importance of the entire life circumstances of each patient must be fostered and given whatever guidance research can provide.

IMPLICATIONS FOR FUTURE RESEARCH

This project was an exploratory study. It did not attempt to test hypotheses; but some sort of systematic testing of the major findings on a large and representative sample of disabled individuals and their families is needed.

Our data are based almost exclusively on the subjects' attitudes toward disability and their perceptions of and expectations for behavior. We have little first-hand knowledge of actual behavior. We do not know to what degree attitudes and perceptions of our subjects are related to their behavior or predict their behavior. This should be an important area for further research.

In this project, the disability of the disabled woman was treated as an independent variable. Concern was with the consequences of the disability. One of the important hypotheses generated out of this type of approach dealt with the relationship of the degree of mobility of the disabled woman and role ambiguity. Certainly this hypothesis is subject to further investigation. But, as it stands, it illustrates the type of analysis which

may be obtained when disability is used as an independent variable.

Maslow's need theory (1954) was useful in relating the everyday problems of the disabled woman to other important variables. However, there are methodological problems involved in this approach. No attempt was made to measure the strength of importance of the need categories to the individual, even though it is generally accepted that individuals differ in this respect. It was also difficult to construct "pure" items which would pertain to only one category of needs at a time. The construction of scales that could satisfy these two requirements would be a major step forward in the study of the motivation of human behavior.

If we understood the dynamics of role ambiguity, our management of its consequences might be greatly improved. The severely disabled person may be subject to several different sets of expectations which conflict with one another. There may be a set of expectations predominant in the culture which a person accepts without much critical thought before being disabled. Or one may have personally known individuals having a particular disability, and expectations may be influenced by this specific knowledge. Another set of expectations is derived from the medical specialists on the case, who may be underestimating or overly optimistic about the abilities of the patient.

Finally, as demonstrated in this study, there are sets of expectations held by each family member for the disabled individual. There may be little consensus among the various sets, particularly when the degree of impairment does not fall at the extremes of the distribution. Role ambiguity suggests the need for research in at least three areas: What are the general expectations promoted by the culture about limitations imposed by the various degrees of impairment? What effect do individual beliefs have on individual expectations? How much influence might the medical team have in setting or altering expectations?

It is our hope that this study will generate a number of ideas for research in practical as well as theoretical areas. We have suggested just a few of the many possible questions which appear to offer exciting opportunities for interesting study and productive research.

REFERENCES

Christopherson, Victor A., and Swartz, F. M. "Role Modifications of the Disabled with Implications for Counseling." Final report, VRA Grant #755, Tucson, Arizona, 1963.

Christopherson, Victor A. "Role Modifications of the Handicapped Homemaker." Rehabilitation Literature XXI: 4, pp. 110–117; April 1960.

Comarr, A. Estin. "Marriage and Divorce Among Patients with Spinal Cord Injury," Journal of Indiana Medical Profession 9: 9, pp. 43–53; December 1962.

Fink, S. L., Fantz, Rainette, and Zinker, J. "Growth Beyond Adjustment: Another Look at Motivation." Paper read at American Psychological Association Meeting, St. Louis, September 1962.

Guttman, L. "The Married Life and Paraplegics and Tetraplegics." Paraplegia II, pp. 182–188; 1964–1965.

Hallenbeck, Phyllis N. "A Study of the Effects of Dogmatism on Certain Aspects of Adjustment to Severe Disability." Unpublished Ph.D. dissertation, Western Reserve University, 1964.

Litman, Theodor J. "An Analysis of the Sociological Factors Affecting the Rehabilitation of Physically Handicapped Patients." Archives of Physical Medicine 45, pp. 9–16; 1964.

Marra, Joseph L. and Novis, Frederick W. "Family Problems in Rehabilitation Counseling." Personnel and Guidance Journal 38, No. 1, pp. 40–42; September 1959.

Maslow, Abraham H. Motivation and Personality. New York: Harper Bros., 1954.

McPhee, W. M., Griffiths, K. A., and Magleby, F. L. "Adjustment of Vocational Rehabilitation Clients." Final report, VRA Grants #178 and #757, University of Utah, September 1963.

Nagi, Saad Z., and Clark, Donovan L. "Factors in Marital Adjustment After Disability." Unpublished, 1962 (mimeograph).

Shontz, F. C. "Severe Chronic Illness," in Garrett, S. L., and Levine, Edna (eds.), Psychological Practices with the Physically Disabled. New York: Columbia University Press, 1962, pp. 410–466.

11 Self-Socialization: Readjustment of Paraplegics in the Community

Betty E. Cogswell

Paraplegics receive little or no professional help for one aspect of the rehabilitation process. In the first phase of rehabilitation, medical teams are available for teaching the physical skills necessary for independent mobility and for assisting patients to accept the reality of their disability. In the final phase, rehabilitation counselors are available to assist with occupational choice, training, and placement. No professional assumes explicit responsibility, however, for assisting paraplegics to learn the social skills necessary to relate successfully with non-disabled people in the community. Many of these skills are acquired during a middle phase of rehabilitation, after paraplegics leave the hospital and before they resume full-time student or work roles.

Physical disability is potentially stigmatizing, and the salience of stigma increases outside of the hospital. To become successfully rehabilitated, paraplegics must learn to diminish this effect. This, however, occurs through self-teaching, for paraplegics are left to chart their own course. This paper presents findings on one aspect of the process—the way paraplegics sequentially arrange their social encounters. It should be noted, however, that the paraplegics studied were essentially unaware that their experiences were sequentially patterned.

PROCESS OF SOCIALIZATION

Rehabilitation may be analyzed advantageously as a process of socialization. In fact, if rehabilitation had not been conceptualized in this way, the present findings might have been overlooked. A socialization model focuses attention on the processes by which individuals acquire new roles and leads to questions on the development of new self-definitions, skills, activities, and associations. Socialization proceeds through interaction among novices (individuals learning a new role) and agents (individuals responsible for training). In the research reported here, socialization was studied from the perspective of the novices, that is, paraplegics' learning the disabled role. Paraplegics were interviewed at repeated intervals about

Reprinted from the Journal of Rehabilitation, 1968, 34:11–13, 35.

The present paper was delivered at the NRA conference in Cleveland in October 1967.

The author wishes to acknowledge the helpful suggestions of Professors Harvey L. Smith, Marvin B. Sussman, and Donald D. Weir, M.D. who read an earlier version of this paper.

their experiences after leaving the hospital. They were asked what they did, who they saw, how they responded to other people, and how other people responded to them. Comparison of the experiences of those studied reveals that the course of socialization was structured in a way that provided opportunities to develop and master social skills for relating to people in the normal world. Medical professionals may give patients gross indications that they will encounter interpersonal problems in the community, but paraplegics mainly discover these problems for themselves and proceed to handle them in their own way. They become their own socializing agents as well as agents for the many people they encounter who are uncertain about proper behavior toward a disabled person.

The data for this paper are taken from a more extensive study which followed paraplegics from the time of injury to the time they resumed roles in the community. Data were collected in a general teaching hospital over a five-year period by means of field observations and interviews with members of a rehabilitation team and with 36 young adult paraplegics. Eleven of these paraplegics were chosen for intensive study through a series of open-ended interviews with both patients and their families. Generalizations were abstracted primarily from the intensive study data. Data on the other 25 paraplegics, however, were used to refine initial hypotheses. The rehabilitation team was composed of physicians, nurses, physical therapists, occupational therapists, and social workers. The study group of paraplegics included both males and females, whites and Negroes, and private and staff patients. The subjects' social class ranged from lower class to upper middle.

MIDDLE PERIOD OF REHABILITATION

Paraplegics need a month or more after leaving the hospital to practice the physical skills necessary to function in the normal world. In theory, after this amount of time, they should be physically ready to resume a job or begin job training. A curious finding is that most paraplegics who do eventually resume full-time training or work roles delay for one to several years. The reasons for this delay are of particular concern for rehabilitation practitioners. Some medical professionals note differences in the way patients respond when they first go home and at that time in the future when they become ready to go back to work, but are unable to give a clear description of these differences. Some suggest that this may be a necessary period of mourning that paraplegics cannot be rushed through.

Compared to pre-trauma life, all of the paraplegics upon returning home had a marked reduction in (a) number of social contacts with others in the community, (b) frequency in entering community settings, and (c) number of roles that they played. All of the paraplegics studied eventually showed some increase in these three activities; however, there is wide variation in the extent of increase. If one takes resumption of a work role as a final indicator of rehabilitation, only six of 26 followed regularly at this hospital had reached this level at the time of last contact.[1] The others who arrested at lower levels along the way appear to have had common socialization experiences up to this point.

All paraplegics face problems which evolve from the stigma of disability. In the hospital, medical personnel help paraplegics develop a self-image of independence and personal worth. Although difficulties are encountered, it is easier to establish and maintain this self-image in the sheltered social environment of the hospital than in the world outside. When paraplegics return to their homes and communities, definitions of their disability as a social stigma reach the height of salience. This common problem apparently orders their course of socialization.

SELF-SOCIALIZATION
INTO A DEVALUED ROLE

In our society the disabled role is socially devalued. Effective socialization results through learning to reduce the stigmatizing effects of disability. Paraplegics must learn the physical and social skills necessary to play the role with sufficient ease to prevent contamination of their identity as well as their performance of other roles.[2] Physical disability, like most stigmas, is not equally stigmatizing in all social situations. Salience of disability as a stigma varies with the type of individual encountered and the type of social setting. It also varies with the paraplegic's definition and projection of self as worthy or demeaned and with his skill in managing others' definitions of his disability.

In learning the skills of stigma management, paraplegics become their own socializing agents. Change which occurs during this period is more apt to occur through day-to-day accommodation to problems rather than through systematic goal-directed behavior. Paraplegics have a diffuse image of a final goal—reintegration into the community as persons of independence and worth. This image was initiated in the hospital by rehabilitation practitioners. There is, however, no awareness of the intermediate steps necessary to attain this goal. There is no agent to spell out these steps nor to structure progress through the sequence.

Paraplegics, seemingly unaware of the long-range process, order their course of socialization in response to

---

[1] Ten of the original 36 did not return to this hospital for their medical care after completing physical retraining. Of the 26 followed here, one died, two were remaining at home on the advice of their lawyer, and one developed a heart condition which prevented his return to work. All of the paraplegics had either worked or had been full-time students prior to injury. The six subjects who did return to work, five men and one woman, are all from middle class families.

[2] See Erving Goffman, *Stigma: Notes on the Management of Spoiled Identity* (Englewood Cliffs, N.J.: Prentice-Hall, 1963), p. 5 for a sociological definition of stigma.

day-to-day problems by avoiding social situations where negative social response can destroy positive definitions of self, by seeking out social situations where demands are not beyond their current level of competence, and by manipulating social encounters to emphasize positive and minimize negative aspects of self. At first, when paraplegics have had little experience in dealing with disability as stigma, the threat of failure is great. Uncertain of what the responses of others will be, paraplegics tend to expect the worst. They are quick to interpret any questionable response as derogatory and rapidly withdraw if they perceive the slightest strain in a social encounter. They are apprehensive that the attention of others may be focused on the disability and that other aspects of self will be treated as irrelevant.

TIME-STRUCTURING
OF SOCIALIZATION

The middle period of rehabilitation begins with a self-imposed moratorium during which paraplegics remain at home. Uncertain about how to proceed, they arrest momentarily. Reentry into the community is gradual and is structured simultaneously in two ways: by sequential choice of social settings and sequential choice of associates. These two sequences begin with social situations which are easiest to handle and proceed to those more difficult. In essence, paraplegics search out the least threatening environments for the trial of new behavior.

Self-imposed Moratorium

On returning home, paraplegics become aware that their once familiar community has become strange. One world is lost, and another is yet to be gained. They are unclear about their own identity, for they must establish new self-definitions for the spectrum of social relationships. These range from casual encounters with waitresses, clerks, barbers, filling station attendants, and dentists to more enduring relationships with friends, dates, teachers, and employers. New definitions of self grow through encounter with others, yet paraplegics are reluctant to resume social contacts. Instead they stay at home for a time in passive avoidance of the outside world. Pretrauma conceptions of self do not apply; new conceptions of self have not emerged; and action is arrested because paraplegics are unable to answer the question, Who am I?

During the first few weeks, a host of friends and neighbors come to visit, but this is not sustained. Very quickly, paraplegics find themselves alone. They describe this period as a time of social isolation and inactivity. When asked, "Who do you see?" they reply, "Nobody." When asked, "What do you do?" they reply, "Nothing." Since there are few social expectations for the disabled role, paraplegics may stay at home for any length of time without arousing negative reactions from family or others in the community. Family and friends may encourage outings; but if the paraplegic is not responsive, these overtures tend to cease.

Sequential Selection of Social Settings

Paraplegics first enter those social settings which require the least amount of physical and social skill and proceed later to those more difficult. In selecting settings, patients used three criteria: (a) physical accessibility, (b) flexibility for leaving the scene, and (c) salience of stigma.

Physical accessibility may be considered in terms of four types of increasingly difficult settings: (a) those where the paraplegic can go and remain in his automobile; (b) those allowing easy wheel chair maneuvering, where surfaces are level and where there are wide doors and aisles; (c) those that can be easily entered by wheel chair but require the paraplegic to change seats, such as a dentist's office, barber shop, or theater; and (d) those where some physical assistance from another person is necessary, such as climbing long flights of stairs or crossing rough terrain.

Regarding flexibility for leaving settings, paraplegics want the option of leaving quickly if stigma should become salient. They are concerned with the socially acceptable length of time one must remain after entering a setting. Public streets provide the most flexibility. Following in order of decreasing flexibility are stores, places where one may have an appointment which lasts for thirty minutes or longer, visits, and parties. The most lengthy time-binding setting and the last to be re-entered is place of work.

Settings vary in the degree to which each paraplegic feels his disability may become stigmatizing. One paraplegic mentioned that "People don't mind you on the street, but they don't like you in their intimate places like bars." Several mentioned that they began going to church and then to church parties long before they had the nerve to go to private parties. They seemed to feel that people in a religious setting had a greater obligation to accept them.

Sequential Selection of Associates

As paraplegics resume social relationship in the community, they choose individuals who will support definitions of them as individuals of independence and social worth. These relationships are sequentially timed. First, paraplegics phase-out and seldom resume relationships with pre-trauma friends; second, they begin to associate with individuals of lower social status; and third, they begin to associate with new individuals of equal status.

The paraplegics maintained very few friendships that existed prior to their injuries, declaring that they did not like to be with people that they had known before the accident. Pre-trauma friends are attached to a conception of the paraplegic as he once was and have difficulty relating to him as a disabled person. Paraplegics find it difficult to establish a new identity with those who view them from a pre-trauma frame of reference. These paraplegics mentioned a number of problems which ensued when they tried to maintain old relationships: expressions of pity frequently contaminated the relationship, the sincerity of overtures made by old friends was questioned, old friends were inclined to offer unneeded physical assistance, and paraplegics felt that old friends made invidious comparisons between the pre- and post-trauma relationship. One of the more articulate paraplegics mentioned the added difficulty in assisting others to readjust to him. In discussing a breakup between him and his girl, he said, ". . . one person can fight it, but to try to carry somebody, to try to rehabilitate them to me at the same time and take the chance of its not working out, that would be a big loss and might make you tend to give up [in your own rehabilitation]."

As paraplegics begin to acquire new friends, they tend to choose people of lower social status than their pre-trauma friends.[3] These friends may be of lower social class, decidedly younger or older than the patient, or less attractive in other ways. By choosing friends of lower status, paraplegics are able to balance the negative definitions of disability against some negative characteristic of the other person. If, in these relationships, paraplegics become successful in projecting themselves as a person of worth and become skilled in eliciting this definition from others, they proceed to more difficult relationships

eventually forming successful relationships with new individuals of equal status. Physical disability will always pose problems for relationships with others, but paraplegics learn to handle these problems with sufficient ease to maintain stable social relationships.

AWARENESS OF PERSONAL CHANGE[4]

Incidents which are here cited as structured in time emerge in interviews as unrelated experiences. Paraplegics do not have a frame of reference for ordering these events into sequences which lead to mastery of the disabled role. Unlike many types of socialization, there were no agents to present the steps involved. Neither was there sufficient contact among paraplegics during this period for them to compare experiences and establish common benchmarks of progress.[4]

From the perspective of the paraplegics, this period of time often lacked meaning: days often seemed wasted and empty and appeared to lead nowhere. It is useful to contrast this experience with socialization in the hospital. Here medical personnel repeatedly listed for paraplegics the sequence of events necessary to achieve physical independence. Ac-

---

[3] Fred Davis, *Passage Through Crisis: Polio Victims and Their Families* (New York: Bobbs-Merrill, 1963), pp. 147–148 found that polio children on returning home established a close friendship with another child whose status and acceptance in the group were also marginal.

[4] Julius A. Roth, *Timetables: Structuring the Passage of Time in Hospital Treatment and Other Careers* (New York: Bobbs-Merrill, 1963) used the term, "benchmarks of progress" to designate events which occur sequentially in a career and which are indicative of movement toward an end-point.

Timetables:

complishments which are meaningless from a normal person's perspective— sitting balance, wheelchair maneuvering, transfer, standing balance, walking with braces and crutches—were symbolized by hospital staff as indicators of progress. Paraplegics accepted this symbolic definition and thereby derived tremendous self-satisfaction from mastery of steps which otherwise they might have considered inconsequential. Due to definitions of the situation presented by the rehabilitation practitioners and accepted by the paraplegics, days had meaning and were filled with purposive activity. Paraplegics knew the steps to be mastered and could assess their own progress.

PRACTICAL IMPLICATIONS

Uncertainty is one of the most threatening experiences a person must face. Any framework for ordering expectations is perhaps better than none. Paraplegics now leave the hospital with only a vague impression of what to expect in their local communities. It would be naive to assume that this uncertainty could be eliminated; but it would appear that it could be reduced, and rehabilitation might be enhanced if each paraplegic left the hospital with a planned sequence of socialization. Obviously this sequence should be geared to the individual life situation of the patient and to his individual goals. Activities appropriate to the life style of a particular paraplegic could be ordered in terms of their increasing social difficulty, and each type of activity could be given symbolic mean-

ing as an indicator of progress toward rehabilitation.

It is perhaps also important to maintain frequent contact with paraplegics during this period. Events since the last contact could be reviewed and assessed. Events for the coming period could be planned and encouraged. The symbolic meaning of social encounters could be reaffirmed. This procedure divides the middle period of rehabilitation into steps of small increments, reducing somewhat the degree of uncertainty. By presenting paraplegics with a framework for ordering this period of socialization and by guiding them through the steps, rehabilitation practitioners might be able to reduce the length of time between hospital discharge and resumption of training or work roles as well as to increase the number of paraplegics who complete the course. Claims for the merit of this procedure, however, must await experimental evaluation.

The findings presented here also have an important implication for present programs of rehabilitation. Rehabilitation counselors should take into consideration that initial stalling by paraplegics is in no way predictive of job success or failure. Some paraplegics stay at home for two to three years, yet eventually they make good social and work adjustments. This suggests that rehabilitation counselors should not despair if a paraplegic is at first unwilling to resume full-time work. It would seem important to maintain contact with this type of client for several years, giving him repeated opportunities for job training or job placement.

These notions on socialization, while applying to young adult paraplegics, may be equally pertinent to other age groups with other types of disabilities. Almost all physical disabilities are potentially stigmatizing, and successful adjustment to these conditions usually requires learning the skills of stigma management. The findings also may have some bearing on the resocialization of released prisoners and psychiatric patients as well as on alcoholics, drug addicts, and other types of deviants.

This paper has dealt with only one aspect of paraplegics' socialization career in the community—ordering social encounters by increasing difficulty. As paraplegics' social skills increased, they attempted to enter more difficult social situations. Further research is necessary to specify the skills which are important and to ascertain the manner in which these skills may be learned. Although our present knowledge of resocialization into the community is limited, it would seem worthwhile for the rehabilitation system to consider assuming greater responsibility for this period of adjustment. Research should be encouraged and the potential role of rehabilitation workers should be evaluated to determine whether professional assistance might enhance rehabilitation.

12 Sexuality in the Handicapped:

Some Observations on Human Needs and Attitudes

Giovanna Nigro

I would like to announce at the outset of my talk that I am not an authority on sexuality in the handicapped. I have no medical or scientific material to present to you. However, I have worked with physically handicapped teens and adults for many years, and I can offer you some observations that may be useful.

I will restrict my comments to a discussion of sexuality in the lives of people who are lifelong handicapped and state simply that the problems of those who become handicapped in adulthood, after sex patterns and relationships have been established, are quite different and require different considerations and solutions.

The lifelong handicapped can be divided into three general categories. Some handicapped people such as the spinal cord-injured, may have, as a result of their disability, an impairment in sexual functioning. Others, such as the cerebral palsied, as far as we know, are not disabled in this area. Still others may have mental deficiency in addition to their physical handicap, which is usually not related to any impairment in sexual functioning. Each of these groups has quite different problems to face in dealing with sex. However, all three categories are composed of people who have *sexual needs* and are *sexual beings* in spite of their sexual functioning or their physical handicap. In addition, all three groups share a problem common to all handicapped people, which is the *attitude* of nonhandicapped people with regard to their sexuality. Unfortunately, not only the general public, but even many professional people working with the handicapped, and certainly the parents and families of the handicapped, frequently overlook or deny the sexual nature of the handicapped, an aspect of living that is the birthright of all people, regardless of their physical condition.

Public attitude that attributes asexual natures to the handicapped seems to be related to cultural values equating physical attractiveness and beauty to sex and romance. This attitude prevails to such an extent that some people find the very thought of an interest in sex among the handi-

Reprinted from Rehabilitative Literature, 1975, 36(7):202–205.

This article is a slightly edited version of a paper presented at the Institute of Rehabilitation Medicine, Fifth Annual Short Course in Pediatric Habilitation, in November, 1973.

capped as indication of perversion. Our society's preoccupation with outward appearance certainly compounds the problems of the handicapped, not only with regard to other people's acceptance of them in every respect, not the least of which is in the area of sexuality. It also makes the usual problems of adolescence more pronounced, so that the handicapped youngster has to cope with not just the concern about acne, or being too fat or too thin, or the wrong color hair, and so on. He or she also has to come to terms with a distorted body, a withered limb, an ugly brace, or a wheelchair cage.

Some justification for the attitude of professionals who "overlook" the sexual needs of the handicapped may be made in connection with the fact that they are so preoccupied with treating the handicapping condition that they lose sight of a concern for other aspects of the person's life. However, in this age of concern for the "whole person" in patient care, this argument cannot be upheld. It is more likely that professionals dodge the sex issue because it is so complex and because of their own hangups and inability to address themselves to helping their patients in the area of sexuality.

The parents of the handicapped, those poor beleaguered souls who bear such a heavy burden in every respect, have perhaps the best excuse for "overlooking" their child's sexual nature. For parents of the able-bodied, the need to recognize and acknowledge their child's interest in sex, and a growing awareness that their child is moving into a life including sexual relationships and sexual activity, though perhaps difficult, are unavoidable. The parents of a handicapped child, however, may be dealing with a dependent person whose relationship to the parents continues to be childlike in many respects, whose time and activities are more likely to continue to be family-centered, whose peer relationships are limited, and whose lack of privacy and physical restriction limit his experimentation with both social relationships and sexual activity. Indeed, many parents of handicapped children never acknowledge their potential adulthood (and eventually their actual adulthood), so it is not hard to understand their reluctance to perceive sexual needs or their inability to prepare themselves and their child for a healthy, happy, sexual future.

All the foregoing is an indication that sex education, in the broadest sense of the word *education*, is essential for all of us, parents, professionals, and the handicapped themselves. For the parents, the initial lessons ought to be concerned with helping their child achieve an appropriate sexual identity, from his or her earliest days. So many of the adults we see are almost "sexual neuters." Their physical handicap has assumed so important a place in their lives that they have little awareness of themselves as boys and girls, men and women. I might say that this seems to be less of a problem with the teens and young adults that I see, than with older adults. However, it is extremely important, and I make mention of it here so that you might emphasize it in your dealings with parents. It is particularly important, perhaps, with severely handicapped boys, whose physical dependence often prevents them from acquiring a masculine self-image and a male orientation. (Perhaps I should not be singling out boys in this era of women's lib and role reversals.) But sexuality is so important to total personality development, and handicapped children ought to be brought up to have a full appreciation of themselves as men and as women in the society in which they live.

Parents of the handicapped, as well as all parents, ought to be educated to treat their child's questions and exploration of his body and curiosity about other people's bodies as opportunities for helping him learn to have as healthy and complete an orientation to his own sexuality, and to human sexuality in general, as is possible within their capacity of handling this area of his education.

The public schools, where sex education is becoming a commonplace part of the curriculum, must be encouraged to include this subject in classes for the handicapped. Too often, special education classes have concentrated on basic academic material, even to the exclusion of such subjects as music and art and physical education. Let's see to it that the handicapped children are not also excluded from sex education courses. And let's recognize that this subject perhaps has more justification for an even stronger emphasis in classes for the handicapped, because handicapped children, due to the limitations on their lives imposed by their own restricted mobility and therefore diminished social outlets, have less opportunity for acquiring this knowledge through self-initiated or peer-initiated activities.

This leads us to the most important, and most debated, area of this discussion—real sexual activity, including dating and courtship and, for some, marriage and family planning. For many mildly handicapped people, the whole business of meeting and mating and marrying may be no different than it is for able-bodied people. There is one important difference, however, which should be noted. Handicapped teenagers and young adults are subject to the same cultural influences that we all are. For the most part, they expect, and desire, to meet and fall in love with beautiful girls or handsome men, not handicapped, who fit their image of the idealized sex object. Some achieve this dream. Others are faced with the agonies of "settling for" something less ideal, perhaps another mildly handicapped person. But the mildly physically handicapped, habilitated, self-supporting person can make his way and find a suitable mate with whom he can establish a home and make family plans that suit himself and his mate. Public opinion and family opposition notwithstanding, he can be the master of his own fate. If his physical disability is one related to genetics, then counseling about family planning is certainly in order. If not, then he and his mate can make plans that suit their circumstances.

The more physically disabled and retarded face other kinds of obstacles. Parents frequently object for an infinite number of reasons, some of which would exist even if their child were not handicapped. But the handicapped adolescent or young adult who is still dependent on his parents physically and financially cannot defy them and go ahead on his own as his able-bodied contemporary might do.

The moderately to severely handicapped young person might look to us for assistance in helping to convince his parents that he has a right to, initially, an opportunity to establish romantic alliances with other young people (usually handicapped also, since those are usually the only people he gets to know and spend time with away from his family). And he does have this right, I hope you'll agree. Parents' objections to their handicapped children's dating (and probably our own objections as well) usually have to do with the fact that the young adult "child" will only be hurt in the long run, because where can a romance lead to but an eventual breakup and heartbreak? Certainly it can't lead to marriage. Or can it?

And this is the real crux of the matter. Who has the right to marry, and who sits as judge to make such decisions? Who decided whether you should marry and whether you would make an adequate parent?

I would first like to say that relationships between two people that don't necessarily lead to marriage can provide enough pleasure to offset the pain of the eventual demise of the relationship. So there is some justifica-

tion for establishing such relationships at all. Furthermore, many long-term alliances or engagements that I have witnessed have given the couples involved, who feel that they could not manage marital life, a semblance of normalcy and many years of satisfaction and emotional fulfillment. Also, of course, not all handicapped people want to marry or find suitable mates, just as is true for able-bodied people. Certainly, I am not advocating that all handicapped people should marry.

But let's examine what marriage is all about. To begin with, sex is one part of marriage, and a very important part. No question about that. However, marriage is far more a way of fulfilling emotional needs. And the right to establish a meaningful intimate relationship with another human being can be the difference between a solitary empty life and a rich sharing partnership between two people, which can make the lives of both of them so much more rewarding. Does anyone have the right to deny this experience to the handicapped, who already have been denied so many other accepted routine experiences that most of us take for granted?

In fact, marriage can be a very satisfying way of life for handicapped people who are too disabled to participate in other human endeavors that most able-bodied people use to give meaning to their lives, mainly their work. Some of the couples I know, before marriage, were dependent or semidependent on their families, felt useless, were isolated, and, in general, were living life in a very marginal way. In their marriage, they have found a meaning and a purpose far beyond that which marriage holds for the average person. And because the marriage is so central to their existence, frequently it is a much stronger, more binding union than we usually see.

One couple I know, both quite handicapped but very resourceful and far from helpless, keep house together, shop for groceries, prepare their food—all, I might add, without regard for the usual male-female roles. They do all this at a snail's pace, because they are so handicapped, and it consumes their day. They take care of each other, share their chores, and when they are finished they relax and make love. What could be more beautiful?

Making love is, for handicapped people as for others, a very private and uniquely worked out practice. If their disability is such that they can engage in sex in the standard or conventional way, they have no more problems than able-bodied people in working toward a good sexual adjustment. If their physical disability prevents them from the usual practices, either because of physical distortions or because of impairment in sexual function, this need not be a barrier to achieving sexual satisfaction. Our book stores and libraries are filled with manuals detailing an infinite variety of methods of achieving sexual pleasure and telling us repeatedly that no practice acceptable to the two parties involved ought to be overlooked. In addition, there is a growing body of literature that rather explicitly describes the methods disabled people with sexual dysfunction have found for achieving success in finding and giving sexual satisfaction. I don't want to imply that no

serious problems in this area may arise, but it is apparent that a loving, determined, and resourceful couple, regardless of their handicap, can find an acceptable way of fulfilling their sexual needs.

Some of the objections to marriage between handicapped people have to do with their inability to support themselves and their inability to bear and raise children responsibly. With regard to financial support, most handicapped people who cannot support themselves are entitled to public assistance. This is true whether they marry or not. And simple arithmetic will prove that it is cheaper to support two people in one apartment than two people in two apartments (and certainly less than two people in a chronic hospital or nursing home). Aside from the simple facts stated here, consider the fact that many people whose circumstances have nothing to do with physical disability are being supported by public assistance. Can we honestly deny marriage to physically handicapped people because they are not self-supporting?

The question of bearing and raising children is perhaps even simpler to deal with. The handicapped couples I know have given, to a large extent, more thought to this question than the average couple has. Their realization of what they can honestly and realistically accomplish and be responsible for has been much more carefully analyzed. Their decision to have children or not to have children has usually been made in relation to the total soul-searching self-examination they have put themselves through in making a decision about whether they could function in a marriage together. Those whose disability is related to heredity have had the best possible professional advice and are acting in accordance with the facts as they perceive them. Most of the couples I know have felt that the most they could expect to accomplish was mutual self-care and that children were out of the question. Even where the desire for children is strong, they have made the decision to establish strong ties to the children of relatives and friends and be satisfied with that.

One couple I know is raising a family. They have two very young children and are managing quite nicely now. They realize they may need help when the children are more active, and they are responsibly planning for the future. But they are loving parents, and their children are healthy and happy.

One young woman I've known for a long time, who had a stormy relationship with her own rejecting mother all of her life, married and had a baby. She had expected that she and her husband would be able to take care of the baby, since the husband was not so disabled. However, the marriage didn't last. The baby was placed in a foster home and is doing well. The mother sees her child regularly, and the child knows she is her mother. Having borne this healthy child (which is something her own mother was not able to accomplish) is probably the single most important achievement in this young woman's life, and she has attained a kind of peace with herself and a purpose for existence she never had before. Sick, you say? Perhaps, but how many other sick reasons have

you heard for people bearing children?

Another couple I know had a baby who, by prearrangement, was to be raised by the childless sister of the wife. They have a beautiful daughter who knows them as aunt and uncle. The child is happy with the parents she knows as her own, and the handicapped couple take great pride in the addition that they have made to their extended family.

I know some midly retarded couples who are raising happy healthy children. Their children are no worse off than the hundreds of thousands of children born to families of marginal people, not designated retarded, whose limitations are known to us all and who are sometimes classified as "culturally deprived." The children of these retarded couples are, in fact, better off by far, for the retarded parents know they have deficiencies and know they must avail themselves of professional advice.

At any rate, there is not a simple solution to the question of whether a handicapped couple, retarded or not, should be restricted in their right to parenthood. Again, who makes the decisions for the rest of us?

In summary, handicapped people are sexual beings. Parents and professionals and the public have no recourse but to accept that fact. With this established, we have an obligation to help them develop appropriate sexual identities, educate them to understand their own sexuality, arm them with information about being responsible human beings, and then allow them to make their own way in life.

Section 4

TREATMENT ENVIRONMENTS

13 Psychosocial Rehabilitation in VA Spinal Cord Injury Centers

Essie D. Morgan,
George W. Hohmann, and
John E. Davis, Jr.

The Veterans Administration Spinal Cord Injury Service, in existence since 1946, has played a leading role in improving medical care and in prolonging life. Largely because of its success in maintaining life and a reasonable degree of good health in patients, new challenges have arisen in the past 10 years. Patient discontent, group hostility, acting-out behavior, organized protest, and exposés in various public media indicated that the VA program was failing to provide the total psychological, social and vocational rehabilitation that would enable patients to achieve productive and satisfying lives.

Although scattered impressionistic observations existed, attempts to answer questions concerning the resources, practices, and effectiveness of psychosocial rehabilitation were hampered by a lack of factual knowledge.

Accordingly, the National Consultants to SCIS, strongly supported by the Chief, Spinal Cord Injury Services, proposed a study of the total psychosocial rehabilitation process within each of the VA SCI Centers. The investigators were given full freedom and responsibility in the design, implementation, and completion of the study reported here.

METHOD

Design

The complexity and diversity of information needed to conduct a comprehensive study of a VA-wide system required that information be gathered not only from staff and patients directly involved in SCI programs, but also from other hospital elements which impact on SCI Services. All data reported here were gathered and recorded on numerical scales by direct, individual interview. Since this type of study had no SCI precedent all scales and questionnaires were designed by the investigators.

Structured and open-ended interview schedules were designed to elicit systematic information from the following:

1. A random sample of inpatients including Vietnam veterans.
2. A small sample of available outpatients.
3. All available physicians assigned to SCI Services.

Reprinted from Rehabilitation Psychology, 1974 21(1)3–33. Copyright 1974, Rehabilitation Psychology.

4. A stratified sample of all staff providing direct SCI patient care.

5. All Service Chiefs who assign personnel to the SCI Centers.

In addition, general unit information concerning patient and staff census data was taken and notes and observations were made of important material not specifically covered in the survey questions and schedules.

Procedure

Data were collected over a one-year period between April, 1969 and March, 1970. Each SCI Center was visited for a two or three day period by two of the three investigators. Individual interviews were conducted, using a standard format, with approximately 350 patients and 225 staff members; responses were recorded at the time of the interview. These figures represented more than one-third of all patients and staff assigned to the SCI Services program at the time of the study.

Interviews also were held with the Hospital Director and Chief of Staff at each hospital having an SCI program.

Upon arrival at a hospital the investigators first explained the purpose of the study to the Hospital Director and then proceeded to the SCI area. A roster of patients was obtained from the office of the Chief, SCI Service, and a *random sample* was selected for interviews. Interviews were conducted in a private office, where possible, or at bedside if the patient's condition so

required. Assurances of confidentiality were given and efforts made to encourage candid, honest responses. Staff interviews were conducted in a similar manner. The utilization of the same interviewers, standard interviewing, numerically rated and immediately recorded responses maximized the reliability of data collection.[1]

RESULTS

Interviews with In-patients

The tables contain much detailed information which may be of interest to the specialist. Attention will be called, however, only to some of the major findings.

Characteristics of the Group

Length of Injury Table 1 shows some characteristics of the inpatient interviewees. It will be seen that 53% of the patients were injured within the previous five years. In fact, if broken down by years, the data show that 44% of the patients were injured in the previous year. On the other hand, a sizeable 18% were injured more than 10 years ago.

Length of Current Hospitalization Two-thirds of the group had been hospitalized for less than two years. One patient in the sample, however, had been hospitalized continuously for 22 years, and the chronicity of the disorders becomes more evident if patients' cumulative length of time in a SCIC is considered.

[1] Assembly of the data in tabular form was completed by Ms. Clare Finlan and the staff of the Biometrics Division, Veterans Administration Central Office.

Table 1. Characteristics of inpatient interviewees (N = 214)

Item	Proportion
Length of current hospitalization	
Months since injury	
Less than one	.08
One to sixty	.53
Over sixty	.39
Months of current hospitalization	
Under one	.11
One to twenty-four	.69
Over twenty-four	.20
Number of readmissions	
One	.78
Two to three	.11
Four to eight	.06
Nine and over	.03
No response	.02
Disability connection	
Service	.54
Non-service	.45
No response	.01
Level of education	
Educational grade attained	
One to eight	.22
Nine to twelve	.72
Over twelve	.06
Work experience	
Full-time employment prior to injury	
Yes	.78
No	.22
Kind of work	
Laborer	.34
Blue collar	.35
White collar–professional	.12
No prior work	.19
Level of injury	
Patients under 30 years of age	
Cervical	.37
Thoracic	.47
Lumbar	.15
Sacral	.00
No response	.01
Patients over 30 years of age	
Cervical	.54
Thoracic	.22
Lumbar	.08
Sacral	.00
No response	.16

For example, 39% of the patients had cumulative hospitalization time of five years or more.

Level of Injury Among the patients under 30 years old, slightly more than one-third were quadriplegic, although more than one-half of patients over 30 years old were quadriplegic.

Education and Employment Educational level was roughly commensurate with the general population: approximately three-quarters of the sample had attended high school and 6% had completed at least one year of college. Similarly, three-quarters of the patients had regular full-time employment prior to injury.

In-Patients' Expectancies for Future Life Table 2 shows the outcome of questions concerning patients' expectations for the next 5–10 years as spinal cord injured individuals. It was believed that such expectancies should reflect to a significant degree, the overt and covert messages delivered by the hospital environment.

Residence It will be seen that more than three-quarters expected to be living at home. Few expected to be in sheltered living quarters or other institutions, although a startling 15% believed they would not leave the hospital during that time. Persons giving the last response, perhaps, were those who did not believe their physical condition would remain stable or improve.

Employment Fifty-eight percent expected to be employed full-time or

Table 2. Inpatient expectations for next 5–10 years (N = 214)

Item	Proportion
Where do you expect to be in 5–10 years?	
Hospital	.15
Other institution or nursing home	.03
Sheltered living other than home	.04
Home	.77
No response	.01
How do you think your health will be?	
Improved	.48
No change	.36
Regression	.12
Death	.03
No response	.01
Employment	
Full-time work in community	.40
Part-time work	.18
Sheltered or home workshop	.04
Avocational only	.07
No work	.31
Preparation needed for employment	
Schooling	.48
On-job training	.11

contd.

Table 2. (*contd.*)

Item	Proportion
Not needed	.12
Non-applicable	.29
Marriage and family	
Not married	.46
Married—no children	.11
Married with children	.37
All other	.06
Need for physical assistance from family	
Quite a lot	.21
Some	.15
Little	.29
None	.35
Relationship to hospital	
Often returning as outpatient	.04
Often returning as inpatient	.17
Routine checkup as outpatient	.26
Routine checkups as inpatient	.26
As necessary for serious complications	.22
Inpatient	.05
Social life	
Active as non-disabled	.33
Active, but less than non-disabled	.43
Restricted to SCI mainly	.11
None	.13
Recreation and pleasure	
Active group	.41
Active alone	.07
Some, but limited group	.27
Some, but limited alone	.06
Very restricted or none	.19
Type of friends	
Other paraplegics	.12
Other handicapped	.01
Special service group (PVA)	.02
Friends, neighbors, or family	.85
Public receptivity	
Overly helpful	.29
Appropriately helpful	.60
Ignoring	.08
No response	.03
Receptivity of employers	
Many special considerations because of disability	.12
Appropriate special considerations because of disability	.69
More difficult because of disability	.14
No response	.05

part-time. Of these, 39% stated that they had an employable skill, 49% stated they needed additional schooling to reach this goal, and 12% expected to need on-the-job training. On the other hand, of the total sample of subjects, 42% had no expectations of returning to gainful employment.

Marital Expectations Almost half of the group did not expect to be married. Of those expecting to have a marriage blessed with children, the impression of the interviewers was that most already had established families.

Physical Independence Two-thirds expected to need at least some physical assistance from their families; one-third expected to need no assistance.

Medical Independence Despite the unpopularity of such an opinion, 5% of the sample declared that they expected to remain hospitalized for the remainder of their lives, and 21% saw themselves closely tied to the SCI Center. Three-fourths, however, viewed the Center only as a source of periodic review or crisis intervention.

Social Life Three-fourths of the patients expected to be socially active, although most of these anticipated a less active social life than others. An alarming 13% believed they would have no social life whatever, and 10% saw their friends and acquaintances restricted to other physically handicapped people.

Recreation and Pleasure Group recreation and pleasure was anticipated by 41%, and an additional 27% envisioned a restricted group. A third, however, expected few or no nonsolitary recreational activities.

Source of Friends The great majority thought they would meet, develop, and maintain friendships through the usual channels of old friends, family, neighbors. A disquieting 14%, however, saw their social circles diminished to other handicapped persons.

Public Attitudes More than one-third expected public attitudes to be overly helpful to the point of interference or not helpful at all. Almost two-thirds anticipated appropriately helpful experiences.

Employer Receptivity The group was optimistic that appropriate (69%), or even special (12%), considerations would be extended by employers.

Patient Needs After stating expectancies for the future, patients were asked to discuss what help was needed to achieve the life anticipated. This line of questioning centered about three areas: The SCI Center, the VA Benefits Program, and the patient, his family and community. The results are shown in Table 3.

Needs From the Center Improved medical care, both inpatient and outpatient; vocational counseling; community activities; and additional physical medicine and rehabilitation therapies were perceived as necessary for goal achievement by approximately 40% of the patients. About one-third saw a need for improved psychosocial climate and preparation for community living, and one-fifth desired personal psychological assistance and assistance with family relationships. They perceived hospital rehabilitation and self-care programs as more strongly oriented to institutional

Table 3. In-patients' perception of help needed to achieve 5–10 year goals (N = 214)

Item	Proportion	
SCI unit and staff		
	Yes	No
Vocational counseling	.44	.56
More community based activities sponsored by the units	.42	.58
Improved medical care in and out of the hospital	.41	.59
More PM&R	.39	.61
More realistic relationship between hospital activities and community living demands	.34	.66
Improved psychosocial climate	.31	.69
Personal, psychological assistance	.22	.78
Other	.21	.77
Removal from other type patients	.12	.88
VA hospital or other VA benefits office		
Adaptive housing	.63	.37
Financial assistance	.60	.40
Academic schooling	.52	.48
Transportation	.47	.53
Job placement	.34	.66
On-job training	.28	.72
Others	.07	.93
Community and self		
More special opportunities for social & recreational activities	.39	.61
More active personal participation in rehabilitation plans	.30	.70
Assistance from family or friends	.23	.77

adjustment than toward achieving independent functioning outside the Center.

The notion, frequently expressed by professional workers, that it is desirable to separate patients according to age, length of injury, etc., was accepted only by 12% of the group. The belief that older patients or those with injuries of longer duration somehow train the newly injured in maladaptive behaviors and attitudes detrimental to goal-achievement was seldom accepted by patients.

Needs from the VA Adaptive housing, financial assistance and academic schooling and transportation were the scope-enlarging assistances identified by half or more of the patients. The proportions specifying need for financial assistance correspond closely to the proportion of non-service-connected patients in the sample and may suggest that nearly all service-connected patients find their compensation adequate. A sizable one-third expressed a definite need for assistance in job placement.

Needs from Self, Family, and Community A disarming 30% admitted a need for more active involvement and participation on their own part. The remainder saw a much greater deficit in unmet community opportunities than in assistance from family or friends.

Psychosocial Services The data shown in Table 4a are not reassuring: 46% of the patients interviewed had never seen a psychologist, 30% had never seen a social worker, 54% had never seen a vocational counselor[2]; and 52% had never seen a staff person

---

[2] The data are not discrete between psychologist and vocational counselor since at some stations this is the same person while at others it is not.

Table 4a. Inpatients' contacts with rehabilitation personnel (N = 214)

Question: When did you last see a	Proportion of sample							
	Never/not applicable	Within last week	2–4 Weeks	2–3 Months	4–5 Months	6–8 Months	9–12 Months	Over 1 yr.
Psychologist	.46	.10	.09	.10	.05	.02	.01	.17
Social Worker	.30	.24	.18	.13	.03	.03	.01	.08
Vocational Counselor for testing or vocational information	.54	Within last month .17 •		.09	.02	.04	.03	.11
VA Benefits Representative	.09	.36 •		.24	.04	.08	.11	.07
Volunteer on ward	.11	.85	.04	—	—	—	—	.05
PVA Representative	.24	.41	.21	.08	—	—	—	.05
Member of your family	.09	.61	.20	.07	—	.01	.01	.01
Friend from outside the hospital	.29	.39	.18	.08	—	.02	—	.04
Staff person about living outside the hospital	.52	Within last month .12 •		.20	.05	.02	.05	.04

• Data breakdown in weeks not available.

Table 4b. Inpatients' principal reason for contact with psychologist and social worker (N = 214)

Item	Proportion
Reason for seeing psychologist	
Did not see psychologist	.46
Vocational assessment and/or counseling	.23
Other	.16
Personal problem	.09
Part of group therapy or observing session	.06
Reason for seeing social worker	
Did not see social worker	.30
Other	.26
Outside living arrangements	.21
Personal problem involving self or family	.17
Financial problem	.06

about living outside the hospital. Among those who had contact with a psychosocial professional person, it is evident from Table 4a that the contact was not frequent.

Table 4b shows that contacts with psychologists were related most frequently to vocational assessment and counseling with relatively few contacts for personal problems or group therapy. A social worker was seen most often for routine social history taking. Counseling for outside living arrangements and on personal and family problems was not infrequent, however.

Contacts with the Benefits Contact Officer and volunteers were reported by approximately 90% of the sample and representatives of the Paralyzed Veterans (PVA) also were active. All but three of the Centers have active PVA chapters within the Center.

The proportion and frequency of family visits to patients were high, but 9% reported that *no* family member had ever visited them in the Center. Visits from friends were much less frequent: 29% had never had a visit from a friend and an additional 4% had not been visited by friends for more than a year.

The interviewers' impression of patients' moods yielded judgments of 52% normative, 37% depressed, and 10% elated.

Interviews with SCI Ward Physicians

Physicians' Evaluations of Needs of Patients Interviewed Table 5 shows the opinions of the ward physicians about appropriate placement of patients. They believed that over one-third of the hospitalized patients had no need for the specialized services of the SCI Center. Lack of community resources and insufficient funds were mentioned most often as the reasons for not moving these patients out of the SCI Center.

Table 5. Physicians' opinion of inpatients' placement needs (N = 30)

Item	Proportion of patients
Patient needs unique services of SCI Center	
Yes	.64
No	.36
Most appropriate living situation	
Hospital	.51
Own home	.24
Independent living away from home	.03
Nursing home	.13
Intermediate care in hospital	.08
Other	.01
Primary reason patient has not been placed	
Needs to stay in SCI unit	.66
Insufficient resources available in the community	.16
Insufficient funds	.05
Insufficient reason for placement	.03
Family objects	.03
Patient objects	.03
Other, don't know	.04

Center's Effectiveness in Meeting Needs of Patients The philosophy and perceptions of thirty physicians directly responsible for the care and treatment of patients were examined by means of a schedule designed to elicit this information. The data in Table 6 show that two-thirds of the physicians interviewed believed that the Centers could do more, or much more, to rehabilitate SCI patients. As they saw it, innate motivation to achieve independent living was the major reason for patient success. About half the interviewees also mentioned assistance from family and friends and the patient's intelligence and capacity. Only 10% attributed significant patient success to the rehabilitation *emphasis* of the unit or the attitudes of the staff. When the rehabilitation *program* was isolated, about 25% of the physicians agreed that most or all of patients' success could be attributed to the program.

These findings should be evaluated in view of the concomitant belief held by more than three-fourths of the respondents that problems of the cord injured for outside living are unique.

Probed with open-ended questions for perceptions of how the rehabilitation and community living prospects of the patients could be improved, the physicians gave highest priority to improved quality staff (46%) and improved counseling (20%). From 10% to 16% mentioned improved orthotic devices, more PM&R, schooling, recreational activities, and research. About 3% cited finding employers, treating alcoholism, better pay for staff and veterans benefits.

Interviews with Staff of SCI Units

Of the 150 SCI staff workers interviewed, 49% were Nursing Service personnel, 34% were from PM&R, 15%

Table 6. Physicians' opinions of SCI Centers' effectiveness (N = 30)

Item	Proportion
In restoring patients to full rehabilitation and community living, SCI unit	
Provides all needed attention	.27
Provides sufficient attention	.07
Could provide somewhat more attention	.20
Should provide a lot more attention	.46
Reasons for varying success of patients in achieving independent living (More than one reason permitted)	
Motivation .	.73
Outside assistance—family, friends, etc.	.57
Inherent characteristics—intelligence, capacity, etc.	.50
Physical and economic resources	.47
Education	.23
Stress placed on rehabilitation by the unit, and staff attitudes	.10
Other	.60
Proportion of patients' success determined by program efforts of the SCI unit	
All	.03
Most	.23
Some	.71
None	.03
Are problems in preparing SCI patients for outside living different from those of other long term disabled patients?	
Yes	.83
No	.17

were Psychologists and Social Workers, and 2% were others. More than a third had been employed on the service more than 5 years, almost half between one and five years, and 17% were relatively new employees. The details of the rather extensive interviews with staff are presented in Table 7.

While the large majority preferred working on SCI and felt that their efforts were important in determining whether a patient would be able to live outside the hospital, there was marked variation in their beliefs about how many patients ultimately would be able to live in the community. About a third thought that most patients could do so; 40% felt that only a few would

ever live independently. This puzzling result suggests that there is little consensus among the staff concerning prognosis in regard to patients' potential for fully caring for themselves. It must be most perplexing for the patients who receive quite contradictory messages about their futures. Perplexity may be accentuated further by staff members' beliefs that other staff are more optimistic than they about patient potential for full restoration.

Other findings from Table 7 deserving special note are the following: Staff felt that SCI patients are different from, and harder to motivate than, other handicapped people.

About two-thirds felt that in-

Table 7. Staff attitudes toward SCI patients (N = 150)

Item	Proportion	Item	Proportion	
How do you feel about working on the SCI unit as compared to working elsewhere in the hospital?		Do you feel that SCI patients are different from other kinds of patients?		
Prefer the SCI	.73	Yes	.71	
Does not matter	.16	No	.29	
Rather work elsewhere	.11			
How many of the patients in the unit do you feel will be living independently in the community within the next three years?		Do you feel that SCI patients are harder to motivate to do things for themselves than other patients?		
Only a few will make it	.40	Yes	.60	
About a half will make it	.26	No	.40	
Most will make it	.34			
How many of the other staff do you feel really believe that most of the patients now on the unit can be successfully rehabilitated to community living?		Which of the following do you feel is most needed on the unit to help patients recover more rapidly?		
		More staff	.64	
		Better methods	.25	
		Better facilities and/or equipment	.09	
Most of the staff	.63	None	.02	
About half of the staff	.14		Yes	No
Few of the staff	.23			
How important is the work you do in determining whether patients will be able to live outside the hospital?		Which of the following do you see the psychologists doing on the SCI unit?		
		Testing	.75	.25
		Vocational evaluation	.72	.28
		Psychotherapy	.66	.34
Unrelated	.03	Assist staff with problem behavior of patient	.65	.35
Little importance	.09	Help motivate patients to want to live independently in the community	.65	.35
Quite important	.30	Job training	.51	.49
Essential	.58	Look after the mentally disturbed	.46	.54

	Yes	No
Which of the following do you see the social workers doing on the SCI unit?		
Help find living arrangements in the community	.95	.05
Help patients being transferred to other places	.93	.07
Listen to patients' problems	.93	.07
Help patients with money	.89	.11
Help patient adjust to his loss and present condition	.66	.34

How important are the psychologist and social workers to the attainment of community living for the SCI patients?	
Only of little importance	.05
Significant but not essential	.23
Essential	.72

Is an effort made to place one patient on the unit next to another patient for the benefit of one and/or the other?	
Planned for psychological or social effects	.53
Don't know	.17
Planned only for physical convenience	.15
No plan usually	.13
Planned for administrative reasons	.02

Do you feel that those in charge of the SCI unit are concerned with the social or psychological aspects of treatment?	
Little if any concern	.12
Somewhat concerned	.28
Quite concerned	.60

Does the Chief of your Service regard your work on the SCI unit as	
Somewhat less important than other assignments	.12
Equally important to other assignments	.48
More important than other assignments	.40

Have you received any formal or in-service training (including lectures) on the social or psychological aspects of being a SCI patient?	
Yes	.60
No	.40

Do you feel you are allowed to provide the full range of services you are trained to provide?	
Most of them	.62
Not as many as I would like	.21
Quite a few restrictions on what I am allowed to do	.17

creased staff is critical to better rehabilitation, while a quarter believed that better methods are what is most needed.

Psychologists were seen by the staff as testers, psychotherapists, and vocational evaluators. Social workers were seen as helping patients with money, finding living arrangements, and being transferred, but having little to do with patient adjustment to loss and present condition. The role of social worker had clearer components than the role of psychologist. Three-fourths of the staff viewed the efforts of social workers and psychologists as *essential* to patient attainment of community living, and most of the remainder said *significant*. Forty per cent of the staff felt that those in charge were little or only somewhat concerned with the social and psychological aspects of treatment. If the leaders of the Centers do regard social and psychological rehabilitation as an important part of the overall treatment process, four out of ten employees are not receiving the message.

The majority of staff felt that their Chiefs viewed their work on the SCI Service as important.

Forty percent of the staff had received no formal or in-service training in the psychosocial rehabilitation of the spinal cord injured, and more than one-third felt that they were restricted from providing the full range of services that they did have training to provide. The major complaints mentioned by two-thirds to three-fourths of the staff, about difficulties in treating and rehabilitating patients, were under-staffing and overwork which often resulted in lack of individual care given to patients. About one-fifth to one-third of the complaints mentioned lack of treatment plans, lack of role coordination among staff, the need for more encouragement to patients, and better placement facilities. Lack of personnel resources primarily was seen as the greatest deterrent to providing good patient care and rehabilitation. The lack of methods, procedures, and other types of resources were secondary.

Interviews with Chiefs of Services Supplying Personnel to SCI Services

An attempt was made to determine the degree of administrative support and attitudes toward assignment of personnel to SCIS by the Chiefs of four Services supplying critical segments of personnel to this program. Thirty-four Chiefs of Nursing, PM&R, Social Work and Psychology were interviewed. At one station no Psychology Service existed and at another the Chief was not available.

The findings, summarized in Table 8, show that about half of the Chiefs said they would assign top priority to SCI if additional staff were available, while approximately a quarter would give it a less than average or low priority. The major reasons for not assigning priority were difficulty in locating personnel and no request for personnel from the SCI unit. In no case did a Chief express feelings of hopelessness about SCI patients or their ability to benefit from services. The latter findings are congruent with the Chiefs' opinion of the "status" of

Table 8. Chiefs of Services' opinions of SCI unit (N = 34)

Item	Proportion
Priority given to assigning any additional staff to SCI unit	
Top	.52
Second	.21
Middle	.15
Low	.12
Reasons for not assigning priority personnel on the SCI unit (N = 12)	
Difficulty in locating personnel willing to work with SCI patients	.50
No request for their service from SCI unit	.42
No request for their service from administration	.08
Status of SCI unit in hospital (professional program)	
High	.47
Moderate	.35
Low	.18
Status of SCI in hospital (administrative support)	
High	.59
Moderate	.35
Low	.06
Judgment by interviewer of Service Chiefs' interest and involvement in SCI unit	
Highly involved and optimistic	.43
Highly involved and pessimistic	.21
Moderately involved and optimistic	.15
Moderately involved and pessimistic	.12
Only minimally involved	.09

the SCI units. Only 18% of the Chiefs believed the SCIS to have lower status than other Services in the hospital, and only 6% felt that the SCIS were poorly supported by the hospital administration.

Similarly it was the investigators' impressionistic judgment that the degree of interest and involvement by the Chiefs in the SCI segment of their responsibility was high. Two-thirds of the Chiefs were seen as highly involved in the SCI program, and more than half of those were optimistic concerning its future.

Interviews with Outpatients

A separate set of questions was asked in interviews with 44 SCI outpatients. Forty-one percent of the men had been out of the hospital from one to three years while the remainder were evenly distributed from four to more than 30 years out of the hospital. Since 37% were non-service connected, it is clear that service-connected benefits are not essential to community living. In this outpatient group, 14 were quadriplegics and 30 were paraplegics.

Obstacles to Leaving Hospital and Remaining in Community The proportions of outpatients mentioning various obstacles to leaving the hospital and remaining in the community are shown in Table 9. Finding suitable living arrangements was the biggest obstacle to leaving the hospital; self-confidence, economic factors, and bowel control also were important problems. In regard to remaining in

Table 9. Outpatients' perceptions of obstacle to leaving hospital and living in community: proportion naming each problem (N = 44)

Problem	Leaving hospital
Living arrangements	.50
Wheelchair maneuvering	.37
Bowel care	.27
Other	.23
Economic support (including work)	.18
Driver training and/or transportation	.16
Bladder control	.11
Fear of idleness	.09
None	.09
Skin care	.04

Problem	Living in community
Other	.39
Wheelchair maneuvering	.32
Living arrangements	.27
Driver training and/or transportation	.23
None	.16
Lack of self-confidence	.14
Economic support (including work)	.14
Bladder control	.14
Bowel care	.09
Fear of idleness	.09

the community, wheelchair maneuvering, living arrangements, and driver training and/or transportation were the most significant problems. For individual patients, however, a large number of idiosyncratic factors—such as fear of idleness—were mentioned as *the* specific reason that made it difficult to leave the Center and live in the community.

Attitudes and Status of Outpatients Table 10 summarizes the rehabilitation experiences and beliefs of the outpatients interviewed. Sixty percent stated that the hospital had done a good or very good job in preparing them for outside living as compared to 22% who felt they were not prepared or were inadequately prepared. Only 5% attributed their successful rehabilitation to efforts made by the hospital or Center. Thirteen percent acknowledged social workers or psychologists as providing help in returning to outside living, but other staff and laymen were mentioned much more frequently. However, most felt that the hospital staff had expected them to make it outside the hospital. The regimentation, confinement, and understaffing were the most negative features relating to thoughts of returning to the hospital.

Of the 18% of outpatients currently employed, almost all felt they were using their full abilities on the job. The number employed must be considered attenuated because all interviews were held during normal working hours. Most striking, however, is the finding that while 30% of those persons working acknowledged some kind of employment assistance from the VA, not one actually found his job through efforts by the VA staff.

The majority of outpatients were living with their wives, and half of these couples had children. Another quarter were living with parents. The SCI outpatients were socially active. Most belonged to the PVA and half belonged to other social or fraternal organizations.

Almost three quarters were taking advantage of some veteran benefits—mostly education, housing, and compensation—and most felt they needed continuing assistance of various kinds from the VA in order to remain in the community. There was considerable spread of opinion as to what could be done by the SCI unit to rehabilitate more veterans for community living. However, almost half attributed their own success in rehabilitation to their own inner motivation or self-drive and 20% gave major credit to their families.

Observations Not Covered in Survey Questions and Schedules

In the structured but "open-ended" interviews, many patients and staff expressed their feelings, attitudes, and perceptions of the treatment and rehabilitation milieus in their Center. The recurring themes of these spontaneous observations were as follows:

Emotional Climate of the Centers In a number of Centers the climate was described as "one of regimentation, confinement, and a prison-like atmosphere," e.g., patients were not allowed in certain public parts of the hospital. In at least two stations a well developed patient-spy-network operating to detect and punish patients who broke rules, was encouraged and rewarded by staff. Patients often expressed the feeling that their treatment was carried out in an assembly-line fashion rather than being prescribed and tailored to their needs. Another almost universal theme of patients and staff alike might be summarized as "nobody talks to me." A feeling on the part of many was that the newly injured and depressed patient had no one to help him come out of his shell. The depressed patient, who tends to be withdrawn, frequently was treated with isolation rather than with support and encouragement. A particular need was expressed by most patients for an opportunity for frank, candid discussion of personal, sexual, marital, vocational, family, and post-hospital living problems. This was expressed most vigorously by one young Vietnam veteran who said: "For God's sake, won't someone talk to me about my sex life and marriage!" In apparent reference to discussion of patients by staff, another said, "Nobody discusses *you* with *you.*" Other patients expressed the notion that when they attempted to discuss personal problems with staff, they "cleverly evade patients." Some believed that the staff created a rather impenetrable barrier between themselves and patients. At times they were extremely patronizing, kept the patients at a distance, and seemed to show little respect for the patient and his status. Patients were told at one Center,

Table 10. Outpatients' rehabilitation experiences and beliefs (N = 44)

Item	Proportion	Item	Proportion
Overall what kind of job did the hospital do in preparing you for outside living?		Are you gainfully employed full or part time?	
Very good	.30	Yes	.18
Good	.30	No	.82
Adequate	.18		
Inadequate	.13	If employed, what is your level of employment in relation to your ability?	
Didn't prepare me	.09	Using my full ability	.80
		Do somewhat less than I could	.20
Which of the following people helped you the most to return to outside living?			
Doctors, nurses or aides	.34	Did the hospital staff assist you in finding work or training in the community?	
PM&R	.30	Yes	.30
Volunteer, friends or family	.21	No	.70
Social worker or psychologist	.13		
None	.02	Do you still see any of the hospital staff at your home or place of work?	
		Yes	.30
Do you feel the hospital staff really expected you to be able to make it outside the hospital?		No	.70
Yes	.80		
No	.20	Where are you currently residing?	
		Own home	.70
If you were to return to the hospital, what about it would bother you most?		Home of friends or relatives	.18
Hospital itself	.27	Boarding house or residential hotel	.05
Regimentation, confinement	.25	Other	.07
Understaffing	.18		
Nothing	.13	Whom do you live with?	
Money	.05	Wife and children	.30
Personal problems	.05	Parents	.23
Inactivity, mental depression	.05	Wife	.20
Pressure to enter, leave	.02	Other relatives	.09
		Friends	.09
		Alone	.09

Are you active in any social or fraternal clubs or organizations other than PVA?

Yes	.50
No	.50

If yes, how many?

One	.30
Two	.09
Three	.11

Are you an active member of PVA?

Yes	.73
No	.27

Of your three cloest friends, excluding relatives, how many are physically disabled?

One	.34
Two	.09
Three	.15
None	.41

Do you take advantage of the Veterans' Benefits program?

Yes	.73
No	.27

If yes, which one?

Compensation	.18
Mortgage and housing	.18
Education	.16
Training	.07
Automobile	.07

Considering your present circumstances, what do you need most from the VA?

Money	.27
Continuation of present situation	.21
Monthly supplies	.18
Treatment	.16
NSC legislation to increase benefits	.09
Nothing	.07
Rehabilitation equipment	.02

What should be done by the SCI unit to increase the number of patients who are successfully rehabilitated for community life?

Nothing	.20
Force, pressure them to be self-sufficient	.20
Trial housing	.16
Improved staff	.16
Improved counseling	.09
Money	.07
Activities	.07
Research	.05

To what do you attribute your degree of success and rehabilitation as compared to others with similar disabilities?

Self-drive	.48
Family	.21
Nothing	.07
Staff, therapy	.05
Education	.05
Employer	.02
Rearing	.02
Physical ability	.02
Religion	.02
Finance	.02
Seeing others succeed	.02
Not rehabilitated	.02

"Don't complain; you could be on a charity ward."

In nearly all of the Centers a pervasive theme ran through the comments of staff and older patients: "Stay in the hospital indefinitely." It set up an expectancy of permanent institutionalization not only for the newly injured, but also for returning patients with older injuries. At one station a physician indoctrinated new patients by telling them to forget their families and life in the community. They were advised that their wives would soon be unfaithful to them, that their families would abandon them, and that the hospital would provide them shelter and care. The expectancy is created that the patient will stay forever. Little, if any, attempt is made in many Centers to move the patient from early depression and self-pity to self-actualization, expectancy of, and effort for, a meaningful life in the community.

Need for Sex Education For many years the Centers avoided discussion of the altered sexual functioning in the cord-injured individual and the interpersonal, psychological, and social implications of this for the patient. Deliberate avoidance has been justified on the grounds that the sexual function of the cord injured is altered almost universally, and it is best to "let repression take its course." This attitude quite clearly is no longer viable. All patients, particularly younger ones, have become increasingly open and frank concerning sexual matters. They seek realistic, factual information regarding not only anatomical and physiological changes

but also the effects of their altered sexual functioning on potential marital, social, and emotional relationships. Several younger patients believed that "the older personnel have too many hangups of their own to talk about sex." They expressed the need for younger personnel who can "face up to the facts of life in discussing with patients matters of sexual relationships, family, and children."

Boredom In every Center patients spoke constantly of the extreme boredom experienced during their rehabilitation and treatment. One patient put it succinctly: "I am so bored I am cracking up!" Others complained of lives consisting of nothing more than going from a boring hospital to a boring home setting. At all Centers, lack of activity and active treatment programs on weekends and evenings was perceived as detrimental. Similarly, lack of social stimulation and intellectual and social deprivation also were mentioned frequently. Programs sponsored by recreational and voluntary services frequently were described as unimaginative. These activities appear to have originated in recreational work with the elderly or senile and reflected extremely stereotyped notions of activities suitable for the severely disabled. One patient expressed this most dramatically: "Bedside bingo don't get it; I am bored stiff!"

Intimidation In the majority of the Centers pervasive intimidation of patients and lower echelon personnel was reported. This oppressiveness led to marked guardedness on the part of patients and personnel at some of the stations. One patient said: "Let me plead the Fifth Amendment; I would rather not talk about that and besides, it won't do a particle of good." Others stated that patients were restricted from prescribed therapies for minor rule infractions; and that personnel were "fired for trying to find ways to help patients; you get put on a blacklist if you speak up, and then you are denied vital services." It appeared that excessive emphasis placed on petty rules led personnel to take leave of good common sense to enforce needless or detrimental bureaucratic rules and regulations. Patients reported being pitted against patients, against nursing assistants, and vice versa. "Patients who do not conform frequently are labeled as 'bad' and given a hard time." Others who are at least superficially conforming become "pets" of the higher echelon staff. The latter frequently are found to be informants in the "spy system" mentioned earlier. An extreme example, reported repeatedly at one Center, was that patients who did not pay privately for attendants' services did not get them. At the same station informants stated that hospital personnel sold intoxicants to patients at exorbitant rates.

Personnel Problems The well publicized "generation gap" was encountered also in the Cord Injury Centers. Numerous reports documented allegations that young, imaginative therapists were harrassed or passively resisted by the older staff. Lacking latitude to try out new methods and techniques, good therapists frequently resigned in disgust. Older staff in many institutions seemed to feel that any kind of personal relationship between staff and patients is "bad and unprofessional." A tone approaching "horrified shock" was used by older nurses who revealed that some of the younger nurses dated patients. This feeling of "impropriety" was surprising if one considers that some of the older nurses had dated patients 25 years ago, and a few had been married to cord injured veterans for two decades or more.

Another problem in several of the Centers was the extremely low status of the nursing assistants and technicians who provided most of the direct patient care. The patients frequently expressed the opinion, and higher echelon staff members confirmed as fact, that the major criterion in employing attendants was "brawn instead of brain." In the majority of the Centers patients expressed apprehension because of the poor qualifications, background, and training in the care of spinal cord injured not only of the nursing assistants but also of the registered nurses and physicians.

A third problem was a shortage and excessive turnover of staff that was prevalent in all disciplines and at all levels: at one station, for example, staff turnover of 80% per year in nursing personnel was reported. Some other frequently mentioned sources of concern were the use of female nursing assistants for bladder and bowel care of men, exploitation of female nursing assistants, and patients' feelings of fear and insecurity about whether a woman nursing assistant would be physically strong enough to give needed assistance.

Methods are needed in education and training of personnel, at all levels, that would inculcate an attitude of responsibility for the favorable outcome of the rehabilitation process. Especially needed is a change in present attitudes of benevolent, but often despotic, expectations of chronic invalidism and dependency in SCI patients.

Program Deficiencies In this section an attempt will be made to elaborate some of the general deficiencies in Center programs as perceived by patients and staff. One of the biggest difficulties seems to be that much of the training in self-care, in physical rehabilitation modalities, and in attitudes and expectancies, is related to the skills needed for institutional living and almost totally unrelated to the kinds of skills the patient will require for community living. For example, most of the self-care clinics have all of the devices that make nursing care in a hospital setting easier for the nurses. Patients are taught self-care with such equipment, and undoubtedly it also makes self-care easier for the patient. When the patient first goes out on pass or is discharged to his home, however, he may not have such assistive equipment and he is unable to manage.

Throughout the system repeated observations were related by staff and patients showing that inpatient care had little relationship to outpatient follow-up. This referred to much more than the physical problems of transition from patienthood to community living. While the patient is hospitalized, the institution plays a sig-

nificant role in disruption of family relationships, sometimes deliberately, but more often unwittingly. There were many complaints about poor contact with family members and the lack of family training in the special needs and problems of the cord injured. Assistance to families in maintaining themselves and in encouraging their involvement with their injured men was meager when it existed at all.

All of the Centers had either personnel in inadequate number or inadequately qualified to assist patients in dealing with personal, family, emotional, and social problems. Sufficient behavioral science personnel were not available even to provide consultation, advice, and program organization to members of other disciplines. An overwhelming need was evident for much more extensive input from the behavioral sciences not only in direct patient services but also and especially in program organization and development. Many statements were made indicating that psychological and social work personnel were restricted by an unduly limited perception of their roles. Psychologists were markedly hampered by patient aversion to the "head shrinkers" stereotype and by staff's attitude that the contribution of psychologists was limited to direct patient services to the severely mentally disturbed only. Similarly, social workers were seen as people who were of value to the program only at the last minute of the patient's rehabilitation process when a need was felt to "clear some of these patients out of here." Where some behavioral scientists' time was available, the psychologists and social workers themselves often had either extremely stereotyped and traditional comceptions of their roles, or they had resigned themselves to the fact that their services would be used in the fashion described above.

Another deficient area was the non-use or non-development of appropriate community resources. Particularly, and most frequently mentioned, were inadequate resources for educational placement, vocational employment, and housing.

Although outside the primary purpose and direction of this study, the frequency and emphasis of so many statements by patients and staff of inadequacies in direct medical care was impressive and—surprising. This study was undertaken with the impression that medical care of SCI veterans was excellent. However, during the course of the study the investigators were bombarded repeatedly by complaints of lack of competence, leadership, and technical knowledge on the part of the medical staff in many of the Centers.

A glaring program deficiency was gross understaffing in every Center. In the time intervening between the collection of data and the writing of this report, much has been done to correct inadequate staffing. However, it should be emphasized here that acquisition of numbers of people alone will not solve the problems described. It is clear from the comments made to us that staffing patterns must be balanced and that staff members must be competently trained in the SCI specialty.

The inculcation of two particular problem attitudes, in our opinion, reflected gross program deficiencies. The first of these we referred to as the "quadriplegic copout"—an attitude held by staff and inculcated in patients that quadriplegics cannot be rehabilitated to meaningful community living. Such an attitude leads to programs for quadriplegics that are devoted to the development of efficient hospital care methods. It essentially precludes the possibility that people with cervical lesions can achieve independent community living. The second mistaken attitude we referred to as the "motivation copout"—the "knee-jerk" labeling by staff and patients alike, of patients who present difficult problems in treatment and rehabilitation as "not motivated." Such an attitude often seemed to be used as a defense against offering the patient the special help that was required. It was evident that staff often believed that "motivation" is some absolute, all-or-nothing, immutable quality that either exists or does not exist "inside the patient," and that "motivation" is unrelated to staff attitudes and performance.

Administrative Support To examine the psycho-social rehabilitation operations of the SCI Centers in a meaningful way, it was necessary to evaluate the hospital environment in which the Centers existed. Patients and staff repeatedly expressed the belief that, in many Centers, the hospital administration held extremely stereotyped views of the program and the SCI veteran. In at least two Centers the hospital director was repeatedly reported to have intervened inadvisably in the discharge plans for individual patients. At other stations we found nursing personnel who were assigned to cord injury service as a punitive measure. At least two hospital directors verbalized to us: "Those paraplegics are all a bunch of bums." At another station a nurse stated, "Nobody on the Service stands up to the Hospital Director in behalf of the patients."

A substantial number of Chiefs of the SCI Services are extremely dedicated to their patients but treat them in a benevolent, paternalistic fashion. Several seemed to see themselves as the protectors, mentors, and all-knowing decision-makers for their patients and staff. They felt neither the need or desirability to delegate responsibility for program planning and treatment. Not only does this kind of attitude hamper innovative program development and the involvement of staff in the challenge of patient care, but also it results in overworked, harried, and ineffective Chiefs of Services.

DISCUSSION

It was evident that patients perceived the SCI Centers as severely deficient in the provisions of physical, psychosocial, and vocational rehabilitation programs. Specifically, vocational assessment and training, both within and outside the Center, were inadequate. In addition, provision for normative social experiences and relearning of the skills necessary for community living were lacking. Not only did patients report inadequacies in staffing, but also they believed that

available staff generally were insensitive to normal desires to live a full life outside the Center. When these desires for community living were hidden or prohibited (as was often the case) degradation of staff as "unfeeling" was even higher.

Some of the data indicate that the behavioral expectations of staff were such as to produce "good patients" rather than productive individuals. Little reinforcement was given to the development of self-sufficiency and assertiveness. The validity of these perceptions is strongly supported by the fact that over half of the patients had never discussed preparation for outside living with any staff member.

The patients were seen by staff as primarily physical care problems. The staff believed that the level of patients' educational, social, and motivational potential could not be altered. They saw little relationship between their attitudes, expectations, and interactions with the patient and whether or not he aspired to or achieved community living. These attitudes were accentuated by the staff's limited perceptions of appropriate community living resources other than a patient's own home. Alternatives generally were not considered. Underpinning these perceptions was the firm belief that SCI patients are different from other handicapped patients and hard to motivate.

Staff often recognized inadequacies. It will be recalled that all levels of staff expressed the opinion that not enough was being done to rehabilitate the SCI patient and many expressed a desire to receive training in psycho-social and vocational rehabilitation.

This survey documents a diminution of emphasis on "comprehensive rehabilitation" in VA SCI Centers in 1969. Inadequate staffing, unbalanced staffing, and the concomitant development of a fatalistic rehabilitation philosophy were probable, causative variables. On the other hand, the patients, reinforced by the influx of younger Vietnam-era SCI veterans, were setting goals for themselves and developing expectations that were different from the institutionally approved ethos, and rather serious cleavage has developed. This cleavage is reflected in impaired communication, cooperation, involvement, and investment of the patients in their own medical and rehabilitation programs, and in dejection and tightening of controls on patients on the part of the staff. The following section lists 14 recommendations for improving the effectiveness of rehabilitation in VA SCI Centers.

RECOMMENDATIONS

The survey results demand broad comprehensive program changes if optimal treatment and rehabilitation are to be achieved. Such changes must include fundamental attitudinal and procedural restructuring for both staff and patients. A vital change in staff orientation must be made which focuses all treatment and patient interactions on patients' positive abilities and potentials for doing, rather than on limitation and deficits. Another change

requires Centers to de-emphasize the role of protector of patients and develop the role of enabler or scope-enlarger. The following recommendations delineate specific courses of action to foster these changes.

1. Staff Training

Training must be provided for SCI personnel at all levels in the philosophy and skills of psychosocial and vocational rehabilitation as well as in technical skills of physical care. This training must be *comprehensive* and *interdisciplinary*.

  a. It is necessary to upgrade existing staff and provide pre-employment training for those who will be employed in the Centers.
  b. Such training should be provided by broad, Central-Office-sponsored, educational programs which are complemented and supplemented by:
    (1) In-Service programs
    (2) Intra-VA detail (i.e., VA sponsored in-service programs between Centers)
    (3) Extra-VA details (i.e., university courses and workshops)
    (4) Use of specialized consultants
    (5) Use of public educational experiences through schools and universities
    (6) Cooperation of the VA Central Office and local stations with community colleges in the development of a curriculum for

the training of para-profes-
sional personnel including
the home health aide.

2. Patient Training

For patients to achieve the goal of
optimal community living, they must
receive purposeful and meaningful
training in the psychological, social,
vocational, and avocational areas in
addition to training for maximal physical self-care. Specific recommendations are the following:

a. An expanded, broad, and
    imaginative program of voca-
    tional preparation must be
    developed which is relevant to
    current and projected job avail-
    ability.
b. Since mobility is crucial, com-
    plete driver training must be
    made available at all Centers.
c. Following careful assessment
    of educational skills and poten-
    tial, a broad range of educa-
    tional options should be made
    available. Elementary school-
    ing as well as advanced educa-
    tional experiences should be
    provided both within and out-
    side the Centers. The VA
    should take leadership in the
    development of unavailable
    but necessary resources.
d. The special challenge presented
    by quadriplegics demands an
    emphasis on training in the use
    of appropriate orthotic devices
    to extend functional inde-
    pendence and self-care.
e. Training in activities of daily
    living should be related di-

rectly to *community living*
rather than to hospital care.

3. Sex Education

Sophisticated, comprehensive, and
clear sex education must be an integral
part of the therapeutic and rehabilitation program of each Spinal Cord
Injury Center. Such information also
should be made available to appropriate family members. Sex education should include psychological,
interpersonal, and social aspects as
well as anatomical, physiological, and
technique-oriented information. This
education program should be a standard part of the Center program and
required of all patients. Training of
staff will be required to implement
this recommendation.

4. Staffing

In 1969, understaffing in all areas was
evident. As more staff is made available, it is imperative that a *balanced*
staffing pattern be achieved. Emphasis
upon personnel in the behavioral sciences is necessary and a comprehensive
psychosocial rehabilitation program is
to be developed.

5. Community Placement Programs

To achieve adequate community living
for a large number of patients, the
following recommendations are made:

a. A wide range of options for
    living must be developed in-
    cluding, but not restricted to,
    the patient's family home.
    Some other alternatives are
    foster homes, halfway houses,

communal living groups, specially-designed public housing, and boarding homes.

b. *Complete* outpatient services, including continuous psychosocial support, must be made available at all Centers.

c. Early and permanent counseling and support programs for families must be developed and maintained.

d. A hospital-based Home Care Program should be available for selected patients at each Center.

e. To avoid unnecessary hospital re-admissions, both pre-admission screening and organized comprehensive follow-up system attentive to both physical and psychosocial problems must be developed.

6. Consumer Involvement

To help overcome the attitude of staff and patients that the role of the patient is simply to be a passive recipient of treatment and services, the following are recommended:

a. Staff must find ways to insure the active involvement of each patient and his family in the planning and implementation of the total treatment and rehabilitation program.

b. All decisions concerning patient life in the Centers (aside from strictly medical regimen) should be made on the basis of group decisions in which the patients are meaningfully represented as patient advocates and planning council

members. Organized veterans groups also should be used.

7. Boredom

This recurring theme must be dealt with definitively through imaginative recreational programs and off-station activities with patient involvement in planning and implementation (e.g., competitive wheelchair sports). Incentive therapy programs and other vehicles for performing meaningful work or services must be developed in the Centers.

8. Use of Behavioral Scientists

The expertise of well-trained personnel in the solution of psychosocial problems must be greatly expanded. Such expertise is needed not only in direct patient services, but more importantly, in the structuring of ward and service programs, and in the development and management of the Center environment.

9. PM&R Activities

These must be made adaptable and relevant to helping the patients attain skills and abilities directed towards maximally independent community living. The use of PM&R activities to occupy or entertain the SCI patients is questionable.

10. Discharge Planning

In view of the shocking fact that over half of the pateints stated that preparation for outside living had never been discussed with any staff member, programs for comprehensive discharge planning must be mandatory. Planning for discharge should begin at the time of patient's admission and continue, in increasingly concrete and specific manner, to and through the point of discharge. Discharge plans, firmly and consistently conveying to the patient the expectation of community living, must be related directly to the altered life style of SCI patients.

11. Motivation

False assumptions concerning patient motivation must be dispelled. Motivation on the part of the patient is as much a malleable, changing quality of a patient's condition as is his physical state. Staff is responsible for providing the positive experiences and expectations which result in patient motivation for recovery and community living.

12. Status of Nursing Assistants

To raise the level of competence and status of the Nursing Assistants on the SCI Services, definitive and specific training in the care of the SCI patient, and certification for this training, should precede assignment to the SCI

Service. Special salary levels should reflect increased expertise.

13. Program Evaluation

It is essential that each station develop a means of auditing and evaluating its own psychosocial rehabilitation program. The formation of a station evaluation committee, utilizing personnel from Central Office or other stations, or by the use of expert consultants are feasible procedures. In any case, the establishment of a procedure and the accountability for its effectiveness should be the direct responsibility of the SCI Center Director.

14. Administrative Training and Support

It is essential that orientation and educational programs be developed to provide an understanding by the Hospital Management and by the Center Directors of the goals of today's SCI program. In addition, if the VA is to meet its obligations to the veterans suffering from spinal cord injury these administrative and professional leaders must be given their active support to the program delineated above.

14 Staff Authority and Patient Participation in Rehabilitation

Lawrence E. Schlesinger

One of the difficulties frequently cited in the rehabilitation literature is the lack of involvement, or participation, on the part of the patient. On this count, we would argue that the fault lies not in the stars but in ourselves. To a very large extent the hospital organization discourages patient participation. Let us examine this claim.

We have previously indicated (6) that the major sociol-psychological impact of severe physical disability to an adult is a loss of social role, a disintegration of personal identity and social relationships. The "patient" role is a deliberately created transitional role to move the person from the "sick" role to some improved level of social functioning (8).

To understand patient motivation for participation we need to have some feeling for his experience in the rehabilitation center. The center is in the class of social organizations that Goffman (2) has described as a "total institution." These are organizations that encompass all aspects of the patients' lives. For the staff, the hospital is a formal organization. For the patients it is a complete residential community, where they carry out their work, play, and recreation in the same setting.

The staff takes total responsibility for the patient, including, as Parsons (3) has delineated, four major categories of activity: custody, protection of the patient, socialization into the hospital, and therapy. The hospital meets all the maintenance needs of the patient; it protects him against himself, from the self-mutilating consequences of depression or aggression; it provides training for the patient in learning the rules of being a full member of the hospital community; and, finally, it provides therapy, the process oriented toward the improvement of patient functioning.

What is expected of the patient in return for these services? In addition to some form of payment, the patient has a task to perform. He contributes to the functioning of the hospital. The positive role of the patient has been stressed by all writers on rehabilita-

Reprinted from Rehabilitation Literature, 1965, 24(8):247–249.

The study reported herein was conducted under a Negotiated Service Contract (SAph 75449) between the Michigan Department of Health and the Heart Disease Control Program, Division of Special Health Services, U.S. Department of Health, Education, and Welfare. The study was made possible through the co-operation of John A. Cowan, M.D., director, Division of Tuberculosis and Adult Health, Michigan Department of Health, and Joseph N. Schaeffer, director of the Rehabilitation Institute of Metropolitan Detroit.

tion. The patient does not just passively receive treatment. He must be adequately motivated to do his part. In one very real sense the patient is employed to play a role in the enterprise. His primary job is to learn to improve his physical, personal, and social functioning (5).

What then is the impact of the "patient" role on the patient's motivation to perform at his "job"? A full understanding of this question requires looking at the organization where the performance of this job takes place. The rehabilitation center is a direct outgrowth of hospital organization in general, just as the body of the first horseless carriage was designed after the buggy that it replaced. And hospitals themselves are organized in the fashion of military and religious organizations. One of the main characteristics of this type of organization is the system of authority, the hierarchy of command that has the patient at the bottom.

THE AUTHORITY SYSTEM

Everyone on the staff has authority over the patient. Since the patient is totally immersed in the institution, this authority is directed toward a multitude of items. In a very real sense he is very closely supervised. The patient is subject to numerous house rules governing all aspects of his behavior, and a system of rewards and privileges can be used by the staff in obtaining conformity to the rules. As Parsons (3) has suggested in describing

patients in a mental hospital, the patient is placed in a situation analogous to that of a child in an adult family, passive and dependent.

The hospital provides little opportunity for mature, autonomous, self-directed responsible behavior. Certainly this complete control over the behavior of the patient is warranted in the phase of recovery from the acute accident, but the question may be raised of its justifiability for longer periods of time.

PATIENT RESPONSE
TO THE AUTHORITY SYSTEM

The possible responses of the patient to the system of authority have been described by Goffman (2) and may be intuitively recognizable. With little opportunity for direct control, the patients may respond to the control apparatus in several different ways: 1) The patient may respond with complete apathy and lack of involvement. 2) The patient may be rebellious and refuse to co-operate with the staff. 3) The patient may be a "colonizer," taking up "permanent" residence in the hospital, a more benign atmosphere for him than the harsher world outside. He will accept the authority system as part of the environment he has to put up with. 4) Patients may become "converts," actively promulgating the party line. These patients take over the official staff picture of themselves and try to act out the role of the perfect inmate. They may even take over the attitudes of the staff toward other patients and urge them to conform to the house rules. This phenomenon has been noted among concentration camp inmates by Bettelheim (1). Many of the older inmates identified with their captors, wore bits of the guards' discarded clothing, and behaved toward the other concentration camp members even more brutally than did the guards. 5) And, finally, the patient may elect to "play it cool." This kind of feigned interest in the program allows the person to participate without undergoing any real change. It has been described as characteristic of the response of American prisoners of war to Chinese indoctrination efforts (4).

In sum, the patient may adopt a variety of methods of responding to the large power differences between himself and the staff. He can identify with the staff's perception of himself or avoid the authority in a number of ways. In either case, the authority system does not develop the personal and social skills of the patient and may violate ego, status, and autonomy needs.

It may well be argued that all decisions need to be made by the staff in order to insure the high quality of decision and that the activities of the patients need to be closely supervised because of the complexity of the tasks and the comparative lack of ability of the patients. Finally, it may be argued that the patients need to be treated standardly in a large institution. To the extent that these arguments are valid, patient participation in the authority or decision-making system cannot be used as an incentive for rehabilitation efforts.

INCREASING PATIENT PARTICIPATION IN DECISION-MAKING

One method of making the patient more active, more productive, and more involved in the rehabilitation process is to increase his participation in the decision-making system. In effect, we are suggesting bringing the patient in on the authority process and reducing the discrepancy between his power and that of the staff. The all-pervasive system of authority that encompasses the patient and which the hospital uses to exert pressure on the patient to learn the patient role, conform to the rules, and accept the therapy may actually backfire by reducing patient participation. Further, it reduces the patient's opportunity for personal and social development.

Research is needed to identify the behavior areas in which the decision-making autonomy of the patient can be increased. If the hospital staff is now discouraged by their inability to get patients to participate, this recommendation may seem paradoxical. However, if the staff has the strengths to leave certain areas of decision-making open and not rush in to fill the power gap, patients will eventually increase their participation (9).

ASSESSING PATIENT READINESS FOR PARTICIPATION

Before deciding what the appropriate time and content of patient participation might be, staff members should assess a number of forces influencing the patient's behavior. The better the staff member understands these factors, the more accurately he can determine what kind of behavior on his part will enable the patients to participate more effectively (7).

Generally speaking, the patient's participation may be increased if the following essential conditions are met.

The Task Itself

Does the patient have the skills necessary to perform the task? It is obvious that patients will be unable to participate in areas where their skills do not equip them sufficiently.

The Pressure of Time

This is perhaps the most clearly felt pressure by the staff member. When time pressures are reduced, patient participation can be increased.

Patients' Independence Needs

It can be expected that patients will respond differently to the opportunity for increased autonomy. Patients who are characteristically passive and dependent and have strong needs for acceptance are more likely to accept the pervasive authority system. Patients who have previously been assertive, controlling, and independent are least likely to conform to the "patient" role.

Patient Interest in Participation

Patients differ in their readiness to assume responsibility. Some feel un-able to perform tasks when they are objectively capable, and others want to perform tasks beyond their current capacities.

Accurate assessment of patient readiness for participation in decision-making is important. To provide the patient with greater freedom than he is ready for at any given time may well tend to generate anxieties and therefore inhibit rather than facilitate the attainment of rehabilitation objectives. But this should not keep the staff member from continuing to confront the patient with the necessity of choice.

CONCLUSION

In summary, there are several implications in the basic thesis that we have been developing. The first is that the patient is not passively treated in rehabilitation but is confronted with a resocialization or learning task. He must learn to improve his physical, personal, and social functioning.

Learning takes place when the patient increases his capability in planning and making decisions for himself, which brings us to our second implication. The hospital organization provides a complete set of plans for the patient's behavior and generally limits his capacity for increasing self-directed behavior.

In a number of ways, patients find a role that is comfortable for them in the hospital and accommodate to the all-pervasive authority exercised over them. Thus, the failure of patients to exercise choice and initiative when they are given the opportunity can be partially explained as a result of their prior conceding of the planning, decision-making function to the hospital staff.

In the process of rehabilitation (as in the socialization of children from infant to adult) a gradual increase in patient participation in decision-making needs to take place. The successful rehabilitation staff is able to allot decision-making freedom to patients in the light of a perceptive assessment of patient readiness for participation. If direction is in order, the staff plans and directs. If increased participation is called for, the staff provides for the exercise of choice. Thus the rehabilitation path through time should indicate a steady increase in the patient's capacity to plan, decide, and control his own behavior.

LIST OF REFERENCES

1. Bettelheim, B. Individual and Mass Behavior in Extreme Situations. In: Newcomb, T. M., and Hartley, E. S., and others. Readings in Social Psychology. New York: Henry Holt & Co., 1947.

2. Goffman, Erving. Characteristics of Total Institutions. In: Stein, M. R., Vidich, A. J., and White, D. M. (eds.). Identity and Anxiety, Survival of the Person in Mass Society. New York: Free Press of Glencoe, Inc., 1960.

3. Parsons, T. The Mental Hospital as a Type of Organization. In: Greenblatt, M., Levinson, D. J., and Williams, R. H. (eds.). The Patient and the Mental Hospital. New York: Free Press of Glencoe, Inc., 1957.

4. Schein, E. H. Reaction Patterns to Severe, Chronic Stress in American Army Prisoners of War of the Chinese. J. Social Issues. 1957. 13:3: 21–30.

5. Schlesinger, L. E. Diagnosing the Social-Psychological Consequences of the Cerebral Vascular Accident. Unpublished manuscript, 1963.

6. Schlesinger, L. E. The Disabled Stroke Patient in the Rehabilitation Center. Lansing, Mich.: State Dept. of Health, 1961.

7. Schlesinger, L. E. Patient Motivation for Rehabilitation. Am. J. Occupational Ther. Jan.–Feb., 1963. 27: 1:5–8.

8. Schlesinger, L. E. Psychological and Social Losses Associated with the Cerebral Vascular Accident. Unpublished manuscript, 1963.

9. Schlesinger, L. E. Staff Tensions and Needed Skills in Staff-Patient Interactions. Unpublished manuscript, 1963.

15 Roots of Prejudice Against the Handicapped

William Gellman

The typical rehabilitation worker feels that the prejudices exhibited by society toward the handicapped do not exist within the rehabilitation facility. By virtue of his constant helpfulness and close association with the severely disabled, he believes that his co-workers and he are immune to the discriminatory attitudes of the outside world. He assumes that when he accepts a handicapped person as a patient he accepts him as a person. He takes it for granted that the semi-insulated world of the rehabilitation facility is free of the forces which lead to discrimination.

Is this contrasting picture of a discriminating society and an unprejudiced facility a reasonable facsimile of the actuality? To answer this question, we should examine the rehabilitation process from the viewpoint of a disabled person. We should ask ourselves what he sees and experiences when receiving service at a rehabilitation facility.

His perception of the facility is colored by his assumption of the social role of a disabled person with its attendant attributes of inferiority and inability. He comes to the facility as an applicant asking whether he can gain or regain the characteristics and abilities of the non-handicapped.

As an applicant, he confronts a closed, self-sufficient subculture with an unfamiliar value system. He is a stranger, an outsider who seeks acceptance from a supposedly omnipotent therapeutic facility. He proceeds through intake, initial screening, and diagnosis; if he meets predetermined selection criteria of potentialities he becomes a patient.

As a patient he occupies a relatively low level in the status hierarchy. He is manipulated by forces over which he has little or no control. His rehabilitation goals are determined by the professional skills of the staff. Time, place, type of activity, and method of treatment are dictated by the needs of the rehabilitation process. Behind a façade of supposed self-determination, choices and decisions are imposed upon him.

Distinctions between staff and patients occur throughout the facility. It is apparent in the antiseptic hospital atmosphere with its orientation toward cleanliness and health and in the white gowns worn by staff. Separation of patients from rehabilitation personnel parallels segregation of the disabled from the nondisabled in the outside world. Both within and without the facility, impairment serves as a symbol of exclusion from the dominant group.

The attitudes of rehabilitation

Excerpted from the Journal of Rehabilitation, 1959, 25(1):4–6.

personnel mirror the division between patients and staff. Buttressed by professional skills and knowledge, they view the patient as a person to be helped. Overt needs and apparent weaknesses strengthen their perception of him as a malleable individual who is to be shaped or educated into health. The teacher-pupil relationship prevalent in the paramedical therapies reinforces the staff's conviction of superiority. Given neurotic tendencies or situational frustration, rehabilitation personnel are transformed into omnipotent therapists who dispense health and succor the helpless.

The social distance between staff and patients is increased by the prevailing middle-class orientation of the rehabilitation sub-culture which sets middle-class stereotypes as goals for patients. Staff values stress health, cleanliness, appropriate dress, proper demeanor, correct speech, occupational achievement, and upward social mobility. Since most rehabilitation patients come from lower-level socioeconomic groups, there is a wide gap between patient behavior and staff expectations. This discrepancy leads to continued efforts to fix patients into middle-class molds. If a sufficiently large proportion result in failure, as is often the case, psychological rejection of non-middle class patients begins to develop.

The preceding picture of a typical rehabilitation facility indicates the presence of prejudice against the handicapped caused by (1) the organizational pattern, (2) the emphasis upon differences between patients and staff, and (3) procedures which accentuate the helper-helped polarity.

16 Professional Antitherapy

Bernard Kutner

The helping professions have a common interest in understanding and promoting the curative process even though each discipline has somewhat different objectives and techniques. The recipient of help may be deranged, disabled, diseased, depressed, displaced or in other ways affected by insult or injury to his person. He seeks—or is brought to a source of aid—a doctor, hospital, clinic, or social agency, and expects that by some previously planned and mutually acceptable system, the process of care will be undertaken to halt or reverse the condition necessitating professional intervention.

To understand the neologism "antitherapy" we must first define what we mean by therapy. Webster's International Dictionary defines therapy as "treatment of disease in animals or plants by therapeutic means." Antitherapy is that treatment which produces non-therapeutic results, contrary to intent. It is almost a contradiction in terms since there is a possible implication here of treatment *designed* to frustrate the aims of therapy. However, antitherapy is a phenomenon of unexpected consequences. A more accurate description of antitherapy would be treatment unintentionally harmful to the patient's long-term interests.

How can antitherapy occur? What are its main features? How may it be prevented or mitigated?

Although most professional-client relationships can develop antitherapeutic aspects, we shall limit our examples and discussion to the professional-patient relationships occurring in the large hospital among seriously impaired patients undergoing rehabilitative treatment. Antitherapy may be presumed to occur when the patient is observed to function well under the eyes of professional therapists but either functions poorly or not at all in the absence of the therapist: for example, a partially paralyzed man who learns to shave one-handed but cannot or will not shave in his room or at home; or the immobilized woman who transfers herself from bed to wheelchair in training for activities of daily living, but requires assistance from her *own bed*; or the amputee who walks well when between parallel bars but is unsteady or falls without them. While such occurrences are commonplace in rehabilitation programs, the source of the difficulty has always been assumed to be an insufficiency of and a need for additional training. Antitherapy can induce equally undesirable end results.

Whatever else therapy may be, and whether psychological or physical in nature, its basic intent is to render the individual more adaptable, more in-

Reprinted from the Journal of Rehabilitation, 1969, 35(6):16–18.

dependent, and free of anxiety to perform normal human activities. "Utilization of full potential," "maximal function of residual capacities," "self-actualization" and other such concepts reflect the therapist's aim: basically, *to increase social competence in the performance of rational activities* (1). To achieve a level of competent behavior in the context of a large hospital presents major problems.

The hospital is generally designed to advance the health and well-being of its clients. Due to its bureaucratic structure, its overriding need for efficient administration, its deployment of manpower in three shifts, and its regulation of patient life, there remains little that can be initiated by patients that could lead to meaningful or significant increments of *social* competence.

Hospital bureaucracy is regulatory both of the behavior of personnel as well as of patients (2, 3, 4). It discourages uniqueness, individuality, and personal preference. Uniformity of procedure, physical facilities, and routine activities promote efficiency of administration and task accomplishment. We need not here document the social sterility of the typical hospital environment. It must be noted, however, that this environment tends to be *deprivational* in character. The patient normally cannot perform the majority of those socially determined acts whose skillful performance are at the heart of normal daily transactions.

The need for efficient administration governs the daily routine of hospital life. Hospital tasks are performed by hospital personnel. The patient is not expected to play more than a passive-receptive role in his status. Policy matters are experienced by the patient as changes in procedure as they filter down from administrative decision-making machinery to the specific nursing unit. The patient is not "involved" in decisions affecting his life as a patient, nor does he expect to be. The gulf between administrative practice and autonomous patient-functioning is so wide in the typical hospital that opportunity for the seriously disabled patient to experience ego-challenging tasks of significance is, for all practical purposes, nearly nil.

The three-shift hospital raises still further the barrier to independence of action by individual patients. Routine tasks of daily life (awakening, dressing, washing, grooming, and eating) are conducted or supervised by the night shift in the early morning hours—usually by a severely understaffed corps. When the patients are disabled and undergoing rehabilitative therapy, these routines are often pressed to completion with or without patient participation so that the patient, paradoxically, can be made "ready" for the "work" of the day, namely, therapy. An equally ironic situation obtains on the afternoon shift culminating in bedtime procedures paralleling those of the morning. The task distributions of the hospital and the manpower deployment are practical compromises to enable the hospital to get on with the job. Routine procedures are completed by staff members since the patient is considered too incompetent to be allowed to do much for himself. By relegating the patient to the status of an onlooker, the hospital is forced to use its staff to carry out tasks which, were they shared by patients, would tend to confront them with realistic life problems and help to close the umbrella of benign protection.

The admixture of a work program that largely excludes patient involvement, and an overprotective, solicitous attitude resulting in non-participation in the pedestrian affairs of hospital life, offers a potential threat to the ego of the patient. They raise serious questions about the role of conventional therapy in increasing his ability to function competently, once he finds himself apart from the hospital.

As part of a larger investigation of the impact of milieu therapy upon the physical and psycho-social status of hospitalized, seriously disabled patients, the patient-staff interactions of a hundred adult in-patients in the rehabilitation service of a large public hospital were studied.[1] Our programmatic efforts were designed to maximize opportunities for patients to engage in group actions centering on the realistic solution of problems constantly facing both patients and staff (i.e., shortages of personnel and material, rigid work and routine schedules, unused and unproductive free time, administrative delays, the communications gap between patients and staff, and the myriad others that afflict hospital life). A comparison group of 100 patients undergoing conventional rehabilitation treatment on an adjacent, identically staffed and equipped ward, were also studied (5, 6).

The milieu therapy (or therapeutic community) group, consisted of about 20–25 patients at any one time. With the aid of a group of social workers, a patient government was formed and a committee structure established, each taking up a major issue. A parallel staff conference (in-service seminar) was organized to discuss the effects upon staff roles of increased patient autonomy and the means to improve patient involvement in the program. When the new structures were appropriately mature, a patient-staff conference was initiated, and the interaction of the two groups functioned as a joint problem-solving endeavor. The main objective of the patient-staff conferences was to normalize social contacts without impairing traditional therapies (physical, occupational, and speech). We will refer to this program again in a moment.

The hospital situation tends to oversimplify the task of being a patient (3). By stripping the individual of all role involvements but those designated as "patienthood," it creates an artificial dichotomy. On the one hand, the patient is taught how to get well again by means of specific techniques of muscle and habit training. On the other hand, this education is carried on in a social vacuum, divorced from

[1] This investigation was supported by the Vocational Rehabilitation Administration under grant #OVR RD-710, by the Russell Sage Foundation, and by the National Institutes of Health under Grants H-3838, M 2562, A-2965.

the hurly-burly of daily life. The patient is taught generically useful habits but is kept from exercising them by a contrived context not remotely approaching the vicissitudes of life in open society. One may learn to ambulate on artificial limbs, but have nowhere to walk; prepare for gainful employment by building endurance and work tolerance, but have no skill in applying for a position; learn to speak, but have no one to communicate with or no drive to use this power to gain useful objectives (e.g., negotiating for a new apartment, arranging for transportation, joining a club or church, developing new friends).

Conventional therapy is antitherapeutic because it emphasizes passivity rather than activity (e.g., walking rather than going, speaking rather than communicating, working rather than seeking employment). It is concerned with ends or with means, but rarely with both together; achievement of goals rather than with coping, the *process of struggle*. For treatment to become therapeutic it must concern itself with the dynamics of individual activity and not with the activity in isolation from its social contexts.

To place these concepts into operation, the rehabilitation service of the hospital must gear itself to utilize hospital facts and situations as the social testing grounds of patient performance (7, 8, 9). If wheelchairs break down (as they seem destined to do) it is the patient who must initiate spontaneous action to seek the means of repairing them. If linens, towels, soap and other shortages occur, the patient must be involved in taking the

first corrective steps. If the food is poor or cold, the rooms too hot or too cold, the staff overzealous or indifferent, the schedules overly rigid; if there are periodic crises of personnel shortages or absences; if recreational programs are too repetitive or pedestrian; if life in the hospital is just too dull and dreary—in any or all of these circumstances, the patient must be personally and heavily involved. These "administrative matters" *are* the real life of the hospital; they resemble the sorts of mundane issues that the disabled individual will be forced to face alone when he leaves the protection of the institution. It is on issues of this nature that he tends to founder in the post-hospital world. To foster involvement, the staff and administration must relinquish a portion of their grip on the patient and on the program. Patient participation in the decision-making process of the unit is an essential step. The patient's voice needs to be heard and, by democratic means, included in determining action. There is a parallel need for staff to make deliberate efforts to avoid domination, unilateral decisions, and exercise of the arbitrary veto. In the project mentioned previously, the patient-staff conferences maintained a one-man—one-vote policy, decisions were by consensus (general agreement without major dissension) and the administrative veto used only with restraint and never without ample explanation. The conduct of such a unit is, almost by its nature, less efficient to administer, capable of making major errors, while exposing both patients and staff to compromises not completely pleasing to either group. It increases the risk of failure in any single venture since patients (who are admittedly less expert in such matters) are given serious responsibilities. The major advance of such a system over traditional hospital programs is that patients are forced to face problems and themselves more squarely, and in so doing, test their capacity to function in real situations prior to discharge. Here they can learn to cope with the sticky business of living with a disability, functioning in a more threatening environment than that provided by the average hospital, and learn how to overcome adversity.

A final issue concerning the process of antitherapy is that of professional intimidation. A subtle aspect of hospital life not often noticed by busy professionals is the influence they exercise over patients by their own presence in the hospital. Patient status is the lowest in terms of their productive usefulness in attainment of the goals of hospital care. They may be viewed both as the objects of treatment and as "social undesirables" since they are "parasitic." The patients are often acutely aware of the gulf separating them from those working around them. Frequently this gap includes social, educational, experiential, age, ethnic, and interest differences which tend to make health differences pale by comparison. In the hospital world, the patient is sick and more or less helpless, a 24-hour per day transient guest in a passive-dependent role set with a questionable future. He is surrounded by others of similar fate. Into this world come, daily (except Saturdays, Sundays and holidays, not to mention

annual and sick leave), a coterie of vigorous, healthy, employed, active, 8-hour per day workers with apparently secure lives and futures. The constant contact of these obvious contrasts is not lost. The patients want and need personal interest and concern from the staff who are trained, from professional school on, to maintain their social and emotional distance. This "conspiracy" of status, role, health, interest, and distance is intimidating since the patient does not want to offend those on whom he must rely while in crisis. Professional intimidation is an aspect of antitherapy.

Especially in the public hospital, where the patient comes to feel the strain of status differences, this unwitting intimidation takes the form of minimal communication on meaningful subjects and institutionalized means of "talking out" the problems of sickness, disability, separation from family and the future (i.e., in sessions with doctor, counselor or social worker) (10). Lives converge socially only on issues affecting the health of the patient. Ego-building experiences depend upon the success of "therapy" rather than on social achievement. Treatment is, in the last analysis, to be judged on the functional uses to which it is eventually put. Yet, there is little in patient-staff interaction that is not stultified by the conventions, customs, and ethics of professionalism. In a sense, professional care appears to the patient as indifferent, cold, and dehumanized. A corrective is patently in order if the patient is to experience other, intact persons as humanly related to him. A number of devices suggest themselves that would tend to reduce the distance between patients and staff and throw patients into normal social interactions. These would include:

1. Elimination of hospital garb for patients and uniforms for staff. (In the context of a rehabilitation program uniforms only serve to call attention to status differences.)

2. A common dining room for both patients and staff.

3. Common recreation rooms, coffee rooms, canteens and the like.

4. Joint social affairs, parties, teas, picnics.

5. Joint problem-solving committees to deal with the overlapping concerns of living and working under the same roof.

These deliberate measures to level the status of the two groups, to encourage fraternal relationships and modify the social structure of the hospital should go far toward reducing the intimidating effects of professional care and decrease their antitherapeutic consequences.

In summary, antitherapy may be conceived of as an undesirable side-effect of professional intervention. It is most easily seen in hospital situations in which the institution itself and those who work in it are unintentionally involved in undoing the benefits of treatment. The patient may consequently become immobilized socially as he becomes mobile physically. The social skills necessary to exercise newly acquired habits of performance may have no useful outlets upon the termination of treatment.

Social therapy, using the human environment of the hospital and its administrative prerogatives as mechanisms to promulgate a deep investment in common social transactions, may be necessary adjuncts to existing forms of hospital-based rehabilitation medicine.

REFERENCES

1. Foote, N., and Cottrell, L. S. Identity and Interpersonal Competence. Chicago: The University of Chicago Press, 1955.

2. Coser, R. L. Life in the Ward. East Lansing: Michigan State University Press, 1962.

3. Goffman, E. Asylums. Chicago: Aldine Publishing Co., 1962.

4. Wessen, A. F. Hospital ideology and communication between ward personnel. In Patients, Physicians, and Illness, ed. E. Gartly Jaco. Glencoe, Illinois: Free Press, 1958.

5. Abramson, A.; Kutner, B.; Rosenberg, P.; Berger, R.; and Weiner, H. A therapeutic community in a general hospital: Adaptation to a rehabilitation service. Journal of Chronic Diseases 16:179–186; February 1963.

6. Kutner, B. Modes of treating the chronically ill. The Gerontologist 4(2):44–48; June 1964.

7. Jones, M. The Therapeutic Community. New York: Basic Books, 1953.

8. Rapaport, R. N. Community as a Doctor. Springfield, Illinois: Charles C. Thomas, 1960.

9. Stanton, A., and Schwartz, M. The Mental Hospital. New York: Basic Books, 1954.

10. Weissman, R., and Kutner, B. Role disorders and extended hospitalization. Hospital Administration 12(1):52–59; winter 1967.

17 Self-Help in Rehabilitation:

Some Theoretical Aspects

Alfred H. Katz

Half a century ago, Prince Kropotkin pointed out that self-help or mutual aid was of great importance in the evolution of society. More recent writers on this theme, like the anthropologist Ashley Montagu and the zoologist Lorenz, stress that cooperation and mutual helpfulness are important not only in the development of civilizations, but in the survival of species as well.

In other writings I have pointed out that there has been surprisingly little interest in self-help social phenomena among American social scientists and in the social welfare field, and I have attempted to account for this omission (1). In the present paper, I wish to discuss some of the social phenomena that seem to me to underlie self-help movements, to relate them to other social trends of the present day, and to examine some ways in which self-help approaches can be employed in understanding and working with the clients of rehabilitation services.

To begin with, let us look at the broader social context of self-help phenomena. Recent health and welfare programs are significantly seeking to grapple with the problems posed by "disadvantaged," "socially deprived" ethnic minorities and other special population groups, who have been little or ineffectively reached by the professional practitioners and agencies. With the growing interest in reaching such clients, professional workers are becoming aware of the potential of technics deriving from self-help principles, e.g., the use of indigenous workers drawn from the same socioeconomic and cultural strata as disadvantaged populations; the use of group approaches on a formally therapeutic as well as an educational and counseling basis; and the principle of "maximum feasible participation of the poor," which is written into the base legislation guiding the antipoverty programs. There are rather striking parallels between the emerging awareness of the need for such approaches to socially deprived, disadvantaged, and minority group populations and the potential for use of self-help approaches with the physically handicapped.

This should not be altogether surprising, for there are some characteristics of these population groups that

Reprinted from Rehabilitation Literature, 1967, 28(1):10–11, 30.

This paper is an adaptation of a speech given at the Western Regional Annual Conference of the National Rehabilitation Association, San Francisco, Calif., April 9, 1966.

suggest they have a number of features in common. First of all, these groups exhibit a *deprivation*, of some material and sociopsychological kind, which results in their partial exclusion and alienation from the "mainstream" of the broader society. Many sociologists use the concept of "deviance" in characterizing diverse social groups such as narcotics addicts, homosexuals, and prostitutes, including as a broad group of "deviants" the physically handicapped (2).

In the current analyses of the "new poor" (as differentiated from the "depression poor" of the '30's), many social scientists believe that their partial exclusion and alienation from the mainstream, and the resultant and concurrent psychosocial behaviors, must be diagnostically taken into account before any effective "treatment" programs can be fashioned.

Deprivation may be physical at base, or emotional, cultural, social, educational, experiential, and so on. The physically handicapped start with a physical anomaly or deprivation but often experience a whole series of psycho-social deprivations that are a response to or a consequence of their environs and are later a conditioning factor in negatively anticipated environmental responses.

Speaking very generally, no matter what the source or origin of their deprivation, the deprived in our society have a hard row to hoe. With all its masterful technological achievements, this society does not have too much tolerance for the deviant, nor does it provide many supporting social groups for their nurture. Individual-istic and isolating tendencies, derived from the socioeconomic environment, pervade social life and individual behavior. The social norms of the society are those of individual achievement in a competitive milieu. Those who, because of a deprivation, do not have the wherewithal to compete without assistance become marked as deviates, sometimes as failures, and frequently their style of life both perpetuates and symbolizes the failure. Social stigma becomes attached to the deprived; it adds to their burdens, raises higher the walls over which they must climb, and by a well-studied process often becomes internalized into a negative self-image. Failure—without outside aid—becomes chronic and cyclical.

When looked at in this way, there is a common thread in some current social phenomena that appears to be quite diverse. Student protest movements on many of the finest American campuses, the civil-rights movement in the South and in northern cities, the self-organization of the poor as in "welfare rights" federations, and the self-organization of groups of former mental patients, narcotics addicts, or persons suffering from a specific disease or physical handicap, all illustrate some ways of countertrending in a society that atomizes, that does not provide much tolerance for deviance or offer many social structures in which deviance can be accepted. When the "mainstream" channels or values reject or are rejected, alternative paths to identity realization must be sought.

For populations of the deviant, deprived, the disadvantaged, and the handicapped, the self-help groups provide a number of advantages. First, they give a sense of rootedness, of identity, of connection with an *appropriate* reference group in the broader society. To be disadvantaged or deprived and to be alone is a double handicap. To be disadvantaged or deprived but to be part of a group may supply a sense of connection, a source from which the vital elements of identity and self-respect can be drawn.

If deviates are rejected by the "mainstream" society or if, for whatever reasons, they choose to reject it, they will seek sources of personal identity elsewhere. "Man is a political animal," said Aristotle, and by political he referred to the basic human need to associate and identify with fellows. Part of the "becoming" of the existentialists is the coming to full awareness of who one is and whom one identifies with.

Further, the self-help groups can provide a locus for action; they can represent a counter to inactivity and passivity. They afford the valuable possibility of participation with others in constructive activity. Psychologically it is a truism that, in times of tension or stress, inactivity or the inability to follow a constructive course of action promotes or at least maintains the experience of anxiety; whereas, activity in and of itself is anxiety- and tension-relieving. Thus the activity component in self-help group membership is enormously important in relation to the problem of motivation to change, crucial for many potential rehabilitees.

The third element that the self-help groups provide is heightened communication. Communication with peers—crossing the barriers of language, style, idiom—has been proved highly effective in contrast to the type of communication that occurs in structured formal relationships where there are status barriers, such as that of pupil to teacher, patient to doctor. The current interest in "indigenous" workers, "subprofessional," "bridge" personnel, and so on attests to the realization that communication between those who wish to give service and the potential recipients of such service requires conscious study and explicit strengthening.

Self-help groups can engender an atmosphere of permissive and open communication, of the sort that psychotherapists believe has the greatest potential usefulness in everyday living, as well as in formal treatment programs for personal problems. Undoubtedly, the greater ease of communicating one's problems to persons who have experienced similar ones has been an important factor in the formation of self-help groups and in their steady proliferation. As Bales and other students of small group interaction have demonstrated, not only communication, but problem solving, is enhanced in the group setting.

An important derivative from self-help group participation is that of securing personal and group satisfactions through engaging in mutually beneficial actions. Creative work with and through the group, whether it involves the painting of a headquarters or a lobbying delegation to a state legislature, enhances feelings of power and competence. For deviant and anomic populations this, as we have noted, is extremely important. One of the least publicized aspects of the handicapped has in fact been their capacities for undertaking constructive action in groups. Public propaganda tends to single out the individual disabled person who has accomplished something unusual—the amputee who learns to play baseball or the paraplegic who becomes a highly skilled architect. Less fully noted are numerous examples of achievements by groups of amputees or paraplegics on a self-help basis. A recent and dramatic example is found in the experience of the Synanon Foundation, which in a few years has created a nationwide network of centers for the rehabilitation of narcotics addicts that has an apparently higher success rate than any other known treatment program. A visit to any Synanon headquarters will convince the observer that group achievement, group morale, and group goals are stressed rather than individual ones.

Because of the vitality and energies that are released through group participation, self-help groups present a potential for innovation, pioneering, and grass-roots expansion in the provision of more effective and new forms of social treatment. They have the potential to innovate, outside the structure of large-scale organization, against the bureaucratic rigidities of the formal treatment "system." Here one can again cite the experience of Synanon and of associations of former mental

patients who have established halfway houses and the major contributions to medical research and professional service programs of such groups as the National Association for Retarded Children and the United Cerebral Palsy Associations.

In traditionally organized programs such as those of institutions and rehabilitation centers, problems may derive from the institutional structure itself. Thus, well-known studies have shown that, in mental institutions, patient initiative is reduced and passivity and "institutionalitis" are increased by the bureaucratic structure. In contrast, institutions organized along "therapeutic milieu" or therapeutic community lines show a higher degree of patient activity, interest, and response. One characteristic of the institutional or formal treatment setting, of course, is that within it therapy is usually divorced from everyday living. That is to say, an artificial environment is created that does not stimulate the conditions at home or in the outside community to which the patient returns and to which he must respond adaptively.

The self-help group, by contrast, can provide a social model that more closely approximates the living situation in the community. It can offer a freer give-and-take, positive and negative interactions with individuals, the structuring of direct comment on a free and open basis without the sanctions, restrictions, or role-playing necessitated by a relationship with professionals. All these can have a positive aspect in preparing the patient for ultimate rehabilitation and return to social responsibilities.

Given these aspects of characteristics of self-help groups, it would seem desirable to utilize them in rehabilitation of the physically and mentally handicapped to a far greater extent than is being done. In another article (3) I have portrayed the operations of an extensive self-help rehabilitation program in Poland in which more than 100,000 persons are engaged in physical rehabilitation, vocational training, and counseling. The program has many workshops, various production activities, and placement facilities. Shortly, I will be undertaking a comparative study of the effects upon patients of this type of participation in relation to such items as the speed of the rehabilitative process, motivation, and self-concept of participants.

It is my belief that such comparative studies will illuminate the possibilities of a much broader application of the self-help principle in treatment activities in the United States. Elsewhere, I have analyzed some of the historic reasons the professional fields, and social work in particular, for which I can speak most directly, have de-emphasized the importance of self-help methodologies (1). Whether or not professional workers wish it, this historic epoch now seems to be drawing to a close, and new methods of structuring service, involving new combinations of professional-client relationships, are now called for and emerging. In such a new pattern of relationships, to me, it seems evident that the self-help approach will be increasingly employed.

LIST OF REFERENCES

1. Katz, Alfred H. Application of Self-Help Concepts in Current Social Welfare. July, 1965. 10:3:68–74.
2. Goffman, Erving. Stigma: Notes on the Management of Spoiled Identity. Englewood Cliffs, N.J.. Prentice-Hall, 1963. [A theoretical work that in my opinion suffers badly from a lack of firsthand data regarding the handicapped.]
3. Katz, Alfred H. Poland's Self-Help Rehabilitation Program. Rehab. Record. May-June, 1964. 5:3: 30–32.

18 Some Viable Service Delivery Approaches in Rural Rehabilitation

James A. Bitter

Rehabilitation as a delivery system emphasizes a planned sequence of services, which are usually purchased by the state agency counselor from rehabilitation resources. Examples of these resources are physicians, hospitals, clinics, rehabilitation centers, workshops, and educational programs. There have been research and demonstration projects undertaken to provide, and determine the effect of, traditional rehabilitation service availability in rural areas (12, 17). Perhaps the most ambitious was the Wood County Project (19). The Wood County Project sought to utilize traditional technics by expanding the availability of resources and examining the impact of saturation coverage in a rural area. The results indicated that rural clients, including the disadvantaged, could be effectively served using the traditional rehabilitation model. A similar project (9), located in the Appalachia region of Eastern Kentucky, was conducted to provide comprehensive rehabilitation services to the disabled in a rural, economically poor area. The results of this demonstration project also suggested that physical restoration and related services were helpful to the rural disabled disadvantaged. The project staff found, however, that "vocational" rehabilitation was difficult to realize due to the unavailability of jobs in Eastern Kentucky.

Though the traditional approach has many merits including its sequential organization, individualization, and concrete goal-orientation, the state-federal rehabilitation program has generally operated on the premise that it is dependent upon the availability of rehabilitation facilities, i.e., traditional resources (10). This approach has worked best in urban areas where rehabilitation services are widely available. It has also worked well in rural demonstration projects when adequate resources were created. However, the traditional resource base is inadequate or nonexistent in rural areas, and will be for a long time to come, and is complicated by great distances between population centers that may have these resources. Yet, the purchase of services from established rehabilitation resources often serves as the approach to service

Reprinted from Rehabilitation Literature, 1972, 33(12):354–357.

Dr. Bitter's paper was adapted from a presentation by him at the American Personnel and Guidance Association Annual Conference held in Atlantic City, N.J., in April, 1971. It was supported in part by Project No. 15-P-5524/8 from the Social and Rehabilitation Service, Department of Health, Education, and Welfare, Washington, D.C. 20201.

delivery in sparsely populated areas. Rural clients are often sent many miles for diagnostic, adjustment, training, and medical services. This utilization of traditional resources by rural counselors generally necessitates relocation of a client to an unfamiliar environment. Though relocation for services can be a very successful approach, particularly when it is strongly related to client goals and motivations, it very often leads to many more adjustment problems for the client than it helps to resolve. Most counselors concede that relocation results, many times, in frustration for both the counselor and the client, and clients tend to return home prior to completion of services. The problem of distance also causes rural client applicants to wait approximately twice as long as urban applicants for acceptance to the state rehabilitation program. In a study conducted by the University of Utah Regional Rehabilitation Research Institute, it was found that contact between counselor and rural client, and the resulting continuity of relationships, is adversely affected by geographic distance (7).

Relocation for services and employment is a natural result of the employment orientation of the state-federal rehabilitation program. The North Star Research and Development Institute in Minneapolis made a literature survey of 291 studies relative to Neighborhood Youth Corps (NYC) programs in rural areas. The survey and a subsequent study led the researchers to conclude that rural projects can be effective only if they help to prepare rural youth for urban occupations and urban living (11). Though the employment objective is one of the real strengths of the public rehabilitation program in general, the widespread lack of rural job opportunities makes it a distinct service delivery problem in sparsely populated areas (5).

Some rehabilitation agencies attempt to overcome the resource and distance obstacles imposed by sparsely populated areas through a greater emphasis on interagency coordination, alternate staffing patterns, and greater utilization of client and nontraditional community resources than is generally found in urban service delivery.

INTERAGENCY COORDINATION

Many counselors successfully use the limited resources available within the client's geographic area for rehabilitation of the client by interagency cooperation. For example, the North Dakota Vocational Rehabilitation Agency places emphasis on coordination with other related agencies through multiagency staffing meetings. The Minot (North Dakota) office participates with representatives from related agencies in client planning sessions. The purpose of these weekly sessions is to discuss individual clients known by each of the agencies and to develop cooperative plans for serving them, utilizing the resources available to each agency. In order to use existing resources and coordinate efforts with other agencies, the Minot office utilizes a specialized caseload (e.g., mentally ill, blind, deaf) and the same geographic territory. The counselors rotate their field work so that contact with existing resources and related agencies has continuity. The advantage of this approach is that it enables at least one rehabilitation counselor to be in the field at all times, each being capable of providing services to the clients. Another example of cooperation between agencies is a collaborative Welfare-Vocational Rehabilitation project in Montana. This project provides intensive services to rural public assistance recipients who can benefit from vocational rehabilitation services and facilitates interagency cooperation by staffing the project in joint offices.

The use of mobile units has been explored as an aid in coordinating agency efforts and eliminating the relocation problems imposed by great distances. The Oklahoma Rehabilitation Service (13) conducted a demonstration project utilizing a mobile evaluation team and found that the use of a mobile unit was a real asset in coordinating services to clients. With staff from various disciplines and various agencies utilized, a very careful evaluation of the needs of the clients and the role of the various agencies in meeting these needs was provided. Mobile units were also found to provide staff opportunity to become acquainted with the client's community environment. The Cincinnati Goodwill Industries (4) conducted a slightly different mobile service approach to serve rural areas in three states (Kentucky, Ohio, and Indiana). Medical, psychological, social, and employment services were provided on a short-term basis for handicapped persons in their own environment by a traveling team from an urban central facility. At various times, physicians, a physical therapist, occupational therapists, psychologist, social workers, nurse, chaplain, and work evaluation personnel were part of the team. The central facility and five branch offices in the three states were utilized as satellite centers for the delivery of services. In some cases the services were provided entirely in the client's local community. The project found this mobile approach improved communications and cooperation between agencies and produced many more appropriate referrals for service.

Public Health nurses are also considered to be good sources of referral of disabled applicants to rehabilitation in rural areas and to be helpful for supportive counseling, identification of community resources, and to some extent, public education. In addition, counselors working with extension agents find them particularly helpful in identifying community resources (16).

ALTERNATE STAFFING PATTERNS

The specialized caseload approach in North Dakota has been cited as one alternative to service delivery problems in sparsely populated areas. Varying use of counselor aides is another approach that has been tried in efforts to overcome the problem of distance and the resulting inefficient use of counselor time. The purpose of the aide generally is to provide more opportunity for the counselor to be service oriented by reducing his involvement in subprofessional activity. In the Wyoming Division of Vocational Rehabilitation, the aide provides outreach and follow-up services in a geographic area that might logically be a subdistrict office. In this way, the distance that counselors have to travel is minimized. The Wyoming aides are usually middle-class women who work part time. On the other hand, some counselor aides in the Utah State Agency work full time and are indigenous to a minority or disability group. The Utah aide serves primarily as communication liaison between the agency and client. Montana also uses indigenous aides in its cooperative Welfare-Vocational Rehabilitation project. However, these aides provide a wider range of case services, including supportive counseling. North Dakota, on the other hand, uses counselor aides to relieve counselors of most intake services, e.g., applicant interviews, obtaining medical information, psychological evaluations.

A unique staffing approach known as the Rehabilitation Service Team (RST) is being utilized in Ohio (6). The RST includes: a counselor-manager, a counselor or two counselor aides, a field medical consultant, and clerical support. The advantage of a team approach to service delivery is the role flexibility of individual team members dependent upon special skills, creative technics, and varying case loads. The special advantage to rural service delivery in Ohio is that time spent in travel as a result of low density population areas is considered in the assignment of RST's.

A recent study (1) also suggests that the role of the rural rehabilitation counselor varies, dependent upon the availability of resources (diagnostic, medical, educational, and rehabilitation services). Counselors with limited support services available find it necessary to work directly with the client and his family and intervene for him in the community. On the other hand, the counselor with many support services at his disposal is more likely to coordinate and delegate responsibilities to these resources. At least moderate availability of resources seems necessary, along with adoption of an advocate role.

CLIENT AND COMMUNITY RESOURCES

As alternatives to traditional rehabilitation services, many rural counselors place greater stress on utilization of client resources and other resources within the client's community. Puth (14) has suggested that abilities and disabilities are contextually relative and are a function of a dynamic relationship between the individual and his environment. The West Virginia Rehabilitation Research and Training Center (18) operates on the hypothesis that rehabilitation potential can be considered only as a combination of two elements: client and environment. The goal of the rehabilitation counselor is to help an individual to increase his ability to respond, integratively and adaptively, to situations in his environment. Thus, it would seem that virtually any type of environment, situation, or test is a potential rehabilitation resource.

Maximum utilization of client resources (i.e., motivation, needs, and knowledge) and the client's environment (i.e., family, friends, and other resources within the client's community: physicians, employers, and other agencies) for the adaptation and development of client functioning seems mandatory in rural areas where traditional rehabilitation services are lacking. Some projects (3, 20) and rural counselors (16) are increasingly using employer environments for evaluation, adjustment, and specific job training.

Though relatively scarce in rural areas, employer environments as a resource have many advantages including proximity. They can be helpful to the counselor in providing: a) a direct, concrete experience and a realistic basis for evaluation; b) a functional appraisal of behavioral dynamics on the job by both the counselor and the employer; and c) an immediate perception of client likes and dislikes, capabilities and limitations (8). In addition, employer environments are especially valuable for work adjustment training because clients can work with normal associates and can experience job changes, various production demands, and different supervisory styles. As a specific job training resource, employer environments also have assets not possessed by most trade schools or rehabilitation agencies. Employers have a reality environment, occupations in which all aspects of a job can

be learned rather than simulated, modern work methods and equipment, and, often times, materials, devices, and facilities, in addition to established performance standards that must be met (2, 15).

Development of community resources and the education of community businessmen are also important to job development and placement (3). Using community resources, particularly employers, for evaluation, adjustment, and specific job training can contribute toward job opportunities for rehabilitation clients, though it would be unrealistic to expect this approach to resolve the immense need for job opportunities in sparsely populated areas. Extensive community involvement by the rural counselor will, however, result in improved public awareness and interest in rehabilitation and in referrals to the state agency, as demonstrated in the Cincinnati Goodwill Project (4).

Of course, specialized services, e.g., physical restoration and other medical services, must continue to be obtained where available in the absence of needed and suitable substitutes in sparsely populated areas.

CONCLUSION

There are, then, some viable approaches to rural rehabilitation service delivery. However, most approaches are limited by the assumption that the public rehabilitation program is dependent upon the availability of traditional rehabilitation resources, which essentially is an urban model for service delivery. A fresh look at rural rehabilitation service delivery seems suggested. In the absence of jobs and traditional support services, rural service delivery is characterized by a need for increased interagency efforts, unique staffing patterns, and innovative use of available community resources. In addition, systematic collaborative efforts between researchers and practitioners in the development of *rural* models for rehabilitation service delivery can, hopefully, reduce the constraints in service delivery to the rural handicapped.

LIST OF REFERENCES

1. Bitter, James A., and Kunce, Joseph T. Counselors' Perceptions of Problems in Delivery of Services to the Rural Disabled Disadvantaged. Rehab. Counseling Bul. Mar., 1972. 15:3:147–153.

2. Bolanovich, D. J. The Role of the Industrial Training Program in Vocational Rehabilitation. Paper presented at the Forty-Seventh Annual International Convention of the Council for Exceptional Children, Denver, April, 1969.

3. Fauber, H. F. Community Resource Development; A Placement Concept. Job Placement Digest. July, 1970. (Professional Supplement, Job Placement Division, National Rehabilitation Association)

4. Cincinnati Goodwill Industries Rehabilitation Center. A Regional Program of Services for the Handicapped; Final Report. (SRS Project no. RD-129) Cincinnati: The Center, 1961.

5. Hulek, Aleksander. Vocational Rehabilitation of the Disabled Resident in Rural Areas. Rehab. Lit. Sept., 1969. 30:9:258–262.

6. Hutchison, Jack. The RST: A Service Delivery System. J. Rehab. Mar-Apr., 1971. 37:2:34–36.

7. Janzen, Frederick V., and others. Interpersonal Relationships: Factors in Rural Rehabilitation. (RRRI Bul. no. 4) Salt Lake City, Utah: Utah Regional Rehab. Research Inst., 1969.

8. Jewish Employment and Vocational Service. Work Experience Center: Habilation of the Retarded; Final Report. (VRA Project no. RD-1525) Prepared by James A. Bitter with assistance from Lawrence P. O'Neil. St. Louis: The Center, 1967.

9. Kentucky Bureau of Rehabilitation Services. Regional Demonstration of Comprehensive Rehabilitation Services in a Rural, Mountainous, Economically Depressed Area; Final Report. (SRS Project no. RD-1642) Frankfort, Ky.: Bureau of Rehab. Services, 1969.

10. National Rehabilitation Association. Delivery of Services. Paper prepared for Citizens' Involvement Training Institute, Washington, D.C., 1969.

11. North Star Research and Development Institute. Final Report on Optimizing the Benefits of Neighborhood Youth Corps Projects for Rural Youths. (U.S. Dept. of Labor, Manpower Admin. Contract no. 41-7-006-25) Minneapolis, Minn.: The Inst., 1970.

12. Northern Montana College. Vocationally Handicapped Montana Indians: Rehabilitation by College Education; Final Report. (SRS Project no. RD-810) Havre, Mont.: The College, 1966.

13. Oklahoma Rehabilitation Service. A Mobile Rehabilitation Evaluation Team in a State Rehabilitation

Agency; Final Report. (SRS Project no. RD-775) Oklahoma City, Okla.: Oklahoma State Rehab. Div., 1964.

14. Puth, A. D. The Rehabilitation Counselor—T.H.E.—Evolving Scientific Humanist. NRCA Professional Bul. Jan., 1969. 9:1:1—6.

15. Rasmussen, William D., Jr. Cosmetology: A Glamour Career for Retardates. Rehab. Rec. Sept.-Oct., 1970. 11:5:1—4.

16. Regional Rehabilitation Research Institute. Regional Exchange (Bul. no. 5) Greeley, Colo.: Univ. of Northern Colorado Regional Rehab. Research Inst., 1972.

17. Saranac Lake Rehabilitation Guild. A Demonstration of Methods of Providing Comprehensive Rehabilitation Services to Residents of Rural Areas; Final Report. (SRS Project no. RD-301) Saranac Lake, N.Y.: The Guild, 1961.

18. West Virginia Rehabilitation Research and Training Center. Annual Report. (SRS Project no. 16-P-56806/3) Institute, W. Va.: Rehabilitation Research and Training Center, 1970.

19. Wisconsin Division of Vocational Rehabilitation. Wood County Project: Total Rehabilitation; Summary Report. Madison, Wis.: Div. of Vocational Rehab., 1969.

20. Worley, B. H. Community Involvement in the Rehabilitation Process, p. 37—43, in: Selected Papers from Professional Program Segments of United Cerebral Palsy's Annual Conference, New Orleans, March, 1967.

Section 5

SOCIAL CONTROLS

19 *To Be Different*

Kaoru Yamamoto

When two strangers meet, an often-forgotten function of language becomes important primarily as a means of preventing silence and establishing communion. The fact that two people are on speaking terms is more revealing than the content of such an interaction. The initial conversation tends to be superficial, and a certain standard format of exchange is expected of the participants. To greet a person by saying, "Hello, how are you?" is to anticipate the familiar answer, "Fine, thank you, and how are you?" To declare, "My, it's a beautiful evening!" is to hear, "Isn't it, though?" This talk is not for transmission of information; accordingly, the topics are preselected to insure an immediate consensus. "With each new agreement, no matter how commonplace or how obvious, the fear and suspicion of the stranger wears away, and the possibility of friendship enlarges [Hayakawa, 1963, p. 72]." The idea is to keep the lines of communication open, to share an experience with one another, and thus to bring forth or reaffirm a sense of social cohesion. Seemingly pointless utterances of social amenities represent an important presymbolic function of language and, together with certain culturally-defined ways of managing one's body, space, time, etc., help make the world go around without too much interpersonal friction.

THE DIFFERENT ONES

Whether expressed in symbolic, presymbolic, or nonverbal languages, the exploratory phases of social interactions allow each participant to gain some information about the other, while leaving him a leeway for easy disengagement. It enables one to assay a potential gold ore, so to speak, without committing himself prematurely for a personal investment. Obviously, this is a precious protective mechanism but it is also a double-edged sword, because this preliminary stage often leads people to separate themselves from certain others on rather flimsy, and frequently erroneous, grounds. The safeguarding process then comes to sunder man from man, instead of bringing them together.

Nowhere can this ironic turn of events be seen so poignantly as in our reaction to those whom we regard as different, or deviant, from ourselves. For example, Kitsuse (1962), in his report on the processes by which certain individuals come to be known and

Reprinted with permission from Rehabilitation Counseling Bulletin, 1971, 14(3):180–189. Copyright 1971 by the American Personnel and Guidance Association.

This article is revised from a paper presented at The Pennsylvania State University Spring Special Education Lecture Series, University Park, Pennsylvania, on May 26, 1969.

treated as homosexuals, points out that specific forms of behavior do not in themselves differentiate deviates from nondeviates. Most people rely on hearsay and other vague notions to identify the alleged homosexuals and then proceed to reinterpret the latter's past actions in this new perspective. Seen in this retrospective and selective light, every bit of "evidence" fits to confirm the now-established picture of deviance. Therefore, the difference is imputed to these individuals, and differential treatment is accorded them. All through this cycle, the actual social contacts seldom go beyond the exploratory phases, and deviance is concluded on the basis of fleeting impressions, gross observations, and loose "everybody-knows" arguments.

Fundamentally, therefore, an imputation of difference from others defines deviance, as well as the deviant roles expected. Looking from the outside in, men in the street classify these individuals for the purposes of social management. Freidson (1966), for example, suggests three possible criteria for such categorization. First, it seems customary for the normals to decide, no matter how tenuous the basis may be, whether the individual involved is to be held personally responsible for the imputed deviance. The judgment of moral accountability determines whether the person should be punished (e.g., execution of a murderer) or merely controlled by other means (e.g., training of the mentally retarded, rehabilitation of the physically handicapped, or correction of the delinquents). Second, a decision is made on the prognosis of the imputed

deviance to resolve the issue of the scope of segregation. For example, lepers and criminals are usually banished from the community for an extended period of time, while the unemployed and the venereal disease patients may be permitted to share many facets of regular social life with other citizens. Third, the degree of status degradation or discrediting is specified to justify the varieties of affective treatment of the deviates. For example, tuberculosis and schizophrenic patients may be loathed, while those suffering from cancer or hearing loss may be handled with less stigma. Epileptics, little people (dwarfs), and the disfigured may be "merely" feared and pitied, but homosexuals and drug addicts can arouse wrathful responses in the nondeviates.

I repeat here that deviance is not inherent in any particular pattern of behavior or physical attribute. Society determines whether some individuals should be regarded as different by selecting certain facets of their being and then attaching to these facets degrading labels and interpretations. Interestingly, most of the designated acts or traits of deviance are themselves not immediately harmful to the group. As in the case of carved demons and pictured gods, the singled-out individuals personify the kinds of experience that fall beyond the boundary of the accepted group norm. In this sense, they preserve stability in society by embodying otherwise formless dangers (Erikson, 1962).

To complete such institutionalization of deviance, society offers various public ceremonies to initiate the chosen people into their distinctly deviant roles. Criminal verdicts, legal definitions of insanity or blindness, professional diagnoses of illness, and referrals to social agencies are some of the dramatic means of pronouncement. The process is essentially irreversible as can be witnessed by the lack of rituals to reinstate deviants into their original roles. It must be conclusive in nature precisely because society is here trying to establish that these individuals are different *in essence* and not merely in the temporary pattern of their life. Their total identity must be so restructured as to demonstrate that their deviance is the basic reality and their former, acceptable identity was but a disguise. It must be shown beyond any shadow of doubt that "these deviant [ones] . . . belong to a fundamentally different class of human beings, or perhaps even a different species" (Scheff, 1966, p. 77).

MEETING THE DIFFERENT

In many cases, ascription of deviance represents a slowly developing process. Beginning with an incomplete inventory of a person's life episodes, an earlier classification and succeeding instances are used to explain each other in a reverberative manner. Thus, when a "slightly odd" fellow is observed to act in a supercilious fashion, this perceived arrogance reinforces the impression of queerness, while queerness itself is in turn used to explain the individual's very behavior. Repeating this circular logic at every occasion of direct or indirect interaction, people weave a pattern ostensibly covering the whole of this man even though the original characterization and label applied to merely a small facet of his total being. Such informal typing and exclusion give way to a new configuration of formal intervention and denunciation at a certain socially defined point—a point not typically corresponding to the actual need of the involved party but rather one at which deviance is most easily and clearly recognized and, hence, most disturbing to the surrounding group. People thus participate in the difference-imputing process and mold the course of the deviate's life.

But why, in this social process of differentiation, are certain characteristics (both attributes and actions) inclined to be singled out? One reason seems to be that the unfamiliar disrupts the established basic rules of social interaction. A disfigured baby, a man in a wheelchair, a blind young girl, an convict, a dying patient, or a homosexual—all present a serious challenge to the accepted rules of conduct in face-to-face settings; the public does not have many alternative modes of action to handle these combinations of man and situation.

Especially when visible impairment is involved, social relations tend to be strained due to a narrow channeling of awareness on the singular physical feature. Not only in terms of incongruence in cognitive gestalt but also as regards lack of affective preparedness, an encounter with a physically impaired person taxes people's social skills. For example, when a highly recommended interior decorator calls on a lady of the house, it tends to spell a shock, both cognitive and affective, for the lady to find the decorator immaculately clad, well groomed, courteous, professional, but perchance one of the little people. A chatty taxi driver who suddenly realizes that his pretty passenger, whom her friends casually helped into his cab, is blind, does not find it easy to regain his carefree volubility.

Typically, the initial phase of the ensuing interaction takes on a fictional character on the form of what Glaser and Strauss (1964) called a pretense awareness context. While each party is fully aware of the other's identity, as well as his own identity in the eyes of the other, both pretend not to be so aware and try to define the situation along dimensions other than those narrowly focused on the impairment itself. In this normalizing process, help is often offered by the impaired themselves in making the normals realize that they are interacting with human beings with as wide a range of interests and capabilities as their own. The connoted "handicap" then recedes into the background, and a spontaneous relationship can be established. Nevertheless, small adjustments must be continuously made by both sides to accommodate the physiological fact of impairment.

Such sophisticated social maneuvers are obviously not easy to accomplish. It has been reported (Barker, Wright, Meyerson, & Gonick, 1953) that in socializing with the physically impaired as opposed to the physically normal, people tend to terminate their interaction sooner, reveal less variability in their verbal behavior, express opinions believed to be closer to those held by the impaired, overcompensate in their impression of favorableness of the impaired, and demonstrate greater motor inhibition. These responses tend to distort the feedback so as to make it all the more difficult for the deviates to learn appropriate social behaviors.

The difficulty in interpersonal relationship is further complicated by esthetic aversion shown by the normals and functional limitations of the deviates themselves. Reactions to these two aspects of physical impairment seem to be crystallized in children's differential preferences among a normal child, a child with crutches and a leg brace, a child in a wheelchair, a child with left forearm amputation, a child with a slight facial disfigurement, and an obese child. While the overall ranking among various age and ethnic groups appears to follow the said order from the most preferred to the least preferred with a remarkable uniformity, it was observed that the obese child (an esthetic impairment) is the least liked by girls and the forearm amputee (a functional impairment) is the least liked by boys (Richardson, 1969). The preference patterns do not change even when a factor of skin color is added to the stimulus drawings (Richardson & Royce, 1968).

Unfortunately, children's negative attitudes seem to increase with age, and the postulate that physical impairment represents only an initial barrier to social relationships does not receive a strong support from available evidence. There is also some indication that the normal child who initiates contact with the deviate is likely to be a socially immature, isolated child. Incidentally, general attitudes in adults and adolescents toward physically disabled persons have been found to show low but positive correlations with attitudes toward members of other "different" groups, including the mentally ill, the aged, and the ethnic minorities (Yuker, Block, & Young, 1966).

The matter of socially defined attitude is also seen in people's reaction to the mentally ill. Studies (Phillips, 1963; Star, 1961) suggest that tolerance is a function more of the social visibility than of the severity of the pathological condition. Thus, the paranoid schizophrenic (suspicious, unpredictable, and violent) is more strongly rejected than the depressed neurotic (touchy, moody, and worrisome), and the latter is in turn more strongly rejected than the simple schizophrenic (quiet, shy, and reclusive). The phobic compulsive seems the least rejected in comparison. For an identical condition, moreover, the kind of help sought has much to do with tolerance. If one goes to see a clergyman about his difficulties, he will be rejected only slightly more than when he does not seek any help from anyone. If, on the other hand, he turns for help to a physician, a psychiatrist, or a mental hospital, he will be subjected to an increasing amount of rejection in the said order. In gen-

eral, men tend to be tolerated less than women for a given condition, and females tend to seek help more openly than males.

WHENCE DOES HELP COME?

In view of the generally negative public reception and of the "looking-glass" nature of self-concepts, it is no wonder that those classified as deviates are inclined to be frustrated, unhappy, and often hostile. For example, discussing upper- and lower-extremity amputees of age 2.5 to 17, Siller (1960) reported that these children are highly sensitive to social appraisal of themselves or of their injury, have a high proportion (40 percent) of inadequate adjustment, and receive low parental acceptance. Both the emotionally disturbed (Rosengren, 1961) and the deaf (Blanton & Nunnally, 1964) children were observed to show deprecating attitudes toward themselves and towards others, especially those who have impairments different from their own.

Understandably, then, the deviates try to avoid contact with others altogether, or at least to "pass" if their deviance has not yet been well established in public. Even after their stigmata have become clearly visible, individuals will attempt to cover them, or to keep them from intruding unnecessarily into social relations. In Goffman's (1963) words, the efforts of the already "discredited" ones go largely into management of social tension, while those of the "discreditable" are expended on management of information. Either way, the extra "performance" required drains the deviates' energy, and many inevitable slips tend to discourage them. It is not easy for the stigmatized to gain any measure of security and status and to retain his sense of balance in recognizing his assets against his liabilities.

Unfortunately, neither the public nor the professionals have been particularly cooperative in helping the different ones overcome their frustration and insecurity. To begin with, in subtle and peculiar ways, the non-deviates seem to be perpetuating the status of deviance in the "chosen" individuals while professing to eradicate it. It was earlier suggested that society may indeed need the deviates as a symbol of evil, intangible dangers.

Within the home itself, a child is often imputed a difference and exploited as a scapegoat for conflicting parental desires (Vogel & Bell, 1965). It is much easier for parents to have a definite object for their own feelings of failure, resentment, rejection, and shame than to admit the emotions and hold themselves accountable.

Those to whom a difference has been imputed grow into the deviant role in response to others' expectations, and this poses another barrier to their resumption of normal roles. In a very true sense, these individuals are under an obligation to remain deviant (Bursten & D'Esopo, 1965), especially after a formal degradation ceremony. To receive a healing treatment in an institution, a deviant must be a "good" patient or client, conforming to the specified patterns of behavior. On the other hand, if a person learns the deviant role too successfully, he will find it quite difficult to revert to his non-deviant role even when he has been pronounced cured and/or exonerated. The tightrope is a difficult one to walk. Moreover, there are some indications that social agencies try to maintain and enhance their service by seeking out certain show cases instead of the neediest deviates (Scheff, 1966; Scott, 1969a).

Consideration of these interactive factors would appear to be quite important in our work with the different ones. A strongly individualistic interpretation of the "unfortunate cases," so typical of psychologically oriented professionals, may hamper them in understanding the basic process of social exclusion and degradation. Likewise, moralistic judgments that underlie much of our allegedly scientific practice and research may be another log in our own eyes.

A corollary of the tendency to look at a phenomenon in isolation is the fact that we tend to ignore the overall figure-ground relationship in the life of the deviates themselves and base our actions on fragmented pieces of information. For example, in working with the mentally retarded, we are more likely than not to regard intelligence as the critical factor in their adjustment and neglect the history of continuous social deprivation that they may have endured. Low IQ is used to "explain" everything in their life, and we overlook the possibility that anyone experiencing such an inordinate amount of failure over many months and years is bound to develop similar patterns of behavior regardless of his intellectual level. We see the figure without paying attention to the ground.

In the same vein, the sighted people often forget that the world of the blind revolves around tactile apprehension. Unlike the ordinary visual image, the resultant haptic schema is temporally, rather than spatially, ordered due to the serial *nature* of tactile input. "A schema is a series of haptic impressions and the temporal changes among them as a hand passes over an object. The schema of an object is based upon the succession, change, and order, among properties of a tactile nature [Scott, 1969b, p. 1027]." If we have been experiencing some difficulties in reaching children of the disadvantaged because of the latter's unfamiliarity with the linear nature of our language and, hence, with the process of sequential translation of spatially-perceived experience, we are observing an interesting reverse case here in our contacts with the blind. In addition, the limited *scope* of tactile explorations open to a blind person is likely to be overlooked. We grow impatient when the blind reveal a blurred distinction of self and nonself, a preoccupation with self as their only reference point, an insensitivity to the details of nonself, or a lack of general model-learning.

Finally, the question of education must be raised in regard to the general public's attitude toward the different and the deviate's reaction to the

normal. While many categories of deviance have attracted professional attention in the past, it may be suggested that no concerted efforts have been expended to inform and prepare people for their interaction with the deviate in various social contexts. Where in curriculum do pupils learn humanely about the deaf, blind, handicapped, emotionally disturbed, mentally retarded, alcoholic, and other unfortunates? Where in school do students learn and appreciate the fact that man lives and dies by his symbols? Where do the young look at their own attitudes to the different ones in relation to themselves? What steps are being taken to influence adults' knowledge, feelings, and actions in this facet of life? Implications for curriculum workers, teachers, counselors, and adult educators must be obvious.

On the other side of the coin, how much have we been doing to help the unfortunate ones recognize their special social status and its ramifications? While there is indeed much shared between certain target groups of current sociopolitical action (i.e., some ethnic minorities and the poor) and the deviates in question here, it must be realized that the latter have little, if any, subcultural support of the kind the former can at least claim. A blind child is typically surrounded by sighted people, and a dying patient remains an island in the sea of living ones. Accordingly, those imputed a deviance have a difficult time learning how to act in general and in relation specifically to the normal majority. No clear guidelines are available, no sharing of experience is immediately possible within a particular generation, and no modeling takes place between generations. To that extent, the different ones are indeed underprivileged even more than most ethnic minority members. Uniqueness and communality must be carefully explored in each case, lest we should fall in the twin traps of easy generalization and specious compartmentalization.

Are we, then, really friends of these unfortunate ones? How can we be of more help to the lonely and afraid? Do we have a helping hand to offer them? This is the challenge confronting us all, the professionals.

REFERENCES

Barker, R. G., Wright, B., Meyerson, L., & Gonick, M. A. Adjustment to physical handicap and illness: A survey of the social psychology of physique and disability, Research Bulletin No. 55. (rev. ed.) New York: Social Science Research Council, 1953.

Blanton, R. L., & Nunnally, J. C. Semantic habits and cognitive style processes in the deaf. Journal of Abnormal and Social Psychology, 1964, 68, 397–402.

Bursten, B., & D'Esopo, R. The obligation to remain sick. Archives of General Psychiatry, 1965, 12, 402–407.

Erikson, K. T. Notes on the sociology of deviance. Social Problems, 1962, 9, 307–314.

Freidson, E. Disability as social deviance. In M. B. Sussman (Ed.), Sociology and rehabilitation. Washington, D.C.: American Sociological Association, 1966. Pp. 71–99.

Glaser, B. G. & Strauss, A. L. Awareness contexts and social interaction. American Sociological Review, 1964, 29, 669–679.

Goffman, E. Stigma: Notes on the management of spoiled identity. Englewood Cliffs, N.J.: Prentice-Hall, 1963.

Hayakawa, S. I. Language in thought and action. (2nd ed.) New York: Harcourt, Brace & World, 1963.

Kitsuse, J. I. Societal reaction to deviant behavior: Problems of theory and method. Social Problems, 1962, 9, 247–256.

Phillips, D. L. Rejection: A possible consequence of seeking help for mental disorders. American Sociological Review, 1963, 28, 963–972.

Richardson, S. A. The effect of physical disability on the socialization of a child. In D. A. Goslin (Ed.), Handbook of socialization theory and research. Chicago: Rand McNally, 1969. Pp. 1047–1064.

Richardson, S. A., & Royce, J. Race and physical handicap in children's preference for other children. Child Development, 1968, 39, 467–480.

Rosengren, W. R. The self in the emotionally disturbed. American Journal of Sociology, 1961, 66, 454–462.

Scheff, T. J. Being mentally ill: A sociological inquiry. Chicago: Aldine, 1966.

Scott, R. A. The making of blind men. New York: Russell Sage Foundation, 1969. (a)

Scott, R. A. The socialization of blind children. In D. A. Goslin (Ed.), Handbook of socialization theory and research. Chicago: Rand McNally, 1969. Pp. 1025–1045. (b)

Siller, J. Psychological concomitants of amputation in children. Child Development, 1960, 31, 109–120.

Star, S. The dilemmas of mental illness. In Joint Commission on Mental Illness and Health (Ed.), Action for mental health. New York: Science Editions, 1961. Pp. 74–76.

Vogel, E. T., & Bell, N. W. The emotionally disturbed child: A family scapegoat. In H. Rodman (Ed.), Marriage, family, and society: A reader. New York: Random House, 1965. Pp. 126–136.

Yuker, H. E., Block, J. R., & Young, J. H. The measurement of attitudes toward disabled persons. Albertson, N.Y.: Human Resources Center, 1966.

20 Correlates of Stigma Towards Physically Disabled Persons

R. William English

The purpose of this basic research paper is to provide information about the anatomy of prejudice towards the physically disabled. "Stigma" refers to an attribute that is deeply discrediting and a stigmatized person is one who is thought to be not quite human or normal (Goffman, 1963). In the final analysis stigma might best be considered to be the negative perceptions and behaviors of so-called normal people to all individuals who are different from themselves. Though the present paper considers stigma in a limited frame of reference as it applies primarily to persons with physical disabilities, in reality most if not all of the content seems readily transferable to other stigmatized groups, e.g., the mentally retarded, mentally ill, socially disadvantaged and religious and racial minorities.

Theoretically, it has been suggested (Barker, 1948; Gellman, 1959; and Wright, 1960) that physically disabled persons are a minority in much the same sense as traditional minority groups, such as Negroes and Jews. Barker was first to suggest that physically disabled persons, like traditional minorities, are subject to group stereotypes, overlapping situations—involving role conflict between acting

normal versus disabled—and an underprivileged social status position. Empirically, this theoretical position has been examined and it has been confirmed that there is a significant relationship between negative attitudes toward traditional minorities and negative attitudes toward the physically disabled. Although the absolute level of the correlation is moderate, approximately .40, the relationship is consistent over time and does suggest that there is credence in the belief that physically disabled persons are perceived in much the same manner as traditional minority groups.

Although it is impossible to specifically document the number or percentage of non-disabled persons who stigmatize the disabled, there is little doubt that stigma does exist and that it is a basic fact of life for nearly all disabled persons. Informally, interpersonal relations between non-disabled and disabled persons tend to follow a superior-inferior model of social interaction or to be non-existent. Numerous accounts (Wright, 1960) exist of disabled persons who have remarked that non-disabled persons treat them as if they were disabled in every way. That is, a blind person may feel that he is often

Reprinted from Rehabilitation Research and Practice Review, 1971, 2(4):1–17.

207

treated as if he were also mentally retarded, socially immature and without feelings, interests or ideas. Results of research by Kleck, Onon and Hastorf (1966) support the notion that non-disabled persons tend to be more emotionally incongruent with disabled persons than with other non-disabled persons. They discovered that non-disabled persons demonstrated stereotyped, inhibited and over-controlled behavior with the disabled. Further, non-disabled *Ss* interacting with a disabled person showed less variability than *Ss* interacting with a normal stimulus person, terminated the interaction sooner and expressed opinions less representative of actual beliefs. In a companion study Kleck (1968) simulated relations between normal-normal and disabled-normal persons. Normal actors interacting with a confederate playing an amputee role showed: greater motor inhibition, distorted positivism toward the disabled, and distorted cognitive agreement with the person acting disabled.

Informally words exist within our language system which describe disabled persons in devaluating terms: words such as "retard," "psycho," "crip" and "dummy" connote stigmatization. Within formal institutional structures words also exist which contribute to separating and stigmatizing the disabled. Instead of the word "retard" we hear the word "mentally retarded" and similarly we hear other words such as "emotionally ill," "psychologically disturbed," "schizophrenic," "orthopedically disabled" and "mentally deficient." Although these terms have professional value in

that they are descriptive, and they are supposedly related to prescriptive rehabilitation planning, they often have a stigmatizing effect (English and Palla, 1971; Jaffe, 1966; Szasz, 1970; Blatt, 1970). I believe that this is inherent in almost all instances, regardless of how well intentioned the labelling process may be.

Behaviorally, a substantial amount of segregation takes place involving disabled persons. While the intent of such institutional segregation may well be to assist individuals, one of the clearest results is that the segregated person feels psychologically apart and inferior to his non-disabled peers, who interact in integrated surroundings (Blatt, 1970 and Dunn, 1968). Although a certain amount of segregation in special classes and institutions may be necessary, it should be minimized wherever possible. For example, orthopedically disabled children without learning disabilities do not need to be placed in special classrooms.

A final example of formal institutionalized stigma is the existence of restrictive legislation which denies disabled persons basic civil liberties such as the right to drive an automobile, vote in elections, marry, become a parent, and the right to secure employment (Schreiber, 1970). The basic premise upon which all this restrictive legislation has been passed, which is to protect society, itself is a foremost example of stigmatization. Furthermore, the fact that restrictive legislation continues to exist in many instances without any moral, philosophical, humanitarian or scientific basis underscores the current American tragedy of stigmatization within formal institutional structures.

In summary stigma exists in the lives of most disabled persons and generally it represents the most salient and frustrating problem to be overcome in rehabilitation. Without negative community attitudes, disabled individuals and their families and human service agents could deal with the basic medical limitations of disabled individuals—what Hamilton (1950) called "disability." With negative community attitudes (stigma), the disabled individual, his family and human service agents must deal with a host of other problems which severely restrict, "handicap," the life space of the disabled individuals and often contribute to severe problems of personal, social and vocational adjustment.

Studies conducted on the attitudes of the general public toward physically disabled persons in general suggest that nearly half of the non-disabled public have primarily negative attitudes toward physically disabled persons. Although this statistic is interesting for practical purposes it is almost useless as an aid to understanding the character and make-up of non-disabled persons who stigmatize the disabled.

Understanding the individuals and institutions that stigmatize the disabled most is an extremely complex problem which can only be arrived at by careful examination of numerous correlates or factors which contribute to overall attitudes. Specifically there appear to be demographic, personality, attitudinal, and experimental and behavioral correlates of attitudes toward disabled persons. These numerous factors interact and account for a particular person's attitudes or tendency to stigmatize the disabled.

DEMOGRAPHIC CORRELATES OF STIGMA TOWARD PHYSICALLY DISABLED PERSONS

Sex

Consistently, females have displayed more favorable, accepting, attitudes toward physically disabled persons than males (Chesler, 1965; Freed, 1964; Jabin, 1966; Lukoff and Whiteman, 1963; Siller, 1964; Titley and Virey, 1969; and Yuker, Block and Campbell, 1960). In contrast to these studies, non-significant differences were reported between males and females in studies by Bell (1962), Freed (1964), Siller (1964), and Siller and Chipman (1965). No studies reported non-disabled males to have more favorable attitudes toward the disabled than non-disabled females.

While the results of tests of sex differences in attitudes toward the disabled may be ego-inflating for women and ego-deflating for men it is somewhat expected given traditional role expectations for the two sexes and the different socialization processes to which men and women have been exposed. These findings are in fact consistent with personality test data which indicates that women are basically more nurturant and less evaluative than men. Perhaps a negative consequence of the current revolution in sexual identity will be that women will become less nurturant, more evaluative and more stigmatizing of disabled persons.

Socioeconomic Status

Surprisingly, researchers have paid sparse attention to examining the relationship between socioeconomic factors and attitudes toward the disabled. The limited data that is available suggests that socioeconomic status is related to attitudes toward particular disability groups but unrelated to attitudes toward the disabled in general. Studies which have compared income groups suggest that higher income groups are more accepting of individuals with intellectual and emotional deficiencies (Farber, 1968 and Jabin, 1966).

It is theorized that this difference in attitudes toward types of disability by socioeconomic group is related to the basic values and life style of lower and higher income groups. Specifically, higher income groups value intellectual and social competence more highly than physique or physical prowess. These values appear to be reversed for a substantial number, if not a majority, of non-disabled persons from lower income groups.

Age

Another demographic variable which has frequently been examined as it related to attitudes toward the disabled is "age." Overall, studies of non-disabled subjects suggest that there is little or no relationship between age and attitudes toward disabled persons. Although significant relationships have been reported which would suggest that young adults hold slightly more favorable attitudes toward disabled persons than adults in general, the size of the correlation has been very low, under .20, and accounts for little of the variance (Auvenshine, 1962; Bell, 1962; Siller, 1963; and Siller and Chipman, 1965).

Education

Examination of the relationship between age and attitudes toward disabled persons is complex, for in the case of young persons the age variable is confounded with education. That is, high school and college students demonstrate more positive attitudes toward disabled persons at each higher grade level (Auvenshine, 1962; Elias, English, Moffet, Simon and Tucker, 1965; Horowitz, Reese and Horowitz, 1965; Jabin, 1966; Knittel, 1963; and Siller, 1964). The most obvious interpretation of this result is that education in general contributes to the development of more positive attitudes towards disabled persons. However, studies of adults who have completed their education and left school suggest that this relationship may be situation-bound. Bell (1962) found no significant differences between dichotomized educational levels and attitudes toward disabled persons, and Cohen (1963) discovered an inverse relationship between the level of employers' education and their willingness to hire mentally retarded persons. In related research Palmerton and Frumkin (1969) discovered that the more college counselors knew about physically disabled the greater was their tendency to be prejudiced towards the disabled.

Because of the contradictions in the data it is hazardous to make inferences about the long term effect of educational grade level on attitudes toward the disabled. However that data are sufficient to permit the theoretical belief that generally there is greater tolerance of individuals who are different in educational settings than exists in non-educational atmospheres, and that probably there is a dissipation in regards to the degree to which disabled persons are tolerated once people leave school. In some respects this suggests that people are considerably suspect to being influenced by situational values and rhetoric, i.e., the liberal college atmosphere versus the more conservative non-college atmosphere.

Disability

Another demographic variable which has received considerable attention by researchers as it relates to the attitudes of non-disabled toward the disabled is that of disability itself. Theoretically, it has been hypothesized by numerous writers that type of disability, extent or severity of disability, hereditary versus acquired diability, and age of onset of disability would be related to the attitudes of the non-disabled person toward the disabled. Although these relationships have been examined rather extensively (Alessi and Anthony, 1969; Wilson and Alcorn, 1969; Wright, 1960; and Yuker, Block and Younng, 1966) results indicate

that there is virtually no relationship between any of these disability variables and stigma. Empirically, this result is consistent with the results of studies which have examined the relationship between disability and the adjustment of disabled persons. While theoretically it has been conjectured that individuals with obvious and severe disabilities acquired after childhood would be more maladjusted no empirical evidence has been found to support this view. In interpreting this data we can conjecture that each individual person has his own perceptions or hang-ups with regards to disability. When counseling and psychology students have been asked to enumerate the types of disability they would personally find to be most crippling they consistently have stated quite different reactions and perceptions (English, 1970; and Wilson and Alcorn, 1969). For one person, the sensory loss derived from blindness may be the most adverse disability and for another it may be a progressive disease like multiple sclerosis or loss of intellectual functioning as represented by brain damage.

Religion

Non-disabled persons from different religious groups have been found (Farber, 1968; Robinson and Robinson, 1965; and Stubblefield, 1965) to differentially accept the mentally retarded. Catholics are significantly more accepting than Protestants or Jews, who are generally approximately equally accepting. English (1971) reported somewhat contradictory results in that the attitudes of non-disabled college students from different religions were nonsignificantly related to attitudes toward blind persons.

These contrasting findings may possibly be explained by differences in dogma or theological beliefs, and a tendency toward less secularization in the Catholic faith. Conjointly, there may be a stereotypic tendency to attribute the etiology of mental retardation to prenatal and paranatal factors versus blindness which is generally associated with postnatal etiology. These inferences must be considered with great caution however given the relative sparseness with which religion has been examined with regard to Attitudes Toward Disabled Persons (ATDP).

Occupation

Investigators have begun to examine the relationship between the occupation of non-disabled persons and their attitudes towards the disabled. Jordan and Cessna (1969) successfully hypothesized that special educators and rehabilitation counselors, teachers, laborers, and managers would show a decreasing tendency toward a progressive and asset value orientation. English and Oberle (1971) found that occupational emphasis upon physique was related to attitudes toward the physically disabled. Specifically, that stewardesses (members of an occupation placing a high emphasis on physique) were significantly more negative, rejecting, of physically disabled persons than typists (members of an occupation placing a low empha-

sis on physique). Mean scores of the two occupational groups indicate that stewardesses fell at the 25th percentile and typists at the 75th percentile level on the ATDP standardization norms.

Although it is premature to draw extensive conclusions with regards to the relationship between occupations and attitudes toward the disabled, the findings of these two studies suggest that this is a promising area for further investigation. Part of the central focus of such future study should be on examining attitudes toward disabled persons as influenced by occupational choice per se versus values derived by the milieu and reinforced by that social structure. The interaction of occupational choice and occupational values should also be examined.

Nonsignificant Demographic Variables

Finally, a number of demographic variables have been found to be unrelated to attitudes of non-disabled persons toward the physically disabled. These include: marital status, urban-rural residence, nationality, and race (Brunswick, 1970; English, 1971; and Yuker, Block and Younng, 1966).

PERSONALITY CORRELATES OF STIGMA TOWARD PHYSICALLY DISABLED PERSONS

Current psychological theory has not yet been able to adequately explain the relationship between personality correlates of non-disabled persons and their attitudes toward the disabled, and relatively few such studies have been attempted. The most salient personality dimensions that have been studied are motivation; self-concept; anxiety; interests; and intelligence.

Motivation

Because it has seemed logical to assume that attitudes, of both non-disabled and disabled persons, toward the disabled are related to motivational factors studies have been conducted relative to operationalizing Murray's (1938) 16 Psychogenic Needs and examining their relationship to attitudes toward the disabled. The instrument used in these investigations is a revision of the Gough Adjective Checklist which was developed by Heilbrun (1958 and 1959). Of the 15 motives that have been studied in various research pieces, only two, aggression and intraception, have been found to be significantly correlated with attitudes toward disabled persons.

Regarding "aggression," it has been hypothesized from theory that less aggressive persons would express more positive attitudes toward disabled persons. This theory has been confirmed and the hypotheses verified in a study by Siller (1964) although nonsignificant results have been reported by Siller and Chipman (1965). No significant contradictory results have been reported by any known studies.

A second psychogenic need that appears to be associated with attitudes toward disabled persons is "intraception." Siller (1964) reported a significant correlation of .13, using a sample of 233 college students and Yuker (1962) reported a correlation of .25 with a sample of 66 college students. Although the correlations are significant, neither accounts for even ten percent of the variance and consequently can be considered as little more than statistical artifacts attributable to the use of relatively large samples. Although the tentative evidence on intraception suggests that persons who see themselves as insightful are predisposed to being empathic and understanding in their interactions with disabled persons, the data is very limited, and clearly more research is called for before any definitive inferences can be drawn.

Numerous motivational factors have been found to be statistically unrelated to Attitudes Toward Disabled Persons. These include: nurturance; affiliation; affect; achievement; dominance; deference; succorance; dependency; need for endurance; order; change; heterosexuality; autonomy; or exhibitionism (Yuker, Block and Younng, 1966).

Self-Concept

In some studies scores from the ATDP Scale have been associated with various measures of self-concept, e.g., Semantic Differential Scale, and the Maslows Security-Insecurity Inventory. The results of these studies consistently show that there is a low but significant correlation between positive self-concept and a tendency to be more accepting of the physically disabled. The correlations coefficients reported in Yuker (1962) and Siller (1964) were .17, .19, .27, and .40, which yield a mean r of .26. Although no studies report contradictory findings, nonsignificant findings are reported in many studies when specific definitions of self-concepts were related to attitudes toward the disabled. For example, Epstein and Shontz (1971) found no relationship between prejudice and body cathexis while Yuker (1962) found "abasement" unrelated to stigma and Siller (1964) found "self-acceptance" to be nonsignificantly associated with attitudes toward the physically disabled.

Anxiety

It has been demonstrated (Jabin, 1966; Siller, 1964; and Yuker, Block and Campbell, 1960) that attitudes toward disabled persons are significantly related to manifest anxiety. Correlations range from a low of .14 to a high of .53. That is, those who accepted the disabled most tended to be lower in manifest anxiety. These results are consistent with the data on self-concept and stigma, which is to be expected, as nearly all prevailing theories of personality suggest that positive self-concept and low anxiety are highly related dimensions.

Although no studies report contradicting results some investigators have reported a nonsignificant association between anxiety and attitudes toward the disabled (Arnholter, 1963; and Siller and Chipman, 1965).

Intelligence

Only one study, involving disabled persons as subjects, has shown there to be a significant positive relationship between higher intelligence and overall attitudes toward physically disabled persons (Yuker, Block, and Campbell, 1960). In contrast to this single study, Knittel (1963), Yuker (1962, 1964), and Block (1962) found no significant relationship between attitudes toward the disabled and intelligence. These results correspond to data, in the area of mental retardation, which consistently shows intelligence to be predictive only to performance in educational situations (Farber, 1968; Koelstoe, 1960; and Robinson and Robinson, 1965).

In addition to studies that have examined the relationship between intelligence and overall attitudes toward the physically disabled, some studies have been more exact and considered the relationship between intelligence and attitudes toward specific disability groups.

Because no studies using non-disabled persons as subjects are known related to this problem it is necessary to extrapolate from studies with disabled Ss. In one such study Bauman (1954) found a significant negative correlation (−.56) between attitudes toward blindness and Wechsler-Bellevue Verbal I.Q., using 443 blind persons as subjects. In subsequent research Bauman, Platt and Straus (1963) replicated this study and obtained a significant correlation of −.43. A tentative conclusion to be drawn from these studies is that persons of higher intellectual capacity tend to be more accepting of blind persons. However, because intelligence and attitudes have not been studied extensively, and because the results are contradictory to the data between intelligence and overall attitudes toward physically disabled persons, the preceding interpretation must be considered with great caution. It is possible, for example, that intelligence may function as a confounding factor in some specific attitude measures. That is, more intelligent individuals may be able to analyze the purposes of a specific attitudinal measure and answer in more socially desirable ways.

Social Desirability

Doob and Ecker (1970), Feinberg (1967), Helson, Blake, Mouton and Olmstead (1956), and Jabin (1966) all found social desirability to be significantly related to positive attitudes, of non-disabled persons, toward the disabled. That is, non-disabled persons with higher needs for social approval were more accepting of the disabled. This is well illustrated by Doob and Ecker's findings which showed that housewives were significantly more compliant to requests to fill out a 70 item questionnaire when the requestor wore an eyepatch. Interestingly, nonsignificant results were obtained when housewives submitted to 15 to 20 minute interviews. This discrepancy in results may perhaps be explained by the differential structural role demands of interviews vs. questionnaires. That is, the interview is acknowledged to demand more personal, direct interaction of persons which may have been more threatening to the housewives studied (Kerlinger, 1965). This suggests that social desirability and anxiety may interact and that avoidance may increase as a response pattern if the possibility of interaction with a disabled person becomes more realistic for the non-disabled.

Tolerance of Ambiguity

Feinberg (1971) administered the Budner Scale of Tolerance—Intolerance of Ambiguity and the Attitudes Toward Disabled Persons Scale to 62 college students and tested for differences in ambiguity among those Ss most positive and negative towards the disabled. His results were significant, indicating that non-disabled persons who are better able to tolerate ambiguity are generally more accepting of physically disabled persons. These findings confirm part of role theory that suggests that a state of ambiguity exists in interactions between disabled and non-disabled persons (English, 1971; Feinberg, 1971; Rochester, 1971; and Wright, 1960) which demands that expectations be modified and new, appropriate, role behavior be learned.

Summary

Overall, there does appear to be a significant relationship between certain personality constructs and attitudes toward the disabled. While the relationships that do exist are not extensive they are sufficient to allow us to conclude that personality does play a part in the attitudes which non-disabled persons hold toward the disabled. Results imply that less aggressive persons, with higher self-concepts, lower levels of anxiety, higher needs for social approval and greater ability to tolerate ambiguity are the most accepting of the disabled.

Interestingly, these results are consistent with the limited amount of information we have with regards to these variables as they relate to the personal and social adjustment of disabled persons. Although the correlational data is even lower in this regard, it is such as to suggest that the best adjusted physically disabled persons are individuals who have more positive self-concepts, are less aggressive, less anxious, and have fewer needs for social approval along with a greater ability to tolerate ambiguity.

ATTITUDINAL CORRELATES OF STIGMA TOWARDS PHYSICALLY DISABLED PERSONS

Overall and Specific Attitudes

Correlational research has shown that overall attitudes toward physically disabled persons, as measured by instruments such as the Attitudes Toward Disabled Persons Scale (ATDP), are closely related to attitudes toward specific types of disabled persons. Siller and Chipman (1965) correlated Attitudes Toward Disabled Persons scores with scores from the Feeling Check List (FCL). They found that overall attitudes, of adults and young adults, were significantly related to attitudes toward these specific disability types: Amputation (.31), Skin Disorder (.36), Cerebral Palsy (.31), Blindness (.34) and Body Deformations (.34). When Attitudes Toward Disabled Persons scores were correlated with scores from the Social Dis-

tance Scale (SDS) the following correlations were found between overall attitudes toward the physically disabled and opinions about these specific disability types: Amputation (.26), Skin Disorders (.28), Blindness (.29), and Body Deformation (.31). These correlations were lower than those obtained associating Attitudes Toward Disabled Persons data with data from the Feeling Check List but all were significant. Overall attitudes toward the physically disabled appeared unrelated to opinions about deafness and paralysis based on correlations between the Attitudes Toward Disabled Persons Scale and the Feeling Check List, and the Attitudes Toward Disabled Persons Scale and the Social Distance Scale (Siller and Chipman, 1965).

Overall attitudes toward the physically disabled are also significantly associated with attitudes toward the aged (Human Resources, 1962, 1964; and McCourt, 1963). McCourt (1963) administered the Attitudes Toward Disabled Persons Scale and the Attitudes Toward Old People Scale (AOP) to a sample of 360 professional and paraprofessional geriatric workers. He made nine statistical tests and found significance in each case with correlations ranging from .33 to .68. Yuker (1964) also correlated scores from the Attitudes Toward Disabled Persons Scale and the Attitudes Toward Old People Scale. The tests were administered to three different samples of disabled employees of Abilities, Inc., and three significant correlations were obtained (.26, .27, .44).

In two studies (McCourt, 1963 and Yuker, 1962) Attitudes Toward Disabled Persons scores and Attitudes Toward Old People scores were non-significantly associated. While the results are not entirely consistent, the weight of the evidence reinforces the belief that there is a significant positive relationship between overall attitudes toward the physically disabled and attitudes toward the aged.

If future researchers derive the same result they will confirm the theoretical view that the greatest amount of public acceptance is extended to severely disabled persons. In one pertinent theoretical study Farber (1968) conjectured that there is considerably more tolerance of the severely intellectually deficient, with IQ's under .50, than of the moderately and mildly retarded. Farber believes that such differential tolerance is based on the belief that lower level retardates are basically incompetent and should not be held responsible for their behavior or their intellectual deficiencies. In contrast higher level retardates are perceived as socially deviant persons who deliberately use their intellectual deficiency in a manipulative fashion to obtain secondary gain(s). Another explanation for differential stigma by severity of disability is that more mildly impaired individuals are more psychologically and economically threatening to non-disabled persons (Doctor and Sieveking, 1970).

Disability Type Preferences: Attitudes Toward Physical Versus Mental Disabilities

Some differences do appear to exist among the attitudes of the non-disabled toward persons with physical versus mental disabilities but the relationships are complex and difficult to analyze. The critical variable that appears to be interacting with disability type, to account for attitudinal differences, is the "context situation."

When a context situation is not specified non-disabled persons express more positive attitudes toward the physically disabled. Freed (1964) reported this finding when he modified the Attitudes Toward Disabled Persons Scale to study attitudes toward the physically disabled versus the "mentally ill" and the "alcoholic." Bates (1965) used similar methodology and had similar, though less striking, results concerning attitudes toward the physically disabled persons who suffered a nervous breakdown. On a continuum this suggests that a generic household label, like nervous breakdown, may be a less adversive symbol of stigma than a more definitive professional label, like "mental illness" or "alcoholic."

Consideration of stigma, towards the disabled, in terms of social and occupational context situations produces more definitive information. Although most research that has related disability type preferences to social context situations has not reported results of statistical tests, the accumulation of data suggests that non-disabled persons find physically disfigured persons less "socially" acceptable than persons who are functionally handicapped by difficulties such as mental illness, alcoholism and diabetes. Present research (English and Palla, 1971; MacDonald and Hall, 1969; MacGregor, 1967; Richardson, Hastorf,

Goodman and Dornbusch, 1961; Siller, 1963; and Whiteman and Lukoff, 1965) suggests that an "aesthetic" factor strongly influences social and personal preferences of non-disabled persons for the disabled. This is well illustrated by a study (English and Palla, 1971) involving the attitudes of non-disabled clerical workers toward a photograph of mildly and severely retarded adolescent boy. Results demonstrated that non-disabled persons hold much more positive attitudes toward persons with intact, so-called normal, body images. The most salient Semantic Differential Scale accounting for individual responses was the "potency" dimension which involved constructs such as weakness, sickness, dependency, and ugliness.

In occupational context situations non-disabled persons, especially employers, appear to choose disabled persons primarily in terms of functional ability or productivity, versus reliance on physical appearance and style in social situations. Data suggests that vocationally the orthopedically disabled, e.g., amputees and paraplegics, are generally preferred as workers over persons with sensory disabilities, e.g. deaf and blind, who in turn are generally more preferred as workers than persons with brain related diabilities, e.g. brain injured, cerebral palsied, epileptic and mentally retarded (Appell, Williams and Fishell, 1963; Bates, 1965; Barker, 1964; Baxt, David, Jaffe and Wang, 1959; Kvaraceus, 1956; Murphy, Dickstein and Dripps, 1960; Nikoloff, 1962; and Rickard, Triandis and Patterson, 1963).

Although definitive data does not appear to be available relevant to the work productivity of different disability groups it may be that many employers prefer persons with organic versus functional limitations because the actions of organically disabled persons may appear to be more predictable, and therefore they might be considered to be more reliable, dependable employees. Certainly the degree of ambiguity increases along a continuum from organic to functional disability and this is likely to contribute to adverse reactions among many non-disabled persons.

Prejudice and Authoritarianism

For some time, it has been theoretically believed that attitudes toward disabled persons are part of a broader constellation of attitudes toward persons who are demographically or psychologically different from prevailing social norms. That is, attitudes toward the physically disabled may be part of a larger constellation of attitudes toward people who are different in any way. To evaluate this concept some investigators have correlated scores of non-disabled persons on measures of attitudes toward disabled persons with scores on measures of general prejudice. In a study conducted at Human Resources, Inc. Chesler (1965) correlated Attitudes Toward Disabled Persons scores with four locally constructed measures of prejudice toward various minority groups. The correlations for the four subscales ranged from −.40 to −.46 and the median correlation was −.44. The overall correlation which included all of the four subgroups was −.52. All five coefficients of correlation were in the predicted direction and all of them were statistically significant beyond the .01 level. These results correspond to those reported in previous research by Cowen, Underberg, Verrillo (1958) and Kogan (1959). Cowen, et al. reported significant correlations between attitudes toward blindness and scores on the California Anti-minority and anti-Negro scales using a sample of college students. In closely related research Kogan (1959) reported significant relationships between ethnocentrism and prejudice towards the aged among college students.

In summary, the results of these studies confirm the theoretical belief that prejudice is a general and pervasive attitudinal characteristic of certain non-disabled individuals which is reflected in a tendency to reject whatever groups they perceive as different from themselves rather than only one or two specific outgroups. Graphically, the results suggest that individuals who reject disabled persons also tend to reject other distinctive groups which may be identified by racial, religious or ethnic terms. In light of the extensiveness and saliency of stigma among certain persons it is easy to comprehend the complexity involved in changing prejudice toward the physically disabled and the different.

Other related studies have been conducted: English (1971) found that the expressed ethnocentrism of college students was significantly associated (r = .41) with attitudes toward blind persons; Cowen, Rockway, Babrone and Stevenson (1967) reported a significant association between antideafness and authoritarian, anti-Negro and antiminority attitudes; and Jabin (1966) indicated that authoritarianism was significantly related to attitudes of pity, hostility and repulsion of nondisabled high schoolers toward the disabled.

In addition to the authoritarianism construct measures of attitudes toward disabled persons have been correlated with various measures of personal and mental rigidity. The latter have included constructs such as Machiavellianism; Intellectual Pragmatism; and Dogmatism. The results of these studies are somewhat contradictory, however the data appears to suggest that low mental and personal rigidity is associated with positive attitudes toward the disabled (Genskow and Maglione, 1965; Rickard, Triandis and Patterson, 1963; Yuker, 1962, 1964; and Yuker and Block, 1964).

Experiential and Behavioral Correlates of Stigma Toward Physically Disabled Persons

Theoretically it has been assumed (Wright, 1960) that the attitudes that non-disabled persons have toward disabled persons are learned and are a function of their past experiences interacting with disabled persons. Yuker, Block and Younng (1966) summarized over 40 studies in this area and report that in general increased amount of contact, time, between non-disabled and disabled persons is related to an improvement in attitude. However, far more important than the mere extent of contact appears to be a consideration of the type or quality of contact that takes place between the two groups. Studies have demonstrated that close and intimate contact produce far more significant and positive changes in attitudes than relatively superficial contact. Particularly in instances where non-disabled persons have had the opportunity to interact with the disabled in relatively equalitarian statuses, not a superior relating to an inferior, there has been an improvement in attitudes toward the disabled. In summary, more positive attitudes have been found to be related to close interpersonal contact with disabled persons in personal, social, educational and vocational settings.

Although the data is inconclusive, tentatively it may be speculated that certain types of contact between the non-disabled and the disabled may actually result in the development of more negative attitudes (stigma) on the part of the non-disabled. Research (Yuker, Block and Younng, 1966) has shown that some hospital and medical workers develop more negative attitudes toward the physically disabled over time. This finding might be explained by the fact that interaction between the non-disabled and the disabled in a hospital setting tends to be generally superficial and involves individuals of unequal status position. Furthermore, hospitalization implies that the disabled person is placed in a dependent position, where materially he contributes less to the non-disabled person than that person does to him. Such a situation could create resentment and hostility towards the disabled if close contact did not take place.

Research by Palmerton and Frumkin (1969) further illuminates the relationship between contact, between helpers and helpees, and attitudes. They found that college counselors had more favorable attitudes toward the disabled when they enjoyed interacting with the disabled, when it was difficult to avoid contact, and when they had alternative job opportunities available with the non-disabled.

In related research Farber (1968) reviewed studies that indicate that on occasion persons have developed more negative attitudes towards the disabled and disadvantaged after visiting them within an institution setting. Thus, the institutional visit which often has been established as a means to improve community attitudes toward the disabled appears in many instances to backfire and result in general repulsion and rejection of the disabled. These feelings may be explained by the psychological reaction people experience at seeing other humans, and themselves as well if they evoke projection, in a dependent status within a total institution. Further, negative reactions may result from the physical conditions of the institution, in addition to unreasonable restrictive policies governing the lives of residents, and the perception that staff hold negative and devaluating attitudes toward the residents.

Vocationally, it appears that persons in certain occupational areas hold more positive attitudes toward the disabled than others. English and Oberle (1971) found that occupations that place a low emphasis on physique, e.g., typists, are more accepting of physically disabled persons in general, than occupations which place a high emphasis on physique, e.g. stewardesses. Related to this finding are studies which have shown that individuals employed in human service occupations are likely to hold more positive attitudes toward the disabled than individuals in other occupational areas, Jordan (1969).

Finally, research (Skelhaus, 1966) has shown that preprofessional educational training contributes to a reduction in negative attitudes, and vocational studies (Yuker, Block and Younng, 1966) indicate that stigma is reduced when non-disabled persons work closely with disabled persons over a long time period.

Work should be regarded as a humanizing experience which provides individuals with dignity and prestige. Specifically, in work individuals have the opportunity and responsibility for displaying competence. Since one of the most prevailing stereotypes of the disabled person is that they are basically incompetent, work can be associated with improving positive attitudes toward the disabled and different.

REFERENCES

Alessi, D. F. and Anthony, W. A. The uniformity of children's attitudes toward physical disabilities. Exceptional Children, 1969, 35(7), 543–545.

Appell, M. J., Williams, C. M. and Fishell, K. N. Interests of professionals in fields of exceptionality. Vocational Guidance Quarterly, 1963, 12(1), 43–45.

Auvenshine, C. D. The development of a scale for measuring attitudes toward severely disabled college students. Unpublished doctoral dissertation, University of Missouri, 1962.

Barker, D. G. Concepts of disabilities. Personnel and Guidance Journal, 1964, 43(4), 371–374.

Barker, R. C. The social psychology of physical disability. Journal of Social Issues, 1948, 4, 29–38.

Bates, R. E. Meaning of "disabled" and "handicapped" their relationship to each other and specific defects. Unpublished doctoral dissertation, University of Houston, 1965.

Bauman, M. K. Adjustment to Blindness: A study as reported by the committee to study adjustment to blindness. Harrisburg, Division of Documents, Department of Property and Supplies, Commonwealth of Pennsylvania, 1954.

_____, Platt, H. and Strauss, S. A measure of personality for blind adolescents. International Journal for the Education of the Blind, 1963, 13(1), 7–12.

Baxt, R., David, P., Jaffe, A. and Wang, D. Survey of employers practices and policies in the hiring of physically impaired workers. Bulletin of the Federation of Employment and Guidance Service, May, 1959.

Bell, A. H. Attitudes of selected rehabilitation workers and other hospital employees toward the physically disabled. Psychological Reports, 1962, 10(1), 183–186.

Blatt, Burton. Exodus from pandemonium. Boston: Allyn and Bacon, Inc., 1970.

Block, J. R. Motivation, satisfaction and production of handicapped workers. Unpublished doctoral dissertation, New York University, 1962.

Bradley, P. A. Generalized rejection: Content or artifact. Proceedings of the American Psychological Association Convention, Miami, Florida, 1970, 5(2), 699–700.

Brunswick, A. F. What generation gap?

A comparison of some generalized differences among blacks and whites. Social Problems, 1970, 17(3), 358–371.

Chesler, M. A. Ethnocentrism and attitudes toward the physically disabled. Journal of Personality and Social Psychology, 1965, 2(6), 877–882.

Cohen, J. Employer attitudes toward disabled persons. American Journal of Mental Deficiency, 1963, 67, 705–713.

Cowen, E. L., Underberg, R. P. and Verrillo, R. T. The development and testing of an attitudes to blindness scale. Journal of Social Psychology, 1958, 48, 297–304.

_____, Rockway, A. M., Babrone, P. H. and Stevenson, J. Development and evaluation of an attitudes to deafness scale. Journal of Personality and Social Psychology, 1967, 6(2), 183–191.

Doctor, R. M. and Sieveking, N. A. Survey of attitudes toward drug addiction. Proceedings of the Annual Convention of the American Psychological Association, 1970, 5(2), 795–796.

Doob, A. N. and Ecker, B. P. Stigma and compliance. Journal of Personality and Social Psychology, 1970, 14(4), 302–304.

Dunn, L. M. Special education for the mildly retarded: is much of it justifiable? Exceptional Children, 1968, 35, 5–24.

Elias, J., English, R. W., Moffet, J., Simon, W. and Tucker, W. Popular conceptions of the civil rights movement. Proceedings of the Midwest Sociological Association Convention, Minneapolis, April 4, 1965.

English, R. W. Differential perceptions of the seriousness of a disability. (Unpublished manuscript, Syracuse University, 1970).

_____ Assessment and modification of attitudes toward blind persons. (Accepted for publication by Psychological Aspects of Disability, 1971).

_____ and Oberle, J. Towards the development of new methodology for examining attitudes toward disabled persons. Rehabilitation Counseling Bulletin, Fall, 1971, 15(1).

English, R. W. and Palla, D. B. Attitudes of non-disabled persons toward a photograph of a mildly and severely mentally retarded adolescent. Training School Bulletin, May, 1971, 68(1), 55–63.

Epstein, S. and Shontz, F. Attitudes toward persons with physical disabilities as a function of attitudes toward one's own body. Paper presented at American Psychological Association, New York, September, 1971.

Farber, B. Mental Retardation: its social context and social consequences. Boston: Houghton, Mifflin Company, 1968.

Feinberg, L. B. Social desirability and attitudes toward the disabled. Personnel and Guidance Journal, 1967, 46(4), 375–381.

_____ Tolerance of ambiguity as a variable in attitudes toward disabled persons. Unpublished manuscript, Syracuse University, 1971.

Freed, E. X. Opinions of psychiatric hospital personnel and college students toward alcoholism, mental illness and physical disability: an exploratory study. Psychological Reports, 1964, 15(2), 615–618.

Gellman, W. Roots of prejudice against the handicapped. Journal of Rehabilitation, 1959, 25(1), 4–6, 25.

Genskow, J. K. and Maglione, F. D. Familiarity, dogmatism and reported student attitudes toward the disabled. Journal of Social Psychology, 1965, 67, 329–341.

Goffman, I. Stigma. Englewood Cliffs, New Jersey: Prentice-Hall, Inc., 1963.

Hamilton, K. W. Counseling the Handicapped in the Rehabilitation Process. New York: Ronald Press, 1950.

Heilbrun, A. B. Relationship between

the Adjective Check List, Personal Preference Schedule and desirability factors under varying defensiveness conditions. Journal of Clinical Psychology, 1958, 24(3), 283–287.

____. Validation of a need scaling technique for the Adjective Check List. Journal of Consulting Psychology, 1959, 23, 347–351.

Helson, H., Blake, R. R., Mouton, J. S. and Olmstead, J. A. Attitudes as adjustments to stimulus background and residual factors. Journal of Abnormal and Social Psychology, 1954, 52, 314–322.

Horowitz, L. S., Reese, N. S. and Horowitz, M. W. Attitudes toward deafness as a function of increasing maturity. Journal of Social Psychology, 1965, 66, 331–336.

Jabin, N. Attitudes toward the physically disabled as related to selected personality variables. Dissertation Abstracts, 1966, 27(2-B), 599.

Jaffe, J. Attitudes of adolescents toward the mentally retarded. American Journal of Mental Deficiency, 1966, 70(6), 907–912.

Jordan, J. E. and Cessna, W. A comparison of attitudes of four occupational groups toward education and physically disabled persons in Japan. Journal of Social Psychology, 1968, 78, 283–284.

Kerlinger, F. N. Foundations of Behavioral Research. New York: Holt, Rinehart and Winston, Inc., 1965.

Kleck, R. Physical stigma and nonverbal cues emitted in face to face interaction. Human Relations, 1968, 21(1), 19–28.

____, Onon, H. and Hastorf, A. H. The effects of physical deviance upon face to face interaction. Human Relations, 1966, 19(4), 425–436.

Knittel, M. G. A comparison of attitudes toward the disabled between subjects who had a physically disabled sibling and subjects who did not have a physically disabled sib-

ling. Unpublished doctoral dissertation, University of South Dakota, 1963.

Koelstoe, O. P. Employment evaluation and training program. American Journal of Mental Deficiency, 1960, 65, 17–31.

Kogan, N. Attitudes toward old people: The development of a scale and examination correlates. Journal of Abnormal and Social Psychology, 1959, 59, 44–55.

Kvaraceus, W. C. Acceptance-rejection and exceptionality. Exceptional Children, 1956, 22, 328–331.

Lukoff, I. F. and Whiteman, M. A summary of attitudes and blindness: components, correlates and effects. Unpublished manuscript, Human Resources Library, 1963.

MacDonald, A. P. and Hall, J. Perception of disability by the nondisabled. Journal of Consulting and Clinical Psychology, 1969, 33(6), 654–660.

MacGregor, F. C. Social and cultural components in the motivation of persons seeking plastic surgery of the nose. Journal of Health and Social Behavior, 1967, 8(2), 125–135.

McCourt, J. F. A study of acceptance of the geriatric patient among selected groups of hospital personnel. Unpublished doctoral dissertation, Boston University, 1963.

Murphy, A. T., Dickstein, J. and Dripps, E. Acceptance, rejection and the hearing handicapped. Volta Review, 1960, 62(5), 208–211.

Murray, H. A. Exploration in Personality. New York: Oxford University Press, 1938.

Nikoloff, O. M. Attitudes of public school principals toward employment of teachers with certain physical disabilities. Rehabilitation Literature, 1962, 23, 344–345.

Palmerton, K. E. and Frumkin, R. M. College counselors attitudes toward education considered a determinant of attitudes toward disabled persons.

Perceptual and Motor Skills, 1969, 28(2), 441–442.

Parsons, T. Definitions of health and illness in the light of American values and social structure, in E. Gartly Jaco (Ed.) Patients, physicians and illness, Glencoe, Illinois: The Free Press, 1958, 165–187.

Richardson, S. A., Hastorf, A. H., Goodman, N. and Dornbusch, S. M. Cultural uniformity in reaction to physical disabilities. American Sociological Review, 1961, 26, 241–247.

Rickard, T. E., Triandis, H. C. and Patterson, C. H. Indices of employer prejudice toward disabled applicants. Journal of Applied Psychology, 1963, 47, 52–55.

Robinson, H. B. and Robinson, N. M. The mentally retarded child: A psychological approach. New York: Mc-Graw-Hill Book Company, 1965.

Rochester, R. K. A consideration of the role theorist's interpretation of mental illness. Unpublished masters thesis, Syracuse University, Summer, 1971.

Schreiber, M. (Ed.). Social Work and Mental Retardation. New York: The John Day Company, 1970.

Siller, J. Reactions to physical disability. Rehabilitation Counseling Bulletin, 1963, 7(1), 12–16.

_____ Personality determinants of reaction to the physically disabled. American Foundation for the Blind Research Bulletin, 1964, 7, 37–52.

_____ and Chipman, A. Personality determinants of reaction to the physically handicapped: II. Projective techniques, Albertson, New York. Unpublished manuscript, Human Resources Library, 1965.

Skelhaus, M. SWEAT project evaluation. Project News of the Parsons State Hospital and Training Center, 1966, 2(10), 10–17.

Stubblefield, H. W. Religion, parents and mental retardation. Mental Retardation, 1965, 3(4), 8–11.

Szasz, T. The manufacture of madness. New York: Harper and Row, 1970.

Titley, R. W. and Virey, W. Expression of aggression toward the physically handicapped. Perceptual and Motor Skills, 1969, 29(1), 51–56.

Whiteman, M. and Lukoff, I. F. Attitudes of the sighted toward blindness and physical handicap. Paper presented at the Eastern Psychological Association, New York, April, 1960.

Wilson, E. D. and Alcorn, P. Disability simulation and development of attitudes toward the exceptional. Journal of Special Education, 1969, 3(3), 303–307.

Wright, B. A. Physical Disability: a psychological approach. New York: Harper, 1960.

Yuker, H. Yearly psycho-social research summary. Albertson, New York, Human Resources, Inc., 1962.

_____ Yearly psycho-social research summary. Albertson, New York, Human Resources, Inc., 1964.

Yuker, H. E. and Block, J. R. Intellectual attitudes and college performance. Paper presented at American Psychological Association, Los Angeles, September, 1964.

_____, Block, J. R. and Campbell, W. J. A scale to measure attitudes toward disabled persons. Human Resources Study Number 5. Albertson, New York. Human Resources, Inc., 1960.

_____, Block, J. R. and Younng, J. H. The measurement of attitudes toward disabled persons. Human Resources Center, Albertson, New York, 1966.

21 Patient Cooperation in a Rehabilitation Center:
Assumption of the Client Role

Edward G. Ludwig and
Shirley Davidson Adams

Assumption of the client role in a rehabilitation setting entails a relationship with medical personnel involving submission to an arduous regimen with only limited assurance of success. Persons whose normal social relationships contain elements of dependency or subordination might be more inclined to assume such a role and successfully complete treatment. Among a population of 406 patients in a rehabilitation center, clients who possessed characteristics of dependency and subordination were found more likely to complete rehabilitation services.

The ultimate success of treatment programs planned and undertaken in behalf of patients hinges largely on the condition that patients will act rationally and cooperate in accord with their own best interests. This study investigates the problem of patients who engage in apparently self-defeating behavior during treatment in a rehabilitation center by failing to cooperate in the medical regimen or by leaving the treatment situation prematurely. The delineation of factors associated with this uncooperative behavior is cast in the framework of role theory with particular emphasis upon the role demands of patients in a rehabilitation setting and the propensity

of individuals to assume that role adequately.

THE CLIENT ROLE

The behavioral expectations of the sick role as outlined by Parsons (1951) involve both rights and duties. The rights include exemption from certain normal role responsibilities and the right to be taken care of. The duties entail the obligation to want to get well as soon as possible and to seek and cooperate with technically competent help to accomplish that end. It is when the individual comes in contact with the technically competent help that the sick role evolves into the patient role with its own set of behavioral demands. Both the physician and hospital confront the patient with a set of role expectations that derive from the notion of the omniscience of the medical community and from the classical model of medical care which "assumes unquestionable obedience to medical authority in order that emergencies of disease may be overcome" (Wessen, 1965:148–178). A number of writers have likened the patient situation to that of childhood where the individual is in a dependent status im-

Reprinted from the Journal of Health and Social Behavior, 1968, 9(4):328–336.

posed by the physical helplessness stemming from his illness (Barker, 1953; Dichter, 1954). Hospital routines tend to enforce passivity and dependency, and the "good" patient is the submissive patient (Blum, 1960:38; Coser, 1960:154–172). The role of the patient in a general hospital differs somewhat from the role of patient or "client" in a rehabilitation setting (Blum, 1960:25; Nagi, 1965: 100–113). Recognizing the variation in role relationships contingent upon elements of the medical setting, Szasz and Hollender (1965) outline three basic models appropriate to varying treatment situations: (1) Activity-passivity, (2) Guidance-cooperation, and (3) Mutual participation. The first is descriptive of the severe emergency situation where the patient is virtually helpless and plays no active, conscious role in his treatment. The second illustrates circumstances of a less desperate nature. The patient is aware of what is going on and able to follow advice and exercise some judgment. The third is the typical approach in the management of chronic illness in which the treatment program is carried out by the patient with only occasional consultation with a physician. None of these models, however, strikes directly at the unique situation of the typical client in a rehabilitation center. He is required to play a much more active role than suggested in any of the three. Yet considerable submission is demanded of him not in terms of restricted activity, but in terms of highly regulated activity, often tedious, fatiguing, physically painful or frustrating. As pointed out by Wessen (1965) rehabilitation procedures frequently involve a painful process of relearning the elementary activities of daily living. The self-respecting adult required to relearn how to tie his shoe, button his shirt, walk with proper balance and gait under the direction of another adult furnishes but a few examples.

The unique aspect of the rehabilitant's role is subjugation to a medical expert who is at times an exasperating taskmaster, who may demand more effort and energy and, above all, patience, than the patient can or believes he can muster. Moreover, the difficulties in accepting such a relationship are increased by the frequently ambiguous nature of the goals. The degree of success of such effort can seldom be assured at the outset, requiring an unusual faith in the medical experts and their vexing procedures.

That patients have difficulty assuming the role of client in a rehabilitation setting is not surprising. Yet many do and are successfully rehabilitated. The question, then, is this: What is it that accounts for some successfully completing treatment while others leave the treatment center prematurely or are discharged as uncooperative? In an attempt to explain at least some of the variation in patient behavior, it is our general hypothesis that certain aspects of the patient's social position and normal role relationships before his illness or disability will aid or impede him in accepting and adequately playing the role expected of him. More specifically, patients whose prior role relationships have required that they take a submissive role, or whose social position places them in a status of dependency or subordination, will be more adept in assuming the client role and continuing treatment to a successful conclusion.

THE STUDY POPULATION

The population of this study is composed of the 406 persons evaluated and accepted for in-patient services during 1957–1961 in a large rehabilitation center attached to a university hospital. Patients admitted for evaluation only, or found in the initial evaluation to be unable to profit from treatment, are excluded from study. The population is predominantly male (87%) white (90%) and middle aged (41% aged 40–59). Of this population screened and accepted for treatment, 43.8 per cent completed services recommended by the staff, while 56.2 per cent either left before services were completed or were discharged by the staff because of failure to make satisfactory use of services. The analysis consists primarily in comparing those who cooperated and completed services with those who did not in respect to their role characteristics and the social positions they occupy. Data were taken from the case histories and medical records of the rehabilitation center accumulated by rehabilitation personnel.

FINDINGS

As has been said, assumption of the client role in a rehabilitation setting entails a relationship with medical personnel involving submission of an arduous regimen with limited assurance of successful outcome. It may be expected that persons whose normal role relationships contain elements of submission, or whose present social position or situation involves dependency or subordination, will be more successful in assuming the client role and completing services recommended by the hospital staff. Table 1 summarizes the relationship between completion of services and variables chosen as indicative of past experience in accepting a submissive role or of social situations which constrain clients to assume such a role: age, sex, race, employment status at time of admission, source of referral, source of payment of services, and degree of handicap. Each will be discussed individually.

Age

The role of patient has been likened to that of childhood by many, while others have pointed up the similarities between childhood and old age. What is held in common, of course, among these three social positions is the lack of loss of independence, the necessity of accepting a subordinate position and submitting to others. It is not surprising, then, to find successful completion of services which requires acceptance of such a position proportionately greater among the very young (78.6%) and the very old (70.6%). The age group with the lowest proportion completing services is the group experiencing that period of life typified by the greatest amount of independence, those aged 40–59, where the proportion completing services is only 48.8 per cent.

Table 1. Proportion of clients who satisfactorily completed services by role relations or social position

Role relations and social positions	Per cent of clients who satisfactorily completed services		
	f	%	Total N
Age			
10–19 years	22	78.6	28
20–39 years	112	58.0	193
40–59 years	82	48.8	168
60 and over	12	70.6	17
			406
(χ^2 = 11.63, 3 d.f., p<.01)			
Sex			
Male	190	53.8	353
Female	38	71.7	53
			406
(χ^2 = 5.28, 1 d.f., p<.05)			
Race			
White	198	54.2	365
Non-white	30	73.2	41
			406
(χ^2 = 4.62, 1 d.f., p<.05)			
Employment before disability			
Not employed	39	78.0	50
Employed	189	53.1	356
			406
(χ^2 = 10.99, 1 d.f., p<.001)			
Source of referral			
Non-agency (self, family, family physician)	115	49.1	234
Agency (B.V.R., Workmen's Compensation, other agencies)	113	65.7	172
			406
(χ^2 = 10.37, 1 d.f., p<.01)			
Source of payment of services			
Private, self insurers	22	55.0	40
Bureau of Vocational Rehabilitation	17	73.9	23
Bureau of Workmen's Compensation	119	47.2	252
Other voluntary and public service organizations	70	76.9	91
			406
(χ^2 = 27.17, 3 d.f., p<.001)			
Severity of handicap			
Slight	79	46.7	169
Moderate	70	53.8	130
Severe	78	74.3	105
			404*
(χ^2 = 20.40, 2 d.f., p<.001)			

*Two cases lacking data concerning severity of handicap excluded from analysis.

Sex

Despite the trend toward equality of the sexes, women by and large are socialized to accept positions of submission and subordination. In keeping with the general hypothesis that persons with experience in accepting such a relationship are more likely to complete services, females (71.7% completion) do better in finishing treatment than males (53.8%).

Race

Another indicator of propensity to accept a submissive role and hence likely to be related to success in rehabilitation is race. It would be expected that non-whites whose social position often necessitates the assumption of a subordinate role would be more likely to cooperate in rehabilitation services. Table 1 indicates that this is the case. Seventy-three per cent of non-whites completed services compared to 54 per cent of whites.

Employment Status

The relationship between employment status at time of admission and ease of accepting the submissive role of client is not readily apparent. It may be argued, however, that a person who is employed is able to exert more independence in his behavior, while the unemployed person is more constrained to cooperate in order to get back to work. More is expected of him, since his deviation from normal roles is the greater. The percentages in Table 1 support this line of argument. Those possessing the security of employment have the lower rate of treatment completion (53.1%), while those constrained by the onus of unemployment have a much higher rate of completion (78.0%).

Inasmuch as it has already been determined that age and sex are similarly related to completion of service and may be expected to be related to employment status as well, Tables 2 and 3 are presented for clarification. It will be noted from Table 2 that the relationship between completion of service and employment status remains regardless of age status, with those employed at time of admission having a substantially lower rate of treatment completion than those unemployed. Those with the lowest rate of completion are the employed in independent

Table 2. Proportion of clients who satisfactorily completed services by employment status and age

| | Proportion of clients completed service Age categories | | | | | |
| | Typical non-labor force 10–19, and 60 years or more | | | Typical labor force 20–59 years of age | | |
Employment status	f	%	Total N	f	%	Total N
Not employed	18	81.8	22	21	75.0	28
Employed	16	69.6	23	173	51.9	333

Table 3. Proportion of clients who satisfactorily completed services by employment status and age

| | Proportion of clients completed services | | | | | |
| | Male | | | Female | | |
Employment status	f	%	Total N	f	%	Total N
Not employed	22	75.9	29	17	81.0	21
Employed	168	51.8	324	21	65.6	32

age statuses (51.9%) while the highest rate of completion is found among the unemployed in dependent age statuses (81.8%). This latter group reflects the influence of the two dependency statuses—age and unemployment—taken together.

On the other hand, the relationship between completing services and age diminishes when employment status is taken into account, reflecting the greater influence of employment status with respect to cooperation in rehabilitation services. This is not surprising, since it is not age *per se* which distinguishes it as a dependent status, but factors concomitant with age, one of the most important being the ability to work or the possession of a job. Understandably, the young and old who have a job appear to behave more like those of middle age, and those of middle age who are unemployed are more likely to resemble those in typically dependent age statuses, more specifically the older age group.

Moreover, the influence of employment status on the likelihood of completing treatment is probably greater than what can be completely or directly explained in terms of the dependency-independency thesis. The

mere fact of having a job waiting while a rehabilitant is in treatment furnishes a strong incentive to question the need for continued treatment and hospitalization. Clearly the group that was employed prior to admission is more likely to have something to go to when they leave the hospital.

Table 3 reveals that the relationship between employment status and likelihood of completion of treatment remains regardless of sex, but appears somewhat stronger among males than among females. The concomitant influence of the two dependency statuses of femaleness and unemployment is reflected in the fact that unemployed females have the highest rate of completion of services, 81.0 per cent, while employed males have the lowest, 51.8 per cent.

The relationship between sex and completion of service is greatly diminished, however, when employment status is held constant, reflecting once again the stronger influence of employment status. The pattern of percentages suggests that among those not employed sex makes little difference in regard to the likelihood of completing services (75.9% of males vs. 81.0% of females completing treatment), while among the employed, females are more likely to complete services (65.5%) than males (51.8%).

In brief summary, employment status makes a great deal of difference in the likelihood of completing services, and age and sex make some difference, particularly among the employed, but are overshadowed when unemployment is a factor contributing to dependency.

Source of Referral and Payment of Services

Presumably persons who have been referred to the rehabilitation center by some agency, or whose treatment is being paid by an agency, feel more constrained to cooperate and complete rehabilitation services. The pattern of percentages in Table 1 suggests that this is the case with the exception of those whose treatment is being paid by the Bureau of Workmen's Compensation. Their rate of success is only 47.2 per cent. Since type of sponsorship is related to prior employment status, Table 4 is presented to weigh the relative influences of these two variables upon the likelihood of completing services. However, due to small frequencies in some of the distributions, only part of the question can be answered.

Table 4 reveals that clients sponsored by agencies other than the Bureau of Workmen's Compensation do well regardless of prior employment status, 79.5 per cent completing treatment among the unemployed and 74.9 per cent among the employed prior to admission. This is in contrast with 44.7 per cent among the prior employed not sponsored by anyone. These percentages suggest that the constraints of agency sponsorship do influence the likelihood of completing service and in addition overshadow the effects of employment status. However, some qualification is in order. The extent to which high rates of com-

Table 4. Proportion of clients who satisfactorily completed services by employment status at time of admission and sponsorship

Employment status at admission and sponsorship	Proportion completed services		
	f	%	Total N
Employed			
Sponsored by Bureau of Workmen's Compensation	116	47.0	247
Private, self-insurers	17	44.7	38
Sponsored by other agencies	56	74.7	75
Not employed			
Sponsored by Bureau of Workmen's Compensation	3	*	5
Private, self-insurers	5	*	6
Sponsored by other agencies	31	79.5	39

*Frequencies too small to compute percentages.

pletion of treatment is the result of the constraining nature of these agencies is debatable. Selective factors also operate whereby those chosen for sponsorship are likely to be those who are found to be more cooperative and submissive by agency personnel.

With respect to the relatively poor performance in treatment of workmen's compensation cases, several things can be said. First of all, no selective factors operate. Clients are entitled to sponsorship by virtue of their job-connected disability rather than by virtue of any other characteristics they may possess. (They were, of course, evaluated prior to admission and the poorest risks were screened out.) Secondly, compensation cases are in an ambiguous situation of attempting to demonstrate their disability to gain reimbursement for financial loss while at the same time being expected to cooperate in efforts to improve their condition. Despite this they appear to perform (47.0% completing service) no differently than those who are not sponsored by anyone (44.7% completion of service). Nothing can be said of the relative influences of sponsorship and employment status among compensation cases and the unsponsored, however, because of the small frequencies in these categories among those not employed.

Severity of Handicap

In keeping with the general hypothesis that dependency facilitates assumption of the sick role, Table 1 reveals that the greater the severity of physical limitation at time of admission, and hence dependency, the greater the likelihood of completing services. Among the slightly handicapped only 46.7 per cent completed services compared to 74.3 per cent of the severely handicapped. This suggests, however, that perhaps the relationship between employment and completion of services is simply a reflection of the relationship between severity and completion of services, since it might be expected that the greater the severity, the greater the likelihood of being unemployed at time of admission. Table 5 clarifies this issue. The more severely handicapped, whether employed or unemployed, have higher rates of success. Moreover, the unemployed have higher rates of success than the employed at each level of severity, with the exception of those slightly handicapped, where there are only five cases

Table 5. Proportion of clients who satisfactorily completed services by employment status at time of admission and severity of handicap

Employment status at time of admission and severity of handicap	Proportion completed services		
	f	%	Total N
Unemployed			
Slight	2	*	5
Moderate	29	85.3	34
Severe	29	85.3	34
Employed			
Slight	77	46.9	164
Moderate	62	52.1	119
Severe	49	69.0	71

*Frequency too small to compute percentage.

among the unemployed, making any comparison at this level impossible.

Attitudes Toward the Medical Profession

The medical records of the population under study included a staff evaluation of the client's attitude (favorable versus unfavorable) toward the medical profession. This makes it possible to examine relationships between: (1) a subjective state, albeit as outwardly manifested and assessed by others, (2) prior role relations and status positions, and (3) success in completing recommended services. It might be assumed that clients with a favorable attitude toward the medical profession would place more faith in the treatment recommendations of medical staff and be more likely to cooperate and complete such treatment. It is not surprising, then, that 67.6 per cent of those with a favorable attitude completed services compared to only 18.8 per cent of those with an unfavorable attitude. Moreover, at least part of this difference may be an artifact of the manner in which attitude was measured. Medical personnel are apt to see clients who are doing well and continuing treatment as having favorable attitudes toward the medical profession.

Table 6 examines the relationship between attitude toward the medical profession and roles and social positions of clients. It will be noted that none of the relationships tested is statistically significant, and percentage differences between categories are not very great. The one exception is the variation in attitude among those with

Table 6. Proportion of clients with favorable attitudes toward the medical professional by selected social position

Social positions	Per cent with favorable attitude		
	f	%	Total N
Dependent ages	35	87.5	40
Independent ages	258	80.1	322
($\chi^2 = 1.23$, 1 d.f., p<.30 and >.25)			
Males	254	80.4	316
Females	39	84.8	46
($\chi^2 = .522$, 1 d.f., p<.50 and >.30)			
White	257	79.8	322
Non-white	36	90.0	40
($\chi^2 = 2.37$, 1 d.f., p<.20 and >.10)			
Unemployed	39	90.7	43
Employed	254	79.6	319
($\chi^2 = 3.01$, 1 d.f., p<.10 and >.05)			
Non-agency referral	161	78.5	205
Agency referral	132	84.1	157
($\chi^2 = 1.75$, 1 d.f., p<.20 and >.01)			
No agency sponsorship	25	73.5	34
BVR sponsorship	23	100.0	23
Workmen's Compensation sponsorship	175	76.5	229
Other agency sponsorship	70	87.5	80
($\chi^2 = 9.83$, 3 d.f., p<.05)			
Slight handicap	119	76.8	115
Moderate handicap	95	81.2	117
Severe handicap	79	87.8	90
($\chi^2 = 4.40$, 2 d.f., p<.20 and >.10)			

different agency sponsorship. In those agencies where attitude plays an important part in screening clients, clients are more likely to reflect favorable attitudes, 100.0 per cent expressing favorable attitude among clients of the Bureau of Vocational Rehabilitation and 87.5 per cent among other agency clients. Among compensation cases where no screening is involved by the agency itself, 76.5 per cent express a favorable attitude. It must be remembered, however, that all clients are evaluated with respect to their likelihood of profiting from treatment, regardless of sponsorship, before being accepted as in-patients of the rehabilitation center. This, no doubt, accounts for the lack of any great variation with respect to attitude among clients in general.

Table 7 attempts to assess the relative influences of expressed attitude and social positions on the likelihood of completing treatment. Because of the small frequencies, nothing can be said regarding the relationship between social positions and likelihood of completing treatment among those with an unfavorable attitude. There are two exceptions, however. First, agency referral and agency sponsorship

Table 7. Proportion of clients who satisfactorily completed services by attitude toward the medical profession and social position

| | Per cent of clients who satisfactorily completed services | | | | | |
| | Favorable attitude | | | Unfavorable attitude | | |
Social position	f	%	Total N	f	%	Total N
Dependent ages	29	82.8	35	2	*	5
Independent ages	169	65.5	258	11	17.2	64
Males	168	66.1	254	11	17.7	62
Females	30	76.9	39	2	*	7
White	168	65.4	257	13	20.0	65
Non-white	30	83.3	36	*	*	4
Unemployed	32	82.1	39	1	*	4
Employed	166	65.3	254	12	18.2	65
Non-agency referral	97	60.2	161	7	15.9	44
Agency referral	101	76.5	132	6	24.0	25
No agency sponsorship	17	68.0	25	1	*	9
BVR sponsorship	17	83.9	23	0	*	0
Workmen's Compensation sponsorship	106	60.6	175	7	13.0	54
Other agency sponsorship	58	82.8	70	5	50.0	10
Slight handicap	72	60.5	119	6	16.7	36
Moderate handicap	61	64.2	95	5	22.7	22
Severe handicap	65	82.3	79	2	18.1	11

*Frequencies too small to compute percentages.

appear to have a constraining effect even among those with an unfavorable attitude. Secondly, unfavorable attitude tends to wipe out the relationship between severity and completion of service.

More can be said with regard to those with a favorable attitude toward the medical profession. Among each of the indicators of dependency-independency, there continues to be ample evidence of an association with treatment performance when attitude is held constant, i.e., all favorably disposed to the medical profession. It would appear that the constraining aspects of roles and social positions, and not attitude, are the important factors in explaining variation in patient behavior in this study population.

SUMMARY AND CONCLUSIONS

This study was concerned with the success of patients in completing treatment at a rehabilitation center. The role of client in a rehabilitation setting was described as entailing submission to an arduous regimen with limited assurance of outcome. It was hypothesized that persons whose normal role relationships and social position contained elements of dependency or subordination would be more inclined to successfully perform such a role and complete treatment. Persons in dependent age statuses: females, Negroes, the unemployed, those referred by or sponsored by agencies (with the exception of Workmen's Compensation sponsorship), and those more severely handicapped, all of which contain ele-

ments of dependency, were found more likely to complete recommended services, thus supporting the general hypothesis. As would be expected, those with a favorable attitude had a much greater rate of success in completing services. However, the relationships regarding roles and social positions remained regardless of the subjective attitude toward the medical profession.

The study was carried out on 406 patients who passed through a rehabilitation center during a five-year period. It must be emphasized that the relationships reported here are between certain role characteristics of clients and completion of recommended treatment, not successful rehabilitation *per se*. The fact that so large a segment of clients do not complete services (56.2%) suggests that patients' conceptions of rehabilitation often differ from those of the medical experts. This type of patient may tend to define rehabilitation in terms of the ability to return to normal social roles, albeit at a reduced or impaired level of functioning, while rehabilitation personnel in the type of setting studied tend to define rehabilitation on the basis of the return of physiological functioning utilizing medical standards rather than social criteria. This discrepancy in defining ultimate goals is likely to be greater with clients who because of their social position and normal role relationships are able to exert a higher degree of independence.

This study raises several questions which cannot be answered with the data at hand: What might be the actual relationship between cooperation in treatment in a medical setting and ultimate successful rehabilitation in terms of return to normal social roles? Do those who remain in treatment actually fare better in the long run? Would the same relationships reported here hold in other types of rehabilitation settings such as sheltered workshops and vocational training centers? The answers to these questions must await further research.

REFERENCES

Barker, R. G., et al. 1953. Adjustment to Physical Handicap and Illness. New York: Social Science Research Council.

Blum, R. H. 1960. The Management of the Doctor Patient Relationship. New York: McGraw-Hill.

Coser, Ruth L. 1960. "A home away from home," in D. Apple, (ed.), Sociological Studies of Health and Sickness. New York: McGraw-Hill.

Dichter, Earnest. 1954. "The hospital-patient relationship." Modern Hospital 83 (September–December) No. 3–6.

Field, M. 1958. Patients are People. New York: Columbia University Press.

King, S. H. 1962. Perceptions of Illness and Medical Practice. New York: Russell Sage Foundation.

Nagi, Saad Z. 1965. "Some conceptual issues in disability and rehabilitation," in Marvin B. Sussman, (ed.), Sociology and Rehabilitation, published by the American Sociological Association.

Parsons, T. 1951. "Illness and the role of the physician: a sociological perspective." American Journal of Orthopsychiatry 21 (July):452–60.

Szasz, T. S. and M. H. Hollender. 1965. "A contribution to the philosophy of medicine: the basic models of the doctor-patient relationship." A.M.A. Archives of Internal Medicine 97 (May). 585.

Wessen, A. F. 1965. "The apparatus of rehabilitation: An organizational analysis," in Marvin B. Sussman, (ed.) Sociology and Rehabilitation, published by the American Sociological Association.

22 Sick-Role Retention as a Factor in Nonrehabilitation

Pearl Davidoff Starkey

This study attempted to devise a measure which would differentiate between men who returned to work following an initial heart attack and those who did not. The 3 variables studied were based on Parson's sick-role theory, current models of aging, and career-pattern classification. The questionnaire was administered to 52 men age 39–55 who had suffered an initial heart attack 5–18 mo. earlier and were medically able to return to work. Two of the 3 variables showed significant differences between the men who retained the sick role and those who did not. Responses on the able-disabled dimension differentiated at .005 level of significance; career-pattern classification differentiated at .025 level of significance.

Some men return to the work role of their prior life following an initial myocardial infarction; others with the same degree of cardiac impairment retain the sick role which their heart attack legitimized. If these men could be differentiated early, better use of rehabilitation resources and professional time might be effected. Minimal service could be provided those men who resembled rehabilitants; maximum effort could be expended early on men whose attitudes resembled nonrehabilitants. This would reverse the current trend (Myers, 1966), which expends rehabilitation service most often on those most likely to be rehabilitants.

This study was an attempt to devise an objective measure for differentiation of those heart-attack patients likely to become nonrehabilitants for extracardiac reasons. The three variables studied used Parsons' (1964) sick role characteristics, current models of aging, and career-pattern classification.

SICK ROLE

In studying the social structure as its mechanisms operate in developing individual personality and the processes which determine a structure of roles which the individual fills, Parsons (1964) became concerned with the personality of the individual in relation to health and illness. Viewing society as interrelating systems, he stressed the major motivational value

Reprinted with permission from the Journal of Counseling Psychology, 1967, 15(1): 75–79. Copyright 1967 by the American Psychological Association.

This article was based on doctoral research submitted to Teachers College, Columbia University. The author is especially indebted to Roger A. Myers, committee chairman, Henry Kavkewitz, and Richard Lindeman. Appreciation is extended to the Nassau Heart Association, Inc., Garden City, N. Y., for considerable assistance in obtaining subjects.

of our society as an emphasis on capacity. The primary obligation of the individual in such a value system is that of achievement.

Parsons (1964) stated: "Somatic health is, sociologically defined, the state of optimum capacity for the effective performance of valued tasks [p. 262]," valued, that is, for the good of the society.

Illness, in this light, is a socially institutionalized role type, characterized by a generalized disturbance in the capacity of the individual for normally expected task or role performance. This role of the sick person in our society bears four distinguishing characteristics:

1. The incapacity is interpreted as being beyond his powers to overcome it by decision making alone; hence, he is not responsible for it. Some therapeutic process is necessary to recovery.

2. There is a legitimate basis for *exemption* of the sick person from his normal role and task obligations.

3. The recognition is present that it is inherently undesirable, and, therefore, the obligation is to "get well."

4. There is an obligation to seek competent help and cooperate with agencies in their attempts to get him well. Implied is the obligation to prevent being ill.

Once the status of being sick is legitimized, dependency is permitted. Yet, included as well are role demands (3 and 4 above) to recognize the role as inherently undesirable and to be obliged to get well. Hence, the emphasis is on active mastery over dependency. Parsons viewed the sick role as deviant behavior.

AGING

Illness in our society is a particularly important form of deviant behavior for older people, Parsons maintained; it legitimizes their status to be useless through incapacitation.

The implications of sick role for older people might be viewed in the light of two current theoretical models of aging. One model of aging revolves around a core of activity (Havighurst & Albrecht, 1953), which emphasizes the maintenance of activities and attitudes of middle age. The other model involves disengagement (Cumming, 1961), a term used to describe the aging individual as gradually changing from a state of full engagement with the world around him (middle age) to a state of disengagement from it (old age).

The Nonrehabilitant

With the nonrehabilitant, the disengagement model may apply. In experiencing an initial heart attack a man is faced with concrete awareness of the aging process. His sick role is legitimized and dependency permitted. If the sick role is maintained as deviant behavior, the close connection between illness, disability, and aging tends to merge into one. This then permits passive withdrawal from normal activities and responsibilities, which Parsons (1964) termed deviance legitimized. Abandonment of Characteristics 3 and 4 of the sick role results in nonconformist behavior and withdrawal from the institutionalized mechanisms and values of his society. Behavior resembles disengagement.

The Rehabilitant

If a man experiencing an initial heart attack views his sick role in institutionally legitimized ways, all four characteristics of the sick role will be binding upon him. For him, illness, disability, and aging represent separate entities which do not merge into one. He will respond to the demands of his sick role in terms of illness, which legitimizes his dependency but places upon him the obligation of active mastery. Behavior continues the activities of middle age.

CAREER PATTERN

An individual's career pattern represents an ongoing development process, as Super's (1957) work emphasized. It might be hypothesized that an individual's career pattern prior to his heart attack would reflect some degree of his commitment to the work role. The influence of such commitment may be a factor in his relinquishing of the sick role.

METHOD

Development of the Measure

To identify possible differences between men who had returned to work and men who had not, a questionnaire for measuring each of the three variables was developed (Starkey, 1966).

Able or Disabled   The first section of the questionnaire consisted of 56 statements describing various aspects of a man's behavior once he had suffered a heart attack and recovered from it. These were placed in a Likert-type form, in which one of four responses, ranging from "agree completely" to "disagree strongly," was to be chosen. The statements reflected able (actively overcoming) or disabled (dependent) behavior. Scoring was in two directions, from 4–1 points on disabled statements and from 1–4 points on able statements. Therefore, the sumscore in this section was a composite of agreement with disabled and disagreement with able statements, as representative of disabled responses, and the reverse composite as representative of able responses. Numerically high sumscores were disabled; numerically low scores were able.

Young or Old   The second section of the questionnaire used adjectives which Bloom (1960) found were chosen significantly more by men 60–69 years old than by men 20–29 years old. These were formed into 20 "I am" statements. The Ss were asked to choose a category for each word which most accurately described them. Five choices were available ranging from "most of the time" to "practically never." This section was scored in two directions, from 5–1 points on adjectives chosen by old men and 1–5 points on adjectives chosen by young men. Again, high scores were viewed as less able than low scores. Two numerical scores were obtained for each S—an old score and a young score.

Stable or Unstable Career Pattern   Sufficient objective biographical data were obtained to enable two trained judges to classify career patterns. Judgments were based on the transfer-of-equity dimension (Gotkin, 1963), by which job or training moves were distinguished as random movement or purposeful behavior. Each judge independently classified all cases as stable or unstable. Agreement was 91%.

Reliability Reliability was obtained by test-related procedure using 100 noncardiac *S*s. Reliability was .89 for Section 1 and .83 for Section 2. The third section consisted of factual vocational information, and was not included in the reliability study.

Subjects

The questionnaire was administered to 52 men age 39–55. Each was chosen by his private cardiologist as physically capable of returning to work; American Heart Association classification was IA or IB, IIA or IIB, indicating minimal or no restriction. All had been employed prior to suffering an initial myocardial infarction 5–18 months earlier. Each was a well-documented case, free of other disability such as hypertension. All were white, married, and able to read at the ninth-grade level.

Being restricted geographically to the Nassau County, New York, area and being completely confined to patients of cardiologists, only 11 nonrehabilitant *S*s were found who fit all the criteria. After careful scrutiny of the economic and demographic characteristics of both the 41 rehabilitants and the 11 nonrehabilitants, it was concluded that both groups appeared to have been drawn from the same general population.

RESULTS

Nonrehabilitants could be differentiated from rehabilitants on at least two of the three dimensions studied. Since sample size was limited, findings should be viewed with caution.

Scores on attitudes reflecting actively-overcoming (able) behavior were significantly different between men who retained the sick role and those who returned to the work role. This difference was in the expected direction. The mean score for rehabilitants was 111; mean score for nonrehabilitants was 125 (Table 1). A *t* test indicated that this difference was statistically significant at the .005 level. Based on the scoring, in which low scores were more able than high scores, the relationship appeared clear.

In addition, none of the scores of nonrehabilitants fell below the median score of 113, while almost 60% of the rehabilitants' scores did. This indicated that men who retained the sick role agreed more often with disabled statements and disagreed more often with able statements. The majority of men who relinquished the sick role agreed more often with able statements and disagreed with disabled statements.

There were no significant differences between the two groups in choice of self-descriptive adjectives which old men had chosen. However, rehabilitants chose adjectives similar to those chosen by young men to a greater degree than nonrehabilitants. Mean scores on the young dimension showed a significant difference between the two groups (Table 1). A *t*

Table 1. Able-disabled and young-old dimensions for rehabilitants and nonrehabilitants

| Dimension | Rehabilitant[a] | | Nonrehabilitant[b] | | |
	M	SD	M	SD	t
Able-disabled	111	14.8	125	12.2	2.76**
Young-old					
Young	16.7	2.8	18.8	1.7	2.19*
Old	32.7	4.5	32.2	3.2	

Note.—Low scores are able; high scores are disabled.
[a] n = 41.
[b] n = 11.
*p < .025
**p < .005.

test indicated that this difference was significant at the .025 level.

It is not clear what the score differences on the young dimension indicate. It is possible that the trauma of experiencing a heart attack confronted all men in the study with concrete awareness of the aging process. Having recovered from such a confrontation, the tendency to describe oneself similarly to old men persisted, even where the sick role was relinquished. Those men able to describe themselves in young terms appeared to be those also able to relinquish the sick role. This might be viewed as behavior reflecting the activity model of aging.

Examination of career patterns made it possible to differentiate between the two groups. Based on the phi coefficient, this difference was significant at the .025 level (see Table 2). Although nonrehabilitants displayed both stable and unstable career patterns, rehabilitants were largely classified as stable. This would support the expectation of greater commitment to the work role by rehabilitants. Since

Table 2. Career patterns for rehabilitants and nonrehabilitants

Pattern	Rehabilitant	Non-rehabilitant
Stable	35*	6
Unstable	6	5

*p < .025, phi coefficient.

career-pattern classification represented ongoing behavior and examined work history longitudinally, this finding appeared to indicate individual differences between men in each group.

Additional Analysis

Although response-set bias had been avoided by scoring responses in both agree and disagree directions, additional analysis was made of yeasaying or naysaying tendencies in each subject's questionnaire. Personality differences between subjects who agreed or disagreed with items had been found in a study by Couch and Keniston (1960). These resembled Gelfand's (1963) descriptions of rehabilitants and nonrehabilitants. Analysis revealed that rehabilitants in the present study disagreed to a greater degree than nonrehabilitants. Using the median test, this difference was significant at the .002 level. It might be hypothesized that the tendency to disagree represented an active rather than a passive stance.

Analysis revealed that chronological age was not a differentiating factor between the two groups. Self-employment, number of dependents, a working spouse, and family incidence of heart disease were other factors which did not differentiate between the groups.

DISCUSSION

Based on the variables studied, a relationship is suggested between sick-role retention and nonrehabilitation following an initial heart attack. That other factors may be involved, though not studied at this time, is readily acknowledged. Those men who retained the sick role displayed nonadherence to its actively-overcoming aspects when asked to evaluate disabled behavior. Regardless of age, they tended to describe themselves in terms unlike young men and behaved in terms of disengagement, that is, withdrawal from the primary activity of middle years, the work role. Their career patterns tended to be unstable or multiple trial. Since all men in the study were physically able to return to the work role, these differences pointed to a conceptual framework within which extracardiac factors might be further investigated.

Limitations

The study was an exploratory one, and its findings must be viewed as tentative, particularly in light of the positive results and limited numbers. All scores on these dimensions were obtained once rehabilitation or nonrehabilitation had become an established mode of behavior. Since the present study afforded no way of measuring the influence of return to work, it is possible to hypothesize that congruence with behavior produced lowering of scores upon relinquishing the sick role. It would be difficult to ascertain whether rehabilitation efforts which permitted return to work, or the actual return itself, could be considered responsible for able and young attitudes. Career pattern, representing predisability behavior, would be difficult to explain on the basis of such a hypothesis. Replication of this study using the questionnaire immediately upon discharge from the hospital and again 1 year later would provide an opportunity to study any incidence of score changes.

The possibility of selection bias must be considered, since the choice of appropriate subjects was entirely controlled by the individual cardiologist. Replication with appropriate subjects assigned from a variety of sources might overcome this limitation.

Implications

The sick-role concept as a factor in nonrehabilitation might alert physicians, rehabilitation counselors, or psychologists to provide early attention to those men most in need of it. Men who most resembled rehabilitants would be expected to relinquish the sick role with a minimum of assistance or none at all. Since procrastination and delay in relinquishing the sick role reduce the likelihood of rehabilitation, it is conceivable that this brief questionnaire, when validated through replication, could provide physicians and rehabilitation workers with early indications of tendencies toward sick-role retention. Prompt and comprehensive attention of such patients could reduce entrenchment of non-rehabilitation.

Of particular importance would be an active educational program to assist the general medical practitioner, particularly with the aging population, in giving early attention to indications of sick-role retention and to prevent his own inadvertent reinforcement of such tendencies. Closer cooperation between medical specialists and generalists and the rehabilitation resources would seem an important and desirable emphasis. Increased research on sick-role retention could be stimulated through these channels.

REFERENCES

Bloom, K. Some relationships between age and self perception. Unpublished doctoral dissertation, Teachers College, Columbia University, 1960.

Couch, A., & Keniston, K. Yeasayers and naysayers: Agreeing response set as a personality variable. Journal Abnormal and Social Psychology, 1960, 60, 151–174.

Cumming, E. Growing old: The process of disengagement. New York: Basic Books, 1961.

Gelfand, D. Factors relating to unsuccessful vocational adjustment of cardiac patients. Philadelphia: Office of Vocational Rehabilitation and Heart Association of Southeastern Pennsylvania, 1963.

Gotkin, E. H. The measurement of career behavior in young men: A preliminary report. United States Office of Education Cooperative Research Project No. 1303, Horace Mann-Lincoln Institute, Teachers College, 1963.

Havighurst, R. J., & Albrecht, R. Older people. New York: Longmans, Green, 1953.

Myers, R. A. The work-motivated client—Paragon, patsy, or pathological. Paper presented at the meeting of the American Personnel and Guidance Association, Washington, D.C., April 1966.

Parsons, T. Social structure and personality. New York: Free Press of Glencoe, 1964.

Starkey, P. Sick role retention as a factor in nonrehabilitation. Unpublished doctoral dissertation, Teachers College, Columbia University, 1966.

Super, D. E. The psychology of careers. New York: Harper, 1957.

Section 6

SOCIAL THEORY

23 Dependent Disabled and Dependent Poor:
Similarity of Conceptual Issues and Research Needs

Marvin B. Sussman

This paper is concerned with rehabilitation of the disabled and the poor as dependent subgroups of our society. Definitions are given for *impairment, disability*, and *handicap*, all of which are distinct conditions of social as well as physical inadequacy. Deviancy, minority status, and marginality are sociological issues which apply to the disabled, as they compete and relate to the nondisabled in our society. The dependent poor are considered as belonging to subcultures, having creative potential to better their condition, but with socioeconomic problems—inadequate socialization and social withdrawal—hampering employment and mobility. The aged are a third subgroup, often characterized by disability and poverty. Multifaceted research is needed about not only the disabled and poor but also the social setting which defines and conditions these dependent subgroups.

As the concept of rehabilitation is broadened, almost every major institutional system in society becomes involved in the varied activities of the rehabilitation system. Thus, the sociologist is provided with an opportunity to examine these activities and relationships and their significance for rehabilitation as an institutional system and a process. The focus of this paper is on the nature of dependency among physically, economically, and culturally deprived populations. Specific attention is directed to current views of the disabled and the poor and to discussion of research needs.

Disability and poverty as phenomena are socially defined and structured. As there are no absolute criteria, problems of dependency are quite susceptible to distortions constructed within the social milieu, in part because of competing goals and needs of institutional systems and their members. Adequate appraisal of dependency thus requires investigation of sociostructural elements; dependency implies a hierarchy, with superordination and subordination of elements. Thus, the dynamics of dependency are related to control; that

Reprinted from The Social Service Review, 1969, 43(4):383–395. Copyright 1969 by the University of Chicago Press. All rights reserved. Printed in USA.

This paper was prepared under contract with the National Institute of Child Health and Human Department. Special appreciation is expressed to Donna R. Siegel, one-time research assistant in the Department of Sociology of Case Western Reserve University, for her aid in its preparation. During 1969–70 the author was visiting professor, Carolina Population Center and Department of Mental Health, University of North Carolina.

is, frequently the superordinate element benefits by keeping another element dependent. Such a relationship represents one way of maintaining order and the status quo; it performs useful stabilizing functions. Some of the problems apparent in any consideration of the nature of dependency come about because of the rationalizations that have developed over time in answer to the needs for stabilization and legitimation of existing organizational relationships. Altering the dependent relationship introduces the factor of competition and changes the "definition of the situation."

The foregoing aspects apply both to the disabled and to poverty groups. Study of the former requires attention to the interaction of the disabled with the nondisabled; to similarities of handicapped and minority groups; to methods of controlling and structuring the dependent-independent relationship, for example, by the "mourning requirement," and by overprotection of disabled children; and to problems of communication between the "normal" and "disabled" worlds. Study of the economically deprived necessitates examination of the varying definitions and perceptions of poverty; the incongruity between goals and structural opportunities; and the subcultures created out of impoverished environments. Emphasis is placed on the need to reappraise the dominant "definitions of the situation," to penetrate stereotypes and stigmatizations of dependent groups, and also to dissect the roles and motivations of the independent elements.

THE DEPENDENT DISABLED

The literature of the rehabilitation field reveals much inconsistency in the use of terms such as *illness, sickness, impairment, disability*, and *handicap*. These terms are treated as synonyms and used interchangeably in discussing rehabilitation issues and problems. Leaving aside illness and sickness which are associated with acute and short-term rather than chronic and long-term disease, it is useful to define impairment, disability, and handicap.

Impairment is defined as any deviation from the normal which results in defective function, structure, organization, or development of the whole or any part of an individual's faculties. Disability refers to any limitation experienced by the impaired individual in comparison with the activities of unimpaired individuals of similar age, sex, and culture. Handicap is used to describe the disadvantage imposed by an impairment or disability upon a specific individual in his cultural pattern of psychological, physical, vocational, and community activities.

One sociological perspective is that impairment becomes disability by defining it as such, and that the act of definition conveys a handicapped condition, one which is deviant and most often stigmatized. Eliot Friedson has noted that "what is common to all acts of defining someone as handicapped and requiring rehabilitation ... is not a set of physical attributes that always 'are' handicaps, but rather *the act of definition itself*, which can be an imputation rather than a statement of fact" (6:71–72).

Disability is thus created and is viewed as a form of deviance in the sense that the individual is disadvantaged in social terms because of "an imputation of an undesirable difference." The impaired person is so defined because he deviates from what is considered normal or appropriate by himself or others. Furthermore, the identification of deviants is a process involving socially structured biases and vague, permissive stereotypes rather than precise, formalized standards. Thus, "the true universe or rate of deviance, whether defined by behavioral or biological criteria, is difficult if not impossible to determine" (6:82).

Social Definitions

Disability, then, is not only a physical fact but also a social fact. Lay and official "normals" are probably much more involved than the handicapped person in carving out a role for the disabled social deviant. How this role is constructed, interpreted, and manifested hinges crucially on perceptions and attitudes toward disability of both the impaired and the nonimpaired. Public definitions and meanings given to the impairment and client-centered institutional systems' insistence on finding, treating, and controlling the impaired individual contribute to the person's self-definition of being handicapped and deviant. Similarly, it will be discussed later how the role of the poor and underprivileged is structured not only by their specific economic and cultural deficiencies, but also by the attitudes of others, especially institutional systems, concerning what it

means to be "lower class"—including the particular stigmatizations attached to poverty.

One of the common obstacles a disabled person encounters in the social world is that he is frequently defined, by himself and others, as a "physically disabled person" rather than a "person with a physical disability." Wright has observed the tendency, where characteristics conveying status implications are involved, for inferiority in one function or activity to spread to total inferiority of the person (17:7–8). Such distortion, although not ill-intended, is both semantic and actual, since in many cases a person's life may be reduced to the disability aspects of his physique. In other words, his behavior is altered, not primarily because of the impairment per se, but because he "experiences" disability because of the social responses to it. Using our definitions of impairment, disability, and handicapped, stated previously, impairment is a deviation which is due to a physical or psychological condition. Disability is a deviation defined by the nondisabled: it is a social condition imposed upon the individual for real or alleged impairments. A person may be handicapped because of his real or alleged impairment; the degree to which he is handicapped depends on his physical and psychological and mental capabilities and the social definition given to his real or so-called impairment.

Minority Group Membership

The disabled are in an inferior position in the status system of society. Various authors have noted that the situation of the disabled individual is somewhat parallel to that of a minority-group member. A single aspect of the individual transforms his self-image and the perception others have of him; the majority emphasize the one facet about him that makes him different from them; being different, he is therefore inferior. By definition, Wright states, inferior status position is something which virtually all disabled individuals experience: "If it does not come about as a result of thwarting due to the inability to achieve a desired goal, then it may result from the discriminations and negative attitudes of the nonhandicapped majority" (17:124).

Being labeled a minority-group member and deviant does not absolve the disabled person from participation in the society. He can neither absent himself, nor can he take part fully. Simultaneously, he is a man of two worlds—the dominant world of the majority and the subuniverse of his minority. His and others' expectations, directives, and personal conflicts are sources of what Wright terms "overlapping situations" (17:16). As a minority group, the disabled are considered different and are thus expected to behave as such. In a similar sense, the poor are often considered by others to be poor because they are inferior; their "lot" is seen as justification for laziness or lack of motivation. That the poor may share the aspirations of the middle class is viewed as inappropriate; attempts at mobility may summon cries to "keep them in their place."

Viewing disability as a regrettable condition and expecting that the unfortunate individual should grieve and mourn exemplifies one institutional method of imposing a devalued role on a person. Wright develops this point:

When a person has a need to safeguard his values, he will either (1) insist that the person he considers unfortunate is suffering (even when he seems not to be suffering) or (2) devaluate the unfortunate person because he ought to suffer and does not. This implies that the devaluer wants the unfortunate person to suffer. He wants him to suffer as a sign that the values denied the unfortunate person are still worthy and important and good [17:242–43].

Thus the incurrence of disability necessitates a period of mourning similar to that of bereavement, regardless of the depth of the psychological shock in the disabled individual. The requirement, which may be a source of extreme perplexity and discomfort for the handicapped person, illustrates the extent to which disability is a socially structured phenomenon.

The initial response of the newly disabled is to be "just like everyone else." This is a common expectation, the desire to get back to a former condition or state. For all illness conditions which are not chronic or long-term, this response is anticipated by both the patient and medical surrogates. Ambiguity and ambivalence surround the expectations of normality involving cultural or physical disability. Attempts at normality by the disabled may, to the dominant group, appear inappropriate or shock-

/ing, in large part because such efforts and motivations conflict with established stereotypes. For example, a handicapped person who declines to participate in some activity because of a realistic appraisal of his limitations may be assumed by others to be "feeling inferior" (17:17).

On the other hand, the disabled individual who attempts to overcome his handicap by superhuman efforts, for example, to take on normal roles, is likely to be rejected by the world of normals as being too aggressive, demanding, and obnoxious. Cowen notes that the fact that lines of demarcation between normality and disability are frequently not sharply drawn results in an enigma for the disabled person concerning what is "proper" behavior: "He is, thus, more often than others, placed in a situation of psychological marginality" (4:126). A marginal situation exists when two sets of behavioral determinants are required simultaneously. In the face of uncertainty the disabled person may, at one extreme, reject his disability and present himself as "normal," or, at the other, exaggerate his handicap and become a caricature of his inferior status. The lower-class person who "acts dumb" in the presence of someone from a higher-status group is also playing along with the dominant stereotype.

Coping with Marginality

The disabled person has two principal techniques for handling the ambiguity surrounding his marginal status. He can confront or "put down" his surrogates; or he can "put them on." Confrontation involves active defiance by an individual or a group organized for this purpose. The person can challenge the system, and, through behaviors that are hostile and obnoxious but essentially embarrassing to the establishment, he may hope to avoid repression while at the same time bringing about a better personal deal. Collective action involves less than model client behavior—bargaining, harassment, and public confrontation—in order to effect a change in policy and practice and even a takeover of control if necessary. Blind employees in sheltered workshops who organize a quasi-union to obtain higher wages and take their case to the public by way of the mass media provide an illustration of the defiance technique.

Individual or group use of a "putting down" technique among the disabled is an infrequent occurrence. A procedure more frequently resorted to is "putting on," a process whereby the disabled person acknowledges publicly the superior power, wisdom, and authority of the surrogate, such as in becoming a "model" patient or client, but privately rejects this state of affairs and often works subtly to subvert the surrogate's authority and control. "Putting on" is basically accommodation to the realities of power and control in order to handle threats to one's self-respect, image, maintenance, and physical and psychological safety. The trick is to "put on" someone without his knowing it.

Mechanisms include playing the stereotyped and expected role of the disabled: playing dumb, nonmotivated, disinterested, and "trying" as a means to indicate unhappiness and discontent. Perceiving situations selectively and hearing only what one wants to in order to sustain one's ego and image; elaborate and detailed acting-out in the learning of disabled roles; abusing privileges as a means of denying the system its due and publicly displaying its weaknesses; staking out a territory in a work system or rehabilitation setting; and adopting unique symbols, mannerisms, habits, clothes styles, and so on—expressions of in-group formation—are other mechanisms of the "putting-on" process.

The "putting-on" procedure is especially suitable to the situation in which a climate is at once positive and negative, in which goals and the approach toward the disabled are uncertain. For example, a recently disabled person, re-encountering the nonhandicapped world in a specific situation, may be unsure of his expected role, his function, his desires, and the path to satisfaction. He lacks a differentiated experiential background and a structured perception of the situation. Another newly disabled person may not define such a situation as "new"; consequently, his impairment would not be a precise "handicap," and his adjustment thus would be more instantaneous. The safest tack in either case is to use the accommodating procedure.

These aspects are, of course, directly related to the problem of dependency. Cowen states that it is not known why some individuals perceive situations as "new psychological situations" and others do not, and she suggests further research in the area of perception and personality. Recent research increasingly substantiates the fact that behavior cannot be directly predicted from disability; individual perception is the critical mediating factor (4:128, 133).

Overprotection of the Disabled Child

When the disabled individual is a child, parents and other siblings play crucial roles in rehabilitation. A common problem encountered in the parent-disabled child relationship is the tendency for the parent to "overprotect" the disabled and "underprotect" the nondisabled one.[1] Overprotection may be founded on feelings of genuine love and concern for the helpless child, the "need" of a parent for a dependent child, or mere impatience. There is insufficient space to elaborate the reasons for or consequences of neglect of the physically or psychologically "normal" child by families with disabled siblings. The important task is how to handle this overprotection.

Beatrice Wright suggests aids for achieving a dependence-independence balance, including observation of other children, parent discussion groups, and familiarization with special techniques and reading materials (17:303–17). One of the most helpful approaches is for the parent to try to create opportunities for specific kinds of experiences. While this approach is one of

---

[1] For further exploration of this problem see Crain (5).

the most promising ways to build real independence, it is a quite difficult method since it frequently involves more work than the alternative of overprotection. Parents must create situations in which the child can assume responsibility commensurate with his ability and also create situations for increasing responsibility. Often family acquaintances will criticize attempts to encourage independence in the handicapped child—they may think the parent is unresponsive to the child's special needs or "expects too much." Another problem is that, while the parents may want the child to mix with a variety of individuals in "normal" situations, the nonhandicapped persons are susceptible to overreaction; that is, they may be unable to relate to the child without emphasizing his disability. The major point is that developing independence in any child—whether or not he is disabled—while at the same time maintaining an expressive relationship, should be the primary goal of the parent, but such a task with a disabled child necessitates extreme patience and a persistent channeling of energies into activities, often without immediate reward and sometimes with ready criticism.

THE DEPENDENT POOR

Dependency and disability are consequences of economic deprivation as well as physical and psychological impairment. In order to examine types of dependency related to economic deprivation, one must first consider:

Who are the poor? A brief review of the literature indicates the difficulty encountered in describing and defining poverty; the general conclusion that emerges is that it is a relative term, varying according to individual, region, and time. One thing is certain: the poor, like the physically or psychologically impaired, are highly susceptible to stereotypes. It is a common occurrence for individuals, when confronted with too grave complexity, to latch onto ever handy labels. The task remains to penetrate the layers of assumptions and stigmatizations that surround the core of poverty. The second task is to ask: Why? What are the mechanisms that perpetuate mass poverty in a rich nation? And what is the nature of the dependency of the poor?

Describing Poverty

Kimmel (8) reports on a project in which it was originally hypothesized that dependent families have fewer middle-class characteristics—such as high achievement motivation, high educational-occupational aspirations, concern with time, and ability to defer gratification—than middle-class and independent poor families. However, it was discovered that poverty could not be given definite descriptions. Research teams, sent to metropolitan, small-village, and rural areas in order to determine social and psychological correlates of economic dependency, found that criteria applied to poverty conditions varied according to the location and background of the respondent. Poverty was thus a "social evaluation," existing "in" the judges as well as in those being judged. It was concluded that the idealization of independence, so pervasive in American society, actually clouds basic understanding and modification of the problems of poverty.

Who is considered poor differs with time and place. Ornati speaks of a new type of poverty now developing—the poverty of the underdog, which differs from the mass poverty characteristic of depression times. Today, structural unemployment strikes a disproportionate number of persons. The concomitant cultural deprivation of these people means that they are often underendowed with skills, education, and health. Ornati suggests that investments in human beings as well as capital goods are essential to deal effectively with the problems of poverty (11).

However, as Coles (2) notes, the poor often feel, not that investments are being made in them, but that they are under attack. Many of the underprivileged are wary of poverty fighters who "talk at them" and insist that they alter their manner of speech and dress. The poor are resentful of unfulfilled promises; what they need first of all are jobs, money, and dignity—but without accompanying degradation.

Coser (3) stresses that poverty can be understood only in terms of social responses to deprivation; that is, only when those who are deprived are given assistance does the sociological category of poverty emerge. One may then examine the terms upon which relief is granted and the effects of aid. The public dispensation of relief often results in degradation of the recipient.

Furthermore, the increasing professionalism of the aid-granters means that personal considerations are suppressed and the status discrepancy between the givers and the receivers is enlarged. Thus, the basic issue involves the relationship between granters-of-aid and the recipients, which is predominantly one of unilateral dependence.

What is preferred is an interdependent relationship in which the deprived person is required and enabled to make a social contribution. For example, the use of nonprofessional workers in the social service professions demonstrates the feasibility of the mutual-aid principle. The critical problem here is: What are the most effective channels for the participation of the poor? The danger is that the entry position becomes the "top" level. It must be recalled that, as with the parent-disabled child relationship, developing new skills and broadening the capacity for responsibility necessitate an extra dose of patience on the part of the helper. Since bureaucracies do not tend to be patient, and by nature focus on efficiency, it is essential to confront directly the problem of building organizational patience into the structural apparatus.

In a review of work on psychological dependency and economic deprivation, Thomas found that usually dependency is viewed as a general psychological state or a global clustering of such traits as lack of initiative and lack of achievement drive, but there are few objective data to support these notions. Thomas pointed out that social workers tend to emphasize diagnosis more than treatment (16). Professional definitions of "desirable behavior" are colored with the societal emphasis upon achievement and individualism; those who differ are labeled immature, dependent, and maladjusted. And obviously maladjustment signifies a personal, as well as a social, problem. A more accurate approach is the behavioral, which focuses on such indicators of psychological dependency as reinforcer reliance, deference, lack of autonomy, and lack of initiative. Each factor manifests particular needs, goals, and consequences.

Available research indicates that welfare recipients display a vast array of psychological traits, and only a minor portion could be labeled "psychologically dependent." The relationship between dependency and maladjustment is not borne out by empirical data. The few studies that are available suggest that social and impersonal factors, such as old age and disability, account for most poverty.

"When individuals or social systems do not perform those role functions normatively ascribed to them and when some other individuals or systems perform those functions for them," dependency is defined as a social problem, writes Spencer (15). This author introduces the concept of "social disability" to refer to those individuals who are mentally and physically healthy, but who are deficient in terms of the values and opportunities essential for independent functioning. An example is the family with an income insufficient to fulfill the instrumental needs of its members; financial assistance can prevent disruption of the familial unit, thereby allowing the family to perform other necessarily emotional and socialization functions.

Poverty Subcultures

Many studies have been directed at lower-class cultures—that array of attitudes, goals, values, and behavior that is thought to characterize the poor. These studies alternatively illustrate the strengths of the poor, arising out of their struggles to adapt to a difficult environment, and document those characteristics of the poor which are considered proof of their inability to lead a middle-class, "higher," existence, even if given a chance.

The operative values of the poor are discussed by Miller (10), who cites the desire to avoid "getting into trouble," physical prowess, smartness, excitement, fate, and autonomy of resentment of controls as areas that command high levels of attention and emotional involvement. It should be noted that these "focal concerns" do not coincide with a view of the poor as chronic dependents. While the lower class may sometimes violate the norms of the middle class, such actions are not necessarily deliberate—in the sense of being motivated by a desire to violate the norms. The culture of the poor has its own traditions and, moreover, its own integrity.

Strengths from Deprivation

Riessman (13) is one who contends that some of the characteristics, developed from efforts to cope with disadvantages, may be cultivated to reduce those disadvantages. He cites the creative potential of the poor and their preservation of ethnic and group traditions which may be channeled into various sectors of work life. Further, a new wealth of materials relating to the skills and aptitudes of the poor is currently evolving from literature on "new careers" and the use of nonprofessional workers. The service professions are beginning to realize that new insights and techniques can be offered by nonprofessional staff members; such staff can contribute to a more comprehensive understanding of the problems of the deprived because of their own experiences.

The continued success of nonprofessional workers contradicts many widespread beliefs concerning the lack of motivation of the lower classes. The acceptance of this myth probably relates fundamentally to a misunderstanding of lower-class culture and a desire to rationalize a superior economic position. As Coser explains, the middle class does not know what a "poor" life is like. The poor culture is alien to the separate worlds of suburbia.

Factors Hampering Employment

Various authors have been concerned with how cultural deprivation lessens chances for employment. Himes (7) distinguishes between "judgmental" and "realistic" deprivation. The first category includes behavior, dress, and level of sophistication; the second, functional illiteracy and lack of education. Examples from the Piedmont region of North Carolina illustrate other deprivations arising from the traditional exclusion of Negroes from certain industries and types of work activity. While children typically learn the ways of the work world and begin to identify themselves with certain jobs through association with adult role models, the Piedmont Negro children have only very limited vision of the job horizon, at least in terms of daily relationships. Further contact with employed adults teaches only that work is unrewarding and uninspiring, and that it has no intrinsic value beyond mere survival. In this particular region, office jobs are barred to Negroes; children are thus unexposed to attitudes and routine associated with this work, as well as denied knowledge concerning labor-union membership. Summarily, deprivation in this community includes lack of work models, exclusion from work ethos, and alienation from job ways.

Genevieve Knupfer discusses how economic underprivilege is linked with psychological underprivilege. She suggests that submission may become a habit and that, when it is linked with the lack of access to information sources and a lack of verbal facility, a person experiences diminished self-confidence. Consequently, the low-status person becomes even more unwilling to participate in various phases of middle-class culture; his refusal to participate goes "beyond what should be a realistic withdrawal adapted to his reduced chances of being effective" (9:210).

Cloward (1) counters with the view that poor motivation among slum youth accounts for the failure of employment training programs. The fundamental problem is that few jobs are available to those who lack skills. Young people are quite acutely aware that few jobs await them upon completion of training; they know that they lack both education and skills for many occupations. Meanwhile, money is poured into programs to improve motivation; a far better method would be to focus on closing educational and skill gaps and preparing these realistically pessimistic youth for occupations which actually have job openings.

The Aged

Sheppard (14) suggests that one measure of the degree to which a society has met the problem of poverty is the status of its aged. In our society the aged are very much a part of both the disabled and the poor groups. While it would be erroneous to conceive of the aged as a homogeneous segment of the population, it is apparent that many older persons share the combined difficulties of declining health and reduced income.

Adequate saving for later years or continued employment after retirement is the lot of only a few. While inflation shrinks savings and the social system demands current employment for well-being, automation and technology eliminate the need for older workers. Furthermore, as Paillat (12) notes, to be downgraded for a fall in personal output due to age is to be penalized psychologically as well as financially. Changes in the nature of job skills mean that older workers increasingly have less to teach younger workers.

Advanced age carries its own particular stigma. In a society marked by concerns for consumption, money, work, and youth, old people represent a specific brand of deviance. They are largely locked in the talons of a fast-moving age that cannot move fast enough to alleviate problems induced by its growth and change. Despite an expanding economy, the older people do not often receive an adequate share of the benefits.

Their situation presents a stark culmination of many types of dependency—their financial and health problems are often heightened by social isolation. Perhaps one of the most shattering adjustments is the sudden loss of roles accompanying withdrawal from the active work sphere. Other social roles tend to revolve around the occupational; one's contacts diminish, and the sense of "uselessness" and isolation sets in. It is particularly important to emphasize that any attempts to alter the material condition of the aged group must also include attention to psychological and social variables.

RESEARCH QUESTIONS

The foregoing discussion has indicated several of the multiple factors involved in dependency and has sought to emphasize that dependency is a process involving both superordinate and subordinate elements. In the past there has been a tendency to focus primarily on the nature of the subordinate; the problems tend to be phrased in terms connoting the inherent inferiority of the dependents. However, examination only of the disabled person, the poor person, or the aged person presents only a partial picture. What must also be considered is the social context within which transactions between the two elements occur. Often dependency is fostered by the independent element—either preservation of a superior status position or conditions built into a structural apparatus, such as a welfare agency, hospital, or family system.

The authors cited above, and others, have pointed out various levels on which further research is needed; some of these suggestions have been incorporated into the Appendix. Moreover, a multifaceted approach is essential; one example of this is that attention must be directed to the family system, both as a unit interacting with other societal institutions and as a system with its own distinct set of internal relationships, values, and structure (2).

It is also important to stress that, aside from particular research and theoretical gaps, much knowledge has already been amassed—knowledge that needs to be synthesized for immediate action. Obviously, the needs of the aforementioned groups are such that both immediate and long-term actions are demanded. Thus, parallel to the following questions of high priority research is the direct necessity for research utilization and dissemination.

REFERENCES

1. Cloward, Richard A., and Ontell, Robert. "Our Illusions about Training." American Child 47 (January 1965):6—10.

2. Coles, Robert. "The Poor Don't Want to Be Middle-Class." New York Times Magazine, December 19, 1965, pp. 7—8, 55—58.

3. Coser, Lewis A. "The Sociology of Poverty." Social Problems 13 (Fall 1965):140—48.

4. Cowen, Emory L. "Personality, Motivation, and Clinical Phenomena." In Psychological Research and Rehabilitation, edited by Lloyd H. Lofquist. Washington, D.C.: American Psychological Association, 1960.

5. Crain, Alan J.; Sussman, Marvin B.; and Weil, William B., Jr. "Family Interaction, Diabetes, and Sibling Relationships." International Journal of Social Psychiatry 12 (1966): 35—43.

6. Friedson, Eliot. "Disability as Social Deviance." In Sociology and Rehabilitation, edited by Marvin B. Sussman. Washington, D.C.: American Sociological Association, 1966.

7. Himes, Joseph S. "Some Work-related Cultural Deprivations of Lower-Class Negro Youths." Journal of Marriage and the Family 26 (November 1964):447—49.

8. Kimmel, Paul R. Identification and Modification of the Social-psychological Correlates of Economic Dependency, Project 199. Washington, D.C.: U.S. Department of Health, Education, and Welfare, Welfare Administration, March 1966.

9. Knupfer, Genevieve. "The Poverty-stricken State of Mind." In Contemporary Society, edited by Jackson Toby. New York: John Wiley & Sons, 1964.

10. Miller, Walter B. "Focal Concerns of Lower-Class Culture." In Poverty in America, edited by Louis A. Ferman, Joyce L. Kornbluh, and Alan Haber. Ann Arbor: University of Michigan Press, 1965.

11. Ornati, Oscar. Poverty amid Affluence. New York: Twentieth Century Fund, 1966.

12. Paillat, Paul. "Old People." Paper

prepared for the International Trade-Union Seminar on Low-Income Groups and Methods of Dealing with Their Problems. Paris, France, Organization for Economic Co-operation and Development, Manpower and Social Affairs Directorate, 1965.

13. Riessman, Frank. "Low-Income Culture: The Strengths of the Poor." Paper presented at the Groves Conference on Marriage and the Family, Knoxville, Tennessee, April 1964.

14. Sheppard, H. L. "Trends Which Affect the Poverty-stricken." Paper presented at the Seminar on Poverty, Institute for Policy Studies, May 5, 1964.

15. Spencer, Gary. A Comparative Study of the Reduction of Dependency in Four Low-Income Housing Projects: A Descriptive and Conceptual Introduction. Monograph No. 4, Northeastern Studies in Vocational Rehabilitation, Rehabilitation in Poverty Settings: No. 1. August 1967.

16. Thomas, Edwin J. "Psychological Dependency and Its Relationship to Economic Deprivation." Paper presented to the National Conference on Social Welfare, Chicago, Illinois, June 1966.

17. Wright, Beatrice A. Physical Disability: A Psychological Approach. New York: Harper & Bros., 1960.

24 Prejudice Against the Disabled and Some Means to Combat It

Constantina Safilios-Rothschild

There is probably no country, and perhaps one has never existed, in which the disabled have not been discriminated positively or negatively in one or more areas. Sometimes this discrimination has taken an extreme form as in ancient Sparta where all babies born with physical defects were thrown into the abyss of Kaida or in the attributing of supernatural powers to epileptics both in Brazil and in some African tribes. At other times discrimination is better disguised by more "civilized" and subtle methods as in the refusal to offer jobs or "normal" social interaction to the disabled. But whatever the form discrimination takes, its presence is always felt.

Prejudice is not unidimensional. An examination of the Attitudes Toward Disabled Persons Scales (1) suggests that attitudes toward the disabled are multi-dimensional variables and that prejudice toward the disabled may be better conceptualized as a continuum. This continuum would reflect the degree of tolerance extended towards disabled people and the degree of social distance that one desires to place between himself and the disabled. Thus, it might range from the lowest point of tolerance of not wishing the disabled (especially the visibly disabled) to be present in public places, entertainment places, etc., to unwillingness to rent apartments to the disabled, or to let them stay in hotels or to give them loans, insurance policies, driver's licenses or to admit them to "normal" schools and universities. Or one might not be discriminating in any of the above areas but would nevertheless be unwilling to employ a disabled individual. Or one might be willing to employ a disabled person but be reluctant to interact socially with him beyond "fictional" acceptance or to become the friend of a disabled person or to ever consider him as a potential lover or marital partner.

When we say that people are prejudiced, we should specify the area or areas of prejudice since very rarely do people discriminate against the disabled in all areas. In this way, the "hard core" areas of discrimination found even in "enlightened" people would become identified, and we would become aware of all the groups which hold different types of discriminatory attitudes. The disabled themselves, especially those who can

Reprinted from International Rehabilitation Reviews, 1968, 19(4):8–10, 15.
The figures in parentheses refer to the Bibliography at the end of the article.

more or less "pass" as normals, seem to discriminate against other disabled, especially in that they are reluctant to interact socially with them, become friends, fall in love or marry another disabled afflicted with the same or a different type of disability (2).

Another continuum which must be also taken into consideration in determining the nature and extent of prejudice relates to the type of disability with which the individual is afflicted. The degree of functional handicap does not solely determine the severity of discrimination to which afflicted persons are subjected. A number of irrational factors intervene. Thus, facial disfigurements, which do not necessarily impair people functionally, still set them apart socially, and they may become the victims of discrimination in many more areas than functionally impaired disabled persons, e.g., amputees. In the case of non-visible disabilities, it is the knowledge of their existence certified by a doctor's official diagnosis that triggers prejudice and intolerance. As long as the non-visible disability is not known and the disabled person can pass for normal he is accepted as such; but usually he cannot pass as normal in all situations or for a long time despite his having developed a wide range of techniques or plain "tricks," which may often be painful, stressful or humiliating to him. Once his true identity is uncovered the seriousness of the discrimination depends upon the nature and the assumed "pervasiveness" of the disability, whether or not it is contagious or considered hereditary, as well as upon the degree and severity of the social stigma attached to it in the particular country in which he is living.

A number of researchers and writers have documented the existence of employment discrimination directed against the disabled in Germany, Holland, Yugoslavia and Argentina (3). Also that there is social prejudice against the mentally retarded and the epileptic in Germany (3) and against the mentally ill in Greece (4). In Greece, for example, the knowledge that a person is mentally ill results in such a potent social stigma that not only can he (she) not work, he will also lose all his friends and have no chance to marry as well. If this person is already married and has children his wife may divorce him (if the pre-illness degree of marital satisfaction was low), and his children will be stigmatized in all their social relationships and usually will not be regarded as potential marital partners. The presence of physical disabilities, on the other hand, in some underdeveloped countries such as Greece, may entail less psychological stress for the afflicted adults (especially the males) because even when their condition renders them unemployable, their status within their family and peer group is not challenged. This occurs because masculinity is defined not in terms of their earning capacity but rather in terms of their "maleness." Their familial and social status would be significantly damaged only if their disability entailed sexual impotence. This definition of masculinity has a special significance since it is most prevalent in the traditional segments of the population; that is, the urban lower and working class where physical disability often brings about serious vocational handicaps.

Prejudiced attitudes toward the disabled may be held not only by the general population but also by the rehabilitation personnel. Some studies have shown that rehabilitation workers in the U.S.A. and Peru were not less prejudiced toward the disabled than other hospital employees (5). Recent studies in the U.S.A., Colombia, and Peru have indicated, however, that the more "modern" the country in terms of a socio-economic-educational point of view, the more positive the attitudes of special education and rehabilitation professionals toward the disabled (6). Of course, in these studies the composition and background of the rehabilitation personnel in each country is so diverse that we cannot be sure about the validity of the results. Also, these cross-cultural differences may be reflecting a greater degree of sophistication and "desirable" answers on the part of rehabilitation personnel, the more developed the country in which they are working.

The natural question that can be asked at this point is how can one combat the discrimination against the disabled practiced by those who are prejudiced. Legislative measures may be helpful in alleviating discriminatory practices in the practical areas of living, but they can never touch the social and affective areas of discrimination. Even in the practical areas, experience with protective legislation in many countries, developed and under-

developed, has shown that legislation can be, at best, only partially successful, mainly in helping the less seriously disabled. For example, in countries where most people work in small family businesses or are self-employed, quota legislation favoring the disabled would be meaningless (7). Also, if people, including employers, are prejudiced against disabled persons as potential workers, the quota legislations may be circumvented by the employers through technicalities in the definition of a "disabled" person. Thus, many people who would not be thought of as disabled and would be working "normally," would tend to become stigmatized as disabled and would then have work problems. Employers would tend to count these people as disabled fulfilling the quota requirements and no progress would have come about in the employment of the disabled.

Thus, while legislation, such as that creating sheltered workshops in countries with high unemployment may be helpful, it must always be remembered that it is not a panacea and that efforts must be directed toward changing the image of the disabled long before as well as simultaneously with the passing of legislation. We must also be aware that many of the efforts to help the disabled often have had as side-effects the creation of greater intolerance and prejudice against them. For example, fund raising campaigns for the rehabilitation of the disabled may, in trying to secure more money by over-dramatizing the condition of the ill or disabled persons, create the image of seriously handicapped persons who are helpless victims, unable to perform any useful activity and thus, reinforce the employers' fears, apprehensions, and prejudices. Or protective employment legislations may make employers more sensitive in differentiating the disabled from the non-disabled workers and lower their level of tolerance of deviations from a "normal" physique. Finally, even educational campaigns aiming at informing the population about a particular illness and disability may also bring about a greater intolerance of mildly disabled persons. One of the interesting observations that seems to hold cross-culturally is a negative correlation between potency of social stigma attached to a disabling illness and the degree of tolerance of a range of symptoms characteristic for this illness (8). Thus, in a country like Greece where a wide range of mentally deviant symptoms are usually tolerated without the individual being labeled mentally ill and stigmatized for life, educational programs and campaigns which would sensitize the public about the meaning of symptoms, could bring about the intolerance of a whole range of presently "normalized" symptoms and the stigmatization of a much larger number of mildly disturbed persons as a result. Unless the seriousness of the social stigma attached to mental illness in Greece is mitigated, educational campaigns may be creating at least as many problems for the mentally ill as they are alleviating.

Also, legislation concerning the construction of housing without architectural barriers for the disabled may lead to the development of a small community for the disabled where they live in their own "ghetto," unless special precautions are taken. Recognizing this danger, the Danish have made special efforts to avoid the isolation of the disabled by requiring that no more than one-third of the inhabitants in such special housing can be disabled (9). However, the social segregation of the disabled and a greater degree of awareness that the disabled are basically different from the non-disabled are the often unintended side-effects of protective legislations as well as of educational campaigns. This may be more so in industrialized societies where "deviant minorities" are usually segregated and little effort is made to integrate them into the larger society. This is probably because it is a faster, more economical and more efficient way to deal with them in the short run, and it relieves the "majority" from having to make any type of adjustment at all. Only the minority members have to adjust to the established "ideal" norms of the majority; that is, they must be willing to accept graciously the benevolently granted segregated facilities and to restrict the satisfaction of their social, emotional, and psychological needs within their group with which they will be "happier." This trend applies in the case of the ethnic, racial and religious groups and to some extent even to women despite the fact that they make up half of the population. However, the disabled of several countries (England, Jamaica and Norway) in a collection of autobiographical essays have very eloquently expressed their protest against the segregation imposed upon them by society in education, recreation, work, and private life, especially their loneliness and sense of "apartness" from the non-disabled (10).

Unfortunately, neither legislation nor educational campaigns can effectively touch or alter the social and effective areas of prejudice. Such prejudice seems to serve a function for the prejudiced person, namely, that of protecting him from the "acknowledgment of unpleasant truths about himself or of the harsh realities of his environment" (11). That is, the non-disabled who live with the perpetual fear of losing their physical integrity become anxious when faced with a disabled person because their fears are then rekindled. Psychological research has shown that the main type of aversion felt by the non-disabled is "aesthetic-sexual," that is, clear-cut feelings of repulsion and disgust for the disabled. These feelings are much stronger for disabilities such as skin disorder, amputation, body deformations (especially, facial disfigurements), and cerebral palsy and less strong for deafness, blindness, and paralysis (12). The guilt brought about by these feelings coupled with the ambiguous norms regulating the disabled-non-disabled social interaction make such interactions uncomfortable, rigid and strained (13). The non-disabled are unsure of the extent to which the disabled may be treated as "normals" and are afraid to make any negative slip or to show their aversion in any way probably because they are afraid that their behavior might "magically"

visit the "affliction" upon themselves. They cannot permit themselves to get angry or to insult a disabled person regardless of how irritating his personality or offensive his behavior might be and, therefore, they cannot act naturally since they have to watch closely every gesture and every word. The consequences of strained social interaction with the non-disabled are of a different nature for these disabled who were born with disabilities or afflicted at an early age and for those who at the onset of the disability, were already married adults between 20—45 years old. In the case of the former, society usually permits them to marry another disabled person but frowns upon "intermarriages" between the disabled and the non-disabled. The non-disabled involved in such "mixed" marriages are looked upon with suspicion and tend to be ostracized. It seems, however, that the disabled greatly value intermarriage with a non-disabled because to them it symbolizes (and rightly so) the ultimate proof of successful integration into the larger society (14).

In the case of married adults 20—45 years old who become disabled it seems that the nature of the pre-disability marital relationship is one of the most significant variables affecting their rehabilitation outcome as well as the outcome of the marriage after the occurrence of the disability. If the non-disabled spouse was quite satisfied with the marriage before the onset of the disability, the chances for the successful reintegration of the disabled person within his family and his circle of friends are excellent. If, however, the non-disabled spouse was not very satisfied with marriage before the onset of the disability, the disability becomes the "last straw" and usually a divorce ensues. How can one change bad marriages into good ones so that the marital partner can be forced to not have affective prejudice against the disabled spouse?

To the extent that legislation and appropriate educational campaigns make it possible for disabled people to work, travel and live in adequate housing, such things as setting them apart and denying them "normal" social intercourse with the non-disabled, as well as the friendship or love of the non-disabled become more acutely felt. They are permitted and encouraged to become self-sufficient, but they are condemned to loneliness and social isolation from the larger society. But how can affective prejudice be diminished? The experience derived from educational campaigns has shown that, except for their operating under the handicap of the label "education" which brings forth resistance especially in those who should be reached, such campaigns cannot be effective because the mass media keep reinforcing stereotypes and discriminatory practices. Possibly, then, the greatest potential for changing the "hard core" affective prejudice on the part of the non-disabled may lie in the effective use of mass media. A change in the image of the disabled in and through the mass media (especially, television and movies), and popular magazines (but also children's stories) should *not* be made through the educational channels or in special educative or informative mov-

ies about the disabled, but in regular movies, "soap-operas," serious movies and comedies in which the hero (or actors in supporting roles) is disabled. Here, the skills of the social psychologists could be applied and through experimentation show us what is the best "formula" for "educating" people subtly, and while they are being entertained, to the fact that a disabled person is not basically different from the non-disabled. That is, he is neither necessarily a hateful, distorted person, a gangster or a murderer, nor an exceptionally gifted or kind and understanding person, but a person who performs his social and familial roles with all the ordinary passions, fears, greatnesses and weaknesses of all humans. The difficulty in such a use of television and popular magazines would lie in persuading the network directors and editors that taking such a "line" whenever a disabled person is cast, would in no way hurt the popularity of their shows or magazines. In countries in which most or all television networks are owned by the government such an image-building effort would be easier to accomplish, and probably these countries should be encouraged to pioneer in this area. There is no valid reason why the content of all mass media must go on completely uncontrolled as to the stereotypes and prejudiced behavior it instills and reinforces in people, especially since the mass media, particularly television, are increasingly playing a very important educative role in the socialization of children and the formation of their values. And the recreational value of a play, a movie, or a book will not be lessened if, at the same time they are eradicating the hard core prejudices of people such as the affecting prejudices directed toward the disabled.

A SHORT BIBLIOGRAPHY

1. The Measurement of Attitudes Toward Disabled Persons. Harold E. Yuker, J. R. Block and J. H. Young. Human Resources Study No. 7, 1966.

2. Stigma. Notes on the Management of Spoiled Identity. Irving Goffman. Prentice-Hall, Inc., Englewood Cliffs, New Jersey, 1963; and The Cloak of Competence. Stigma in the Lives of the Mentally Retarded. University of California Press, Berkeley, 1967.

3. Industrial Society and Rehabilitation Problems and Solutions: Proceedings of the Tenth World Congress of the ISRD, Wiesbaden, Federal Republic of Germany, September 11–17, 1966. Deutsche Vereinigung für die Rehabilitation Behinderter e.V., Heidelberg-Schlierbach, Federal Republic of Germany, pp. 36–40 and 34–36.

4. Deviance and Mental Illness in the Greek Family. Constantina Safilios-Rothschild, Ph.D. Family Process, Vol. 7, No. 1, March, 1968, pp. 100–117; A Preliminary Report of a Research Concerning the Attitudes of the Families of Hospitalized Mental Patients. G. Alivisatos and G. Lyketsos. International Journal of Social Phychiatry, Vol. 10, No. 1, 1964.

5. Attitudes of Selected Rehabilitation Workers and Other Hospital Employees Toward the Physically Disabled. Howard A. Bell. Psychological Reports, 1962, pp. 10 and 183–186; and Nature and Determinants of Attitudes Toward Education and Toward Physically Disabled Persons in Colombia, Peru, and the United States. Eugene W. Friesen. Unpublished doctoral dissertation, Michigan State University, East Lansing, Michigan, 1966.

6. Attitudes of Rehabilitation Personnel Toward Physically Disabled Persons in Colombia, Peru, and the United States. John E. Jordan and Eugene W. Friesen. The Journal of Social Psychology, 1968, pp. 74 and 151–161.

7. Relations with Employers, Job Induction and Follow-up. Manual on Selective Placement of the Disabled, International Labour Office, Geneva, Switzerland, October, 1965, chapter IX.

8. The Sociology of Disability and Rehabilitation. Constantina Safilios-Rothschild, Ph.D. 1968.

9. Housing for the Disabled in Denmark. Frank Knudsen. Rehabilitation, No. 52, January-March, 1965, p. 21.

10. Stigma. The Experience of Disability. Paul Hunt (ed.). Geoffrey Chapman, London, England, 1966.

11. Attitude Formation and Change. David S. Abbey. Paper presented at the Canadian Association for Retarded Children's Tenth Annual Conference on Mental Retardation, Quebec City, Quebec, September, 1967.

12. Perceptions of Physical Disability by the Non-Disabled. Jerome Siller and Abram Chipman. Paper presented at the American Psychological Association Meetings, September, Los Angeles, California, 1964.

13. Deviance Disavowal:: The Management of Strained Interaction by the Visibly Handicapped. Fred Davis. Social Problems, IX, No. 2, Fall, 1961, pp. 120–132.

25 Societal Rehabilitation:

Changing Society's Attitudes Toward the Physically and Mentally Disabled

William A. Anthony

Individuals who bear the labels physically handicapped, mentally retarded, or mentally ill often are the targets of prejudicial attitudes and discriminatory practices which in many instances hamper their chances of becoming fully functioning members of society. The present survey reviews three traditional ways in which researchers have attempted to change attitudes toward disabled persons: (a) contact with disabled persons, (b) information about disabled persons, and (c) an experience combining both contact and information. Results of the survey followed a seemingly consistent pattern: Neither contact nor information alone is sufficient to effect positive attitude change toward disabled persons, but experiences which involve both contact and information do appear to have a favorable impact on attitudes. The research reviewed was remarkably consistent. Similar results were reported regardless of inter-study differences in subjects, assessment procedures, type of contact and information experience, and type of disability.

Physically and/or mentally disabled individuals, who bear such labels as the mentally ill, physically handicapped, or mentally retarded, often are the targets of prejudice and dis-

criminatory practices. Researchers have shown that this discrimination is least apparent in relatively impersonal situations and most blatant in contemplating either close interpersonal or business situations, such as marriage and employment (McDaniel, 1969; Rusk & Taylor, 1946; Whatley, 1959). It would appear that society is least tolerant of the disabled individual in areas of functioning which in our culture are of critical importance to mental health.

With the growing interest in preventive or community psychiatry, mental health professionals have increased their concern about the impact of the community's negative attitudes on the mental health of the mentally and physically disabled (Bindman & Spiegel, 1969; Caplan, 1964; Caplan, 1970; Iscoe & Spielberger, 1970; Lamb, Heath, & Downing, 1969). Various researchers have theorized that society's attitudes and expectations for the disabled may be of critical importance in maintaining the mental health of the physically handicapped and in restoring quickly the mental health of the mentally ill (Anthony, 1970; Centers & Centers, 1963; Roehrer, 1961; Scheff, 1963; Spitzer

Reprinted from Rehabilitation Psychology, 1972, 19(3):117–126. Copyright 1972, Rehabilitation Psychology.

& Denzin, 1968; Yamamato, 1971). If society's attitudes are indeed so crucial to the functioning of the physically and mentally disabled it would seem incumbent upon mental health professionals to attempt to influence these attitudes in a positive direction.

In this survey *societal rehabilitation* refers to efforts which attempt to reduce the general public's prejudicial attitudes toward the disabled individual. *Societal rehabilitation* is to be distinguished from *individual rehabilitation*. The latter is designed to restore or reintegrate the disabled individual into society (Jacques, 1970).

Although efforts at societal rehabilitation have been varied, it seems both possible and legitimate to group these attempts into three broad categories on the basis of the procedures emphasized: (a) contact with the disabled individual, (b) information about the disabled individual, and (c) a combination of both contact and information.

CONTACT

One procedure designed to induce attitude change is to arrange contacts between the general public and members of a disabled group. Studies investigating the contact dimension do so in two different ways. One method is to divide the subjects into groups simply on the basis of their self-reports about the amount of contact which they have had with a member of a disabled group and determine if differences exist in the attitudes of subjects differing in amount of self-reported contact. The second method exposes the subjects to a specific contact experience and assesses the effects of this observable contact experience on the subjects' attitudes.

Results of studies of the first type are fairly divergent. If one struggles to find a consensus it appears that individuals who report contact tend to have slightly more favorable attitudes than those who report no contact. Evidence of the facilitative effects of contact has been provided by Semmel & Dickson (1966) who found that as the amount of contact reported by college students increased, attitudes toward handicapped people became more positive. Another study also provided evidence of a moderate tendency toward more favorable attitudes by individuals who said they had had contact with the physically disabled (Gaier, Linkowski, & Jacques, 1968). A further example of the mild effects of contact was provided by Jaffe (1967). He found that high school students who reported some contact with the mentally retarded showed a more positive attitude on one of three attitudinal measures.

Slightly negative effects of contact also have been reported (Cowen, Underberg, & Verrillo, 1958). These researchers found that individuals who had had contact with the blind tended to have more negative attitudes than individuals reporting no contact.

A recent monograph summarized the results of over twenty studies of the relationship between reported contact with the physically disabled and attitudes toward physically disabled persons. Similar to the results presented previously, the studies exhibited a wide range of findings, but a slight majority of studies reported a significant relationship between amount of contact and favorableness of attitude (Yuker, Block, & Younng, 1966).

These retrospective contact studies are methodologically deficient in several important ways that may account for their conflicting results. First, it is the individual subject who defines what is meant by *contact*: the type of contact experience no doubt varies from subject to subject. Also, the contact experience for many subjects may have contained informational components as well, and the independent effects of contact and information may not be isolated.

These deficiencies are overcome in the more experimental type of contact study, and as a result the divergent findings disappear. Studies of the effects of specific contact experiences with a wide variety of disabled groups consistently have found no consistent changes in the subjects' attitudes as a result of their contacts with disabled persons.

Physically Disabled

Anthony & Cannon (1969) found no effect on physically normal children's attitudes toward physical disability as a result of attendance at a 2-week summer camp with physically handicapped children. The findings indicated a nonsignificant tendency for children who had negative attitudes to become even more negative. Similarly, Centers and Centers (1963) found that children who attended class with amputee children had significantly more rejecting attitudes toward the amputee children than toward a matched group of nonhandicapped children. In a study of adult attitudes, Granofsky (1966) was unable to improve the attitudes of volunteer hospital workers toward the physically disabled by arranging eight hours of social contact between the volunteers and a group of physically disabled men.

Mentally Retarded

Studies which attempted to change attitudes toward the mentally retarded through contact experiences have met with equally discouraging results. These studies typically involve assessing the attitudes of school children toward mentally retarded classmates who have been integrated into the non-mentally retarded children's class or school. The findings are unanimous in indicating that contact is not sufficient to produce positive attitudes toward mentally retarded children (Lapp, 1957; Rucker, Howe, & Snider, 1969; Strauch, 1970).

Mentally Ill

The unique effects of a contact-only experience with mental patients recently have been investigated (Spiegel, Keith-Spiegel, Zirgulis, & Wine, 1971). College students visited mental patients for 1–3 hours per week for a semester but received no supervision or information. At post-testing the students saw the typical mental patient as significantly more depressed and irritable, less neat and less interested in socialization. Their scores on the Opinions about Mental Illness scale (OMI) changed on only two of the five scales—the students became significantly less authoritarian but also less benevolent toward the mentally ill.

Of peripheral interest is one other study which examined the specific effects of contact with the mentally ill (King, Walder, & Pavey, 1970). Rather than assessing attitude change this investigation assessed pre-post personality changes in college students who volunteered for a semester-long, companion program in a mental hospital. While some personality changes did occur, it was more circumscribed than the changes brought about by a similar contact plus information experience to which it was compared.

In summary, while a dearth of experimental studies on the effects of contact exist, those that have been done are in general agreement—contact in and of itself does not significantly change attitudes toward persons with a disability. The unique effects of contact on changing attitudes toward the physically handicapped, mentally retarded, or mentally ill have yet to be demonstrated.

INFORMATION

Attempts also have been made to change attitudes by providing the non-disabled person with information about disabled people. This information may take the form of a book, a course lecture or discussion, or a film or institutional tour. General agreement seems to exist in the literature that regardless of the way in which the information is presented, the power of information alone to produce positive attitude change is negligible.

Several studies investigated the attitude change of college students enrolled in an abnormal psychology course (Altrocchi & Eisdorfer, 1961; Costin & Kerr, 1962). The first study compared students in classes of abnormal psychology, personality development, and industrial management. As would be expected, abnormal psychology students increased their information about mental illness; however their attitudes toward mental illness as measured by a semantic differential did not change.

Costin and Kerr (1962) compared students in an abnormal psychology class with a comparable group of controls. They reported some changes for the abnormal psychology students on the OMI, but these changes appeared to reflect informational increases rather than attitudinal changes. For example, the students increased their belief that mental illness is caused by interpersonal experience (Interpersonal Etiology scale), but they did not change their opinion about how different the mentally ill are from normals (Mental Hygiene Ideology). Furthermore, their scores on a scale of benevolence toward mental patients decreased.

Semmel and Dickson (1966) compared seniors in elementary education who had taken a course in special education with those who had not. No significant difference was found in attitudes measured by the Connotative Reaction Inventory, a scale designed to assess how comfortable a person says he would be in 10 social situations with a physically disabled person. Two studies on the combined effects of contact plus information have used as a control group an information-only sample—typically psychology majors or introductory psychology students (Chinsky & Rappaport, 1970; Smith, 1969). Neither study reported significant, positive changes in attitudes as a result of didactic coursework in psychology.

Another way to present information about disabled people is by means of film or institutional tour. Staffieri and Klappersack (1960) examined the effect of viewing a favorable film on cerebral palsy on college students' attitudes. The authors found no change in attitudes as measured by a social distance scale. An attempt to modify high school and college students' attitudes toward the mentally retarded by providing them with a tour of a state school for the mentally retarded did result in attitude changes, "but not necessarily of a positive nature" (Cleland & Chambers, 1959). While the students became more open in praise of the institution and employers, they tended to see the mentally retarded children as "better off in the institution."

Carbin and Mancuso (1970) recently reviewed various educational programs designed by mental health professionals which attempted to influence the general public to consider mental illness with the same nonrejecting attitudes as somatic illness. Similar to the results of the informational studies reviewed in this survey, they concluded that mental health education campaigns have been notably unsuccessful in their objective.

In conclusion, it would appear that providing individuals with information about disabled people has demonstrated only the obvious effect—it increases a person's knowledge about disabled people. However, merely having more and more information about persons with a disability does not enable the nondisabled person to evaluate the disabled person more positively. An as yet untested possibility remains that the information presented by the professional is faulty and that some other kind of information would be effective in facilitating attitude change.

CONTACT PLUS INFORMATION

Many researchers have attempted to change attitudes toward disabled individuals by combining the contact experience with some type of information about the disability. The findings of these studies appear to be remarkably consistent: Regardless of the type of disability studied, and seemingly independent of the type of contact and information experience provided, all studies reported that a contact-plus-information experience had a favorable impact on the nondisabled person's attitudes.

Physically Disabled

Anthony (1969) studied the attitudes of counselors employed at a summer camp for handicapped children. The camping experience provided the counselors with information conveyed by the professionals on the camp staff as well as continuous contact. The findings indicated that at the beginning of the camping experience new counselors had significantly less positive attitudes than counselors who had worked at the camp previously, and that by the end of the summer the new counselors had significantly improved attitudes toward physically disabled persons.

In a cross-sectional study of the effects of rehabilitation counselor training, Anthony and Carkhuff (1970) found that advanced students, who generally had more contact and information about physical disability, had more positive attitudes toward physically disabled individuals than beginning students, whose attitudes did not differ from graduate students in a non-helping profession.

Rusalem (1967) attempted to change the attitudes of a group of high school girls toward the deaf-blind. A unique aspect of this study was that the students were preselected from a larger group to form two groups: one with the most positive attitudes and one with the least positive. In addition, the students did not volunteer but were required to participate in the research. The contact and information experience consisted of six 1-hour group sessions that involved information about deaf-blindness, instruction in the manual alphabet, and the opportunity to communicate with deaf-blind individuals. Measures of attitude change were self-reports, a sentence completion test, and behavior.

Results showed that students with the most positive attitudes did not change on the self-report or the sentence completion test, probably due to a ceiling effect, but that the group with the poorest attitudes improved on both the attitude and behavioral measures. Measures of behavioral change included self-initiated volunteer work and reading about deaf-blindness.

Mentally Ill

The studies concerned with changing attitudes toward mental illness have used only two groups of subjects—student nurses in psychiatric training and college students concurrently working part-time in a mental hospital and enrolled in courses which provided them with an opportunity to discuss their work. The college students were participants in programs which ranged from 30 hours (Chinsky & Rappaport, 1970) to 2 years (Smith, 1969) and varied in intensity from 40 hours per week (Kulik, Martin, & Scheibe, 1969; Scheibe, 1965) to several hours per week (Holzberg & Gewirtz, 1963; Keith-Spiegel & Spiegel, 1970). Using a variety of measures such as the Adjective Check List, Opinions about Mental Illness Scale, and the Custodial Mental Illness Ideology Scale, all of the above studies reported favorable effects on attitudes toward the mentally ill.

Of related interest some researchers also investigated the effects of contact-plus-information experiences on volunteers' descriptions of themselves. The results have been inconsistent. Both positive effects (Scheibe, 1965; Holzberg, Gewirtz, & Ebner, 1964) or no effects (Chinsky & Rappaport, 1970) as a result of the contact-plus-information experience have been reported.

The effects of psychiatric-nurse-training on the attitudes of student nurses have been investigated repeatedly (Altrocchi & Eisdorfer, 1961; Hicks & Spaner, 1962; Lewis & Cleveland, 1966; Smith, 1969). Within a time span of 8–16 months, the psychiatric nursing experience provides the student nurse with extensive opportunities for contact as well as exposure to the professional literature in psychopathology. The research has shown consistently that this type of experience has positive effects on attitudes toward mental illness.

Mentally Retarded

A study of attitudes toward mental retardation, while not a pre- post-test design, compared a group of student teachers and teachers of the mentally retarded with teachers and students in general education and professionals in other fields. The findings indicated that student teachers and teachers of the mentally retarded had the most positive attitudes (Efron & Efron, 1967). If one can assume that training to teach the mentally retarded involves both contact and information, this result is consistent with the previously reported positive effects of a contact-plus-information experience.

CONCLUSIONS AND IMPLICATIONS

1. The attitudes of nondisabled persons toward persons with a disability can be influenced positively by providing the nondisabled individual with an experience which includes contact with disabled persons and information about the disability. Neither alone is sufficient, significantly and consistently, to have a favorable impact on attitudes toward disabled persons. It appears that without information contact has only a limited positive effect or may even reinforce existing negative attitudes. Similarly, information without contact increases knowledge about the disability only but appears to have little or no effect on attitudes.

The consistency of the research is all the more remarkable when one considers that the present survey examined attitudes toward three different disability groups assessed with a variety of attitudinal measures. In addition, the type of contact-plus-information experience varied from study to study. While it is conceivable that a researcher could deliberately arrange a destructive contact-plus-information experience and obtain negative results, it is impressive that of the variety of contact-plus-information experiences which researchers have so far investigated, all have yielded positive results.

2. The research conclusions on the contact-plus-information experiences must be limited because almost all the studies have been done on either college students who volunteered to undergo a contact experience or trainees in the helping professions. A dearth of research exists on other age groups, non-helping professionals, and non-volunteers.

3. Little is known about how much time is needed to change attitudes. The programs presented in this survey varied in length from 6 hours to 2 years. Smith (1969) suggested that

attitude change occurs early in a semester-long contact-plus-information experience. The fact that Rusalem (1967) was able to bring about both attitude and behavioral change toward the deaf-blind in only 6 hours suggests that an extremely short but intensive contact-plus-information experience is capable of producing favorable attitude change.

4. Professionals involved in community mental health and rehabilitation possess sufficient knowledge to begin to design broad societal rehabilitation programs based on a contact-plus-information experience. Mental health professionals who work in the schools could devise a societal rehabilitation program consisting of a required course, at the high school level, similar to the kind of program conducted by Rusalem (1967). Such courses should include contact with physically disabled and formerly mentally disabled individuals, as well as reading and discussions which facilitate student understanding of their reluctance to interact with disabled persons. College instructors of abnormal psychology courses also might include a contact-plus-information experience as part of their course requirements.

Other professionals could run programs designed to change the attitudes of employers. Perhaps such a course could be required in-service training for personnel directors of government agencies. The attitudes of private employers might be changed by training disabled persons to conduct job development interviews, thus insuring a contact-plus-information experience for each employer interviewed.

All of these societal rehabilitation programs should be based on the principles of program development which emphasize the development of simple steps to achieve a complex goal such as attitude change (Carkhuff, Friel, & Berenson, 1972). In addition, such programs must evaluate their efforts not just in terms of attitude change but ultimately in terms of behavioral criteria. For example, if the attitude change program was directed at employers the real measure of success might be the number of disabled persons subsequently hired. Or, if the target population was high school and college students, behavioral measures might include variables such as the number of individuals who subsequently volunteered to work in agencies serving disabled persons, or the amount of information about disabilities obtained on the students' own initiative, or the frequency of contact with disabled persons.

REFERENCES

Altrocchi, J. & Eisdorfer, C. Changes in attitudes toward mental illness. Mental Hygiene, 1961, 45, 563–570.

Anthony, W. A. The effect of contact on an individual's attitude toward disabled persons. Rehabilitation Counseling Bulletin, 1969, 12, 168–171.

Anthony, W. A. The physically disabled client and facilitative confrontation. Journal of Rehabilitation, 1970, 36(3), 22–23.

Anthony, W. A. & Cannon, J. A. A pilot study on the effects of involuntary integration on children's attitudes. Rehabilitation Counseling Bulletin, 1969, 12, 239–240.

Anthony, W. A. & Carkhuff, R. R. The effects of rehabilitation counselor training upon trainee functioning. Rehabilitation Counseling Bulletin, 1970, 13, 333–342.

Bindman, A. J., & Spiegel, A. D. (Eds.) Perspectives in community mental health. Chicago: Aldine, 1969.

Caplan, G. Principles of preventive psychiatry. New York: Basic Books, 1964.

Caplan, G. The theory and practice of mental health consultation. New York: Basic Books, 1970.

Carkhuff, R. R., Friel, T. & Berenson, B. G. The art of program development. Amherst, Mass.: Human Resource Development Press, in press, 1972.

Centers, L. & Centers, R. Peer group attitudes toward the amputee child. Journal of Social Psychology, 1963, 61, 127–132.

Chinsky, J. M., & Rappaport, J. Attitude change in college students and chronic patients: A dual perspective. Journal of Consulting and Clinical Psychology, 1970, 35, 388–394.

Cleland, C. C., & Chambers, W. R. Experimental modification of attitudes as a function of an institutional tour. American Journal of Mental Deficiency, 1959, 64, 124–130.

Costin, F., & Kerr, W. D. The effects of an abnormal psychology course on students' attitudes toward mental illness. Journal of Educational Psychology, 1962, 53, 214–218.

Cowen, E. L., Underberg, R. P., & Verrillo, R. T. The development and testing of an attitude to blindness scale. Journal of Social Psychology, 1958, 48, 297–304.

Efron, R. E., & Efron, H. Y. Measurements of attitudes toward the retarded and an application with educators. American Journal of Mental Deficiency, 1967, 72, 100–107.

Gaier, E. L., Linkowski, D. G., & Jacques, M. E. Contact as a variable in the perception of disability. Journal of Social Psychology, 1968, 74, 117–126.

Granofsky, J. Modification of attitudes toward the visibly disabled. Unpublished doctoral dissertation, Yeshiva University, 1966.

Hicks, J. M., & Spaner, F. E. Attitude change and mental hospital experience. Journal of Abnormal and Social Psychology, 1962, 65, 112–120.

Holzberg, J. D., & Gewirtz, H. A method of altering attitudes toward mental illness. Psychiatric Quarterly Supplement, 1963, 37, 56–61.

Holzberg, J. D., Gewirtz, H., & Ebner, E. Changes in moral judgment and self-acceptance as a function of companionship with hospitalized mental patients. Journal of Consulting Psychology, 1964, 28, 299–303.

Iscoe, I., & Spielberger, C. D. (Eds.) Community Psychology: Perspectives in training and research. New York: Appleton-Century-Crofts, 1970.

Jacques, M. E. Rehabilitation counseling: Scope and services. New York: Houghton Mifflin, 1970.

Jaffe, J. Attitudes and interpersonal contact: Relationships between contact with the mentally retarded and dimensions of attitude. Journal of Counseling Psychology, 1967, 14, 482–484.

Keith-Spiegel, P., & Spiegel, D. Effects of mental hospital experience on attitudes of teenage students toward mental illness. Journal of Clinical Psychology, 1970, 26, 387–388.

King, M., Walder, L. O., & Pavey, S. Personality change as a function of volunteer experience in a psychiatric hospital. Journal of Consulting and Clinical Psychology, 1970, 35, 423–425.

Kulik, J. A., Martin, R. A., & Scheibe, K. E. Effects of mental hospital volunteer work on students' conceptions of mental illness. Journal of Clinical Psychology, 1969, 25, 326–329.

Lamb, H. R., Heath, D., & Downing, J. J. (Eds.) Handbook of community mental health practice. San Francisco: Jossey-Bass, 1969.

Lapp, E. A. A study of the social adjustment of slow learning children who were assigned part-time regular classes. American Journal of Mental Deficiency, 1957, 62, 254–262.

Lewis, D. L., & Cleveland, S. E. Nursing students' attitudinal changes following a psychiatric affiliation. Journal of Psychiatric Nursing, 1966, 4, 223–231.

McDaniel, J. W. Physical disability and human behavior. New York: Pergamon Press, 1969.

Roehrer, G. A. The significance of public attitudes in the rehabilitation of the disabled. Rehabilitation Literature, 1961, 22, 66–72.

Rucker, C. N., Howe, C. E., & Snider, B. The participation of retarded children in junior high academic and non-academic regular classes. Exceptional Children, 1969, 35, 617–623.

Rusalem, H. Engineering changes in public attitudes toward a severely disabled group. Journal of Rehabilitation, 1967, 33(3), 26–27.

Rusk, H. A., & Taylor, E. J. New hope for the handicapped. New York: Harper, 1946.

Sarbin, T. R., & Mancuso, J. C. Failure of a moral enterprise: Attitudes of the public toward mental illness. Journal of Consulting and Clinical Psychology, 1970, 35, 159–173.

Scheff, T. J. The role of the mentally ill and the dynamics of mental disorder: A research framework. Sociometry, 1963, 26, 436–453.

Scheibe, K. E. College students spend eight weeks in mental hospital: A case report. Psychotherapy: Theory, Research, and Practice, 1965, 2, 117–120.

Semmel, M. I., & Dickson, S. Connotative reactions of college students to disability labels. Exceptional Children, 1966, 32, 443–450.

Smith, J. J. Psychiatric hospital experience and attitudes toward "mental illness." Journal of Consulting and Clinical Psychology, 1969, 33, 302–306.

Spiegel, D., Keith-Spiegel, P., Zirgulis, J., & Wine, D. B. Effects of student visits on social behavior of regressed schizophrenic patients. Journal of Clinical Psychology, 1971, 27, 396–400.

Spitzer, S. P., & Denzin, N. K. The mental patient: Studies in the sociology of deviance. New York: McGraw-Hill, 1968.

Staffieri, R., & Klappersack, B. An attempt to change attitudes toward the cerebral palsied. Rehabilitation Counseling Bulletin, 1960, 3, 5–6.

Strauch, J. D. Social contact as a variable in the expressed attitudes of normal adolescents toward EMR. Exceptional Children, 1970, 36, 495–500.

Whatley, C. D. Social attitudes toward discharged mental patients. Social Problems, 1959, 6, 313–320.

Yamamato, K. To be different. Rehabilitation Counseling Bulletin, 1971, 14, 180–189.

Yuker, H. E., Block, J. R., & Younng, J. H. The measurement of attitudes toward disabled persons: Human Resources Study No. 7. Albertson, N. Y.: Human Resources, 1966.

26 Cross-Cultural Rehabilitation

D. Corydon Hammond

The Vocational Rehabilitation Act of 1965 extended rehabilitation services to the socially and culturally handicapped. Up to the present time, however, little more than lip service has been given to providing rehabilitation and helping services to a forgotten population, the American Indian. With conditions of extreme poverty, unemployment rates often reaching forty percent on reservations, a frequent inadequacy of educational and employment skills, a considerable lack of awareness of employment opportunities, alcoholism, and cultural, language and experiential barriers, probably no other group in American could profit more from or has a more pressing need for the services provided by rehabilitation agencies. This article will examine problems which have contributed to this void in assistance to the native Americans and make some recommendations for the future of rehabilitation with this population.

DIFFICULTIES IN REHABILITATION

The remoteness of many Indian reservations from urban areas and existing facilities and the low population density of rural reservations discourage rehabilitation efforts. The very magnitude of such problems as poverty, unemployment and educational deficiencies may also have been disheartening. These factors and the isolation of reservation living have contributed to a reluctance of professional workers to enter reservation rehabilitation.

Cultural difference is the label I would attach to the other broad problem area which has hindered rehabilitation efforts.

The modern Anglo-American, as Ruth Benedict has pointed out, knows little of ways of life except his own. He has been protected because of the wide diffusion of western civilization and has been led by this to accept a belief in the uniformity of human behavior. He has been culturally conditioned, and he often projects his own absolutes to all other men (2).

Research reveals that the majority of psychotherapists in our society come from middle class backgrounds (8, 9, 16), and I suspect most rehabilitation workers also come from these circumstances. Having developed in this environment, helping services have clustered in metropolitan areas, and both psychotherapeutic approaches and rehabilitation agencies have become oriented to the dominant culture and race. It is possible that some therapeutic principles we take for granted

Reprinted from the Journal of Rehabilitation, 1971, 37(5):34–36, 44.

may even be culture specific and inappropriate for use with other populations.

Lending support to this possibility is evidence that the majority of the clients our middle class counselors see also come from the middle and upper classes (3, 4, 17) and that duration of stay in psychotherapy has likewise been found to favor clients from these socioeconomic strata (1, 6, 10, 12, 19). It seems likely that these relationships also apply to rehabilitation counseling.

Culturally biased samples have typically made up treatment and research groups, and from these limited samples unjustified overgeneraliztions have been drawn about helping principles and services. Therapeutic formulations derived from such narrow samples are of dubious reliability in rehabilitation and therapy with divergent populations.

A statement by Devereux two decades ago about the cultural relativity of our helping professions seems relevant to rehabilitation services today:

> Unfortunately, in the formulation of the techniques and goals of therapy, ethnocentrism still plays a preponderant role, and psychotherapy is still inspired by the motto, 'How to be more like *me*—or at least more like *us*.' (5)

VALUE DIFFERENCES

It should be remembered that the value system of Anglo-America is based on Judeo-Christian philosophy, whereas Indian traditional values generally contrast with such tenets as original sin, blind faith in a heaven after death and a reward for righteous living, proselyting, the death of a man atoning for sins and a Sunday religion (14).

In the dominant culture, time is like a flowing river coming out of the past into the present and the future. We are tied to schedules, and indeed, often the present hardly exists. To the Indian, time tends to be a relative thing. In fact, among the Hopi Indians there is not a three tense language system; there is only the present tense.

Typically, tribal views of nature and concepts of life-space also differ from Anglo orientations. Instead of seeing nature as something to be mastered, most Indians believe man must live in harmony with nature. Where the white man views nature as something to be controlled and prevented from destroying, the Indian feels nature will take care of him if he lives as he should.

In the United States, "youth" is glamorized. Millions of dollars are spent annually for makeup and hair dyes. Indian cultures tend to have more respect for "the elders" and their wisdom, and to stress following the old ways and de-emphasize innovation and change. Attempts to hide white hair or conceal signs of age are not as often seen.

The middle class American believes in the prime importance of the biological family. However, in Indian cultures the extended family assumes more importance, and a large number of relatives may effect the socialization of the children, live together, and be referred to by biological family names, such as "father."

In our society, men should strive to be "the best," the "first" and climb toward success. Indian cultures, on the other hand, usually stress cooperation instead of competition, and anonymity rather than individuality.

"A penny saved is a penny earned," expresses a prominent value most counselors hold. Saving is not seen as a virtue in native American societies, however, and respected men are men who share their wealth and possessions.

CROSS-CULTURAL COUNSELING

Perhaps these few generalizations have served to illustrate the problem: we see the world not as it is but as we are. In rehabilitation across cultures, where a client views the world from an unfamiliar and different frame of reference, the counselor will find communication and empathy difficult, and the interview may be frustrating and threatening for both participants.

From 1963 through 1966, a special Navajo Rehabilitation Project was funded at Flagstaff, Arizona. The technical reports indicate the magnitude of the problems of isolation, poverty and cultural-linguistic differences in rehabilitation counseling with members of the nation's largest Indian tribe. The project staff noted seven particular difficulties in the establishment of a counseling relationship (7).

1. There was a high rate of unkept appointments, and when the client returned, it was often for assistance with something unrelated to the original contact problem.

2. Navajo clients perceived the counselor as a solver of immediate practical problems and not as an agent of psychological or interpersonal change.

3. Navajos viewed the counselor as an authority figure and seemed to expect him to be much like other Anglo authorities they had known.

4. Rehabilitation counselors found the language barrier insurmountable with most of the Navajo Indians. The staff did use interpreters, but they felt it made the establishment of rapport almost impossible.

5. More time was needed to acquire rapport, and they found that "Navajos generally withdraw psychologically when they are anxious rather than covering up the anxiety by talking" (7). The clients were more withdrawn than Euro-American clients in the early interviews.

6. The counselors seemed disturbed because their Indian clients did not disclose their inner thoughts or portray their behavior in psychologically meaningful terms. They did not perceive the counselor's role as that of an insight facilitator.

7. Navajo Rehabilitation Project counselors found educational, economic and social disadvantages frustrating for both them and their clients.

Osborn (13), in evaluating his counseling experience with Paiute Indians, commented on the infrequency of self-analysis and self-inspection by his trade school clients. He found that they were present oriented, wanted help with immediate problems, did not anticipate the future or show concern with making long range plans, distrusted federal programs and were willing to try to manipulate authority figures. He interestingly observed that he saw the situation of some of the Indians as a problem, but because they did not recognize the circumstances as a problem it might be said that for them no problem existed.

Despite the obstacles to Indian rehabilitation, the Navajo Rehabilitation Project staff at the conclusion of three years of reservation rehabilitation sounded an optimistic note:

> If the cultural-personality differences are anticipated and accepted, and if stereotyping is avoided, constructive, warm and satisfying counseling relationships develop (7).

RECOMMENDATIONS
AND OBSERVATIONS

My personal experiences on Indian reservations also indicate that very gratifying and productive relationships may be established with Indian clients. However, my own experience and that of others would prompt me to make the following recommendations which should assist in facilitating successful counseling among American Indians.

1. It is very difficult to talk about "the Indian." I believe one of the primary causes of failure among Anglo innovators on the reservation has been stereotyping. There are over two hundred and fifty Indian tribes in the country, each with its own culture and background. Tribes, even when separated by only a few miles geographically, may have cultural differences as great as between Anglo and Indian. Therefore—and this should be taken

as a qualification of this article also—anyone speaking about "the Indian," is speaking with questionable generality in many cases.

2. Become familiar with the local tribal culture and history. Understanding cultural values may often aid in understanding and communicating with the individual. But, again, beware of stereotyping the Indian or the culture concept will work against you and mask clients instead of promoting the understanding of unique individuals (11).

Particularly recommended are home visits, attendance at local functions and knowledge of common phrases in the native language. This communicates respect and interest. If possible, the counselor should live on the reservation.

3. Analyze your own attitudes, values and background. What are your emotional reactions to their culture and traditional, native religion? What are your reactions to setting "dirty," perhaps ill clad, runny-nosed Indian children on your lap? How comfortable do you feel in an Indian home; eating Indian food? Do you feel superior to the Indian adults?

At the Pine Ridge Sioux reservation, Wax, in describing teachers, described (in my experience) most white men on the reservation when he noted that "very few of the Day School teachers actively dislike their pupils; quite a few seem fond of them; very few respect them. . . . The most common attitude is condescension, sometimes kindly, often well-meant, but always critical" (18).

I have seen many Indians who have

grown tired of hearing sonorous rhetoric from white people about their "love" for the Indians as they condescendingly look down their noses at them. I'll pass on the advice an Indian friend once gave a missionary: "Don't love us, respect us!"

4. I believe informality and personal contact are required. The Flagstaff study has also recommended providing a sustained relationship, using the same counselor for intake interviewing and counseling. This seems essential if a longer time is needed to establish rapport.

5. In my experience, a lot of communication takes place nonverbally with some Indians. The reservation counselor will need to increase his sensitivity to these cues and learn to discriminate their nonverbal communications. If they do not develop ability in this, middle class counselors who are verbally oriented may miss a lot of what is going on, especially with clients who do not seem talkative.

The counselor will also need to take care that Indian clients are not telling him what they think he wants to hear. Also, superficially, some Indian clients may seem to share your values, but this may be illusory. The client may be trying to please you and to fulfill your expectations, or perhaps he is ashamed or reluctant to admit his true feelings.

Care should also be taken to differentiate between actual problems and what may appear to be difficulties because of cultural bias and comparisons to Anglo, middle class culture.

6. Become aware of opportunities and services available to Indians. For example, I understand that a university in Pennsylvania has had a nursing scholarship for Indian students for a couple hundred years which has seldom been used. Rehabilitation personnel will also need to become acquainted with Public Health Service facilities, the Bureau of Indian Affairs Branch of Welfare and their Branch of Employment Assistance, tribal agencies, scholarships, money available for Indians through foundations, university Indian education programs and programs such as the Thiokol Chemical Roswell (New Mexico) Indian Employment Training Project.

7. A counselor working on the reservation will no doubt meet Indians who will stereotype him. Their reactions to you may have little to do with you as a real person. If you experience hostility, cool receptions or suspicions which seem unwarranted, try not to take it personally. Years of experience with "white men" and Anglo authorities are bound to have their carryovers. It may take time to establish yourself as being different from those who have gone for decades before you.

8. Rehabilitation and counseling services may be entirely new to many reservation residents. The problem of role expectations has already been mentioned. There will probably be a need for community education about your program, precounseling orientations and structuring. Indian case aides may be almost essential, and certainly more Indians should be encouraged to enter rehabilitation counselor training programs.

Remember on the reservation that you are an alien. Just because you have a degree or title does not make you an "expert." Listen to and seek out local advice; they have learned something about their own people in a lifetime on the reservation.

9. My experience would recommend an active orientation toward casefinding. Do not expect clients to flock to you because you have established an office, or you may end up sitting in that office alone a mighty long time. You will probably need to "beat the bushes" and engage in an active outreach program. Hospitals may be an excellent place for establishing contact.

The responsibility for establishing contact and a relationship should be placed on the counselor rather than the client. The counselor should show an active caring by trying to meet the client's immediate needs (such as for transportation) and by activity on his behalf. Care should also be taken to set up short-range goals besides your long-range planning.

10. I view role-playing as a potentially very useful technique with Indians in developing assertive behaviors and building new behavioral repertoires, such as in social interactions and for job interviews.

11. Frank Riessman has made the following recommendations about counseling with the "culturally deprived":

Psychotherapeutic methods that stress authority, directiveness, the physical aspect, the group and the family, action rather than talk alone, are likely to be far more successful than introspective depth orientations. The educationally deprived person in therapy is more likely to see his problems as exter-

nally-caused, to want a doctor's prescription, to prefer action to words, and to want his "symptoms" cured rather than to submit to a complete overhauling of his personality (15).

I partially agree and partially disagree with Riessman. A more active and behavioral approach seems to have merit to me. However, we must be careful to affirm the self-determination of Indian clients. This may be very difficult for the counselor when, from the frame of reference of his middle class values, the client seems to be making wrong choices.

I would warn the behaviorally oriented counselor not to manipulate clients into behaviors and goals in accordance with his frame of reference which may be unacceptable to the clients and their culture. It may be useful to present the client with alternatives from which to choose, but remember that different ways of life may lead to constructive goals and happiness. Don't be just another white man condemning the Indians' way and telling them yours is the only way.

In accordance with Riessman, however, I would caution the insight oriented rehabilitation worker that many Indians are not concerned with introspection and self-examination. They will probably want to concentrate on behavior and actual experiences rather than vicarious experiences.

But whether or not you use behavioral methods, I believe a relationship with the Indian client is very important. I believe skill in establishing a relationship with empathic understanding, acceptance of the client where he is and unconditional positive regard are almost essential to success with the Indian client. My experience also testifies to the importance of counselor genuiness. I have found that if you play a role and are not real, most Indians will see through it.

My recommendation would be to remain flexible in your therapeutic approaches and be willing to innovate. Consider the needs of the client first and not your own. If your therapeutic model is rigid, ask yourself if it is meeting your needs or those of your client.

CONCLUSION

Probably no other population in the United States has such a desperate need for rehabilitation services as the American Indian. The magnitude of the poverty-related problems which exist on the reservations, the isolation of reservation residents and cultural-linguistic differences may have accounted for the paucity of services. However, with the aid of staff recruitment incentives and the recommendations cited, it is the author's conviction that profitable and fulfilling cross-cultural rehabilitation can be carried out in the virtually untouched area of Indian reservations.

REFERENCES

1. Bailey, M. A.; Warshaw, L.; and Eichler, R. M. "A Study of Factors Related to Length of Stay in Psychotherapy." Archives of Neurology and Psychiatry 15 (1959):442–444.

2. Benedict, Ruth. Patterns of Culture. Boston: Houghton Mifflin, 1934.

3. Brill, N., and Storrow, Hugh. "Social Class and Psychiatric Treatment." Archives of General Psychiatry 3 (1960):340–344.

4. Cole, N.; Branch, C. H. Hardin; and Allison, R. "Some Relationships Between Social Class and the Practice of Dynamic Psychotherapy." American Journal of Psychiatry 118 (1962):1004–1012.

5. Devereux, G. "Three Technical Problems in the Psychotherapy of Plains Indian Patients." American Journal of Psychotherapy 5 (1951): 420.

6. Frank, J. D.; Gliedman, L. H.; Imber, S. D.; Nash, E. D.; and Stone, A. R. "Why Patients Leave Psychotherapy." Archives of Neurology and Psychiatry 77 (1957):283–299.

7. Henderson, N. B., and Avallone, V. L. "Problems in Counseling Navajo Rehabilitation Clients." Navajo Rehabilitation Project Technical Report No. 4. Flagstaff: Northern Arizona University, 1967.

8. Hollingshead, A. B., and Redlich, R. C. Social Class and Mental Illness. New York: John Wiley and Sons, 1958.

9. Holt, R. R. and Luborsky, L. Personality Patterns of Psychiatrists, Vol. 1, New York: Basic Books, 1958.

10. Imber, S. D.; Nash, E. H.; and Stone, A. R. "Social Class and Duration of Psychotherapy." Journal of Clinical Psychology 11 (1955): 281–284.

11. Leacock, E. "The Concept of Culture and Its Significance for School Counselors." Personnel and Guidance Journal, May, 1968, pp. 844–851.

12. Lorr, M.; Katz, M. M.; and Rubinstein, E. A. "The Prediction of

Length of Stay in Psychotherapy."
Journal of Consulting Psychology 22
(1958):321–327.

13. Osborn, Jr., H. B. "Evaluation of
Counseling with a Group of Southern Paiute Indians." Unpublished
doctoral dissertation, University of
Utah, 1959.

14. Reichard, G. "The Navajo and
Christianity." American Anthropologist 51 (1949):66–71.

15. Riessman, Frank. The Culturally
Deprived Child. New York: Harper
and Row, 1962, p. 24.

16. Roe, Ann. The Psychology of Occupations. New York: John Wiley
and Sons, 1956.

17. Schaffer, L., and Meyers, J. K.
"Psychotherapy and Social Stratifi-
cation." Psychiatry 17 (1954):
277–292.

18. Wax, M., et al. Formal Education
in an American Indian Community.
Kalamazoo, Michigan: Society for
the Study of Social Problems, 1964,
p. 73.

19. Winder, A. E., and Hersko, M.
"The Effect of Social Class on the
Length and Type of Psychotherapy
in a Veterans Administration Mental
Hygiene Clinic." Journal of Clinical
Psychology 11 (1955):77–79.

27 Personal Space as a Function of the Stigma Effect

Mary Emmons Worthington

In this experiment, measurement of personal space, or the invisible boundary surrounding an individual into which another may not come, was investigated as a function of visibility of stigma. Stigma was defined as a discrediting attribute that is highly visible; the stigmatized person has a "spoiled identity."

Edward Hall (1959) described the "organism's territory" as a nonphysical boundary surrounding both animals and man; this territory is claimed and defended by the organism and, although spatial cues are often meager, spatial invasion may cause emotional reaction. Hall stated that the dynamics of spatial interaction arise because they are related to interpersonal action. "Proxemics" is the term coined by Hall (1966) for man's use of social and personal space. Territoriality is behavior by which an organism claims an area and defends it against members of its own species. Heidiger (1961) applied the term "personal distance" to the normal spacing maintained by noncontact animals, and his term "critical distance" is the zone which separates flight distance from attack distance. Social distance is a psychological distance which is not rigidly fixed, but shifts with the situation and varies from species to species.

Hall (1966) measured personal distance in terms of intimate, personal, social, and public (each with its close and far) phases. How people feel toward each other is a decisive factor in the distance used. Intimate distance varies from physical contact in the close phase to 6–18 inches in the far phase. Personal distance in the close phase is 1½ to 2½ feet, and in the far phase 2½ to 4 feet. Social distance in the close phase is 4 to 7 feet, and 25 feet or more in the far phase, with 30 feet around important public figures. The specific distance depends on the nature of the interpersonal transaction.

Studies by Robert Sommer (1969) focused on the concept of personal space or the portable territory that a person carries with him, which does not extend equally in all directions. This space varies with the relationship between individuals. Leipold (1963), for example, reported that college students given stress instructions seated themselves at a greater distance from the professor than those given neutral instructions. The results of McBride et al.'s (1965) study on human spatial

Reprinted from Environment and Behavior, 1974, 6(3):289–294, by permission of the publisher, Sage Publications, Inc.

behavior using the galvanic skin response as an index of emotionality showed that the GSR was greatest when an individual was approached frontally.

Goffman (1963) stated that the person with a highly visible stigma has a "spoiled identity." His physical defect may transform an individual into a "faulty interactant," from both his own and others' points of view. Encounter may evoke a situational impropriety with the shamed person being ashamed to be ashamed but still withdrawing from contact with the discredited one as a means of adjustment. Tension management is involved, as the stigmatized and the normal are part of each other; the normal and the stigmatized are perspectives in a two-role social process. In his balance theory of sentiments, Heider (1958) stated that there is a negative reaction to the different and strange. Deferential avoidance may be of a self-protective kind. A discredited individual may be avoided so that the other may not be polluted or defiled by him. MacGregor et al. (1953) found that negative character traits are imputed to persons with facial disfigurements.

The purpose of this experiment was to discover whether by measurement of the amount of personal space selected by the subjects, a different degree of spatial separation would be chosen in interaction with a "normal" experimenter compared to an experimenter with a "spoiled identity." If it was true that encounter with an individual possessing highly visible manifestations of impairment caused the subject in the experimental group to maintain a greater distance from the stigmatized person than in the control group (encountering an individual possessing no visible signs of impairment) and to spend less time imparting aid, a contamination effect was considered to be operative. If, however, personal space was not increased or if the personal distance remained the same, no contamination was considered to be operative; if personal space actually decreased, it was assumed that the subject was demonstrating empathy or helping behavior.

Personal space, sex differences, and time spent in encounter were measured in a randomly selected experimental group by the experimenter, simulating a stigma, and the same factors recorded in a randomly selected control group by the nonstigmatized experimenter.

METHOD

Subjects

Subjects were chosen at random in the lobby of the Long Beach, California, Airport. Individuals were not questioned who appeared to be in physical distress or highly gravid—that is, in the late stages of pregnancy. Children below adolescence were not among the subjects used.

Apparatus

An empty area of the airport lobby, approximately thirty feet in diameter, was used between the airport entrance and the boarding ramp. The floor surrounding the location of the experimenter was marked, in advance, with strips of cream-colored paper tape which closely approximated the color of the lobby floor. The strips of paper tape were one inch wide and one foot long, and were placed at distances from the experimenter of 1½ feet, 2½ feet, 4 feet, 7 feet and 12 feet which corresponded to Hall's (1966) designation of personal distance in the close and far phase, and social distance in the close and far phase. His extremes of intimate distance and public distance were not used, because personal contact could be measured without a floor marker and the element of noise in the lobby was such that public distance (or a distance of more than 12 feet) precluded verbal communication. A wheelchair was used in the experimental part of the study.

A street map of Long Beach with a stopwatch concealed in the palm beneath the map was held in the right hand of the experimenter, who wore street clothes. An opaque rubber tube, one-quarter inch in diameter and 12 inches long, inserted in the left nostril and terminated under the suit jacket lapel, was used in the experimental phase of the study; in the control portion of the experimenter, the experimenter was dressed in the same street clothes without visible stigma.

Procedure

In the control condition, the experimenter was seated in the previously described location of the airport lobby, surrounded by the marked measurements of distance on the lobby floor, in street clothes, with a Long Beach street map and concealed stopwatch in the right hand. Random subjects were hailed by eye contact and a wave of the right hand. The question, "Which way is it to the San Diego freeway?" was asked of each subject. In both experimental and control conditions, the point of nearest approach to the experimenter by the subject was recorded as well as the sex of the subject and the length of time spent in reply.

In the experimental condition, the stigmatized experimenter was seated in a wheelchair in the same place of the airport lobby when questioning the second randomly selected group of subjects. The Long Beach street map with concealed stopwatch beneath it were held in the right hand. The rubber tube was inserted in the left nostril, terminating under the left lapel. Subjects were contacted in an identical manner to the preceding group and the same inquiry made. It was judged that the number of people in the lobby were approximately the same for the two conditions as the same day of the week used in both cases, and the same time of the afternoon was chosen. Weather conditions were similar.

Results

Twenty-nine people were included in the control group, 16 men and 13 women. The mean approach distance was 10.4 inches (standard deviation = 2.85). Control Ss spent an average of 27.55 seconds in the encounter (standard deviation = 5.79).

Thirty-four Ss were included in the experimental group, 19 men and 15 women. The mean approach distance was 19.5 inches (standard deviation = 3.90). Experimental Ss spent an average of 19.21 seconds in the encounter (standard deviation = 5.65). A t-test of the difference between the means for approach distance indicated a significant difference between conditions (t = 3.05, p < .01). There was no significant difference in the amount of time spent with the experimenter in the two conditions (t = .99, p > .05).

The present study lends support to Goffman's (1963) hypothesis of "spoiled identity." A contamination effect was considered to be operative since the amount of personal space was quite significantly increased from the visibly stigmatized experimenter. The amount of time spent in encounter was not significantly less or greater, which indicated that the subjects were equally willing to help, but did not want to catch whatever it was that the stigmatized experimenter had. It was felt by the experimenter that older subjects were less affected by signs of visible stigma. There was one black subject included in the experimental group and the nearest point of approach was 4 inches, well below the average number of inches of 19.4, which led the experimenter to question if this subject felt his own identity was "spoiled." Helping behavior was observed when one female subject offered to obtain a better map of the area than the one the experimenter was using, obtained such a map from the PSA Airline office in the airport, returned, and gave it to the experimenter. (This was an experimental subject.)

It was felt by this experimenter that this was a heuristic study, suggesting future studies among subjects who had "spoiled identities" themselves, located perhaps in a paraplegic ward of a Veterans Hospital, a convalescent hospital, or ghetto, to see if use of space would deviate significantly among such subjects.

AUTHOR'S NOTE

The author would like to express profound appreciation to Diana Solar, Ph.D. Pepperdine University for her encouragement and help in this study.

REFERENCES

Argyle, M. and J. Dean (1965) "Eye contact, distance, and affiliation." Sociometry 28:289–304.

Goffman, E. (1967) Interaction Ritual. Garden City, N.Y.: Doubleday.

——— (1963) Stigma. Englewood Cliffs, N.J.: Prentice-Hall.

Hall, E. T. (1966) The Hidden Dimension. Garden City, N.Y.: Doubleday.

——— (1959) The Silent Language. Greenwich, Conn.: Fawcett.

Heider, F. (1958) The Psychology of Interpersonal Relations. New York: John Wiley.

Heidiger, H. (1961) "The evolution of territorial behavior," in S. L. Washburn (ed.) Social Life of Early Man. New York: Viking Fund Publications in Anthropology.

Leipold, W. E. (1963) "Psychological distance in dyadic interview." Ph.D. dissertation. University of North Dakota.

McBride, G., M. G. King, and J. W. James (1965) "Social proximity effects on galvanic skin response in adult humans." J. of Psychology 61: 153–157.

McDowell, K. V. (1970) "Violations of personal space." Dissertation Abstracts International Vol. 31 (1-A) (July):467.

MacGregor, F. C., T. M. Abel, A. Bryt, E. Lauer, and S. Weissmann (1953) Facial Deformities and Plastic Surgery. Springfield, Ill.: Charles C Thomas.

Sommer, R. (1969) Personal Space. Englewood Cliffs, N.J.: Prentice-Hall.

Wright, B. A. (1960) Physical Disability—A Psychological Approach. New York: Harper & Row.

Part III

PSYCHOLOGICAL ASPECTS OF DISABILITY

Editorial
Introduction

Joseph Stubbins

Psychology makes many different kinds of contributions to the understanding of disabled persons. But it is scarcely possible to over-emphasize that the disabled person must be understood as a human being serving as a background to the study of disability. There are several branches of psychology that are relevant to appreciating the disabled in this broad sense. To mention a few:

1. Personality theories or models of human behavior that enlighten aspects of behavior referred to as motivation and drives
2. Developmental psychology, which is concerned with the continuities of behavior over time and how events at one stage of life influence behavior at subsequent stages
3. Social psychology, which studies the behavior of individuals in groups and the dynamics of group behavior
4. Differential psychology, or the study of individual differences in interests, aptitudes, and intellectual traits

Professionally trained psychologists study such subjects and others in the spirit of science. This requires public disclosure of the bases on which findings were made, an assumption that behavior is substantially predictable and follows discoverable laws or regularities, and the willingness to specify the conditions or evidence which one would accept as refutation of a scientific conclusion. In this spirit, psychologists learn about how psychological knowledge is generated. At the highest level of training, they engage in research. They learn techniques of applying the knowledge for the benefit of their clients. Partly as a consequence of self-understanding and partly through trained judgment, they practice the helping role as an *art*—something difficult to define but which most practitioners agree is important in applied psychology.

In Part I, our understanding of disability was developed by viewing disablement from the perspective of the unfiltered experience of the injured person. This could be called phenomenological psychology. Part II interpreted the impact of disability as social experience and as socially generated. This, too, could be claimed as a branch of psychology, viz., social and community psychology. But psychologists are relative newcomers to this approach so it was more appropriate to title Part II, *Sociological Aspects of Disability*. In Part III, we use the terms "psychological" and "disability" in a limited sense. Disability is analyzed as an *intra*-personal system. There are many words in the English language that point to the reality of the individual as a more or less self-contained unit; words such as personality, self, character, temperament, and individual. In line with this definition, we can expect the authors of the articles in Part

295

III to approach disability from an individualistic standpoint and to seek solutions to disability by tapping the resources of the individual client. The other restriction in our use of "psychological" is the limited range of subjects covered—all referrable to disability. This limitation is unfortunate since it presents the subject of disability divorced from the other life concerns of disabled but well adjusted persons. We know of no way out of this dilemma, except to point it out with emphasis.

The articles dealing with the psychology of disability are grouped as follows:
Section 7 Reactions to Severe Disability
Section 8 Mechanisms of Coping with Disability
Section 9 Body Image
Section 10 Sexuality
Section 11 Prevention of Disability

REACTIONS TO SEVERE DISABILITY

Each of the four articles in this section approaches the problem of trauma from a different point of view. Siller reviews a range of psychological reactions to traumatic injury and the way hospital personnel deal with it. He is clearly at home in his psycho-analytic theory. This aspect of his article should be of special interest to younger professionals who may believe that psychoanalysis is only of historical interest.

The next article attempts a developmental theory of the process of adjustment to disability. Cohn stipulates five stages: shock, expectancy of recovery, mourning, defense, and adjustment. This kind of thinking can be helpful in setting realistic expectations for severely disabled persons and avoiding unnecessary disappointments.

The brief paper by English is eclectic in style. It should remind us that the psychology of disability has borrowed generously and adapted much from the broad field of psychology—from Freud, Adler, Schilder, and numerous social psychologists. Preoccupation with specialization may obscure the basic ties to psychological science that makes reactions to disability comprehensible.

The last article of this section is an excellent summary of the issues relating personality theory to disability, with emphasis on the research support for the various theories. Shontz finds little support for characteristic reactions to amputation, blindness, and other specific disabilities. Thus, he puts to rest the notion that each type of disability generates identifiable personality reactions. He concludes also that individuals' reactions to disability bear no simple relation to severity of injury based on the evidence to hand.

Each of these four articles attempts to deal with reactions to trauma in a generic way, and in this respect differs from the mainstream literature of disability which discusses specific disabling conditions. There is a compelling need to break down these barriers and to determine the commonalities that would contribute to a broad-based psychology of traumatic disablement.

MECHANISMS OF COPING WITH DISABILITY

Despite the strain toward and utility of a limited number of principles with which to understand disability, experienced clinicians are ever ready to deal with exceptions to such principles and to confront individuality. Not every severely injured person goes through a period of depression. An early coping attitude of a patient is not necessarily denial nor a failure to fully grasp the seriousness of a drastically changed life.

In this section are a group of five articles on the longer-term reactions to disability and those referrable to individual life styles of the disabled. Here the focus is on the differences among disabled persons and on habituated ways of reacting that most students of the subject agree existed before disablement. A brief survey of these articles will illustrate the meaning of mechanisms of coping.

The first article, by Wright, elaborates on her concept of "spread," which she first discussed in *Physical Disability: A Psychological Approach* (1960). This concept is more commonly known in psychological literature as "the halo effect." However, I much prefer "spread" because it is neutral in value. Spread is the tendency of some perceived important characteristic of the self to influence the evaluation of other unrelated characteristics. For example, a popular actor or actress might give opinions on the causes of the economic depression, thereby showing that his or her superiority in acting has greatly influenced the self-estimate in other spheres. With respect to handicapped persons, such unjustified attributions tend toward the exaggeration of their deficits.

The next article, by Gray, Reinhardt, and Ward, discusses the factors making for successful rehabilitation of heart patients, but it has a broader based significance. Heart patients tend either to spread their impairment or to deny it, both of which impede rehabilitation. But once heart patients realistically accept their impairments, they recover at a rate comparable to others. The findings of this study may explain why psycho-social professionals have had relatively little contact with recovered heart patients; they are either back at their usual activities too soon (denial) or completely retired (spread).

Denial of impairment is not a univocal phenomenon. It may be stated directly by the patient, or it might be inferred from behavior. The varied forms in which denial is manifested are detailed in the article by Nathanson, Bergman, and Gordon and are the most useful aspect of it. The authors partly attribute denial to the intellectual deterioration resulting from brain damage. In the light of later studies, it is now known that some of the "organic" type behavior results from the shock effects of hospitalization in a large impersonal public institution, which was the locale of this study.

There are reasons other than spread and denial for unsuccessful rehabilitation. Some of these reasons are the secondary benefits of disability. Secondary benefits are the advantages that go with the disabled role not ordinarily enjoyed by the unimpaired. These advantages or benefits may be intra-psychic, as when a disabled middle-aged man is relieved of family responsibilities which he secretly resented. They may be related to the dynamics of family life where the wife, for instance, has gained some measure of independence not available before her husband's disability. Secondary benefits may be generated by the welfare and insurance systems, whose rewards are greatest for permanently disabled persons.

The psychological function of denial is not necessarily counter-productive. Denial may blend imperceptibly into hope, which can be motivating. The patient without hope may be quite realistic about his condition but be unable to project himself into a more promising future. In recounting his experiences in a Nazi concentration camp, Victor Frankl recalled the sustaining virtues of the denial of reality in extreme situations and of the capacity to project through imagery. In the context of hemodialysis patients, Short and Wilson see constructive roles for denial in facilitating coping in the patient while pointing out that members of the family and those attending the patient must admit the medical realities. The critical judgment of denial must be sought in its impact on the patient's daily activities. As Short and Wilson point out, denial can give coherence, purpose, and dignity to a person with a poor prognosis for recovery. More frequently, however, denial results in the patient's failure to engage in new learning and rehabilitation activities that would provide him or her with increased satisfactions. For this reason, rehabilitation personnel have assumed that denial is the enemy. The role of denial, hope, and faith as factors in recovery from disability has not been given the attention it deserves at the hands of psychologists. Is it more functional, for example, for the disabled person to recognize his reduced status in the eyes of others and to suffer the resulting pain, or is it more functional to deny this? The mechanistic trend in scientific psychology has ignored the notion that current behavior might be significantly influenced by man's capacity to project. This very belief is viewed by some psychologists as an obstacle to the development of scientific psychology.

The final article by Fogel and Rosillo demonstrates that measured intelligence is not related to physical rehabilitation. The inclusion of this article could provide the occasion for reflecting on the proper function of intelligence testing in the rehabilitation process. There are, of course, many appropriate uses of intelligence testing, as in vocational evaluation and planning and in the clinical assessment of unusual deficits. But as I scanned the many publications reporting test results on rehabilitation patients, I concluded that this one approach to assessment was over-used. In some settings, patients are routinely tested. It is regrettable that the short supply of psychological services is not used more diversely and imaginatively, e.g., in the direct observation of behavior on the ward, consulting with various personnel who have contact with the patient, speaking with members of the patient's family, and the evaluation of work capabilities through activities in work stations in the rehabilitation center. The modes of assessment suggested have a certain basic face validity. As psychologists gain more self-confidence in their scientific status, they will likely use a wider range of assessment procedures.

BODY IMAGE

Each of us takes his body and his relations to objects in the surrounding space so much for granted that it is difficult to visualize the consequences of disturbances in these areas. The personal picture of the body, its various organs, and their relations to the space about is called the body image or body schema. The physiological seat of the body image is the brain, and we might think of the brain as possessing traces that roughly parallel the subjective experiences of the body image. Injury may result either in a disturbance in the body image or the continuation of impressions of the body and spatial relations no longer corresponding to the changed states.

It would help to make the transition to body image problems of disabled persons to realize that there are many individuals whose assessments of their body parts deviate from reality. A very tall young man might think of himself as awkward, whereas others might view him as graceful. A pretty girl may think of herself as ordinary. In an extreme case, a disturbed person might believe that in the space occupied by the intestines, there is a radio receiver and sender. Less extreme deviations in the awareness of the organs are so common as to be everyday events. In the case of the psychiatric patient cited, there is a perceptual disturbance in the absence of any sensory or motor loss. There are various psychological theories which attempt to explain the discrepancies between the experienced body image and the organic state.

The disturbances in body image resulting from injury are the subject of Section 9. The article authors take a naturalistic viewpoint and avoid making psychopathological interpretations of the lack of correspondence between physical conditions and patients' reports of sensations. The phantom limb phenomenon was once thought to be a delusion. But now it is regarded as normal and reflecting the persistence of body schema in the brain—a phenomenon which usually disappears with time. Body image disturbances are becoming normalized in the light of an expanded knowledge of the subjective experiences of physically disabled persons. Evans' report was based on a study of the subjective reports of seven paraplegics, and he compares their experiences with those of amputees.

The article by Fink and Shontz continues the discussion and introduces the concept of substitute avenues to compensate for breaks in the sensory feedback loop. The paraplegic who examines the areas beneath a table in which to position his legs is engaged in visual feedback to compensate for loss of sensation.

The correct mapping of residual sensory and visual skill and potential compensations for losses are of importance in understanding what the person can and cannot perform. Such understanding is a practical help in relating to disabled persons and helping in their vocational rehabilitation. A practical illustration is presented in the last article of this section. Bardach examined the reasons why certain disabled persons had unusual difficulty in learning how to drive a car. She considered body image, perceptual motor skills, cognitive impairments, and emotional characteristics in accounting for the learning difficulties encountered.

Some rehabilitation personnel regard body image problems as engaging subjects of purely theoretical interest. While much remains to be discovered in this slowly developing field, there is already a body of knowledge with pragmatic implications, as the Bardach article demonstrates.

SEXUALITY

The articles on body image alerted us to the value of viewing disturbances in the body schema as naturalistic rather than pathological phenomena. The phantom limb need not be viewed as a weird experience but as normal to the physiological circumstances of amputees. Another way in which disabled persons are being normalized is through the sympathetic understanding of their sexual needs. Until recently, disabled persons were often regarded as unsexed creatures.

Personality and behavioral disruptions are usually associated with difficulties in obtaining sexual satisfaction. To the extent that sex involves sensitive adaptations to ambiguities between two persons, it is peculiarly vulnerable to disruptions among both non-disabled and disabled persons. Because disability is itself a major personality upheaval, we can expect that the capacity to cope in the sexual area would be affected.

The two articles in this section, the first by Diamond and the second by Singh and Magner, are major contributions to the subject of sex. Both are free of jargon and of the glamorization of sex. Diamond makes the point that talking about sex does not come naturally to many professionals. If the latter are to be successful helpers, they must have an appropriate philosophy of sexual satisfaction that goes beyond the belief that "the only satisfactory means of expressing oneself sexually and achieving satisfaction is with an erect penis in a well-lubricated vagina." While the Singh and Magner article deals with persons with spinal cord injuries, its generic implications are clear. Like Diamond, they too do not promise professionals instant success in helping disabled persons to enlightenment and sexual satisfaction. The specific knowledge they provide and the kinds of research they suggest indicate the value of specific techniques for helping disabled persons in this area.

The proliferating literature on sexuality in the United States makes one wonder whether we have moved from inhibition to total preoccupation. But surely one of the benefits might be to help professionals concerned with disabled persons move out of the era of silence on sex. The changing cultural climate is broadening the definition of sexual gratification and should have a constructive impact on both the surround and personal dynamics of handicapped persons.

PREVENTION OF DISABILITY

It seemed incomplete to write about disability without taking note of the fact that most disabilities are preventable. Yet, there is relatively little on this subject in psychological and rehabilitation journals.

Prevention could focus on accidents in factories, on highways, and in homes. Another aspect of prevention concerns the improvement of the delivery of medical services so that latent and incipient medical problems may be diagnosed early and treated. The prevention of cancer is an example. There is a prevention referrable to disabling conditions arising from stressful life styles, of which heart disease, stroke, and psychosomatic conditions are examples. Finally, we must mention the prevention achievable through improving the quality of the environment, particularly the air and water.

Stambler's article on coronary-prone persons is typical of the accumulating evidence that implicates heart disease with life styles and psychological factors. It is now possible to predict with some accuracy the probabilities of a person having a cardiac incident based on psychological information. The contribution of stress to creating disability and to enlarging its problems is the subject of the next article by Stubbins. Breakthroughs in genetics are now yielding practical results that are useful in the prevention of some types of disabilities. Swinyard's article on genetic counseling states that there are some 40 genetically determined disabilities.

The three articles of this section indicate the potentialities of prevention. The millions of newly disabled persons each year should not be thought of as victims of nature or a wrathful God. They are uniquely human failures. Knowledge and technology have reduced some types of disabilities, the most dramatic being those caused by infectious disease. Progress in prevention has occurred through the reduction of malnutrition, public health measures, industrial safety, and government regulation of the automobile industry. On the other hand, "progress" has increased many types of disabilities, for example, those resulting from the increased use of machine-driven appliances in the home and the abuse of alcohol and addictive drugs. People everywhere are much more open to the creature comforts produced by science and technology than they are to the education and wisdom necessary to live with them. It is easier to learn to drive a car than to become fully cognizant of its destructive potential.

As we observe the changes in the incidence of the sources of disability brought on by progress, we need no longer think of it as caused by God. Disability is, indeed, a creation of men and women. Nevertheless, the tendency among the majority is still to regard the happening of a severe injury or disabling disease as bad luck. Others consider disability as retribution for wrong-doing or as something wrought by an inscrutable fate. Perhaps that is why preventive programs have trouble gaining widespread support.

Before concluding this introduction to Part III, I am sharing my impressions of the numerous articles examined that did not find their way into this book. Many quality papers simply did not fit the purpose and scope of this book. As to the poor and mediocre ones, most suffered from *scientism*, that is, a blind faith in the value of data, the pursuit of scientific rituals, and an inhibition in the faculty of wisdom and judgment. Writers seemed unaware that the particular level of development of their subject was ill-suited to the scientific orthodoxy into which they boxed themselves.

It is unfortunate, too, that the literature tells us little about successful coping with disability based on persons with little or no contact with public agencies. Subjects discussed in the literature are heavily weighted on the side of the poor and those who tended to lack the psychological resources to overcome disability. We need more information about the many disabled persons who use little or no professional help and yet resume fulfilling lives. The study of such successes under naturalistic conditions could be as helpful as the insights from the psychopathology of coping. Abraham Maslow (1971) made a major contribution to psychology by introducing a similar dimension through his studies of self-actualized persons. By directing our energies to exploring the dynamics of successful adaptation, we might learn about the organic defenses of disabled persons under ordinary conditions of living.

REFERENCES

Maslow, A. 1971. The Farther Reaches of Human Nature. The Viking Press, New York.
Wright, B. 1960. Physical Disability: A Psychological Approach. Harper & Row, New York.

Section 7

REACTIONS TO SEVERE DISABILITY

28 Psychological Situation of the Disabled with Spinal Cord Injuries

Jerome Siller

I am always impressed with the contrast between the verbalization of the importance of a team approach and the actual operations in rehabilitation settings. One is reminded of a nursery school for two-year-olds where despite physical proximity everyone is busy with his independent play.

I think that the latent purpose of interprofessional meetings is to reduce our professional provincialism and to recognize that, like the four blind men with the elephant, we all have a piece of the action. My present objective is to sensitize others to issues that I, as a psychologist and psychoanalyst, believe to be of general importance.

Although cast as a survey of aspects of the psychosocial situation of a person with spinal cord injuries, many matters of concern to rehabilitation in general will be considered. It can be flatly asserted that the job of *properly* rehabilitating patients is impossible without giving full cognizance to the impelling psychosocial problems that they face. It is regrettable that treatment of persons with such conditions should have become fixed within an essentially medical rather than a more general rehabilitative mode because, except for the initial period and for the subsequent maintenance of good physical health, the predominant problems are emotional, interpersonal, functional, and vocational. Now, lest physicians and other directly medically involved persons become offended at this point, let it be understood that when the term *psychosocial* is used it does not refer to the activities and concern of any particular profession.

Referred to are the perceptions of the patient of himself and of his immediate and extended interpersonal environment, which should be understood and responded to by all personnel, professional and nonprofessional alike. This point should be stressed because, although specific specialists—psychologists, psychiatrists, social workers, rehabilitation counselors, and others—may enter at particular stages in terms of specific foci of their profession, *all* must consistently and responsibly attend to the particular needs of the person. This means that, even when conducting a procedure such as a physical therapy exercise,

Reprinted from Rehabilitation Literature, 1969, 30:290–296.

Part of the work underlying this article has been supported by research grants from the Division of Research and Demonstration Grants, Social and Rehabilitation Service, Department of Health, Education, and Welfare, Washington, D.C. The paper is an extension of presentations made at conferences at Hillside Hospital, Warren, Ohio, and the Woman's Christian Association Hospital of Jamestown, N.Y.

one's job is to respond to (treat) the person in the terms just noted.

I will be ranging over a wide variety of topics, hoping thereby to jog associations in the future. Thus, considered will be whether spinal cord damage has a unique effect on personality structure, immediate and long-term adjustment patterns to disablement, and psychological implications of losing a body part or function. This latter issue will be discussed in terms of mourning phenomena and related to early prosthetic fitting. The proposition is advanced that the focus in rehabilitation should lie in helping the person reconstitute his self-image in approving terms. Finally, staff reactions to patient needs are considered and a suggestion offered for the role of the professional in dealing with chronic conditions.

IS THERE A UNIQUE SPINAL CORD PERSONALITY?

Can one observe a unique constellation of personality characteristics that can be attributed to the consequence of spinal cord injury? In a word—no. As with all other disability groups, there is no direct relationship between type of physical condition and personality structure. The absence of such an inherent relationship will, of course, come as no surprise to those oriented toward the field of somatopsychology (1), where an important principle has long been that somatic abnormality as a physical fact is not linked in a direct and clear-cut way to psychological behavior. To put it in a deceptively simple way: Unlike the medical area

where one may for many purposes appropriately refer to specific diagnostic conditions, in psychology the proper emphasis is on the person rather than on the condition. Accordingly, physical injury is but another stress situation to which the person brings a repertoire of response patterns characteristic of him. Thus, all of our insights into the bases of human behavior are applicable. The more attuned we are to a psychological level of functioning and the more capable of sensing our own feelings in past stress situations, the better we are able to help our patients.

Although reaction to disability is idiosyncratic, a particular kind of condition, such as cord damage, restricts certain functions while leaving others untouched. It is feasible to isolate certain functional issues as being fairly specific to the condition and to look for personalized reactions to these common problems. Foremost among these problems are control of excretory functions, decubiti, sexual response, and severe mobility and muscular restrictions.

Highly charged self and social reactions are evident in relation to these difficulties. Taking excretory functions as an example, we find a highly irrational area, not just for persons with spinal cord damage, but for persons generally. Great privacy and elaborate rituals are set up around excretory functions. Strong infantile elements influence our behavior as adults, e.g., people giggle, make jokes, and otherwise show their tension and anxiety. When there is a distinct disturbance in this area the individual feels responsible, regardless of the physical facts, and much shame, guilt, and anxiety are aroused. Therefore, we not only must help the patient to overcome these unfortunate attitudes in himself, but also counter our own feelings in this regard.

Decubiti not only are medically serious but create strong aversive reactions on the part of viewers. The work of my research group clearly shows that sores and oozing ulcerous type conditions elicit some of the strongest aversive reactions shown to any disability (7). We, as well as others, have made the connection between surface sores and imputations of dirtiness, contagion, and venereal disease.

A tremendously important area of anxiety for those with spinal cord damage (as well as others) is sex. The physical question of "Can I perform sexually?" Is transformed for many males into the basic psychological problem of "Am I a man?" Observers have noted that feminization and passivity not infrequently occur among spinal cord damaged and other handicapped patients. Unchecked, these tendencies promote depression, low self-esteem, and other destructive reactions that undercut rehabilitation efforts. Technics that will be helpful to patients need to be worked out.

The severe mobility and muscular restrictions that are involved in cord damage can be brought up in a context that might be overlooked. Obviously, such a person is limited in the ways in which he can achieve most significant life goals (as being a father to a growing son, companion to a wife).

With the combination of sexual, muscular, and vocational problems, there is a resultant high rate of divorce among persons so traumatized. Not so apparent, perhaps, is the problem of expression of anger, particularly in those who are used to expressing it through physical means. Imagine, if possible, the situation of being so restricted motorically that one's muscular apparatus is substantially bypassed and the physical ability to relieve tensions is almost nil.

Ordinarily, when one has a "fight," it is possible to gesture, pace, stamp, throw something, or even walk out. These are all distinct, relatively socially feasible outlets. Walking out may prevent a lot of trouble. What happens when one can't readily walk out? Well, one might "swallow it," and "swallow it," and "swallow it," and many persons do just that. At times the satiation point for swallowing is reached and an eruption results. So, there may be an irascible, explosive quality associated with a person who has not had his characteristic opportunity to keep the general level of anger down by letting some of it be diffused through relieving physical movements.

IMMEDIATE REACTIONS TO TRAUMATIZATION

Some of the principal immediate reactions to physical traumatization are now briefly considered. Not knowing of any unique reactions that apply to spinal cord injuries in this respect, the following discussion may be taken to apply to severe disability of any origin. Clinically, the reactions of anxiety and depression are the foremost reactions to physical traumatization and usually are observed readily. On occasion these affects are displaced, delayed, or otherwise disguised so that the superficial clinical picture suggests their absence. Careful and more extended observation generally does reveal their operation. However, one should go beyond observing the obvious—that cord injury and amputation create anxiety and depression in the patient—and try to understand what a particular patient is anxious and depressed about. That is, what does his particular condition mean to him? What are his expectations for treatment, recovery, and future life? By joining the patient at a level of specificity of affective as well as cognitive functioning, we can accelerate the restitutive process.

Occasionally a newly disabled person does not seem to be particularly depressed, and this should be a matter of concern. In almost all instances something inappropriate is taking place. A person should be depressed because something significant has happened, and not to respond as such is denial. Such obvious denial is rare except in the case of a retarded person or in the very young. Mostly what is operating is a denial of functional loss or of the social implications—a denial that one's life likely will substantially change in important respects. Because denial goes in the face of reality, there can be negative repercussions since the patient is not making necessary adjustments to his situation. Denial can be useful as a temporary solution, as a transient or provisional form of adaptation, but it becomes a problem if it persists as an

important mechanism. Rehabilitation personnel will have much trouble trying to train and otherwise interact with a person who has a great deal of investment in denying the implications of what has happened to him.

There is one other immediate reaction to physical traumatization that will be stressed—that of grief and related mourning behavior. This is a crucial phenomenon in any kind of severe disability. One mourns a loved one who dies or who departs, and a period of time is needed until he can be worked out of our systems (withdrawing cathexes from the loved object). Meerloo (4, p. 214), in recounting his experiences at the end of World War II with concentration camp victims, indicates amazement and surprise that their most tragic complaint was "that they were not permitted to mourn over their dead. . . ." Similarly, loss of a body part or of an important function activates mourning reactions, and time also is needed to get over this kind of loss. Time, to a good extent, is the healer, and Freud (2) has brilliantly described this process when he defined the "work of mourning."

In this context the present trend toward early postoperative fitting of prosthetic devices as well as the increasing use of operant conditioning technics for modifying behavior might be examined. These devices are an effort to quicken the rehabilitation process as well as to make it more effective. While these procedures may be very effective in many respects, there is an inherent danger in intruding upon the usual vicissitudes of the mourning process. When this occurs people are not permitted to get a feeling of themselves in new terms and *at their own pace*. We may be missing the cue: "I'm overwhelmed; give me a chance to grab hold of myself before you ask so much of me." The rapid insertion of rehabilitative devices and technics undoubtedly can be functionally and psychologically highly constructive. However, I would suggest that we really don't know what we are doing. It is not enough to observe immediate successes because what we may have done is to reinforce patterns of denial that we share. What is jointly being denied is recognition that the experience of loss inevitably is accompanied by diminished self-regard and intrinsically intertwined with meanings dating from early childhood.

Instead, we try to be reasonable and to comprehend the emotional situation basically in terms of the reality of the loss. But as Rochlin (5) and others have noted, this attitude is misleading in that it could not possibly account for the "regularly observed responses of denial, increased egocentricity, hypochondriasis, and regularly altered relationships . . ." (5). The ties to the lost part or function are represented by hundreds of separate memories; for each of these memories, the dissolution of the tie is carried through separately, and this is what Freud meant by the concept of the "work of mourning." Working through the myriad of meanings that a part or function has for the person cannot be hurried, nor should it be, for the reaction of grief is adaptive in that it prevents the complete breakdown of the ego.

Does this mean that the affect associated with physical traumatization necessarily will be repressed for later emergence or displaced into other channels by early rehabilitation efforts? This need not be so if the specific efforts are based upon a conception of restitution that puts primary focus on emotional rather than just physical rehabilitation. Later, in discussing a conception of "Rehabilitation Focus," more will be said on this point. Right now, and speaking specifically to the issue of immediate prosthetic fitting, it can be reiterated that we really do not know what we are doing. There may be delayed effects one, two, and three years afterwards.

This is really a problem of empirical research, but I know of no sophisticated research as of this time. In the next few years we are likely to get some useful information on this problem. It is my guess that, as knowledge is systematized in regard to the psychological effects of immediate postoperative prosthetic fitting, it will be realized that, like all other promising panaceas, it will have to be individualized. One might expect that for some this procedure will offer the sufficient replacement for the lost part or function necessary for overcoming the melancholic reaction. For others the prosthetic manipulations will be false coin in that no substitute will be sufficient. For the vast majority of persons I predict that what will be done will be to leave the emotional experience unexplored and unresolved, and to reinforce instead the tranquilization and denial tendencies dominant in our society. As a nation we are anti-direct experience. We prefer to reduce and to blunt affect rather than to plumb its depths and emerge richer and more complex persons. Thus, although there is no intrinsic reason why sensitive handling of the early fitting procedure could not be beneficial to a large set of patients, it is doubtful whether this will happen. Instead, I gloomily foresee that the functional success of this .procedure will enable those rehabilitation personnel who prefer to bypass the emotional domain (and they are legion) to do so. Sets of statistics will be provided demonstrating the brilliant new ways of dealing with rehabilitation problems measured in such unimpeachable objective terms as length of time hospitalized and early job placement. (And those would be good criteria of success if they were supplemented by other criteria that are equally or even more relevant but which are more attuned to the subjective state of the individual.)

A false analogy might be made with those suffering from traumatic neuroses, as in combat situations, where the person has been overwhelmed by the total overstimulation of the situation to the point where the ego is in danger of being overwhelmed. Here replacement in the combat situation, or near it, can serve a distinctly therapeutic role in that one is responding to a discrete and focused threat. When physical traumatization occurs the threat is nowhere as delimited as with traumatic neuroses as the initial psychological trauma in the former becomes compounded by a complex of character, social, familial, vocational, and other variables. To judge the success of rehabilitation by whether one uses a prosthetic or whether employed or not is a gross oversimplification.

LONG-TERM REACTIONS TO TRAUMATIZATION

It would be desirable for persons who have gained their experience with the newly disabled to be exposed to persons with the same kinds of conditions 5, 10, and 20 years post-trauma. This would serve as a healthy corrective for overgeneralization for many. Reactions, central affects, attitudes, expectancies, life situations, and so on are so different as almost to suggest a different kind of psychological analysis. One might shift from a conception of trauma → anxiety → defense to more pervasive and less focalized characterological adjustment patterns. (I have suggested elsewhere that a similar sequence differentiates persons suffering from traumatic conditions from that of congenital origin (6).) It will be feasible to mention only a few long-term (or characterological) behavioral patterns, and discussion will be restricted to passivity, dependency, aggression, and compensation.

Passivity has been defined as a mode of adaptation to one's environment that involves going back from it (3). The opposite would be, of course, activity. In popular terms we talk of the passive person, the one who essentially waits for things to come to him rather than initiating action, responding to situations as they develop. For the disabled person this mechanism can be useful to the extent that it protects him from embarrassing situations. It can also be felt that "I'm not going to initiate action because I am afraid that I might fail. Rather than trying and finding out that this, too, I can't do, I would rather not try too much." So passivity can serve—some people are quite willing to survive on that basis.

We probably can agree that rehabilitation must respect such passivity, if the person can be offered nothing better. But with others who are resistant to treatment, resistant to doing better for themselves, we might have to overcome the passivity and be ready to assume the initiative. Inability to accept the responsibility for one's own rehabilitation should not be mistaken for unwillingness to be rehabilitated.

A very prominent form of adjustment is that of dependency. Dependency is not a phenomenon unique to disability, of course, but rather a basic condition of higher organisms. We all start out being dependent. Leave the one-week, one-month, or two-year-old child by himself and he won't survive. The same is true of animals. Residuals of this dependent condition exist in all of us. What we have done is to have resolved it more or less and in one way or another. Its developmental course has ramifications for all subsequent interpersonal relations. It governs the kind of person one marries, the ambitions one has for one's children, and the relations with one's boss. Spinal cord injury obviously imposes a state of actual dependency regardless of the particular manner in which one has resolved such matters in the past.

As clinicians it is our problem to comprehend sufficiently how the real restrictions of one's condition interacts with the particular manner in which one has passed from biological dependency to psychological dependency. The variety of ways in which spinal cord injuries, and for that matter any serious trauma, are absorbed into the ongoing dependency condition of the person is almost unlimited.

Let us consider briefly just two general possibilities—overdependence and underdependence (pseudoindependence). The overdependency phenomenon is characterized by such behavior as excessive questioning, fearfulness in trying things, looking for approval, self-derogation, need for proximity with personnel, inability to make decisions, and leaning on others. One might understand overdependency behavior as representing a sense of being overwhelmed by catastrophe, without hope of being able to grab hold of things, at least as yet.

For some such persons, temporarily relieving them of any sense of responsibility is a mercy that is completely justified. In time they can relinquish the dependency. What they need is time. For others the great moment has arrived. They have finally received natural dispensation from the burdens of being self-reliant and self-supporting. If we are not too imbued with the cultural values of achievement and independence, we might even be able to let these people alone and let them become rehabilitated on their own terms.

The pseudoindependent phenomenon can be seen behaviorily as expressed in obstinancy, inappropriate confidence, inability to accept appropriate offers of help, and unrealistic goal setting. It should be clear that these behaviors do not reflect successful long-term adaptive operations, although superficially they may appear to do so. It might seem that "This guy really has courage," but this form of adaption fails because too much of reality is denied to be sustained over an extensive period of time.

Since the phenomenon of secondary gain, a topic that might be seen as related to dependency, is well known, it will not be discussed here. Obviously, the secondary gains of the physical condition can be so enormous that rehabilitation in self-sustaining terms is prevented. The emotional blackmail that might be provided over members of the family is considerable. Considering the opportunities for special advantages, certain persons will hang on to their dependency and value it.

Aggression is another of the possible long-term adjustment patterns. Aggression as a reaction can be seen in many different forms. Of course the simplest and obvious form is striking out—directly assaulting someone physically—but this doesn't usually happen. For social reasons other means are generally used, e.g., "constructive" criticism of someone else's paper or style of dress. Thus verbal expression of aggression is frequent,

far outnumbering physical expression. Interestingly enough, the signs of aggression in patients (aggressive behavior, aggressive attitudes), while obnoxious to us as persons, may very well be indications that a person is fighting. He is trying. He hasn't given in; he has not come to the passivity mentioned earlier. Although it may be galling, one tries to refrain from counterhostility in the recognition that for the patient it might also be quite constructive. The prognosis may be better for such persons than for those who are more docile.

There is a different kind of aggressive behavior that is not as constructive and that is passive-aggressiveness. Passive-aggressive behavior takes such forms as not taking medicine when one is supposed to and misinterpreting what is said. Frequently the relationship is switched so that the person, rather than doing for himself, is doing for you. Hostility is expressed through spite and deviousness.

As the last pattern of adjustment, let us consider compensation. Although compensatory behavior might be thought of as a specific adaptive action, it is best considered as a more generalized orientation of the person whose purpose is to maintain feelings of significance and effectiveness. Compensatory behavior probably is one of the most frequent and most effective of the restitutive mechanisms. Although, as Alfred Adler has shown in great detail, compensation is defensive in origin in that it is rooted in an attempt to overcome feelings of inferiority, its effects are generally productive. Compensatory behavior becomes problematical mostly when it is overdone and leads to impoverishment in other aspects of functioning.

A STATEMENT OF REHABILITATION FOCUS

I will paraphrase to some extent a thesis advanced in another context (7). It is clear that an overriding problem for one who incurs a severe disability is the belief that life as known cannot continue. Among the nondisabled a primary reaction of many asked to contemplate the possibility of crippling is that they would rather be dead. Perhaps the fuller statement should be, "As a cripple I would no longer be my recognizable self and therefore I am horrified at the possibility of losing my ego. For all practical purposes I would then be dead, because the self that I know would not exist."

This has implications for where the focus of rehabilitation should lie. The aim is to assist the person toward reformulating a self that approves of continuing to be, despite important discontinuities with its past identity. Specifically, this means the promotion of a new self-image predicated on worth, rather than on deficiency and self-contempt. (Dembo and associates' analysis of enlarging the scope of values is most relevant here. See the discussion in Wright (8).)

The goal of rehabilitation therefore never changes—it is *always* directed toward promoting ego integrity and feelings of self-worth—but the specific operations of the rehabilita-

tion unit must constantly shift, being coordinated with the physical, psychological, and social realities of the rehabilitant. The danger arises when these operations are mistakenly identified as being the ultimate goal. Thus, one speaks of prosthetic rehabilitation, vocational rehabilitation, and so on, as entities real in themselves. It is my position that these are partial processes, the timing of which is governed by a strategy designed to foster the ego-integrative qualities of the rehabilitant.

This position might be made clearer by an illustration using functional effectiveness and independence training. It is natural for a person newly disabled to have great anxiety about the extent to which he will be functionally capable. Independence training in the early stages is most valuable as a prod toward the enhanced self-esteem necessary to undo the narcissistic insult generated by the disability. It is a misplaced emphasis, *at this point* in the rehabilitation regime, to be literally concerned about how well the patient is doing so far as specific functions are concerned. On the other hand, at a later point activities of daily living may very well be a specific focus and charts of progress and the like seriously attended to. Early rehabilitation should be directed to shaping basic life goals with later rehabilitation focused on providing the emotional, physical, and technical resources for their accomplishment. Foremost among early rehabilitation goals would be facilitation of a restitutive orientation so that recrystallization of the self is in terms of acceptance rather than hate. The direction of this recrystallization will be a major determinant of response to later specific rehabilitation procedures. Rejection of prosthetic restoration by certain amputees or of aids by the blind or deaf well illustrate the consequences of resolution of the self in the direction of hate. Aspects of this process have been discussed earlier in terms of a dichotomy organized around the concepts restitution versus avoidance of loss (6). Wright's (8) discussion of "coping-succumbing" in many respects describes the later stages of this process.

The nebulous phrase *acceptance of loss* might be defined in terms of the foregoing discussion as being the extent to which the reconstituted self is oriented toward self-approval (i.e., recovered from the narcissistic wound) and responsive to reality (i.e., relying on protective mechanisms that are essentially nonpathological).

Some of the above can be restated in more concrete and descriptive terms. Some persons are restitutively oriented following disablement, attempting to compensate for their condition. Others are not directed toward positive gratifications, seeking instead avoidance of the implications of their condition, and their primary motivation is to ward off anxiety, shame, and other noxious affects. This latter resolution is the basis for residual self-hate. Our job is to extend every aid possible to help the patient feel that he, as a personality, still continues. The obligation to give functional aid should be seen in the larger context of enhancing self-respect. Functional and physical progress therefore can be ef-fective as ego-builders, but functional efforts in early treatment should be seen as specific strategies designed to help the rehabilitant feel that such things are possible and thus serve as a promise for the future. One need not be overly concerned with graphs of achievement, although they can serve as objective cues of the rehabilitant's internal state. As indicated earlier, my fear is that emphasis on function serves as a ready way of avoiding the affective implications of disablement.

STAFF REACTIONS TO PATIENT NEEDS

A body of research literature is being built up demonstrating the importance of professional attitudes, social-religious-cultural background of the professional, and many other variables for treatment outcome. An early awareness of the importance of such factors was achieved by psychoanalysts in their extensive analyses of the phenomenon of countertransference, i.e., irrational feelings in the analyst (professional) activated by unconscious needs or conflicts in oneself. To illustrate counter-transference effects in the rehabilitation process, one might attend to common countertransference reactions to dependency in patients.

Whether dealing with overdependent or pseudoindependent patient resolutions, many patient-staff difficulties arise because of the professionals' own unresolved dependency needs. It is vitally important to examine our own attitudes in regard to achievement and independence. For example, one might consider the operation of reaction formations, wherein one must compulsively do the opposite of what one unconsciously desires. For people with this type of defense, independence, which is generally a culturally valued trait, might be serving an unconscious function as a defense against dependency. The diagnostic tip-off resides in the compulsive and uncompromising quality of the independence—no one need, or even dare to, help such a person. For staff members with such an adjustment to their own dependency needs, contact with patients who by disposition require a great deal of support and help cannot be tolerated and they are looked upon with contempt, labeled "babies," and treated disparagingly. I suspect that many professionals who are made anxious by their own dependencies either leave the area entirely or go on to administration, teaching, or research.

Unresolved conflicts of our own might, on the other hand, lead to permitting too much patient dependency, or even perhaps to preventing patient autonomy. This might be seen in highly authoritarian persons (or even settings) who are most comfortable when completely in charge of a situation. Even more important, I suspect, is the fact that such patients feed our sense of omnipotence. Isn't it seductive to be looked upon as having God-like qualities? (This idolatry becomes less palatable when one realizes the job requirements of God—one might then want to resign the post.) Overdependency might also be encouraged by those who feel guilty because they have personalized the gap that exists between patient expectation-fantasy and what they really can do. Then, of course, there is also the more idiosyncratically based sense of guilt, derived from some of the perverse occurrences that overtake people as they develop, which leads us constantly to do more than we really should do, which makes us accept responsibility that more properly resides in the patient.

THE ROLE OF
THE PROFESSIONAL
WITH CHRONIC CONDITIONS

It is my contention that the proper role of the physician, the psychologist, the nurse, and the physical therapist is as an assistant to the patient. We simply have too much professional conceit. While justified to some extent—we did go to school for many years and really do know a great deal—the working model of most rehabilitation settings seems inappropriately fixed in the acute medical situation. In such a setting, particularly when immediate emergency service is required, the passivity of the cadaver might be recommended and strong authority may have a place. But passivity and authoritarian direction are completely inappropriate for persons with chronic conditions. The principal investment must be theirs, and we should be ready to define our role as being secondary (which does *not* mean unimportant). To the extent that we abandon our own sense of omnipotence and see ourselves as being assistive personnel, we support the self-enhancement of the patient that was indicated earlier to be so necessary. It is well to face up to the reality not only that we cannot be with a person 24 hours a day but that this would probably be an unmitigated disaster that would serve only to perpetuate the patient's status as patient.

The trend toward the development of therapeutic communities and self-help procedures seems to be a promising one. Psychotherapy, particularly of the supportive sort, has an important role in the rehabilitation process. We are grossly negligent in discharging persons without adequate orientation as to reality problems generated by interaction with family and the community. Sensitivity trainings can be recommended. But, to conclude, regardless of the specific steps taken, basic changes are required in our orientation toward rehabilitation patients. The changes should be from the passive mode to the active mode for the patient and from the active mode to a more "passive" mode for the professional.

ACKNOWLEDGMENTS

The observations of the author's colleagues, Mrs. Linda T. Ferguson, Mr. Bert Holland, and Mr. Donald H. Vann, on this final paper, which is an extension of presentations made at conferences, are appreciated.

LIST OF REFERENCES

1. Barker, Roger G., in collaboration with Wright, Beatrice A., Meyerson, Lee, and Gonick, Mollie R. Adjustment to Physical Handicap and Illness: A Survey of the Social Psychology of Physique and Disability. New York: Social Science Research Council, 1953. (Bul. 55, rev. 1953).
2. Freud, Sigmund. Mourning and Melancholia, p. 243–258, in: Strachey, James, ed. The Complete Psychological Works of Sigmund Freud, Standard Edition. Vol. XIV. London: Hogarth Press, 1957.
3. Hinsie, Leland Earl, and Campbell, Robert Jean. Psychiatric Dictionary. (3rd ed.) New York: Oxford University Press, 1960.
4. Meerloo, Joost Abraham Maurits. The Two Faces of Man: Two Studies on the Sense of Time and on Ambivalence: New York: International Universities Press, 1954.
5. Rochlin, Gregory. Griefs and Discontents: The Forces of Change. Boston: Little, Brown and Co., 1965.
6. Siller, Jerome. Psychological Concomitants of Amputation in Children. Child Development. Mar., 1960. 31:1:109–120.
7. Siller, Jerome, and Chipman, Abram. Attitudes of the Nondisabled Toward the Physically Disabled. New York: New York University School of Education, 1967. (Final Report, VRA Project, RD-707, May, 1967)
8. Wright, Beatrice A. Physical Disability: A Psychological Approach. New York: Harper & Bros., 1960.

29 Understanding the Process of Adjustment to Disability

Nancy Kerr

Counselors working with the handicapped generally agree that there is a relationship between the patient's attitude toward his disability and the success of his physical or vocational rehabilitation. Disabled people who refuse to accept their impairment, or who are bitter, critical, and unmotivated, frustrate those who are trying to help and, in addition, fail to gain maximum benefit from rehabilitation services. Such people are not simply stubborn, ornery, or ungrateful. Rather, they are responding to some difficult reality situations created for them by the loss of parts or functions of their bodies.

Clearly, then, knowledge about the process of adjustment to loss is valuable not only to the counselor, but to all workers in the field. The concepts discussed here are empirically based on interview material obtained from orthopedic patients under treatment in a large rehabilitation center. Experience with these people indicates a remarkable similarity in their progressive changes in attitude and behavior.

It is convenient to talk about these changes in terms of stages of adjustment, if several restrictions are kept in mind: The stages are not discrete categories, but points on a continuum. There is no implication that the person mysteriously and inevitably evolves through a sequence of "stages." It is common, but by no means inevitable, for disabled persons to experience similar need conflicts and to be exposed to comparable environmental situations. Finally, this discussion refers to permanently disabled persons whose physical conditions are not likely to improve appreciably.

The stages of adjustment may be isolated and illustrated as follows:
1. Shock—"This isn't me."
2. Expectancy of Recovery—"I'm sick, but I'll get well."
3. Mourning—"All is lost."
4. Defense—A. (Healthy) "I'll go on in spite of it."

   B. (Neurotic) Marked use of de-

Reprinted from the Journal of Rehabilitation, 1961, 27(6):16–18.

This article placed second in NRA's 1961 Graduate Rehabilitation Literary Awards competition.

This investigation was carried out during the tenure of a Predoctoral Fellowship in Somatopsychology from the National Institute of Mental Health, United States Public Health Service.

The author wishes to express particular gratitude to Dr. Lee Meyerson, her advisor, whose excellent training made this paper possible.

fense mechanisms to deny the effects of the disability.

5. Adjustment—"It's different, but not 'bad.'"

SHOCK

Behavior

This stage is seen during the early diagnostic and treatment period. The person has not yet comprehended that his body is sick. Initially he may be so unaware of his physical condition that he fails to show any anxiety. For example, a young mother lying in the hospital with her body totally paralyzed was mildly amused when told the lab report had confirmed the diagnosis of polio. She said to a bystander, "They think I have polio! But they got the lab reports mixed up. I hope it doesn't take them long to correct the error, because I have to get home in time to feed the baby supper."

As reality becomes more inescapable, the reaction is, "This can't be me. It's all a bad dream; I'll wake up soon." Some people have described feeling numb or dazed.

Finally, the person is apt to blame the hospital and the people around him for his inability to function as usual. One woman became very irritated because they wouldn't let her out of her iron lung to keep a luncheon engagement. The feeling is, "If only I could get out of here, I'd be all right." The person doesn't realize that he needs the care he's getting in the hospital.

Psychological Situation

Psychologically, he is still a normal person. He is able-bodied and striving for the same goals and doing the same things he did yesterday. This "normal" life space may be diagrammed as follows [Figure 1]:

The incompatibility between the person's physical situation and the mental picture he holds of himself accounts for his inappropriate verbal behavior. Initially, his body image is more potent than his perceptions and he rejects perceptions incompatible with his self-image.

Conditions for Change

When the person almost inevitably tests reality and finds he can no longer function as he did previously, the psychological situation is restructured.

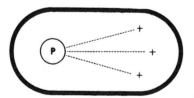

Figure 1. P, The person, with his needs and abilities. +, Positive goals or activities which the person values. For example, earning a living, being a good mother, building a radio. −, Path to goal.

The reality situation is so potent that "denial of illness" is recognized as clearly pathological, and few previously psychologically healthy individuals remain in this stage.

EXPECTANCY FOR RECOVERY

Behavior

Eventually the person realizes he is "sick," but he thinks he will soon get well. In the beginning of this stage he *knows* he will recover. He may say, "As soon as I get well," or "As soon as I get out of the hospital, I'm going to do such and such." The assumption of a normal body is implicit in any discussion of future plans. The only thing that is important is to get well. His search for a cure may lead him from one doctor to another. He is preoccupied with his physical condition and is apt to overestimate the meaning of any small improvement.

He is apt to relate stories of other people who had late and miraculous recoveries long after the doctors had given up hope. He will conclude such stories by saying, "I know it's going to take a long time, but I still haven't given up hope." Recovery is his only goal and he will be motivated to do any work perceived as aiding recovery; he will not be motivated to learn to function with his disability.

Psychological Situation

In the person's mind, and quite often in reality, too, the disability creates a barrier [Figure 2], cutting him off from everything that he considers worthwhile in life. So far as he can see, he needs a whole body in order to attain the goals he held as a normal person. It is therefore essential that he get well before he can do anything else.

Conditions for Change

Any stimulus condition that is more similar to "normal living" than to "being temporarily ill" may help to induce the next stage—mourning. Being transferred from the hospital ward to a more home-like unit of the rehab center, being sent home in a wheelchair, having therapy withdrawn or directed at teaching the person to function with a permanent disability, being told by the doctor that he won't get well—all these are associated with the start of mourning.

The shift from expectancy for recovery to mourning is essentially that of realizing the disability may be per-

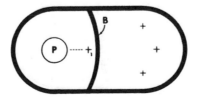

Figure 2. B, The barrier of disability, blocking the path to the goals the person had valued. +, Recovery, which the person feels he must attain before other goals are accessible.

manent. For many, this realization is too difficult to face. Putting the person in a therapeutic situation such as counseling, where he can have support and understanding when he "cries it out," may enable him to re-examine his feelings and move forward.

MOURNING

Behavior

The person is in acute distress. All is lost. He feels he can never attain any goals that are valuable to him. He is not motivated to cope with the disability in any way. He's ready to give up—and thoughts of suicide are not uncommon.

In situations where the person is severely reprimanded for "feeling sorry for himself," he may avoid talking about how he feels and display extreme hostility toward those who keep him from expressing himself. Then he becomes a "problem" patient who won't work and spends his time complaining about the hospital and its personnel.

Sometimes the person resigns himself to his fate and remains at this point. Such a person believes he is worthless and inadequate. He simply exists and remains dependent and, perhaps, hostile.

Psychological Situation

The picture is the same as that in expectancy for recovery, except that the goal of recovery is too unrealistic to hold, and now the barrier is impermeable and cannot be moved. [Figure 3.]

Conditions for Change

The person's psychological situation will change to the degree that the barrier of disability can be pushed back. Situations can be created artificially, if necessary, in which the person attains a goal that he held as a normal person. It should be emphasized that such activities as feeding and dressing were probably taken for granted before the disability occurred, and hence are often not positive goals for the adult.

It is common for the person in this stage to start mourning also the loss of some psychological characteristic in addition to his physical loss. Gradually the fact that he has lost his "fight," his pride, his faith, or his ability to cope with the situation distresses him more than the loss of the physical tool.

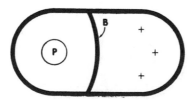

Figure 3. B, The barrier is perceived as nonpermeable, and therefore, nothing can be attained that is valued.

When this occurs, it is possible to put the person into situations in which he can learn that a disabled person can have "fight," be proud, have faith, etc. In this way, he begins to realize that the disability is irrelevant for the attainment of some of his more basic goals.

DEFENSIVE STAGE A: HEALTHY

Behavior

The person begins coping with the disability. He goes on in spite of it. He is motivated to learn to function as a disabled person, and will work at anything that will improve his physique. He is pleased with his accomplishments and takes an active interest in learning to be as normal as possible.

Psychological Situation

The psychological barrier of disability is being pushed back. Some goals held as a normal person are still accessible. The first goals attained are often little things: for example, a mother may be permitted to sit on the hospital lawn one balmy evening and rock her baby to sleep. From this she may learn that at least some experiences she treasured are still possible.

The barrier is still present, however—an enemy to be fought and conquered. In addition to the goals directly accessible, some may be reached by going around the barrier [Figure 4]. That is, the person may achieve a "normal" goal, such as preparing meals, by functioning in a disabled way, i.e., cooking from a wheelchair.

Other goals are still blocked completely and the person remains distressed by the areas he perceives as closed to him. The difference between healthy defenses and neurotic defenses is that, in the former, the person is very much aware that the partial barrier still exists.

Conditions for Change

1. From Defensive A to Defensive B: Probably the most potent environmental factor causing the person to adopt neurotic defenses is having those around him reinforce him highly for "looking on the bright side," for focusing on the attainable goals—and reprimanding him any time he starts feeling bad about the areas blocked by

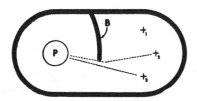

Figure 4. B, Partial barrier. $+_1$, Goal still blocked by the barrier, e.g., keeping house. $+_2$, Goal may be reached by functioning as a disabled person, e.g., cooking from a wheelchair. $+_3$, Goal is directly accessible, e.g., rocking the baby and enjoying a spring evening.

the barrier. This situation appears conducive to denying that any barrier exists.

2. From Defensive A to adjustment: A changed need system is necessary if one is to progress to adjustment. This may occur in one of two ways: In the simplest case, the need for a whole body is relinquished; the second way involves a more complex reorganization of the need system.

An example of the first process is illustrated by a man whose major goals were to earn an adequate income, marry and raise a family, and go hunting and fishing. He discovered all these goals were attainable. The disability was irrelevant and as a result the barrier was not felt to be present. He no longer felt a need for a whole body, since his more basic needs, goals, and values could be gratified or attained.

The second process must occur in cases where the physical impairment actually prohibits attainment of a major goal. It is assumed that the goal was held originally because it satisfied one or more needs. In order for the goal to be relinquished, the person must learn that there are other equally good ways of satisfying those needs. An example is that of a housewife who must relinquish the goal of keeping house and taking care of her children. This may have been her way of satisfying her need to be a good mother. However, in exploring the other characteristics of a good mother, she can learn that there are alternative ways to satisfy this need. For example, a good mother always has time to spend with her children, is interested in their trials

and victories, helps them with their homework, gives them love and emotional support. In fact, it is objectively possible for everyone to feel that these are more important characteristics of a good mother than ironing children's clothes and cooking their meals.

DEFENSIVE STAGE B: NEUROTIC

Behavior

The defensive stage may be considered neurotic if the person employs defense mechanisms to deny that the partial barrier still exists.

Diverse behavior may arise, depending on the particular defense mechanism employed. The person may try to conceal his disability. He may rationalize that he doesn't want the things he can't have. He may project his own negative feelings and complain, "I've accepted my disability . . . but no one else will." He may spend much time trying to convince others that he is well adjusted, and become greatly concerned if others do not see him as such.

Psychological Situation

This is basically the same as for Defensive A except that he denies the existence of the barrier.

Conditions for Change

It is not uncommon, even after several years of disability, for a person's defenses to fail under some additional stress. He may regress permanently to an earlier stage, or, after a temporary regression, he may progress to an adequate adjustment.

ADJUSTMENT

Behavior

The person who has made an adjustment to permanent physical impairment considers the disability as merely one of his many characteristics. Excerpts from an interview illustrate the part that disability plays in the life of such a person. The following comments were made in answer to an interviewer's questions by a man who had been confined to a wheelchair for four years:

> Oh, I guess there are some things I'd like to do and can't ... Well, I just hired the decorators to do some painting in the house. Now, if I weren't in a wheelchair, I'd like to do it myself. ... Oh, sure, I know I *could* do it now. In fact, you can do just about anything from a chair, if you want to bad enough. But it would take a lot more effort ... and I'm not *that* crazy about painting walls.
>
> I suppose the thing that bothers me most is these people who insist on giving me a pep talk—you know, 'Don't give up hope. Some day you'll walk again.' And then they try to get me to go

to some doctor they heard about. It's so hard to explain to them that it just doesn't make that much difference. Oh, sure, it would be nice to be able to walk ... but maybe I'm crazy or something. I'm happy.

Psychological Situation

The person is psychologically normal again. The disability is no longer a barrier to be fought. It is one of his characteristics and moves with him, along with his other assets and liabilities [Figure 5]. He has found satisfactory ways to satisfy his needs.

Conditions Necessary for Adjustment

There is a danger that one may assume that teaching a person to do everything he did prior to disability will automatically insure adjustment. It should be emphasized that there are at least two goals held by many people that are not necessarily attained when the person learns to "do things."

The first lies in the area of religion or philosophy. If the person has religious beliefs, and wants to be "right with God," he must feel that a disabled person *can* be right with God.

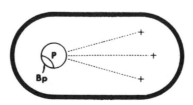

Figure 5. Bp, Disability-connected regions of the person which have been internalized as one of his characteristics.

The disability stands as a barrier between him and God as long as he feels a disabled person is being punished or that God will surely heal those who love Him.

Second is the goal of feeling that he is an adequate person. Normally, this goal is attained by reaching the more concrete goals of earning a living, etc. There is a common belief in our society, however, that a disabled person is automatically inferior. Regardless of his accomplishments, a person holding such a belief will consider himself inferior. One way of handling this problem is to create situations in which the person is forced to make the discrimination between adequate and inferior people on the basis of characteristics other than physique.

It is essential that the paths to these more "abstract" goals be structured if the person is to make a genuine adjustment.

30 The Application of Personality Theory to Explain Psychological Reactions to Physical Disability

R. William English

In spite of a considerable increase, in recent years, in efforts to research many areas of rehabilitation psychology, virtually nothing has been done to relate salient personality theories to a developing psychology of disability. Although a little is known as to "why" physically disabled persons react as they do to disablement (McDaniel, 1969), even less is known about "why" the physically disabled are stigmatized (Yuker, Block and Younng, 1966, and English, 1971).

In this sense, the paper that follows is something of a pioneering effort, where precedents are lacking. Because this is a theoretical study, the goal will be to develop a manuscript that is basically descriptive and hypothesis generating.

SALIENT THEORIES IN THE PSYCHOLOGY OF DISABILITY

Certain major theoretical principles and positions have obtained popularity in the psychology of chronic illness and disability and have more potential value than others. Occasionally these theories have been used to try and explain the impact of disablement on disabled persons per se; however, it seems possible to apply the same constructs to explain stigma. The theories that will be examined are: (1) Psychoanalytic Theory; (2) Individual Psychology; (3) Body Image Theory; and (4) Social Role Theory.

Psychoanalytic Theory

The earliest theory of personality which has applicability to explaining a psychology of disability is that of psychoanalytic theory developed by Sigmund Freud in the late 1800's and early 1900's. Freud conceptualized a duality of existence, where people are humans and animals. Within this model, he believed that people exist at different levels of growth and development, the lowest levels corresponding to the basic animal side of man. At lower maturational levels, psychoanalytic theory suggests that man operates in accordance with basic instinctual drives involving sex and security needs where only the fittest individuals survive. A central tenet of psychoanalytic theory seems to be that "competition" rules the lives of

Reprinted from Rehabilitation Research and Practice Review, 1971, 3(1): 35–41, 47.

men. Where there is little if any security, the struggle between men may be very physical, resulting in the death or injury of combatants. However, even when physical security is virtually assured, as has generally been the case since the industrial revolution, men continue to compete for "psychological superiority." Psychoanalytic theorists believe that most behavior is unconscious and that learned behavior occurs in the formative preschool years.

If this bird's eye view of psychoanalytic theory is applied to stigma, we might hypothesize that a nondisabled person who is prejudiced towards the disabled is a relatively immature individual with unexpressed hostilities and a need to feel psychologically superior. In terms of the disabled themselves, psychoanalytic theorists would believe that disablement almost always has an adverse effect on personality, especially if it occurs in early childhood. They are likely to be immature and passive-aggressive types. Persons disabled after school begins probably would not experience any substantial change in personality, according to psychoanalytic thinking.

Individual Psychology

A neo-psychoanalytic theory of personality which is often mentioned by students of disability is termed "individual psychology." Its author was Alfred Adler (1927), who studied psychiatry with Freud after practicing ophthalmology and general medicine in Vienna. Adler's personality theory departed from Freud's psychoanalytic theory in its emphasis on social motivation and individuality, rather than sexual impulses.

The most relevant of Adler's constructs that relate to the stigmatization of the physically disabled are "striving for superiority," "inferiority," "compensation" and the idea of the "life style." Adler believed that all people possess an innate drive to strive for superiority. He felt this drive evolved into a pattern or life style from early childhood and that it was motivated to compensate for certain innate feelings of inferiority. Stigma, in the view of individual psychology, is part of the life style to achieve superiority—even at others' expense—by nondisabled persons.

Proponents of individual psychology believe that physically disabled persons attempt to compensate for a defective organ by strengthening it. In their view, physical or mental deformities are principal causes of a "faulty" life style. Individual psychology theorists probably believe there is a higher incidence of emotional disturbance among the disabled than the nondisabled (McDaniel, 1969).

Body Image Theory

Another neo-psychoanalytic system prominent in explaining the psychology of disability is "body image theory." The idea of the body image and its disruption due to chronic illness and physical disability has become nearly as popular a construct among rehabilitation practitioners as the construct of "inferiority" (McDaniel, 1969).

The individual who has contributed more than anyone else to body image theory is Paul Schilder (1950), as far back as 1935. Schilder and others believe that people respond to each other substantially in terms of nonverbal and physical cues and images.

Followers of Gestalt Psychology believe that, over time, most people have come to recognize that there is frequently an inconsistency between verbal and cognitive behavior and nonverbal body behavior (Kohler, 1947). This aspect of our humanness seems recognized both within ourselves and in others. To illustrate, we know there are times we have told companions we are very satisfied while at the exact same moment our gestures and expressions communicated something else. As an aside, it is interesting to note that frequently we are less sensitive to our own incongruence than are others. Based on self-perceptions, it is usually the rule that we place most of our faith in what we see and not what we hear.

Related to this, body image theorists believe that the attitudes individuals have towards themselves and others is viewed as being shaped substantially in terms of their perceptions about physique. Although it is somewhat oversimplified, "body image" can be viewed as a construct existing on a continuum, where those who are most acceptant of their own bodies will be most acceptant of the bodies of others and vice versa.

Theoretically, the construct "body image" is of course closely related to that of the "self-concept," although proponents of Body Image Theory believe they are not equivalent concepts, but, rather, that body perceptions reflect generalized feelings of self (Wapner and Werner, 1965). In Freud's early writings he argued that the body image is closely related to the development of the ego. Freud thought the self-core followed first and foremost from a body ego, that the ego is derived from bodily sensations which can be thought of as a mental projection of the surface of the body (Fisher and Cleveland, 1968).

Many body image theorists believe that body attitudes are often the result and reflection of interpersonal relationships. Cleveland (1960) discovered that body attitudes appear to change during psychotherapy, and Popper (1957) showed that body images are differentially affected by previous success and failure experiences. In related research, Cleveland and Fisher (1965) have observed that body feelings are often correlated with various personality measures. Abel (1953) discovered that more severely facially disfigured persons make more distorted figure drawings. Abel's (1953) findings, however, are contradicted by a study by Silverstein and Robinson (1956), who found that judges were unable to distinguish between the self figure drawings of paralytic and normal children.

Some objective data has come forth with regard to persons' objective body image, that is, how they are viewed by others, and attitudes towards physically disabled persons. In one study, English and Oberle (1971) had psychiatrists identify the extremes in occupational groups believed to employ women with a high and low emphasis on physique. Using the Attitude Towards Disabled Persons Scale, they found that the high physique group, airline stewardesses, were significantly more rejecting of disabled persons than the low physique group, typists. In another study, Witkin, Lewis, Hertzman, Machover, Meissner and Wapner (1954) demonstrated fairly convincingly that body image is important in determining perceptual functioning. They observed that persons who produced more field dependent figure drawings reflected a lower evaluation or confidence in their own bodies, whereas persons who drew less field dependent figures had more self-body confidence.

Social Role Theory

A relatively recent trend of thought which is valuable to the study of psychological responses to disability and rehabilitation is social role theory. The major contributor in this area has been Talcott Parsons, a sociologist (1951 and 1958).

A basic construct in role theory is that of a "status" which is simply a collection of rights and duties (Linton, 1936). A role represents the dynamic aspect of a status where individuals put the rights and duties which constitute a particular status into effect. Obviously roles and statuses are quite interdependent, there being no statuses without roles or roles without statuses (Davis, 1949, and Gordon, 1966).

The basic notion underlying Role Theory is that people interact according to learned expectations of behav-

ior. This represents the individualized side of Role Theory which is of greatest interest to psychologists, counselors and other students of disability. Whereas the rights and duties attributed to statuses are generally well understood, role expectations are not as well understood. This seems attributable to the fact that there are many more roles than statuses to learn and that people are exposed to differential socialization experiences for role learning.

The fact that individuals enact roles in different ways is not completely understood but seems attributable to a number of factors: First is that people are exposed to an unequal number of roles, which influences the knowledge of role expectations; Second, people learn role expectations with a relative degree of accuracy, depending primarily on the relative teaching abilities of significant role models; Third, people possess differential role taking skills, dependent on learning and heredity and constitution; Finally, role enactment is influenced by unknown factors, "X" if you will, such as motivation or personality.

Related to successful role enactment is the concept of role reciprocity (Sarbin, 1954). This is the construct that every role is closely interwoven with one or more others, e.g., girl-woman, father-son, winner-loser, and so on. It is believed therefore that people must understand role reciprocity if they are to accurately act out individual roles. In a general frame of reference, it might be argued that the most successful people in life are those who accurately know the expectations for the greatest number of roles, have the most outstanding role skills, and the greatest drive to engage in role taking activities.

In terms of disability, it has been hypothesized that persons primarily enact roles according to their expectations, or role set, for and about the so-called "sick-role" (Gordon, 1966). Parsons (1951) believed that Role Theory affords an ideal model for evaluating the reciprocal interaction of disabled and nondisabled persons. In Parson's view, the major dyadic relationships influencing disability roles are between the physician and the patient and the patient and his family. Parsons (1951) goes on to state that these relationships must be viewed in terms of four behavioral presumptions of the sick role. First is the presumption that sick persons are exempt from social responsibility. Second is the presumption that the sick person cannot be expected to take care of himself. Illness or disability produces incapacity and consequently limits or inhibits the performance of routine duties. In this sense the sick person is viewed as incompetent, and not accountable for his actions. That is, he is in a condition that must be cared for. Parson's third behavioral presumption is that sick persons should wish to get well because health is viewed as necessary for the optimal performance of most important life tasks. Fourth, there is the presumption that society demands that sick persons should seek medical advice and cooperate with medical experts.

A psychological construct that is closely related to Parson's behavioral presumptions about the sick role is that of "the requirement of mourning" developed by Barker, Wright, and Gonick (1946) and Wright (1955). They feel that there is an expectation or demand made on disabled persons to act sick, like it or not, for a time following disablement. This expectation, to be depressed over his loss of functionality and to brood or mourn, is believed to be almost universally imposed on the disabled person. The role demands represented by the "requirement of mourning" can be considered to be infectious and applicable to nearly all disabled and nondisabled persons. On the part of the disabled persons, mourning has frequently been observed, especially closely after disablement, along with such related affective dimensions as self-devaluation and spread or the generalization of dysfunctional anxiety (Wright, 1960). Significant others, that is, those persons who are closest to and psychologically most important to the disabled, also experience the "mourning" response in what can be viewed as a sympathetic response due to a case of overidentification with the disabled person. Finally, some nondisabled persons who are not significant others— they may, in fact, not even personally know the disabled person—may require the disabled individual to mourn his loss because they are personally threatened by the person's medical condition or have a pathological need to feel psychologically superior.

In addition to the statements already made, Role Theory can be extended still further to explain the psychological impact of disability on so-called disabled and nondisabled individuals. In terms of the disabled themselves, it has been hypothesized that the response to disablement is quite individualized (Gordon, 1966). It has further been hypothesized (Parsons, 1958) that illness or disability disrupts established role patterns and leads to a reorganization of roles, which is also applicable to rehabilitation treatment or service which is designed to restore or maximize the person's ability to enact roles appropriately. These hypotheses have all been studied to some extent and are generally supported by research findings (McDaniel, 1969, and Wright, 1960).

As might be anticipated, given the embryonic development of a psychology of disability, not all hypotheses put forth by role theorists have been supported by research findings. For example, Parsons (1958) predicted that the severity of disability or illness would be directly related to the degree of individual psychopathology expressed by a disabled person. The conclusions of English (1968), McDaniel (1969) and Wright (1960), who have all written extended literature reviews on this topic, dispute this hypothesis.

Apart from those hypotheses, derived from Role Theory, which have or have not found support, there are many which apply to both the reciprocal disabled and nondisabled actors which simply have not been researched sufficiently to allow for definitive conclusions. It is assumed, for example, that disablement promotes a higher incidence of role conflict among the disabled and the nondisabled with whom they interact. The disabled, for exam-

ple, are believed to be placed in the ambiguous situation of having to choose between acting "as if" they were healthy or sick, and the nondisabled encounter similar problems in wrestling with the question of how to treat the so-called disabled person. Related to this, it is believed, without substantiation as yet, that much of the negative interaction that has been observed as taking place between disabled and nondisabled persons, after traumatic disablement, can be ascribed to uncertainty about what are appropriate role expectations and role enactments. Theoretically, again this hypothesis has yet to be adequately tested; this explains why the disabled and nondisabled have unsatisfactory interactions and why the disabled promote "prejudice by invitation" and why the nondisabled inadvertently stigmatize the disabled (Wright, 1960). As a final example, more research needs to be forthcoming with regard to the concept of "stigma by association." This refers to the notion, developed by Olshansky (1965), that nondisabled persons—especially nonfamily members such as counselors or teachers—are often themselves victims of prejudice and devalued simply because of their interaction with the disabled.

OVERVIEW

Up to this point, the focus of this article has been on presenting in rather straight-forward terms the relative merits of four prominent and, I believe, promising personality theories as they apply to a psychology of disabil-

Table 1. The effect of heredity and early childhood on the psychological adjustment of the physically disabled

Personality theories	(1) Heredity influences the psychological adjustment of the physically disabled	(2) Early childhood education influences the psychological adjustment of the physically disabled
Psychoanalytic theory	Very definitely	Very definitely
Individual psychology	Very definitely	Very definitely
Body image theory	Definitely	Definitely
Role theory	Slightly or not at all	Somewhat

ity. At this juncture, all the theories will be cast into a common conceptual model and briefly analyzed. The article will end after some succinct concluding remarks.

In Table 1, the relative effects of two etiological conditions are considered, within the framework of four personality theories, as they apply to the psychological adjustment of the physically disabled. The subjective judgments that are made are solely those of the author. Evaluations made involved analysis on a five point scale: very definitely; definitely; probably; somewhat; and slightly or not at all.

The theoretical data contained in Table 1 suggest that heredity and early childhood are believed to be very critical factors, influencing the psychological adjustment of physically disabled persons, by psychoanalytic theorists and Adlerians, while Body Theorists believe they are only critical and Role Theorists believe they are relatively inconsequential.

Conceptually these differences reflect the basic character of these theories. That is, they range on a continuum from the most pure psychological theory (psychoanalytic) to refined psychological theories (individual psychology and body image theory) to one of the most pure of sociological theories (role theory). These differences are, of course, only logical, given their historical origins. Considering that Freud and his protege Adler were medical men most active around the turn of the twentieth century, it is hardly surprising that they developed basically psychogenic theories of personality. In related fashion, Body Image Theory and Role Theory reflect the times in which they were written as well as the backgrounds of their major protagonists. Most body theorists have been psychologists, and nearly all of their work has been done since 1930. Most role theorists are sociologists or social-psychologists, and nearly all of their work is post World War II.

REFERENCES

Abel, T. A. Figure drawing and facial disfigurement. American Journal of Orthopsychiatry, 1954, 23, 253–264.
Adler, A. The practice and theory of

individual psychology. New York: Harcourt-Brace, 1927.

Barker, R., Wright, B. & Gonick, M. Adjustment to physical handicaps and illness: A survey of the social psychology of physique and disability. New York: Social Science Research Council, 1946.

Cleveland, S. E. Body image changes associated with personality reorganization. Journal of Consulting Psychology, 1960, 24, 256–261.

Davis, K. Human society. New York: MacMillan Co., 1949.

English, R. W. Assessment of change in the personal-social self-perceptions of vocational rehabilitation clients. Unpublished doctoral dissertation, University of Wisconsin, Madison, 1968.

_____ Correlates of stigma towards physically disabled persons. Rehabilitation Research and Practice Review (Accepted for publication, Fall, 1971).

_____ & Oberle, J. B. Toward the development of new methodology for examining attitudes toward disabled persons. Rehabilitation Counseling Bulletin 1971, 15 (2), 88–96.

Fisher, S., & Cleveland, S. E. Body image and personality. New York: Dover Publications, Inc., 1968.

Gordon, G. Role theory and illness. New Haven, Conn.: College and University Press Services, Inc., 1966.

Hall, C. S. & Lindzey, G. Theories of personality. New York: John Wiley and Sons, 1957.

Kohler, W. Gestalt psychology. New York: Mentor, 1947.

Linton, R. The study of man. New York: Appleton-Century-Crofts Co., 1936, pp. 113–114.

McDaniel, J. W. Physical disability and human behavior. New York: Pergamon Press, 1969.

Olshansky, S. S. Stigma: Its meaning and some of its problems for vocational rehabilitation agencies. Rehabilitation Literature, 1965, 26, 71–74.

Parsons, T. The social system. Glencoe, Illinois: The Free Press, 1951.

_____ Definitions of health and illness in the light of American values and social structure. In E. G. Jaco (Ed.) Patients, physicians and illness. Glencoe, Illinois: The Free Press, 1958. Chapter 20, pp. 165–187.

Popper, J.M. Motivational and social factors in children's perception of height. Doctoral dissertation, Stanford University. Palo Alto, California, 1957.

Sarbin, T. R. Role theory. In G. Lindzey (Ed.) Handbook of social psychology. Cambridge, Massachusetts: Addison-Wesley Publishing Co., 1954, p. 223.

Schilder, P. The image and appearance of the human body. New York: John Wiley and Sons, 1950.

Silverstein, A. B. & Robinson, H. A. The representation of orthopedic disability in children's figure drawings. Journal of Consulting Psychology, 1956, 20, 333.

Wapner, S. & Werner, H. (Ed.) The body percept. New York: Random House, 1965.

Witkin, H. A., Lewis, H. B., Hertzman, M., Machover, K., Meissner, P. B. & Wapner, S. Personality through perception. New York: Harper and Row, 1954.

Wright, B. Physical disability: A psychological approach. New York: Harper and Row, 1960.

_____ The period of mourning in chronic illness. In R. Harrower (Ed.) Medical and psychological teamwork in the care of the chronically ill. Springfield, Illinois: Thomas, 1955.

Yuker, H. E., Block, J. R. & Younng, J. H. The measurement of attitudes toward disabled persons. Human Resources Center, Albertson, New York, 1966.

31 Physical Disability and Personality:

Theory and Recent Research

Franklin C. Shontz

This survey agrees with previous studies of the literature by others, in that it discloses no evidence to support the hypothesis that many forms of somatic disability are associated with particular forms of personality or the hypothesis that the extent of the psychological effects of disability are proportional to the severity of the disability. Theoretical alternatives are available, but are infrequently applied in research. Basic personality structure appears to be stable even when somatic change is severe. Absence of anxiety is usually interpreted as evidence of denial, but it may be a sign of good and realistic adjustment in many cases. Negative emotional experiences are associated with improvement in somatic status as well as with the onset of disability or disease; the crucial factor seems to be change in an enduring somatic state, rather than illness or health, *per se.* Future research should focus on relations among psychological variables, naturalistic observations, and experimental rather than purely descriptive techniques.

Opinion about the relationship between disability and personality has generally reflected uncritical acceptance of two assumptions. The first assumption is that specific forms of somatic disorder commonly are associated with specific types of personality. The second is that some types or degrees of disability constitute sufficient causes of psychological maladjustment.

Psychologists with an objective interest in the study of disability and personality have expended a good deal of effort to assess the merits of these entrenched and appealing notions. It is not generally realized how firmly and with what consistency the notions have been discredited by the evidence.

The first comprehensive reviews were published by Barker, Wright & Gonick in 1946 and by Barker, Wright, Meyerson & Gonick in 1953. These monographs (especially the 1953 revision) surveyed the available psychological literature, supplied critiques of research, and summarized findings to date. In her later book on the psychology of disability, Beatrice A. Wright (1960) credited these sources for her conclusions that there is no evidence that particular personality characteristics are associated with particular disabilities or that severity of disability is correlated with level of psychological adjustment. (No authority claims that disability never affects personality; individual reactions frequently are profound and intense. What is denied is

Reprinted from Psychological Aspects of Disability, 1970, 17(2):51–69. Copyright 1970, Psychological Aspects of Disability (formerly Rehabilitation Psychology).

the systematic and universal correlation of type or degree of disability with type or degree of personality adjustment.)

Disenchantment with the two hypotheses was not confined to those who dealt broadly with the issues. It was evident in the writings of experts on particular disabilities as well. Specific personality characteristics were not found to be associated with paraplegia (Berger, 1953), amputation (Fishman, 1962), epilepsy (Tizard, 1962), tuberculosis (Harris, 1953), or coronary heart disease (Whitehouse, 1962; Mordkoff & Parsons, 1967). Even when authorities claimed some degree of similarity of personality in persons with a particular form of disability, they carefully qualified their claims by noting that reactions are by no means identical, individual differences are marked, and maladjustment is far from universal.

What has been uniformly regarded as crucial is the personal meaning of his disability to each individual client. Such conclusions have been drawn for patients with ophthalmic conditions (Young, 1953), for the deaf (Levine, 1953, 1962) and hard of hearing (Lane, 1953), for patients with facial disfigurement (Abel, 1953; Madan, 1962), for the blind (Lowenfeld, 1953; Raskin, 1962), for patients with cerebral palsy (Garrett, 1953; Allen, 1962), poliomyelitis (Seidenfeld, 1953), multiple sclerosis (Harrower, 1953), cancer (Cobb, 1962), rheumatoid arthritis (Seidenfeld, 1962), language disorders (Wepman, 1962) and hemiplegia (Diller, 1962), and for exceptional children in general (Kaplan and Lotsof, 1968; Pringle, 1964). Virtually all these authors have cautioned that psychological treatment must be directed toward individual situations and reactions rather than toward psychological processes that can be assumed to be constant from patient to patient.

The negative character of disability effects. Physical disability is commonly supposed to inflict only negative, disruptive, and disturbing psychological consequences. Wright (1960) has pointed out, however, that disability may generate opportunities and gratifications as well as frustrations and grievances. In an analysis of the contents of 31 first person accounts of disability experiences, Shontz (unpublished) found that statements describing satisfactions occurred slightly more frequently than statements describing dissatisfactions. Wright and Schontz (1968) have shown how hope exerts a strong counterforce against despair. Such positive phenomena are all but ignored in most studies of the psychological aspects of disability.

THEORETICAL ALTERNATIVES

Fault-finding alone does not solve the theoretical problem. Discredited hypotheses must be replaced eventually by more attractive possibilities. Several such possibilities have been proposed. Some of these are considered briefly in the following discussion.

Interpersonal Theory

Probably the best developed theoretical ideas are those that have grown out of the work of Barker and his colleagues (Barker, Wright, & Gonick, 1946; Barker, Wright, Meyerson, & Gonick, 1953; Meyerson, 1955; Dembo, Leviton, & Wright, 1953; 1956; Barker & Wright, 1953; Wright, 1960). These theorists regard the body as a value-impregnated stimulus to the self and others. They trace the self concept and personal values back to a primary source in interpersonal relations, particularly to evaluations by others. This group of theorists has generated and applied a number of useful descriptive concepts, such as spread, value loss, containment of disability effects, comparative and asset values, expectation discrepancy, new and overlapping situations.

Body Image Theory

Typically, body image theory applies psychoanalytic or psychoanalytically-derived principles to explain the development in each individual of a conception of and set of attitudes toward himself as a bodily entity (Schilder, 1935; Frank, 1959; Menninger, 1953; Fisher and Cleveland, 1968). The oral, anal, phallic, latency, and genital stages of psycho-sexual development work their effects through the body image, and it is by way of the body image that castration anxiety, arising initially during the Oedipal conflict, influences personality in persons with physical disabilities (Murphy, 1957).

The concept of the body image is not specific to the explanation of disability effects, but it serves a useful purpose by enabling practitioners in rehabilitation to express in a few words the nature of a client's difficulties and by providing a rational basis for making decisions about treatment (Shontz, 1969).

Motivation Theories

Maslow's (1954) theory of motivation has led to the distinction between lower level (hygiene or security) needs for physiological satisfactions and safety, and higher level (growth) needs for interpersonal gratifications and self esteem. Motivational distinctions such as those proposed by Maslow are implied in discussions of disability reactions by Shontz (1962) and by Shontz, Fink, and Hallenbeck (1960). Barry and Malinovsky (1965) used Maslow's theory for organizing their comprehensive review of the literature on client motivation. Patterson (1964) expressed a preference for a unitary theory of motivation in the counseling situation. For Patterson, the unitary motive is self-actualization, a term used by Goldstein (1959) as well as by Maslow.

Keith (1968) called for greater emphasis on autonomous activity in theories of motivation in rehabilitation. He objected to the assumption that disability is equivalent to illness and that the proper role for the person with a disability is therefore the sick role (Parsons, 1954; Parsons and Fox, 1952) in which dependency and childlike behavior are expected and fostered by the environment.

McDaniel (1969) has suggested that the concept of achievement motivation (Atkinson and Feather, 1966) might be useful in rehabilitation, especially in work-oriented settings.

Attitudes Toward Disability

The idea that attitudes of others affect attitudes toward self is succinctly expressed by Siller, Chipman, Ferguson and Vann (1967):

> A person with a handicap reflects prevalent social attitudes of self-depreciation and self-hate. In the newly disabled, on the other hand, negative attitudes previously focused on members of a devalued outgroup may refocus on the self with devastating results.

The interests of many investigators have been directed most clearly toward attitudes held by the nondisabled (Kleck, 1966; Yuker, et al., 1960; 1966; Wright, 1968). However, MacDonald and Hall (1969) have correctly pointed out that evidence of consistency in attitudes of others toward people with disabilities does not tell what the attitudes of the disabled themselves are. Nor does knowledge that a person holds certain attitudes toward disability prove that these attitudes would determine his reaction to personal disability. The study of devaluating attitudes toward disability is important in its own right, but it does not tell the whole story of disability and personality.

Crisis Theory

Several authors have expressed the view that disability may be considered a crisis-inducing event. Davis (1963), Cohn (1961), and Fink (1967) have provided analyses of the crisis experience into stages (e.g., shock, defensive retreat, acknowledgment, and adaptation—Fink, 1967). Fink tied his analysis to motivational theory by specifying that the early stages of reaction involve primarily security needs, while the last stage is growth oriented and can result in increased self actualization. Shontz (1965) simplified the analysis by describing the adjustment process as a succession of approach-avoidance cycles. In the early stages of reaction, these cycles recur rapidly and reach high levels of emotional intensity. With time, a dampening process reduces both their frequency and intensity until, in adjustment, the cyclical nature of the process becomes virtually unnoticeable.

Crisis theory is not fully developed. It needs more careful and elaborate delineation of the stages of reaction and ways to determine, in individual cases, where the client is in the process of adjustment and how he can be best helped through it.

Miscellaneous Specific Proposals

Comparison Level The comparison level (CL) is the level of payoff or reinforcement a person experiences as neutral in value, i.e., as appropriate and reasonable. Outcomes exceeding the CL are experienced as good and satisfying. Outcomes below the CL are experienced as bad and dissatisfying (Thibault and Kelley, 1959). In disability, mourning occurs when outcomes drop below the CL. If the CL changes appropriately, or if outcomes return to their previous level (e.g., as a result of rehabilitation) adaptation takes place and mourning ceases. If outcomes are not grossly affected by disability, or if the CL was chronically below outcome level before disability (if the person always underestimated his own potential) mourning does not occur at all (Kelley, Hatsorf, Jones, Thibault & Usdane, 1960).

Comparison level theory points out that adjustment is a joint function of the actual situation (outcomes) and the way in which the situation is experienced (CL). Unfortunately, few investigators have used comparison level theory in actual research on personality and disability.

Stress Cowen (1960) suggested that recent research on psychological stress might provide leads that would enable us to understand reactions to disability. Unfortunately, again, little seems to have come of this suggestion. Perhaps this is partly because adequate summaries of the complex literature on the subject of stress have not been available until recently (Appley and Trumbull, 1967; Lazarus, 1966). Certainly, no coherent psychological theory of stress response existed before Lazarus' book appeared. Perhaps the future will see a more significant application of stress theory to the explanation of relations between disability and personality.

Traditional Theories of Personality Few traditional theories of personality have had much to say specifically about the impact of physical disability. Adlerian theory is most explicit, because Adler was concerned about the person's attempts to compensate for somatic defect (organ inferiority). However, the problem of reaction to disability seems far too complicated to be explained by a few sweeping concepts like inferiority

complex and style of life. At the same time, Adler's theory does not lend itself to research because the theory is so strongly individualistic that it makes definitive empirical investigation of general laws applying to groups of subjects seem impossible.

The contributions of psychoanalytic theory appear largely in concern for the concept of the body image and for personality defenses (especially denial). Psychosomatic medicine has been strongly influenced by psychoanalytic thought, and some contributions to the study of disability and personality have been made by investigators of psychosomatic phenomena. However, despite its claim to concern for all aspects of organismic functioning, only a small percentage of psychosomatic research deals with the process of adaptation to disability once it has occurred.

AN EXAMINATION OF RECENT LITERATURE

Subsequent sections of this report summarize a review of the recent literature on personality and disability. The sources examined were primarily recognized psychological journals (such as the *Journal of Abnormal Psychology, Clinical Psychology,* and the *Journal of Personality*), although several medical-psychiatric sources were also reviewed (such as the *American Journal of Psychiatry,* and the *Journal of Nervous and Mental Disease*). In addition, certain specialized publications, such as the *Journal of Chronic Diseases* and the *Archives of Physical*

Medicine and Rehabilitation, were examined for relevant articles. Most of these sources were surveyed for five years of publication, from 1965 through 1969.

In the following sections, examples from this literature are used to demonstrate that evidence in support of the two popular hypotheses described above is still lacking (though the hypotheses themselves seem not to have been abandoned), and that interpretations of findings continue to be dominated by the preconceived idea that disability is a source of psychological maladjustment. Useful by-products of this demonstration are the proposal of some rather important generalizations about disability effects and the opportunity to comment on methodological issues.

Kidney and Heart Disease

Published reports on the psychological aspects of illness and disability tend to reflect developments in the field of medicine. Consequently, several reports have described the psychological effects of kidney and heart failure and responses to treatment of these conditions with artificial or transplanted organs. Although specific behavioral responses are associated with renal or cardiac failure, these are toxicity or deficiency effects (fatigue, anorexia, cognitive disturbances) which generally disappear when normal body functioning has been restored (Kemph, 1966). Emotional responses to treatment are varied and individualized, but many patients experience fantasies of rebirth as well as guilt over taking ad-

vantage of the death of the donor, when transplant is involved (Kemph, Bermann, & Copolillo, 1969). Patients sometimes think of themselves as zombies who have returned from the dead and are therefore not quite human (Abram, 1968; 1969). The most common postoperative psychiatric complication is depression (Kemph, 1967).

Lunde (1969) expressed the fear that personality disturbances will be frequent as transplants become more common. However, it has been observed that most psychiatric symptoms in such cases either can be prevented by adequate preoperative preparation and sympathetic postoperative care (H. R. Lazarus and Hagens, 1968) or successfully treated with psychotherapy or drugs (Kemph, 1967) when they do occur. Even catastrophic responses with severe behavioral effects have been found to last but a few days. They are replaced by mild depression which tends to lift spontaneously after a period of time (Abram, 1965).

Preoperatively, anxiety or denial are common (Abram, 1969). Weiss (1966) found that, in general, high preoperative scores on the MMPI correlated with poor reactions to open heart surgery, although no specific standard MMPI scales (except the Barron Ego Strength Scale) correlated significantly with postoperative reaction. Henricks, MacKenzie and Almond (1969) found that preoperative MMPI data from survivors of open heart surgery generally resembled MMPI profiles of patients with other medical diagnoses. (The almost universal MMPI profile associated with medical illness of any type shows elevations on Hs, Hy, and D.) Men who did not survive were more agitated than men who did. Women who did not survive were more over-controlled and more concerned with bodily complaints. To some investigators (Kimball, 1969; Eisendrath, 1969) it appears that the best predictor of favorable response to radical surgery is a history of previously successful adjustment and coping.

The Coronary Personality

A large number of studies has attempted to determine whether a specific personality is associated with predisposition for, or presence of, coronary heart disease. The "coronary" (or Type A) personality is usually described as aggressive, competitive, ambitious, and prone to a sense of urgency or time pressure. Some instruments have been devised for detecting this type of personality (Bortner and Rosenman, 1967; Jenkins, Rosenman, & Friedman, 1967) and a few studies have revealed differences in massed data between appropriately selected groups on personality test scores (Caffrey, 1968; 1969; Keith, Lown, & Stare, 1965; Ibrahim, Jenkins, Cassell, McDonough, & Hames, 1966; Miller, 1965; Klein & Parsons, 1968; Mordkoff & Golas, 1968; Mordkoff and Rand, 1968). Nevertheless, nearly all investigators who found such differences in grouped data placed heavy qualifications on their interpretations. Keith et al. (1965) noted that more than half their coronary patients did *not* show pattern A behavior. Mordkoff and Rand (1968); Klein and Par-

sons (1968), and Miller (1965) observed that many patients with heart disease gave responses that are typical of responses given by patients with other illnesses (i.e., elevation of Hs, D, and Hy on the MMPI). Some investigators (Klein et al., 1965; Ludwig and Wysong, 1969) found discriminations among groups to be statistically significant only for younger persons. Others noted that personality test data usually correlate at least as well with social class measures as with the presence or absence of coronary disease (Keith et al., 1965; Mordkoff and Golas, 1968). However, Antonovsky (1968) reviewed 56 studies and concluded that, if there is a relationship between heart disease and social class, it is not a simple one and its presence has not been convincingly demonstrated.

Rheumatoid Arthritis

The list of personality attributes ascribed to patients with arthritis is long. They have been said to have weak egos, to repress hostility, to be compliant and subservient, to be potentially psychotic, to be depressed, dependent, conscientious, masochistic, emotionally labile, compulsive, introverted, conservative, perfectionistic, moody, nervous, worried, tense, over-concerned about personal appearance, and prone to express psychopathology in physical symptoms.

Evidence exists that patients with rheumatoid arthritis behave differently from people who are not physically ill (Moos and Solomon, 1964; 1965a; 1965b), although even these findings have not gone uncontested (Nalven and O'Brien, 1968). Geist (1969) reported finding differences between arthritics and patients with other illnesses, but none of the differences was statistically significant. Warren and Weiss (1969) studied MMPI scores of patients in nine disability groups (including arthritis) and found no way to classify subjects into meaningful disability clusters.

Obesity

Atkinson and Ringuette (1967) found no distinguishing MMPI features in the records of 21 obese persons, nor was there evidence of homogeneous psychological, biographical, or familial factors that distinguished these subjects from any others. Crumpton, Wine, and Groot (1966) found that obese subjects produced generally flat MMPI profiles and showed less psychopathology than neuropsychiatric patients. Werkmann and Greenberg (1967) characterized the obese as self-satisfied and concerned with giving socially acceptable responses. High suggestibility (Glass, Lavin, Henchy, Gordon, Mayhew, & Donohoe, 1969) and field dependence (Karp & Pardes, 1965) have been reported in obese subjects. Glass et al. found, however, that underweight subjects also were highly suggestible. It is likely therefore that the critical factor in these studies is deviance rather than obesity per se.

Overview

The results summarized above are typical. Similar conclusions are justified by studies of asthma (Aaron, 1967; Green, 1965; Knapp, 1969), hemophilia (Mattsson and Gross, 1966), Huntington's chorea (Werner and Folk, 1968), leprosy (Ponomareff, 1965; Weigand and Dawson, 1967), systemic lupus erythematosus (Guze, 1967), epilepsy (Ferguson and Rayport, 1965; Kleck, 1968; Schwartz, Dennerll, & Lin, 1968; Meier and French, 1965); Small, Small, & Hayden, 1966); cancer (Fras, Litin, & Pearson, 1967; Goldfarb, Driesen, & Cole, 1967; Koenig, Levin, & Brennan, 1967), pulmonary emphysema (DeCencio, Leshner, & Leshner, 1968). Wilson's disease (Goldstein, Ewert, Randall, & Gross, 1968), ileostomy and colostomy (Dlin, Perlman, & Ringold, 1969), hemicorporectomy (Frieden, Gertler, Tosberg, & Rusk, 1969; DeLateur, Lehmann, Winterscheid, Wolf, Fordyce, & Simons, 1969); mastectomy (Jarvis, 1967), deafness (Fiebert, 1967), multiple sclerosis (Hovey, 1967), brain damage (Krug, 1967; Lansdell, 1968; Shaw and Matthews, 1965; Watson and Thomas, 1968), blindness (Zunich and Ledwith, 1965), gastric ulcers (Thoroughman, Pascal, Jarvis, & Crutcher, 1967; Wolowitz, 1967), diabetes (Swift, Seidman, & Stein, 1967), cleft palate (Gluck, McWilliams, Wylie, & Conkwright, 1965; Palmer and Adams, 1962; Ruess, 1965), essential hypertension (Hardyk, Chun, & Engel, 1966), paraplegia and quadriplegia (Kunce and Worley, 1966; Mitchell, 1970).

The recent literature provides no support for the hypothesis that particular disabilities are associated with particular personality characteristics or for the hypothesis that disability is a sufficient cause of maladjustment. Such group differences as have been found are weak and are usually subject to interpretation in terms of contaminating factors. In massed data, the somatically ill consistently show higher levels of depression and concern for body functions than do the somatically healthy or the psychiatrically disturbed. However, the somatically ill show no evidence of marked or enduring psychopathology.

IMPORTANT GENERAL ISSUES

Stability of Personality

Radical changes in body structure frequently have little or no prolonged effect on personality. Procedures such as hemicorporectomy (Frieden, et al., 1969; DeLateur, et al., 1969), bilateral hip disarticulation (Hirschenfang, Cosla, & Benton, 1966), ileostomy and colostomy (Dlin, et al., 1969), and the introduction of cardiac pacemakers (Gladstone and Gamble, 1969) involve gross alterations of the body. Yet, investigators report little or no evidence of radical, permanent personality change as a result of these interventions. Stone, Rowley, and MacQueen (1966) found that MMPI data from adolescents with physical symptoms having an organic (as opposed to a functional) basis were virtually the same as those from the normative sample for the test. Even patients with intractable cancer (Koenig, et al., 1967) or pulmonary emphysema (De-Cencio, et al., 1968) show no signs of

serious disorders of behavior. Personality structure may be temporarily disorganized by somatic crisis, but it seems capable of reestablishing itself by drawing on pre-existing resources for integration of the crisis experience into the self.

Depression and Somatic Improvement

Ferguson and Rayport (1965) described five persons with epilepsy whose seizures had been arrested. In all five cases, a crisis followed improvement and depression set in. In the preceding discussion of surgery for kidney and heart disorder, it was noted that depression is a common postoperative reaction. Depression and guilt have also been observed in survivors of atomic bombings (Lifton, 1967) and concentration camps (Krystal, 1968).

The common sense view of disability as a negative psychological experience does not prepare us for the possibility that improvement from illness or that removal of disability or threat to life may produce depression. Neither does it prepare us to accept the fact that personality disturbance is more likely to occur when disability is mild or marginal than when it is severe; yet, such seems to be the case (Cowen and Bobrove, 1966).

DeWolfe, Barrell, and Cummings (1968) found that older patients with more severe illnesses expressed less discomfort than younger patients with milder disabilities. Schwab, Marder, Clemmons, and McGinnis (1966) found that patients with psychiatric diagnoses were more anxious than patients with somatic illnesses and that lower anxiety was generally associated with more severe medical conditions. These findings were substantially confirmed in a related study by Goldman and Schwab (1966).

A balance theory of expectations (Heider, 1958) may be devised to explain these and related findings. According to this view, severe pain or suffering is subjectively equated with punishment or trial by ordeal, while the expectation of relief is subjectively equivalent to purification, exoneration, rebirth, or release from confinement. Negative explanations for suffering are balanced by positive expectations for states of relief. When relief actually occurs, and the person who has suffered finds himself basically unchanged, no more free of problems than he was before (indeed, he may have more problems than he did previously), the expected balance is disconfirmed and disruption of behavior follows.

Denial

The concept of denial is used in two distinctly different ways in the literature. On the one hand, it is used in the traditional way, to refer to a pathological defense against overwhelming affect, which is avoided by distorting or rejecting the harsh facts of reality. On the other hand, denial is sometimes regarded as an effective mode of adjustment, in which a person becomes capable of realistic present action by refusing to allow himself to anticipate necessary sufferings of the future. Thus, for example, when investigators find that families of children with cardiac pacemakers are well adjusted and realistic, the interpretation of denial is offered in explanation (Gladstone and Gamble, 1969). Similarly, when patients with myelopathy are found to be better adjusted on a test of personality than the normal population on which the test was standardized, it becomes "evident that some form of psychologic denial is in operation" (Weiss and Diamond, 1966, p. 75). Investigators do not seem to consider the possibilities that absence of anxiety may sometimes be taken as a sign of good adjustment, that suffering may be concealed without being denied, that hope is as real as despair, or that suffering may produce genuine psychological growth and maturity. This is a serious lack in virtually all studies of personality and disability.

COMMENTS ON RESEARCH METHODS

Case Studies and Impressionistic Reports

Several new ideas have been suggested by case studies. The case study also provides the investigator with a vehicle for describing rare and unusual patients or conditions. As might be expected, most of the work on the effects of radical surgery is reported in case study or impressionistic form.

The least impressive case studies are those in which intuitions are offered as if they were something more than suggestive evidence or illustrations of a theoretical position. It is not possible to prove that disability and personality are related or that psychiatric symptoms are more frequent in people with disabilities than in other groups, by simply communicating clinical impressions in a professional journal. Unfortunately, much of the literature still attempts to do this.

Test-based Studies

A large number of studies employ psychological tests. However, many such studies do not provide contemporaneously obtained data from comparison groups. It cannot be assumed that test norms (which have usually been obtained from persons without disabilities, tested months or years previously under quite different examination conditions) or that data obtained by others, who have tested subjects in different institutions, provide satisfactory standards for comparison of results obtained with a given sample at a given time and place.

One notes the lack of factor analytic research in this literature. Properly replicated, basic, intensive and extensive multivariate research, using a variety of psychological measures with subjects having a variety of somatic conditions, could go a long way toward clarifying the descriptive problem and identifying the most important variables for future study.

Evidence and Inference What evidence ultimately would be needed to show that personality and disability are, in fact, related in some systematic way?

First, groups of patients with virtually nothing in common except the disability in question must be shown to differ in performance on some measure of behavior from persons without disabilities.

Second, patients with one disability must be shown to differ from groups of patients with other disabilities.

Third, within groups of persons who have the disability, degree of manifestation of relevant personality characteristics must be shown to correlate appropriately with severity, duration, or some other medical feature of the disability.

None of the studies cited in the literature comes anywhere close to meeting any (except, perhaps, the first) of these requirements.

Even a satisfactory demonstration that personality and disability are correlated cannot establish the existence or directionality of a cause-effect relationship between them (Keith, 1966; Lahav, 1967; McFarland and Cobbs, 1967). Cause-effect relationships can be established only by longitudinal study of the same subjects over a period of time.

Longitudinal data also must be interpreted with caution. If a third factor (say, malnutrition) produces, first, personality changes and only later produces bodily disease, longitudinal tests would show predictive validity for personality tests and still fail to reveal the true cause of the illness. Similar cautions apply to the study of somatopsychological relations, in which the demonstration that given personality follows the onset of a particular disability must be accompanied by evidence that other factors cannot be adduced to explain them both.

Psychological Variables Future

research will be more productive if it concentrates more heavily on relations between psychological variables than on relations bewteen somatic variables and behavior. An instance of the type of research that ought to be done more often is a study which found that dogmatism (Rokeach, 1960) in blind subjects correlated positively with denial and negatively with depression (Hallenbeck, 1967). These findings suggest that denial of illness is not an isolated defense mechanism but is embedded in the matrix of the whole personality structure. Findings such as these can provide useful leads to counselors and therapists, who are in a position to influence belief systems in ways that will promote favorable client reactions.

Naturalism In conjunction with increased emphasis on psychological variables, it would be highly desirable for investigators to develop more naturalistic techniques. In this respect, one of the most interesting studies in the literature was conducted by Belmont, Benjamin, Ambrose, and Restuccia (1969). These investigators observed patients' task-oriented activities in the presence of and in the absence of the therapist. Level of activity was found to remain high when the therapist was absent from patients without cerebral damage but to drop significantly when the therapist was absent from patients with hemiplegia.

This study operationally defined motivation as "continuing to work when the therapist leaves." The definition is naturalistic, easily objectified, and intuitively appealing. With it, one can study motivation in a variety of behavior settings and can look for correlations between motivated behavior and a variety of measures, including those derived from psychological tests. The investigator can be sure his results will reveal something of interest not only to himself but also to those who work directly with clients. The naturalistic approach (Willems and Raush, 1969) offers many possibilities for fruitful research on disability, nearly all of which remain open to exploitation by ingenious investigators.

Experimental Methods

If the word experiment is taken to mean only research in which a carefully operationized independent variable is manipulated under rigidly controlled laboratory conditions, there are practically no experimental studies in the literature on disability and personality. Given a broader conception of the term, however, it is possible to identify a few (though not many) investigations that can be called experimental in spirit, if not in actual design.

An example of experimentation using naturally occurring events as the independent variable is a study by Riklan, Levita, and Cooper (1966) of the psychological effects of bilateral subcortical chemosurgery and cryosurgery for Parkinson's disease. These investigators administered a battery of cognitive, perceptual, and personality tests to 22 patients who had undergone surgery from five to 23 months before testing. A comparison group consisted of patients with the same disease who had not experienced surgery. Lack of significant differences between groups led the investigators to conclude that these forms of surgery have no lasting effects on cognitive or perceptual functioning, on body image or personality.

In a more obviously contrived investigation, Roberts, Dinsdale, Matthews, and Cole (1969) used operant methods to modify undesirable self-care behavior in a hemicorporectomized patient. The patient was successfully taught to prevent decubitus ulcers by being given reinforcement for proper care of his own skin. Operant methods are deservedly becoming more popular in rehabilitation settings (Michael, 1970; Shontz, 1970) as a means for managing client behavior. Whether these methods exert a significant influence on personality processes as well as on overt behavior remains to be seen.

The overall lack of experimental research is a serious deficiency in the literature on personality and disability. Investigators must ask less often "what are people with disabilities like?" and more often "what effects do specific events have upon the behavior of people with disabilities?" This requires an experimental attitude.

SUMMARY AND CONCLUSIONS

Two hypotheses dominate the literature on disability and personality. One hypothesis is that many (if not all) forms of somatic disability are associated with particular forms of personality. The other hypothesis is that the extent of the effects of disability on personality is proportional to the severity of disability. Both hypotheses are derivable from the assumption that all psychological effects of disability are negative, i.e., disruptive, dissatisfying, and disorganizing.

Previous reviews of the literature have concluded that there is virtually no support for these hypotheses or for the assumption with which they have so much in common. The present survey discloses no evidence to challenge that conclusion.

Several generalizations are suggested by the recent literature:

First, basic personality structure appears to be remarkably stable even in the face of serious somatic change. Such disorganization as occurs is generally transient, even though it may be severe in many cases.

Second, illness and disability (regardless of type) produce general increases in depression and somatic concern, but they do not necessarily raise the level of manifest anxiety. Absence of anxiety is often a sign of good adjustment and is not always presumptive evidence of the operation of the mechanism of denial.

Third, negative emotional experiences, such as depression and despair, are sometimes associated with improvement in somatic status as well as with the onset of disability or disease. The crucial factor seems to be sudden change in an enduring somatic state rather than illness or health, per se.

Methodologically, there is a need for descriptive research that is sufficiently comprehensive in scope to provide necessary information in compact and usable form. More attention should be paid to relations among psychological variables, and less effort should be devoted to the search for correlations between somatic variables and behavioral responses. Few studies are sufficiently naturalistic in design to permit ready application of findings to the rehabilitation situation. There is a paucity of needed experimental research with a psychological orientation.

Studies of disability and personality often appear to be investigations of convenience, rather than programs of investigation designed to pursue to the end the answer to some particular question. As a result, much valuable time and talent are wasted, not only in the conduct of unproductive research, but also in the rapid accumulation of uninstructive reports which others must periodically take the time to review.

REFERENCES

Aaron, N. S. Some personality differences between asthmatic, allergic, and normal children. Journal of Clinical Psychology, 1967, 23, 336–340.

Abel, T. M. Facial disfigurement. In J. F. Garrett (Ed.) Psychological aspects of physical disability. (Rehabilitation Service Series No. 210.) Washington, D. C.: Office of Vocational Rehabilitation, Department of Health, Education and Welfare, 1953. Pp. 112–124.

Abram, H. S. Adaptation to open heart surgery: A psychiatric study of response to the threat of death. American Journal of Psychiatry, 1965, 122, 659–667.

Abram, H. S. The psychiatrist, the treatment of chronic renal failure, and the prolongation of life: I. American Journal of Psychiatry, 1968, 124, 1351–1358.

Abram, H. S. The psychiatrist, the treatment of chronic renal failure, and the prolongation of life: II. American Journal of Psychiatry, 1969, 126, 157–167.

Allen, R. M. Cerebral palsy. In J. F. Garrett and E. S. Levine (Eds.) Psychological practices with the physically disabled. New York: Columbia University Press, 1962. Pp. 159–196.

Antonovsky, A. Social class and the major cardiovascular diseases. Journal of Chronic Diseases, 1968, 21, 65–106.

Appley, M. H., & Trumbull, R. Psychological stress. New York: Appleton-Century-Crofts, 1967.

Atkinson, J., & Feather, N. A theory of achievement motivation. New York: Wiley, 1966.

Atkinson, R. M., & Ringuette, E. L. A survey of biographical and psychological features in extraordinary fatness. Psychosomatic Medicine, 1967, 29, 121–133.

Barker, R. G., & Wright, B. A. The social psychology of adjustment to physical disability. In J. F. Garrett (Ed.) Psychological aspects of physical disability. (Rehabilitation Services Series No. 310.) Washington, D. C.: Office of Vocational Rehabilitation, Department of Health, Education and Welfare, 1953. Pp. 18–22.

Barker, R. G., Wright, B. A., & Gonick, M. R. Adjustment to physical handicap and illness: A survey of the social psychology of physique and disability. New York: Social Science Research Council, Bull. 55, 1946.

Barker, R. G., Wright, B. A., Meyerson, L., & Gonick, M. R. Adjustment to physical handicap and illness: A survey of the social psychology of physique and disability (rev. ed.) New York: Social Science Research Council, Bull. 55, 1953.

Barry, J. R., & Malinovsky, M. R. Client motivation for rehabilitation: A review. Gainesville, Fla.: Regional Rehabilitation Research Institute, University of Florida, 1965.

Belmont, I., Benjamin, H., Ambrose, J., & Restuccia, R. D. Effect of cerebral damage on motivation in rehabilitation. Archives of Physical Medicine and Rehabilitation, 1969, 50, 507–511.

Berger, S. Paraplegia. In J. F. Garrett (Ed.) Psychological aspects of physical disability. (Rehabilitation Service Series No. 210.) Washington, D. C.: Office of Vocational Rehabilitation, Department of Health, Education and Welfare, 1953. Pp. 46–59.

Bortner, R. W., & Rosenman, R. H. The measurement of pattern A behavior. Journal of Chronic Diseases, 1967, 20, 525–533.

Caffrey, B. Reliability and validity of personality and behavioral measures in a study of coronary heart disease. Journal of Chronic Diseases, 1968, 21, 191–204.

Caffrey, B. Behavior patterns and personality characteristics related to prevalence rates in coronary heart disease in American monks. Journal of Chronic Diseases, 1969, 22, 93–103.

Cobb, B. Cancer. In J. F. Garrett and E. S. Levine (Eds.) Psychological practices with the physically disabled. New York: Columbia University Press, 1962. Pp. 231–260.

Cohn, N. Understanding the process of adjustment to disability. Journal of Rehabilitation, 1961, 27(b), 16–18.

Cowen, E. L. Personality, motivation, and clinical phenomena. In L. H. Lofquist (Ed.) Psychological research and rehabilitation. Washington, D. C.: American Psychological Association, 1960. Pp. 112–171.

Cowen, E. L., & Bobrove, P. H. Marginality of disability and adjustment. Perceptual and Motor Skills, 1966, 23, 869–870.

Crumpton, E., Wine, D. B., & Groot, H. MMPI profiles of obese men and six other diagnostic categories. Psychological Reports, 1966, 19, 1110.

Davis, F. Passage through crisis: Polio victims and their families. New York: Bobbs-Merrill, 1963.

DeCencio, D. V., Leshner, M., & Leshner, B. Personality characteristics of patients with chronic obstructive pulmonary emphysema. Archives of Physical Medicine and Rehabilitation, 1968, 49, 471–475.

DeLateur, B. J., Lehmann, J. F., Winterscheid, L. C., Wolf, J. A., Fordyce, W. E., & Simons, B. C. Rehabilitation of the patient after hemicorporectomy. Archives of Physical Medicine and Rehabilitation, 1969, 50, 11–16.

Dembo, T., Ladieu-Leviton, G., & Wright, B. A. Acceptance of loss—amputations. In J. F. Garrett (Ed.) Psychological aspects of physical disability. (Rehabilitation Service Series No. 210.) Washington D. C.: Office of Vocational Rehabilitation, Department of Health, Education and Welfare, 1953. Pp. 80–96.

Dembo, T., Leviton, G. L., & Wright, B. A. Adjustment to misfortune—a problem of social psychological rehabilitation. Artificial Limbs, 1956, 3, 4–62.

DeWolfe, A. S., Barrell, R. P., & Cummings, J. W. Patient variables in emotional response to hospitalization for physical illness. Journal of Consulting Psychology, 1968, 30, 68–72.

Diller, L., Hemiplegia. In J. F. Garrett and E. S. Levine (Eds.) Psychological practices with the physically disabled. New York: Columbia University Press, 1962. Pp. 125–158.

Dlin, B. M., Perlman, A., & Ringold, E. Psychosexual responses to ileostomy and colostomy. American Journal of Psychiatry, 1969, 126, 374–378.

Eisendrath, R. M., The role of grief and fear in the death of kidney transplant patients. American Journal of Psychiatry, 1969, 126, 381–387.

Ferguson, S. M., & Rayport, M. The adjustment to living without epilepsy. Journal of Nervous and Mental Disease, 1965, 140, 26–37.

Fiebert, M. Cognitive styles in the deaf. Perceptual and Motor Skills, 1967, 24, 319–329.

Fink, S. L. Crisis and motivation: A theoretical model. Archives of Physical Medicine and Rehabilitation, 1967, 48, 592–597.

Fisher, S., & Cleveland, S. E. Body image and personality (rev. ed.) New York: Dover, 1968.

Fishman, S. Amputation. In J. F. Garrett and E. S. Levine (Eds.) Psychological practices with the physically disabled. New York: Columbia University Press, 1962. Pp. 1–50.

Frank, L. K. Image of the self. In G. Leviton (Ed.) The relationship between rehabilitation and psychology. Washington, D. C.: U. S. Department of Health, Education and Welfare, 1959. Pp. 26–35.

Fras, I., Litin, E. M., & Pearson, J. S. Comparison of psychiatric symptoms in carcinoma of the pancreas with those of some other intra-abdominal neoplasma. American Journal of Psychiatry, 1967, 123, 1553–1562.

Frieden, F. H., Gertler, M., Tosberg, W., & Rusk, H. A. Rehabilitation after hemicorporectomy. Archives of Physical Medicine and Rehabilitation, 1969, 50, 259–263.

Garrett, J. F. Cerebral palsy. In J. F. Garrett (Ed.) Psychological aspects of physical disability. (Rehabilitation Service Series No. 210.) Washington, D. C.: Office of Vocational Education, Department of Health, Education and Welfare, 1953. Pp. 60–67.

Geist, H. Psychological aspects of rheumatoid arthritis. Proceedings, 77th Annual Convention, American Psychological Association, 1969. Pp. 769–770.

Gladstone, R., & Gamble, W. J. On borrowed time: Observations of children with implanted cardiac pacemakers and their families. American Journal of Psychiatry, 1969, 126, 104–108.

Glass, D. C., Lavin, D. E., Henchy, T., Gordon, A., Mayhew, P., & Donohoe, P. Obesity and persuasibility. Journal of Personality, 1969, 37, 407–414.

Gluck, M. R., McWilliams, B. J., Wylie, H. L., & Conkwright, E. A. Comparison of clinical characteristics of children with cleft palates and children in a child guidance center. Perceptual and Motor Skills, 1965, 21, 806.

Goldfarb, C., Driesen, J., & Cole, D. Psychobiologic aspects of malignancy. American Journal of Psychiatry, 1967, 123, 1545–1552.

Goldman, J., & Schwab, J. J. Medical illness and patients' attitudes: Somatopsychic relationships. Journal of Nervous and Mental Disease, 1966, 141, 678–683.

Goldstein, K. What can we learn from pathology for normal psychology? In G. Leviton (Ed.) The relationship between rehabilitation and psychology. Washington, D. C.: U. S. Department of Health, Education and Welfare, 1959. Pp. 36–61.

Goldstein, N. P., Ewert, J. C., Randall, R. V., & Gross, J. B. Psychiatric aspects of Wilson's disease (hepatolenticular degeneration): Results of psychometric tests during long-term therapy. American Journal of Psychiatry, 1968, 124, 1555–1561.

Green, R. Asthma and manic-depressive psychosis—simultaneously incompatable or coexistent? Journal of Nervous and Mental Disease, 1965, 140, 64–70.

Guze, S. B. The occurrence of psychiatric illness in systemic lupus erythematosus. American Journal of Psychiatry, 1967, 123, 1562–1570.

Hallenbeck, P. A. Dogmatism and visual loss. (Research Series No. 17.) New York: American Foundation for the Blind, 1967.

Hardyk, C. D., Chun, K., & Engel, B. T. Personality and marital-adjustment differences in essential hypertension in women. Journal of Consulting Psychology, 1966, 30, 459.

Harris, D. H. Psychological aspects of tuberculosis. In J. F. Garrett (Ed.) Psychological aspects of physical disability. (Rehabilitation Service Series No. 210.) Washington, D. C.: Office of Vocational Rehabilitation, Department of Health, Education and Welfare, 1953. Pp. 97−111.

Harrower, M. R. Psychological factors in multiple sclerosis. In J. F. Garrett (Ed.) Psychological aspects of physical disability. (Rehabilitation Service Series No. 210.) Washington, D. C.: Office of Vocational Rehabilitation, Department of Health, Education and Welfare, 1953. Pp. 68−79.

Heider, F. The psychology of interpersonal relations. New York: Wiley, 1958.

Henrichs, T. F., MacKenzie, J. W., & Almond, C. H. Psychological adjustment and acute response to open heart surgery. Journal of Nervous and Mental Disease, 1969, 148, 158−164.

Hirschenfang, S., Cosla, H. W., & Benton, J. G. Anxiety in a patient with bilateral hip disarticulation: Preliminary report. Perceptual and Motor Skills, 1966, 23, 41−42.

Hovey, H. B. MMPI testing for multiple sclerosis. Psychological Reports, 1967, 21, 599−600.

Ibrahim, M.A., Jenkins, C. D., Cassell, J. C., McDonough, J. R., & Hames, C. G. Personality traits and coronary heart disease. Journal of Chronic Diseases, 1966, 19, 255−271.

Jarvis, J. H. Post-mastectomy breast phantoms. Journal of Nervous and Mental Disease, 1967, 144, 266−272.

Jenkins, C. D., Rosenman, R. H., & Friedman, M. Development of an objective psychological test for the determination of the coronary-prone behavior pattern in employed men. Journal of Chronic Diseases, 1967, 20, 371−379.

Kaplan, M. F., & Lotsof, E. J. Are the principles of behavior of "exceptional children" exceptional? Psychological Reports, 1968, 23, 1207−1213.

Karp, S. A., & Pardes, H. Psychological differentiation (field dependence) in obese women. Psychosomatic Medicine, 1965, 27, 238−244.

Keith, R. A. Personality and coronary heart disease: A review. Journal of Chronic Diseases, 1966, 19, 1231−1243.

Keith, R.A. The need for a new model in rehabilitation. Journal of Chronic Diseases, 1968, 21, 281−286.

Keith, R. A., Lown, B., & Stare, F. J. Coronary heart disease and behavior patterns. Psychosomatic Medicine, 1965, 27, 424−434.

Kelley, H. H., Hatsorf, A. H., Jones, E. E., Thibault, J. W., & Usdane, W. M. Some implications of social psychological theory for research on the handicapped. In L. H. Lofquist (Ed.) Psychological research and rehabilitation. Washington, D. C.: American Psychological Association, 1960. Pp. 172−204.

Kemph, J. P. Renal failure, artificial kidney and kidney transplant. American Journal of Psychiatry, 1966, 122, 1270−1274.

Kemph, J. P. Psychotherapy with patients receiving kidney transplants. American Journal of Psychiatry, 1967, 124, 623−629.

Kemph, J. P., Berman, E. A., & Coppolillo, H. P. Kidney transplant and shifts in family dynamics. American Journal of Psychiatry, 1969, 125, 1485−1490.

Kimball, C. P. Psychological responses to experience of open heart surgery: I. American Journal of Psychiatry, 1969, 126, 348−359.

Kleck, R. Emotional arousal in interaction with stigmatized persons. Psychological Reports, 1966, 19, 1226.

Kleck, R. Self-disclosure patterns of the nonobviously disabled. Psychological Reports, 1968, 23, 1239–1248.

Klein, H. P., & Parsons, O. A. Self descriptions of patients with coronary disease. Perceptual and Motor Skills, 1968, 26, 1099.

Knapp, P. H. The asthmatic and his environment. Journal of Nervous and Mental Disease, 1969, 149, 133–151.

Koenig, R., Levin, S. M., & Brennan, M. J. The emotional status of cancer patients as measured by a psychological test. Journal of Chronic Diseases, 1967, 20, 923–930.

Krug, R. S. MMPI response inconsistency of brain damaged individuals. Journal of Clinical Psychology, 1967, 23, 366.

Krystal, H. (Ed.) Massive psychic trauma. New York: International Universities Press, 1968.

Kunce, J. T., & Worley, B. H. Interest patterns, accidents and disability. Journal of Clinical Psychology, 1966, 22, 105–107.

Lahav, E. Methodological problems in behavioral research on disease. Journal of Chronic Diseases, 1967, 20, 333–340.

Lane, H. S. The hard of hearing. In J. F. Garrett (Ed.) Psychological aspects of physical disability. (Rehabilitation Service Series No. 210.) Washington, D. C.: Office of Vocational Rehabilitation, Department of Health, Education and Welfare, 1953. Pp. 147–161.

Lansdell, H. Effect of extent of temporal lobe surgery and neuropathology on the MMPI. Journal of Clinical Psychology, 1968, 24, 406–412.

Lazarus, H. R., & Hagens, J. H. Prevention of psychosis following open-heart surgery. American Journal of Psychiatry, 1968, 124, 1190–1195.

Lazarus, R. S. Psychological stress and the coping process. New York: McGraw-Hill, 1966.

Levine, E. S. The deaf. In J. F. Garrett (Ed.) Psychological aspects of physical disability. (Rehabilitation Service Series No. 210.) Washington, D. C.: Office of Vocational Rehabilitation, Department of Health, Education and Welfare, 1953. Pp. 125–146.

Levine, E. S. Auditory disability. In J. F. Garrett and E. S. Levine (Eds.) Psychological practices with the physically disabled. New York: Columbia University Press, 1962. Pp. 279–340.

Lifton, R. J. Death in life: Survivors of Hiroshima. New York: Random House, 1967.

Lowenfeld, B. The blind. In J. F. Garrett (Ed.) Psychological aspects of physical disability. (Rehabilitation Service Series No. 210.) Washington, D. C.: Office of Vocational Rehabilitation, Department of Health, Education and Welfare, 1953. Pp. 179–195.

Ludwig, E. G., & Wysong, J. Work, heart disease and mental health. Journal of Chronic Diseases, 1969, 21, 687–689.

Lunde, D. T. Psychiatric complications of heart transplants. American Journal of Psychiatry, 1969, 126, 369–373.

MacDonald, A. P., & Hall, J. Perception of disability by the nondisabled. Journal of Consulting and Clinical Psychology, 1969, 33, 654–660.

Madan, R. Facial disfigurement. In J. F. Garrett and E. S. Levine (Eds.) Psychological practices with the physically disabled. New York: Columbia University Press, 1962. Pp. 261–278.

Maslow, A. H. Motivation and personality. New York: Harper, 1954.

Mattson, A., & Gross, S. Adaptational and defensive behavior in young hemophiliacs and their parents. American Journal of Psychiatry, 1966, 122, 1349–1356.

McDaniel, J. W. Physical disability and

human behavior. Elmsford, N.Y.: Pergamon Press, 1969.

McFarland, D. D., & Cobbs, S. C. Causal interpretations from cross-sectional data. Journal of Chronic Diseases, 1967, 20, 393–406.

Meier, M. J., & French, L. A. Some personality correlates of unilateral and bilateral EEG abnormalities in psychomotor epileptics. Journal of Clinical Psychology, 1965, 21, 3–9.

Menninger, K. A. Psychiatric aspects of physical disability. In J. F. Garrett (Ed.) Psychological aspects of physical disability. (Rehabilitation Service Series No. 210.) Washington, D. C.: Office of Vocational Rehabilitation, Department of Health, Education and Welfare, 1953. Pp. 8–17.

Meyerson, L. Somatopsychology of physical disability. In W. M. Cruickshank (Ed.) Psychology of exceptional children and youth. Englewood Cliffs, N.J.: Prentice-Hall, 1955, 1–60.

Michael, J. L. Rehabilitation. In C. Neuringer and J. Michael (Eds.) Behavior modification in clinical psychology. New York: Appleton-Century-Crofts, 1970.

Miller, C.K. Psychological correlates of coronary artery disease. Psychosomatic Medicine, 1965, 27, 257–265.

Mitchell, K. R. The body image variable and level of adjustment to stress induced by severe physical disability. Journal of Clinical Psychology, 1970, 26, 49–52.

Moos, R. H., & Solomon, G. F. MMPI response patterns in patients with rheumatoid arthritis. Journal of Psychosomatic Research, 1964, 8, 17–28.

Moos, R. H., & Solomon, G. F. Psychologic comparisons between women with rheumatoid arthritis and their nonarthritic sisters: I. Personality tests and interview rating data. Psychosomatic Medicine, 1965, 27, 135–149. (a)

Moos, R. H., & Solomon, G. F. Psychologic comparisons between women with rheumatoid arthritis and their nonarthritic sisters: II. Content analysis of interviews. Psychosomatic Medicine, 1965, 27, 150–164. (b)

Mordkoff, A. M., & Golas, R. M. Coronary artery disease and responses to the Rosenzweig Picture-Frustration Study. Journal of Abnormal Psychology, 1968, 73, 381–386.

Mordkoff, A. M., & Parsons, O. A. The coronary personality: A critique. Psychosomatic Medicine, 1967, 29, 1–14.

Mordkoff, A. M., & Rand, M. A. Personality and adaptation to coronary artery disease. Journal of Consulting and Clinical Psychology, 1968, 32, 648–653.

Murphy, W. F. Some clinical aspects of the body ego, with special reference to phantom limb phenomena. Psychoanalytic Review, 1957, 44, 462–477.

Nalven, F. B., & O'Brien, J. F. On the use of the MMPI with rheumatoid arthritic patients. Journal of Clinical Psychology, 1968, 24, 70.

Palmer, J. M., & Adams, M. R. The oral image of children with cleft lips and palates. Cleft Palate Bulletin, 1962, 12, 73–76.

Parsons, T. Social structure and personality. New York: Free Press of Glencoe, 1964.

Parsons, T., & Fox, R. Illness, therapy, and the modern urban American family. Journal of Social Issues, 1952, 8, 31–44.

Patterson, C. H. A unitary theory of motivation and its counseling applications. Journal of Individual Psychology, 1964, 20, 17–31.

Ponomareff, G. L. Phenomenology of delusions of a case of leprosy. American Journal of Psychiatry, 1965, 121, 1211.

Pringle, M. L. K. The emotional and social readjustment of physically handicapped children: A review of the literature between 1928 and 1962. Educational Research, 1964, 6, 207–215.

Raskin, N. J. Visual disability. In J. F. Garrett and E. S. Levine (Eds.) Psychological practices with the physically disabled. New York: Columbia University Press, 1962. Pp. 341–375.

Riklan, M., Levita, E., & Cooper, I. S. Psychological effects of bilateral subcortical surgery for Parkinson's disease. Journal of Nervous and Mental Disease, 1966, 141, 403–409.

Roberts, A. H., Dinsdale, S. M., Matthews, R. E., & Cole, T. M. Modifying persistent undesirable behavior in a medical setting. Archives of Physical Medicine and Rehabilitation, 1969, 50, 147–153.

Rokeach, M. The open and closed mind. New York: Basic Books, 1960.

Ruess, A. L. A comparative study of cleft palate children and their siblings. Journal of Clinical Psychology, 1965, 21, 354–360.

Schilder, P. The image and appearance of the human body. New York: International Universities Press, 1950. (Orig. publ. 1935.)

Schwab, J. J., Marder, L., Clemmons, R. S., & McGinnis, N. H. Anxiety, severity of illness and other medical variables. Journal of Psychosomatic Research, 1966, 10, 297–303.

Schwartz, M. L., Dennerll, R. D., & Lin, Y. Neuropsychological and psychological predictors of employability in epilepsy. Journal of Clinical Psychology, 1968, 24, 174–177.

Seidenfeld, M. A. Psychological problems of poliomyelitis. In J. F. Garrett (Ed.) Psychological aspects of physical disability. (Rehabilitation Service Series No. 210.) Washington, D. C.: Office of Vocational Rehabilitation, Department of Health, Education and Welfare, 1953. Pp. 33–45.

Seidenfeld, M. A. Arthritis and rheumatism. In J. F. Garrett and E. S. Levine (Eds.) Psychological practices with the physically disabled. New York: Columbia University Press, 1962. Pp. 51–84.

Shaw, D. J., & Matthews, C. G. Differential MMPI performance of brain-damaged vs. pseudo-neurologic groups. Journal of Clinical Psychology, 1965, 21, 405–408.

Shontz, F. C. Severe chronic illness. In J. F. Garrett and E. S. Levine (Eds.) Psychological practices with the physically disabled. New York: Columbia University Press, 1962. Pp. 410–445.

Shontz, F. C. Reaction to crisis. Volta Review, 1965, 67, 364–370.

Shontz, F. C. Perceptual and cognitive aspects of body experience. New York: Academic Press, 1969.

Shontz, F. C. The problems and promises of psychological research in rehabilitation. In E. P. Trapp and P. Himelstein (Eds.) The exceptional child: Research and theory. New York: Appleton-Century-Crofts, 1970.

Shontz, F. C., Fink, S. L., & Hallenbeck, C. E. Chronic physical illness as threat. Archives of Physical Medicine and Rehabilitation, 1960, 41, 143–148.

Siller, J., Chipman, A., Ferguson, L., & Vann, D. H. Studies in reactions to disability. XI: Attitudes of the nondisabled toward the physically disabled. New York: New York University, School of Education, 1967.

Small, J. G., Small, I. F., & Hayden, M. P. Further psychiatric investigations of patients with temporal and nontemporal lobe epilepsy. American Journal of Psychiatry, 1966, 123, 303–310.

Stone, F. B., Rowley, V. N., & MacQueen, J. C. Using the MMPI with adolescents who have somatic symptoms. Psychological Reports, 1966, 18, 139–147.

Swift, C. R., Seidman, F., & Stein, H. Adjustment problems in juvenile diabetes. Psychosomatic Medicine, 1967, 29, 555—571.

Thibault, J. W., & Kelley, H. H. The social psychology of groups. New York: Wiley, 1959.

Thoroughman, J. C., Pascal, G. R., Jarvis, J. R., & Crutcher, J. C. A study of psychological factors in patients with surgically intractable duodenal ulcer and those with other intractable disorders. Psychosomatic Medicine, 1967, 29, 273—283.

Tizard, B. The personality of epileptics: A discussion of the evidence. Psychological Bulletin, 1962, 59, 196—210.

Warren, L. W., & Weiss, D. J. Relationship between disability type and measured personality characteristics. Proceedings, 77th Annual Convention, American Psychological Association, 1969. Pp. 773—774.

Watson, C. G., & Thomas, R. W. MMPI profiles of brain-damaged and schizophrenic patients. Perceptual and Motor Skills, 1968, 27, 567—573.

Weigand, E. L., & Dawson, J. G. Response patterns of Hansen's disease patients on the perceptual reaction test. Journal of Clinical Psychology, 1967, 23, 452—454.

Weiss, A. J., & Diamond, M. D. Psychologic adjustment of patients with myelopathy. Archives of Physical Medicine and Rehabilitation, 1966, 47, 72—76.

Weiss, S. M. Psychological adjustment following open-heart surgery. Journal of Nervous and Mental Disease, 1966, 143, 363—368.

Wepman, J. M. The language disorders. In J. F. Garrett and E. S. Levine (Eds.) Psychological practices with the physically disabled. New York: Columbia University Press, 1962. Pp. 197—230.

Werkman, S. L., & Greenberg, E. S. Personality and interest patterns in obese adolescent girls. Psychosomatic Medicine, 1967, 29, 72—80.

Werner, A., & Folk, J. J. Manifestations of neurotic conflict in Huntington's chorea. Journal of Nervous and Mental Disease, 1968, 147, 141—147.

Whitehouse, F. A. Cardiovascular disability. In J. F. Garrett and E. S. Levine (Eds.) Psychological practices with the physically disabled. New York: Columbia University Press, 1962. Pp. 85—124.

Willems, E. P., & Raush, H. L. (Eds.) Naturalistic viewpoints in psychological research. New York: Holt, Rinehart and Winston, 1969.

Wolowitz, H. M. Oral involvement in peptic ulcer. Journal of Consulting Psychology, 1967, 31, 418—419.

Wright, B. A. Physical disability—A psychological approach. New York: Harper and Row, 1960.

Wright, B. A. The question stands: Should a person be realistic? Rehabilitation Counseling Bulletin, 1968, 11, 291—296.

Wright, B. A., & Shontz, F. C. Process and tasks in hoping. Rehabilitation Literature, 1968, 29(11), 322—331.

Young, M. A. C The partially seeing. In J. F. Garrett (Ed.) Psychological aspects of physical disability. (Rehabilitation Service Series No. 210.) Washington, D. C.: Office of Vocational Rehabilitation, Department of Health, Education and Welfare, 1953. Pp. 162—195.

Yuker, H. E., Block, J. R., & Campbell, W. J. A scale to measure attitudes toward disabled persons. Albertson, N.Y.: Human Resources Foundation, 1960.

Yuker, H. E., Block, J. R., & Young, J. H. The Measurement of attitudes toward disabled persons. Albertson, N.Y.: Human Resources Foundation, 1966.

Zunich, M., & Ledwith, B. E. Self-concepts of visually handicapped and sighted children. Perceptual and Motor Skills, 1965, 21, 771—774.

Section 8

MECHANISMS OF COPING WITH DISABILITY

32 Spread in Adjustment to Disability

Beatrice A. Wright

The terms "spread" and "spread phenomenon" are used in this paper to refer to the tendency of persons perceiving one characteristic of another person (such as lameness or physical beauty) to develop other perceptions about that person which tend to be positive or negative according to the attitude generated by the first impression received. The "halo phenomenon" is another term used to describe the positive aspects of this process. Thus if one is favorably impressed by the pleasing appearance of a person, it is easy to believe that he has other positive attributes such as good character and intelligence. The same phenomenon may occur with a negatively toned trait. If the person's appearance is viewed as displeasing or disturbing, as is sometimes true if he has a disability, then the observer's tendency may be to infer other negative attributes, such as emotional instability or intellectual limitation. The spread phenomenon is difficult to escape because it seems to be cognitively easier to integrate like-sign attributes than an admixture of positive and negative ones.

The spread phenomenon becomes manifest not only in the perceived effects of disability. It may extend to a negative concept about the cause of disability. It is as though there were some kind of "requiredness in cause-effect relations" whereby an effect which is perceived as negative and unwelcome "requires" a cause which is also perceived as negative. For example, one of the difficulties in relating the blindness associated with retrolental fibroplasia to the use of oxygen for the premature infant may well have been due to the fact that oxygen, the provocative agent, had almost always, in the past, been seen in positive contexts. Oxygen did not evoke the negative affects, the antipathy, which were aroused by the disability of blindness.

It is also necessary to recognize that the spread phenomenon occurs not only with respect to the perception of others, but also with self-perception. In the discussion that follows, the target or object of this spread will not be specified when the process has relevance for both self and interpersonal perception.

THE POWER OF PHYSIQUE IN SPREAD

Physique, more than many other characteristics of the person, wields an enormous power in bringing about the

Reprinted from the Bulletin of the Menninger Clinic, 1964, 28:198–208.

Presidential Address of Division 22 presented at the 1963 Annual Convention of the American Psychological Association, Philadelphia, Pa., August 30, 1963.

spread phenomenon. Using Asch's conceptualization (1), we may say that physique is a highly central characteristic of the person.

There are two basic reasons for this. First: Physique is intimately connected with the identity of the person. Very early in life, one's physical attributes become intricately a part of the "I," the self-concept. Moreover, other people recognize a person by his appearance. His identity is established by his physique even though his behavior may be highly variable. A person may startle others by acting unexpectedly or in unaccustomed ways. He may then be excused for "not acting like himself," but he is not viewed as "being someone else." On the other hand, if an individual's behavior remained characteristic and unchanged, but his appearance were markedly altered, recognition would be difficult. Although time makes for many changes in appearance, physical features are generally among the most stable of the dispositional characteristics of a person.

A second reason for the potency of physique in generating the spread phenomenon is that of stimulus primacy. By its visibility, physique becomes quickly apparent and pre-empts the field of stimuli in influencing what the first impression of the person will be. It sets up a direction for thinking and feeling about the other person that exerts a continuous effect upon the development of other impressions about that person. That the order in which the characteristics of a person are perceived does influence the total personality impression of that person has been experimentally demonstrated (2).

Conditions Facilitating Spread

There are three conditions that seem to facilitate the phenomenon of spread. The first of these, stressed by Dembo (3), is the *comparative frame of reference* of the evaluator. This means, succinctly, that a standard of comparison is used in the evaluation which causes him to emphasize status implications. For example, a person may be judged to be bright or stupid and concomitantly admired or disgraced, with little concern about the value of what he can do within his limitations. In contrast, an "asset frame of reference" focuses on the qualities inherent in the object of judgment itself. For example, a musical performance may be enjoyed or suffered for what it offers without comparing it to the performance of anyone else.

The theory about the influence of the comparative frame of reference upon the process of spread hypothesizes that if normalcy is taken as the standard, and a disability is viewed as far below that standard, then other vague characteristics of the person, as well as the person as a whole, will be regarded as below standard. In some diffuse sort of way, the person who has been judged comes to be regarded as being inferior. Dembo (4) explains the dynamics as follows: In comparing a person with a standard, one is interested only in a particular characteristic (such as physique or intelligence). Because these characteristics are within the main field of concern, they acquire considerable potency, and influence the perception and evaluation of other characteristics which, not being compared at the time, are therefore vague and unstructured. Thus, the evaluator, be he the person with the disability, the parent, or outsider, when judging the disability against the standard of the nondisabled state, is prone to generate a broad array of negative perceptions about other attributes which are only arbitrarily connected with the disability. Where the comparative frame of reference is a pervasive pattern of thinking, that is, where a person characteristically functions within this outlook, then it is to be expected that he will be more highly susceptible to the spread phenomenon and more apt to overestimate the inadequacies and inferiority of a person with a disability. This theory has been experimentally supported in a study (5) in which a significant correlation (r = .37) was found between comparative mindedness and spread scores, as measured by specially devised tests.

A second condition facilitating spread has to do with emotional factors which engender *dedifferentiation* and fluidity of cognitive processes. By dedifferentiation is meant a primitivization in which parts of a system become less defined. To put it another way, the parts become more global in structure. Thoughts become dedifferentiated when richness of ideation is supplanted by a paucity. In the motor sphere, an example is the substitution of the finely coordinated prehensile grasp by the cruder palmer

grasp. Fluidity refers to the ease with which boundaries within a system are crossed. For example, thought processes are said to be fluid when the cognitive system is without firm boundaries, when ideas freely influence each other and blend together. Both fluidity and dedifferentiation are assumed to characterize heightened emotionality, and therefore it is predicted that such a state would give rise to spread effects, which, in the case of disability, would encase the person in an overwhelming undifferentiated devaluation. This may be a meaningful basis for understanding the early reactions of some people to severe traumatic injury when they experience the deep depression of a feeling of total loss of self and capabilities. It is after the spread has had a chance to become differentiated that the process of reconstitution can begin and the total devaluation diminished. Similar undifferentiated, yet pronounced effects of spread can be expected in persons who have a deep fear, resentment, or guilt about disability, whether the disability is theirs or another person's.

The third condition has to with *wish forces* within the evaluator. It can be postulated that spread will proceed more readily and with less restraint when it is in accord with the wishes of the perceiver than when it is in opposition. Thus, when there is a wish to devalue a person with a disability in order to maintain one's own uncertain status, negative spread can be expected to be particularly clear. This is sometimes seen, for example, in a parent of a normal child, who "feels so sorry" for the crippled child next door, all the while attempting to reassure herself that her own child meets all specifications. In such instances the need to devaluate has been labeled the "requirement of mourning." Facilitation of spread may also appear in the person with a disability himself through masochistic satisfactions or thoughts of secondary gain. Where the wishes run counter to the direction of spread, on the other hand, the restraining forces of reason, rationalization, denial, and other processes may be expected to enter.

PROCESSES GIVING SPREAD CONTENT

What gives content to the personal attributes encompassed by spread? How do *particular* characteristics become ascribed to the person? It is true that under some circumstances an undifferentiated, generalized devaluation or adulation of the person occurs. But more frequently, there is a specification of traits. Moreover, spread is not to be regarded simply as an inundating process that captures all traits bearing the same sign as the propelling one. On the contrary, not all like-sign traits are included. Typically there is a selection among innumerable traits which could have been subsumed by the spread phenomenon. For example, a person may believe that cripples tend to be bitter, irritable and indigent, but not sneaky, conceited or selfish.

The spread phenomenon appears to establish an orienting framework within which certain adjunctive processes operate to bring about trait selection. It is as if the perceiver, sensitized by his reaction to a potent negative characteristic of a person, activates additional processes within himself to guide the selection of traits from among many negative ones which have become candidates for admission by the original sensitization. We shall try to identify four such processes, and it should be noted that the last two of these not only serve to give content to the impugned personality characteristics, but also serve to justify them.

The first of these adjunctive processes concerns the *Gestalt properties of personality traits*. As an illustration, let us examine such trait attributes as impulsiveness, anger, and suspiciousness from the point of view of their figural properties.

In one pilot study, a subject was asked to select the two trait attributes which he could represent most nearly by the same set of geometrical lines. He chose impulsiveness and anger, and represented them with sporadic spikes over a distance of three-fourths of an inch, followed by a plateau of two inches. He contrasted these traits with suspiciousness which he represented as a band extending across the page with unchanging direction. He also added that he would color impulsiveness and anger red, and suspiciousness black. It is here proposed that traits with similar Gestalt properties, such as might hold true for impulsiveness and anger, are predisposed toward being assimilated by the spread process by virtue of this factor, as compared with dissimilarly figured traits, such as impulsiveness and suspiciousness. In Gestalt perceptual terms, this hypothesis parallels the principle of similarity as a factor in unit formation.

A more complex exploration of Gestalt properties would have to consider other sense modalities in addition to the visual, *e.g.*, synesthesic patterns as provided by such dimensions as smooth-rough, heavy-light, etc. The semantic differential techniques developed by Osgood (6) may be one approach to the determination of important Gestalt properties of personality traits.

The second factor in trait specification is an immature cognitive process characteristic of children between two and four years of age, but persisting as a form of archaic thinking throughout life. It is here designated the *DW power of disability* after the type of response on the Rorschach in which a detail of the blot (D) becomes the key for perceiving the whole blot (W) even though the other features of the blot do not support the percept. For example, children will commonly call Card VI a cat, primarily because the side projections, seen as whiskers, dictate the concept. As applied to the present discussion, a single fact of disability, like the cat's whiskers, has the power to reinstate a previous experience involving it, even though the rest of the existing conditions ill fit it.

The present situation then becomes analogous to the reinstated one. Moreover, because analogous reasoning gives added potency to the similarity of the situations being compared, the very act of drawing the analogy makes detection of flaws difficult.

To take an example from the area of disability, consider the pos-sibility that disability evokes thoughts of someone who was an invalid during the person's childhood. At that time the invalid may have been seen as bitter, irritable and indigent. It is these traits, then, that become attached to the meaning of a present disability by way of the DW process. Even more subtle meanings of disability may be captured by the DW process. For example, the omnipotence of infantile thinking may have led the child to attribute the invalidism to his own wishes, with consequent fear of retribution. He therefore, as an adult, sees the need for revenge as a complement to disability. It does not matter that the present situation bears little actual resemblance to the earlier one of invalidism, just as it does not matter that the rest of the Rorschach card does not look like the tail, paws and head of a cat.

What does seem to matter is the salience of the part as a symbol for the whole. Because of unique figural properties, the whiskers suggest a cat. Because of the central position of physique as a personal characteristic, a disability, too, is salient. And where a disability has been the focus of highly charged emotional meanings, especially as these were experienced during childhood when dramatic and even terrifying misconceptions about disablement so easily are formed, the saliency is even further enhanced.

The third adjunctive process lends *moral support* to the spread contents. As expressed in Heider's balance theory (7), man has a tendency to bring into harmony conditions as they exist with conditions as they ought to be. In short, the "ought" and "is" approach congruency. In order to satisfy the moral requirements, a disability, as a reality, "needs to be deserved." Thus, the cause of disability is so often associated with wrongdoing and sin. The negative spread to the cause of disability is given a moral significance. Once such a casual attribution has been effected, a guiding influence is exerted on the further selection of personality traits within the spread process. It should be noted that the same need for moral balance may, under certain conditions, hamper spread effects. If, for whatever reason, it is difficult to perceive the disability as deserved, negative spread may be expected to be limited. Thus, it is our prediction that, because of the presumed innocence of childhood, there would be a tendency to perceive children within a far more restricted negative spread than would be true of teenagers or adults.

The fourth process to be considered provides *rational support* for the spread phenomenon. From the total array of negative possibilities, a selective process occurs that seems to make some sense. For example, when someone has the idea that persons with a disability tend to be bitter and irritable, but not sneaky or conceited, the former may fit into a constellation made cogent by a certain view of the effects of misfortune. Moreover, it is likely that not only does the rational integrating process guide the selection, but also that it serves to rationalize the spread array that has been brought about by other processes. Whether the attempt at reason comes before or after the negative array has been differentiated, we may say that the spread phenomenon sets up a preju-diced orientation within which man's rational efforts function. As we shall soon see, there also are instances of the reverse. That is, rational consideration may define the sign, either positive or negative, of the orienting framework within which the spread phenomenon will then proceed.

NEGATIVE TRAIT— POSITIVE SPREAD

Thus far, we have considered disability as a negative fact from which a negative spread ensues. This sequence may be complicated by the possibility that a disability, in spite of its being negative, may also spark a positive spread through the interpolation of other processes. It is a fact that an admixture of positive and negative personality impressions is typical of those generally reported. Thus it is that the man pictured in the wheelchair in one study (8) was not only perceived as unhappier than when pictured in the nondisabled state, but also as more conscientious and generous.

One such interpolated process is a rational one which links a particular conception about disability to positive effects, which effects, in turn, give a positive direction to the spread that follows. For example, the belief that deep understanding is a by-product of disability may be sufficiently potent to initiate a positive spread in connection with disability.

It is also proposed that, although it is cognitively easier to integrate like-sign personal attributes, there are certain nonrational predispositions toward grouping traits of opposing sign. We do not feel comfortable for long with a person who is either all good or all bad. Thus, the person who aspires to the purity of God is soon damned. At the other extreme, even the most despised are raised a notch by the awakening of compassion. It is as if some counterpoint is required in which a more complex, but more interesting, picture of the person emerges whose features are both positive and negative. The all good—all bad percept tends to be reserved for the condition of dedifferentiation such as occurs with heightened emotionality.

The nature of the nonrational predisposition toward bringing traits of unlike sign together offers challenging speculation. Possibly a need to be fair, to balance the score, may be at work. Possibly there is an aesthetic appeal in the more complex personality impression. Not to be discounted is the possibility that traits of unlike sign may have similar figural properties that make for a stable personality structure in the Gestalt sense. Finally, this type of balance tendency may be related to the kind of free association process in which the stimulus word elicits its opposite instead of a halo proliferation of like-sign associations. Love evokes hate, hot evokes cold, and so on. As applied to person-perception, the idea of disability would then predispose the evaluator toward ability connotations. He may see the person as able in special ways, perhaps made cogent by a theory of compensation for misfortune. For example, the person who is blind may be said to have a sixth sense, the person who is crippled, a depth of understanding, and so forth.

SPREAD AND ADJUSTMENT

It is of interest to consider the way spread is related to certain principles of adjustment to disability. These principles characterize adjustment as a process that encourages the person to view himself as a person with a disability, rather than as a disabled person, the latter syntax epitomizing the spread phenomenon.

The principle known as *enlargement of the scope of values* is especially applicable in the case where the person has become so overwhelmed by his disability that nothing else exists but his loss, and his suffering seems boundless in extent and time. The spread effects have become so diffuse that they have inundated all of his life, even obliterating the variety of meanings and possibilities that life has to offer. Whatever the person thinks about he is filled with pain and gloom. The main problem for that person is to begin to see meaning and potential in those aspects of life which are not touched by the disability or closed off to the person. It requires a renewal of values that have been submerged by the disability, as well as an appreciation of new ones.

The principle, *containing disability effects*, attacks the spread phenomenon directly by indicating that the adjustment process involves a new look at the implications of disability, so that they can become confined to those areas which in fact are disability-connected.

Subordinating physique, as a principle, challenges the hegemonious position which disability commands in the spread phenomenon. It affirms that body-whole and body-beautiful are often overrated as values, and implies that if physique becomes a less central personal characteristic, its spread effects will be less.

Finally there is the *change from comparative to asset values*, a change which has been regarded as essential to fully accepting a disability as non-devaluating. Since physique as a value is of substantial importance, the negative effects of disability will tend to show considerable spread when viewed from a comparative standpoint. On the other hand, an asset frame of mind can be expected to retard spread.

In addition to the above principles, I would like to consider the role of *denial* in the adjustment process. It is discussed here because denial often seems to arise as a counter reaction to spread. Both spread and denial alter reality, spread by exaggerating disability effects and denial by overly containing them.

In its extreme form, denial is seen as anosognosia, a term first introduced by Babinski in 1914 to denote denial of paralysis, and since applied more generally to all extreme cases of denial of illness (9). The person who is blind insisting that he can see, or the individual who is paralyzed, that his limb can be moved, are dramatic examples. To account for the apparent discrepancy between his assertion and reality, the person rationalizes. Thus, one patient, having denied that his limb was paralyzed, attributed his difficulty in moving it to the fact that it was "sore from injections." Another patient who denied his blindness said he could not see because there were

"tears in his eyes." It is noteworthy that anosognostic patients typically have some form of brain damage, this condition evidently facilitating the necessary suspension of reality testing. Anosognostic denial has been interpreted to be a mode of adjustment to avoid catastrophic reaction (10). I do not know of anyone who recommends anosognostic denial even as a useful or necessary first step in the process of adjusting to disability. When it occurs, however, there is some question as to whether it should be directly challenged, or whether the patient should be allowed to reconstitute himself at his own pace.

A second form of denial has been labeled "as if" behavior. Unlike the case of anosognosia, the person is aware of his disability, but acts "as if" it does not exist. He attempts to conceal it and avoid reference to it. This mode of adjustment has been criticized on the grounds that such pretense forces the person to become hypervigilant lest his disability be inadequately concealed. It therefore tends to reinforce physique as a dominant value in all situations, rather than allowing disability-connected matters to be restricted to relevant situations. It proves the paradox that deliberately trying to forget haunts the memory and thereby tends to increase spread effects. "As if" behavior has also been criticized as leading to estrangement in interpersonal relations. On the other hand, there may be some situations in which "as if" behavior is used to advantage, as when one wishes to avoid intrusion into one's privacy. Further complexities of "as if" denial, including a consideration of its possible positive value, have been elaborated elsewhere (4, 11).

A third form of denial may be called "denial by decathexis." This involves the intellectual admission of disability effects but the affective denial of any emotional investment in them. The blindness is recognized, for example, but in a totally bland or startlingly objective way. It is as if the negative sign were removed from the spread effects. This is not unlike man's efforts to deal with the overwhelming horror of nuclear warfare. Man deals with the idea of his own death in much the same way. We know that such numbing of affect often occurs in early reaction to trauma and allows the person time to regain the necessary strength to cope with the misfortune.

Spread and denial—two opposing tendencies. How effectively they succeed in limiting each other or indirectly reinforcing each other needs a good deal more analysis. When and how these tendencies can be pressed into serving the adjustment potential of the person also need further investigation. The four principles of adjustment previously discussed neither attempt to deny or exaggerate difficulties but rather to effect an acceptance of disability through important value changes. Spread and its opposite, denial, however, may some day become part of psychological strategy when we have more understanding of the conditions which indicate that a person needs to be temporarily jarred into realization of his difficulties through facilitating

spread, or lulled for awhile through encouraging denial.

REFERENCES

1. Asch, S. E.: Social Psychology. New York, Prentice-Hall, 1952.
2. _____: Forming Impressions of Personality. J. Abnorm. Soc. Psychol. 41:258–290, 1946.
3. Dembo, Tamara: Devaluation of the Physically Handicapped Person. Paper presented at the Annual Meeting of the American Psychological Association, Cleveland, Ohio, Sept. 4–9, 1953.
4. _____, Leviton, G. L. and Wright, B. A.: Adjustment to Misfortune—a Problem of Social-Psychological Rehabilitation. Artificial Limbs 3:4–62, 1956.
5. Butts, S. V. and Shontz, F. C.: Comparative Evaluation and its Relation to Coping Effectiveness. Abstract in Amer. Psychologist 17:326, 1962.
6. Osgood, C. E., Suci, G. J. and Tannenbaum, P. H.: The Measurement of Meaning. Urbana, University of Illinois, 1957.
7. Heider, Fritz: The Psychology of Interpersonal Relations. New York, Wiley, 1958.
8. Mussen, P. H. and Barker, R. G.: Attitudes Toward Cripples. J. Abnorm. Soc. Psychol. 39:351–355, 1944.
9. Weinstein, E. A. and Kahn, R. L.: Denial of Illness. Springfield, Ill., Charles C Thomas, 1955.
10. Goldstein, Kurt: The Organism: A Holistic Approach to Biology Derived from Pathological Data in Man. New York, American Book Co., 1939.
11. Wright, B. A.: Physical Disability—A Psychological Approach. New York, Harper, 1960.

33 Psychosocial Factors Involved in the Rehabilitation of Persons with Cardiovascular Diseases

Robert M. Gray,
Adina M. Reinhardt, and
John R. Ward

One of this nation's major health problems concerns the growing number of severely disabled persons (1). For example, it has been estimated that several million persons in this country are disabled today and a sizeable proportion of these will remain disabled for the rest of their lives, taxing medical facilities and welfare rolls unless something is done to improve this situation (2). Adding to the seriousness of the problem is the general agreement that the number of disabled persons will increase in the future, thus becoming a greater problem and creating a situation that could have serious consequences unless alleviated (3).

This paper will deal specifically with persons with cardiovascular disease who make up a sizeable proportion of the disabled population. Contributing to the interest in this group is the fact that rates of rehabilitation among these persons are lower than is the case with other disabled persons (4). Further emphasizing the extent of this problem are the disclosures that heart and other cardiovascular diseases are responsible for a sizeable proportion of the total number of disabled, in the United States, with over 16 million cases (5). A final observation of importance in the present context is the recognition that the death rate in coronary disease of the United States is among the highest in the world (6).

The specific purpose of the present paper is to report findings of a recent research endeavor that investigated several dimensions of cardiovascular patients' willingness or ability to accept their physical impairments and the effect of this behavior on their involvement in a rehabilitation program. A basic premise underlying the study is: The process of rehabilitating patients is psychosocial as well as being a physical process—one reason cardiovascular patients are rehabilitated less frequently than other disabled persons is their being less willing or able to accept their impairment realistically. It is further assumed that, once cardiovascular patients can be helped to accept their impairment and

Reprinted from Rehabilitation Literature, 1969, 30(12)354–359, 362.

participate in a rehabilitation program, they can be rehabilitated as successfully as are other disabled patients.

CONCEPTUAL FRAMEWORK

The conceptual framework upon which this study is based takes as its starting point the position that psychosocial factors play a significant role, especially in the lives of cardiovascular patients. The reasoning here is: These patients undergo profound social and psychological alterations once they perceive that they have a cardiovascular ailment; the effect on their ego structure is such that a sizeable proportion of these persons simply give up and resign themselves to a life of dependency and incapacitation. The acceptance of this role is further reinforced, according to Parsons, by societal values communicating to these persons that they are useless and that the obvious way to make their status legitimate is to "act out" their feelings of uselessness through the incapacitation of illness (7). Thus, it is to be expected that a sizeable proportion of cardiovascular patients will have resigned themselves to their fate and given up hopes of resuming their role as functioning, contributing members of society.

A further assumption of the present framework is: Persons with cardiovascular impairments, in addition to resigning themselves to their fate, will reinforce this mental state by denying the fact that they are ill more frequently than other severely disabled

persons do so. In this connection Whitehouse has pointed out that:

> The first reaction to a heart attack is fear of death, a condition of psychic shock, and this feeling may continue to remain prominently in the picture. The succeeding reaction may be either an obvious depression, which may persist in conjunction with other modes of maladjustment, or a masked depression covered by various regressive or denial patterns. Fears are also present. They are often expressed in questions as to whether normal living will be regained. Most fundamental and often unexpressed is the threat to the self, one's basic self-image and ego structure: Am I the same person? Did this really happen to me? Will this change me? Am I now less worthy, a different kind of person? Shall I lose the regard of my wife, my family, my friends? . . (8).

Karl A. Menninger gives further insight on this subject when he writes:

> Another class of patient who is likely to reject his disability is the patient with the internal disability, for example, the cardiac patient. With this patient, it is not false hope of eventual recovery, but the possibility of masking the defect which may render him resistive to rehabilitation measures (9).

Thus, it is to be expected that cardiovascular patients will tend to deny that they are ill due to the sequelae of a heart attack—psychic shock, fears, depression, and denial patterns, as previously suggested.

It is further assumed that cardiovascular patients will be less willing to adopt the sick role than will other severely disabled persons because a decisive element in assuming the role of a patient is the recognition by the affected person that he needs help in coping with his condition. In developing this latter point, it is important that the distinction between the disabled person's adopting the sick role and his taking a dependent and passive posture be kept clear. Adopting the sick role involves the recognition by the patient that he is ill and acceptance of the fact that he needs professional assistance in getting better. It further involves the understanding that the person is willing to seek competent medical services and cooperate in the treatment process.

The foregoing observations are of special pertinence in view of the fact that several recent reports and studies (10) have suggested that a reluctance to adopt the sick role inhibits the treatment process. R. N. Wilson pointed this out as follows:

> ... No one is "born" as a patient. ... The decisive element in assuming the role of patient is probably not the sheer fact of sickness or accident, but the recognition by the affected individual and/or certain other people of a particular need for help in coping with the condition. ... The decision to become a patient, whether it is autonomous or imposed, is conditioned by many factors including the urgency of symptoms, degree of experience with the sick role, and availability of help (11).

Consistent with these observations is the further assumption that cardiovascular patients will be not only less inclined to adopt the sick role but also less willing to respond to a prompting to participate in a rehabilitation experience. This expectation is based on the growing recognition that the acceptance of illness and disposition to seek aid in recovery is a key prerequisite to successful treatment.

Finally, it is assumed that, if persons with cardiovascular impairments can be helped to accept their disablement and become motivated to participate in a rehabilitation program, they can be rehabilitated as frequently and as successfully as other severely disabled persons.

A test of these assumptions follows through the balance of this paper.

RESEARCH PROCEDURES

The data analyzed in this study are from two sources: a national sample and a community sample of severely disabled persons. Throughout the remainder of this paper these samples will be identified as the "national" and the "community" samples. Subjects in both samples were severely disabled persons who had been allowed Social Security Disability benefits because of their disablement.

The National Sample

The national sample was made up of severely disabled persons who participated in a Vocational Rehabilitation Administration and Office of Social Security project located in 11 rehabilitation centers throughout the United States (12). The projects located in these centers, which were representative of all such centers throughout the country, were developed to: 1) study the feasibility of lowering the threshold for eligibility of Social Security Disability beneficiaries for rehabilitative services, and 2) determine the efficacy of intensive rehabilitation services when applied to severely disabled persons.

The national sample consisted of 4,463 severely disabled persons who were considered, after screening, to have some rehabilitation potential even though they previously had been awarded Social Security Disability benefits (12). The sample subjects, representing a broad range of disabili-

ties, were invited to participate in the rehabilitation programs at one of the 11 centers cooperating in the project. The mean age of the subjects in the national sample was 52.9 years with a standard deviation of 12.1 years. Their ages ranged from a low of 20 to a high of 68 years.

Those subjects adjudged as "persons with cardiovascular disease" had a primary disability meeting criteria established by the staff of the national study (12). These criteria included all heart disabilities as well as other impairments of the cardiovascular system. A breakdown of the community sample subjects with cardiac

Table 1. The etiologic cardiac diagnosis therapeutic classification and functional class of community sample subjects disabled by heart disease

Cardiac diagnosis	Functional class	American Heart Association functional class and therapeutic classification*				
		Therapeutic classification				
		A	B	C	D	E
Hypertensive cardiovascular disease	I.					
	II.		1	1	1	
	III.					
	IV.					
Rheumatic heart disease	I.					
	II.			1		
	III.			1		
	IV.					
Arteriosclerotic heart disease	I.					
	II.		4	4		
	III.			4	4	
	IV.					
Arterial disease	I.					
	II.		1			
	III.			3	2	
	IV.					

*Classifications taken from: Criteria Committee, New York Heart Association, Nomenclature and Criteria of Diagnoses of Diseases of the Heart and Blood Vessels, 5th Ed. New York: New York Heart Association, 1953.

impairments who are representative of the national sample participants relative to their cardiac diagnosis and functional class is contained in Table 1.

The Community Sample

The community sample was composed of 109 disabled persons, aged 55 years and over, who were contacted in their homes and encouraged to participate in the program of a rehabilitation center located in a medical school of a western state that was cooperating in the national study. This sample differs from the national sample in that only those persons 55 years of age and over were included for the purpose of analysis and also in that it included persons who did not come to the rehabilitation center as well as those who did, which was not the case for the national sample. These differences introduce no bias into the study inasmuch as the two samples are not used for comparative purposes. The mean age of the community sample was 62.6 years with a standard deviation of 5.0 years. Ages ranged from a low of 50 to a high of 68 years.

Self-Perception of Health Status

In testing the adequacy of the conceptual framework developed in this paper as a partial explanation as to why rehabilitation success rates are lower among persons with cardiovascular disease than among other disabled persons, the first factor to be investigated concerned the subjects'

perception of their physical health. It was hypothesized that cardiovascular patients would tend to deny their illness more frequently than would other severely disabled persons. A test of this hypothesis was made using the subjects' responses to a questionnaire of Burgess and others (Your Activities and Attitudes (13)) which was designed to measure personal adjustment in later maturity. The subjects' responses to the health subscales and other health items in this inventory were used in this analysis.

As may be seen in Table 2, the cardiovascular patients in the community sample perceived themselves as less sick, reported that they spent fewer days in bed, and said they were troubled with fewer physical and emotional difficulties than were the severely disabled persons in the comparison group. This was not an unexpected finding and it is consistent with the conceptual foundation upon which this study is based.

Attitude Toward Disability

Another important dimension hypothesized to be instrumental in influencing the participation in rehabilitation of cardiovascular subjects was related to their attitudes toward their disabilities. A basic supposition underlying this premise was that disabled persons with cardiovascular disease are not rehabilitated as often as are other disabled persons because they more frequently become resigned to living with their disablement rather than accepting it realistically. In other words, we hypothesized that subjects with

Table 2. Comparison of community cardiovascular patients and all other severely disabled community patients in terms of self-perception of health status (N = 109)

Self-perception of health status	Cardiovascular patients		All other severely disabled		χ^2
	N	%	N	%	
Current health status					
Poor health	7	26	54	66	13.4*
Fair to good health	20	74	28	34	
Serious physical problems					
Few	12	44	20	24	3.94**
Three or more	15	56	62	76	
Number of days spent in bed					
A few or none	19	70	27	33	11.68*
Two or more weeks	8	30	55	67	
Physical or emotional difficulties					
A few	19	70	36	44	5.69**
Many	8	30	46	56	
Self-report of having serious physical difficulties					
One or less	9	33	5	6	
Two or more	18	67	77	94	13.46*
Health attitude subscale Burgess activities and attitude scale					
Health "very poor"	0	0	25	30	10.68*
Health "fair to good"	27	100	57	70	

*p .01.
**p .05.

cardiovascular impairments would express attitudes of passive hopelessness and resignation more frequently than would comparable persons disabled by other physical conditions.

Data contained in Table 3 relative to the national sample (where the rehabilitation center teams evaluated the patients as to their attitude toward disability) indicate that a significantly larger proportion of the cardiovascular patients were resigned to living with their impairment. This was in comparison with all other severely disabled patients, who more frequently were evaluated as having accepted their disablement realistically. This was an expected finding.

Table 3. Comparison in national sample of cardiovascular patients and all other severely disabled patients in terms of attitudes toward disability*

Attitude toward disability	National sample patients			
	Cardio-vascular patients		All other severely disabled patients	
	N	%	N	%
Accepting realistically	277	36	1042	45
Resigned	372	48	768	33

$\chi^2 = 42.99$ p .01.

*Variations between sample size and figures reported above and in Tables 6 and 7 occurred because these data were not collected on all subjects due to persons leaving project, noncooperation, or data not applicable.

Adoption of Sick Role

An additional factor examined in this study that assumably was related to the cardiovascular subjects' rehabilitation experience was related to their willingness to accept the sick role. It was hypothesized that these persons would accept the sick role less often because this would involve their acceptance of the fact that they were impaired and that they had an obligation to try to get better. Data relative to this hypothesis were obtained by administering a questionnaire to the community sample subjects, which contained Mechanic's measurement of a person's tendency to adopt the sick role (14). The resulting data, contained in Table 4, indicate that, as

expected, the cardiovascular patients in the community sample adopted the sick role less frequently than did the other disabled patients. This is an especially significant finding when it is considered that a person's willingness to adopt the sick role is usually a functional prerequisite to rehabilitation and treatment.

Participation in Rehabilitation Program

The next phase of the study was determining if there were any differences in the rehabilitation rates between persons disabled by cardiovascular diseases and comparable persons disabled by other physical conditions. A basic assumption of the conceptual framework developed in this paper was that the cardiovascular patients would be less willing to accept an invitation to participate in a rehabilitation center program than would other severely disabled persons. This assumption was

Table 4. Comparison of community cardiovascular patients and all other severely disabled patients in terms of adoption of the sick role (N = 109)

Adoption of the sick role	Community sample patients			
	Cardio-vascular patients		All other severely disabled patients	
	N	%	N	%
Low tendency	14	52	27	33
High tendency	13	48	55	67

$\chi^2 = 3.10$ p .05.

tested by comparing the response rates of the two groups of disabled persons in the community sample, all of whom were contacted in their homes and urged to participate in the rehabilitation center program. The findings resulting from this comparison are contained in Table 5 and these data indicate that, consistent with the study conceptual framework, cardiovascular patients did not respond to an invitation to participate in a rehabilitation center program as frequently as did the other subjects.

Rehabilitation Success Rates

The final hypothesis of the study was that cardiovascular patients, once they were able to accept their impairment realistically and were motivated to participate in a rehabilitation program, would be rehabilitated as frequently as would other severely disabled persons.

This hypothesis was borne out, as may be seen by viewing Table 6. These data are relative to the proportion of the national sample who were rehabilitated to employment once they entered into a rehabilitation program that emphasized helping subjects accept their impairments and adopt the sick role. These data disclose that, while a higher percentage of the severely disabled persons as compared to the cardiovascular subjects were rehabilitated to employment, the difference between the two groups was not statistically significant.

These data are further buttressed by the findings reported in Table 7, which disclose the fact that cardiovascular patients in the national sample were rehabilitated to productive competitive or self-employment rather than homebound or sheltered workshop employment more frequently than were the other disabled sample subjects. These findings, which are in agreement with the study hypothesis, lead to the acceptance of the notion that severely disabled cardiovascular patients can be rehabilitated as frequently as other severely disabled persons once they enter into a re-

Table 5. Comparison of community cardiovascular patients and all other severely disabled patients in terms of their willingness to participate in a rehabilitation program (N = 109)

| | Community sample patients | | | |
| | Cardiovascular patients | | All other severely disabled patients | |
Participation in rehabilitation program	N	%	N	%
Participants	9	33	47	57
Nonparticipants	18	67	35	43

x^2 = 7.16   p .01.

Table 6. Comparison of national sample of cardiovascular patients and all other severely disabled patients in terms of frequency of successful rehabilitation

| | National sample patients | | | |
| | Cardiovascular patients | | All other severely disabled patients | |
Success of cases being rehabilitated	N	%	N	%
Closed employed*	54	39	300	46
Closed unemployed*	83	61	356	54

$x^2 = 1.83$ p = NS.
*These statuses are respectively interpreted as successful and unsuccessful rehabilitation.

habilitation activity that includes a program of helping subjects accept their impairment and adopt the sick role.

A note of caution needs to be inserted at this point concerning the findings reported in this study. The subjects in this study, first, are severely disabled persons, all of whom had previously been examined and rated poor rehabilitation risks. Therefore, these data are limited to severely disabled persons and as such are not necessarily applicable to persons with less serious impairments. Furthermore, it is quite possible that after one gets beyond a certain point of disablement relative differences of impairment are functionally meaningless. These observations document an important limitation of the data resulting from a comparison of severely disabled cardiovascular persons and comparable persons disabled by other impairments. Notwithstanding these limitations the foregoing findings are of pertinence, especially in view of the growing numbers of disabled cardio-

Table 7. Comparison of national sample of cardiovascular patients and all other severely disabled patients in terms of their employment status after successful rehabilitation

| | National sample patients | | | |
| | Cardiovascular patients | | All other severely disabled patients | |
Employment status after rehabilitation	N	%	N	%
Competitive and self-employment	44	81	180	60
Homebound or sheltered workshop	10	19	120	40

$x^2 = 9.36$ p .01.

vascular persons who are not being rehabilitated.

SUMMARY

The purpose of this study was to test the assumption that one reason cardiovascular patients are rehabilitated less frequently than other disabled persons is their being less willing or able to accept their impairment and the sick role realistically. A further test was made of the parallel assumption that, once cardiovascular patients can be helped to accept their impairment and participate in a rehabilitation program, they can be rehabilitated as successfully as can other disabled patients. A test of these assumptions was made utilizing data obtained from two sources: 1) a national sample of 4,463 severely disabled persons and 2) a community sample of 109 severely disabled persons who had been allowed Social Security Disability benefits because of their disablement.

The study analysis resulted in findings supporting the above assumptions. It provided additional insights as to why persons with cardiovascular impairments are rehabilitated less frequently than are other disabled persons. The resulting data disclosed that the severely disabled cardiovascular subjects tended to deny their illness more frequently than a comparable group of disabled persons. These patients also tended to be less willing to accept their illness realistically or adopt the sick role as compared to the other disabled persons.

Once the persons disabled by cardiovascular impairments entered a rehabilitation program that emphasized helping them accept their impairments and adopt the sick role they were rehabilitated comparably to other severely disabled persons.

These findings, together with the recognition that persons with cardiovascular impairments constitute one of the largest groups of disabled persons in the nation, emphasize the need and desirability of further research and application in this area.

Our findings support the conclusion that psychosocial factors may be partially responsible for the differential rehabilitation success rates found between subjects impaired by cardiovascular and those having other disabling conditions.

LIST OF REFERENCES

1. Switzer, Mary E. Vocational Rehabilitation in the United States. Internatl. Labour Rev. Mar., 1958. 77:3:189–208. Also see: U.S. Office of Vocational Rehabilitation. An Introduction to the Vocational Rehabilitation Process. Washington, D.C.: Govt. Print. Off., 1961. p. 10.
2. National Easter Seal Society for Crippled Children and Adults. 1963 Annual Report. Chicago: The Society, 1964. p. 2. For additional supporting information, see: Kelman, Howard R. Evaluation of Rehabilitation for the Long Term Ill and Disabled Patient: Some Persistent Research Problems. J. Chronic Diseases. July, 1964. 17:7: 631–639. Community Responsibility for Disability Prevention and

Rehabilitation, a staff paper prepared for the Office of Vocational Rehabilitation and Public Health Service Joint Task Force on Rehabilitation, Sept., 1961. p. 1–2. Rusk, Howard A. Background Paper on Rehabilitation of Disabled Middle-Aged and Older People, prepared under direction of White House Conference on Aging, Planning Committee on Rehabilitation, Washington, D.C., Apr., 1960. p. 3–4.

3. For example, see: Switzer, Mary E. Rehabilitation a Decade Hence. Rehab. Record. July–Aug., 1964. 5: 4:19–24. Whitten, E. B. The Road Ahead. J. Rehab. Sept.–Oct., 1964. 30:5:38–40. Gray, Robert M., Kesler, Joseph P., and Newman, W. R. Elton. Social Factors Influencing the Decision of Severely Disabled Older Persons to Participate in a Rehabilitation Program. Rehab. Lit. June, 1964. 25:6:162–167. Gray, Robert Mack, and others. Stress and Health in Later Maturity. J. Gerontol. Jan., 1965. 20:1:65–68. Krusen, Frank H. Physical Medicine and Rehabilitation for the Chronically Ill. J. Am. Geriatrics Soc. Feb., 1954. 2:2: 75–85.

4. White House Conference on Aging. Background Paper on Research in Gerontology: Psychological and Social Sciences. Washington, D.C.: Dept. of Health, Education, and Welfare, Apr., 1960.

5. Facts on the Major Killing and Crippling Diseases in the United States Today, 1966. New York (866 United Nations Plaza): National Health Education Committee, Inc., 1966.

6. See, for example, Puffer, Ruth R., and Verhoestraete, Louis J. Mortality from Cardiovascular Diseases in Various Countries, with Special Reference to Atherosclerotic Heart Disease, a Preliminary Analysis. Bul., World Health Organization. 1958.

19:2:315–324. Bronte-Stewart, B. The Epidemiology of Ischaemic Heart Disease. Postgrad. Med. J. (Brit.) Apr., 1959. 35:402:180–185.

7. Parsons, Talcott. Toward a Healthy Maturity. J. Health and Human Behavior. Fall, 1960. 1:3: 163–173.

8. Whitehouse, Frederick A. Cardiovascular Disability, p. 85–124, in: Garrett, James F., and Levine, Edna S., eds. Psychological Practices with the Physically Disabled. New York: Columbia Univ. Pr., 1962. p. 95.

9. Menninger, Karl A. Psychiatric Aspects of Physical Disability, p. 8–17, in: Garrett, James F., ed. Psychological Aspects of Physical Disability. Washington, D.C.: Dept. of Health, Education, and Welfare, [1952]. (Rehab. Serv. Ser. no. 210)

10. Lederer, Henry D. How the Sick View Their World. J. Social Issues. 1952. 8:4:4–15. Gray, Robert M. Adoption of the Sick Role and Rehabilitation of Severely Disabled Older Persons. Rocky Mountain Soc. Sci. J. 1965. 2:194–199. Mechanic, David, and Volkart, Edmund H. Illness Behavior and Medical Diagnoses. J. Health and Human Behavior. Summer, 1960. 1:2:86–94. Mechanic, David, and Volkart, Edmund H. Stress, Illness Behavior, and the Sick Role. Am. Sociological Rev. Feb., 1961. 26:1:51–58.

11. Wilson, Robert N. Patient-Practitioner Relationships, p. 273–295, in: Freeman, Howard E., Levine, Sol, and Reeder, Leo G. Handbook of Medical Sociology. Englewood Cliffs, N.J.: Prentice-Hall, 1963. p. 274, 275.

12. See Gray, Robert M., and others. The Severely Disabled Person Is Rehabilitated. Salt Lake City, Utah: Univ. of Utah College of Medicine, Div. of Physical Medicine and Rehabilitation, Mar., 1966.

13. Cavan, Ruth Shonle, and others.

Personal Adjustment in Old Age. Chicago: Science Research Associates, 1949. (Appendix A)

14. Mechanic, David, and Volkart, Edmund H. Stress, Illness Behavior, and the Sick Role. Am. Sociological Rev. Feb., 1961. 26:1:51–58.

34 Denial of Illness:

Its Occurrence in One Hundred Consecutive Cases of Hemiplegia

Morton Nathanson,
Philip S. Bergman, and
Gustave G. Gordon

Many descriptions of the phenomenon of denial of illness have been published.[1] The literature contains little, however, concerning the frequency of its occurrence. The purpose of this investigation was to determine the incidence of denial of illness in patients with hemiplegia. We chose hemiplegia because of its prevalence and extensive somatic involvement and for historical reasons. The study also permitted us to observe denial of illness in relation to the mental state of the patient, the side of the body involved, and other factors.

The term anosognosia, introduced by Babinski in 1914,[1e] referred to two cases of left hemiplegia, but it has subsequently been used by others to denote denial of other illnesses as well.

Reprinted from Archives of Neurology and Psychiatry, 1952, 68:380–387. Copyright 1952 by the American Medical Association.

[1] (a) Weinstein, E. A., and Kahn, R. L.: The Syndrome of Anosognosia, Arch. Neurol. & Psychiat. 64:772–791, 1950. (b) Henson, R. A.: On Thalamic Dysesthesiae and Their Suppression by Bilateral Stimulation, Brain 72:576–598, 1949. (c) Head, H., and Holmes, G.: Sensory Disturbances from Cerebral Lesions, ibid. 34:102, 1911. (d) Hemphill, R. E., and Klein, R.: Contribution to the Dressing Disability as a Focal Sign and to the Imperception Phenomena, J. Ment. Sc. 94:611, 1948. (e) Babinski, J.: Contribution à l'étude des troubles mentaux dans l'hémiplégie organique cérébrale (anosognosie), Rev. Neurol. 22:845–848, 1914. (f) Barkman, A.: De l'anosognosie dans l'hémiplégie cérébrale: contribution clinique à l'étude de ce symptome, Acta med. scandinav. 62:235, 1925. (g) Alajouanine, T.; Thurel, R., and Ombredane, A.: Somato-agnosie et apraxie du membre supérieure gauche, Rev. neurol. 41:695, 1934. (h) Egas Moniz; Almeida Lima, and de Lacerda, R.: Hémiplégies par thrombose de la carotide interne, Presse méd. 45:977, 1937. (i) Nielsen, J. M.: Gerstmann Syndrome: Finger Agnosia, Agraphia, Confusion of Right and Left and Acalculia, Arch. Neurol. & Psychiat. 39:536, 1938. (j) Nielsen, J. M., and Sult, C. W.: Agnosias and the Body Scheme, Bull. Los Angeles Neurol. Soc. 4:69, 1939. (k) Olsen, C. W., and Ruby, C.: Anosognosia and Autotopagnosia, Arch. Neurol. & Psychiat. 46:340, 1941. (l) Spillane, J. D.: Disturbances of the Body Scheme: Anosognosia and Finger Agnosia, Lancet 1:42, 1942. (m) Gerstmann, J.: Problem of Imperception of Disease and of Impaired Body Territories with Organic Lesions, Arch. Neurol. & Psychiat. 48:890, 1942. (n) Sandifer, P. H.: Anosognosia and Disorders of Body Scheme, Brain 69:122, 1946. (o) Schilder, P.: The Image and Appearance of the Human Body: Studies in the Constructive Energies of the Psyche, Psyche Monographs No. 4, Kegan Paul, Trench, Trubner & Company, Ltd., 1935. (p) Weber, F.P.: Agnosia of Hemiplegia and of Blindness After Cerebral Embolism, Lancet 1:44, 1942. (q) Roth, M.: Disorders of the Body Images Caused by Lesions of the Right Parietal Lobe, Brain 72:89–111, 1949.

Another phenomenon, the denial of existence of a part of the body, sometimes called autotopagnosia or somatoagnosia,[1g] has at times been confused with anosognosia. For the sake of clarity, we decided to abandon both these terms and refer to the phenomenon simply as denial of illness. We considered that a patient with a completely paralyzed extremity who maintained (1) that he could move the involved limb, (2) that it was not paralyzed or weak, or (3) that there was "nothing wrong" with it had denial of hemiplegia. In this report, although the terms "lack of awareness" and "denial" are often used interchangeably, they actually may have different implications, a point which will be discussed later.

MATERIAL AND METHOD

One hundred consecutive patients with hemiplegia were interviewed in Bellevue Hospital Center (Third and Fourth Divisions, Medicine, Neurology and Psychiatry). All were asked the same questions and given the same commands from a prepared form, which is reproduced here. The answers to the questions were recorded exactly as offered by the patient, and detailed descriptions of their responses to these commands were made. The ages ranged from 29 to 86 years, with an average age of 61.

Part 1.
1. Why are you here?
2. What is the matter with you?
3. Is there anything wrong with it (part involved)?

4. Is there anything wrong with it? (Examiner either points to or raises it.)
5. Can you move it? Raise it? etc.
6. Is it weak, paralyzed, numb? How does it feel?
7. What is this? (Examiner holds up part involved and shows it to patient.)
Part 2.
The questions concern orientation in time and space, ability to understand commands, general information, and attempts to elicit confabulation ("Have you ever seen me before?"; "Where were you last night?")

The questionnaire consisted of two parts. Part 1 was aimed at determining the patient's awareness of his illness, and Part 2, at determining his orientation and ability to understand and carry out commands. The questions were simple and direct and varied in wording, in order that cultural and educational differences should be eliminated. The interview began with general questions, such as, "Why are you in the hospital?" "Are you sick?" etc., and proceeded to more specific questions, such as, "Anything wrong with your arm?" "Anything wrong with it?" (examiner touching and lifting the involved part), and, "Can you move it?" This part was followed by questions to elicit evidence of an organic mental syndrome.

The same series of questions and commands was given to all patients with aphasia except those whose speech disorder was so severe that no contact could be made.

In this report, the term hemiplegia is used to mean complete paralysis of one or both extremities on one side of the body. When movement was present to the extent that the arm could be raised,[2] the case was not included. Patients with less severe abnormalities also may have denial of illness, but in order that the significance of responses to specific questions, such as "Can you move your hand?" should be interpreted more accurately, the criterion of complete paralysis was necessary.

The clinical diagnosis in more than 95% of this series was cerebrovascular accident, either intracerebral hemorrhage or occlusion of a major cerebral vessel. The remaining five patients had cerebral neoplasm (one primary and one metastatic), syphilis of the nervous system, and traumatic encephalopathy.

RESULTS

Patients with
Denial of Illness (Group 1)

Of the entire series of 100 patients with hemiplegia, 28 had denial of illness. This included five patients who, although they sometimes gave evidence of awareness of their illness, for the most part denied their defects. For example, two of the patients admitted that they had had a "stroke" but insisted that they could move or walk. The others fluctuated in their responses from awareness to total denial. Twenty-three patients of this group unequivocally and consistently denied

that they were ill, denied that their extremities were weak or paralyzed, and claimed that they could move them.

Patients with
Full Awareness of Illness (Group 2)

Forty-eight patients were able to indicate clearly and promptly the nature and extent of their illness. They were aware of their paralysis and of the reasons for hospitalization and readily admitted the extent of their disability. As will be shown later, this awareness was not always complete, and, on being further questioned, several patients gave hints of minimizing or ignoring their defects.

Patients with Whom No Verbal
Contact Could be Made (Group 3)

This group consisted of the remaining 24 patients, who presented right hemiplegia and severe aphasia.

ANALYSIS OF
FACTORS IN DENIAL

In the groups in which denial of illness was unequivocally present (Group 1) or absent (Group 2), analysis of the following factors was made: (1) presence of organic mental syndrome; (2) side of the body involved and, if the dominant side was involved, presence of aphasia, and (3) length of time the hemiplegia had been present.

---

[2] Since we did not encounter any patients whose lower extremity was paralyzed and the upper relatively spared, the questions were referred mainly to the upper extremity.

Mental Status

In Group 1 (with denial of illness) all the patients showed some degree of disorientation. The spheres of orientation most involved were time and place. Memory defects were less apparent, possibly because the patients' responses were more difficult to verify. This finding contrasts strikingly with that in Group 2 (patients who did not deny illness). In this group only 31% (15 of 48 patients) had an organic mental syndrome, whereas 56% (27 of 48 patients) did not have this defect, by the criteria described. In 12% (6) of the patients it was difficult to determine whether or not an organic mental syndrome was present, although they readily indicated awareness of their illness. Almost one-third (8 of 28) of the patients with denial of illness were in the psychiatric wards, whereas of those who did not deny illness, only one-ninth (5 of 48) came from the psychiatric pavilion.

Patients on whom repeated observations could be made presented denial of illness in direct relation to their degree of disorientation. The patient who denied his hemiplegia when grossly disoriented often admitted the defect when more alert and better oriented. In a series of 58 consecutive disoriented patients examined by Weinstein,[3] 52 had denial of illness.

Side of Involvement

A comparison of the groups showed a striking difference in regard to the side of the body involved. (Since there was only one patient with left hemiplegia and aphasia in the entire series, the term "dominant side" will not be used in this discussion.) Of the 28 patients who denied illness, 19 (69%) had left hemiplegia; 6 (21%) had right hemiplegia with aphasia, and 3 (11%) had right hemiplegia without aphasia. Of the 48 patients without denial of illness, 18 had left hemiplegia, 17 had right hemiplegia with aphasia, and 13 had right hemiplegia without aphasia.

Presence of Aphasia

The problem arose of classifying the patients with severe aphasia, who had to be included in an unselected series. The distribution of right and left hemiplegia in the two groups may be artificial because there is no way of knowing whether the patients with global aphasia denied their defects or not. There is no satisfactory way of evaluating the severely aphasic group, but it is reasonable to assume that some of them had denial of illness.

It is evident that the presence of aphasia is not incompatible with denial of illness. While a reliable evaluation of denial of illness is usually impossible in patients who have a predominantly receptive aphasia, such an evaluation can be made in most patients with motor aphasia. All the aphasic patients (24) with whom adequate communication could be established had expressive aphasia. Seventeen of these 24 patients fully realized and indicated the extent of their defects, and 7 gave

---

[3] Weinstein, E. A.: Personal communication to the authors.

equally convincing evidence of denial of illness.

Time Factor

In all the groups the hemiplegia had existed for periods ranging from one day to several years. There were representatives from each of the three groups in all periods in time. The individual numbers, unfortunately, were too small for statistical evaluation.

The factor of age proved not to be significant in this study, since the average age of the patients with denial of illness was 60, as compared with 62 for those who were aware of their illness.

Other Factors Observed
in Patients with Denial of Illness

The nature and character of the remarks made by the patients with denial of illness, either spontaneously or in response to various questions, suggest some of the underlying mental processes involved in this phenomenon.

Several of the explanations offered for their present situation involved other persons, usually members of their own families or the physician—for example, "My brother told me my hand was paralyzed," or "Well, that's what I was told by the doctors; I suppose the doctors know what they say." One patient, when asked whether he was paralyzed, said, "I have no way of determining that; I'm not a physician." Another, when asked whether her right hand was paralyzed, said, "Well, the doctors say it is; so I

guess it is," or, "I was told it was weak."

Rationalizations were common and often grossly unrealistic. One patient, when asked why she could not move her hand, said, "Somebody has a hold of it." Another patient, asked if anything was wrong with her hand, said, "I think it's the weather; I could warm it up, and it would be all right." One woman when asked whether she could walk said, "I could walk at home, but not here. It's slippery here." One patient, when asked if anything was wrong with his arm, said, "It's just a little stiff—from the cold or something." When asked why he couldn't raise it, he said, "I have a shirt on." A common explanation was "stiff joints," one which could have been accepted if the same patients had not claimed that they could move their paralyzed extremities.

Another said she entered the hospital "because I lost a lot of weight." Others gave a variety of unrelated somatic complaints.

Patients occasionally used facetious expressions, such as, "I came here to see you," when they were asked to explain their coming to the hospital. One woman who was almost moribund, dyspneic, and cyanotic stated, "I came for a vacation." Another said, "I guess New York State has a lot of money to waste."

Others were hostile throughout the examination and made statements like, "If I weren't sick I wouldn't be here, would I?"

Some of the responses given by the patients were frank confabulations. One patient claimed she was "here at home last night." Another said she was in church last night. Others stated that they knew the examiner from previous contacts.

Denial of Existence of Affected Extremity: Several of the patients in this group denied the existence of their affected extremities or were unable to identify parts of their involved extremities correctly. This phenomenon, called, among other things, autotopagnosia, was never the sole defect present and was not the defect upon which the evaluation of denial of illness was based. All these patients also had denial of illness. Even though they may have denied that the extremities were theirs, they stated that the ones they had were normal. The patients either could not identify the extremity when it was held up for their inspection or identified it as belonging to the examiner or someone else. One said, "I don't know what the hell it is!" They occasionally referred to it in inanimate terms, such as "dead wood." This defect sometimes took the form of an inability to identify fingers on the affected side. Taken by itself, such a finding suggests a finger agnosia or other aphasic or agnostic phenomenon, but the same patients give correct responses in regard to the unaffected side.

Absence of Aphasia: The patient may seem to have aphasia when the affected side is discussed. He may be unable to find the correct words, fail to carry out commands, become mute, or use neologisms or gibberish. When the normal side is tested, however, this apparent aphasia disappears. These phenomena did not occur in the patients who were aware of their illness. It is improbable that a disorder in language function, in the usual sense, can be implicated here. Furthermore, some patients with definite aphasia and right hemiplegia can clearly demonstrate, either verbally or by performance, that they are acutely aware of their physical defects. Weinstein has described "nonaphasic language disturbances" in patients with denial of illness.[4]

Denial of Associated Illnesses

This phenomenon was not studied in the same detail as denial of the hemiplegia, but the patients generally did not deny other illnesses that could be verified, such as heart disease, arthritis, or hypertension. For example, several patients stated correctly that they had heart disease, while denying the more obvious and more recent hemiplegia. One patient had had a Parkinsonian tremor in the left upper extremity for 20 years as the result of carbon monoxide poisoning. With the onset of his hemiplegia the tremor disappeared, but he said he was in the hospital "to try to get rid of the tremor I have." Many of our patients were incontinent of urine, but only an occasional patient denied this symptom. As a matter of fact, although there were a few bizarre explanations for wetting the bed, some of the answers were

---

[4] Weinstein, E. A., and Kahn, R. L.: Nonaphasic Misnaming (Paraphasia) in Organic Brain Disease, A. M. A. Arch. Neurol. & Psychiat. 67:72–79, 1952.

astonishingly frank. One patient said, "I just let go, and I don't give a damn."

Denial of Illness by Others

It is often stated, usually by the laity, but occasionally by physicians, that denial of illness occurs only because the patient has never been told that he is paralyzed and the sensory impairment in the involved limb prevents his becoming aware of this fact. In almost every case our patients were told directly and repeatedly that they were paralyzed, but this had no effect upon the response. The daughter of one patient, overhearing her mother deny the existence of her hemiplegia in answer to our questions, interrupted the interview to explain why the patient answered as she did. "We told her she was all right, and she believes us. If I told her she was paralyzed, then she would answer your questions right." She talked to her mother, demonstrated to her that she was paralyzed, and invited us to repeat the questions. Again the patient stated she could move her left extremities and denied that they were paralyzed.

Denial of illness is also encountered in persons related to, or closely associated with, the patient. One of our patients was so aphasic that he could respond only to the simplest commands, but his physician insisted that he had normal speech function, saying, "He's really a nice guy. He's only excited and nervous now."

Patterns of Disorientation

Weinstein and Kahn[5] found that disorientation in space and time usually follows a certain pattern in patients with brain disease. The directions of error were generally toward the patient's home, toward a happier time of day, or toward a time in which the patient was, or hoped to be, well. These patterns, in combination with the denial of illness itself, suggest a tendency toward a state of well-being exemplified by the home as contrasted with the hospital, the past as contrasted with the present, and absence of disease as contrasted with the current status. These findings were amply confirmed in this study, in which spatial disorientation, when it occurred, was always in the direction of the patient's home or toward a location less suggestive of illness than a hospital. That these patterns represent denial, and not lack of awareness, is evident from the spontaneous slips that occur in the conversation of these patients. One woman, aged 83, persistently claimed that she was home with her mother and father, but said spontaneously, "Doctor, will you come home with me and be my doctor when I get out of here?" Another woman maintained repeatedly, when questioned directly, that she was at home. In her conversation on other subjects, however, she indicated that she knew she was in a hospital. We asked her why she said she was at home when she knew she was in the

[5] Weinstein, E. A., and Kahn, R. L.: Patterns of Disorientation in Organic Disease of the Brain, A. M. A. Arch. Neurol. & Psychiat. 65:533–534, 1951; Patterns of Disorientation in Organic Brain Disease, J. Neuropath. & Clin. Neurol. 1:214–225, 1951.

hospital, and she replied, "Because I *want* to be home."

Another claimed that the hospital, which she named correctly, was in Buffalo, where she lived, and maintained that she was now "a couple of blocks from where I live." When told she was in New York City, she denied it. Later in the conversation, she was again asked where she lived, and she said, "Buffalo, when I'm home." This patient also showed "duplication," as observed by Weinstein in his series.[5] She maintained that there were several parts of Bellevue Hospital. One part she located correctly; the other part, "where I am now," she said was close to her home.

Some of these phenomena also occurred in the group without denial of illness. However, they were less common, did not take such bizarre forms, and were more susceptible of correction.

COMMENT

From the data presented, it is evident that denial of illness is fairly common. More than a quarter (28%) of the patients with hemiplegia showed this phenomenon. The actual incidence, however, is probably higher, since rigid criteria for a single illness were used and many of the patients could not be tested because of severe aphasia. The percentages presented here merely represent the incident of denial in a group of 100 consecutive patients ob-

served under the conditions stated above. Observations on another group of hemiplegic patients, with the same methods of testing, might yield a lower or a higher incidence of denial of illness, depending on the number of cases of left and right hemiplegia, the number of cases of severe aphasia, the type of hospital (psychiatric or general), and, to a certain degree, the attitude of the investigators.

Expressions of denial of illness by the patient are often overlooked by the physician because they do not interest him or do not appear relevant to the symptoms of which the patient does complain. Many of our patients readily admitted that they were "sick" and described many unrelated symptoms, but stated flatly that nothing was wrong with their extremities, even when confronted with the fact that they were paralyzed.

From sporadic case reports that appear in the literature, one gains the impression that denial of illness is a rarity, although Gerstmann[1m] had already suggested that many patients may be found to show this abnormality if the examiner looks for it. By its very nature—denial—it will rarely appear spontaneously in the history but mut be elicited by specific questions.

The difference in incidence of right and left hemiplegia was striking (3:1). Nielsen[6] classified this phenomenon among the symptoms of the "minor" hemisphere, although he stated that he had seen it in disease of

[6] Nielsen, J. N.: Agnosia, Apraxia, Aphasia: Their Value in Cerebral Localization, Ed. 2, New York, Paul B. Hoeber, Inc., 1946, pp. 82–84; 137–138.

the "dominant" side. In the present series, seven patients with right hemiplegia without aphasia expressed denial of illness. It is probable that this phenomenon is commoner in cases of severe aphasia than even these data indicate. Dattner,[7] by observing the imitation of gestures, showed that patients with severe aphasia are "confused" about the right side of the body and suggested that they lacked awareness of its defects.

Weinstein and Kahn indicated that the disorientation which occurs in these patients may merely be part of the whole pattern of denial of illness. Offhand remarks by many of our patients suggested that they actually knew where they were; yet when questions formally as to orientation, they claimed that they were either in their homes or in other places more familiar to them than the hospital. It appeared, at least in some cases, that these patients were literally denying their location in time and space, rather than being actually unaware of it. Pointing out the patients' defects in the most concrete manner failed to alter the stated conviction that their extremities were normal. Weinstein and Kahn showed that all the phenomena observed—the denial of illness, disorientation, confabulation, and language difficulty—are part of an over-all pattern of behavior which appears at certain levels of defective brain function.

Often when other illnesses were present in addition to the hemiplegia, only the hemiplegia was denied. One patient, whose long-standing Parkinsonian tremor disappeared with the onset of the hemiplegia, denied the paralysis and maintained that he still had the tremor. On the other hand, denial of illness, deafness, incontinence, and other symptoms can occur in association with denial of hemiplegia. We do not have sufficient information for worth-while speculation on this point.

In general, the productions of the patients with denial of illness closely resemble those in normal persons when explaining away or rationalizing any defect. The only differences are in degree and in susceptibility to correction.

SUMMARY

1. The incidence of denial of illness was found to be 28% on investigation of 100 consecutive cases of hemiplegia due to organic disease of the brain.

2. Denial of illness was always associated with an "organic mental syndrome" and occurred in a much higher proportion of cases of left hemiplegia. It also occurred, however, with lesions of the "dominant" hemisphere.

3. Associated phenomena, such as rationalizations, confabulations, duplications, denial of the existence of an extremity, denial of other illnesses, patterns of disorientation, and denial of the patient's illness by others, were observed and described.

---

[7] Dattner, B.: Body Image Disturbances with Lesions of the Dominant Hemisphere, Tr. Am. Neurol. A. 75:141–143, 1950.

35 Roles of Denial in Chronic Hemodialysis

M. J. Short and
W. P. Wilson

During the past decade, hemodialysis has become an established treatment for chronic renal failure. The use of long-term intermittent hemodialysis is now successful in maintaining the lives of individuals who otherwise, in the past, would have succumbed to a uremic death. With this procedure, these patients are sustained to return to their home, and assume a more or less usual life.

With the beginning of treatment, two to three times weekly, the dialysand (hemodialysis patient) is initiated to the endless series of accommodations and compromises that are to follow. These not only involve the dialysand, but also significantly affect members of his family and community. The early adjustments may require moving his home closer to the dialysis center, modifying his employment, or changing his responsibilities in the home. These initial modifications may be major changes, but they generally prove to be the least of the many accommodations that he will face during the course of hemodialysis. The continuing sequence of events will tax the dialysand, his family, and even the dialysis team to the limit. When faced with the recurrent physical and psychological stresses, these individuals will utilize the mental mechanism of denial in a manner characteristic for a chronic dialysis regimen.

DIALYSAND'S DENIAL

During the early period of adjustment to the dialysis program, the dialysand comes to admit or recognize the fact that his life is dependent upon dialysis. He recognizes that if dialysis should be terminated, he would cease to live. Cramond and associates (1) have pointed out that during the first weeks or months in the dialysis program, the dialysand ceases to deny his illness, accepting that his future and financial security arc uncertain. Most patients are able to achieve this level of insight, simply because of the undeniable reality of being hooked-up to the "machine" several times a week. Occasionally, a patient will avoid other dialysis patients with the implication that his condition is different.

Patients that are receiving hemodialysis as an interim treatment while they are awaiting renal transplantation do not make even this level of recognition of their life situation. They reject the idea of having to conform to the dietary regulations, etc. thinking that "all will be over once the transplant is in place." This, too, is a naive attempt

Reprinted from the Archives of General Psychiatry, 1969, 20: 433–437. Copyright 1969 by the American Medical Association.

to deny the significance and existence of their physical condition.

Typically, at this point, the dialysand accepts those limitations and attempts to "carry-on as usual." This response is a rather typical "flight into health." However, the dialysand comes to the prompt awareness that he has not the energy, and that his physical capacities do not meet his expectations. To handle these disappointments, he minimizes the significance of his limitations, only to begin again the reinforcement processes of denial that are to continue throughout the remainder of the dialysis program.

Psychological testing demonstrates the changes occurring in the personality of the dialysand during the course of dialysis. Using the Minnesota Multiphasic Personality Inventory (MMPI), Wright and associates (2) have demonstrated changes in scales 1, 2, and 3 which are frequently interpreted as representing the presence of denial. We have used supplementary scales for the MMPI (3) specifically designed to appraise repression, ie, the unconscious derivative of denial (4). Initial MMPI profiles on dialysis patients have not been unusual for our hospital population (Figure 1). In time, changes develop in scales 1, 2, and 3 of the MMPI (Figure 2), reflecting increasing denial. The index for appraisal of repression (R) also becomes significantly elevated. Coincident with this is a lowering of the anxiety (A) scale, demonstrating the effectiveness of the denial. These changes are rather typical for our dialysis patients. During periods of acute stress, when additional physical crises develop, the MMPI configuration becomes even more pronounced (Figure 3), demonstrating their capacity to mobilize even more denial.

The capacity for denial in these

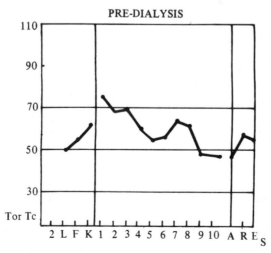

Figure 1. MMPI profile of patient prior to institution of hemodialysis. This profile is consistent with the general population of our hospital. The supplementary scales A, R, and Es represent indices for anxiety, repression, and ego strength, respectively. In this and subsequent figures the horizontal lines at 70 and 30 represent the boundaries of 2SD.

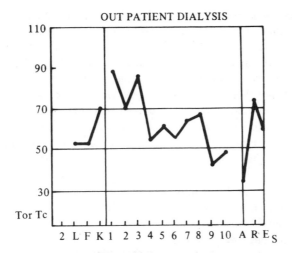

Figure 2. During the course of hemodialysis the MMPI profile of the patient reflects the increasing presence of denial. The so-called hysterical "V" formed by the elevation of scales 1 and 3 associated with a lower value for scale 2 has been interpreted as demonstrating the presence of denial. Elevation of scale R supports the increasing intensity of repression, the unconscious derivative of denial.

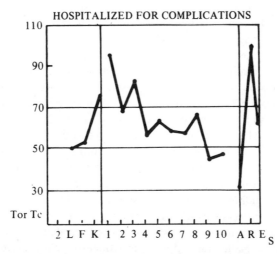

Figure 3. The capacity for these patients to mobilize additional resources for repression is demonstrated in this MMPI obtained from the patient when he was hospitalized for surgery. The R scale is markedly elevated. The K-F ratio, KF, may be interpreted as an attempt on the part of the patient to present himself as appearing better than he is.

patients is phenomenal, but what are they denying? Previously, it was pointed out that these patients accept their condition and the inevitability of its outcome. What is denied is that it is happening now. When their bones become bowed from osteomalacia, and they go from a cane to a walker, and then to a wheelchair, they continue to expect and to hope that this process will be reversed. When clotting, bleeding, or infection occurs at the cannula site, they accept this as a singular occurrence, only to have it happen again.

The dialysis patient not only has renal failure, but with time, he may develop a variety of medical complications that further compounds his condition. To continue in life with chronic infections, hypertension, peripheral neuropathy, anemia, and secondary hyperparathyroidism, all at one time, most certainly would require a special capacity to repress. Such a combination of problems is not uncommon in a dialysis patient.

In addition to the complications of treatment that may affect the dialysand's psyche, there are repeated shifts of plasma electrolytes affecting the brain. The blood urea nitrogen (BUN) may be dropped from 180 to 60 mg per 100 cc in the course of an eight-hour dialysis. There may also be profound shifts in potassium and sodium electrolytes. The brain's response to shifts of this magnitude at times produces clouding of the sensorium during the process of dialysis. In time, most patients develop a significant degree of "organic brain" dysfunction. These changes are readily demonstrated by Bender-Gestalt figures, and the performance level on the Wechsler Adult Intelligence Scale (WAIS) falls appreciably below the verbal level, indicating "organicity" (M. J. Short, MD, and A. D. Krugman, PhD, unpublished data).

In view of the foregoing, it would appear that increasing denial would be an inevitable consequence of chronic hemodialysis. However, in actuality, it may be necessary that these patients be allowed to maintain their capacity to repress in order to cope with their life situation.

FAMILY DENIAL

At the beginning of the dialysis program, there are usually a number of accommodations that the family has to make in order to adapt to the treatment program. They make these changes in good faith and with sincere motivation; however, the demand to adjust to continuing changes imposed by dialysis complications does not stop. As the dialysis patient continues to decline, the home responsibilities that he maintained at the beginning of dialysis are slowly given up. These concessions occur over a period of months to several years, but it is a continuous process of decay for the patient and his home situation. The dialysand becomes more and more a spectator in home activities, and in time, he may no longer be involved in family decisions, since his presence in the future is far from certain.

The repeated stresses and disappointments encountered by the dialysand are shared by his family. The continual uncertainty for the future wears on the spouse. The initial hope that comes with the beginning of dialysis is slowly transformed into a weary accommodation to a situation, where the dialysand is living on "borrowed time."

Marital roles previously established in the marriage become altered and the closeness of marital life becomes more distant. These changes are most pronounced when the dialysand is the husband, who had been the authority figure in the family. His usual masculine vigor declines with loss of sexual capacity. The physical changes in stature, and particularly the desquamating skin changes, minimize intimate contact. By the natural consequence of events, he becomes a dependent member of the family. These changes are slowly arrived at, and are truly disappointing consequences of the unabated progression of physical as well as psychological changes occurring in the marriage.

In order to maintain a degree of self-protection, the spouse, who initially supports the dialysis program for the mate, begins to question the validity of the decision to continue the dialysis. They recognize the changes occurring in their loved one, who is no longer the person they married. They see their children moving away from the disabled parent, making decisions at the exclusion of the dialysand. Initially, attempts are made to correct these reactions, but the problem persists. In an effort to maintain some degree of balance in the household, these changes become ignored and situations producing them are avoided by the family. All of which establishes a pattern of denial for the family.

It becomes evident that the family is also paying a big price for the "borrowed time." These hostile feelings are rationalized, that the patient's suffering is so great that he might be better out of his misery, or the family may project their guilt onto the dialysis team by criticizing the management of the patient.

In contrast to the dialysand who maintains himself with the support of denial, the family cannot continue effectively with this attitude. Assistance during the early phases of treatment will significantly improve the handling of problems as they occur, and at the end of dialysis, the family will hopefully be prepared to handle a normal grief reaction, free from excessive guilt feelings.

COMMUNITY DENIAL

Dialysis patients tend to give up their activities and recreational pursuits. Their loss of energy and apathy contribute to this; however, many patients comment that they are avoided by their friends and associates. These patients perceive the subtle rejections by once close friends who become uncomfortable in the presence of the dialysand. People feel ill at ease with these patients. A dialysis patient acquires a definite "sick appearance" early in the course of treatment. Not only does he look thin and apathetic, but his skin acquires a pallid gray hue, and his sclera becomes icteric. As a consequence, these patients give up playing cards with their former "poker buddies" and drop out of their civic activities. Members of the community tend to avoid or even reject the dialysis patient, reinforcing the process of denial in the dialysand.

TEAM DENIAL

During the course of intermittent hemodialysis, close relationships develop between the dialysand and the nursing staff. The dialysand will often see the nurse as his most confidential friend. The nurse attends to him during his most dependent hours, when he is "hooked-up to the machine." At this time, the dialysand is more inclined to regress, expressing more complaints when his frustration and pain thresholds are at their lowest. Regression slowly increases with more and more demands placed on the nurse, until it is no longer possible to satisfy the patient. At this point, the noble, well dedicated nurse becomes frustrated; she wants to meet the patient's needs, but cannot satisfy his demands. This is a critical period in the course of hemodialysis, for a conflict develops between the two most significant people in the program, the dialysand and the dialysis nurse. Unless the nurse can recognize this situation when it occurs, she will fall into one of two pitfalls. She will either cater to the dialysand's every beckon and call, or she will ignore them. Should either occur, she will feel guilty, then angry, and finally reject the patient; however, when these situations are recognized for what they are, ie, requests for attention, and not just unreasonable demands, she will be more effective in caring for the patient. Because these situations recur repeatedly, it may do well for the

dialysis nurse to assume the role of an understanding mother.

As mentioned earlier, the dialysand not only has chronic renal failure, but many superimposed major medical problems. A physician caring for these patients will be recurrently taxed to manage an admixture of pathological conditions within one patient. It is not an oversimplification to say that these patients are never well. As a consequence of the constant chronic diseases in the patient, the physician tends to accommodate to the fact that his patients are "walking textbooks of medicine." In time, he comes to recognize that his patients are destined to live with several simultaneous illnesses, and that he will have to accept this fact.

For some physicians, this is difficult to accept. The doctor who is able to handle a medical situation such as this is a special breed. However, he too has a trap waiting for him at some time during the management of chronic hemodialysis patients. The physician must be able to accept the presence of multiple chronic diseases in his patients, realizing that these conditions can smolder until they reach proportions of significant magnitude. When managing chronically debilitated patients, a thin line separates clear clinical judgment "to wait," from that of avoiding the situation and denying the magnitude of the condition.

A dialysis physician becomes used to being "between the Scylla and Charybdis," when managing the medical complications of dialysis patients. The problem is to recognize when it is time to act upon a compromised situation; it is easier to make a choice between the lesser of two rights, than the lesser of two evils (compromised situations).

The life and death problems of the dialysand do not confront the psychiatric member of the dialysis team as they do the internist; however, in the course of caring for the dialysand, the psychiatrist soon finds that there are too few approaches to the solution of the psychosocial problems confronting the dialysand. What life adjustments or modifications that were possible to make for the dialysand and his family were done during the early phases of dialysis, leaving few resources to cope with during the later stages of treatment. However, the emotional and social problems persist throughout the period of dialysis, and he is to manage these problems with as much insight as the patient is still able to mobilize and the family can handle. At this time, it would become convenient to spread out the visits with the patient, when there remains no alternative and nothing new to add to the situation. Should this occur, then he too has weakened under the unrelenting stress of the dialysis situation, yielding to the ubiquitous presence of denial. To counter such inclinations when faced by this immutable medical situation, it is well to remember the admonition, *guerir quelquefois, soulager souvent, consoler toujours* (to cure sometimes, to relieve often, and to comfort always)(5).

CONCLUSIONS

To say the least, chronic hemodialysis is a problematic therapeutic endeavor.

Repeated dialysis does substitute for diseased kidneys but at the present level of development, dialysis does so only to a limited degree. The variety of metabolic complications occurring in dialysis patients attests to the fact that this approach to chronic renal failure is only an acceptable substitute for normal kidney function.

Inherent in the dialysis program are many unusual demands placed upon the patient, family, community, and dialysis team. Often times, a convenient and expeditious response to these problems is denial. When this occurs in the dialysand, it may serve as an effective mental mechanism helping him to cope with a continuing unsatisfactory situation. Denial is ineffective for the family and community and inappropriate for the nurses and physicians responsible for the care of the dialysand.

REFERENCES

1. Cramond, W. A.; Knight, P. R.; and Lawrence, J. R.: The Psychiatric Contribution to a Renal Unit Undertaking Chronic Haemodialysis and Renal Homotransplantation, Brit J Psychiat 113:1201–1212 (Nov) 1967.
2. Wright, R. G.; Sand, P.; and Livingston, G.: Psychological Stress During Hemodialysis for Chronic Renal Failure, Ann Intern Med 64: 611–627 (March) 1966.
3. Welsh, G. S.: "Factor Dimensions A and R," in Welsh, G. S., and Dahlstrom, W. G. (eds.): Basic Readings on the MMPI in Psychology and Medicine, Minneapolis: University of Minnesota Press, 1956, pp 264–281.
4. Fenichel, O.: The Psychoanalytic

Theory of Neurosis, New York: W. W. Norton and Co., Inc., 1945, p 148.

5. Strauss, M. B. (ed.): Familiar Medical Quotations, Boston: Little, Brown & Co., 1968.

36 Relationships Between Intellectual Factors and Coping in Physical Rehabilitation

Max L. Fogel and
Ronald H. Rosillo

Investigations of the significance of intellectual functioning for improvement in physical rehabilitation have yielded inconclusive results (Anderson, Bourestom & Greenberg 1970; Freed et al. 1971; Lorenzo & Cancro 1962). The most effective prognostic indicators have generally been found among perceptual-spatial-motor types of tasks, but even these have not yielded strongly reliable relationships with improvement parameters (Boone 1959; Gruen 1962; Shontz 1957; Wood 1955). One factor contributing to the inconsistency in these results has been a lack of specificity in using the term "rehabilitation." This concept may refer to any of several broadly construed social, vocational, functional, or physical reconstructive treatment activities, or to subunits of one of these major activities such as self-care or ambulation.

Another problem contributing to confusion in this research area is the wide variety in the types of patients selected for evaluation. Differing types of lesions with their attendant disabilities often lead to differing functional effects upon intellectual capacities. Anderson, Bourestom, and Greenberg

(1970) found that certain performance tests of the Wechsler Adult Intelligence Scale (WAIS) evidenced some degree of prognostic validity in respect to rehabilitation outcome, for example, digit symbol in relation to improvement in self-care and block design in relation to improvement in functional communication. Lorenzo and Cancro (1962) reported that impaired performance on block design and object assembly were negative indicators for the recovery of self-care in hemiplegic patients. Ben-Yishay and others (1968, 1970, 1971) and Diller and others (1971) have also evaluated block design along with other tests of cognitive integration in hemiplegic patients undergoing rehabilitation.

Choice of different types of criterion variables for assessment of physical rehabilitation outcome is a third major issue which has led to difficulty in interpretation of studies of the association between intelligence and rehabilitation (Shanan, Cohen & Adler 1966).

The approach adopted in the present investigation was to undertake an overall evaluation of intellectual factors with particular reference to global indices of physical improvement in rehabilitation, using as subjects a wide variety of patients undergoing rehabilitation in two separate facilities. The only aspect of rehabilitation rated was that of physical improvement. Criterion measures consisted of global ratings of improvement by a team of physiatrists and length of hospital stay.

METHOD

Subjects were 122 physically disabled patients hospitalized at the Piersol Rehabilitation Center, University of Pennsylvania (n=98) or at the Veterans Administration Hospital in Philadelphia (n=24). The 93 male and 29 female subjects ranged in age from 16 to 76, with a mean age of 44.8. Their mean level of education was 10.1.

The patients were also categorized into four major groups (Rosillo & Fogel 1970a) consisting of: 32 braindamaged, including 17 left and 10 right hemiplegics (mean age, 49.1; mean level of education, 10.3); 30 amputees (mean age, 49.3; mean level of education, 10.8); 27 spinal cord lesions (mean age, 39.3; mean level of education, 10.2); and 33 miscellaneous (mean age, 43.4; mean level of education, 9.2), including patients with severe disabling pelvic and lower extremity fractures, peripheral neuropathies, severe burns, and systemic diseases such as rheumatoid arthritis. The hemiplegias were caused in all cases by cerebrovascular accidents occurring six weeks or more prior to admission for rehabilitation.

Soon after admission for rehabilitation the patients were administered seven WAIS subtests, and prorated IQ scores were calculated. Some patients could not be administered all of the tests.

At discharge each patient was rated on the degree of overall physical improvement since admission by a team of physiatrists who evaluated on a 5-point scale ranging from "markedly improved" to "worse." Only the degree of improvement during hospitalization was rated. Thus a single change score was obtained for each patient (Rosillo & Fogel 1970a).

All variables were analyzed by chi-square technique. In order to minimize the number of low frequency cells, and to sharpen trends for heuristic value, the data was condensed into 2 X 2 or 2 X 3 tables for chi-square analyses.

RESULTS

IQ Scores

The findings shown in Table 1 indicate nonsignificant relationships between IQ scores and physical improvement. IQ and improvement rating cutoff levels other than those shown in the table were also applied, resulting in no appreciable differences.

Subtest Scores

No subtest score significantly discriminated physical rehabilitation progress. Trends toward mild positive relationships did occur in the 3 performance tests, two of which are shown in Table 2.

Table 1. Frequency classification of prorated WAIS scores and physical improvement ratings of patients in rehabilitation

Level	Full scale IQ			Verbal IQ			Performance IQ		
	$\leqslant$90	90+	Total	$\leqslant$90	90+	Total	$\leqslant$90	90+	Total
4 to 5	29	46	75	33	51	84	28	47	75
1 to 3	15	15	30	14	21	35	15	15	30
Total	44	61	105	47	72	109	43	62	105

Note: Numbers vary according to ability to take tests.
p = ns.

Table 2. Frequency classification of performance subtest scores and physical improvement ratings of patients in rehabilitation

Level	Test		
	Picture completion[1]		
	2–8	9+	Total
4 to 5	35	46	81
1 to 3	21	15	36
Total	56	61	117

	Picture arrangement[2]		
	0–6	7+	Total
5	18	28	46
1 to 4	32	27	59
Total	50	55	105

Note: Numbers vary according to ability to take tests.
[1] Chi-square = 2.28; $p < .20$.
[2] Chi-square = 2.36; p = ns.

Age and sex were analyzed for all scores and were found not to alter the findings.

Diagnostic Groups

The brain-damaged, amputee, spinal cord lesion, and miscellaneous group results may be seen in Table 3. The brain-damaged groups' scores were lower than those of the other groups except on comprehension and verbal IQ. The spinal cord group achieved the highest scores in all tests but picture arrangement. F-tests revealed significant group differences in four subtests. Comparisons by t-test, shown at the bottom of Table 3, indicated that the brain-damaged group contributed heavily to the significant variances.

Relationships between WAIS scores and improvement ratings were inspected separately for each diagnostic group. Considering the two small hemiplegic subgroups first, verbal score differences were found favoring the left hemiplegics (LH) over the right hemiplegics (RH) (LH prorated verbal IQ = 100.9; RH verbal IQ = 79.8). Contrary to trends typically obtained, the LH group also had slightly higher prorated performance IQs (LH = 89.5; RH = 81.9). Another finding not anticipated was that in the left hemiplegics improvement was negatively associated with verbal scores. These relationships were nonsignificant but consistent. For example, there were nine high improvers with a

Table 3. Mean subtest and WAIS IQ scores for subgroups of physically disabled patients

Subgroups	Comprehension	Arithmetic	Similarities	Digit span[1]	Picture completion[1]	Block design[1]	Picture arrangement[1]	Verbal IQ	Performance IQ[1]	Full-scale IQ[2]
									IQ scores	
Brain-damaged	9.2	7.9	7.5	7.6	7.1	5.6	5.6	92.8	87.2	89.5
Amputees	9.8	8.4	8.4	8.5	9.2[3]	7.4[3]	6.7	92.7	98.0	96.7
Spinal cord lesions	10.6	8.7	9.5	9.9[3]	9.8[3]	8.8[3]	7.7[3]	99.6	98.3	99.6
Miscellaneous	9.1	8.4	8.7	8.9	8.9[3]	8.2[3]	8.7[3]	94.1	99.1	96.5
Total group	9.6	8.4	8.5	8.7	8.7	7.3	7.2	94.6	95.5	95.2

[1] One-way analyses of variance yielded significant ($< .01$ or $< .025$) between-groups' F-tests.
[2] F-test approached significant, $p < 10$.
[3] Significantly different from the brain-damaged group. All significant t-test results involved brain-damaged group.

verbal IQ under 100 and four with a verbal IQ over 100, while only one low improver had a verbal IQ under 100 and five had verbal IQs over 100. This apparent reversal was not found in the performance scores.

In the amputee and spinal cord lesion groups, IQ scores showed positive but nonsignificant relationships with improvement, except for picture arrangement which was positively ($p <$ .05) related to improvement in both groups. In the miscellaneous group, as in the LH group, improvement was negatively related to verbal scores. The chi-square tests were significant ($p <$ .05) for the similarities and digit span subtests and verbal IQ.

Length of Stay

Ben-Yishay and others (1968) obtained negative rho correlations between length of stay in months and seven WAIS subtests in 24 left hemiplegic patients. The correlations were significant for digit span ($-.38$), block design ($-.53$), digit symbol ($-.56$), and object assembly ($-.45$).

To obtain a larger range and to enhance precision, length of stay in the present study was measured in weeks rather than months, permitting the use of Pearson correlation coefficients. The findings are presented in Table 4. The correlations were mainly low and nonsignificant.

Although the numbers were quite small, contrasting trends between the two hemiplegic groups in the correlations between IQ and length of stay may be observed. Lumping the hemiplegic subgroups along with four additional patients into one group simply called brain-damaged masks correlation discrepancies between LH and RH in the four verbal tests and block design.

The inverse relationships between verbal scores and improvement ratings in the left hemiplegics did not occur in the verbal score-length-of-stay data. In our study length of stay and improvement ratings show an essentially zero correlation. Table 4 reveals that no subtest was consistently related to length of stay over a majority of subgroups.

Age

The IQ subtest scores were used in this study without age corrections, even though significant ($p < .01$) between-group differences were demonstrated by analysis of variance. Both the brain-damaged and amputee groups were significantly older than the spinal cord group. In this patient population it has been found that age is nonsignificantly related to ratings of improvement (Rosillo & Fogel 1970a). Nevertheless, all previous analyses were recomputed using age-corrected scores. No noteworthy changes in trends were observed. Even if such had been found, the essential question in any case had to do with how differences in intellectual abilities, whether age-related or otherwise, affect rehabilitation progress. The issue was whether each patient's current level of functioning would influence his ability to cope with the rigorous challenges of a rehabilitation program.

Table 4. Pearson correlation coefficient between length of stay and WAIS subtest scores in physically disabled groups

Subgroups	Comprehension	Arithmetic	Similarities	Digit span	Picture completion	Block design	Picture arrangement	Verbal	Performance	Full-scale
			Subtests						IQ scores	
Brain-damaged	−.11	−.06	−.29	−.14	.13	−.18	.03	−.17	.22	.07
Left hemiplegic	−.29	−.22	−.39	−.22	.09	−.36	−.05	−.15	.18	−.07
Right hemiplegic	.39	.04	.02	.07	.06	.10	.22	.09	.20	.15
Amputee	−.01	.00	−.41**	−.26	−.19	−.39**	−.38**	−.09	−.22	−.14
Spinal cord lesions	.20	−.40	−.05	−.13	−.37	−.20	−.09	−.13	−.53**	−.54**
Miscellaneous	.28	.06	.27	.01	.08	.19	.22	.21	.08	.19
Total group	.09	−.10	−.13	−.13	−.08	−.14	−.06	−.04	−.08	−.07

Note: Subtest scores were not age-corrected; prorated IQ scores were. Hence a few subtest correlations appear slightly inconsistent with reference to their respective prorated IQ scores.
**p .05.

Expected versus Actual Length of Stay

The physician who provided the ratings of disability and improvement also estimated each patient's expected length of stay based on several years of his experience with similar patients in two rehabilitation services. Discrepancy scores were then calculated at the time of discharge, expressing in weeks the difference between the expected and actual length of stay for each patient. Most of these discrepancies fell within an interval ranging from −15 weeks (discharged earlier than expected) to +5 weeks (discharged later than expected). Six patients were discharged 16 or more weeks earlier than predicted, thus coming at the minus end of the continuum. Nine patients were discharged 6 or more weeks later than predicted, or on the positive side of the continuum. For exploratory purposes the mean IQ scores of these two groups were computed. The early dischargees had a mean full scale IQ of 104.5, and the late dischargees' mean IQ was 95.5. The difference was nonsignificant.

DISCUSSION

The results indicate that WAIS intelligence scores were not significantly related to prognosis in physical rehabilitation. Performance test scores showed suggestive relationships. These findings essentially corroborate other work (Anderson, Bourestom & Greenberg 1970; Shontz 1957) indicating that intellectual functioning generally does not play a clearly defined role in physical rehabilitation, particularly in respect to group scores.

An initially tenable hypothesis might be that higher intelligence should facilitate success in coping with the stresses posed by the rehabilitation process. However, there are factors which might modify this expectation. One is that the majority of tasks in physical rehabilitation at most require merely an average level of intelligence. From a purely cognitive standpoint there is little to be gained from intellectual abilities beyond this minimal level.

One might also postulate a dynamic interplay between negative and positive effects of intelligence, two potentially opposing effects. On one hand, cognitive abilities can be used for constructive, goal-directed purposes, in the same way in which drives aroused by negative affects can be channeled in support of effective coping maneuvers (Rosillo, Fogel & Freedman 1971). For example, previous findings have suggested that habit patterns of dominance can be used in support of either positive or negative goals. Whether constructive or destructive uses of intelligence predominate depends upon the total personality in combination with the external resources available (Rosillo & Fogel 1970b).

On the other hand, patients with higher intelligence have a potentially greater capacity to hinder their therapy, whether intentionally or without awareness. Brighter patients also may become more readily bored with the more rigid or repetitive aspects of a rehabilitation program. Moreover, differences in intelligence could prompt variable interactions with respect to the changeable expectations of patients concerning their recovery prospects. These idiosyncratic interactions may result in overall positive or negative individual or group influences on such factors as motivation for recovery and acceptance of the consequences of the disability. Categorical predictions concerning the effects of intelligence in rehabilitation are therefore difficult to make.

Inverse relationships were observed between verbal scores and improvement in the left hemiplegic patients and to a lesser extent between verbal scores and improvement in the miscellaneous group. Deficits in verbal abilities in left hemiplegic patients could be expected to be transient, since verbal abilities have been found to be predominantly associated with left hemisphere functions (Fogel 1964). That is, patients are classified as left hemiplegics because of a primary motor disability stemming from right hemisphere damage. Obviously, the patients with left hemiplegias had histories of cerebrovascular accidents essentially involving the right hemisphere. In the left hemiplegics, symptoms of left hemisphere dysfunction should not be as pronounced as should symptoms of right hemisphere dysfunction. Regression upwards toward the mean of an expected population base rate of left hemisphere functioning should occur.

Although still brain damaged, in time the left hemiplegics should nevertheless arrive at a more normal level of those abilities primarily mediated by the left hemisphere. The extent to which left hemiplegics display below average group verbal scores presumably provides an indication of their deficit in the left hemisphere. If the deficit is pronounced, it may be anticipated that many who evidence such a deficit will show spontaneous improvement during the period of rehabilitation (Marshall & Wilkinson 1971). This does not preclude the possibility that some patients in this group may have transient disturbances in left hemisphere functions. In many of the latter patients the left hemisphere functions will restabilize. In all probability there will then be exhibited an attendant general physical and emotional improvement, ultimately to be reflected in the ratings made at the time of discharge.

The reasoning just detailed also leads to the question of a possible analogous relationship with respect to low performance scores in right hemiplegic patients. That this did not occur may simply reflect an increasing awareness in recent years of the importance of implicit verbal medication in performance test activities.

Reversals, i.e., lower verbal scores in high improvement patients, also occurred to some extent in the miscellaneous group, but not in the spinal or amputee groups. Eleven of the miscellaneous patients had peripheral neuropathies associated with diabetes or chronic alcoholism. Of these patients, several who had low verbal scores may have had mild or moderate circulatory disturbances at the time of admission which temporarily depressed cerebral functioning. During the course of their hospitalization, these patients could have experienced improvement in their circulatory deficits due to spontaneous remission or to therapeutic management consisting of improved nutrition, more adequate rest, appropriate exercises, avoidance of toxic substances, and other factors.

Age did not play an important role in the findings. The groups differed in age, but the relationships between intelligence and rehabilitation outcome remained essentially unaltered by the age factor.

There was consistent evidence (Table 4) that length of stay was inversely related to level of intelligence, as had been found by Ben-Yishay and others (1968). That study was restricted to 24 left hemiplegics; in this study they numbered 17. In this present group two negative correlations higher than .30 (nonsignificant) were obtained. Thus the significant inverse relationships between stay and intelligence as found by Ben-Yishay and others (1968) were not confirmed in this study. Population differences, subtle variations in techniques of test administration or scoring, and statistical unreliabilities due to the small numbers of subjects in both studies may account in part for the differences in findings. In the amputee and spinal cord groups a few significant negative correlations were found, but no consistent trends were observed.

A small group analysis was performed on extreme early and late dischargees, as defined by discrepancies between estimates of expected length of stay and actual length of stay. The results of this analysis were nonsignificant, but raised the possibility that intelligence may be related to the phase of rehabilitation when discharge occurred, since those discharged early averaged 9 points higher in full scale IQ. Larger group analyses are needed to evaluate the reliability and import of this possibility.

REFERENCES

Anderson, T. P.; Bourestom, N.; & Greenberg, F.R. Rehabilitation predictors in completed stroke. Final Report, HEW Project No. RD-1757-M-68-C3. Minneapolis, Minn.: Kenney Rehabilitation Institute, 1970.

Ben-Yishay, Y.; Diller, L.; Gerstman, L.; & Haas, A. The relationship between impersistence, intellectual function and outcome of rehabilitation in patients with left hemiplegia. Neurology, 1968, 18, 852—861.

Ben-Yishay, Y.; Diller, L.; Mandleberg, I.; Gordon, W.; & Gerstman, L. J. Similarities and differences in Block Design performance between older normal and brain-injured persons: A task analysis. Journal of Abnormal Psychology, 1971, 78, 17—25.

Ben-Yishay, Y.; Gerstman, L. J.; Diller, L.; & Haas, A. Prediction of rehabilitation outcomes from psychometric parameters in left hemiplegics. Journal of Consulting and Clinical Psychology, 1970, 34, 436—441.

Boone, D. R. Communication skills in right and left hemiplegics. Journal of Speech and Hearing Disorders, 1959, 26, 261—268.

Diller, L.; Ben-Yishay, Y.; Weinberg, J.; & Goodkin, R. Studies in cognition and rehabilitation in hemiplegics. Final Report VRA Project No. RD-2666-P. Washington, D.C.: United States Government Printing Office, 1971.

Fogel, M. L. The intelligence quotient as an index of brain damage. American Journal of Orthopsychiatry, 1964, 34, 555–562.

Freed, M. M.; Palmer, J. D. K.; Anstine, L. A.; & Isaacs, L. I. Diagnostic, predictive and operational significance of self-care (dressing) problems in hemiplegia rehabilitation. Final Report, VRA Project No. 13-P-55005/1-03. Washington, D.C.: United States Government Printing Office, 1971.

Gruen, A. Psychological deficit as a pre-existing factor in strokes. Journal of Nervous and Mental Diseases, 1962, 134, 109–116.

Lorenzo, E. J., & Cancro, R. Dysfunction in visual perception with hemiplegia: Its relation to activities of daily living. Archives of Physical Medicine and Rehabilitation, 1962, 43, 514–517.

Marshall, J., & Wilkinson, I. M. S. The prognosis of carotid transient ischemic attacks in patients with normal angiograms. Brain, 1971, 94, 395–402.

Rosillo, R. H., & Fogel, M. L. Correlation of psychologic variables and progress in physical rehabilitation: I. Degree of disability and denial of illness. Archives of Physical Medicine and Rehabilitation, 1970, 51, 227–233. (a)

Rosillo, R. H., & Fogel, M. L. Emotional support. Psychosomatics, 1970, 11, 194–196 (b).

Rosillo, R. H.; Fogel, M. L.; & Freedman, K. Affect levels and improvement in physical rehabilitation. Journal of Chronic Diseases, 1971, 24, 651–660.

Shanan, J.; Cohen, M.; & Adler, E. Intellectual functioning in hemiplegic patients after cerebrovascular accidents. Journal of Nervous and Mental Disease, 1966, 143, 181–189.

Shontz, F. C. Evaluation of intellectual potential in hemiplegic individuals. Journal of Clinical Psychology, 1957, 13, 267–269.

Wood, N. E. A comparison of right hemiplegics with left hemiplegics in visual perception. Journal of Clinical Psychology, 1955, 11, 378–380.

Section 9

BODY IMAGE

37 On Disturbance of the Body Image in Paraplegia

John H. Evans

If the body image is defined as an individual's total awareness of his body, "awareness" implying the availability of information to consciousness, it may be claimed that disturbance of the body image is a necessary accompaniment of any disease which is apparent to the sufferer, because the disturbance which he observes is the symptom of which he complains. As a rule the disturbance of the body image described by the patient correlates sufficiently well with the physical evidence of disease that the distinction between the subjective world of symptoms and the objective world of physical signs is scarcely appreciated. In certain conditions, however, there is such a disparity between the body image as described by the patient or expressed in his non-verbal behaviour and the objective picture of his body that the disparity itself is a prominent physical sign. This is strikingly seen in patients with cerebral disease who deny the existence of blindness or disown their hemiplegic limbs.

Awareness of the body is, however, dependent on information from many different sources and if the information is contradictory an individual may become aware of discordant imagery. The commonest situation in which this arises is following amputation of a limb, provided that this occurs after early childhood, when the patient develops a phantom image of the absent limb.

The body image is composed of perceptual images derived from immediate sensory experience, and memory images derived from previous knowledge. The perceptual image of the body is dependent on two sources of sensory data, those providing information from outside the integument, chiefly visual or tactile from contact of one part with another, and those providing information wholly from within the body: tactile and kinaesthetic sensations. These two different sources may be called external and internal sensory data as convenient, if inaccurate, terms. The external nature of the visual data is obvious but the distinction between external and internal tactile data is not easy to define and may be clarified by an illustration. If the left hand grasps the right wrist, then the left hand is enriching the perceptual image of the right wrist from external tactile data and simultaneously, from its contact with the wrist, is providing tactile data about its own position which are entirely internal.

In the case of the amputee with a phantom limb memory, vision and palpation (providing external tactile data) are continually challenged by

---

Reprinted from Brain, 1962, 85:687–700, by permission of Oxford University Press.

internal tactile and kinaesthetic sensory data which seem to arise from within the absent limb. One might expect a similar perceptual discord to occur in patients with functional division of the spinal cord, and after hearing a spontaneous description of an internal perceptual image by a patient with a complete paraplegia, the writer was prompted to enquire into the body image in seven patients with clinically complete interruption of the spinal cord above the first lumbar nerve roots.

REVIEW OF THE LITERATURE

In contrast to the extensive literature on the phantom limb phenomenon in amputees the reports of contradictory perceptual images after interruption of the spinal cord are comparatively scanty.

The earliest reference to this subject is in Riddoch's classical study (1917) of the reflex function of the spinal cord in man, which was made on patients whose spinal cords had been transected by gunshot wounds. He described the patients' body image in four instances. One patient, twenty-five days after injury, felt as though his body ended at the sixth rib but, by the fifty-seventh day after injury, he felt as though his hamstrings were aching and he had a tingling sensation in his feet. Reviewing his patients, Riddoch drew attention to the variation of the mental image of the limbs, its fragmentary nature, and the apparent shortening of

the legs from knees to ankle. Painful sensations which were observed by his patients were frequently referred to the hamstrings. With regard to the clarity of the image he concluded that the proximal part of the leg was more easily identified than the lower leg with the exception of the foot. He believed that the internal perceptual image of the legs was not present immediately after the injury and he related its appearance to the onset of flexion spasms.

Kuhn (1950) reported 25 patients with complete division of the spinal cord. Eight had no sensations referable to below the level of the cord injury. In the remainder burning "hot tingling" or warm sensations predominated, and resembled those described by Davis and Martin (1947) in a large series of patients with injury, but not necessarily complete division, of the spinal cord. These authors made no reference to any other kinds of perceptual imagery in their patients.

A more extensive review of the body image in fifty patients with traumatic interruption of the spinal cord was made by Bors (1951). He found that all his patients had internal perceptual images of the legs which were usually fragmentary and the frequency with which the distinct parts of the image were identified diminished from the toes to the hip with the exception of the knee. He emphasized the absence of distortion of the perceptual image or of telescoping in any of his patients.

Reference to this subject was made by Li and Elvidge (1951) and Cook and Druckemiller (1952) who reported the appearance of phantom limbs after amputation of a leg in patients whose spinal cords had previously been transected. These authors indicated that the perceptual image of the amputated leg might be more vivid than that of the remaining leg, but Bors did not find this difference in the three of his patients who had had a leg removed surgically after the spinal cord injury.

Reports on the internal perceptual image in health are also infrequent but Schilder (1935) has discussed the matter in some detail and the following is a summary of his description which the reader may care to verify from his own experience. If the eyes are closed and the limbs kept well supported and motionless to exclude external sensory data, one is aware of a mental image of the limbs which is fairly accurate in position, form and detail. However, if an attempt is made to reject the memory image by attending only to the immediate internal sensory data the resultant perceptual image is surprisingly vague. With the legs resting on a couch one is aware of the position of the larger joints, a sense of mass and length, but one has no direct information about the contours of the limbs or the number of toes. Exploratory movements increase the detail and enhance the vividness of the kinaesthetic image but it is not until the skin of the limb is brought into contact with a firm object that any idea of contour and surface can be obtained. In health and full consciousness any attempt to dissociate the body image from reality by attempting

to alter the kinaesthetic image without moving the physical limbs is probably impossible (Kanner and Schilder, 1930).

METHOD

The subjects were all inpatients at Claremont Street Hospital, the City Hospital or the Royal Victoria Hospital, Belfast. They were selected on the basis of having a paraplegia of at least three months' duration with complete sensory and motor loss below the first lumbar segment. None of the patients had clouding of consciousness or intellectual deterioration at the time of the interviews. The clinical pictures are summarized in Table 1.

The patient was interviewed in an informal manner and no set questionnaire was used but enquiry was made into the following points:

(1) The predominant sensations referred to the regions of complete anesthesia.

(2) The extent and continuity of the internal perceptual image.

(3) The presence of any distortion of volume, length, or contour of the perceptual image.

(4) The position of the image in phenomenal space.

(5) The ability to alter the position of the image by voluntary effort.

To facilitate the patient's task and to ensure the greatest possible accuracy attention was paid to the following details. The examiner was known to the patient before the inter-

Table 1.

Case no.	Initials	Sex	Age	Diagnosis	Duration of paraplegia	Tone	Bladder	Upper level of cutaneous sensory loss	Sensation of joint position
1	E.B.	F	26	Probable multiple sclerosis	18 mo.	Spastic	Automatic	T.8	Absent in legs
2	J.C.	M	48	Possible multiple sclerosis	2 yrs.	Spastic	Automatic	L.1	Absent in legs
3	C.H.	F	59	Angioma of spinal cord	3 mo.	Spastic	Retention	T.12	Absent in legs
4	S.H.	F	27	Probable multiple sclerosis	18 mo.	Spastic	Automatic	T.7	Absent in legs
5	M.L.	F	28	Probable multiple sclerosis	6 yrs.	Spastic	Automatic	T.12	Absent in legs
6	C.M.	F	72	Vascular occlusion of spinal cord	6 mo.	Flaccid	Automatic	L.1	Absent in legs
7	M.M.	F	34	Acute encephalomyelitis	11 yrs.	Flaccid	Retention	T.8	Absent in legs

view, which was conducted at a time when the patient was neither fatigued, nor hungry, nor emotionally disturbed. Motivation was increased by a simple explanation of the object of the enquiry and by inviting the patient's co-operation. Comprehension was aided by a gradual introduction to the subject in simple words. To aid concentration on internal perceptual data the patient was instructed to lie still and keep his eyes closed. Encouragement was given in moderation but at the same time the reproducibility of the patient's answer was tested by further questions and by repeating the same question later on in an attempt to bring up inconsistencies. Every patient was interviewed three times. With the exception of Cases 3 and 5 the interval between the second and third interviews was over a year. The patient's replies were recorded on a tape recorder or taken down verbatim in longhand.

RESULTS

Predominant Sensations

The most vivid components of the perceptual images were abnormal sensations which seemed to originate in the anesthetic lower limbs.

Case 1 described a "pain in my knees as if I had fallen down and bruised myself" and a similar pain in her heels and the soles of her feet. This pain was continuous but it varied in intensity and was accentuated by passive movements of her limbs. There was no sensation of contact. The sensation of temperature varied with the environmental temperature so that her legs seemed warm when she was warm, and cold when she was cold.

Case 2 described a "smarting" at the back of the knees. It varied in severity but there were no obvious aggravating factors. He also had sensations of contact which seemed to restrict movements of the perceptual image—"you feel there's a bar across the bed" or, referring to his foot, "it seems to be caught in the bedclothes."

Case 3 had no painful sensations but the "left foot—you would think there was a bandage, awful, awful tight" with a similar, but less intense, sensation in the right foot. "Sometimes I feel a beat in my right foot, like when you are tested for blood pressure." There was no sensation of contact with the bedclothes. The sensation of temperature varied unpredictably, but was occasionally intense—"yesterday they seemed to be on fire."

Case 4 also had no painful sensations. About twice a day, particularly when her feet were warm, she had a "tingling" in the foot "as if the tuning fork were on my ankle." This lasted for four to five seconds. She also was aware of a pressure at the backs of the thighs, calves and heels as though they were in contact with the bed. The sensation of temperature varied without reference to her general feeling of warmth.

Case 5 felt a "smarting" in the knees and a feeling of pressure behind the buttocks, calves and heels. There were no painful sensations and the legs usually felt warm, sometimes "roasting."

Case 6 denied painful sensations but said "you would think my feet were bandaged up so far as my boots would come; and my knees are bandaged—separately, the legs are not together." In addition there was a sensation in the fronts of both thighs "like pins and needles working—like worms." She also felt as though the backs of the thighs, knees, calves, heels and soles were touching the bedclothes. After a warm bath the whole of both legs would tingle, "not painful, pleasant really because they feel alive."

Case 7 described her legs as feeling "straight down and tied tight together." The predominant feeling was a "stinging feeling" in the hips, just above the patella, on the outside of the ankles and in the balls of the feet, "and if I am wakened out of sleep it makes it worse." This feeling was also accentuated by nervousness, attempted movement of her perceptual image, or by someone sitting on her bed near her legs. The stinging was always present, usually it was "a nice comfortable feeling" but "if I'm waked up suddenly it goes wild." She described her legs as feeling "as if they are tied tight together ... tight at the knees and tight at the ankles ... as though something was wrapped round them." She felt as though the knees and ankles were pressing upon each other but there was no sensation of contact with the bedclothes. As regards temperature, they were sometimes warm, sometimes cold and sometimes neutral.

In spite of the variety of sensations reported by different patients three points of similarity can be detected.

(a) The use by 4 patients of adjectives which are normally applied to pains (bruised, smarting, stinging) although in fact no patient ever spontaneously complained of pain or behaved as though he was suffering pain. Although the sensations were at first described as continuous, all patients later said that they were unaware of them at times, so that it may be concluded that it was the availability of the sensation to consciousness that was continuous, not the sensation itself.

(b) Sensations of contact either with the bedclothes or with the opposite limb, or of a tight constricting sensation were described by 5 patients.

(c) A noticeable sensation of temperature was observed by 5 patients, with an abnormal feeling at times in 2 patients ("on fire" and "roasting").

These sensations of heat, pain and pressure resemble those described by Kuhn and by Bors but in this series they were never severe enough to cause discomfort. The accentuation of the pain by nervousness or by attempted movement of the perceptual image has been noted by Davis and Martin, but the influence of sudden waking from sleep seems to be unique.

Extent and Continuity

In assessing the extent of the perceptual image of the lower limbs the patient was presented with a list of the main anatomical parts of the legs which he then tried to identify in his perceptual image. His answers were checked by repeating the questions at least once. The answers obtained by this method of enquiry were much less consistent than the patient's spontaneous description of their predominant sensations. Under repeated checks the extent of the image tended to become more complete but whether this was due to suggestibility or increased attention to the perceptual data can only be surmised. Furthermore the replies became less reliable. Case 3, for instance, could not be moved from an illogical claim that she was not aware of the hips, thighs, calves, or the lateral four toes on each side and she denied that there was a gap between the body and the knees, and between the knees and the feet, yet she maintained that the feet were a normal distance from her body.

It was also difficult to get a description of the basic sensation by which the patient was aware of the parts identified in the image but not carrying any of the abnormal sensations described in the preceding section. On further questioning the patient either extended the area of the abnormal sensation or implied an indescribable awareness. Case 6 said of her toes "I can feel that they are there even when I am not moving them; it's quite vivid, as vivid as my fingers." The validity of this statement as a description of an internal perceptual image unembellished by memory is questionable, because as has been discussed the normal internal perceptual image of the fingers is anything but vivid.

Two patients, however, gave spontaneous and consistent accounts of gaps in their perceptual images. Case 5 was unable to identify the lower legs between knee and ankle and said "you would think there's a space, you know." Case 7 was unable to identify the foot and the lateral four toes on the left side and said of the left hallux "it feels all on its own and cold."

The extent of the perceptual image was, therefore, difficult to assess in every patient owing to the unknown part played by memory images and suggestibility. This difficulty suggests that the anatomical components of the image are by no means clear and in this respect resemble the normal internal perceptual image of a motionless limb.

In 2 patients the image was fragmentary and gaps were clearly appreciated. This phenomenon has been reported by Riddoch and by Bors.

Distortion of Size and Shape

The general outline of the perceptual image was reported as normal and while again this may have been due to memory filling in a gap in the perceptual data there were certainly no feelings of increased or decreased size or abnormal contour.

Two patients noticed small differences in the length of the two limbs.
Case 2 was asked:
Q. What about the size of the legs?
A. . . . . . It seems as though it's longer right enough
Q. Which one?
A. The right.

Q. How much longer?
A. . . . . . About an inch.

Case 7 said "the right ankle feels further up the leg than it should be and the toes feel further from the ankle than they should be."

In each case the overall length of the perceptual legs was always approximately normal and there was no evidence of shortening even in the patient with a paraplegia of eleven years' duration (1). This is in agreement with the findings of Bors who emphasized the absence of telescoping in paraplegia.

Position

On enquiring into the proprioceptive aspects of the image all the patients were able to give convincing descriptions. Some had previously noticed the disparity between the position of the image in phenomenal space and the physical position of the actual limb. "When I was at the X-ray department I thought I had my legs out straight but when I looked the right one was bent up on my tummy" (5). Two patients had also noticed this particularly vividly in hypnagogic states. "Just as I'm going to sleep I feel as though I am lying in my normal position with the knees bent up" when in fact they were straight out (6). "Sometimes at night when I'm in bed asleep I think the left leg has fallen over the edge of the bed" (this had happened twice). "I put my hand down to feel it and it wasn't there, it was in bed" (7).

Usually the position of the perceptual image during the interview cor-

responded to the position of the physical legs. Case 7, however, immediately after pulling herself into a sitting position on the side of the bed said that her legs "feel straight up and down through the bed." A few minutes later she reported that the image had adopted a natural sitting position.

Mobility

All patients noticed an involuntary change in the position of the image from time to time and only one patient (3) was unable to move the perceptual image on request. The remainder could move at least one part of the perceptual image (Table 2).

The kinaesthetic sensation was not the same as that of a normal movement and most patients experienced some impediment to their efforts. Case 1 said "its not terribly easy." Case 2 found great difficulty and his demeanour reflected this because in the

Table 2. False internal perception of voluntary movement

Case no.	Hips	Knees	Ankles	Toes
1	0	+	++	+
2	+	+	+	++
3	0	0	0	0
4	0	0	+	+
5	+	+	+	+
6	+	+	+	+
7	0	0	+	On rt. only

0 = No sensation of movement.
+ = Sensation of movement reported.
++ = Sensation of movement obtained more easily than at other joints.

effort of concentration he held his breath and gripped the sides of the bed with his hands—"the foot is jammed against a pillow, prevents you getting it shifted." Case 4 found no difficulty in moving her perceptual toes and feet. Case 5 was familiar with this kinaesthetic image, "I have a habit of exercising them, well I always feel that I am moving them. The first or second time nothing happens but at the third time it seems to move a bit." On further effort "it sort of gets tired." No sense of effort was found in maintaining the kinaesthetic image in its new position—"until I push them back they stay there, at least that's what I imagine it." Case 6 also denied any effort in making the movement but said that it was a slow process lacking the quickness of a normal movement—"not as free as they should be." Case 7 found it difficult to make the movements of her perceptual left toes and feet and she also said that the process was painful due to an accentuation of the stinging sensation.

Thus, while 6 patients were able to move at least some part of their perceptual image, only 1 felt that the movement was unimpeded. Movement at the peripheral joints was more frequently reported. These findings are in agreement with those of Bors.

DISCUSSION

Reliability of Evidence

As the above descriptions are based on statements made by persons unused to this particular form of introspection, it would be reasonable, at the outset, to question the assumption that each patient's statement is an accurate account of his perceptual image. Three reasons can be advanced in support of this assumption.

(*a*) The patient's manner. The behaviour of a patient while trying to describe a percept was typified by slow thoughtful speech and an expression of concentration on his face, and was easily distinguished from the rather bewildered expression and the hesitant doubting manner of a patient who had not grasped the point of the enquiry. Indeed, while explaining the object of the enquiry and telling the patient how to distinguish the various types of imagery, the moment of comprehension was often accompanied by a visible "Aha!" effect and sometimes the patient spontaneously distinguished between the perceptual image and the memory image by some expression such as "I know my legs are bent up as I have seen them, but they feel as if they are straight out in front of me" (6).

(*b*) An overall consistency was apparent from one interview to another, sometimes after an interval of a year, in the descriptions of the sensations, the kinaesthetic image and the mobility of the image.

(*c*) The similarity between descriptions by different patients as in the quasi-painful quality of the sensation, in the ability to move the image and the curiously stiff quality of the sensation of movement. The variability of each patient's description of the extent of the image, while in contrast to the reliability of the other evidence, was in itself a consistent feature from one patient to another.

Surviving Afferent Neurons

Another justifiable criticism is that the evidence for complete discontinuity of spinal cord function at some level above the first lumbar segment is only based on the clinical finding of complete anaesthesia in the lower limbs, and that a few remaining fibres may be stimulated by continued pressure on the skin or continued movement of the joints and contribute to the perceptual image.

The fact that Case 1 developed more severe pain in the legs on repeated passive movement of her limbs is not in itself evidence of spinal cord continuity for one of Riddoch's patients, with a complete transection of the cord visualized at operation, felt a pain referred to his legs when they were passively moved. Kuhn has described a patient with previous division of the cord at the third thoracic segment, who invariably felt a burning sensation referred to a decubitus ulcer when 70 per cent alcohol was applied to the granulating surface of the ulcer. This observation suggests that some sensory pathway runs outside the spinal cord to join it at a higher level than the majority of the sensory fibres. This view is supported by the animal experiments of Kuntz and Saccomanno (1942) which suggest that the sympathetic chain is the site of this alternative pathway. They divided the spinal cord in cats at the level of the upper lumbar nerve roots and one of the sympathetic chains at a similar level. Strong stimuli to the legs on the side where the sympathetic chain was intact then caused dilatation of the pupils but not response when the opposite leg was stimulated.

Complete functional dissociation of central structures from the peripheral nerves cannot therefore be claimed even if the division of the spinal cord is known to be complete. In the patients described here some afferent fibres may have been preserved within the spinal cord, but, if so, their integrity could not be demonstrated by clinical examination.

Comparison with Phantom Limb Phenomenon

The internal perceptual images of paraplegic patients may be compared with the phantom limb phenomenon following amputation of a limb. Both constitute a contradictory perceptual image whether of limbs which are still in continuity with the body but separated from the higher centres by functional division of the cord or of a limb which has been removed with a division of the peripheral nerves.

The material for this comparison is taken chiefly from the reviews of Henderson and Smyth (1948) and Cronholm (1951). The sensations referred to phantom limbs were as varied as those found in this series. Cronholm noted the frequent occurrence of pins and needles, burning pain, cramps, aching pains, momentary pains, and a feeling of compression in which the limb felt "bound up" or "in plaster." All these sensations are recognizable in the descriptions given above. On the other hand the basic sensations of tingling or numbness which Henderson and Smyth felt to be an almost invariable accompaniment of a phantom limb were not present in this series.

When investigating the extent of the phantom limb Cronholm found considerable variation from day to day or even in a single interview. Nevertheless he concluded that the phantom was often incomplete and that the peripheral parts were more often perceived. Henderson and Smyth also had difficulty in getting a clear account of the extent of the phantom and confirmed its patchy nature but found that the feet and larger joints were usually the most vivid. The unreliability of the descriptions of the extent of the perceptual images was a feature of the cases reported here but in two instances the perceptual images were incomplete.

A major difference between the perceptual image in paraplegics and the phantom limb phenomenon is the tendency for the latter to become progressively foreshortened. Henderson and Smyth regarded this telescoping as a natural property of a phantom. Cronholm found foreshortening in 48 out of 81 amputees. In this series of paraplegics, while minor variations in length were found, foreshortening did not occur even after eleven years in one instance (7).

The proprioceptive image is equally well described by paraplegics and by amputees. The sense of voluntary movement is also very similar in the two groups both in its distribution, the peripheral joints of the image being more readily moved, and in the sense of restriction which accompanies attempted movement. Henderson and Smyth noted, however, that this sense of effort on moving the phantom increased over the months following the amputation. In paraplegics the sense of effort did not increase. The attempted movement of a phantom was always accompanied by contraction of the stump musculature. In paraplegics the proximal limb girdle muscles were paralysed and no associated movements were observed but one patient (2), in attempting to move his perceptual image, held his breath and gripped the sides of the bed as if he were attempting a difficult physical movement.

It may be concluded that the internal perceptual image of paraplegics bears a close resemblance to a phantom limb, but differs from it in the absence of telescoping and of the increasing difficulty in moving the phantom.

A possible explanation of this difference is that the paraplegic has frequent visual experience of his real legs with which to correct any changes in his mental imagery, whereas the amputee has no such check. Expressing this in practical terms, a paraplegic who wheels his chair up to a table has to take care that his legs do not get in the way of the table legs. His mental image is of positive use to him and one might expect it to be sustained. An amputee who is not wearing an artificial limb need not concern himself with his lost leg when he sits at table. In his case a phantom limb of normal size is therefore not only superfluous but misleading. It is a useless percept which one might expect to be modified.

The Anatomical Basis of the Perceptual Image

Discussion of mental imagery in terms of cerebral anatomy and physiology is hazardous because of the difficulty in finding common terms of reference, but one assumption that has stood the test of time is that the immediate perceptual image and the memory of previous images are dependent on activity in closely related, if not identical, regions of the brain. This was supported as long ago as 1886 by Ferrier when he was discussing the "sensory centres," but his statement could be cast in modern terms without any loss of meaning. He wrote "Each (sensory centre) is the substratum of consciousness of its own special sensory impressions, and each is the organic basis of the memory of such impressions in the form of certain cell-modifications, the reinduction of which is the representation or revival in idea of the individual sensory characters of the object."

Although not susceptible to proof this hypothesis does not contradict clinical experience and is still accepted today (see, for example, Brain, 1950). The hemiplegic patient with a lesion of one cerebral hemisphere who has a complete loss of sensation in his paralysed limbs has lost not only the internal perceptual image of the affected limbs but all memory of sensory data arising in those limbs. The perceptual image of his paralysed limbs is dependent on external sensory data supplied by vision and palpation. The inadequacy of his incomplete image may be revealed by neglect of the affected limbs when attention is directed elsewhere, or by hemi-asomatognosia when consciousness is clouded.

After damage to the spinal cord, however, these cerebral mechanisms are intact and still function in providing, when called upon to do so, an internal perceptual image which may bear no relation to the actual position of the limbs because of the absence of a normal sensory input. It is probable that some afferent impulses do reach the cerebrum from the anesthetic limbs via intact fibres within the spinal cord or through the sympathetic chain but their spatial and temporal pattern is so abnormal that they are responsible for the sensations of pain, heat and pressure which are described by these patients.

The similarity between the phantom limbs of amputees and the contradictory perceptual images of paraplegic patients suggests a common basis for each phenomenon. After amputation of a limb the sensory projection areas are intact but deprived of all sensory information except abnormal patterns of afferent stimuli which arise in the cut ends of the peripheral nerves.

To summarize these speculations: it is proposed that the contradictory perceptual images in paraplegic patients depend on continued activity in the sensory projection areas of the cortex that have incurred deprivation of afferent stimuli by damage to the spinal cord, and that the quasi-painful quality of the basic sensations referred to the anaesthetic limbs is due to the distorted pattern of afferent impulses reaching the brain through extra-spinal pathways or via surviving fibres within the spinal cord.

SUMMARY

Seven patients with a complete paraplegia of at least three months' duration were encouraged to give a detailed account of subjective sensations referred to their legs.

The predominant sensations, although described in terms connoting pain, heat or pressure, were not distressing.

The length of the perceptual image of the legs did not decrease with the passage of time. Reports of the extent of the image tended to be vague but gaps in the anatomical continuity of the image were clearly described by 2 patients.

The postural image was vividly described by all the patients and could be altered by voluntary effort in six.

The difficulties inherent in such an investigation are discussed.

The findings are compared with reports of phantom limbs in amputees. It is concluded that the images are similar except that telescoping and progressive difficulty in moving the image do not occur in paraplegia.

Reasons for these differences are proposed and the anatomical basis of these images is discussed.

ACKNOWLEDGMENTS

It gives me great pleasure to record my thanks to the late Dr. H. Hilton Stewart, and to Dr. R. S. Allison, and Dr. J. H. D. Millar in allowing me access to these patients and in providing me with encouragement and helpful criticism in the preparation of this paper.

REFERENCES

Brain, W. R. (1950) Brain, 73, 465.

Bors, E. (1951) A.M.A. Arch. Neurol. Psychiat., 66, 610.

Cook, A. W., and Druckemiller, W. H. (1952) J. Neurosurg., 9, 508.

Cronholm, B. (1951) Acta psychiat., Kbh., Suppl. 72.

Davis, L., and Martin, J. (1947) J. Neurosurg., 4, 483.

Ferrier, D. (1886) "The Functions of the Brain." London. (Smith, Elder) p. 427.

Henderson, W. R., and Smyth, G. E. (1948) J. Neurol. Neurosurg. Psychiat., 11, 88.

Kanner, L., and Schilder, P. (1930) J. Nerv. Ment. Dis., 72, 489.

Kuhn, R. A. (1950) Brain, 73, 1.

Kuntz, A., and Saccomanno, G. (1942) Arch. Surg., Chicago, 45, 606.

Li, C-L., and Elvidge, A. R. (1951) J. Neurosurg., 8, 524.

Riddoch, G. (1917) Brain, 40, 264.

Schilder, P. (1935) "The Image and Appearance of the Human Body." London.

38 Body-Image Disturbances in Chronically Ill Individuals

Stephen L. Fink and
Franklin C. Shontz

The importance of understanding the nature of the body-image, from both a theoretical and practical point of view, was emphasized by Fisher and Cleveland (4) when they stated that "the body-scheme may function as a basic standard or frame of reference which influences some of the individual's modes of perception and also his ability to perform certain skills." In the field of rehabilitation of the chronically ill, study of the body-image has become especially important, since the process of rehabilitation requires that a patient relate his body to objects in the environment (e.g., a wheelchair, crutches, parallel bars, etc.) and, therefore, requires that he be aware of his body and of the relative positions of the various parts of his body.

A number of investigations of body-image disturbance have employed groups of hemiplegics as the subjects (1–3, 6, 7, 9–11). Most of these studies have attempted to interpret observed disturbances in terms of the organic brain deficit known to occur in hemiplegia. Very few have attempted to control for disturbance which may be associated more directly with the overall loss of body functioning characteristic of chronic illness. In hemiplegics, as well as in almost any other group of disabled persons, the amount of physical activity and interaction with the environment is markedly lowered by the limitations imposed by the physical disability. Schilder (8) emphasized, "We can have a postural model of our body only when we get sufficient data. . ." While the body-image itself is presumably a central process, the data upon which it depends may come by way of peripheral avenues, and disruption of these avenues will certainly affect the central process. The same point of view has recently been emphasized and elaborated in an article by Gerstmann (5). Therefore, in any study of body-image disturbances in hemiplegics it is crucial to evaluate possible effects of chronic disability in general before

Reprinted with permission from the Journal of Nervous and Mental Diseases, 1960, 131: 234–240. Copyright 1960 by the Williams & Wilkins Co.

This paper is a condensed version of a research report submitted by S. L. Fink in partial fulfillment of the requirements for the degree of Doctor of Philosophy, at Western Reserve University. A report of this research was presented at the 1959 meeting of the Midwestern Psychological Association in Chicago, May, 1959. The project was carried out at Highland View Hospital, Cleveland, Ohio, and was financially supported by the Cleveland Foundation.

423

drawing conclusions about brain damage specifically.

The present investigation was designed to test certain hypotheses regarding alleged differences between physically healthy and chronically ill individuals in body-image functioning. This paper represents a report of the findings in regard to two major research hypotheses:

1. Hemiplegic individuals show greater body-image disturbance than non-hemiplegic non-brain-damaged persons; and

2. Chronically ill non-hemiplegic non-brain-damaged persons show greater body image disturbance than physically healthy persons.

The two hypotheses together predict an ordering of body-image disturbance, from least to most, which places the three groups in the order: physically healthy persons, chronically ill non-hemiplegic non-brain-damaged persons, and hemiplegics. It should be noted that the question of the presence or absence of brain damage in the group had to be considered in a relative sense only. The diagnosis for each subject was dependent upon available medical and psychological information; where this information failed to indicate the presence of measurable brain damage it was assumed that gross damage of this type was not present. Although it was recognized that varying degrees of cortical deterioration are likely to be present in the kinds of subjects employed in this study, especially since they represented the upper age brackets, it was felt that the groups, as groups, were fairly distinct in this respect.

The investigation employed double simultaneous tactual stimulation as the stimulus variable and judgments of related visual distance as the response variable. It was assumed that the process of translating a stimulus presented to the body into a visual dimension (viz., distance), when direct visual contact with the body is not permitted, is a function of the individual's ability to picture the stimulus on his body; i.e., it is a function of the individual's body-image. It is important to emphasize that the present study focuses upon the *pictorial* aspects of the body-image concept. No attempt was made to include measures of feelings or attitudes toward the body; the primary interest was in measuring the ability of the subjects to picture, or represent along a spatial dimension, their own physical bodies.

METHOD

Subjects

The physically healthy group was composed of twelve male and twelve female members of the Golden Age Club of Cleveland; the mean age was 69.2 (SD = 6.5). The non-hemiplegic patient group was composed of twelve males and twelve females with a mean age of 71.0 years (SD = 10.2). It consisted of sixteen patients with hip or limb fractures, four arthritics, one person with a lower leg amputation, one with arteriosclerosis, one with multiple sclerosis, and one with Charcot's disease. Every patient was wheelchair-bound at the time he was seen and none had been diagnosed as brain-damaged. The hemiplegic group contained twelve left and twelve right hemiplegics, evenly split into males and females. Only those patients who were capable of perceiving and indicating that they could perceive tactual stimulation in all body areas relevant to the experimental measures were included in the study. It was necessary to exclude right hemiplegics who suffered from receptive aphasia and thus were not capable of comprehending the instructions of the examiner. It was also necessary to exclude patients suffering from hemionopsia. As a result, the sample was somewhat biased in favor of hemiplegics who were not grossly deteriorated. The mean age of the group was 67.1 (SD = 11.6).

In order to provide some control for the factor of intelligence in comparing the groups, the Columbia Mental Maturity Scale was administered to each subject. This particular test was selected for several reasons. It purports to measure an individual's abstract conceptual abilities, which is especially relevant to the present study; it requires a minimum of both verbal and manual functioning, thereby permitting evaluations of all subjects without posing any special handicap for patients with motor and/or verbal expressive difficulties; and it may be administered in a relatively brief period of time and, therefore, tends not to impose excessive demands upon patients who fatigue easily. The mean Columbia score for the physically healthy group was 65.1 (SD = 8.5); for the non-hemiplegic patient group it was 58.4 (SD = 13.8); and for the hemiplegic group it was 63.2 (SD = 8.9). In an analysis of variance on the Columbia scores the between-groups variance was not statistically significant. It might also be noted that the hemiplegic group, which could be expected to show a deficit in Columbia performance, fell closer to the physically healthy group than did the non-hemiplegic patients.

Experimental Situation

A table which could be adjusted to various heights was placed at a distance of forty-four inches from a blank wall. The subject was seated behind the table facing the wall. A flashlight designed to focus a vertical strip of light on the wall was attached to the table, with a handle for turning the light within easy reach of the subject. The arrangement permitted the light to be turned in a horizontal direction. A strip of white tape, the same size as the strip of light, was fastened to the wall, opposite the center of the table. The room was in a semidark state, and both the light strip and tape strip were clearly visible to the subject. A cloth sheet was attached to the table and tied around the subject's neck, so that he could not see any portion of his body below the neck. A pair of wooden calipers was used as the stimulus; the caliper setting under each condition of the study served as the objective standard for each subjective response.

Procedure

The body-image test consisted of requiring each subject to adjust the distance between the two visually perceived points (the light strip and the tape strip) to correspond to the distance between two points indicated (with the calipers) on his body. Three different stimulus sizes, eight, twelve and eighteen inches, were distributed among eighteen body-region combinations. Left unilateral, right unilateral and bilateral body areas were sampled and equally balanced throughout. The order of the conditions was randomized for each subject. A test of visual perceptual discrimination, using the same three caliper settings, was employed in order to control for possible disturbances in this sphere. In this test, the task consisted of presenting the two-point stimuli visually and requiring the subject to make the same response as in the body-image test.

The measures of interest were the deviations of the light setting responses from their corresponding stimulus values. A logarithmic transformation was performed on all responses in order to render deviation values perceptually equivalent on an equal interval scale. The transformation formula was $100 \log X/18$ where X was the raw score response in inches. This transformation converted the 8, 12, and 18 inch raw values into equi-distant values (5, 6, and 7) on the transformed scale. The method is consistent with general psycho-physical methodology where it is necessary to transform perceptual discrimination responses, which occur on a ratio or geometric scale, into an equal interval or arithmetric scale. The logarithmic values were considered, in the present study, to be the "raw data" of the project. The groups were compared, by means of analysis of variance, on both constant and average errors from the visual perception and body-image tests. It should be added that in order to obtain an average error for a given subject, it was necessary to analyze the raw data for the presence of possible systematic effects associated with the experimental conditions (the body locations and stimulus sizes) and to correct the data for these effects wherever they proved to be significant. An analysis of variance applied to the raw data provided the means of evaluating these effects and for correcting the scores accordingly. Only after these corrections were made was it legitimate to average the deviations around their respective means.

The research hypotheses applied to the average error values, which were assumed to reflect the *stability* of the responses. It was assumed that larger average errors indicated greater disturbance, i.e., less stability. No predictions were made regarding the constant errors, but it was recognized that this variable might also serve as an index of disturbance. It remained to be determined whether chronic illness tended to result in an *inflation* of judgments about the body (i.e., a constant error in a positive direction), in a *constriction* of the judgments (i.e., a constant error in a negative direction), or in no change of this kind.

In the analysis of the constant errors, the values which were entered into the cells were the subjects' mean constant errors in the visual perception and body-image tests, a total of 114 scores. The analysis of the average errors involved analogous values, again a total of 144 scores. Inspection of the data revealed that the between-subjects variances within the groups were not homogeneous or normally distributed; this was true of both the constant and average errors. It was necessary to apply a square root transformation to all the scores in order to meet the assumptions of analysis of variance.

RESULTS

Table 1 shows the results of the analysis of the constant errors; the term "Conditions" refers to the two types of tests, the visual perception and body-image tests. All three groups differed significantly in the body-image scores, but not in the visual perception scores. This finding is reflected in the fact that the interaction of "Groups by Conditions" was significant, while the term "Groups" was not; i.e., the differences among the groups was significant for one condition (body-image) and not for the other (visual perception). The physically healthy group had the highest constant error, the hemiplegics had the lowest constant error, and the non-hemiplegic patients fell in the middle on the body-image test, reflecting a progressive *constriction*, from group to group, in the responses. Figure 1 shows the mean response (on the logarithmic scale) of each group on both tests. The mean stimulus value for all conditions was twelve inches, which was 6.0 on the log scale. Relative to this value it may be noted that the physically healthy group tended to overestimate the stimulus, while the disabled groups showed underestimations of the stimulus. It should be pointed out that the physically healthy group's responses were employed as the standard for interpreting the responses of the other groups, and, therefore, the term "constriction" applies to the responses of the disabled groups taken relative to the healthy standard. To employ the actual stimulus values as the "standard

Table 1. Analysis of variance results: constant errors*

Source of variance	df	Mean Sq.	F	p
Groups	2	59.0	2.7	ns
Conditions	1	56.0	8.4	<0.01
Groups by conditions	2	62.5	9.3	<0.01
Subjects within groups	69	22.0	3.3	<0.01
Error	69	6.7		
	143			
Physically healthy vs. non-hemiplegic patients (body-image scores)			11.2	<0.01
Physically healthy vs. hemiplegics (body-image scores)			34.9	<0.01
Non-hemiplegic patients vs. hemiplegics (body-image scores)			6.6	<0.025

*Based upon values obtained after square root transformation.

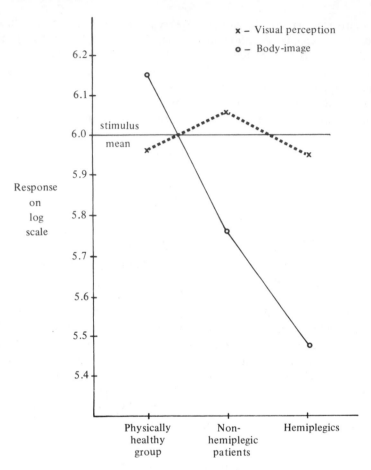

Figure 1. Mean response of each group on visual perception and body-image tests.

of reality" would require the evaluation of the effects upon perception of various testing conditions, particularly the conditions chosen for this study, as well as making assumptions about the relationship between measured distance and perceived distance. It may be noted that the differences among the groups fell almost on a straight line, indicating approximately equal intervals of body-image constriction.

Table 2 shows the results of the analysis of the average errors. Again all three groups differed significantly in the body-image scores and not in the visual perception scores. This finding is reflected in the significant interaction of "Groups by Conditions." The fact that the term "Groups" tested out as significant was evidently an artifact of the data related to a trend in the visual perception average errors which paralleled the body-image average errors. The groups fell in the order predicted,

Table 2. Analysis of variance results: average errors*

Source of variance	df	Mean Sq.	F	p
Groups	2	13.57	10.6	<0.01
Conditions	1	73.10	54.3	<0.01
Groups by conditions	2	4.82	3.8	<0.05
Subjects within groups	69	1.23	1.0	ns
Error	69	1.28		
	143			
Physically healthy vs. non-hemiplegic patients (body-image scores)			10.2	<0.01
Physically healthy vs. hemiplegics (body-image scores)			26.3	<0.01
Non-hemiplegic patients vs. hemiplegics (body-image scores)			3.8	<0.05

*Based upon values obtained after square root transformation.

on the body-image values, supporting both hypotheses. The physically healthy group had the smallest average errors, the hemiplegics had the largest, and the non-hemiplegic patients fell in the middle on the body-image test. Figure 2 shows the mean average error (on the logarithmic scale) for each group on both tests. Again the differences fell along an almost straight line, reflecting approximately equal intervals of body-image instability.

The significant difference between the conditions in the constant errors could be accounted for by the changes, from group to group, which occurred in the body-image values while the visual perception values remained fairly constant. This same factor operated in the average errors, but it may be observed in Figure 2 that the body-image test yielded larger average errors than the visual perception test in all three groups.

No significant relationships were found between body-image disturbances and age or body-image disturbance and intellectual level.

DISCUSSION

The present study demonstrates clearly that chronic disease tends to have associated with it measurable disturbances in the body-image, and that these disturbances occur even where there are no indications of serious cerebral damage beyond that attributable to age alone. The nature of the disturbance seems to involve a loss of stability in judgments about distances between body parts and in a tendency toward constriction of the size of these judgments.

Even though the hemiplegics exhibited greater body-image disturbance than the other patient group, this finding can only tentatively be interpreted to be the result of actual cerebral

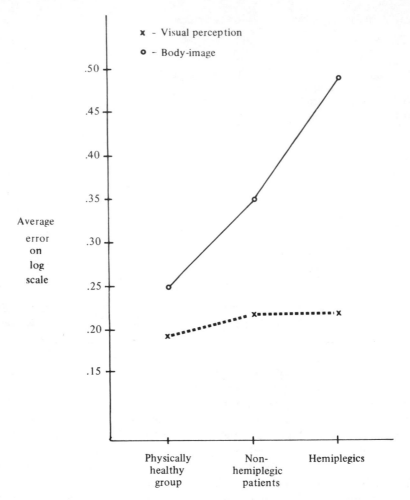

Figure 2. Mean average error of each group on visual perception and body-image tests.

damage. It is the authors' impression that hemiplegia tends to be a more functionally disabling illness than those illnesses that were characteristic of the non-hemiplegic patient group. On this basis one would expect to find greater body-image disturbance in hemiplegics even after correcting for that which might be due directly to central deficit.

The best theoretical analysis of the present results is that the body-image is the product of mutually communicating central and peripheral processes. The peripheral processes obtain and deliver the raw data of active and passive sensation to the central system. The central system processes and integrates this data and, in turn, provides feedback and control for the peripheral nerve network. Gerstmann (5) suggests the parietal or parieto-occipital area as the possible locus of the central system in this type of analysis.

The body-image phenomenon may, therefore, be expected to be altered by either central or peripheral changes in the overall system. Disturbance in the body-image may result from either direct damage to the central mechanism or damage to any of the peripheral sources of information. Conceivably, this latter type of damage results in a weakening, or eventual loss, of central associative connections; and this weakening becomes manifested in a reduction in stability of judgments about distances between body parts. The phenomenon of *constriction* may be construed to represent a shrinking of the overall body-image, the process occurring because of the loss of sustaining input to the central processing mechanism.

Implicit in this interpretation is the possibility that in those cases where the central system may be assumed to be relatively intact substitute peripheral avenues may serve to provide data in compensation for the loss of input associated with the relative disuse of sensory-motor pathways. In other words, the central processes may be strengthened or, perhaps, reactivated by supplying information through sources other than the damaged ones. Where chronic disease destroys muscular functioning and thus eliminates feedback from behavior dependent upon this functioning, the stability of the body-image conceivably may be maintained by increasing, for example, the amount of direct visual contact the individual has with his own body. Over and above the theoretical implications, there is probably little question as to the potential practical value research in this area has in relation to the rehabilitation of the chronically ill.

REFERENCES

1. Bender, M. B., Shapiro, M. F., and Fink, M. Patterns of perceptual organization with simultaneous stimuli. A.M.A. Arch. Neurol. Psychiat., 72: 233–255, 1954.
2. Cohn, R. Role of the "body-image concept" in the pattern of ipsilateral clinical extinction. A.M.A. Arch. Neurol. Psychiat., 70: 503–510, 1953.
3. Denny-Brown, D., Meyer, D., and Horenstein, S. The significance of perceptual rivalry resulting from parietal lesion. Brain, 75: 433–471, 1952.
4. Fisher, S., and Cleveland, S. Body Image and Personality. Van Nostrand, Princeton, 1958.
5. Gerstmann, J. Psychological and phenomenological aspects of disorders of the body image. J. Nerv. Ment. Dis., 126: 499–512, 1958.
6. Jaffe, J. and Bender, M. B. The factor of symmetry in the perception of two simultaneous cutaneous stimuli. Brain, 75: 167–176, 1952.
7. Prater, G. F. A comparison of the head and body size in the drawing of the human figure by hemiplegic and non-hemiplegic persons. Unpublished master's thesis. Univ. of Kentucky, 1950.
8. Schilder, P. The Image and Appearance of the Human Body. Routledge, London 1935.
9. Shontz, F. C. Body concept disturbances of patients with hemi-

plegia. J. Clin. Psychol., 12: 693–295, 1956.

10. Shontz, F. C. and Fink, S. L. The measurement of body concept disturbances in hemiplegic individuals. Unpublished study. Highland View Hospital, Cleveland, 1956.

11. Teitelbaum, H. A. Psychogenic body image disturbances associated with psychogenic aphasia. J. Nerv. Ment. Dis., 93: 581–590, 1941.

39 Psychological Considerations in the Driving Skills of the Handicapped Person

Joan L. Bardach

Of 520 patients who have participated in the driver training program at the Institute of Rehabilitation Medicine, 31 have been listed by the driver-educator as "difficult." Fourteen were women and seventeen were men. The operational definition of "difficult" seemed to be the large number of training sessions that each of these patients required. For instance, patients whose training was considered to be routine spent 20 to 25 sessions in the program, a figure comparable with that of the normal population (Gimpelson), but patients considered difficult took almost twice that number of training sessions.

At the end of each driving session, the driver-educator wrote brief comments on that day's lesson. As a preliminary investigation of the training program, the comments on the difficult cases were read. Those comments, judged by the present author to be contributory to the difficulty, were recorded for each patient, along with such objective data as name, age, sex, disability and total number of training sessions. The author then recorded what she judged to be the central difficulty and this judgment was compared

with the driver-educator's judgment of the primary difficulty. The two independent judgments have been remarkably similar.

The individuals in the group of difficult cases can be classified into those with brain injury and those without. It is useful to make this division because the nature of the difficulties encountered in the driver training program appears to be different in the two groups. The non-brain-injured group consisted primarily of quadriplegics, paraplegics and amputees. In general, their difficulties in completing the driver training program were either the severity of their disabilities or their emotional problems.

In driving, severely disabled patients had problems with both movement and strength, some of which were so severe that special equipment had to be designed for them. This process involves numerous trials and many modifications of equipment, and it results in long delays. It necessitates, therefore, much perseverence, ability to withstand disappointments and to withstand frequent reminders of the extent of one's injuries on the part of patients. The design of individualized

Reprinted from Psychological Aspects of Disability, 1970, 17(1): 10–13. Copyright 1970, Psychological Aspects of Disability (formerly Rehabilitation Psychology).

equipment also requires much perseverance, patience, and creativity on the part of staff.

The second major source of problems for the non-brain-injured patient, who was rated "difficult" to teach to drive, appeared to be emotional. Among the factors mentioned in the records were "family problems" that created considerable tension. Patients under tension found it difficult to perform more than one operation simultaneously while driving or to follow instructions with adequate speed. Another factor that appeared in some charts was authority problems. Individuals with such problems object to restrictions placed on their actions. These people are often quickly aroused to anger; some may be irrationally competitive. The need to gratify emotional demands of this sort takes precedence over meeting the conditions of the driving task. Such emotional patterns produce situations that further car accidents.

Marked egocentrism also results in a kind of rigidity that makes the driver unresponsive to the varying conditions of the road. The need for flexibility is necessary if one is to be a safe driver. Authority problems are not the only kind of maladaptive personality that produced marked egocentrism. It was found in an hysteric, for instance, who exhibited the classic "la belle indifference." This young woman did not consider the consequences of her acts with regard to a hazardous traffic situation that her own driving behavior might impose. Similarly anger, especially in a setting of impulsiveness, can produce egocentrism that can be hazardous on

the road. One man of thirty-three had sustained an injury in an industrial accident. Despite his obvious skill, this patient's temper was aroused in a flash and was acted upon with almost no restraint.

Although severity of motor disability and emotional factors appeared to be primary contributors to the difficulties the non-brain-injured patients encountered in the driver education program, there is one other factor, body image, that might be investigated in more detail. A young woman behaved as if she were unsure of the limits of her body parts when they were extended in space. For instance, she tended to watch her feet while driving. Moreover, it may be that not knowing her own body limits in space increased her difficulty in incorporating the car into her body image. Such incorporation is necessary if the driver is to know the spatial limits of his car. The driver-educator wrote in the record of this woman "trouble judging distances between her car and parked cars." A sense of equilibrium (Bardach, 1965) is an important component in body image. The patient under discussion is a triplegic so that sensations from her body are asymmetrical. Such asymmetry also might contribute to a sense of imbalance, which, in turn, might produce problems in body image.

Although severity of motor disability, emotional maladjustments and body image problems may be factors in the difficulties encountered in training the brain injured to drive, results suggest so far that these factors are generally less salient in the brain damaged group than in the non-brain-injured group. Instead, achievement of competence in the driver training program for the brain-injured individuals seemed to be affected primarily by perceptual-motor or by cognitive problems, with, perhaps, a scattering of cases whose difficulties might be attributable to disinhibition leading either to panic reactions or marked impulsiveness. So far, these latter problems have been seen only in patients with cerebral palsy or head injuries due to external accidents.

Of 49 hemiplegics who have participated in the program, 17 were right hemiplegics and 32 were left hemiplegics. So far, despite language problems that were sometimes quite severe, not a single right hemiplegic has been rated by the driver educator as "difficult." Although the number of cases is small, these results seem to corroborate the growing literature (Diller, 1963; Bardach, 1963; Diller & Weinberg, 1968; Reitan, 1959) on the psychological differences between right and left hemiplegics. The verbal impairments of the right hemiplegic do not appear to be central to the task of driving. By contrast, the perceptual-motor impairments of the left hemiplegic do seem central to the driving task. As Diller and Weinberg (1968) have pointed out, the styles of cognition, at least so far as memory and attention are concerned, are different in right and left hemiplegics. It may be that the differences in cognitive styles between these two groups account in part for the fact that no right hemiplegics have thus far been rated as having difficulty in the driver education program. Of course, it may be that those right hemiplegics who would have had difficulty with the program were weeded out beforehand, but that the left hemiplegics were not.

The cognitive difficulties that the left hemiplegics had consisted of inadequate scanning of the environment with consequent poor planning, inability to shift according to the changing demands of the driving task, distractibility, poor judgment, and confusion. Their perceptual-motor impairments resulted in such things as reduced awareness of traffic conditions, confusion between right and left directions and inadequate use of space. Limitations of the visual field also may account for poor behavior in driving. Use of peripheral vision is important in calling attention to outlying objects (Duke-Elder, 1949). Perusal of notes taken while the author rode in the back sear of the training car revealed that some left hemiplegics tended to ignore their environment on the affected side. For example, a number of them failed to look left when crossing an intersection, when pulling out from a parked position, or when making turns.

The conclusions in the present paper must be regarded as suggestive only, for data from control groups have not been obtained. Nevertheless, it seems useful to assess in what direction the findings seem to be heading.

It is obvious from the examples given of the driving behavior of the disabled patients rated difficult that the factors of severity of motor disability, emotional problems, body-image problems, perceptual-motor impairments and cognitive deficits are not mutually exclusive categories. Moreover, they interact with each other in ways that are not understood. How should these factors be weighted? Are their weights different in different kinds of people, as is suggested here? What are the conditions other than individual differences that affect the weighting of variables operative in the course of driving? Are there other factors that result in change of their weights? What other factors are important? What are the consequences of the complex interaction of variables in driving?

All the factors mentioned probably contributed to the difficulties encountered by both groups of patients in the driver education program. However, the impression that the saliency of some factors is different in the one group from that of the other suggests that studying the pattern of interaction of variables is more relevant than the study of each variable separately, if one wishes to understand the nature of the driving task. Research in teaching the disabled to drive carries with it the potentiality for contributing to two important areas of much needed knowledge; namely, the nature of specific disabilities, and a further understanding of the nature of the driving task.

REFERENCES

Bardach, J. L. Psychological factors in hemiplegia. Journal of American Physical Therapy Association. 43, 792–797, November, 1963.

Bardach, J. L. Psychological considerations in bracing. Orthopedic & Prosthetic Appliance Journal. 26–29, March, 1965.

Diller, L. Sensorial and psychological factors in stroke. Read at "Stroke Conference," Chicago, 1963.

Diller, L. & Weinberg, J. Attention in brain-damaged patients. Journal of Education. Boston University School of Education, 150 (3), 20–27, February, 1968.

Duke-Elder, Sir W. S. Textbook of Ophthalmology, Vol. IV, The Neurology of Vision, Motor and Optical Anomalies. St. Louis; C. V. Mosby, 1949.

Gimpelson, Morris: Personal Communication.

Reitan, R. M. The effects of brain lesions on adaptive abilities in human beings. Indianapolis, Indiana University Medical Center, 1959.

Section 10

SEXUALITY

40 Sexuality and the Handicapped

Milton Diamond

Professional recognition of the sexual problems and concerns of the handicapped has been developing and expanding for the last several years. To date, however, little has been formalized in print and what has been done is primarily directed toward making the professional aware of the area as one of legitimate concern. For this presentation, I would like to formalize some specific matters to be considered, offer specific recommendations for handling problems, and develop a directness with dealing with some of the more controversial issues involved. This is now appropriate, since during the past several years many excellent people have contributed their knowledge and efforts to make the sexual problems of the handicapped a respectable issue of concern and have awakened many to the disrespect that must be attached to ignorance and nonconcern with the subject (e.g., Comarr; Gochros and Schultz; Kempton). These positive efforts have further engendered a desire for professionals to have working models and ideas to follow the general attitudinal changes stressed previously.

My presentation will be divided into several portions. First, I will indicate how the perspective of various individuals or groups color the way this subject is treated. Then I will deal with some specific problems and issues in sexual expression and follow this with recommendations for handling problems that fall into associated areas. My concluding comments will contain several general rules for improving sexual functioning that are pertinent for all, able-bodied and handicapped, but more so for the handicapped.

First, I would like to make clear just how many levels I think are involved with sexuality and how these must be distinguished. It must be understood that when one considers sexuality, one must not think only of genitals or bedroom activity, although that is usually what first comes to mind. At least two broad areas must be considered: public and private sexuality.

Public. How does the person act in public; what role is played by these actions? Will a handicap interfere with the individual's personal or public appraisal of his or her masculinity or femininity? For example, can a telephone lineman with a paralyzed leg accept, without loss of masculinity, the job of a telephone operator? Can

Reprinted from Rehabilitation Literature, 1974, 35(2):34–40.

This paper is an edited version of an address presented at the National Rehabilitation Association, Pacific Region Conference, June 14, 1973, Honolulu, Hawaii.

the arthritic housewife accept the loss of her hands and deft touch without considering it a reflection of her femininity?

Sexual patterns and roles are our public demonstration of socially recognized sexual expressions. Public concerns may manifest themselves in the choice of how the individuals interact with society.

Private. Here we refer to the genital sexual responses and those inner problems not usually discernible. This includes the ability to maintain an erection, have orgasm, receive and give genital and sensual pleasures, and reduce sexual tensions in oneself or partner.

Naturally, these public and private concerns might be combined.

Next, I would like to make clear that we must not confuse genital satisfaction, love, reproduction, and marriage. These four areas are quite distinct, although they may go together or be related. We must clearly keep them separate in our own minds and in the minds of our clients, certainly to insure just what is being communicated. The four areas of genital satisfaction, love, reproduction, and marriage offer different rewards and present different problems. For example, a client wanting genital satisfaction doesn't necessarily want marriage and one wanting marriage doesn't necessarily want children or sex. If this seems like too radical a concept, just recall that it is only a few generations back when our ancestors had marriages that were arranged so sex and marriage were started without love, most

present-day marriages are not entered into by virgins, and birth control and family planning are facts of life. In a very practical vein, we must insure that children are to be considered on their own merits not as visual proof of masculine or feminine abilities; reproduction is not sexual identity and neither is genital gratification. A handicapped person might be more disadvantaged than an able-bodied person in having a child who is not wanted for himself but rather as an affirmation of masculinity or femininity.

It is appropriate here to distinguish between the different stages during which persons may become handicapped. These may be considered: prepubertal, adolescent, marriageable, married, separated, divorced, widowed, and senescent. A teenager is obviously involved with different concerns than is a senior citizen and obviously the attendant concerns of one with memories of the past and lost demonstrated abilities would differ from those of one who never had experiences to draw from. While this will not be dealt with in detail now, it is well to reflect on how each stage has its specific concerns.

PERSPECTIVES AND ISSUES

At least five different perspectives have to be considered in any professional situation. These viewpoints are those of: 1) the client; 2) the professional dealing with the client; 3) the agency represented by the professional; 4) the family in which the client resides; and 5) the "second person" involved, i.e., the individual to whom the client's attention is or might be focused.

These five different perspectives all have a similar focus but they may differ quite markedly. There may even be many areas of wide disagreement and friction among these five factions although theoretically they should all be working together.

Client

The client generally looks at his or her problem as quite personal and private. The client may consider the sexual situation as separate from the handicap or part of the handicap but generally thinks it's a problem to be borne in silence and one that should not concern the professional. This is doubly so for the handicapped compared to the able-bodied. Both the able-bodied and handicapped have, first of all, been taught that sexual matters are private and not to be honestly discussed, so this is a common problem. But the handicapped also has or is given the feeling that any interest or effort that doesn't focus most directly on the handicap should be considered minor. For example, the blind should worry only about seeing and the paralyzed only about walking.

Professional

The professional quite often looks at sexual problems as outside both the professional's scope and the client's area of legitimate concern. The professional's training has generally been toward getting the individual back on the job, capable of caring for a family and generally self-supporting. Regardless of whether the professional has been trained as a physician, psychologist, social worker, or other type of therapist, until quite recently sexual counseling was never considered as within the legitimate scope of activities. Therapists were not taught the clues to which to attend in this area. Often, even if the client does bring up concern regarding the subject, the professional quite often avoids the issue entirely by not replying to the clues or defends himself by saying words to the effect of, "You should be worried about not being able to walk or not being able to see or not being able to hear rather than worrying about your sexual concerns." It's as if the sexual concerns have to be of lower magnitude than the other abilities. The professional more than anyone must realize that meeting an individual's sexual concerns can go a long way in reestablishing or establishing a general feeling of self-worth conducive to general rehabilitation.

It must be mentioned here, in contrast with what I've just said, that an overzealous professional should in this area, as in others for which he has been trained, be careful to be attuned to client sensitivities. One should not project concerns on patients that are not there, since many handicapped handle their sexual concerns quite well.

Agency

Agencies, most often, are interested only in those factors that they consider leading to job placement or getting the person functioning in the home. They think in terms of productivity or income and their distance from the client makes them even less aware than the professional counselor of some of the human sexual concerns of the client. Agencies change even more slowly than do individual professionals. So, even though the professional (physician, social worker, counselor, or psychologist) might be interested in the individual client's sexual abilities, the agency frequently takes a dim view of these concerns. Often, the agency is most concerned with image and thinks that being concerned with an individual's sexual problems is inappropriate for a state, foundation-supported, or religion-affiliated organization. Again, I think these views are changing and it's slowly becoming apparent, to both the professional and the agency, that, once an individual's worth as a complete person is reestablished, he or she is much more apt to be educable, hirable, and self-content with himself and his situation.

Family

Next, we have the family perspective. Here the issue is quite different. To be sure, the family, too, thinks the sexual problems are private and not to be discussed in public. They think they are also outside the province of the agency or professional dealing with the client, yet the family is quite often ambivalent about the situation. While they recognize that these are valid issues, they generally wish the sexual concerns to be ignored; they want them to sort of "go away," since they are ill at ease dealing with them and don't really know how to handle the issues. They, too, are beset with the societal value that sex is private and not to be discussed in public.

Quite often, the family would imagine that if, especially in younger people, sex is not discussed, it would never come up in a person's experiences. As with the able-bodied, they don't know how to deal with overt sex, whether it be masturbation or displays of affection toward possible sexual partners. They have strong conflicts. On the one hand, they want to consider the handicapped family member like everyone else and thus allow all opportunities. On the other hand, they don't want to, as they consider it, raise false expectations and hopes. Lastly, it is difficult for the family to recognize that children or parents can be sexual. Regardless of age, elderly parents are often considered "beyond it" and children "not yet ready."

Second Person

Last is the "second person." This is the perspective of the one on whom the client focuses his or her sexual attention. This is also considered to be personal and private, but here the individual definitely is concerned with how the handicap may be involved, although the concern may not be shown. There is the question of just what the partner can do or not do and can this be discussed openly or will the issue be too sensitive for probing? Often both of the parties involved seek advice and counsel from others, lay and professional, instead of speaking with each other about sexual feelings, concerns, capabilities, and expectations.

SPECIFIC ISSUES

With my broad introduction and talk of perspectives, I will now present three specific issues that must and can be dealt with within these perspectives. These issues are: 1) performance and expectations, 2) guilt, and 3) communication. While my remarks are directed mainly toward dealing with the concerns of the handicapped, it will be obvious that they apply equally as well to the able-bodied.

Performance and Expectations

Too many individuals view their sexual expression as a performance to be rated and graded on some sort of consensually agreed upon scale. It is as if there were a "right" and a "wrong" way to be sexual and anything less than "right" is to be criticized. Our society certainly fosters these expectations and we live with them in Archie Bunker fashion every day. For our clients, in a realistic and nonjudgmental manner, we have to realign the performance expectations with performance capabilities, so that the only allowable criteria for concern are

based on what the couple or the individuals prefer within their abilities. The capabilities naturally will limit the expectations, but it must be made clear that the value systems that an individual puts on a particular type of love relation, or sexual relation, or reproduction relation, or marriage relationship, should be on an individual level or a couple level, so long as public society is not disturbed. Private acts have no standards that are immutable or written in stone. As we ourselves don't ask society's blessings on our private activities, let's help our clients to be encouraged in arriving at their own acceptable solutions with our blessings. Not only should we sanction their solutions, regardless of how novel, but we must encourage experimentation so that many possibilities are attempted to achieve a maximum of satisfaction.

Guilt

Here it is appropriate to introduce the issue of guilt. Too often the clients have enough problems with considering themselves different. In the area of sexuality, we must honestly stress that being different may be of small actual matter, because what one does in the privacy of the bedroom is of concern only to the individuals involved. If the function of sexual expression is private genital satisfaction, then that takes precedence over public approval and, if the purpose is to give or receive love, then that is not dependent upon certain formulas of performance or public acceptance.

With these concepts, the client

should realize that guilt is an inappropriate feeling, not because the individual is less able, but because no standards for anyone, able-bodied or not, are legitimately imposed. One needn't worry about being different sexually because anything goes that is functional and mutually acceptable. Oral-genital stimulation, manual stimulation, anything that the couple or the individual can find satisfaction in doing is okay and we as professionals and agencies have to make our permission and sanction (because we have the power to grant such) very clear. We must not put a negative value on any practice found acceptable, whether it involves masturbation, oral-genital relations, a female superior position, or anything else that satisfies the couple.

For this we have to train ourselves against being judgmental and considering some practices preferable to others. This doesn't mean that we have to force on any client any practice he or she may find objectionable. We also shouldn't force our own or society's guilt-laden values on the person or couple. We may encourage experimentation into previously personal or societally taboo areas. We should do all we can to help remove whatever inappropriate guilt feelings may exist in the achievement of sexual satisfaction.

Communication

Lastly, here it is appropriate to talk about communication. There are practically no sexual concerns or situations that cannot benefit from increased communication by and between the individuals involved. Expectations and performance capabilities can be more realistically appraised with good communication and false impressions can be minimized. The handicapped, as do many able-bodied, often attach a magnified value to certain suspected deficiencies without ever testing the reality of the situation with the "second person." For example, in the realm of sexuality, most of us are concerned with something in our physical makeup. In this regard the handicapped and able-bodied again are alike. Consider that an individual may be concerned personally with being bald, having small breasts, or being deaf, blind, or elderly. Only by communication with the "second party" can one find out if the concern is mutual or the magnitude of the concern. Communication between the individuals involved will reduce hesitancy in finding out just what is and is not possible and what is or is not acceptable.

As professionals, we must thus encourage open, frank discussions of sexual matters as legitimate topics of conversation (often this means removing guilt in talking about sex). We must realize, parenthetically, that communication may be nonverbal as well as verbal. A touch, glance, smile, or grimace may speak loudly. However, for most, an adequate vocabulary still provides the best means of transmitting ideas and feelings. Regrettably, not everyone has an adequate vocabulary and we as professionals may help in providing one. For the deaf, for example, we might remedy the lack in acceptable universal signs for many sexual and reproductive ideas. We hope a satisfactory vocabulary is available soon.

We then come full circle. Good communication can help the other issues, linking performance and expectations and reducing guilt as well as helping in its own way. With this brief introduction, I'd like to present a dialogue and see how it exemplifies some of the issues at hand.[1]

JERRY: Well, I don't really think that I had any idea that things were going to be so different after the operation on my back. I thought my sexual life was going to be the same as it always was and it turned out to be completely different.

MICKIE: I think at first I felt a sense of desolation that the emotional side of my life was all over with and that I've been condemned to the life of a robot or a zombie.

FRANCIS: I feel embarrassed when I talk to girls because I drool a lot and I spit when I talk. And during the conversation, I keep on drooling; I feel like a waterfall.

GEORGE: A heart attack is a massive insult to the body, and to myself as a person. And because of this, the relationship between myself and others— the alienation, the depression—is a whole area of related phenomena that we ought to study very carefully; an area of which we know very little about.

BILL: I've been paralyzed for over 20 years and it's been so long ago that I've forgotten what "normal" sex was. But as I recall, it had to do with sex being pretty much equated with an orgasm. But since I've been paralyzed and had a few chances for sex, I've realized that orgasm is not so important in sex; in fact, it actually hinders the enjoyment of it because when you don't worry about the orgasm and don't think about the orgasm, sex just continues on and on and it's never over.

DR. DIAMOND: When we think of the functions that sex serves, we have to think in terms of giving and getting pleasure, of reducing tension, of sharing intimacies. If we keep that in mind we can remove ourself from the stereotype that "good" sex involves only an erect penis in a vagina; that that's the only way or right way. Do you feel that the value of an orgasm is part of the myth, Bill?

BILL: Well, very much so. In fact, before you kinda work up to something, and then it's over. This way, you just keep going on and on.

DR. DIAMOND: What do you find the most pleasurable thing now?

BILL: Well, still touching the penis, but just touching the nipples and breasts and the sides. I'm very sensitive under the arms.

DR. DIAMOND: So you could find your own way of giving and getting

---

[1] At the 1973 regional National Rehabilitation Association conference in Hawaii, a half-hour video recording of various participants discussing sex and the handicapped, made with the aid of the Rehabilitation Association of Hawaii, was presented. This dialogue is a slightly modified portion of the tape. A full copy of the tape is available from the Public Television Library, 512 E. 17th St., Bloomington, Ind. 47401, under the title When Illness Strikes, Program 21 of the Human Sexuality Series, moderated by Dr. Milton Diamond.

pleasure and that solves your own needs.

BILL: Yeah, but it's much better when somebody else does it.

DR. DIAMOND: Well, that's what I assumed.

BILL: You just have to try—find the right partner and I guess the right partner is just about anyone who shares your feelings toward each other.

DR. DIAMOND: Mickie, how about yourself?

MICKIE: Well, since being paralyzed and getting out of the more severe part of it, I find that I am perfectly normal except that the mechanics of the thing are different. My legs and back are totally paralyzed. As far as feelings are concerned, if anything, they're heightened because the type of polio I had made me hypersensitive. I find that it's just mostly the mechanics that interfere. And, of course, the preconceived idea that, because you're in a wheelchair, "Don't bother with her—she can't do anything anyway."

DR. DIAMOND: Well, we find that even able-bodied persons begin to find that there is more than one way to skin a cat and probably the handicapped find this out a lot quicker. George, how about you and your heart condition?

GEORGE: Well, I feel like there isn't that comfort that I'm getting from the rest of the people here about my relationship with sexuality. When I had my heart attack, the doctor told me to stop having sex for awhile but he never told me when to come on again. I feel a profound kind of lack of knowledge and hesitancy . . .

MICKIE: George, do you feel a sense of fear in this area?

GEORGE: Oh, yeah. I think that the fear that accompanies this kind of activity is very profound because it's a deep insult to the body. There's a great hesitancy and I think this leaves a feeling of separation.

DR. DIAMOND: How about with your wife? Obviously, you can look at it both ways. You may want love but she doesn't want to lose you. Francis, how about yourself with cerebral palsy? How do you see your condition now?

FRANCIS: Well, I'd like to be like any normal guy. I had this cerebral palsy since back in my preschool years. There came a time when the doctors over there wanted me to progress and I didn't progress rapidly. Now, I could do almost anything any normal person could do.

DR. DIAMOND: But now, are you dating now? Are you married now?

FRANCIS: Oh, no. I'm still dating girls.

DR. DIAMOND: Jerry, how about yourself with your back condition?

JERRY: With me, it was a problem, I believe, of creating a new self-image. I thought that I had to be the virile male and live up to my wife's expectations (which she didn't have) of me. She was perfectly satisfied with what I was able to give her after the accident but I was always trying to do more, and finally I just sat back and enjoyed it, and it was great!

DR. DIAMOND: Why couldn't it have been this way before?

JERRY: Yeah, why did I have to go through all this misery of thinking that I wasn't performing and that I had lost my capabilities?

DR. DIAMOND: Isn't that a problem

with all of us—we become spectators, rather than participants. We ask, "What am I supposed to be doing?" rather than, "What can I do?" Shouldn't we concentrate on what we have, rather than on what we don't have?

BILL: This business about fear—it can be emotional fear, too. With fear that, once you are handicapped, you're not going to be able to live up to the expectations that you've been taught in the past other people have of you and you have of yourself. Being in a wheelchair, they don't have the same expectations; they kind of wonder if you can or you can't. Once you show that you can have intercourse you can also show them what would normally be progressing steps to intercourse. You can show them that you've had good experiences and pleasurable experiences, and the orgasm doesn't become important anymore—or the typical intercourse methods.

DR. DIAMOND: Did you have different experiences as you went through different ages? Many of you have had your handicaps for quite some time.

MICKIE: I've had a rather different type of life. I lost my first husband because of my illness. He couldn't face up to having a disabled wife and two small children. The second time around, it was great. However, before my husband died, he was, for the last two or three years, so very ill that for us there was no more sex as most people think of it. But there was still a deep affection between us. I built my life around different types of activities, so I can't say that I really felt too great a lack in my life because he was still very affectionate, very sweet to me, and showed me lots of love and attention, and I tried to do the same for him. That was important. The fact that we no longer had typical sexual relations just ceased to be of any importance to either one of us.

DR. DIAMOND: Do any of you get the feeling that either the spouses or lovers, or what have you, are hesitant in initiating sex because of the handicap? How do you overcome that?

GEORGE: I feel that one of the greatest difficulties with my whole family is lack of being able to say it's all right. We begin to have a profound doubt of our own feedback mechanism. You know what I mean—an acceptance. That I'm okay where I'm at is kind of cut off because of this regression. You know, when you're on your own, you lose that trust in yourself.

DR. DIAMOND: Is there anybody that you can communicate with? Your physician or your spouse?

GEORGE: Somewhat; I think more would be helpful.

DR. DIAMOND: Francis, whom do you talk to when you have problems?

FRANCIS: I sometimes talk to my parents, counselors, or probably with the girl I'm dating. I find that the girls are understanding. I talk about the problems that I have and they feel compassion about my problems and I feel that they understand.

DR. DIAMOND: What is your biggest problem that you think you've had and overcome? Jerry, how about that?

JERRY: I really believe that the biggest problem was living up to an expectation that wasn't expected at all.

DR. DIAMOND: But now you don't worry about it at all?

JERRY: No, I don't worry about it. That's just the way it is. My wife is a wonderful woman. She's very loving and we've established a new relationship on a different level.

DR. DIAMOND: You just don't have the movements.

JERRY: Right.

DR. DIAMOND: Bill, how about yourself?

BILL: I agree with that. That the most important thing is to get your own self-confidence and just do what comes naturally when you're with your girl.

DR. DIAMOND: How do you do that?

MICKIE: Well, you throw your inhibitions out the window and let it all hang loose.

DR. DIAMOND: How do you do that though? How do you throw out your inhibitions if you've got them?

BILL: It's just a matter of confidence. The first time you may not take advantage of what you later perceive to be the girl's willingness, then you verbally kick yourself in the rear end. The next time, by God, you're not going to make the same mistake twice! You're going to go ahead and do it.

DR. DIAMOND: Mickie, you said something I think is crucial about getting rid of your inhibitions. How about those feelings with guilt? That you may be doing something that somebody else says is not normal?

MICKIE: That is a very hard thing to overcome, but you've got to make up your mind; either you're going to take happiness now while it's there waiting for you or forget it because you're not going to come back and do it again. You know—it's that simple. It isn't like having a piece of cheese in the "refrig" and a week later going and getting it out. There's no way that you're going to be able to do that. So you've just got to say—maybe we'll try something else.

DR. DIAMOND: Sex, in terms of genitals, is important but, in terms of personal worth, getting along with somebody and self-worth are perhaps more important.

MICKIE: Oh, I think so!

What does the discussion illustrate? The dialogue demonstrates how the separation of expectations and capabilities is narrowed when guilt feelings are lessened. It goes further, as we must, in reducing guilt and lessening the gap between expectations and capabilities by legitimately doing away with false expectations. For example, we do away with the "myth," which, in essence, states that the only satisfactory means of expressing oneself sexually and achieving satisfaction is with an erect penis in a well-lubricated vagina. For the able-bodied as well as the handicapped, sexual satisfaction is possible without these practices and, in fact, may even be more satisfying. Hands, mouth, feet, any body part may be used any way to achieve satisfaction, and one means is not, a priori, to be preferred over another. Presenting this concept in a positive way can be very helpful to clients.

Further, we should do away with the "marriage manual" formula and concept, which views some activities as foreplay, some as afterplay, and only coitus as "the real play," each "play" with a prescribed time allotment and sequence. We must advocate that anything goes, for however long or in whatever sequence. This is as true for those whose motor functions are compromised as for those with a sensory loss. Persons should be encouraged to maximize the use of those functions that remain, rather than bemoan the nonuse of those functions that are lost.

We can do even more to lessen the gap between capabilities and expectations by suggesting the use in sexual expression of some of the same types of devices we would offer to lessen the gap in job performance between capabilities and expectations. I'm referring to the use of prostheses. We certainly encourage the use of and recommend artificial, arms, legs, or eyes where they will serve a function, even a cosmetic one. We can do similarly in a sexual situation. While the use of false breasts has become common for women with mastectomies, we might encourage or at least recommend the use of dildos, vibrators, or anything that the client might find usable, functional, or cosmetic, in his or her sexual relationships.

While this might strike some as inappropriate, I think we have to realize that the same reasons other prosthetics are used in normal, everyday life apply to their sexual use. This actually should be seen as quite appropriate for the handicapped since many able-bodied use them routinely; in fact, the able-bodied provide the major market for their present use. The aged and arthritic and hand amputees can certainly use vibrators where they have lost hand function, and an artificial penis or vagina also has its use, for either solitary or mutual pleasure. While it may take some education on the part of both the client and the partner to accept these devices, with professional encouragement they can accept or reject them without the connotations of guilt that might otherwise go along with their use or consideration. It is to be emphasized that these devices are presently available and are most often used by the able-bodied, so they should not carry a special stigma for the handicapped. These should legitimately be sold in surgical supply stores as freely as in the porno supply shops, where they are presently sold.

Prostheses help those with motor problems. For those with a sensory loss, I will offer a suggestion that is also helpful for those with reduced motor abilities, i.e., maximize the use of all possible senses. If a person is deaf or blind, then obviously maximal use is made of other input means. A soft touch or caress or kiss on a sensitive area may be quite stimulating, and we can increase or multiply the use of available senses by reading or viewing explicit, sexually oriented material or pornography, by the use of perfume, good food, fancy candles, music, and the like. Certainly it should be reiterated here that talking and touching, the most basic means of communicating, must be increased. Eye contact and language are to be encouraged. Novelty and spontaneity also have erotic overtones that should be exploited for maximum sexual satisfaction.

The dialogue also stressed another

major point made earlier. That is, satisfaction is quite different from orgasm. Further, sex is, itself, usually used as a means of communicating deep feelings. These feelings can be provided with simple touches, glances, and personal interchanges, which don't require elaborate gymnastics or idealized anatomy. Satisfaction is most often a result of good sexual communication and shared intimacy and is independent of orgasm. Satisfaction and orgasm may be simultaneously sought after but separately achieved. If we make this idea acceptable to our clients, I think we will have helped them in a major way.

In conclusion, I would like to apologize for not discussing, in detail, special problems associated with pregnancy or contraception, or dealing with the special issues and concerns of the mentally retarded. These must await a subsequent publication. What I did hope to do, however, is alert your attention to: 1) the difference between public and private sexuality; 2) the separate concerns attendant to genital satisfaction, love, reproduction, and marriage; 3) these aspects as different, dependent upon the client's life stage; and 4) sexuality as viewed from various perspectives. Further, I tried to show how to deal conceptually with several overriding issues for the handicapped, i.e., expectations and performance, guilt, and communication. Lastly, I tried to provide some specific ideas to help meet these issues.

I would reiterate that everyone's sexual life can be improved by 1) increased communication; 2) decreased guilt with anything mutually satisfying; and 3) education and ease in dealing openly with sexual issues, so that expectations are more realistically in line with performance capabilities. All of this serves the human need for satisfaction in self-assessment and interpersonal relationships. This satisfaction is seen as the first stage in a person's successful road to rehabilitation specifically, but contentment with life's lot generally.

What I am offering for you to master are concepts that don't take a large budget or special, elaborate training. What it does take is empathy, and those in rehabilitation, by virtue of the career choice, have usually demonstrated an ample supply of this.

41 Sex and Self:

The Spinal Cord-Injured

Silas P. Singh and
Tom Magner

Injuries to the spinal cord or cauda equina frequently cause partial or complete loss of sensory and motor function below the lesion. Paralyzed patients have to face many difficult physical and psychological problems, including the belief of the patient or his family that he has completely lost his sexual function. Up until several years ago, the view held by most physicians was that the less said about sexual function, the better. Paraplegics and quadriplegics were encouraged to substitute interest for their sex drive (20). Today, after a great deal of research, it has been determined that most people with spinal cord injuries can have sexual activity; however, it probably will be limited to some extent, depending on the level and extent of the injury (109).

Lesions can occur at one of four levels: cervical, upper thoracic, lower thoracic, and lumbar. Generally, the higher the lesion, the better the chances for the male's being able to have erections and to ejaculate; however, with a high level of injury, often there is more neural damage and it is more difficult to carry out coitus (22).

In a study at Hines Veterans Hospital in Chicago in 1957, of the 100 patients, 33 had cervical lesions. Of these 33, 27 (82%) were able to have complete erections, 2 (6%) were not able to have any type of erection, 14 (42%) attempted intercourse, and 11 (33%) were successful. Of the total of 100, 21 had upper thoracic lesions. Of these 21, 15 (71%) had complete erections, 4 (19%) had incomplete erections, 2 (10%) had no erection at all, 8 (38%) attempted intercourse, and 6 (29%) were successful. In the next group, 39 with lower thoracic lesions, 18 (46%) had complete erections, 12 (31%) had incomplete erections, 9 (23%) had no erection, 12 (31%) attempted intercourse, and 6 (15%) were successful. In the last group, 7 with lumbar lesions, 4 (57%) had complete erections, 2 (29%) had incomplete erections, 1 (14%) had no erections, 4 (57%) attempted intercourse, and 3 (43%) were successful (114).

These figures show that, in general, the lower the injury, the less the chance for the spinal cord victim to have erections and ejaculate; however, each individual is so unique in his injury that it is nearly impossible to predict the extent to which a person can have sex.

A spinal cord victim may have a

Excerpted from Rehabilitation Literature, 1975, 36(1): 2–10.

complete or an incomplete lesion. If the lesion is complete, the cord is transected and there is no feeling below the level of the transection (94). With this type of injury, there is a possibility of erection, but very little chance of ejaculation. With an incomplete lesion, there still may be partial feeling beneath the level of injury, and both erection and ejaculation are possible (94).

For the male, the sex act consists of three major occurrences, desire, erection, and ejaculation (89). Desire can be built up in a number of ways, one of which is through fantasy. The male may have dreams in which he is fully functioning sexually; to many this will give sexual desire. The need to prove to himself or to his mate that he can perform is another factor in building up desire (72). Erection occurs when the blood vessels of the cavernous bodies actively dilate by parasympathetic stimulation to engorge and stiffen the penis. The center for erection is located in the sacral portion of the cord and may be activated reflexly by sensory impulses reaching the center over the pudendal nerve from the numerous sensory nerve endings in the glans and prepuce. Erection is also often activated by psychic stimuli descending from the cerebral cortex through the spinal cord (89).

A male should be able to have erections and ejaculate if the sacral cord, cauda equina, and thoracolumbar sympathetic outflow are intact. Because these two centers are far apart, a lesion may affect one and leave the other intact, which means that many times the injured man can have erections but cannot ejaculate (89).

In the female, the problem of sex has not been studied as extensively as in the man. In a woman, the problem is not so traumatic. She plays the passive role in sex relations usually (109). The penis enters the vagina and, with the contraction of her sphincter muscles, the male is able to reach ejaculation. It can be a relatively simple process for the woman; therefore, with a spinal cord injury, it is still possible for her to have coitus. She may lack feeling but not function. She may even become pregnant and deliver a child normally (79).

While it has been proved that up to 70 percent of all spinal cord patients are capable of having some degree of sexual activity (114), many do not indulge in any type of sex and actually have a poor attitude toward the whole idea of a person with this type of injury engaging in sex. There are many reasons for this attitude, all of which go back to the idea of self-concept, which is: 1) how a person perceives himself, 2) what he thinks, 3) how he values himself, and 4) how he attempts through various actions to enhance or defend himself (98). In spinal cord injury, the self-concept many times is low (43). Many factors account for this. Physical disability is one. Loss of bladder and bowel control and inability to walk causes great shame and feelings of inferiority. Increased dependency is another factor, and body image is the final and most important one. The concept of body image or body schema refers to the mental idea and/or basic attitudes a person has towards his own body and reflects how he perceives himself physically, esthetically, and socially. It also provides a clue as to how he sees himself in relation to his world and hence reflects his style of life (74) and

> ... in working with disabled individuals, one is frequently impressed not with their depression, as one would imagine, but with their complete inability to understand what the disability is all about. ... There is a veritable struggle that takes place. ... They cannot find a place in their body image for the deformity (74, p. 155).

The study of sexual abilities in spinal cord injury is relatively new, but its importance cannot be overly stressed. The main concern of a spinal cord patient after the frustration and bitterness of the first few months is the ability to live as a functioning person in society. For so long, society was interested solely in the physical rehabilitation of these people, but that is not enough. They need help in accepting what has happened to them and learning to live with it; hence the creation of a "wholeman concept" (81). Sex is a major part of this acceptance because it involves marriage and raising a family, which is both normal and fulfilling to most. Cord-injured patients today are not willing to settle for physical rehabilitation. Many are demanding to know what their sexual limitations are and how to realize their full sexual capacity (90). Most physicians are educated to handle the physical problem of sex with the spinal cord-injured, but they are not educated to handle the emotional problems going along with them. This constitutes a major problem. Patients very much need counseling in this area.

It is especially important to correlate the positive relationship between self-concept and sexual attitudes in the spinal cord-injured. If a counselor were to know a person's self-concept, there is a greater chance he could learn how that person feels about himself and the world around him. With this knowledge, the counselor should be better equipped to handle the recovery problem. If problematic sexual attitudes are a result of self-concept, the counselor would assist in solving a person's sexual problem through encouraging gradual acceptance of a positive self-concept by the client.

SELF-CONCEPT: SOCIAL INTERACTION

The self-concept of a person summarizes all that he is and serves as a supermoderator of his functioning (30). It is the type of vital and relevant data about a person that supersedes other things in importance to the individual and thereby expresses his true raison d'être. What an individual feels, how he acts or reacts, and how others react to him is a direct result of his individual self-concept.

James (53) described the infant without a self at birth. He suggested that the self develops to become the sum total of "I," the knower or experiencer, and "Me," the self that is known or experienced.

Charles Horton Cooley (25), in considering the meanings of "I" described a social self since labeled the "Looking Glass Self." Cooley's basic premise was that the self imagines a perception of itself in the mind of another and this affects behavior. Cooley's self idea has three basic elements: 1) the imagination of one's appearance to the other person; 2) the imagination of the other person's appraisal of that appearance; and 3) some kind of self-value feeling such as pride or shame.

Later, George Herbert Mead (71) described the features of self-conception from the stance of a social interactionist. Mead's theory proposed that an individual will conceive of himself as he believes significant others conceive of him and that he will tend to act in accord with expectations he projects to significant others. He will act the way "people like him" should act. Thus, Mead departed from the single notion of self-as-experienced and placed the emphasis on social interaction as an integral part of the development of self-concept.

Self has figured prominently in social control, economic behavior, social deviance, personal aspirations, psychological development, interpersonal attraction, social influence, psychopathology, and psychotherapy.

John Kinch (56) offers a general theory of self-concept in one sentence: "The individual's conception of himself emerges from social interaction and, in turn, guides or influences the behavior of that individual." The following are implicit in most considerations of the self-concept that take this stance and are suggested as basic pos-tulates of the theory: 1) the individual's self-concept is based on his perception of the way others are responding to him; 2) the individual's self-concept functions to direct his behavior; and 3) the individual's perception of the responses of others toward him reflects the actual responses of others toward him.

The self is a very unique phenomenon. It can be divided into three types of self: 1) the identity self, 2) the behavioral self, and 3) the judging self (30).

The identity self is perhaps the most basic aspect of the self-concept. This includes the labels he places on himself. As a young child, the labels are few and simple. "I am John"; "I am cute"; "I am ugly." These elements of identity continue to expand with the growth and broadening of the individual's abilities, activities, group memberships, and services for identification.

The behavioral self probably precedes the identity self. It is the action of the individual. An example of this would be riding a bike. The actual riding of the bike is the action or behavior. If a child masters it, he becomes a "bike rider," this becoming part of the identity self.

The third type of self is the judging self. The interaction between identity self and behavioral self and their integration into the total self-concept involves the judging of self. This self functions as an observer, standard setter, dreamer, comparer, and, most of all, evaluator. It also serves as mediator between the two selves and ultimately judges the self and determines the self-concept.

Self-concept is a complicated term that includes many different ideas of self, two of which are self-esteem and self-actualization. Self-esteem is essential for any individual (30). He must feel he has worth. Self-esteem is derived from two main sources: the self and other persons. Esteem is earned as one achieves certain goals, operated by certain values, or measures up to certain standards. These goals, standards, and values may be internal, external, or both. They may be established, regulated, and applied by the judging self, by others, or by both.

Maslow (69) assigns a position of central importance to self-esteem. In his hierarchy of needs, a positive level of self-esteem is the final prerequisite for self-actualization; once self-esteem is achieved, the individual is free to concentrate on actualizing his potentials.

Maslow perceives self-actualization as the striving of man to become in actuality what he is potentially—to become everything he is capable of becoming—to do what he is best suited for.

Another area of self vital to self-concept is the body image. The body image is the composite picture the individual has of his own body. The picture is a multiply determined, continuously developing, and constantly changing condensed representation of the individual's current and past experiences of his own body. Berger (7), in reference to paraplegic patients, emphasizes the necessity for the integration of the disability into the body image and further hypothesizes that the long period of withdrawal, depression, and lack of interest following the bodily insult is due to the great amount of psychic energy needed for this reintegrative process. Similarly, Grayson wrote: The image has to be reorganized so that the deformed, absent, or useless member of the body can somehow fit itself into the individual's image of himself (43). He states that many patients who display a complete inability to understand what the disability is all about do so because they cannot find any place in their body image for the deformity. He attributes such symptoms as depersonalization, feelings of unreality, and resistance to the use of orthopedic appliances to a defense the ego unconsciously sets up to maintain its integrity in the face of body-image disturbance.

In the spinal cord-injured, self-concept is very important. It influences whether he will desire, seek, cooperate with, participate in, or successfully utilize rehabilitation services (74). After the trauma, the patient goes through a series of changes. He changes from a state of independence to one of almost helpless dependence. He is dependent on others for movement, nourishment, and bodily care. Physically he has regressed to the level of an infant. He experiences three types of pain in the early stages of his paralysis—root pain, which is sharp, is excruciating and radiates along the distribution of nerve roots; burning pain, which is poorly localized and diffuse and does not follow any root distribution; and visceral pain, which is dull and poorly localized and has a sickening quality (74).

Because his mind is not affected by the injury, he is acutely aware of his disabilities. This awareness results in temporary or situational depression. This is natural; in fact, if the spinal cord-injured does not go through this depression, many times he is denying the injury and this could be a severe problem. Along with feelings of depression, he also goes through such a phase where he is very dependent. Such patients are forced to become dependent for their bodily needs but sometimes they become dependent on others for all their needs, physically and emotional. Autistic thinking can obstruct rehabilitation. Facing reality regarding loss of function is most difficult for the paraplegic patient. Every paraplegic patient, it is safe to say, believes that sooner or later he will recover his lost functions and will walk again. Frustration can also be a result of the trauma. These frustrations may vary from trivial slights to absolute blocking of goals (74).

These phases can make the cord-injured person feel abnormal and not at all accepting of himself. It is believed one who is not self-accepting will also have a poor self-concept. The sexual limitation of a spinal cord victim is probably the most frustrating and serious of all his disabilities (94).

It has been established that sex is important to spinal cord victims, as well as to walking persons; in fact it is so important to one with cord injury that he would rather have this func-

tion than walk (94). It is important, however, that he learn the extent and limitations of his abilities and desires. This takes much adjustment. He must accept a rather passive role in sexual relations. The female mate must be the aggressor (89). It is up to her to stimulate the penis to erection and ejaculation.

The spinal cord-injured person also must make adjustment to a change in sexual desire. In a study by Weiss and Diamond (110) on sexual desires and activities, prior to disablement, 92 percent of the male population reported desire, and 96 percent of them reported some form of sexual activity. After disablement, 81 percent reported desire, and 69 percent of them reported sexual activity—a decrease in both desire and activity. In the same study, of the female population, 48 percent reported desire before disablement and 52 percent reported some sexual activity. After disablement, 62 percent reported desire and 62 percent reported sexual activity. These reactions show an increase in both desire and activity in the female, and compared to the results of the male study all the reactions show a "convergence effect" (110).

Another adjustment that is difficult for the spinal cord victim lies in his continued sexual interest and fantasy. It has been reported that, while his sexual abilities have been limited somewhat, his drive is as strong as ever (110). Obviously, this is frustrating to the individual. This drive is many times fulfilled through fantasy and dreams. Usually the dream or fantasy is on a par with the type of sex life before trauma. If the individual had an extremely active, fulfilling sex life before trauma, his dreams tend to follow that trend (72). In a study by Bors and others (12) of 35 patients, 10 remembered complete, dry dreams; 14 remembered incomplete, dry dreams; and only 10 remembered no dreams (no correlation between dream and type of injury). In an overall study, 46 percent of paraplegic males have some type of sexual dreams, and in none of them did the paraplegic see himself disabled in any way.

Another obvious obstruction that most spinal cord victims find difficult to overcome is inability to discuss the problem of sex openly. For many it is an embarrassing topic and, instead of discussing it, they ignore the matter entirely and whatever sexual ability there might be goes unrealized.

For many paraplegic males to engage in sex, the penis must be forced to an erection by either manual or oral manipulation. Many find the latter "dirty" and against their moral principles and therefore will not engage in this type of sex. But after talking and learning more about sex, many realize it is natural and necessary for sex.

It is the author's belief that attitudes toward sex will undoubtedly revert to the upbringing of the individual and are extremely difficult to change. If a child is raised in an atmosphere where there is little affection shown between parents or between parents and children, chances are a child will begin to feel that sex is a "dirty" thing. On the other hand, if a child is raised in a home where there is love shown all around, he will acquire an attitude that sex between people who love each other is good.

Those from the first group, who believe that sex is "dirty," feel this way because they have a rather negative view of themselves in a sex role. They cannot function on a sexual level because their attitude toward themselves is poor. A spinal cord victim will sometimes take a dim view of himself because he has not integrated his disability into his body image. His handicapped body looks ugly to him, so he feels that a person as unattractive as he is should forego any type of sex activity (7).

RESEARCH

Although the cultural trend has been toward a more open, less inhibited outlook on sexual material, the scientific aspect of that same culture has, with some exceptions, remained chastely distant from investigating things remotely connected with sexuality.

Gebhard (37) notes that, prior to World War II, almost no research had been done in the area of human sexuality. He comments on the problems that arose, mentioning the fact that the stigma attached to such research not only dissuaded some scholars from undertaking it but also at times prevented the publication of work already completed.

With today's society so much more open to sex it is impossible to repress it; spinal cord victims want to know and are entitled to know, since their own sexual functioning must be altered. It can be asserted that the job of properly rehabilitating patients is impossible without giving full cognizance to the impelling psychosocial problems that they face.

Adjusting to sexual limitations is an important part of the rehabilitation of the patient to his maximal physical and emotional level. Any effective rehabilitation program must consider the whole person, for the greatest resource in the rehabilitation of any individual is that individual himself.

At a workshop conducted by Dr. Theodore Cole from the University of Minnesota (94) the great need for research was expressed. Dr. Cole's goal was to change attitudes of physicians and hospital staff as well as spinal cord patients and their mates about prospects for sexual fulfillment. Dr. Cole and his wife, Sandy, stressed that spinal cord victims have many sexual problems and that physicians are often handicapped by their own taboos and fears but that solutions can be found with research (94).

Bucy (15) emphasizes that attitudes of members of the medical profession and the ignorance and indifference of the general public have made the United States the most backward, negligent major civilized country of the world in providing adequate care for civilians who have been paralyzed by spinal cord injury. England has had a spinal cord center for over 25 years.

Mueller (74), as cited previously in this article, has pointed out that one is impressed less often with the disabled's depression than with their complete inability to understand what the disability is all about. The most intelligent persons, even those having medical training, frequently are genuinely puzzled as to what the disability means to them. In their struggle to comprehend, these disabled persons need an explanation, or some form of counseling.

Counseling about sex should include positions, special techniques of foreplay, and stimulation and feeling by couples on such matters. Cole and his wife Sandy tried to explain what paraplegics and quadriplegics can and cannot do sexually and stimulated the open and honest exchange of views and feelings.

Talbot has outlined in philosophical-historic terms the necessity for dealing with psychosocial aspects of sexuality in cord-injured patients but little has been written about the actual counseling of the cord-injured man regarding his sexual function.

Hohmann (51) has worked for 30 years in accumulating information in relation to counseling about sex. Hohmann states the most effective counselor is one with warmth, gentleness, and personal interrelationships. The counselor should know all about the neurological urology and psychology of sex relationships before taking this on. The counselor should be relatively free of sex hangups; if not, he could exploit the patient with this feeling. The counselor must know something about typical male and female sex attributes in our society.

The ideal research setting would be a cord center that would provide both physical and emotional rehabilitation. This cord center could provide prompt and adequate care and also an atmosphere of hope, initiate a demand for research, and provide a clearinghouse for the exchange of information about existing curricula or those being planned in medical school for counselors.

LIST OF REFERENCES
AND BIBLIOGRAPHY

1. Ashcraft, Carolyn, and Fitts, William H. Self-Concept Change in Psychotherapy. Psychother. May, 1964. 1:3:115–118.
2. Auerback, Alfred. The Battle of the Sexes. Medical Aspects of Human Sexuality. Dec., 1967. 1:4:6–11.
3. Barker, Roger G., and others. Adjustment to Physical Handicap and Illness: A Survey of the Social Psychology of Physique and Disability. New York: Social Science Research Council, 1953.
4. Baum, William C. Neurogenic Vesical and Sexual Dysfunction Attendant on Trauma to the Spinal Cord: Observations on Management. J. Michigan Med. Soc. Mar., 1962. 61:5:574–584.
5. Bell, Robert R. Some Emerging Sexual Expectations Among Women. Medical Aspects of Human Sexuality. Oct., 1967. 1:2:65–67, 72.
6. Bensman, Alan, and Kottke, Frederic J. Induced Emission of Sperm Utilizing Electrical Stimulation of the Seminal Vesicles and Vas Deferens. Arch. Phys. Med. & Rehab. July, 1966. 47:7:436–443.
7. Berger, Stanley. The Role of Sexual Impotence in the Concept of Self in Male Paraplegics. Dissertation Abstracts. 1952. 12:4:533.
8. Bolles, M. Marjorie, and Landis, Carney. Personality and Sexuality of the Physically Handicapped Woman. New York: Paul B. Hoeber, 1942.
9. Bors, Ernest. Spinal Cord Injuries. Veterans Administration Tech. Bul. TS10-503. Dec. 15, 1948. p. 26–27.
10. Bors, Ernest. The Spinal Cord Injury Center of the Veterans Administration Hospital, Long Beach, California, U.S.A.: Facts and Thoughts. Paraplegia. Nov., 1967. 5:3: 126–130.
11. Bors, Ernest, and Comarr, A. Estin. Neurological Disturbances of Sexual Function with Special Reference to 529 Patients with Spinal Cord Injury. Urolog. Survey. Dec., 1960. 10:6:191–222.
12. Bors, Ernest, and others. Fertility in Paraplegic Males. J. Clinical Endocrinol. Apr., 1950. 10:4:381–398.
13. Boyarsky, S. Management of the Genito-Urinary Problems of the Paraplegic. Alabama J. Medical Sciences. Apr., 1967. 4:119–122.
14. Brady, John Paul, moderator. Roundtable: Frigidity. Medical Aspects of Human Sexuality. Feb., 1968. 2:2:26–27, 30–31, 36–37, 40.
15. Bucy, Paul C. Paraplegia: The Neglected Problem. Physical Therapy. Mar., 1969. 49:3:269–272.
16. Caprio, Frank Samuel. Variations in Sexual Behavior. New York: Citadel Pr., 1955.
17. Cavanagh, John R. Rhythm of Sexual Desire in Women. Medical Aspects of Human Sexuality. Feb., 1969. 3:2:29, 34–35, 39.
18. Cibeira, Jose B. Some Conclusions on a Study of 365 Patients with Spinal Cord Lesions. Paraplegia. Feb., 1970. 7:4:249–254.
19. Coffin, T. The Sex Kick: Eroticism in Modern America. New York: Macmillan, 1966.
20. Colbert, James N. Philosophia Habilitatus: Towards a Policy of Human Rehabilitation in the Post-Institutional Phase of Disability. J. Rehab. Sept.-Oct., 1969. 35:5:18–20.
21. Comarr, A. E. Sexual Function Among Patients with Spinal Cord

Injury. Urologia Internationalis. 1970. 25:2:134–168.

22. Comarr, A. Estin. Sexual Concepts in Traumatic Cord and Cauda Equina Lesions. J. Urol. Sept., 1971. 106:375–378.

23. Comarr, A. Estin, and Bors, Ernest. Spermatocystography in Patients with Spinal Cord Injuries. J. Urol. Jan., 1955. 73:1:172–178.

24. Congdon, C. S. Self-Theory and Chlorpromazine Treatment. (Unpublished doctoral dissertation) Vanderbilt Univ., Nashville, Tenn.: 1958.

25. Cooley, Charles Horton. Human Nature and the Social Order. New York: Charles Scribner's Sons, 1902.

26. Desmond, John. Paraplegia: Problems Confronting the Anaesthesiologist. Canadian Anaesthetists' Soc. J. Sept., 1970. 17:5:435–451.

27. Ellis, Albert. The American Sexual Tragedy. New York: Twayne, 1954.

28. Ellis, Havelock. Psychology of Sex: A Manual for Students. New York: Emerson Books, 1964.

29. Fitts, W. H. Manual for the Tennessee Self Concept Scale. Nashville, Tenn.: Counselor Recordings and Tests, 1965.

30. Fitts, William H. The Self Concept and Self-Actualization. (Research Monograph 3) Nashville, Tenn.: Dede Wallace Center, 1971.

31. Ford, Amasa B., and Orfirer, Alexander P. Sexual Behavior and the Chronically Ill Patient. Medical Aspects of Human Sexuality. Oct., 1967. 1:2:41, 57–61.

32. Fordyce, W. E. Psychological Assessment and Management, chap. 6, p. 168–195, in: Krusen, Frank H.; Kottke, Frederic J.; and Ellwood, Paul M., Jr., eds. Handbook of Physical Medicine and Rehabilitation. Philadelphia: W. B. Saunders, 1971.

33. Frankel, Alan. Sexual Problems in Rehabilitation. J. Rehab. Sept.-Oct., 1967. 33:5:19–21.

34. Fried, Edrita. The Ego in Love and Sexuality. New York: Grune & Stratton, 1960.

35. Friedland, Fritz. Rehabilitation in Spinal Cord Injuries, chap. 17, p. 460–535, in: Licht, Sidney, ed.: Rehabilitation and Medicine. New Haven, Conn.: Elizabeth Licht, Publ., 1968.

36. Gagnon, John H., and Simon, William. The Sexual Scene. Chicago: Aldine Publ. Co., 1970.

37. Gebhard, Paul H. Human Sex Behavior Research, Chap. 23, p. 391–410, in: Diamond, Milton, ed. Perspectives in Reproduction and Sexual Behavior. Bloomington, Ind.: Indiana Univ. Pr., 1968.

38. Goldberg, M. Viewpoints: What Do You Tell Patients Who Ask about Coital Positions? Medical Aspects of Human Sexuality. Dec., 1968. 2:12: 43, 46–48.

39. Goldberg, Martin, moderator. Roundtable: When Patients Ask About Various Sex Practices. Medical Aspects of Human Sexuality. Feb., 1969. 3:2:54–55, 58–61.

40. Goldman, George D., and Milman, Donald S., eds. Modern Woman: Her Psychology and Sexuality. Springfield, Ill.: Charles C Thomas, 1969.

41. Göller, Herta, and Paeslack, Volkmar. Our Experiences About Pregnancy and Delivery of the Paraplegic Woman. Paraplegia. Nov., 1970. 8:3: 161–166.

42. Gorer, Goeffrey. Sex and Marriage in England Today: A Study of the Views and Experience of the Under 45's. London, Eng.: Nelson, 1971.

43. Grayson, Morris, in collaboration with Ann Powers and Joseph Levi. Psychiatric Aspects of Rehabilitation. New York: Inst. of Med. and Rehab., N.Y. Univ.-Bellevue Med. Center, 1952.

44. Gross, Mortimer D. Marital Stress and Psychosomatic Disorders. Medical Aspects of Human Sexuality. Jan., 1969. 3:1:22, 24–25, 30, 32–33.

45. Guttmann, Ludwig. The Married Life of Paraplegics and Tetraplegics. Paraplegia. Oct., 1964. 2:182—188.

46. Guttmann, Ludwig, and Walsh, J. J. Prostigmin Assessment Test of Fertility in Spinal Man. Paraplegia. May, 1971. 9:1:39—51.

47. Henry, J. The Self-Concept of Paraplegics and Quadriplegics: A Counseling Variable. (Master's dissertation) Carbondale, Ill.: Southern Illinois University, 1972.

48. Herman, Myron. Role of Somesthetic Stimuli in the Development of Sexual Excitation in Man: A Preliminary Paper. Arch. Neurol. & Psychiat. July, 1950. 64:1:42—56.

49. Hetrick, William Robert. Sexuality Following Functional Transection of the Spinal Cord. Dissertation Abstracts. June, 1968. 28:12: 5206B—5207B.

50. Hohmann, George W. Considerations in Management of Psychosexual Readjustment in the Cord Injured Male. Rehab. Psychol. Summer, 1972. 19:2:50—58.

51. Hohmann, George W. Some Effects of Spinal Cord Lesions on Experienced Emotional Feelings. Psychophysiol. Oct., 1966. 3:2: 143—156.

52. Horne, Herbert W.; Paull, David P., and Munro, Donald. Fertility Studies in the Human Male with Traumatic Injuries of the Spinal Cord and Cauda Equina. New England J. Med. Dec. 16, 1948. 239: 25:959—961.

53. James, William. The Principles of Psychology. New York: H. Holt & Co., 1890.

54. Jochheim, K.-A., and Wahle, H. A. Study on Sexual Function in 56 Male Patients with Complete Irreversible Lesions of the Spinal Cord and Cauda Equina. Paraplegia. Nov., 1970. 8:3:166—172.

55. Kessler, Henry H. Rehabilitation of the Physically Handicapped. New York: Columbia Univ. Pr., 1953.

56. Kinch, John W. Experimental Factors Related to Self-Concept Change. J. Social Psychol. Apr., 1968. 74: 2nd half:251—258.

57. Kinsey, Alfred, and others. Sexual Behavior in the Human Female. Philadelphia: W. B. Saunders, 1953.

58. Kinsey, Alfred C.; Pomeroy, Wardell B.; and Martin, Clyde E. Sexual Behavior in the Human Male. Philadelphia: W. B. Saunders, 1948.

59. Kuhn, Robert A. Functional Capacity of the Isolated Human Spinal Cord. Brain. Mar., 1950. 73: Pt. 1:1—51.

60. Labenne, Wallace D., and Greene, Bert I. Educational Implications of Self-Concept Theory. Pacific Palisades, Calif.: Goodyear Publishing Co., 1969.

61. Levy, Ronald B. Self-Revelation Through Relationships. Englewood Cliffs, N.J.: Prentice-Hall, 1972.

62. Lewis, J. M. Impotence as a Reflection of Marital Conflict. Medical Aspects of Human Sexuality. June, 1969. 3:6:73—75, 78.

63. Lief, Harold I. New Developments in the Sex Education of the Physician. J. Am. Med. Assn. June 15, 1970. 212:22:1864—1867.

64. Lindner, Harold. Perceptual Sensitization to Sexual Phenomena in the Chronic Physically Handicapped. J. Clin. Psychol. Jan. 1953. 9:1:67—68.

65. Lipkin, K. Michael, and Daniels, Robert S. The Role of Seduction in Interpersonal Relationships. Medical Aspects of Human Sexuality. June, 1969. 3:6:79, 82—83, 86, 88.

66. Long, Charles, H. Congenital and Traumatic Lesions of the Spinal Cord, chap. 25, p. 566—578, in: Krusen, Frank H.; Kottke, Frederic J.; and Ellwood, Paul M., Jr., eds. Handbook of Physical Medicine and Rehabilitation. Philadelphia: W.B. Saunders, 1971.

67. MacDowell, Fletcher H. Sexual Manifestations of Neurologic Disease. Medical Aspects of Human Sex-

uality. Apr., 1968. 2:4:13, 16–17.
20–21.

68. Marshall, Donald S., ed., and Suggs, Robert C. Human Sexual Behavior: Variations in the Ethnographic Spectrum. New York: Basic Books, 1971.

69. Maslow, Abraham Harold. Motivation and Personality. New York: Harper, 1954.

70. Masters, William H., and Johnson, Virginia E. Human Sexual Response. Boston: Little, Brown, 1966.

71. Mead, George Herbert. Mind, Self, and Society, from the Standpoint of a Social Behaviorist. Edited by Charles W. Morris. Chicago: Univ. of Chicago Pr., 1934.

72. Money, John. Phantom Orgasm in the Dreams of Paraplegic Men and Women. AMA Arch. Gen. Psychiat. Oct., 1960. 3:373–382.

73. Morgan, Clifford T., and Stellar, Eliot. Subcortical Centers and Pathways, in: Morgan, Clifford T. Physiological Psychology. (ed. 2) New York: McGraw, 1950.

74. Mueller, Alfred D. Psychologic Factors in Rehabilitation of Paraplegic Patients. Arch. Phys. Med. & Rehab. Apr., 1962. 43:4:151–159.

75. Munro, Donald. Clinical Problems in Paraplegia: Paraplegia Then and Now and What Can Be Learned from the Comparison, chap. 5, p. 196–205, in: French, John D., and Porter, Robert W., eds. Basic Research in Paraplegia; A Conference Sponsored by the California Spinal Cord Research Foundation under the auspices of Los Angeles Society of Neurology and Psychiatry. Springfield, Ill.: Charles C Thomas, 1962.

76. Munro, Donald; Horne, Herbert W.; and Paull, David P. The Effect of Injury to the Spinal Cord and Cauda Equina on the Sexual Potency of Men. New England J. Med. Dec. 9, 1948. 239:24:903–922.

77. Nagler, Benedict. Psychiatric As-

pects of Cord Injury. Am. J. Psychiat. July, 1950. 107:1:49–56.

78. Nickerson, Eileen Tressler. Some Correlates of Adjustment of Paraplegics. Dissertation Abstracts. Aug., 1961. 22:2:632–633.

79. Oppenhimer, William M. Pregnancy in Paraplegic Patients: Two Case Reports. Am. J. Obstet. & Gynecol. July 15, 1971. 110:6: 784–786.

80. Pfeiffer, Eric. Geriatric Sex Behavior. Medical Aspects of Human Sexuality. July, 1969. 3:7:19, 22–23, 26, 27.

81. Physician's World. Nov., 1973. p. 24.

82. Popenoe, Paul. Sexual Inadequacy of the Male. Los Angeles: Am. Inst. of Family Relations, 1950.

83. Powys, J. C. Psychoanalysis and Morality. San Francisco: Jessica Colbert, 1924.

84. Riddoch, George. The Reflex Functions of the Completely Divided Spinal Cord in Man, Compared with Those Associated with Less Severe Lesions. Brain. 1917. 40: 264–402.

85. Rossi, Romolo, and Conforto, Carmelo. 3rd Annual Convention on the Subject: Sexual Impotence: Psychotherapeutic Problems in Organic Sexual Impotence. Rivista di Psichiatria. 1969. 4:4:326–329.

86. Rossier, A. Problems Raised by the Rehabilitation of Spinal Cord Injury Patients. (French) Schweiz. Arch. Neurol. Neurochir. Psychiat. 1969. 103:1:117–136.

87. Rossier, A. B.; Ruffieux, M.; and Ziegler, W. H. Pregnancy and Labour in High Traumatic Spinal Cord Lesions. Paraplegia. Nov., 1969. 7:3: 210–216.

88. Rusk, Howard A. Rehabilitation Medicine. St. Louis: C. V. Mosby, 1964.

89. Rusk, Howard A., moderator. Roundtable: Sex Problems in Para-

plegia. Medical Aspects of Human Sexuality. Dec., 1967. 1:4:46–50.

90. Ryan, James H. Dreams of Paraplegics. Arch. Gen. Psychiat. Sept., 1961. 5:3:286–291.

91. Salzman, Leon, moderator. Roundtable: Female Orgasm. Medical Aspects of Human Sexuality. Apr., 1968. 2:4:37–38, 42–43, 46–47.

92. Saunders, Douglas, and Yeo, John. Pregnancy and Quadriplegia— The Problem of Autonomic Dysreflexia. Austral. & New Zealand J. Obstet. & Gynaecol. Aug., 1968. 8: 3:152–154.

93. Schimel, John L. The Fallacy of Equality in Sexual Relations. Medical Aspects of Human Sexuality. Aug., 1969. 3:8:15–22, 24.

94. Sex and the Paraplegic. Medical World News. Jan. 14, 1972. 13:2:35, 38.

95. Sherman, Julia A. What Men Do Not Know About Women's Sexuality. Medical Aspects of Human Sexuality. Nov., 1972. 6:11:138, 141–142, 144–147, 151.

96. Siller, Jerome. Psychological Situation of the Disabled with Spinal Cord Injuries. Rehab. Lit. Oct., 1969. 30:10:290–296.

97. A Survey of Medicine and Medical Practice for the Rehabilitation Counselor. Washington, D.C.: U.S. Vocational Rehabilitation Administration, 1966.

98. Symonds, Percival M. The Ego and the Self. New York: Appleton-Century-Crofts, 1951.

99. Talbot, Herbert S. A Report on Sexual Function in Paraplegics. J. Urol. Feb., 1949. 61:2:265–270.

100. Talbot, Herbert S. Sexual Function in Paraplegia. J. Urol. Jan., 1955. 73:1:91–100.

101. Talbot, H. S. The Sexual Function in Paraplegics. (Society Transactions) AMA Arch. Neurol. & Psychiat. 1951. 66:650–651.

102. Thom, Douglas A.; VonSalzen, Charles F.; and Fromme, Alan. Psychological Aspects of the Paraplegic Patient. Med. Clin. North Am. Mar., 1946. 30:473–480.

103. Thompson, Warren. Correlates of the Self Concept. (Research Monograph 6) Nashville, Tenn.: Dede Wallace Center, 1972.

104. Trainer, Joseph B. Emotional Bases of Fatigue. Medical Aspects of Human Sexuality. Jan., 1969. 3: 1:59, 63–65.

105. Tsuji, I., and others. The Sexual Function in Patients with Spinal Cord Injury. Urologia Internationalis. 1961. 12:4–5; 270–280.

106. Van Stolk, Mary. Man and Woman. Toronto, Can.: McClelland and Stewart, 1968.

107. Wahle, H., and Jochheim, K.-A. Studies on Neurogenic Disorders of Sexual Functions in 56 Paraplegic Men with Complete Irreversible Injuries of the Spinal Cord or the Cauda Equina. (German) Fortschr. Neurol. Psychiat. und ihrer Grenzbebiete. Apr., 1970. 38:4:192–201.

108. Warter, C. and Gonzáles, J. On Sphincteric and Sexual Disturbances in Paraplegics. (Spanish) Neurocirugia. Jan.-June, 1970. 28:72–76.

109. Weber, Doreen D., and Wessman, Henry C. A Review of Sexual Function Following Spinal Cord Trauma. Physical Ther. Mar., 1971. 51:3: 290–295.

110. Weiss, Aaron J., and Diamond, M. David. Sexual Adjustment, Identification and Attitudes of Patients with Myelopathy. Arch. Phys. Med. & Rehab. Apr., 1966. 47:4: 245–250.

111. Whitelaw, George P., and Smithwick, Reginald H. Some Secondary Effects of Sympathectomy with Particular Reference to Disturbance of Sexual Function. New England J. Med. July 26, 1951. 245:4: 121–130.

112. Williams, J. G. Sex and the Paralyzed. Sexology. 1965. 31:453–456.

113. Winston, Arnold, and others. Patterns of Psychological Decompensation in Patients with Spinal Cord Syndromes. Diseases of Nerv. System. Dec., 1969. 30:12:824–827.

114. Zeitlin, Austin B.; Cottrell, Thomas L.; and Lloyd, Frederick A. Sexology of the Paraplegic Male. Fertility and Sterility. July–Aug., 1957. 8:4:337–334.

Section 11

PREVENTION OF DISABILITY

42 The Coronary Prone

Jeremiah Stamler,
David M. Berkson,
Howard Lindberg, and
Monte Levinson

The concept of the coronary prone has come to the fore in recent years because of its great implications with respect to the etiology, pathogenesis, and prevention of the arterosclerotic coronary heart disease (CHD). The concept has great import, particularly for practicing physicians. From 30 to 40% of first myocardial infarctions terminate fatally during the first six weeks of illness. About 15 to 20% of first attacks are sudden deaths, terminating within 60 minutes of onset (1, 4, 5). Survivors of acute myocardial infarction have a shortened life expectancy under the best of circumstances.

Major progress must therefore be made in preventing the first attack—in achieving primary prevention. The key to such a preventive effort lies in the new knowledge of risk factors associated with proneness to atherosclerotic disease and their responsiveness to therapy.

PRONENESS AND RISK FACTORS

The coronary risk factors are those habits and abnormalities known to be associated with significantly increased risk of developing the disease in subsequent years. They include hypercholesterolemia (also hyperbetalipoproteinemia and hypertriglyceridemia), hypertension, cigarette smoking, diabetes mellitus, over-weight, a family history of premature vascular disease, and abnormalities in the electrocardiogram (ECG)—resting, exercise, and post-exercise. A diet high in total calories, total fats, saturated fats, cholesterol, refined carbohydrates, and salt can contribute to the development of hyperlipidemia, obesity, hypertension, and diabetes.

Several other abnormalities have also been implicated as coronary risk factors: hyperuricemia, decreased vital capacity, thyroid dysfunction, renal disease, sedentary living habits, personality, and behavior patterns. Limited data have also suggested others: arcus senilis, arteriovenous nicking in the eye grounds, aortic calcification on X-ray, dental calculus, ballistocardiographic abnormalities, history of peptic ulcer or gall bladder disease, "noncardiac" chest discomfort, chronic cough, shortness of breath, slow or rapid pulse, high hematocrit, certain somatotypes, and large coffee intake.

Evaluation of persons for the major known risk factors permits assessment of proneness to coronary disease on a probability basis, i.e., a given per-

Reprinted from the Journal of Rehabilitation, 1966, 32(2): 18–20.

son's chance of developing clinical CHD before age 60 or 65. The new information on coronary risk factors is relevant as well for secondary prevention, i.e., the long-term care of persons with established clinical atherosclerotic disease, to prevent recurrent episodes and progression of the disease.

HYPERCHOLESTEROLEMIA, HYPERTENSION

Risks in experiencing a clinical episode of coronary disease in middle age is a function of serum cholesterol level. Persons with hypercholesterolemia experience three to four times as many heart attacks as those with low-normal serum cholesterol levels.

Since hypercholesterolemic persons have sizeable increases in risk of developing premature clinical CHD, it is important to determine the frequency of this abnormality, alone and in combination with other risk factors. In our study with the Peoples Gas Co. of employed men aged 40 to 59 without definite or suspect CHD in 1958 (the year of initial examination), the prevalence rate of frank hypercholesterolemia (250 mg/100 ml or greater) was 37% (6). If the above criteria were used, then a large majority of middle-aged Americans do not fall in the normal range. And a majority with frank hypercholesterolemia are totally unaware of its presence.

Elevated blood pressure is a second major risk factor for premature clinical atherosclerotic disease (1). As shown by the data of several investigations,

so-called "minor" blood pressure elevations (diastolic levels in the range of 90–94 mm Hg) and even high normal values (80–89 mm Hg) are associated with increases in risk, compared with optimal levels (less than 80 mm Hg). Hypertension is also a frequently encountered abnormality in the U.S. middle-aged adult population. The prevalence rates are higher in women, and much higher in Negroes than in whites.

DIABETES MELLITUS, OBESITY

Diabetes mellitus is a third major risk factor for atherosclerotic disease (1, 2, 3). Diabetic men have a risk of myocardial infarction 2–4 times greater than men free of clinical diabetes. Recent studies also indicate that persons with manifestations of atherosclerotic disease exhibit abnormalities in glucose tolerance more frequently than do clinical controls. Moreover, abnormalities in response to the glucose tolerance test tend to be associated with abnormalities in serum β-lipoproteins and with hyperlipidemia, hypertension, and overweight (1).

Data from life insurance actuarial studies indicate that overweight persons have an increased risk of dying of coronary and cerebrovascular diseases. The findings of one study revealed an 8 to 37% higher mortality rate from coronary artery disease in overweight men, the range being a function of the degree of overweight (8). When minor impairments were present together with overweight, the increased risk of mortality ranged from 31 to 76%.

Obesity is unquestionably associated with increased risk of hypertension, evidently with diabetes and hyperlipidemia, as well as with the high-risk combination of hypercholesterolemia plus hypertension, and with increased risk of so-called minor, nonspecific T-wave abnormalities in the ECG of both hypertensive and normotensive persons (1).

It is possible that "pure and simple" obesity is by itself unrelated to susceptibility to coronary disease. This distinction is of limited significance, however, since obesity combined with other risk factors occurs frequently in our middle-aged population; "isolated" obesity is relatively infrequent.

DIET, SMOKING, PHYSICAL INACTIVITY

The contemporary eating habits of the vast majority of adult Americans add up to nutrient intakes excessive in total calories, total fats, saturated fats, cholesterol, sugars, and salt. These patterns can contribute significantly to the development of hypercholesterolemia, hypertension, diabetes, and obesity.

In the U.S., the increase in coronary risk from cigarette smoking is currently two- to six-fold. CHD risk is a function of the number of cigarettes smoked. In contrast, use of pipe or cigars in moderation is associated with only slight increases in coronary proneness. A majority of middle-aged men in the U.S. are cigarette smokers. Of the men in the Peoples Gas Co. study, in 1958, 56.7% were smoking

10 or more cigarettes per day; 43.1% were smoking 20 or more a day. Several studies unequivocally demonstrate that men who quit smoking while still free of overt evidence of coronary disease experience a significantly lower CHD rate in the ensuing years, compared with men who continue to smoke (1, 9).

Studies in Great Britain and the U.S. reveal a correlation between habitual physical inactivity of work and susceptibility to CHD. From a practical point of view, some considerations need emphasis. First, any partial protective effect of habitual physical activity demonstrated in populations eating foods high in saturated fats and cholesterol has been shown only with moderately heavy or very heavy physical work, involving the daily expenditure of hundreds or thousands of calories above the sedentary level. But heavy physical work is rapidly becoming an anachronism, and sedentary habits—in work and in leisure—are becoming the rule. Literally no data are as yet available as to whether light or moderate exercise is protective, at least when combined with reasonable alterations in diet and smoking patterns.

THE PACE OF MODERN LIFE

The idea that "stress" induces heart attacks is unquestionably valid regarding one aspect of the problem: an acute psychologically stressful experience can precipitate a clinical episode of CHD in persons with severe advanced atherosclerosis of the coronary arteries. However, scientific understanding is far less clear about the role of psychological stress, tension, personality, behavior pattern, and the pace of modern life in the basic pathogenesis of atherosclerosis itself. Several studies have demonstrated that acute psychological stress tends to raise serum cholesterol levels. Other findings suggest that the long-term state of the higher nervous activity may also play a role in the long-term regulation of serum cholesterol levels.

Recent data indicate that a high-drive, overly-ambitious personality-behavior pattern is a significant risk factor for premature clinical CHD in middle-aged American men. Social and cultural factors, occupational stress—including long hours of work and little sleep—have also been implicated as possible risk factors.

The valid assessment of such variables as stress, tension, etc. is complex. Data continue to accumulate, however, supporting hypotheses that personality-behavior patterns and psychocultural factors play a significant role in the etiology and pathogenesis of premature atherosclerotic disease. Although great gaps in knowledge and disagreement as to the significance of these factors continue to exist, the trend of research development indicates that they cannot be dismissed.

ELECTROCARDIOGRAPHIC ABNORMALITIES

Recent epidemiologic studies have consistently shown that ECG abnormalities are frequent in presumably healthy middle-aged American men. In our study of a male labor force aged 40–59, over 10% had abnormal resting ECG's. The ECG response to exercise also gives information relevant to coronary risk. A significant percentage of middle-aged adults with normal resting ECG patterns exhibits an abnormal ischemic response to exercise. Long-term studies demonstrate that such persons have an increased incidence in subsequent years of frank clinical CHD (including myocardial infarction), compared to persons with a normal ECG pattern in response to exercise. The increase in risk ranges from three- to eight-fold.

FAMILY HISTORY OF VASCULAR DISEASE

Available research findings confirm the impression that a familial predisposition to premature CHD (prior to age 60) exists. A history of premature CHD is especially significant in indicating increased risks for blood relatives, particularly brothers and sisters. A familial tendency also exists in hypertension, hypercholesterolemia, diabetes, obesity, and cigarette smoking. With the probable exception of smoking, the familial tendency is at least in part genetically influenced and conditioned.

These findings have great practical import. It is not possible thus far to influence genetic background; however, the patient with a positive family history of premature disease should be approached in a positive way by the physician. When the patient reveals no evidence of abnormalities with respect to hypertension, hypercholesterolemia, diabetes, obesity, or smoking, but rather exhibits optimal findings, it is possible to reassure him as to his risk status—provided he maintains his optimal situation by deliberate long-term adherence to sound nutritional-hygienic practices.

When one or more of the cited risk factors is present, early detection permits effective sustained intervention, particularly when these factors occur against the background of a positive family history. Since contemporary medicine can treat every one of the cited abnormalities making for coronary proneness, it is undoubtedly sound to attempt to head off the effect of a poor family background.

COMBINATIONS
OF RISK FACTORS

Large-scale prospective epidemiologic studies have made it possible to assess the impact of two or more key risk factors present in combination. In the Peoples Gas Co. study, for example, initial assessment was made of several pairs of abnormalities, e.g., hypercholesterolemia and overweight, hypercholesterolemia and hypertension, hypercholesterolemia and cigarette smoking (1, 6). With this last combination, a 16-fold increase of risk was observed.

The Albany study (10) also recorded, in an analysis of findings with respect to both weight and serum cholesterol, that the range of risk was about sevenfold. The Framingham and Los Angeles studies recorded similar findings when the combined effects of hypertension and hypercholesterolemia were evaluated (11, 12). In a study of San Francisco longshoremen, hypertensive smokers of 20 or more cigarettes a day had a many-fold increase in 10-year CHD mortality rate compared with normotensive non-smokers—13.6 times for men originally age 45–54, and 35 times for those 55–64 (13).

In the Los Angeles and Framingham studies, analyses were made of the relationship between any combination of three factors and CHD incidence. Again, the tendency emerged for the effects of abnormalities to be compounded when present in combination. In the Peoples Gas Co. study, simultaneous evaluation of four risk factors—hypercholesterolemia, hypertension, overweight, and cigarette smoking—again demonstrated a range of risks.

The Framingham study showed that it is possible to identify a truly coronary-resistant group in our middle-aged male population, based on optimal findings, with respect to the known risk factors. Unfortunately, such men are the exception, rather than the rule. With use of only three measurements, the vast majority of middle-aged American men are quickly excluded from the low or optimal risk group. Our study of the Peoples Gas Co. men yielded similar findings.

Associations among the multiple risk factors have been demonstrated between overweight and hypertension, diabetes, hyperlipidemia, etc. All are in turn related to caloric intake—and, of course, caloric balance is in turn related to energy expenditure. Further, composition of the diet is of key importance in relation to hyperlipidemia.

Space limitations make it impossible to discuss here the theoretical questions of disease causation posed by the demonstration that multiple abnormalities are significantly related to risk of premature clinical CHD. Further, this statement is by no means exhaustive, in terms of a profound delineation of the etiologic aspects of atherosclerotic disease.

PREVENTIVE
TREATMENT OF RISK FACTORS

Early detection of susceptibles is important in the effort to achieve primary prevention of disease. Medicine now has the means—nutritional, hygienic, and pharmacologic—to correct and control the cardinal coronary risk factors in most persons harboring them.

Several long-term research studies in progress since the 1950's have accrued significant experience in this area. We have been engaged since 1958 in an expanding long-term study to assess ability to achieve primary prevention of clinical CHD in high-risk men aged 40–59. This program entails close work with the participants and their wives in an effort to control and correct the key risk factors, chiefly by nutritional and hygienic means. The aim is not only to correct abnormalities, but also to establish new habit patterns.

It has been possible to maintain participation for a majority of the middle-aged men volunteering for this program. Hypercholesterolemia has been reduced, the mean over-all decline being about 15% (1). Overweight and hypertension have also been corrected in significant numbers. About 30% of the men who were cigarette smokers have either given up tobacco altogether or switched to pipe or cigars. A significant percentage of the men who were formerly sedentary have adopted habits of regular frequent exercise—walking, swimming, etc.

The ability to control the major coronary risk factors by medical means holds out the possibility of achieving effective primary prevention of premature clinical atherosclerotic disease—coronary, cerebral, and peripheral. It also has obvious implications for the long-term therapy (secondary prevention) of disease in patients who are already clinically ill. Undoubtedly medicine and public health will accrue extensive further experience in the years ahead, as the expanding effort unfolds to master the nation's main contemporary health problem.

REFERENCES

1. Stamler, J., Lectures on Preventive Cardiology. New York: Grune & Stratton, in press.
2. Katz, L. N. and Stamler, J., Experimental Atherosclerosis. Springfield, Ill., C. C Thomas, 1953.
3. Katz, L. N., Stamler, J., and Pick, R., Nutrition and Atherosclerosis.

Philadelphia: Lea and Febiger, 1958.

4. Dawber, T. R., et al, The Prediction of Coronary Heart Disease. Paper read at 72nd Annual Meeting of Association of Life Insurance Medical Directors of America, October 1963.

5. Stamler, J., et al, Prevalence and incidence of coronary heart disease in strata of the labor force of a Chicago industrial corporation. J. Chronic Dis., vol. 11, p. 405. 1960.

6. Stamler, J., Atherosclerotic coronary heart disease—The major challenge to contemporary public health and preventive medicine. Conn. Medicine, vol. 28, p. 675. 1964.

7. Pell, S. and D'Alonzo, C. A., Acute myocardial infarction in a large industrial population—Report of a 6-year study of 1,356 cases. J.A.M.A., vol. 185, p. 117. 1963.

8. Build and Blood Pressure Study, 1959—Vol. 1. Society of Actuaries, Chicago, 1959.

9. Doll, R. and Hill, A. B., Mortality in relation to smoking: Ten years' observations of British doctors. British Med. J., vol. 1, p. 1399, 1460. 1964.

10. Doyle, J. T., et al, A prospective study of degenerative cardiovascular disease in Albany: Report of three years' experience—I. ischemic heart disease. Amer. J. Public Health, vol. 47, no. 4, part 2, p. 25. 1957.

11. Paul, O., et al, longitudinal study of coronary heart disease. Circulation, vol. 28, p. 20. 1963.

12. Drake, R. M., et al, An epidemiological investigation of coronary heart disease in the California health survey population. Amer. J. Public Health, vol. 47, no. 4, part 2, p. 43. 1957.

13. Rifkind, B. M., The incidence of arcus senilis in ischaemic heart disease. Its relation to serum lipid levels. Lancet, vol. 1, p. 312. 1965.

43 Stress and Disability

Joseph Stubbins

Environmental forces such as heat, cold, and inadequate nutrition constitute threats against the physical integrity of the body. Where people live at a subsistence level, such stresses continue to be a threat to life. But in the United States the major sources of stress are social and psychological. Some conditions are universally stressful. Conditions that are directly threatening to life such as being shot at are experienced as stressful by everyone. At the other end of the continuum of stress are conditions that very few would find threatening, such as being in open spaces or looking out of the window of a tall buiding. In between these extremes are the conditions of everyday life of the vast majority of the American people. They experience their everyday circumstances of work, family life, or social existence stressful to one degree or another.

Most business executives are able to manage their work without adverse health effects. However, some suffer from various psychosomatic illnesses and neurotic behaviors. Other persons working and living under rather adverse psychological conditions still manage to do so without physical or psychological symptoms. There is a wide range of individual differences in what is experienced as stressful. A major sign of such differences, says

Selye (1974), is the variable rate at which persons age.

It is easy to grasp the idea that the body is maintaining an internal equilibrium in a physical sense. A person can feel comfortable only within a very limited temperature range unless equipped with special clothing. He can do without water for only a few days. The composition of the air he breathes may not vary very much without ill effects. But the notion that a person requires certain psycho-social conditions for well-being is more difficult to comprehend. Perhaps this difficulty arises from the non-specificity of what is required for psychic well-being. It is easier to pinpoint a bodily discomfort than a psychological one. A person whose self-esteem has been damaged or who feels blocked in realizing ambitions may not locate the sources of his unhappiness; he simply feels bad all over or he may attribute his malaise to the wrong source. In his classic book, The Stress of Life (1965), Hans Selye defines stress as any threat to the integrity of the organism. We know that disease is counteracted by the production of anti-bodies; bleeding, by the production of coagulants. But how does the organism defend itself from the conflict of, on the one hand, being humiliated by a powerful person and, on the other, the fear of expressing hate and anger? Despite the

---

This essay was written for this book.

insights of dynamic psychology, there is no reduction in the incidence of neuroses, psychoses, or in the psycho-somatic illnesses that are implicated with stress.

Statistics on the incidences of various kinds of disability tend to be received with the same fateful attitude as natural calamities. While much has been accomplished in the prevention of accidents, one rarely sees mention of this where rehabilitation is concerned. But there is relatively even less attention to the prevention of disability contributed to by stress. Stroke, cardiovascular disease, and gastrointestinal conditions are a class of disabling conditions strongly implicated with faulty reactions to stress. There is general agreement that stress lowers the immunological defenses against infectious diseases. There is a theory of cancer that stipulates that the body also has natural defenses against tumors which are rendered useless under conditions of stress. There are the psychological disorders that send their victims to psychotherapists, clinics, and mental hospitals—regarded by psychologists as resulting from inadequate interpersonal skills. Those who work with the traumatically and severely injured have observed the disproportionate number of them who are under 25 years of age and with a history of impulsive behavior. Finally, we must admit that attempted suicides and homicides disable many persons, and such behaviors by definition are ineffectual solutions to problems. At any rate, this impressive array of the sources of disablement might justify a closer examination that stress plays.

These sources of disablement are considered types of adaptive failures. When a defense proves inadequate to cope with the threat posed, the original problem remains or it becomes worse. Another way of conceptualizing the adaptive failure is to refer it to a particular life-style. The life-style of most cardiac-prone persons has been well documented; they are ambitious, aggressive, impatient, hard working, and with a well-practiced tendency to ignore bodily symptoms of malaise, or the opposite of hypochondriacs. Similarly, the hypertension associated with stroke has pointed to a life-style of frustration and hostility and inadequate socially sanctioned outlets for expressing these emotions. There are many theories of the formation of schizophrenia. But one which has substantial research to back it is that it arises from a developmental history characterized by conflicting aggressive impulses which could find no outlet in normal communication. But, few conditions resulting in disablement have been studied in the manner of the predictive studies of cardiovascular disease, that is, with large unselected samples and followed up for many years.

Despite the scarcity of hard data on which to build preventive programs, the disciplines of sociology, psychology, and psychiatry have generated an impressive collection of studies and clinical and pragmatic evidence supporting the critical part played by stress and adaptive failure in filling our clinics and hospitals.

How can an expanded awareness of stress contribute to prevention?

There are many programs aimed at improving the environment both by physical and psychological means. But in this essay, we are considering stress as an individual rather than as a social problem. The issue then becomes: How can anyone learn to manage stress so as to avoid the consequences that might lead to disability? First, there is evidence that Americans have already made some progress along this line if the recent decline in the death rate may be considered as an index of reduced stress. There appears to be a widespread readiness among Americans to listen to suggestions on how to manage stress more efficiently.

Some stress is a necessary aspect of existence. We need not always consider stress as harmful. Clearly, there are those who manage their lives so as to avoid virtually all stress. But such a life comes too close to a vegetative existence to commend. The management of stress means working toward a style of living congenial to one's individual capacity for coping. It is preferable to consider stress management before the onset of symptoms such as headaches, sleeplessness, and upset stomach. The fact that disturbing symptoms occur indicates that the person has become habituated to disattending to the source of trouble.

Many could benefit from periodic medical and psychological assessment which would reveal the current reactions to stress and uncover trends that could be interrupted before they ran their course. For instance, working long hours may or may not be harmful. But sometimes this is an ineffectual way of dealing with some conflict that itself is a source of stress. Typically, persons who deal with anxiety and stress by intensifying their activities do not go to therapists or clinics to explore the source of their uneasiness. The development of low-cost bio-feedback apparatus has opened up an avenue for reaching such persons. This mode of representing what is happening to the body and the prospects of moderating ill effects appeals to many clients who are otherwise unreachable.

Those who seek to avoid all stress need to learn improved modes of coping. They have stabilized a way of life based upon an unrealistically low estimate of their capacity to cope. They can be taught to take on more stressful engagements if they would lend themselves to the necessary remedial learning. Sometimes, they have stereotypes and inflexible perceptions of the environment carried over from childhood experiences. This type of mental health problem and the necessary corrective measures have been frequently dramatized in the popular media. The learning involves providing them with a broader repertoire of ideas with which to interpret what happens to them. A larger repertoire also increases the prospects that happenings seemingly unfavorable to self-esteem can be interpreted in some other way. Those whose life has been built too much around escaping from stress may lack social skills. They may have alienated others or have given up trying to attract friends because they have simply not learned how to make themselves attractive enough to warrant the attention of the other. A fair number of such persons come to the attention of helping agents and are, in fact, helped.

But a more difficult group to reach with a preventive message are those who stretch their resources by failing to respect their physical and psychological limits. These persons are victims of an unexamined life that puts inordinate emphasis on ambition, competitiveness, and success to the exclusion of other enjoyments. They need to adopt a new life-style that places greater emphasis on the here-and-now, simple joys, and a genuine sense of humor. I suspect that if these persons were reached, they could contribute significantly to the reduction of disablement. Just as hypochondriacs must learn to disattend to organic states, others must be taught to disattend periodically to their blind strivings and singleness of purpose that make them vulnerable.

Because the average person spends considerable time watching television, it is reasonable to assume that he learns some of his coping styles from T.V. shows. What makes a good show is entertainment, excitement, and holding audience attention. Much of the daily fare is romantic, unrealistic, and more optimistic than the realities of life suggest. It is said that those who watch it benefit from the escape from the real world and come away from it better prepared to take on the harsher realities of their life. I believe that the contrary is the general rule, viz., that television watchers are left less competent to cope—especially with disappointment, stubborn difficulties, and tragedy. Ordinary people find precious

few models on television from whom they learn adaptive ways of dealing with their life's problems. Almost everything is so telescoped in the interests of time and attention-holding that the viewer is left with the image of a world of highly competent persons which the viewer vaguely senses he can never enter. What is projected on that screen ultimately is not viewed as the contrivance dreamed up by an imaginative playwright in the comfort of his study, and carefully plotting what the audience shall experience. *It is life.*

Sociologists have written about the increasing alienation that characterizes human relations. But the ultimate in alienation is the abrupt discontinuity between life as it is experienced by real men and women and what is seen on television. In an era when there are more opportunities for constructive leisure activities than ever before, so many people are dulled by the anodyne of television. Television watching reinforces the frequently occurring maladaptations to stress such as withdrawal, denial, and distortion of reality, and potentiates disability by robbing people of their native capacity to live wisely and productively— especially in the presence of stress.

If any threat to the organism constitutes stress, then certainly disability itself is a source of stress. Disabled persons experience more than an ordinary amount of frustration, and in permanent disability the adaptive potential is subject to severe tests.

The course of a disease is not only determined by its causes but by the individual's reaction to it. Similarly, in disability, persons show a wide range of reactions. It is useful to understand unsuccessful defenses against the stress of disability. An unsuccessful defense is one that has run amok. A moderate rise of body temperature in the presence of infection enables the body to mobilize and counteract alien microorganisms. A drastic rise might be fatal. Bodily reactions that normally are functional to survival can get out of control.

Psychological reactions are similar both in their utility and in their potential to become dysfunctional. The initial reaction to trauma is frequently withdrawal and depression. On the positive side, such a reaction enables the disabled person to reassess his condition, to mourn, to reflect, and after a period to resume the struggle. But some patients remain in the depressive phase for so long that it threatens their residual capacities and becomes the major focus of concern. Often it is helpful to understand the developmental history of such patients for clues on how to trigger their interest and involvement. The disability may acquire a symbolic significance far beyond its actualities; it may indicate that the conditional love the patient had received from his parent is now lost.

Certain personality types are prone to weak defenses against the stress of disability. The criteria by which threats are judged are acquired in the course of psychological growth and development and are built into one's personality. The adolescent with a diffuse identity lacks the criteria by which to measure what has befallen him through disablement. If he had

been disabled at a later phase of his development, he might have reflected that he could still carry on his occupation, he could depend on the loyalty of his family, and he could still be guided by the life purposes he held before injury. Most adolescents lack such reference points that might place the disability in some kind of perspective.

Disability poses special threats to the authoritarian personality. This is the type of person who desires to perceive everything in black-and-white terms and tends to convert the grays into either black or white. He is intolerant of ambiguity, contradictions, and pluralism. As the physical and psychological course of disability is typically uncertain and because the social reactions to his visible disability are ambiguous, the authoritarian person suffers and distorts the feedback in order to simplify it.

Finally, the disabled person with articulated personal values has a great asset with which to contain the threatening aspects of his situation. He tends to imbue with worth, goals that are attainable, and thus he has a sense of purpose. Values serve as a brace against adversity and they provide a context within which to reduce the negativity of disability to its proper proportions.

If indeed the person with a crystallized self-concept, capable of tolerating ambiguity, and possessing more or less stable values manages the stress of disability more readily, then there are implications in this for helping handicapped persons. It suggests that some persons do and others do not possess the competencies necessary for dealing with the extraordinary stresses of disability. Diagnostically, such determinations can be made by means of psychological tests and interviews. As to treatment, rapidly evolving technologies of learning should enable professionals to develop appropriate teaching devices to impart the necessary personal skills. Techniques of learning and teaching are not to be found in the psychological literature on disability but in the broader field of behavioral and cognitive studies.[1] The latter have

the merits of providing step-by-step methods that are readily acquired by professionals; they provide for follow-up and assessment; and possess the beginnings of a science of coping with disability.

REFERENCES

Selye, H. 1965. The Stress of Life. McGraw-Hill, New York.
Selye, H. 1974. Stress Without Distress. New American Library, New York.

---

[1] See, for instance, Behavior Change, edited by G. R. Patterson et al., and published annually by Aldine Publishing Company, Chicago, which contains an excellent sample of reprints of journal articles.

44 Genetic Counselling in Rehabilitation Medicine

Chester A. Swinyard

Many of the most significant advances in medicine during the last two decades have extended our understanding of the mechanisms and importance of the role which heredity plays in human disease.

A large percentage of the patients who require rehabilitation services have chronic diseases which are either hereditary or strongly influenced by hereditary mechanisms. All of those working professionally in the field of rehabilitation should, therefore, have some understanding of the general features of human inheritance. It is, in fact, impossible to understand the rationale behind genetic counseling without such basic information. The objective of this paper, therefore, must be twofold; first to review briefly in nontechnical language the basic concepts of human inheritance and indicate how these biological principles affirm and justify advice given in counseling sessions.

BASIC CONCEPTS OF HUMAN INHERITANCE

Virtually all literate human beings are aware that each of us begins life as a fertilized egg cell (zygote) about the size of a grain of sugar. At the end of 280 days of gestation, the newborn infant produced is a complex living being with marvelous potential, weighing approximately seven pounds and consisting of millions of cells (the structural and functional units of the body) organized into tissues, organs and systems. It is obvious that, during this time, the single cell and its daughter cells divided and redivided many times in prenatal life. The complex process of cell division (mitosis) assures that the vital material which transmits hereditary characteristics (deoxyribonucleic acid [DNA]) is shared equally by the two daughter cells. This process is illustrated in Figure 1.

Note that, timewise, the process is divided into stages or phases. The visible division may require only one hour, but preparation for the change may require 10–12 hours. Also observe that the essential part of the process requires formation of a specific number of elongated blocks of condensed hereditary material (DNA) known as chromosomes which are duplicated during the middle of the process and each daughter cell normally receives the same number of chromosomes which were in the par-

Reprinted from International Rehabilitation Review, 1971, 22(1):3–7.

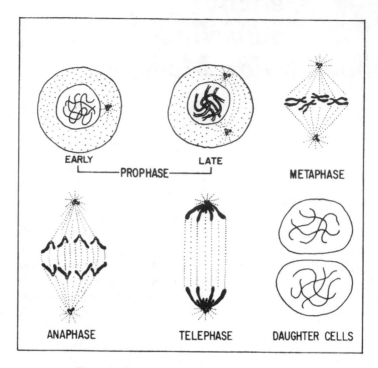

Figure 1. Diagrammatic representation of mitosis.

ent cell. The cells of every animal and plant species contain a specific number of chromosomes. All normal men and women have 46 chromosomes; the male (spermatozoon) and the female (ovum) sex cells must divide in a special way so that these sex cells, when mature, have but 23 chromosomes. During cell division in the ovary and testis, respectively, a special type of cell division (reduction division or meiosis) results in reducing the chromosome number to 23. Thus, when the sex cells fuse at fertilization, the characteristic number for body cells (46) is restored.

The sex of an individual is determined by specific chromosomes. The mature ovum has one sex chromosome called an "X" chromosome. The mature spermatozoa are of two types: One half have an "X" sex chromosome and one half possess a chromosome of different shape designated as "Y." There is an equal chance for an egg to be fertilized by an "X"- or "Y"-containing spermatozoon. Sex of the newborn is determined at the moment of fertilization (Figure 2).

The chromosomes specifically concerned with sexual development are designated as sex chromosomes; the remaining 44, concerned with all other aspects of development and function, are called autosomes.

In Figure 1, all chromosomes are

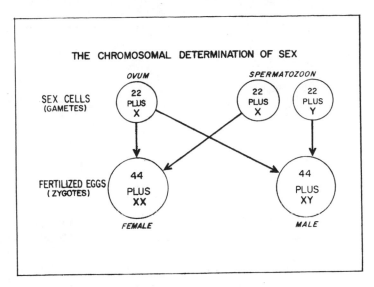

Figure 2. Diagrammatic representation of chromosomes in mature sex cells and restitution of the full number in fertilized eggs.

shown almost the same size and shape; however, during the past fifteen years, it has become possible to study each individual chromosome separately. We have learned that each pair of chromosomes differ from the others in size, shape and biochemical activity. If one stains the chromosomes of a human dividing cell, photographs them through a microscope, enlarges the picture, cuts each chromosome out of the picture with a scissor, then arranges them by size on a sheet of paper, one has prepared what geneticists call a Karyotype (Figure 3).

Note that the forty-six chromosomes are arranged in twenty-three pairs. One member of each pair was derived from the father and the other from the mother. Each individual chromosome is composed of the complex substance (DNA) which transmits all hereditary traits, initiates and maintains numerous biochemical processes which are essential to life. The discovery of the biochemical composition and molecular configuration of the hereditary substance comprises a fascinating chapter in the history of modern medicine. Five investigators have become Nobel Prize Laureates for their contributions to this knowledge.

Tiny subunits of the DNA molecule are the genes which determine particular traits by influencing production of enzymes or protein units which initiate and sustain specific biochemical processes essential to health. The existence of genes was predicted on an empirical basis long before the characteristics of the hereditary material were known.

There are many thousands of genes in each of man's 46 chromosomes,

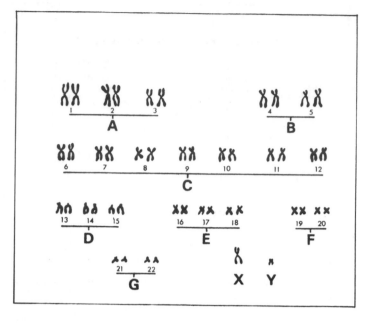

Figure 3. Normal human male karyotype.

each one responsible for initiating or influencing a specific biochemical activity. For example, even a relatively simple trait such as eye color is determined by a gene which determines how many pigmented cells will be formed in the iris of the eye (heavy pigmentation = brown eyes; light pigmentation = blue eyes). Thus, geneticists sometimes refer to single gene activity with reference to production of an enzyme in succinct terms. In a positive sense, this concept can be phrased: One gene → one enzyme → specific normal process; or negatively, one missing or defective gene → absent or defective enzyme → defective biochemical or developmental process. This is, of course, a gross oversimplification, but the illustration does indicate that the vast majority of the hereditary conditions with which we are concerned in rehabilitation medicine are gene defects.

A second category of defect in hereditary material which accounts for a much smaller number of patients with serious rehabilitation problems is related to defects in all or part of a chromosome. A complete chromosome may be lost or an extra one gained by a cell at the time of division, or a fragment of one chromosome may become attached to another one. This means that the individual concerned does not have the normal number of chromosomes (46), but may have 47 or 48 or 45. Many variations in total number have been reported.

We shall illustrate this category of hereditary defect (chromosomal defect) with two examples. The first is the child with mental retardation, commonly a heart defect, characteristic palm and finger prints and facial appearance. This is the child with Down's Syndrome or Mongolism. This child has 47 chromosomes because there is an extra chromosome number 21 (trisomy 21). This error in cell division occurs once in 600 live births among mothers 25 years of age and occurs forty times more frequently in mothers over 45 years of age.

The second example might be the diminutive girl who does not menstruate and is sterile, may have an abnormality of the great artery leaving the heart (aorta) and has webs of loose skin on the side of the neck. This patient (Turner's Syndrome) has only 45 chromosomes because one of her two "X" chromosomes has been lost. There are many varieties of sex chromosomal abnormalities, all of which affect sexual development in various ways.

It is generally agreed that about 1% of all newborn babies have a chromosomal malformation and about one fourth of these affect the sex chromosomes ("X" or "Y").

There is still a third type of change in the hereditary material which is of great importance. We prefer here to refer to this condition as genetic influence. More technically, it might be termed "polygenic or multifactorial inheritance." Many chronic diseases belong to this category. This is not a single defective gene causation, but represents the influence of many genes. Diseases initiated by this type of defect in the hereditary material are not transmitted in a pattern as are the single gene defects.

At this point, it should be clear that more frequent appearance of a chronic disease in a family might be produced by either single gene defects, which may be transmitted as dominant, recessive or sex-linked traits, chromosomal defects, or gene influence (polygenic or multifactorial inheritance).

Patients always want to know immediately if a given condition is hereditary. It should now be apparent that this is often not an easy question to answer since many diseases which are under multifactorial gene influence occur more frequently in certain families than in others, but are not transmitted in definitive ratios.

We should remember that environmental influences may affect the hereditary material deleteriously during prenatal development, and that some genetic constitutions are more or less resistant to environmental change than others. When looked at from this broad perspective, one could assume that all chronic diseases or developmental defects have some hereditary aspect. When one examines the entire spectrum of interrelationships between heredity and environment, it becomes possible to catalogue a large list of diseases which range from a condition which is entirely environmental in origin (irradiation damage) to those which are completely genetic and apparently not influenced by the environment (Duchenne progressive muscular dystrophy, Figure 4).

Perhaps, one example will suffice to show how environmental factors can influence the expression of a gene defect. For example, around the Mediterranean area, there is a high incidence of hereditary deficiency of a blood enzyme which we shall call

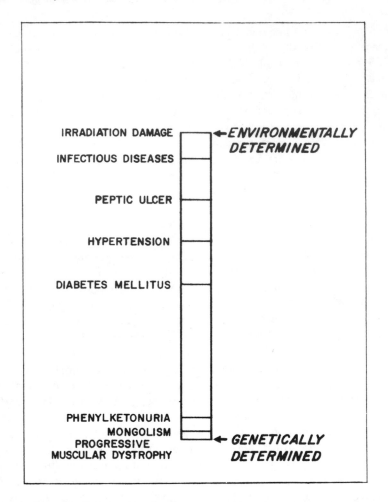

Figure 4. Relationship of environment and heredity to human disease.

G6PD. This deficiency occurs more frequently in this area because blood of such individuals appears to be more resistant to infection by the malarial parasite. On the other hand, when individuals with this enzyme deficiency inhale the fumes of moth balls or eat fava beans, they become acutely ill with a serious blood crisis, while individuals without such a gene defect are not affected.

The popular concept of hereditary disease is based on awareness of the occurrence of certain types of defect appearing in given families with certain frequency. This concept is derived from the classical work of the Austrian monk, Gregor Mendel, who carefully recorded the effect of cross breeding certain types of sweet peas in his monastery garden at Brno, Czechoslovakia. Mendel published his work in the Transactions of the Natural History Society of Brunn in 1866, but his paper was ignored until 1900 when it was rediscovered and confirmed by three investigators. We now refer to the mechanisms of inheritance as Mendelian inheritance and have already mentioned the physical basis upon which it rests (gene defect). On this basis, hereditary transmission of certain physical traits or diseases can be classified as being passed to future generations as a dominant, recessive or by sex-linked type of transmission. The genes for dominant and recessive inheritance are located on the autosomes (non-sex chromosomes), while the sex-linked transmission is related to a gene defect on one of the sex chromosomes ("X" or "Y"). Criteria for recognizing these types of Mendelian ratios are given in the following table [Table 1].

Two final points need mention before indicating the importance of this information with respect to genetic counselling. In the data on criteria for recognizing Mendelian ratios, the word "heterozygous" is mentioned. We have noted that, for each trait every individual possesses, two determiners (genes) are located at the same point in each member of a pair of chromosomes. If these genes are the same in each member of a chromosome pair, the individual is referred to as homozygous; if they are different, he is heterozygous for a given trait or disease. If the gene expresses itself in heterozygous state, it is said to be dominant; if both members of a chromosome pair must have the gene before it expresses itself, it is transmitted as a recessive trait. This is a vital point

because in establishing a complete genetic diagnosis, it is important to detect the carriers of recessively inherited traits.

There are methods of detecting carriers of many types of recessively inherited diseases. The methods are generally biochemical assessments of the amount of certain biochemical compounds in either blood or urine. Not infrequently, it is necessary to give the suspected carrier a certain "load" of a compound which is suspected to be metabolized imperfectly because of the gene defect. Carriers of Duchenne progressive muscular dystrophy can be detected by measuring an enzyme in the blood serum (creatinephosphokinase), and mild exercise of the suspected carrier prior to taking the blood sample aids in detecting a larger percentage of the carriers.

We must not assume that every newborn affected with a gene-defect disease has received this defect from his parents or other ancestors. There are both external (environmental) and internal pressures which cause gene defects to originate in a given individual. The occurrence of a new gene defect is termed a "mutation." There are relatively simple methods to determine how frequently certain mutant genes arise. We should appreciate that the new mutation of a given gene which results in disease is transmitted to future generations in the manner characteristic of the disease.

Finally, it is hoped that this extremely brief, essentially non-technical, account of a number of very complex processes which form the basis for hereditary transmission of disease will assist the reader in under-

Table 1. Criteria for recognizing several types of Mendelian ratios

A. Simple dominant inheritance.
  1. Every affected person has an affected parent.
  2. Affected persons married to normal persons have affected and normal offspring in equal proportions.
  3. Normal children of affected parents, when married to normals, have only normal children.
  4. An affected parent is assumed to be heterozygous, and inheritance from one parent only is assumed.
  5. Whenever the defective gene is present, its effect is produced.

  4. Mating of heterozygous parents produces a ratio of three normal (one without the defective gene and two heterozygous for the defective gene) and one affected individual (homozygous for the defective gene).
  5. Affected individuals who marry affected individuals have only affected children—provided the abnormality is due to the same gene defect.
  6. Generally speaking, the average defects due to recessive genes are more serious than those of dominant gene defects.

  5. The female has two X chromosomes; therefore the sex-linked trait may express itself in either the single dose (heterozygous) or double dose (homozygous) situation depending on its degree of dominance.
  6. Most of the human sex-linked genes are recessive.
  7. Marriage of a heterozygous female (normal) to a normal male produces a ratio of three normal and one affected male.
  8. Marriage of an affected male to a normal female results in all normal children, but the females are heterozygous carriers. An affected male

6. When two affected persons marry, the ratio of affected to normal children is 3:1.

B. Recessive inheritance.

1. The trait appears only if the individual received the defective gene from both parents (i.e., is homozygous).

2. If the trait is at all rare, the great majority of affected persons have normal parents.

3. The affected person must have received the defective gene from both parents.

C. Sex-linked inheritance.

1. There are many ordinary genes in the X chromosomes affecting many structures and functions not related to sex.

2. For practical purposes, sex-linked transmission is related to X chromosome. Evidence for Y gene inheritance is poor.

3. Since the male has only one X chromosome, the defective gene is unpaired and no question of homozygous or heterozygous state exists.

4. If the male carries the defective gene on the X chromosome, he is abnormal.

cannot transmit to a son, nor to a subsequent generation through the son, but only through the unaffected daughter.

9. Marriage of affected men and heterozygous (carrier) women produces the following ratio: 25% affected males, 25% affected females. 25% normal males, 25% unaffected females (heterozygous carriers).

10. Marriage of affected women and normal men results in 50% affected males and 50% normal females (heterozygous carriers).

11. Marriage of affected men and affected women produces all children affected.

standing the rationale of genetic counseling.

GENETIC COUNSELLING IN REHABILITATION

It should now be apparent that the prelude to effective genetic counselling is, first, an accurate medical and genetic diagnosis. Patients with hereditary chronic disease require counselling, not only with reference to the medical and genetic problems but also psychosocial and vocational counselling. The psychosocial and vocational counselling cannot be done effectively in ignorance of the medical and genetic diagnosis and its implications for family mental health, interrelationships and anxieties relative to the patient's siblings, future children and prognosis for the patient. Effective psychosocial and vocational counselling is, therefore, utterly dependent on proper understanding of both the medical and genetic diagnosis, and the latter, in turn, is dependent on at least an elementary understanding of the mechanisms of inheritance.

Ideally, genetic counselling should be done by a geneticist who should make at least the initial approach to the family concerned, but, more importantly, would discuss with the evaluation and treatment staff the genetic counselling implications pertinent to the family. As a practical matter, however, there is such a shortage of professional geneticists that only a small percentage of the rehabilitation centers will have professional genetic counselling available.

Under these circumstances, it becomes the obligation of the physician concerned to acquire by training and/or reading sufficient background in cellular and genetic aspects of reproduction to understand the genetic aspects and implications of at least several of the categories of hereditary disease which he most frequently encounters. He should also maintain a consulting arrangement with a professional geneticist to enable him to cope with unusual problems which arise. Under these circumstances, the physician must take the responsibility for assuring that those professionals who provide essential specialized counselling will do it with understanding of both the medical and genetic problems that confront the patient and his family.

The anxieties of parents who learn that their child has an hereditary disease are enormous. The father questions the mother about her family background and she, in turn, gives much attention to her husband's ancestors. One of the first questions in their minds is: *"What are the chances of having another child like this one?"* or *"Would you advise us to have more children?"*

If the condition is one which is transmitted quite clearly in one of the Mendelian ratios, the answer is relatively easy, and the frequencies for recurrences are given in Table 1 for autosomal dominant, recessive and sex-linked inheritance. On the other hand, if the disease is polygenic or multifactorial inheritance, the problem becomes much more difficult. There is, however, a distressing tendency for some physicians, who lack understanding or appreciation of the genetics of the problem, to take a chance with the parent and give a quick response such as "not a chance in a million" or "Lightning never strikes the same place twice." It is a sober fact that parents who have had one child with a congenital anomaly may be much more likely to produce a second, similarly involved child than parents who have not produced such a child. For example, unaffected parents in the general population have approximately an 0.10 to 0.15 per cent chance of having a child with a cleft lip. If unaffected parents have a child with a cleft lip, there is a 5.0 per cent chance of each subsequent child being affected. If a second child is born with a cleft lip, the chances of a subsequent child being so affected rise to about 10 per cent. Approximately the same situation pertains with respect to children born with spina bifida (myelomeningocele). Such figures imply a considerable risk and are actually so-called risk figures, which are empirically determined average figures. Carefully computed risk figures have clinical usefulness, but there are many pitfalls to be avoided in their use.

Can Anything Be Done for a Child with an Hereditary Disease?

This frequently-asked question reflects the relatively common public attitude of defeatism and helplessness which prevails with reference to hereditary diseases. The answer is a very positive affirmation that much can be done to preserve life, reduce morbidity and enable the patients with many types of hereditary diseases to become independent, contributing members of society. This does not mean that the defective gene or group of genes can be identified and replaced with new ones, nor that the condition can be cured. It does mean, however, that in spite of the basic gene defect alone or in combination with an unknown environmental factor, it is possible by utilization of a comprehensive medical rehabilitation program to enable many children to live an effective independent life. For example, twenty years ago, virtually all newborns with spina bifida (myelomeningocele) (multifactorial inheritance plus unidentified environmental factor) died, but advances in control of infection, neurosurgical, urological and orthopedic surgical technics have reduced the mortality by more than 50% and the survivors are socially acceptable and perfectly capable of obtaining an education and working within the limits dictated by their lower limb muscle weakness. Another example is the single gene recessive trait of galactosemia (a disorder of carbohydrate metabolism). These newborns have vomiting, diarrhea and fail to develop. Later, they develop cataracts, mental retardation and liver complications. The genetic block is deficiency of the enzyme (Gal-1-P uridyl transferase) necessary to utilize the sugar galactose. The serious consequences of the disease can be prevented by feeding a milk substitute which contains neither galactose nor lactose (lactose forms galactose during metabolism).

The outlook for control of the

disease consequences of gene defects improves almost monthly. Recently an announcement was made of a new way to control an inherited intolerance to another sugar (fructose). This condition has been known for fifteen years.

Is it Possible to Detect the Presence of Disease before My Baby is Born?

This question comes to minds of ever-increasing numbers of parents as social attitudes toward legal abortion change. Investigation of methods for determining whether or not a young fetus is carrying a given hereditary disease is being conducted intensively in many medical centers. It has now been demonstrated that a skilled physician can enter the fluid-filled sac inside the uterus in which the fetus is suspended (amnionic sac) and, between the 12th and 16th week of pregnancy, can remove a sample of fluid (amniotic fluid) without significant discomfort to the mother and with small chance of interfering with the pregnancy. The procedure is called amniocentesis.

The amniotic fluid contains biochemical products of fetal metabolism and cells shed from body surface. By chemical and cellular study of the fluid, it is possible to make a medical and genetic diagnosis of hereditary disease in human fetuses between the 13th and 18th week of pregnancy. If the fetus in question has the disease, the mother may elect to have a legal abortion. Not all hereditary diseases can be detected at this stage of development, but at the present time, about forty hereditary conditions can be recognized by utilizing this technic. If this procedure is used completely, it theoretically changes the answer to the parents' question about "having another baby like this one" because under these circumstances, the chances of recurrence are essentially zero.

Since virtually all human diseases are influenced by the hereditary composition of the body, it is apparent that one must predicate the counselling on the specifics of the particular condition of concern. Even genetic counselling is not a one session affair because different facets of genetic implication come into sharper focus as the patient becomes older. It is therefore essential for those doing the psychosocial and vocational counselling to consult periodically with a professional geneticist or physician adequately trained to fill this essential function.

Because of the widespread interest in cerebral palsy, many readers might wonder why we have come to the end of this discussion without mention of it. There are two reasons for this: First, cerebral palsy is not a hereditary condition; it is the result of defect or injury to the brain and is non-progressive. We do, however, occasionally see examples of hereditary progressive neuromuscular diseases which are quite similar to cerebral palsy, but most of these are known under other names and are not cerebral palsy as the word is generally used. Secondly, cerebral palsy is only one of hundreds of human disabilities which are of special interest to particular groups.

There is an enormous literature available for reference. The following reading list was selected as representative of the subject matter discussed and is easier to read than some of the more detailed volumes and should enable the reader to obtain information about a condition which is of special interest.

SELECTED REFERENCES

Bergsma, D. (Editor) 1968 Human Genetics. 124 pages. National Foundation Original Article Series IV, No. 6.

Butler, J. A. V. 1959 Inside the Living Cell. Basic Books, Inc., New York.

Emery, A. E. H. 1968 Heredity, Disease and Man: Genetics in Medicine. 247 pages. University of California Press. Berkeley, California.

Hammons, H. G. 1959 Hereditary Counseling. 112 pages. Paul B. Hoeber, Inc., New York.

Nadler, H. L. and Gerbie, A. B. 1970 Role of amniocentesis in the intrauterine detection of genetic disorders. New England J. of Med., 282: 596–599.

Reed, S. C. 1963 Counselling in Medical Genetics, 2nd Edition, 278 pages. W. B. Saunders Co., Philadelphia.

Roberts, J. A. F. 1967 An Introduction to Medical Genetics, 4th Edition. Oxford University Press, London.

Swanson, C. P. The Cell, 3rd Edition. 150 pages. Prentice Hall, Inc., Englewood Cliffs, New Jersey.

Valentine, G. H. 1966 The Chromosome Disorders: An Introduction for Clinicians. William Heinemann, Ltd., London.

Williams, P. L. and Wendell-Smith, C. P. 1966 Basic Human Embryology. 136 pages. J. P. Lippincott Company, Philadelphia.

Part IV

NORMALIZATION OF DISABLED PERSONS

Editorial
Introduction

Joseph Stubbins

Part IV consists of ten articles which elaborate the principle of normalization. This principle stipulates that disabled persons should be treated the same as the non-disabled, except with regard to their specific needs arising from deficit or disability. It seems simple enough. But applying the principle presents many difficulties and honest differences of opinion. There would be no dispute about physically disabled persons being entitled to special aids to enable them to enter public buildings. But once in the building, they should not be entitled to move to the head of a queue nor entitled to other considerations unrelated to their handicap. Normalization would aver that begging is no less reprehensible when done by a disabled person than by a non-disabled one. Between these clear illustrations are numerous gray areas in which differences arise as to the proper application of normalization. Subsidized special housing for group living for severely disabled persons is an example. Some maintain that is in compliance with normalization because it provides the material and social means for near-normal living denied to severely handicapped persons elsewhere. Others would say that it is in violation of normalization because of the segregation involved and the subsidization not available to other disadvantaged groups.

The principle of normalization has been most fully elaborated in the professional literature dealing with mentally retarded persons. This group has been victimized by the tendency of others to view them almost exclusively in terms of their limited intellectual ability. This halo effect, or "spread," (Wright, 1960) has resulted in the mentally retarded being over-protected, under-developed socially, and denied jobs well within their capabilities. The practice of viewing a disabled person's behavior and potentiality in terms of a single dimension such as a missing limb and making interpretations of behavior in terms of amputation have been most unfortunate for the personal development and rehabilitation of disabled persons. Normalization counteracts this practice and demands a justification of any special treatment from those who would deal with disabled persons in a special way.

Some professional workers who subscribe to the normalization principle would like to retain for disabled persons prerogatives of the disabled status. These prerogatives may be advantages mandated by law or granted by the community's largesse. The advantage may be a pension, educational grant, or preference in employment. Normalization requires the abandonment of many special privileges based on diagnostic labeling. For this reason, normalization is being regarded as a mixed blessing, particularly by those whose efforts on behalf of disabled persons were directed toward lobbying for special benefits. This aspect of normalization is not fully appreciated even by some of its advocates. The conflict between normalization and privilege based on diagnostic labeling can be illustrated by the movement toward mainstreaming handicapped children in the public schools.

In the course of the development of special educational services, handicapped children came to enjoy advantages such as the following: small classes, specially trained teachers with technical skills for overcoming learning handicaps, counseling services, specially constructed buildings, free transportation to a centrally located school, and so on. There was a price to be paid for such advantages, and there is a growing consensus that the price was too great. The social cost was segregation, so that handicapped children spent their most formative years primarily with other handicapped children, depriving normal children of the experience of relating to them. This system continued through the high school level. By the time handicapped young men and women entered college or university, many lacked any sustained contact with the non-disabled outside of their immediate family. In the course of trying to undo the estrangement that developed between handicapped and non-handicapped persons and in opting for mainstreaming, parents and their handicapped children will have to become adapted to a world in which many substantial advantages of segregation are no longer present. The larger competitive world to which normalization would admit them lacks many props built into the segregated world.

Community and legislative activities on behalf of disabled persons have usually involved selling the idea of supportive services for disabled persons to be paid for by the public. No doubt much of this will continue, and properly so, because there are still special needs that do not violate normalization. However, if normalization is to be realized, there ought to be a shift in focus from "What is the maximum the disabled can get from the public purse?" to "What kind of services and in what amounts will optimize the dignity and independence of the disabled?" We can expect a long period of transition during which the physical and social barriers of the normal world will be removed. During this period, the temptation to retreat to the comforts of old perquisites and segregation will be great. The readings of Part IV provide coverage of the many-sided features of implementing normalization. The articles have been divided into the following three sections: Section 12, "Work and Leisure," Section 13, "Architectural Barriers," and Section 14, "Civil Rights."

WORK AND LEISURE

Normalization does not preclude pensions for permanently disabled veterans, industrially injured persons, or for those too old to work. However, there is still the question of how such disabled persons would maintain meaning in their lives in the absence of work. The Larson and Spreitzer article deals with these issues. The article reflects conditions in this country in the late sixties when continued affluence was taken for granted and the erosion of the work ethic was less clear. Nevertheless, the issues they raise are still timely, e.g., the alternatives to work for filling time and providing purpose in daily existence.

Providing for the constructive use of free time has now become a major industry in this country. While normalization places major emphasis on maximizing the opportunities for leisure under mainstream conditions, it would also sanction special facilities to meet the needs of disabled persons. From the larger perspective of his international observations, Lancaster-Gaye reviews on-going projects that provide leisure activities for severely handicapped persons in Great Britain and several European countries. Since many forms of leisure are social, planning and organization are necessary.

The research study reported in the article by Rickard, Triandis, and Patterson revealed a hierarchy of prejudice in the attitudes of employers toward hiring handicapped persons. The greatest prejudice was expressed toward epileptics, ex-offenders, and recovered mental hospital patients. These findings are corroborated by rehabilitation counselors involved in job placement. Physicians who rate disabilities on the basis of organic impairment are often unaware of the differential social significance of disabilities as revealed by the actions of employers and others. The Rickard et al. study sheds light on the obstacles to normalization and the necessity for temporary expedients such as financial benefits for persons victimized by social exclusion.

Because sheltered workshops are at the crossroads between the competitiveness of business and industry and the protectiveness accorded disabled persons, they encompass many of the problems and contradictions of normalization. This theme is taken up in the article by Power and Marinelli as they apply the normalization principle to the sheltered workshop. The proliferation of workshops in the last decade has created the illusion that much was being done to compensate for the handicapped person's inability to find employment. The forthright discussion of the pit-falls of workshops contained in the article illustrate, how remedies for disabled persons can become frozen into dead-end patterns. Insofar as workshops simulate the conditions of industry, pay wages to the trainees, and produce goods that find their way into the marketplace, they comply with the principle of normalization. But workshops have other practices that violate the normalization principle. They may pay wages below the legal minimum; they accept contracts that necessitate low wages; and their productive workers tend to subsidize the less productive. The sheltered workshop is a very interesting institution to study for it is the microcosm of society with its reality principle of production and marketing and its conflicting humanistic principle of providing for human needs.

The most difficult area in which to apply the normalization principle is with homebound persons. To some extent, homebound persons are homebound because some disabilities are so severe that human ingenuity has been unable to improve their condition or we have failed to invest enough in bio-engineering. To some extent, they are homebound because the world of the non-disabled is not ready or able to receive them. This is the subject of the article by Rusalem, chosen as the last one of this section. He reviews some recent progress and points up the many unmet needs of severely disabled persons. The article concludes with recommendations that would contribute to the normalization of homebound persons, with particular emphasis on enhancing possibilities for social contacts.

The cumulative impact of technological change can no longer support the optimism of a decade ago: that somehow an enlightened society would eventually provide work for even severely disabled persons. At a time when substantial unemployment seems more and more a steady feature of our society and work alienation is more and more a stable characteristic of the work place, the issues of work and leisure illustrate how closely the fate of disabled persons is tied in with that of the larger society.

ARCHITECTURAL BARRIERS

The restricted mobility of severely handicapped persons is a major obstacle to their normalization. Lack of mobility makes them dependent and limits their options in making contacts with others. The modification of cars so that they can be driven by persons with lower extremity dysfunctions provides a glimpse of the possibilities of improving mobility. Inability to enter a building is, in effect, blocked mobility. Thus, even if great advances were to be made in enabling disabled persons to get around, architectural barriers would still constitute a major block to normalization. The three articles in this section address themselves to advancing normalization through removing architectural barriers.

Park opens up an aspect of normalization that too often is ignored, viz., the risks involved. Every advance in normalization incurs more risks. In this article Gunnar Dybwad is quoted as saying, "Normal on our earth is trouble and strife, trial and tribulation, and the handicapped person has a right to be exposed to it. Normalization thus includes the dignity of risk." Nowhere is this more apparent than in enhancing mobility through adaptive transportation and housing. This moving article concludes with a challenge to disabled persons themselves to participate in the removal of barriers.

The next two articles, one by Jeffrey and the other by Stock and Cole, point up critical issues in housing for severely disabled persons. The impulse to over-protect disabled persons encourages excessive dependence on families and institutions, both of which stifle personal development. More faith in their self-care potential would stimulate creative adaptive housing, which is at an early stage of development. Clearly, there is room for much experimentation in this area. The Co-operative Living Project in Texas described by Stock and Cole is such an experiment. These authors concluded that the experience of living among themselves raised the self-esteem of these disabled persons and enhanced their employability and independence. The ideological position that special housing for handicapped persons would impede their integration into society was not supported by this pragmatic test, possibly because that position under-estimates the degree of prejudice against disabled persons. Though special housing falls short of the ideal of normalization, it may be viewed as a transition to a more complete integration.

When one considers that until about 30 years ago, severely disabled persons were rarely seen in public places, great advances in normalizing disabled persons have occurred. However, when this progress is measured against the medical breakthroughs that keep an increasing number of severely disabled persons alive, the picture looks less satisfying.

The inclusion of the articles on architectural barriers and mobility implies that the subject has psychological significance. In what sense is this true? The constricted life space of the disabled person is both a physical fact and a social psychological fact. Similarly, the difference for the severely disabled person between living in a nursing home and in a cooperative housing project architecturally adapted for disabled persons has far-reaching psychological significance. But psychologists have no influence in such decisions. Their influence is largely palliative rather than fundamental. Physically handicapped persons are guaranteed few particular rights based on their disablements, but they share with other citizens certain natural rights. There is a considerable gap between such abstractions and the real lives of disabled persons, which brings us to the final section of this book.

CIVIL RIGHTS

Psychology has lived a double life. In *one* world—the moral and ideological one—it aspired to discover the keys to human behavior and to contribute dynamically to human welfare, or, as stated in Article I of the bylaws of the American Psychological Association, "The objects of the American Psychological Association shall be to advance psychology as a science and as a means of promoting human welfare...." It is not accidental that the pursuit of knowledge and its application to welfare were stated in the same sentence; the presumption is that they should be inseparable. In the *other* world, the generation of psychological knowledge is considered to be best advanced by separating it from applications. It is maintained by some that the pursuit of practical goals impedes discovery.

This ambivalence about the responsibility of psychologists to use their knowledge and skill to intervene in the affairs of society is a continuing divisive force in the Association. It has its counterpart at the local clinical level where some psychologists prefer the scientific role, with priority given to discovery, and other psychologists prefer the applied and advocacy roles. The issue of research and practice is considerably more complex than stated here. What gets researched and the roles taken by psychologists are not quite matters of individual choice but are laid out by institutions and their power structures. The psychologist coming into a rehabilitation facility finds that his or her role has already been delineated and laid out. Psychological services have been remedial and palliative. Psychologists have accepted the position of disabled persons in society as givens and have helped severely disabled persons to become reconciled to their lessened existence. The same evaluation could be made of other psycho-social professionals in the rehabilitation field. Whether their roles should extend beyond this conservative function is moot. At any rate, professionals have not played a remarkable role in advancing the fundamental interests of handicapped persons.

The article by Thoben reminds us that the position of disabled persons is similar to that of persons disadvantaged by racial origin, color, or sex. These groups have made progress through political action that led to corrective legislation. The employment provisions of the Rehabilitation Act of 1973 implicitly recognize the grave limitations of increasing employment of handicapped persons by persuasion and education alone. The final article by Abramson and Kutner constitutes an agenda for a civil rights program for disabled persons.

Psychologists and other psycho-social professionals promised disabled persons more than they delivered. This may be attributable to their training which placed so much emphasis on the reconstructive value of a one-to-one relationship. Probably, this is most evident at the fringe of professional respectability, where psychologists, social workers, and pretenders offered disabled persons increased self-awareness and narcissistic self-interest as a panacea. The mainstream of professionals have also been dispassionate and emotionally antiseptic in their daily relations with disabled persons and uninvolved in the fundamental issues affecting the welfare of disabled persons. Concluding this book with civil rights placed the contribution of psychology in a balanced light. In addition to a well-ordered psyche, the disabled person needs food, clothing, adaptive housing, access to public places, and other things not within the power of psychologists to provide. How much and how soon disabled persons come by them will be determined in the community and political arena and other places where resources are allocated.

REFERENCES

Wright, B. 1960. Physical Disability: A Psychological Approach. Harper & Row, New York.

Section 12

WORK AND LEISURE

45 The Disabled Role, Affluence, and the Meaning of Work

David L. Larson and
Elmer A. Spreitzer

The general objective of this paper is to discuss the relationship of the disabled role with the level of economic affluence and with the cultural meanings attached to work. The first section of the paper involves a conceptual analysis of the disabled role. The second section makes a case for the United States as a society of abundance and suggests some implications of this affluence for the role of the disabled. The basic thesis presented is that the absence of an institutionalized role for the disabled is inconsistent with a society of relative abundance. A third section of the paper analyzes the meaning of work from the perspective of the Protestant ethic and delineates some ramifications for the role of the disabled. It is proposed that the conception of work as a moral imperative militates against a legitimated role for the disabled.

A working hypothesis of this paper is the following: The disabled role will become increasingly legitimated to the extent that (1) our society comes to accept affluence as an accomplished fact, and (2) our conception of work becomes less and less that of a moral duty and a virtue in itself. Since we do not have statistical data pertaining to

these variables, our treatment of the relationships will be confined to the conceptual level. However, such a hypothesis could be empirically tested on the attitudinal level, for example, by correlating the willingness to endorse a legitimated role for the disabled with both the opinion of whether affluence has been achieved and attitudes concerning the meaning of work. Ideally, an empirical test of the hypothesis would involve a cross-cultural design and would include an analysis of structural arrangements as well as attitudes and beliefs.

THE CONCEPT OF THE DISABLED ROLE

Talcott Parsons' conceptualization of the sick role is one of the most widely discussed concepts of medical sociology. Parsons posits four basic dimensions of the sick role: the exemption from usual role obligations, holding the patient not responsible for his condition, the perception of sickness as an undesirable state to be relinquished as soon as possible, and the obligation to seek and cooperate with competent assistance (1). Although

---

Reprinted from the Journal of Rehabilitation, 1970, 36(4): 29–32.

subjected to numerous criticisms, Parsons' analysis of the sick role has been of considerable value in that it has stimulated much discussion and some empirical research (2).

Perhaps the major criticism of the sick role concept is that it is too abstract and idealized; consequently, it is not applicable in a large number of situations. Freidson maintains that it is necessary "to construct a number of sick roles so as to be able to discriminate the characteristics of behavior expected from a person who is believed to have a minor, a major or a fatal illness, a curable or an incurable illness, a short-term or a long-term illness, and an ordinary or a stigmatized illness" (3).

For purposes of the present paper, it is necessary to emphasize that the sick role is not appropriate for persons with chronic and disabling conditions. Such conditions are, almost by very definition, not temporary; consequently, the expectation that the patient should want to get well and to abandon the sick role as soon as possible is largely irrelevant. Generally speaking, these persons will not totally escape their condition regardless of how motivated they may be to do so. In short, the position of disabled people is rendered ambiguous by the fact that the institutionalized sick role does not fit their situation. Their conditions are usually not so much curable as they are improvable. In addition, the motivational factor does not count as heavily in their situation since they are more commonly the victims of accidents, infections, and contingencies of inheritance, rather than the psychosomatic conditions where motivation is more relevant (4).

This absence of an appropriate, clearly articulated role for those who are disabled is the focal point for this paper. In using the concept of the disabled role, we refer to the position of being disabled as well as the behavior expected of one who occupies that status. An institutionalized role for the disabled, as conceived in this paper, would include among other aspects the expectations that (1) disabled persons would not be obliged to seek conventional employment, and (2) a humane standard of living would be provided to them from public programs as a matter of right. Admittedly, this conception of a disabled role emphasizes the economic aspects; however, this somewhat restricted conception is not completely out of place in that disability is commonly defined as the inability to perform to one's usual productive roles. One might also reason that if disabled persons could achieve freedom *from* economic insecurity, they would be more likely to have the freedom *to* pursue self-actualization in non-economic spheres.

At this point, it is important to distinguish two aspects of the sick role: the individual and the social. From the individualistic perspective, one might inquire into the motivation of an individual to seek out or avoid the disabled role. The concept of secondary gains is relevant here; it has frequently been observed that certain individuals make a psychological investment in the exemptions provided by this role (5). For example, an injured person may seek the disabled role as a refuge from the competitiveness of our achievement-oriented society. It has frequently been noted that for one person an objectively minor impairment can produce serious behavioral aberrations, whereas another person with a severely debilitating impairment will make an excellent adjustment. There seems to be little parity between cause and effect; widely different impairments can produce relatively similar reactions and vice versa. This psychological mode of analysis is quite prevalent in the literature on disability (6).

A more sociological perspective concerns the conditions under which the disabled role is granted to an impaired person. That is, what factors are taken into consideration, other than the purely medical, when professionals and laymen define someone as disabled? Agents of social control, such as physicians and disability determiners for cash benefit programs, play a particularly important part as gatekeepers to the disabled role. The course of an individual's life can be greatly affected by their decision of whether or not to approve one for the disabled role, i.e., to grant disability benefits. Consequently, one can see that the routine approval or denial of cash benefits has enduring consequences for an individual's self-conception. At this point one might raise the question as to what explains the relative availability of the disabled role in different societies. From a sociocultural point of view, it can be hypothesized that the availability of an institutionalized role for the disabled is likely to be related to (1) the societal level of economic affluence and (2) the dominant cultural meanings attached to work and leisure.

SCARCITY AND ABUNDANCE

In a subsistence economy there is little surplus to allocate for the maintenance of those who cannot (or will not) perform a productive role. On the other hand, where productivity is so great that efforts are required to match consumption with this production, it would seem logical to grant freely a legitimate status to the disabled. Since productivity is not problematic in an affluent society, one might reason that the lack of a productive contribution by the disabled would not be dysfunctional for the economy, their support would not be a burden to society, and they could still function as needed consumers. As will be seen, however, such purely economic reasoning is too simplistic.

The central focus of economics historically has been on productivity and the allocation of scarce resources. Up until the present era, man has constantly faced the specter of scarcity and the niggardliness of nature. All things being equal, increased economic productivity has been a result of expanded human labor, either qualitative or quantitative. Labor was the necessary ingredient to provide the physical sustenance of human life. Although there have been many secondary reasons why men work, the primary purpose was to maintain life with varying degrees of comfort. Consequently, St. Paul's dictum has received virtually universal acceptance: "If anyone will not work, let him not eat." The contemporary version might read, "If anyone will not work, let him have only a subsistence standard of living." This traditional view of work has been challenged by the affluent society theorists who work with an abundance model rather than one of scarcity.

In 1958 John Kenneth Galbraith published his famous book entitled *The Affluent Society*. One of Galbraith's main theses is that "production for the sake of the goods produced is no longer very urgent" (7). Our national preoccupation with maintaining and increasing productivity is vestigial from an earlier era of scarcity. Galbraith strongly criticized the conventional wisdom which sees no reduction in the urgency of consumer needs with increasing affluence. He makes a telling argument that one cannot defend production as satisfying wants if the production itself creates the wants. "For then the individual who urges the importance of production to satisfy these wants is precisely in the position of the onlooker who applauds the efforts of the squirrel to keep abreast of the wheel that is propelled by his own efforts" (8).

Other writers have also addressed themselves to the presence and problems of the affluent society. David Riesman, for example, suggests that in such a society there is a tendency for people to lose their zest for bounteous consumption (9). The law of diminishing utility is in operation for all goods in the aggregate and not for just one kind of commodity. Riesman explains the reasons why this process has not

been more apparent in our society: "Enormous expenditures for research and development of new, or seemingly new, products along with ever larger advertising budgets, have helped postpone the specter of satiation ..." (10).

C. Wright Mills has an interesting analysis of the "life styles" of an underdeveloped society as compared to industrial ones. He points out that when the economy has developed to the point of providing the basic necessities, and then some, the people begin to struggle for prestige through the quantity and style of their consumption. "Here the style of life is *dominated* by the standard of living" (11). Mills emphasizes that in an overdeveloped society there is much production for meeting luxury needs, as well as conspicuous consumption and conspicuous waste. The dictates of fashion and planned obsolescence become central features in such a society.

The general conclusion to be drawn from these analysts is that the United States economy can provide a relative abundance of consumer goods. Affluence has been achieved in the sense that production is no longer problematic: the major concern presently is to maintain effective consumer demand (12). However, it seems that the proposition that our expanding economy will employ progressively fewer workers is still an empirical question. The present high rate of employment could be cited as counterevidence for this important proposition, but it could also be argued that this is merely a temporary phenomenon due to the fact that the full impact of automation has not yet descended upon us. The resolution of this question will, of course, have serious consequences for the position of disabled people.

If the analysis of the affluence theorists turns out to be accurate, the characteristic orientation of disability and rehabilitation programs with employment and economic productivity will be anachronistic. Terrence Carroll is one of the few writers who has pointed up this paradoxical situation of the disabled:

> Since it seems inevitable in the immediate future that we will have a persistent pool of unemployed, there is little logic in insisting on individuals entering the labor market when they are physically or emotionally unable to compete on relatively equal terms with most other workers, if socially and personally acceptable alternatives are available to them (13).

In short, it seems logical to Carroll, and probably many others, that an institutionalized role for the disabled is compatible with an affluent society. We now appear to have the interesting situation where economic needs are harmonious with a humanitarian motive of providing a decent standard of living for disabled people. The belief that everyone must work in an economy of abundance may increasingly produce ambivalence in both the minds of the disabled and in the gatekeepers of public programs for the disabled. A seriously impaired person may consider it paradoxical to be told he should seek work in order to pull his own weight when he is aware of the frivolity and waste in the economy, and when he realizes that the major problem is consumption, not production. The Social Security determiner, for example, might sense a paradox in denying a claim for cash benefits when the claimant was not quite impaired enough to quality, while at the same time being aware of our increasing economic productivity without the manpower needs of an earlier era. The basic question may be formulated in the following manner: Why should those seriously impaired be coerced to obtain unneeded productive roles in order to qualify for needed goods and services which exist in such quantity that a major industry has evolved solely to entice people into consumption?

The typology below [Figure 1] represents the intersection of the two variables that we have been discussing: the degree of legitimation of the disabled role and the level of economic affluence. These two variables are hypothetically distributed along a continuum, but they are dichotomized in this typology for purposes of illustration.

Cell B probably characterizes contemporary American society, although there is evidence of movement toward Cell D. Cultural lag may be a way of conceptualizing this situation where a society has the capacity to produce a plethora of material goods for all but still demands that the disabled should fill productive roles in order to justify their share of these surplus products. In the following section, an attempt is made to explain this seemingly inconsistent stance toward the disabled in our society. It will be argued that the

	Scarcity	Affluence
No legitimated disabled role	(A) Consistent type	(B) Inconsistent type
Presence of legitimated disabled role	(C) Inconsistent type	(D) Consistent type

Figure 1. Intersection of the degree of legitimation of the disabled role and the level of economic affluence.

cultural meanings attached to work are very important factors in this area.

THE MEANING OF WORK

The cultural meanings attached to work appear to affect the availability and degree of legitimation of the disabled role. One could hypothesize that in a society where work serves only an instrumental function—as a means to an end—the disabled role would be more likely to be institutionalized. On the other hand, in a society where work is defined as a moral duty, or as an end in itself, a legitimated role for the disabled is less likely to evolve. In the latter case, the withdrawal from work involves much more than an economic loss; it involves a most important way of meaningfully relating to the larger society. Consequently, since the work role has this latent function, disability results in a twofold loss: a diminuition of income and the loss of a major means of integration

into a larger network of social relationships.

Adriano Tilgher, in his *Work Through the Ages* has analyzed the various meanings that have been attached to work in various cultures (14). To the Greeks and Romans of the classical period work was perceived as more or less of a curse and something to be avoided. For the ancient Hebrews, however, work offered man a way to atone for sin and a means to regain lost spiritual dignity. To the early Christians no particular intrinsic value was recognized in labor. In early Catholicism work was not exalted as something of value in itself but rather as an instrument of purification, expiation, and charity. Calvinism represents an interesting viewpoint in that here work was seen as the will of God; diligence, industry, and prosperity came to be considered as signs of God's grace. For the Calvinist a dislike of work might suggest that election to God's grace was doubtful. To pursue one's vocation with all of one's conscience was a religious duty. This so-called Protestant ethic was held to be instrumental in the development of capitalism by Max Weber in his classic study, *The Protestant Ethic and the Spirit of Capitalism.*

The modern era, according to Tilgher, shows a decline in the religious meaning of work. Unlike the era of the Protestant ethic, when consumption and indulgence were proscribed, the present period has been characterized as sensate and "pleasure seeking." The modern period shows tendencies toward a religion of the body, and Tilgher describes it as an age of sport. A number of other writers have also focused on the increasing importance of leisure and the decline of the work ethic in the United States. Max Kaplan suggests that "we are in an age of leisure" (15). Herman Loether, in a study of attitudes toward the meaning of work, concludes that "the importance of the Protestant ethic has declined among American workers" (16). Robert Dubin concludes from his research that work is no longer a central life interest for most Americans (17). Terrence Carroll maintains that the "ideology of work" is dysfunctional in a society growing ever more affluent:

> There is no intrinsic virtue in work in and of itself; virtue is attached to it by individual attitudes that have been learned, and the fact that a great many individuals in our society share that attitude does not mean either that all people should share it, or that it is even a healthy attitude for all who do (18).

It is important to note, however, that a number of other writers believe that work is still accorded a very high value in our society. Peter Berger, for example, suggests that an ethical attitude toward work has persisted in America albeit in a worldly form: "The conception of vocation persists in a secularized form, maximally in the continued notion that work will provide the ultimate 'fulfillment' of the individual, and minimally in the expectation that, in some shape or form, work will have some meaning for him personally" (19).

Robert Blauner also points out the existence of a transmuted Protestant ethic in our present society:

> But work has significant positive meanings to persons who do not find overall satisfaction in their immediate job. A still viable consequence of the Protestant ethic in our society is that its work ethic (the notion of work as a calling, an obligation to one's family, society, and self-respect, if no longer to God), retains a powerful hold (20).

Sebastian DeGrazia also concludes that the importance of work shows no sign of disappearance, and that the habits of work and its prestige persist at the present time. As DeGrazia states, "The men who go to work in the morning and come home at night are still the pillars of society, and society is still their pillar of support" (21).

CONCLUSION

The working hypothesis of this paper was that the degree of legitimation and availability of the disabled role is directly related to the level of economic affluence and the cultural meanings attached to work. We have suggested that an institutionalized role for the disabled should be compatible with an affluent society under the condition that work is defined in an instrumental manner. We have also emphasized that the dominant definition of work has profound implications for the social and psychological situation of the disabled person.

It is important to point out that even if the link between employment and an adequate income could be severed by enactment of generous disability benefits, the life situation of the disabled would still be problematic because of the integrating functions provided by work. Although the societal level of affluence may eventually preclude the employment of every willing hand, it is likely that work will be sought because of its social and psychological consequences. As Nosow and Form have written,

> Work continues to be the driving force giving direction and meaning to contemporary living. While it is true that work satisfaction tends to decrease with level of occupational skill, work still occupies a central role in the lives of most people. The primary reason for this is that there is no other activity which provides as much social continuity to life as does work. Certainly leisure has not yet replaced work as a central organizing principle of life. It is work, not leisure, that gives status to the individual and his family (22).

It is somewhat ironical that the very time that our economic situation makes it possible to provide the dis-

abled with a decent standard of living, a countervailing trend emerges on the psychological level. Some observers believe that one of the distinguishing features of industrialized societies is the conscious expectation to derive meaning from work. "Whereas in earlier eras family, community, and religious activities were expected to give meaning to work, today we expect work to give meaning to other areas of life" (23). This position receives considerable support from a survey conducted by Morse and Weiss which showed that 80 percent of the employed men questioned would prefer to keep on working even if by some chance they inherited enough money to live on comfortably (24).

This line of reasoning suggests a need to develop alternatives to the work role such that the disabled will not be condemned to live on the periphery of society in a status that is socially and psychologically marginal. The discussion above concerning the latent functions of work suggests that it will not be easy to find an equivalent integrative force that work provides in an urban setting. A number of writers hold that recreation and consumption, the entire leisure sphere, could serve as a functional alternative to work. This is an important and optimistic hypothesis that truly deserves additional research.

In a related context, William Goode has raised the interesting question of whether society can or should reward equally those who are known to be less productive (25). His answer to this question deserves consideration in the context of our present discussion, despite its high level of idealism, simply because we seem to have so few other "practical" alternatives:

> On a different level of values, though we may feel the less able performer ought not to be given more rewards, some of us may also assert that the performances properly to be rewarded are not those of automobile protection and billboards, or even moon-rockets, but the far less easily measurable performances of warmth and loving, truth—note that the problem here is not one of ineptitude but simply a total lack of demand—beauty and taste, laughter, compassion, courage, generosity, or the support of variety in men and women (26).

REFERENCES

1. Talcott Parsons. 1958. Definitions of health and illness in the light of American values and social structure. In Patients, Physicians, and Illness, edited by E. Gartly Jaco. New York: Free Press, pp. 165—187.
2. Gerald Gordon. 1966. Role Theory and Illness. New Haven: College and University Press.
3. Eliot Freidson. 1961—1962. The sociology of medicine. Current Sociology 10(3): 129.
4. Eliot Freidson, n.d. Disability as social deviance. In Sociology and Rehabilitation, edited by Marvin Sussman. Washington: American Sociological Association, pp. 71—99.
5. Parsons, "Definitions of health and illness."
6. See, for example: Beatrice Wright. 1960. Physical Disability: A Psychological Approach. New York: Harper.
7. John Kenneth Galbraith. 1958. The Affluent Society. Boston: Houghton Mifflin Company, p. 197.
8. Ibid., p. 153.
9. David Riesman. 1964. Abundance for What? Garden City, New York: Doubleday and Company.
10. Ibid., p. 304.
11. C. Wright Mills. 1963. Power, Politics, and People. New York: Ballantine Books, p. 150.
12. For an extended analysis, see: Gerard Piel. 1961. Consumers of Abundance. Santa Barbara: Center for the Study of Democratic Institutions.
13. Terrence Carroll. 1965. The ideology of work. Journal of Rehabilitation 31(4): 26.
14. Adriano Tilgher. 1930. Work: What It Has Meant to Men Through the Ages. New York: Harcourt, Brace and Company.
15. Max Kaplan. 1960. Leisure in America. New York: John Wiley and Sons, p. 3.
16. Herman J. Loether. 1964. The meaning of work and adjustment to retirement. In Blue-Collar World, edited by Arthur Shostak and William Gomberg. Englewood Cliffs, New Jersey: Prentice-Hall, p. 521.
17. Robert Dubin. 1956. Industrial workers' world: A study of the "central life interests" of industrial workers. Social Problems 3(1): 131—142.
18. Carroll, "The ideology of work," p. 26.
19. Peter Berger. 1964. The Human Shape of Work. New York: The Macmillan Company, p. 221.
20. Robert Blauner. 1960. Work satisfaction in modern society. In Labor and Trade Unionism, edited by Walter Galenson and Seymour Lipset. New York: John Wiley and Sons, p. 353.
21. Sebastian DeGrazia. 1962. Of Time, Work, and Leisure. Garden City, New York: Doubleday and Company, p. 385.
22. Sigmund Nosow and William Form. 1962. Man, Work, and Society. New York: Basic Books, p. 11.

23. Ibid.

24. Nancy Morse and R. S. Weiss. 1955. The function and meaning of work and the job. American Sociological Review 20(2):191–198.

25. William J. Goode. 1967. The protection of the inept. American Sociological Review 32(1):5–19.

26. Ibid., p. 18.

46 What About Leisure?

Derek Lancaster-Gaye

Work is highly valued in most societies for most people: as a means of economic independence, as a status symbol, as a virtue in itself. Traditional concern to integrate persons with a disability into the work force has therefore continuing validity for many disabled. However, a single-minded concern for work to the neglect of other human values does not give full weight to the many possible dimensions of human life.

Rehabilitation Guidelines
for the Future

Leisure is one of those relative words that means different things to different people. To the vast majority it probably implies something that stands in marked contrast to their work. Leisure to the office worker might well be seen as a challenge with the elements; to the factory worker an opportunity to stay at home and create order our of the chaos of his garden. To the compilers of the Oxford Dictionary, leisure is seen as "an opportunity for time in which to do something."

Just how significant this is becomes evident when we think about leisure in terms of disability, no matter how slight, provided one's ability to enjoy change in some form or another or the opportunity to engage in some activity of one's choice is impaired or perhaps denied altogether. Unfortunately this impairment applies to the vast majority of disabled people, not so much because the disabled person does not have the capability but because he is either unaware of or we fail to provide the opportunities that he needs.

Of course this sounds all very trite, but is it? We live in a society that places increasing value on leisure time; we work hard to be allowed to do our own thing one or two days a week and in the evenings. And soon we shall be dealing with three days a week at leisure. In anticipation of this moment, which for some has already arrived, books are being written [as part of the system devised] to educate us how to use all this time we shall have. But if we believe the compilers of the Oxford Dictionary then we must accept that at least one section of the community already has all the time in the world but, alas, so often without the means or the opportunity that are so fundamental to leisure itself. That section is, of course, the severely disabled.

The fact that our life style is work-oriented has in some measure dictated the attitudes both of the disabled person himself and of those who have to care for him. Dignity and status are achieved through work and through accomplishment. A man is judged by others by what he achieves.

Reprinted from International Rehabilitation Review, 1973, 24(2): 6–11.

And so we have tended to transfer these attitudes to the life style of those who by reason of severe physical handicap have to live in a care situation. How valid this argument is and how realistic this approach is are matters of opinion. You either go along with the idea or you oppose it. If you accept the necessity for productive work in such a situation it is possible that you do not see the charade that must accompany the exercise to provide the "worker" with the feeling that his productivity is an essential part of the local community. And so frequently this productivity is related to simple repetitive procedures providing little if any stimulation to those of average intelligence.

Often we assume that the disabled person in care has the opportunity to take part in leisure pursuits and to choose which pursuits. In all probability we just don't think about it at all and if we do, we fail to recognize that there are opportunities provided only if we can educate the community at large and the disabled themselves. Leisure is not something that comes naturally; it is something we learn and without opportunity there is nothing to learn. In an essential "care" environment in which upwards of twenty handicapped adults live together, the individual has had little if any choice about who his fellows will be; friendships are dictated by necessity regardless of the intellectual compatibility of his co-residents. For the majority the opportunity to make those simple day to day decisions that we take for granted is usually not there, and the privacy of a single room or small sitting rooms that are fundamental to the non-institution are by and large still "privileges" rather than the norm in residential provision.

This environmental picture is further colored by the fact that economics dictate how many staff are available to provide care facilities and indeed by the existence of staff at all. It is almost inevitable that so long as we have two groups, those who are being cared for and those who are providing the care, the former will inevitably see themselves as inferior to some degree.

It is not surprising, therefore, that our attitudes and those of the disabled resident have done so little to progress leisure participation either on an individual basis or as a communal activity. And with so much time available, what a great pity it is that the vast possibilities for participation in limitless leisure pursuits are not more widely appreciated. This fact became very evident at the "Sports and Leisure Seminar" held this summer by the International Cerebral Palsy Society in Sweden, a seminar attended by delegates from as far afield as Europe, USA, Canada and Western Australia.

Naturally, we encounter man-made obstacles as well as man-contrived attitudes. How many more disabled people could bowl, golf, could attend concerts, meetings and community get-togethers if man had produced buildings without architectural barriers. But this is a story in itself; we are concerned here rather more with attitudes.

For many disabled people, with or without aspirations to the four minute mile, sport is a leisure and great strides appear to have been made in recent years to provide sport facilities for disabled people that will at least provide opportunities for effective competition. The Paraplegic Games of Stroke Mandeville have been emulated the world over. More recently, the Spastics Games started in England have spread to other European countries and 1974 is to see the first International Spastics Games in London.

What about the non-competitive sports? Horse riding, sailing, canoeing, swimming, climbing, camping—these are not new activities, yet lack of finance and lack of opportunity still seem to limit their popularity. Yet from the USA and England we have stories of gliding and sail planing. One young athetoid man recently qualified as a glider pilot and became a full member of a gliding club. No doubt, ability, a lot of guts and the financial backing helped, but more important the local gliding club was sufficiently realistic not to regard disability as an automatic disqualification. Of course, few severely disabled people will ever qualify as pilots, but the experiences and the thrills of gliding are still available to them through clubs with a little imagination.

Camping and the open-air life have gained in popularity during recent years and now we have an exchange bureau in London, one of whose functions is to introduce parties of disabled people to each other for exchange visits, often on the basis of a camping holiday. At least these provide opportunities to visit other countries and to make new friends; for many disabled people this may well be a first experience. But, again we seem to have the isolationist approach, an approach that presupposes that disabled; people have a great deal in common; enough in common not only to live together but to want to go away together. Whereas, in logic, it does not necessarily follow that disabled people have anything in common apart from the difficulties of being disabled.

And here is probably one of the most fundamental points about leisure in terms of severe disability. For the less disabled person living in the community, he is at least able to recognize and understand the leisure pursuits available whether he is the out-door enthusiast or the stay-at-home type. For him integration and opportunity go hand in hand with a little help from the community. But for the more severely disabled person living in a care situation, life is not quite like that. He is already dependent upon others charged with the responsibility of looking after him. The chances are he will have spent much of his life in such an environment and his leisure experiences will have been limited to this small community, his understanding and knowledge of leisure directly proportional to that of the staff who care for him. How then do we try to overcome these obvious limitations?

Sweden has an interesting experiment in which small "centres" are provided in the main urban areas; in these centres both disabled people from "care" situations and those living in the community meet with others trained in this area of activity to provide the necessary knowledge and experience so that the disabled person may himself decide just what is his thing and what is not. These visits offer opportunity to meet others with perhaps similar interests living outside the "institution." Opportunity is then a short step away given a little understanding by the disabled person himself and rather more by the staff with whom he is involved.

Leisure is not to be equated with a box of chocolates, a visit to the seaside and an evening's TV; as adults we grow out of that before we reach our teens. Perhaps it is because we do not always see handicapped adults as adults that these attitudes persist. Leisure is a serious business and we need to learn how to provide the opportunities and to teach the severely disabled person how to choose those opportunities that appeal to him most. Let there be no doubt at all—they have all the time in the world.

COURSES OF DANCING LESSONS FOR PHYSICALLY DISABLED YOUNG PEOPLE IN CZECHOSLOVAKIA

by Otto Knizek

Between November 1970 and April 1971, the Youth Chapter of the municipal Council of the Czech Association of Invalids Unions in cooperation with the Committee of Parents and Friends of Handicapped Children and Youth, of the Central Board of the Czech Union of Physically Disabled, organized a course of dancing lessons for physically disabled young people.

The weekly classes of three hours'

duration, were attended by fifty young men and women ranging in age from 15 to 36 years. In their course the students learned a number of dances, among others the waltz, polka, mazurka, blues, slow-fox, beat, tango, rhumba, swing-buggy, la bostela, cha-cha and shaker. It would pose no special problem to teach these dances to youngsters paralyzed in the upper part of the body only. But the classes were also frequented by those whose disabilities included various forms of post-cerebral palsy conditions and amputation of lower limbs, even by a boy who had lost both legs.

Yet all the participants learned the above-named dances, though sometimes with modifications authorized and introduced by the dance master, Mr. Josef Markvart. A former Czechoslovak representative in international dancing competitions, Mr. Markvart, member of the Czech Union of Dancing Masters, combined his practical experiences and pedagogical talent with a sensitive approach to each individual to make the learning of the dances accessible to all. By somewhat altering the more difficult steps and by teaching each dance in three versions according to the degree of disability, he succeeded in arousing in all his students, even those with impaired hearing and vision and one totally blind, an interest to learn every new dance to the best of their abilities and to improve on those already known. And what is more, he managed to create from a group of very diverse personalities a comradely team grateful for the opportunity of being able to acquire a new skill under professional guidance. For his part, Mr.

Markvart admits that these classes, his first attempt at work with handicapped youth, have given him more satisfaction than regular dancing lessons, for he, too, felt the friendly relationships that eventually came into being between his students, their parents and himself.

The dancing lessons attracted attention of many professionals. They were visited several times by MUDr. J. Kraus, neurologist of the rehabilitation centre of the Faculty Hospital in Prague, MUDr. Kraus was very explicit in praising not only the psychological and social aspects of the classes but also the direct rehabilitational effect they have, particularly on postcerebral palsy cases, many of whom he had treated as children. In his opinion, the dancing lessons represent a practical application of treatment by music and movement, which he himself employs and refines in his practice. Doc. MUDr. V. Janda CSc, the chief of the same rehabilitation centre, decided to watch some participants in his institute.

In autumn 1971 dancing classes for beginners were again opened at the same place and under the same conditions. Judging by the number of young people attending them, they are even more popular than they were last year. The event is attracting increased attention on the part of professional people who are beginning to follow it systematically, and on a social level. Their findings and conclusions are a valuable guide for the dancing master, and his present partner, a student nurse working in rehabilitation and taking courses in psychology.

Everyone directly or indirectly connected with this highly rewarding undertaking, hopes that dancing classes for physically handicapped youth will become a yearly event not only in Prague but also in other cities and towns. We would be delighted to share our existing experience with anyone interested in such a project.

SPORTS FOR THE HANDICAPPED IN INDONESIA

by P. Manurung

The Foundation for the Promotion of Sport for the Disabled in Indonesia was founded in 1962, following the success of several national sports demonstrations in conjunction with professional rehabilitation seminars. Originally formed under the auspices of the Professor Soeharso Rehabilitation Center in Solo, the Foundation is now under the direction of the handicapped themselves. It was felt sporting activity would be further effective as a medium of rehabilitation, if its implementation were the responsibility of the participants. On the occasion of each national sports activity, the working program, organization and general policy for the following period are determined. The most recent national meetings were attended by 400 participants from 11 regions of Indonesia, held July 29-August 4, 1972 in Bandung, West Java.

Organizationally, the Foundation has developed rapidly with 11 regional representatives in Central Java, Jogyakarta, Metropolitan Jakarta, East Java, West Java, North Sumatra, West Sumatra, South Sumatra, South Celebes, North Celebes and East Borneo. The

Foundation is also a member of the International Sports Organization for the Disabled, which has its headquarters in London.

The Foundation for the Promotion of Sports is interested in regional cooperation through the Association of South East Asian Nations (ASEAN), of which Thailand, Malaysia, Singapore, the Philippines and Indonesia are members. Initial contacts towards this end have been made and positive response is expected.

Each national sports meeting includes contests in badminton, handball, soccer, volley ball, table tennis, swimming, shooting, archery, bridge and skill in the use of prostheses. In addition to competing for locally contributed prizes, all teams strive to win the Doctor Soeharso Cup for the best overall performance. This cup was contributed by the late Dr. Soeharso, founder of the Solo Rehabilitation Center, and pioneer of rehabilitation in Indonesia.

Recognizing that sporting activities have proved a positive influence on overcoming the psychological handicaps of disability, the Foundation for the Promotion of Sports for the Disabled in Indonesia hopes to continue expansion and development of its programs.

HOLIDAYS FOR DISABLED CHILDREN IN THE GERMAN DEMOCRATIC REPUBLIC
by Prof. Dr. Karlheinz Renker

The organization of holidays for disabled children in the German Democratic Republic is carried out by district health departments and the district committees of the German Red Cross in cooperation with local rehabilitation centers, institutions and social services. In most cases, financing of holidays is the responsibility of the State Health Department.

Special holiday camps are available as follows:

(1) Each district organizes a holiday camp for physically handicapped children attending upper schools and schools for backward children, who, due to disability or the effects of long-term diseases, are not yet eligible for admission into the holiday camps of their schools. Generally, 100–140 pupils participate in a camp of this nature, enjoying a three-week stay. In addition to the above mentioned authorities, the rehabilitation commissions of the relevant health departments participate in this program.

(2) A central holiday camp is organized annually at Pepelow on the Baltic Sea by health or social institutions or by special schools which are not in a position to carry through holiday camps of their own, or, due to the wide range of the children's disabilities, can operate only local camps. Children who would most benefit from the hydrotherapeutical and climatic advantages of the seaside camp are given priority.

(3) A central holiday organization for pupils suffering from metabolic disorders is carried out in a home for diabetics in Garz (Isle of Rugen). The selection of pupils for this camp, which can accommodate 50–70 participants, is the responsibility of the diabetics council offices.

(4) Holidays are also organized by special schools in institutions of the health department and rehabilitation centers for vocational education. The institutions of the State Health Department are responsible for special medical-professional preparations, which are carried out in accordance with pedagogical tasks of the special schools.

It is felt that this recreation has strengthened the self-confidence of the disabled children involved and that these programs will in this way contribute to preparing them for their future positions in society.

PHAB, UNITED KINGDOM
by Wendy Francis

PHAB is a coined word, coined as a mis-spelt adjective when everything was "fab" amongst the younger set in Great Britain. It stands for Physically Handicapped/Able Bodied, which was a very new idea about 15 years ago. Now there are many clubs and movements in various countries with similar ideas of integration and the atmosphere provided by society is better able to nurture them.

PHAB is not *for* the disabled. The able bodied are not there to act as helpers; they are there for themselves.

Those running Youth Club holiday projects found an increasing number of severely handicapped youngsters were applying for places. They were accepted on their own merits and found to have an ability to participate in the course as well as offering something new in the way of understanding and tolerance, of perseverance and patience, which was quickly taken up by able-bodied young people.

Youth Club courses and, equally, PHAB courses, have grown in number and in range of subject matter each year. The courses are essentially times of learning to know and understand the many facets of society and of other people's backgrounds through sharing a week of living under conditions which are different for everyone—perhaps camping in an old country manor house or in a school empty for the vacations. At the same time, as with youth clubs in other countries, part of the time is spent on an activity or line of study not usually covered by a tighter school curriculum, such as: drama, stage craft, photography, film making, field work and nature craft, art in various forms, geology and history of the immediate vicinity, and sports and other reactions.

The essential point is that there can be equal participation as the numbers of physically handicapped and able-bodied young people are near enough equal not to give emphasis to either. Each young person learns a great deal more of the problems of others. Able-bodied children and physically handicapped children are very quick to accept each other and find a mutual meeting point.

This year there have been "junior" PHAB courses abroad, in France and Belgium; there have been many PHAB "holidays," including members from Wales and Northern Ireland combining to go to Eire; and the older PHAB group (ex "25") attended the International Edinburgh Arts Festival with participants also from Holland and France.

LEISURE TIME AND ACTIVITIES OF THE MENTALLY HANDICAPPED
by Constantina Safilios-Rothschild

The following points were emphasized at the Conference of Experts concerning "Leisure Time and Activities of the Mentally Handicapped," held in Cologne, Germany in November, 1972 by the International Catholic Child Bureau. Seventy specialists from 15 countries attended the Conference.

(1) Every human person, and, consequently, the mentally deficient person is called upon to develop his potentialities and to take part in the development of others.

(2) Leisure time and activities, insofar as they are a factor of self-expression and of social development are means of achieving this. Leisure activities are disinterested and therefore, they liberate; they foster relaxation, self-knowledge, knowledge of others; they integrate play, culture and festive celebration.

(3) It is, therefore, the mentally deficient person's right and duty, just as it is anyone else's, to engage in leisure activities and to have access to a state of leisure in which he will be able to find well-being and to become personally involved.

LEISURE AS MEANS OF INTEGRATION

"It seems that the only area of 'integration' that the institution of rehabilitation has universally endorsed is that into the occupational world; an integration that must be accomplished on the terms of the non-disabled . . . these terms are equal efficiency, speed, productivity and ability.

"However, occupational integration represents only one life sector, when a number of other sectors such as leisure, entertainment, social life, community life and marriage and the family are extremely important aspects of one's life. Integration in these areas has not advanced very far. Furthermore, most probably the advances will be slow unless the disabled themselves succeed in creating a genuine social movement and demand such integration.

"It is the integration of the disabled in such life sectors as social and community life, friendship and marriage that would entail the complete social acceptance of the disabled. Such an acceptance is hindered by the social and affective prejudice often held by the non-disabled. This prejudice is deep-rooted and potent and cannot be eradicated by legislation or educational programs. It requires a rather drastic change in the non-disabled person's value and emotional structure in such a way that they could accept the disabled as human beings with abilities and shortcomings, passions and weaknesses, virtues and faults."

47 Indices of Employer Prejudice toward Disabled Applicants

Thomas E. Rickard, H. C. Triandis, and C. H. Patterson

A scale to measure prejudice toward disabled applicants for employment, based upon the multi-factor stimuli method for Triandis, was developed. The scale was used with 2 samples, a group of 18 personnel directors and a group of 87 school administrators, who rated applicants for the position of accountant and 3rd grade school teacher. 6 types of disability, as well as absence of disability were included in the scale. All disabled groups were subject to expressed prejudice. The disabilities could be ranked in terms of the amount of prejudice expressed toward them. Competence and sociability were also influential in ratings, the former being more significant and complementary with disability. The method can be used to measure prejudice of various groups toward various disabilities in various settings.

It is generally accepted that unwarranted discriminations exist in the employment of the disabled (Federation Employment and Guidance Service, 1959; Jennings, 1951; Noland & Bakke, 1949; Schletzer, Dawis, England, & Lofquist, 1961). Since such discriminatory attitudes and practices are unwarranted in terms of the actual performance of the disabled (see, e.g., United States Department of Labor, 1948), they constitute prejudice. It was the purpose of this study to develop an instrument for measuring the extent of employer prejudice.

METHOD

Instrument

An assumption underlying the concept of prejudice toward the disabled is that where two persons apply for a job, and are equal in all characteristics except for the presence of a disability in one of them, the nondisabled person will be hired in preference to the disabled. In actual practice, such a situation seldom, if ever, exists. It is possible, however, to control or hold constant other variables than disability by the construction of a questionnaire or scale to which employers may respond.

The instrument is a modification of the questionnaire used by Triandis (1961) in a study of factors affecting employee selection in Greece and the

From an unpublished dissertation entitled "Indices of Employer Prejudice: An Analysis of Psychological Aspects of Prejudice Toward Disabled Workers," completed by the senior author at the University of Illinois for the PhD degree in the College of Education, January 1962.

United States and developed by Triandis and Triandis (1960) in a study of social distance. The essence of this approach is that it describes the stimulus persons in terms of a number of characteristics simultaneously, rather than by the use of one characteristic as does the Bogardus Social Distance scale. Results are thus less ambiguous, since a particular characteristic can be measured while holding constant other characteristics. In the present study the instrument was developed to include four characteristics: disability (deaf, confined to a wheelchair, epileptic, discharged from a mental institution, discharged from prison, discharged from a tuberculosis sanatorium, and with no physical defect), sex (male or female), competence (barely competent, highly competent), and sociability (sociable, unsociable). Utilizing these characteristics in all possible combinations, 56 stimulus items were constructed. For each disability (and for no physical defect) the items were as follows, using deafness as an example:

Deaf, male, highly competent, unsociable

Deaf, female, highly competent, unsociable

Deaf, male, barely competent, sociable

Deaf, female, barely competent, sociable

Deaf, male, highly competent, sociable

Deaf, female, highly competent, sociable

Deaf, male, barely competent, unsociable

Deaf, female, barely competent, unsociable

The 56 items were randomized and presented with instructions requiring the subject to indicate his feeling about hiring each subject by circling a number on a seven-point scale from "I would *strongly recommend*" to "Would *strongly oppose.*" Competence and sociability were defined. Judgments were to be made assuming a file on the applicant, but no personal interview.

This instrument may be used in relation to any job title. If the results are to be considered as relevant to prejudice, however, the position should be one which can be performed by persons with the disabilities included, that is, the disability is irrelevant to the performance of the position. The position of accountant was selected as one which would be common to a large number of work establishments, whose job requirements would be generally understood, and one which would also meet the requirement that it could be performed by a variety of disabled persons. The position of third grade teacher was used as a second position for one group of subjects to allow for a study of stability of rejection in positions with different requirements, and of stereotypes.

The instrument may be scored in a number of different ways. The primary interest in this study was employer prejudice, and therefore scores relevant to this were obtained. Two types of scores were obtained: prejudice scores of individual employers toward each disability, and prejudice scores for a group of employers. These are designated, respectively, as Index of Individual Employer Prejudice (IIEP) and Index of Group Employer Prejudice (IGEP). The individual scores for each disability are obtained by subtracting the sum of the eight ratings for a given disability (rejection score for the disability) from the sum of the ratings for the eight no physical disability items (rejection score for the nondisabled). The IGEP is the mean of the IIEP distribution for the group being studied. Both scores may thus be computed for any given disability and any given position.

Samples

Two widely different groups of potential employers of disabled persons were sampled. The first sample consisted of 32 personnel directors contacted by mail, of whom 25 returned the questionnaire, of which 18 were usable. The second sample consisted of 140 school administrators and potential administrators enrolled in classes in school administration at the University of Illinois, of whom 102 completed questionnaires, of which 87 were completed in full and were thus usable. The personnel directors completed the questionnaire only in regard to accountant, while the school administrators did so in regard to both accountant and third grade teacher.

Hypothesis

Employers, on the basis of preinterview knowledge, will reject disabled applicants more strongly than they will nondisabled; i.e., the Indexes of Employer Prejudice will be positive for all disabilities.
1. There will be differences among the six disabilities in the amount of employment prejudice expressed.

2. There will be some differences between the prejudice expressed toward the disabled who are being considered for the position of accountant and those who are being considered for the position of third grade teacher. Some disabled groups, such as the deaf, and the person in a wheelchair will experience more prejudice because of the relevance, or assumed relevance, of the disability to the job requirements. In other cases, such as the epileptic and the ex-prisoner, stereotypes are fixed, so that there will be little change of rejection with change of job title.
3. Competence, sex, and sociability, as well as disability, will affect employers' ratings.

RESULTS

Table 1 presents the Indexes of Group Employer Prejudice for both samples for accountant and for the school administrators for third grade teacher. The scores for each disability were significantly higher than the scores for the nondisabled for all three groups of comparisons ($p < .01$, one-tailed test) except for the difference between the tuberculous and the nondisabled for the personnel directors. The differences between the scores for accountant and teacher for the school administrator sample were significant ($p < .01$) for the deaf, the epileptic, and those in a wheelchair. In each case there was greater prejudice when the applicant was being considered for the position of teacher.

Table 2 shows the results of analyses of variance of the factors influencing the employment ratings of the

Table 1. Indices of group employer prejudice for samples of personnel directors and school administrators

| | Personnel directors* | | School administrators** | | | |
| | Accountant | | Accountant | | Third grade teacher | |
Disability	Mean	Variance	Mean	Variance	Mean	Variance
Epileptic	12.8	55.3	9.1	54.6	14.3	41.3
Prison	9.7	66.7	11.2	66.2	11.2	45.5
Mental hospital	9.0	66.7	8.5	55.4	11.1	45.9
Deaf	8.8	61.8	5.8	27.4	13.0	44.9
Wheelchair	7.4	61.2	3.7	21.5	7.9	36.4
Tuberculosis	2.8	15.8	3.3	17.0	4.9	22.9
Nondisabled	0.0		0.0		0.0	

*$N = 18$.
**$N = 87$.

personnel directors. The F for each disability is significant, indicating that disability was a significant factor in ratings. Ranking of the disabilities on the basis of the percentage of the total sum of squares attributable to disability yields the same order as that obtained from the IGEP scores. Competence was also significant in each case. Competence and disability are roughly complementary, that is, as the percentage of the total sum of squares due to disability increases, the percentage attributable to competence decreases.

DISCUSSION

The hypothesis that employers are prejudiced toward disabled applicants was supported. Disabled applicants were rejected more strongly than nondisabled applicants. The strength of the prejudice varies among the disabilities. Employers are more prejudiced toward the epileptic and persons dis-

charged from prison than toward the person discharged from a tuberculosis sanatorium. Persons discharged from a mental hospital, the deaf, and persons confined to a wheelchair fall in between. The results were similar for a sample of personnel directors and a sample of school administrators. The school administrators rejected the person discharged from a prison more strongly than the epileptic, but in general their prejudice appeared to be somewhat less than that of the personnel directors, except toward the tuberculous.

However, school administrators showed greater prejudice toward applicants for a position as third grade teacher than for applicants for a position of accountant, except in the case of persons discharged from a prison. The higher prejudice toward the deaf and persons in a wheelchair may be related to the relevance of the disability to the position. The greater prejudice toward the epileptic and the person discharged from a mental insti-

Table 2. Analyses of variance of factors influencing employment ratings of various disability groups by personnel directors

Source	Ex-tuberculars		Deaf		Wheelchair		Ex-mental patients		Epileptics		Prison parolees	
	SS	F	SS	F	SS	F	SS	F	SS	F	SS	F
Competence	50.5	405.4**	44.7	371.2**	43.5	357.1**	43.2	363.7**	35.6	316.0**	43.4	354.1**
Disability	.9	7.5**	7.4	61.3**	5.8	47.6**	7.6	64.3	17.3	153.8**	8.2	67.1**
Sex	.1	.5	.2	1.8	.1	1.2	.5	4.2*	.1	1.3	.3	2.4
Sociability	7.4	59.5**	6.0	50.09**	7.5	61.9**	7.1	60.1**	4.8	42.9**	5.4	44.1**
Interaction	3.1	2.3**	5.1	3.86**	6.0	4.5**	5.3	4.1**	7.9	6.4**	5.4	4.0**
Within cells	37.9		36.6		37.0		36.2		34.2		37.3	

Note. $N = 18$.
*$p < .05$.
**$p < .01$.

tution (the latter not significant, however) may indicate the presence of stereotypy in regard to these disabilities. However, to the extent that school administrators are concerned with the psychological adjustment of teachers the ratings of the ex-mental patients may not represent prejudice. The hypothesis that there would be differences between the prejudice expressed toward the disabled being considered for the position of accountant and those being considered for the position of third grade teacher, related to apparent relevance of the disability and stereotypes, thus tends to be supported. Hiring officers probably attempt to take into account the job requirements and the nature of the disability in making their decisions, although misinformation and stereotypy may still be present.

The hypothesis that competence, sex, and sociability would be significant factors in rating applicants was also supported, except for sex in the case of ex-tuberculars, persons confined to wheelchairs, the deaf, and epileptics. It appears that sex is not an important factor in qualifying for an accounting position for persons with these disabilities, while it is for persons who are prison parolees or ex-mental patients, with the females being at a disadvantage.

The F ratios for sociability were significant in all cases. It appears to be about as important as disability as indicated by the percentages of the total sums of squares in the case of persons in wheelchairs, the deaf, ex-mental patients, and parolees; and somewhat more important in the case

of the tuberculous and less important in the case of the epileptics. These latter two are the cases in which disability has the least and the greatest weight, respectively, as a factor in the hiring decision. It is probable that the importance of the sociability factor would vary with different positions.

In every case, however, competence exerted the greatest influence in the hiring decision, contributing from 35.6% (for epileptics) to 50.5% (for the ex-tuberculars) to the total sums of squares. While competence was thus the major consideration in the decisions made by the personnel directors, the other factors were also significant. It appears that where the influence attributed to the disability is high, the variance is taken primarily from competence and secondarily from sociability.

In this study all variables (characteristics) were held constant for each disability group as a whole. This method allowed us to compare the influence of disability variables on the employers' decisions. It is possible to design studies to evaluate the influence of the competence or sociability variable with the disability variable held constant. Under such conditions it is possible that we would find that an increase in the level of competence would offset the prejudicial effects of the disability. Such an investigation would experimentally examine a current dispute in the field of rehabilitation (Cruickshank, 1958, pp. 124–125; Patterson, 1962, p. 278). The present study demonstrates the importance of the competence factor in the employment of the disabled. It thus supports Patterson's idea that increased competence, perhaps obtained by so-called "overtraining," may compensate for the general prejudicial attitude of many employers toward the disabled applicant.

REFERENCES

Cruickshank, W. M. The exceptional child in the elementary and secondary schools. In W. M. Cruickshank and G. O. Johnson (Eds.), Education of exceptional children and youth. Englewood Cliffs, N. J.: Prentice-Hall, 1958.

Federation Employment and Guidance Service. Survey of employer's practices and policies in the hiring of physically impaired workers. New York: FEGC, 1959. (Mimeo)

Jennings, M. Twice handicapped. Occup. Psychol., 1951, 30, 176–181.

Noland, E. W., & Bakke, E. W. Workers wanted: A study of employers' hiring policies, preferences, and prac-

tices in New Haven and Charlotte. New York: Harper, 1949.

Patterson, C. H. Counseling and guidance in schools: A first course. New York: Harper, 1962.

Schletzer, Vera M., Dawis, R., England, G. W., & Lofquist, L. H. Attitudinal barriers to employment. In, Minnesota studies in vocational rehabilitation. No. 11. Minneapolis: Industrial Relations Center, 1961.

Triandis, H. C. Factors affecting employee selection in two cultures. In, Fourteenth International Congress of Applied Psychology. Copenhagen: Munksgaard, 1961. Pp. 223–224. (Abstract)

Triandis, H. C., & Triandis, Leigh M. Race, social class, religion, and nationality as determinants of social distance. J. Abnorm. Soc. Psychol., 1960, 61, 110–118.

United States Department of Labor. The performance of physically impaired workers in manufacturing industance. J. Abnorm. Soc. Psychol., States Government Printing Office, 1948.

48 Normalization and the Sheltered Workshop:

A Review and Proposals

Paul W. Power and
Robert R. Marinelli

The frame of reference from which many rehabilitation and helping services are provided is to create a controlling environment that will, hopefully, stabilize sickness or deviancy. This rehabilitation effort wishes to achieve the goal of stopping certain behaviors without instilling new, positive directions. Within this atmosphere and with these goals, new, healthy life-styles are not therapeutically created and nourished. These beliefs have been previously emphasized by Leitner and Drasgow (12), as well as by others (6, 13).

With less than normal expectations, in an environment provided by many sheltered workshops that is more in harmony with deviancy than normalcy, the handicapped are only being contained in their weakness. The entire so-called "therapeutic atmosphere" is not enabling people to grow from their strengths. Program results reflect the program itself. The rapid turnover of many clients, clients seeking a haven in the terminal workshop when there is measured capability for competitive employment, few competitive job placements—all bear evidence that, if our expectations in the workshop and in rehabilitation are considerably less than normal, we will achieve less than normal results.

Relevant to the necessity for a change in our rehabilitation philosophy are a renewed examination of the nature of work and a brief look at what workers think of their jobs. The *Occupational Outlook Quarterly* (23) reported that in a survey conducted by the Department of Labor, where a representative sample of the nation's labor force was interviewed, most workers were happy enough at what they were doing, and only 3 percent said they were not at all satisfied. The article explained that employee contentment depends on the inter-relationship of what a worker wants and what he gets. Almost three-quarters of those interviewed felt it was very important to be doing interesting work; 17 percent felt this was "somewhat" true and only 4 percent replied "not at all." About 85 percent of the workers said that opportunities to develop their special abilities was "very" to "somewhat" important. Yet only 70 percent could say such opportunities existed at all on their jobs.

Experience alone testifies to the discrepancy between the types of work found in a workshop setting and

Reprinted from Rehabilitation Literature, 1974, 35(3): 66–72.

in competitive industry. The dull, routine, monotonous type of work seems to be the backbone of the workshop setting. We cannot avoid monotony and routine in work. But does it mean that, because we feel that most of the handicapped can perform only such tasks, the potential for higher type tasks cannot be explored? Many a rehabilitation client has received a poor work rating, implying that he is unmotivated. Perhaps, through an extended time of monotonous work, he has become bored.

Hudson (11) writes that the actual meaning a worker derives from his occupation has decreased. He explains that, because the job a man performs has become further alienated from its resultant product, it has become meaningless; in former times the fact that a man could see the finished product of his efforts produced a significant satisfaction. We can thus surmise that for the average working man it becomes necessary to learn ways in which to cope with this dilemma and attempt to solve it.

For the handicapped and the disabled, such satisfaction becomes all the more important. Recovery of independence and self-functioning status becomes an extremely strong motivation in the lives of the disabled. It would seem that workshop training programs, with work as the main therapeutic tool, would attempt to develop pride and a desire for craftsmanship in those clients who are offered the opportunity. Unfortunately, the workshop may mirror the feeling that most handicapped and disabled are not capable of independence and self-functioning status.

Reflecting today's emphasis on mainly stopping and controlling deviancy, rather than creating environments for the building of positive, healthy behavior, is society's attitude toward deviancy. Wolfensberger (25) explains that handicapped persons are frequently perceived as deviant. Yet the attitude that we may see expressed toward a person with a certain deviancy may not really be specific to that deviancy at all. Such an attitude is very apt to be part of a more generalized attitude-complex about a group of deviancies, or perhaps about deviancy in the hardest sense. English (10) provided evidence that negative attitudes toward blindness were related to similar attitudes toward racial and ethnic minorities.

Wolfensberger (25) writes that when a person is perceived as deviant he is cast into a role that carries with it powerful expectancies. Strangely enough, these expectancies take hold not only of the mind of the perceiver, but also of the perceived person as well. Wolfensberger believes it is a well-established fact that a person's behavior tends to be profoundly affected by the role expectations that are placed upon him. Our experience only reinforces the truth that people will play the roles they have been assigned. Consequently, role-appropriate behavior, dictated by environmental events and circumstances, will often be interpreted to be a person's "natural" way of acting.

What happens, therefore, is that,

when the handicapped person is seen as different and sometimes offensive, he is separated from the mainstream of society and placed on its sidelines. The aged are placed in special homes, and many of the handicapped are told to go to a sheltered workshop, often located on the periphery of a respectable population center, and are supposedly rehabilitated in far from a normal situation.

The environment of the workshop today, the nature of work and its pervading unappealing aspects to the handicapped, the subhuman expectancies both in the disabled and in the mind of the perceiver—all have created a lack of growth in our rehabilitation efforts and, more importantly, have caused harm to the client. There is time for change; there is a necessity for change. To achieve this final goal of client change, change itself must be explored and a proposal presented as to how this can alleviate many problems accruing from the rehabilitation atmosphere.

THE WORKSHOP AS A REHABILITATION MEDIUM

Generally workshops want to provide a variety of services in order to meet a wide diversity of client needs. This wide variety provides, in turn, a complex pattern for an observer to understand. Though one can delineate a dominant service offered in the workshop setting, such as vocational evaluation, at the same time this service will display many different forms and shapes according to the facility staff, the "type" of clientele, the purpose of the facility, and the work offered. Yet, with this diversity one can still detect, from a brief examination of the available literature, certain problems that arise from the current rehabilitation approach of the sheltered workshop.

Wolinsky and Kase (26) write that the production function of the sheltered workshop is meant to be ancillary to the main theme of rehabilitation, but it has often dominated the scene. Production is seen by these writers as the prod that moves the workshop into the area of marketing its products. It is in marketing, the writers believe, that the rehabilitation agency is found crossing swords with the other participants in our economic movement. An agency, therefore, commits a disproportionate amount of its resources into marketing with little skill in this area. In competition, sale prices are reduced and because of this condition in the midst of the rehabilitation effort the alarm goes out, "We must get something, anything, into the workshop to keep the clients busy" (26, p. 41).

To accomplish this and to compensate for the price drop, the writers state that the client's wages may be reduced below their full production value. Because of cost and money crises, opportunities for client services within the workshop deteriorate. Even necessary improvements, improvements that could make a work station, for example, look similar to that found in competitive industry, are put aside. Old machinery is used. The client's opinion that he is in an "unreal" atmosphere is reinforced.

The director of a workshop does not have an easy job. Asfahl (3) believes that usually his job can be made easier than it is and difficulties avoided if effort is directed to establishing effective system management. These authors also believe that system management can be an effective tool, but only if used in a way that considers that many clients are or can be qualified to assume responsibility. Usually the staff takes over the management responsibilities and systematically orders the responsibility down to the foreman. But does such responsibility have to stop there? Generally it does, often because the client is lost in system management. Rusalem and Baxt (19) write that delivery of rehabilitation services and work involvement should be decentralized and returned to the people through procedures that guarantee professional freedom and the over-all participation of everyone concerned. Wendland (24) adds that present programs must be revised in order to accommodate persons who have a greater capacity for and need to expand their physical and emotional energies. His survey, in presenting views expressed by administrators from some of the larger rehabilitation centers, indicates that many potential client problems can be prevented by sharing and giving a greater degree of confidence to the handicapped worker.

A common occurrence in vocational rehabilitation is for handicapped persons to seek and obtain employment with other handicapped people.

Unfortunately, counselors often have no choice but to encourage such employment. This practice is defended by believing that the handicapped can spend their time profitably and productively and be rehabilitated by it. Yet Wolfensberger (25) writes that, when deviant individuals work for and with other deviant persons, or when deviant persons socialize intensively and perhaps exclusively with each other, it is almost inevitable that a climate or subculture is created that increases rather than reverses the deviancy of those within this climate or subculture.

He further suggests, moreover, that at a given time a person generally has the potential of forming a limited number of social ties and meaningful relationships. Thus, if deviant workers are surrounded by deviant workers, the chances for the workers to socialize with nondeviant persons are lowered. In fact, it is the author's experience that many workshops will hire only handicapped supervisors or foremen to work with handicapped workers. The possibility that deviancy could be enhanced in such a situation seems to be great.

The lack of achieving two of the important integrations in life, namely, the physical and social, constitutes one of the main limitations arising from the sheltered workshop environment. Placed in facilities that are removed, even geographically, from the mainstream of life, working in surroundings almost exclusively comprised of deviant people, it is no wonder that a subculture of the handicapped is maintained, a subculture that brings with it ridicule and subnormal role expectations. Olshansky (16) believes that for some clients the workshop may serve as a negative agent because it is to them a symbol of their failure and hopelessness. It is further seen as a stigmatized institution, much like prison or a mental hospital, and a continuing reminder of their defeat, ill fate, and plight. We can surmise safely, therefore, that the clients who perceive the shop in these terms are likely to be hurt by the workshop experience.

Though we are aware of the limitations, it does not mean that they cannot be overcome, or even eliminated. To achieve the latter would enhance the rehabilitation of the handicapped. Fortunately, some people in rehabilitation believe that it is necessary to introduce change. At the present time it appears that this change is in the form of a principle called *normalization,* a principle that can have far-reaching ramifications for all the handicapped.

NORMALIZATION

History and Meaning

Wolfensberger (25) writes that until about 1969 the term *normalization* had never been heard by most workers in human service areas. He explains that the concept of normalization owes its first promulgation to Bank-Mikkelsen (4), head of the Danish National Service for the Mentally Retarded, who phrased it in terms of his own field as follows: "to let the mentally retarded obtain an existence as close to the normal as possible" (25, p. 27).

A review of the literature indicates, however, that in the United States normalization, though not precisely referred to by this name, had been suggested as early as 1958. Beatrice Wright (27) set down a set of statements derived from a conference on psychology and rehabilitation, now known as the "Basic Dozen." The statement included such principles as: 1) every human being has an inalienable value and is worthy of respect for his own sake; 2) every person has membership in society and rehabilitation should cultivate his full acceptance; 3) the assets of the person should be emphasized, supported, and developed; 4) each person should assume as much initiative and participation as possible in the rehabilitation plan and its execution. Allen (1) writes that legal decisions enacted as early as 1966 were closely related to the principle of normalization.

These decisions (*Kent v. U.S., 383 U.S. 541, 1966; in re Gault, 387 U.S. 1, 1967*), which Allen feels may be termed the *principle of fairness,* require that in decision-making affecting one's life, liberty, or vital interests, the elements of due process will be observed. He adds that the principle of respect for the dignity and worth of the individual has been supported by legal decisions and suggests in his paper that, as reference had been made at several points to the principle of normalization, so it is important in the context of legal rights. The handicapped person, Allen explains, is to be accorded all the rights that any other citizens may enjoy, excepting only such rights as have been taken away lawfully, for good reasons, and under fair and appropriate procedures.

It was not until late in 1969, though, that the principle was systematically stated and elaborated in the literature by Nirje (15, p. 181), who was then executive director of the Swedish Association for Retarded Children. He phrased the principle as follows: "making available to the mentally retarded patterns and conditions of everyday life which are as close as possible to the norms and patterns of the mainstream of society." Wolfensberger (25) proposes, for purposes of a North American audience, and for broadest adaptability to human management in general, the following definition: "Utilization of means which are as culturally normative as possible, in order to establish and/or maintain personal behaviors and characteristics as culturally normative as possible."

From the latter definition it is apparent that as much as possible human management should be typical for our own culture and that a potentially deviant person should be enabled to emit behaviors and an appearance appropriate (normative) within that culture for persons of similar characteristics, such as age and sex. Wolfensberger's formulation implies both a process and a goal, suggesting that, in as many aspects of a person's functioning as possible, the human manager will aspire to elicit and maintain behaviors and appearances that come as close to being normative as circumstances and the person's behavioral

potential permit. Greatly stressed is the fact that some human management means will be preferable to others.

In attempting to translate this principle in action, we discover that it can have many dimensions and implications. Wolfensberger (25) believes that one dimension is concerned with the structure of interactions that involve deviant or potentially deviant persons directly, while another dimension is concerned with the way such people are interpreted to others. The dimensions themselves involve both the person and social systems. In the person area, according to Wolfensberger (25), the normalization principle would dictate "that we provide services which maximize the behavioral competence of a 'deviant' person." It would demand that a person should be taught, as much as it is feasible, to walk with a normal gait and to use normal, expressive behavior patterns. The social dimension implies that "we teach a person to exercise habitually those behaviors which elicit social judgment, even if they have little practical problem-solving value." These behaviors include such normative skills as grooming, dressing, walking, talking, and eating.

Nirje (14) explains that the normalization principle implies normalization of the total environment and of the activities, attitudes, and atmosphere surrounding the handicapped to such a degree that life in the open community will have become understandable to them. As a result the mentally subnormal, for example, will appear to the normal population less deviant, which in turn will lessen the pressures on the mentally subnormal and thus make him surer of himself. The application of the principle will not make the subnormal normal, but will make life conditions of the mentally subnormal normal as far as possible, bearing in mind the degree of his handicap, his competence, and maturity, as well as the need for training activities and availability of services.

Normalization further means that choices, wishes, and desires of the handicapped have to be respected and taken into consideration as much as possible. Isn't it true, for example, that many clients are only coming to a particular workshop because they are forced by the referring agency? This affects assessment, training, and possible placement. But through a personal involvement in the selection of a workshop, the choice process can be an opportunity for the client to gain some needed freedom and self-respect.

The Literature and Normalization

In reviewing the literature related to the normalization principle, it became obvious to these authors that most of its application has been directed toward the mentally retarded. As the principle originated from concerns over the poor treatment of the mentally retarded, the dominance of this particular implementation is not surprising. The literature strongly suggests, moreover, that the principle is today finding more of a home in the care and rehabilitation of the mentally retarded.

Ethel Temby (22) an Australian writer, has been urging the administrators of facilities in her country to grant equal rights to the mentally retarded, unless they show themselves incapable of using these rights. Quoting the International League of Societies for the Mentally Handicapped, which has interpreted rights spelled out in the United Nations Declaration of Human Rights, she has encouraged the institutions to believe that the needs of the mentally retarded and his independence must be respected by the community, if the mentally retarded are to live satisfactorily in one.

Shearer (20) responded to two local conferences in the Middle West which were exploring the normalization of the mentally retarded living in society in the light of Scandinavian ideas and experiences. She believes that the Swedish concept changes the manner of housing mental retardates to one of domiciling them in small, family-style dwellings near the center of towns, where they have a minimum of supervision and have added opportunities to work and live normally. Ames (2) reports on an Institute and Workshop in New York City that has developed a program enabling mentally handicapped young adults (16 years of age and over) to move from dependent to relatively independent living and employment. An adjustment center gives counseling and guidance in problem-solving and develops social, communication, and employment skills. The atmosphere of the Institute and Workshop is as normal as possible. A follow-up study of 100 clients indicated 20 percent made limited gain, 39 percent significant gain, and 39 percent achieved success.

Bridges (5) writes about centers operated by the Marbridge Foundation of Austin, Texas. Community living centers provide such services as housing, meals, job placement, social and recreational programs, and money management. A center should be attractive, near a main bus line to ease transportation problems, and have a capacity for 15 to 40 residents, while the clients must cooperate in housekeeping and in maintaining grounds, wear clean clothes, and launder and iron their own clothing. Clients are placed on a weekly budget with surplus earnings deposited for emergencies and savings. When a client has demonstrated the ability to spend money wisely, maintain a job, practice healthful living and accumulate savings, he may be discharged to assume a position of independent living within the community.

Shulman (21) conducted an interesting study, attempting to identify those variables that contribute to or may hinder the success of the youngsters at the Jewish Vocational Service in Chicago, in their efforts to become successfully functioning adults. The findings of his three-year study include: 1) A workshop rehabilitation program did not appear to accelerate the vocational development of experimental group subjects when compared to their control group counterparts. 2) The environment from which handicapped adolescents come is a major influence on their vocational development.

His conclusions reflect Collins' (7) statement that it is important to understand that each mentally retarded person is a human being first and only incidentally retarded. Olshansky (17) adds that a totally new approach should be undertaken to allow the mentally retarded person to prove himself as an individual rather than as a member of a special group. He feels that segregation of the mentally retarded should be minimized as much as possible and workshop assessment should emphasize situations that would encourage more effective responses.

Though much of the literature suggests that more attention has been given to the mentally retarded, the applications of normalization are also found today in other helping services. Normalization is implicit in much of the mental health movement. The attempts to "get the patient out of the hospital" and into the normal atmosphere of the community are but a ramification of normalization. The further attempts on the part of some sheltered workshops to pay a decent, living wage to their handicapped employees constitute another dimension of normalization. The attempts from the facility staff to raise their expectations of the disabled are still another aspect of normalization.

The studies and the literature reviewed either express the practical implications of the normalization principle or suggest possible effects if it would be used. The studies reviewed are more of the survey type, and to this date there have been no attempts to do an experimental study, comparing those disabled who have been exposed to normalization with those who have not. Such a study would provide us with more tangible evidence of the effects of normalization. Because the principle was really only implemented into facilities for the mentally retarded in the late Sixties, perhaps it is too early for a feasible follow-up research.

SUGGESTED IMPLEMENTATION OF NORMALIZATION INTO WORKSHOPS

Rose and Shay (18) wrote that the first thing to remember about a handicapped youth is that he is "more *like* his peers than unlike them." The same can be said of handicapped adults. It appears, however, that our efforts to rehabilitate these adults contradict this dictum. As has been shown previously in this article, if our rehabilitation frame of reference is deviancy, our restorative treatment efforts will be inhibited. It is our intention, though, to show how normalization, when implemented into the workshop setting, can alleviate many of the problems accruing today from the rehabilitation atmosphere of sheltered workshops.

Crowe (8) states that the times are exerting a great pressure upon the field of rehabilitation evaluation. The emphasis upon consumer involvement, the rights of the consumer, and the emphasis upon the client's "signing off" his own remediation plan illuminate the indicative that research in evaluation must be done from the perspective of the client's needs, rather than the needs of the professional or of the delivery system. It appears most appropriate, therefore, to begin any implementation with the client himself.

If the client is given more decision-making power, starting from giving him an opportunity to visit several workshops in his area and including his involvement in the choice of training within the workshop he selects, then the client's feelings of resentment and anger stemming from his work incapacity, dependency, and sense of failure could be minimized. Assessment and training, moreover, generally mean judgments from the professional. But observations from the client and an opportunity from him to express his feelings about what occurs during assessment can become just as important, especially when a decision is going to be made for more specific training.

Within the workshop it is also important that there should be a wide variety of work tasks that stimulate interest. Often what many workshops accomplish is only to establish that a person is capable of performing stupid and trivial tasks. Both allowing the client to rotate to various jobs, when feasible, until he decides on a job area that will prepare him for either "terminal" or competitive employment and giving him challenging tasks as part of his workshop experience would help the person to develop some good feelings about himself.

If the client's needs for both self-respect and the desire to lead as normal a work life as possible are placed into a more enlightened perspective, the purpose of workshop training will be brought into sharper focus and the exploration of job capability will be enhanced. This does not imply that the goals of the workshop are undermined when considering client needs. Too often workshop practitioners believe this is so. It actually becomes a question of priorities. As rehabilitation professionals, if we try to assist the client to a greater understanding of himself and provide steps toward giving him back some important self-worth, we will then achieve an appropriate balance between the aims of the respective workshop and the client's uniqueness.

To implement normalization effectively into the workshop presupposes changing the attitudes of the workshop staff. Regardless of the past performance of a client, if the workshop treats the individual with normal expectations, he might try to conform to working demands. A client often brings to the facility an unmotivated or nonconforming past, shaped by those who expected him to act differently. Expectancies can strongly influence behavior. If a workshop expects and accepts poor performance, clients will perform poorly.

In a workshop, of course, some clients will violate rules for a variety of reasons. Many will perform consistently below even minimum production expectations. Though the entire workshop concept can be implemented to be as normal as possible, still many will not be helped in such an atmosphere. One can consider behavior modification and implement certain principles of behavior change

without violating or limiting the normalization principle. It can be demonstrated that behavior is continually modified as a result of daily interaction with the environment. Both in structured learning situations and in everyday life, the principles of behavior modification are continually in operation. Olshansky (16) suggests that within the workshop, for example, positive reinforcement, in terms of pay increments, even on an increased piece-rate basis, might spark motivation. Time-out procedures for those who continually violate the shop rules could be used. He feels that, if one responds to violations by a handicapped worker as violations that won't be tolerated, the punishment could be appropriately painful without ever being humiliating. The punishment should be based on the capacity of the client to understand and benefit from his punishment, the status of the client within the shop, the nature of his disability, and his age.

In implementing the normalization principle, it becomes apparent that both attitudes and behaviors are considered. In normalization, attitudes should begin with the workshop staff, and these attitudes can be expressed in staff behavior. Staff behavior, moreover, can influence positively client performance. And normalization, in attempting to create more normal working conditions and raise staff expectations, is directed to changing behavior. When a person is accomplishing something in a normal atmosphere, usually the attitudes toward self, and hopefully toward the job, will change.

With pleasant working conditions and appropriate, normal expectations from the staff, the importance of pay is additional. Workshops have the notorious reputation for paying substandard wages. Yet these authors know of a workshop that, because it is doing production work necessary to meet the needs of the community, is able to receive federal and state grant money. This money enables the workshop to pay at least the minimum wage. In such a workshop the workers appear to have respect for themselves and are generally treated with respect by others on the workshop staff. Yet, if a workshop is not able to receive grant money, and, because of low production or falling consumer purchases, deems it impossible to pay the minimum wage, a system could be worked out where each worker is paid at least the minimum amount, for example, $1.25 an hour, and then allowed to earn over that minimum through piece rate. One workshop in Northern California follows this procedure, and it seems that more workers are entering competitive employment from this workshop, rather than looking at their workshop as refuge for their so-called deviancy. Other variables exist, of course, but a fair wage for a good day's work is certainly a strong incentive.

The location of a workshop is very important in eliminating many psychological factors of the handicapped in a workshop setting. Buildings can be symbols and, though used for service, can be an effective medium for public relations. Buildings should be located in a first-rate business building that is also used by nondisabled workers. It should be accessible to public transportation and the equipment and machinery used should not be obsolete. Community Workshops in Boston is just one illustration of how both a building and facilities can serve normalization goals.

Referring to a problem already mentioned in this article, namely, production competition, Wolinsky and Kase (26) suggest one way to alleviate this difficulty. Workshops feel that to survive they must strongly compete in the market place. This usually has negative results, affecting wages and even the growth of the facility. But there are ways to cope with this production mania. Rehabilitation and sheltered workshops as a whole are seen by Wolinsky and Kase as being a benefit to society as a whole. Society as represented by government should provide an incentive to the private sector of the economy through the provisions of a tax credit. This credit would be an incentive for the commercial world to use the workshop and its resources. With the plan proposed by Wolinsky and Kase, the workshop could maintain production and continue to offer a variety of suitable jobs to its employees, preparing them for more competitive employment.

CONCLUSIONS

Though the importance of the normalization principle may be obvious to many, roadblocks to enlightened care for the handicapped are still rooted in mass cultural attitudes reflected in traditional institutional regimes. Dybwad (9) believes that the prejudical attitude toward the handicapped in the professional community, the inadequate management and rigid administrative structure of institutions, and the inattention to appropriate client programing portray a dismal picture. Such a picture may suggest that the implementation of normalization into the sheltered workshop is in the indefinite future. Yet a review of the literature indicated that a change in sheltered workshop philosophy is necessary. It remains for administrators, rehabilitation counselors, and other rehabilitation professionals to become convinced that a change means needed growth for the client.

It has been mentioned that a totally new approach should be undertaken to allow the mentally retarded to prove himself as an individual rather than as a member of a special group. A new approach should be undertaken to allow all disabled persons to prove themselves as individuals. Perhaps in these days of limited funds for vocational rehabilitation, both the administrator and the rehabilitation counselor will once again become aware of the importance of accountability. What are the client's needs? How involved will he be in the decision of his own rehabilitation? As a transitional workshop is our shop really preparing him for competitive employment? Professionals will have to answer these questions. And in attempting to answer, perhaps change will be born.

LIST OF REFERENCES

1. Allen, Richard C. Legal Rights of the Disabled and Disadvantaged. Washington, D.C.: U.S. Govt. Print. Off., 1969 [SRS-117-1969]

2. Ames, Thomas-Robert. Independent Living for the Mentally Handicapped: A Program for Young Adults. Mental Hygiene. Oct., 1969. 53:4:641–642.

3. Asfahl, C. Ray. Sheltered Workshop Management. J. Rehab. Sept.-Oct., 1971. 37:5:17–19, 40.

4. Bank-Mikkelsen, Niels E. A Metropolitan Area in Denmark: Copenhagen, p. 227–254, in: U.S. President's Committee on Mental Retardation. Changing Patterns in Residential Services for the Mentally Retarded, edited by Robert B. Kugel and Wolf Wolfensberger. Washington, D.C.: U.S. Govt. Print. Off., 1969.

5. Bridges, J. E. Philosophy and Need for Community Living Centres Based on the Experience of the Marbridge Foundation. Deficience Mentale/Mental Retardation. 1970. 20:3: 8–11.

6. Clark, Ramsey. Crime in America: Its Nature, Causes, Control and Correction. New York: Simon and Shuster, 1970.

7. Collins, Dean T. General Principles of Training Programs for the Mentally Retarded, p. 241–248, in: Poser, Charles M., ed. Mental Retardation: Diagnosis and Treatment. New York: Harper and Row, 1969. Also in: Menolascino, Frank J., ed. Psychiatric Aspects of the Diagnosis and Treatment of Mental Retardation. Seattle, Wash.: Special Child Publications, 1971. (p. 371–378). Reprinted from: Modern Treatment. July, 1967. 4:4:827–834.

8. Crowe, S. The Vocational Evaluation Project. Washington, D.C.: National Rehabilitation Assn., 1973 (unpublished).

9. Dybwad, Gunnar. Roadblocks to Renewal Care, p. 552–574, in: Menolascino, Frank, ed. Psychiatric Approaches to Mental Retardation. New York: Basic Books, 1970.

10. English, R. William. Assessment, Modification and Stability of Atti-

tudes Toward Blindness. Psychological Aspects of Disability. July, 1971. 18:2:79–85.

11. Hudson, David W. Rehabilitation Philosophy and Middle-Class Values. J. Rehab. Sept.-Oct., 1972. 38:5: 34–35, 42.

12. Leitner, Lewis A., and Drasgow, James. Battling Recidivism. J. Rehab. July-Aug., 1972. 38:4:29–31.

13. Menninger, Karl. The Crime of Punishment. New York: Viking Pr., 1968.

14. Nirje, Brengt. Symposium on "Normalization": I. The Normalization Principle: Implications and Comments. J. Mental Subnormality (Birmingham, Eng.). Dec., 1970. 16:31, Pt. 2:62–70.

15. Nirje, Brengt. The Normalization Principle and Its Human Management Implications, p. 179–195, in: U.S. President's Committee on Mental Retardation. Changing Patterns in Residential Services for the Mentally Retarded, edited by Robert B. Kugel and Wolf Wolfensberger. Washington, D.C.: U.S. Govt. Print. Off., 1969.

16. Olshansky, Simon. Behavior Modification in a Workshop. Rehab. Lit. Sept., 1969. 30:9:263–268.

17. Olshansky, Simon. An Examination of Some Assumptions in the Vocational Rehabilitation of the Mentally Retarded. MR/Mental Retardation. Feb., 1969. 7:1:51–53.

18. Rose, Edward F., and Shay, Harold F. The School Unit Counselor, p. 336–350, in: Cull, John G., and Hardy, Richard E. Vocational Rehabilitation: Profession and Process. Springfield, Ill.: Charles C Thomas, 1972.

19. Rusalem, Herbert, and Baxt, Roland. The Delivery of Rehabilitation Services. Rehab. Record. Sept.–Oct., 1969. 10:5:22–26.

20. Shearer, Ann. We Want to See Their Faces. Parents Voice (London). 1971. 21:1:16–17.

21. Shulman, Lee S. The Vocational Development of Mentally Handicapped Adolescents: An Experimental and Longitudinal Study. Chicago, Ill.: Jewish Vocational Service, 1967. (Research Monograph No. 6)

22. Temby, Ethel. Rights of the Retarded. Australian Children Limited. Aug., 1970. 3:11:328–340.

23. U.S. Department of Labor. Occupational Outlook Quart. Winter, 1972.

24. Wendland, L. V. Integrating the Disadvantaged into the Residential Vocational Rehabilitation Center. Pittsburgh, Pa.: Research and Training Center in Vocational Rehabilitation, School of Education, University of Pittsburgh, 1970.

25. Wolfensberger, Wolf. The Principle of Normalization in Human Services. Downsview (Toronto) Can.: Natl. Inst. on Mental Retardation, 1972.

26. Wolinsky, Daniel, and Kase, Harold M. Human Resource Credit— A Product Marketing Aid to the Rehabilitation and Sheltered Workshop. J. Rehab. Jan.–Feb., 1973. 39:1:41–42.

27. Wright, Beatrice A. Psychology and Rehabilitation. Washington, D.C.: Am. Psychological Assn., 1959.

49 Exploring the Widening Circle:

Recent Developments in the Rehabilitation of Homebound Persons

Herbert Rusalem

When *Rehabilitation Literature* printed its first review of the literature on rehabilitation of homebound persons (Rusalem (45)), the outlook for this client group was doubtful, at best. With the exception of a few small islands of creative homebound rehabilitation activity, the United States was a vast wasteland of apathy and neglect. Hidden behind the walls of family residences, institutions, boarding houses, and hospitals, hundreds of thousands of persons, unable to leave their homes regularly with available resources to participate in community rehabilitation and employment activities, unwound the mainspring of their lives in desperate idleness and isolation. There was little in the 1967 social context to suggest that the years ahead would be any different. From that vantage point, nothing loomed on the horizon to suggest better days ahead.

Basing his conclusions on the content of 103 publications, Rusalem observed that:

1. A large majority of homebound people in the United States are not receiving adequate rehabilitation service. To some extent, this is due to important information gaps in our knowledge about homebound persons and their rehabilitation potential.

2. The psychosocial component in homeboundedness is one of the most vital and yet one of the most unexplored aspects of the problem.

3. The homebound condition can be likened to a narrowing circle in that isolation and neglect breed further isolation and neglect until inward-turning results in extensive personal and social disengagement.

4. Although homebound persons seem to be vulnerable to mental health problems, no data are available concerning the emotional status and needs of members of this group.

5. Progress in service to the homebound is most evident in the field of education where extensive and imaginative service programs using electronic and other aids have been developed in many parts of the nation.

6. A second area of marked progress

This paper was presented at the National Conference on the Rehabilitation of Homebound Persons held at Arden House, Harriman, N.Y., Feb. 19–21, 1971.

Reprinted from Rehabilitation Literature, 1971, 32(7): 194–207, 209.

is that for home care, in which health-related (but not necessarily psychosocial) services have achieved a gratifying level of acceptance and sophistication.

7. In the years just preceding the 1967 review of the literature, therapeutic recreation specialists had expressed a lively interest in the homebound and were developing innovative activity programs for them in institutions, rehabilitation centers, sheltered workshops, and long-term care facilities.

8. Although limited mainly to creative arts and crafts and industrial homework, vocational rehabilitation of the homebound had been demonstrated successfully by a small number of agencies. However, in 1967, a generalized spill-over into the total field had not yet occurred and such programs were the exception rather than the rule.

9. Group residence programs for the homebound had been under discussion for a number of years but organized attempts to demonstrate such facilities were very slow in developing.

10. From the viewpoint of the homebound client, existing services in most parts of the United States were unsatisfactory. The then current practice of whittling away at the problem through uncoordinated and partialistic local efforts seemed to hold limited promise for early alteration in the desperate situation of most homebound persons.

On the basis of his review, Rusalem offered the following recommendations in 1967.

1. One or more federally funded programmatic research projects designed to open the whole area of homebound rehabilitation to intensive investigation and experimentation should be initiated soon.

2. Research and demonstration projects in this area should move away from the traditional approaches to the problem into imaginative and innovative programing that tests new social arrangements and new rehabilitation techniques. Although crafts and industrial programs have merit and should be expanded, their usefulness is restricted to certain clients and locales.

3. An effort should be made to report homebound rehabilitation programs that have not yet been described in the literature. Many of these programs have pioneered exciting new methods but the heavy commitment of their staffs to service and their avoidance of reports and other forms of paper work have mitigated against wider dissemination of their experiences.

4. Although continuing concern should be maintained for the urban-based homebound person, research and demonstration are needed relative to other groups, including the rural, the institutionbound, the neighborhoodbound, and homebound persons with intellectual and emotional conditions.

5. Firm evidence is needed concerning the efficacy of remedial rehabilitation services for this group. Data confirming the extent of rehabilitation potential and response to rehabilitation service of this group will be useful in efforts to extend the national commitment to them.

As 1971 dawns, just three-and-a-half years after the publication of the first review of the literature on the rehabilitation of the homebound, one senses that the rehabilitation movement is abandoning its long-standing detachment from the homebound. Although this generalization is, in large part, a "gut reaction," some factual base does exist to substantiate it.

1. In 1968, two meetings on the homebound were scheduled for national conventions of professional organizations. One of these attracted 6 participants, the other 12. In September, 1970, a meeting on the homebound conducted at the annual convention of the National Rehabilitation Association in San Diego, Calif., attracted almost a hundred professional rehabilitation workers.

2. In 1967, even the most patient and persevering researcher would have found fewer than 10 references in the literature concerning the vocational rehabilitation of homebound persons. During the 1970 calendar year alone, three of the leading rehabilitation journals in the United States carried articles on this subject.

3. In the decade preceding 1967, perhaps one or two new rehabilitation programs for the homebound were launched. A little more than three years later, no less than 6 new programs for this group were started in various parts of the country in a single 12-month period.

4. Since 1967, federal grants have been awarded to the Federation of the Handicapped for its Programmatic Research Project for the Rehabilitation of the Homebound and to Abilities, Inc., and George Washington University for the development of new occupational opportunities for the homebound.

5. Practical rehabilitation workers are increasingly accepting of the concept that homebound persons can constitute feasible rehabilitation clients, despite the fact that rehabilitation, in general, is passing through a crisis period of reduced funding.

6. A growing number of general community agencies such as the Mount Carmel Guild, in Newark, N.J., are embarking upon service programs for the homebound in the belief that the problems of the members of this group are so complex and difficult that solutions may be found most readily in settings that have extensive mental health, family counseling, housing, welfare, and vocational resources.

7. A number of institutions for the aging, the chronically ill, and severely retarded have re-evaluated their programs and are adding rehabilitation components that improve institutional adjustment and promote re-entry into the community.

8. A rising tide of research materials is emerging from the field of special education and vocational rehabilitation. For example, in the former field, the Research and Demonstration Center for the Education of Handicapped Children at Teachers College, Columbia University, has just completed a status and attitude study of 116 graduates of a home instruction program. In rehabilitation, the Programmatic Research Project on the Rehabilitation of the Homebound of Federation of the Handicapped (supported, in part, by a grant from the Social and Rehabilita-

tion Service) is finishing an extensive survey of the rehabilitation experiences of homebound clients at a state vocational rehabilitation agency.

9. A series of special conferences concerning the homebound will be conducted in 1971. With grant funds provided by the Rehabilitation Services Administration and the Social and Rehabilitation Service, the Federation of the Handicapped held a National Conference on the Rehabilitation of Homebound Persons at Arden House, Harriman, N.Y., in February, 1971, to be followed by five regional conferences in various sections of the United States to disseminate current findings about the rehabilitation potential of the homebound.

The remarkably quickened pace in service and research for the homebound should be attributed in large part to the forward-looking and courageous posture adopted by the U.S. Social and Rehabilitation Service and the Rehabilitation Services Administration for their sponsorship of the Programmatic Research Project and other programs for the homebound. Although the work of these agencies constitutes a "great leap forward," the present status of the field should be regarded only as an early stage in an evolutionary process. The decade of the 70's could well be the decade of the homebound. Perhaps, when the rehabilitation history of 1970–1980 is written, the homebound will have ceased to be one of the most disadvantaged groups in American life. If that is to come to pass, it will be important for rehabilitation planners, practitioners, and researchers to be up

to date concerning the current status of this group. Such information could well provide a baseline for further action on behalf of the homebound. This review of recent literature and observations (1967–1970) may contribute to this baseline and stimulate further thinking about homebound persons in America.

REHABILITATION POTENTIAL

The most cogent data concerning the rehabilitation potential of homebound persons has been derived from the day-to-day experience of rehabilitation agencies and institutions serving this group. During the middle and late 1960's not only did new programs for the rehabilitation of homebound persons emerge, but older ones such as those conducted by the New York State Office of Vocational Rehabilitation, the Wisconsin Division of Vocational Rehabilitation, and the Federation of the Handicapped enlarged and extended their services. In view of the economic and social pressures under which such agencies functioned during this period, one can only conclude that their continued involvement in homebound programs was justified by the rehabilitation therefrom.

Specific findings concerning rehabilitation potential among the homebound still are rare. However, a growing literature suggests that limited mobility constitutes only one component in defining the rehabilitation potential of this group. For example, Hoyt (23) found that 42 percent of the homebound persons on a home care caseload ambulated without assistance, suggesting that psychosocial factors should be considered in determining the rehabilitation potential parameters of homebound persons. Similarly, Nash (34) reported that 22 percent of the patients in an institution for long-term chronic care were potential candidates for community living with the aid of local health care services. However, most of this rehabilitation potential remained undeveloped because 90 percent of these high rehabilitation potential patients did not have community homes to which they could return or were rejected by their families. In these cases, the social factors contributing to homeboundedness were as important as health in determining the degree of realization of rehabilitation potential.

In conjunction with the Programmatic Research Project on the Rehabilitation of the Homebound, a five-year project sponsored by Federation of the Handicapped, New York, with a grant from the Social and Rehabilitation Service, a long-term study was made of four subsamples of homebound persons: 1) those who were accepted by a state rehabilitation agency, 2) those who could not or did not use the services of a state rehabilitation agency constructively, 3) residents of long-term care institutions, and 4) graduates of high school home instruction. In reviewing the multidisciplinary diagnostic team findings for this group in the first three Project Progress Reports, Rusalem and Cohen (unpublished) noted the following:

1. More than 90 percent of the community-based and more than 60 percent of the institutionalized home-bound persons participating in this Project retained sufficient physical capacity to engage in some form of employment.

2. More than half of these homebound persons had a need for early mental health interventions, especially supportive or group, as opposed to depth, therapy.

3. Prolonged experience as a homebound person or as a resident of an institution tends to depress intellectual level.

4. Most of these homebound persons were characterized by limited manual dexterity. For example, 45 percent had such severe restrictions in this area that they could not take standard manual dexterity tests.

5. Among community-based homebound clients, only 12 percent were unsuitable for any type of employment activity. The comparable percentage for institutionalized home bound persons was 32 percent.

6. Disrupted and unstable family situations were found in the current relationship patterns of 43 percent of the community-based sample and 65 percent of the institution-based sample.

7. Financial distress prevailed in all the samples of the homebound group with 62 percent of the community-based sample and 100 percent of the institution-based group being recipients of welfare and/or social security disability benefits.

8. Homebound persons, as a group, have almost limitless unobligated time that is filled by sedentary activities such as television, reading, conversation, and ruminating about the past. Prolonged isolation had impoverished

the interest life of these people to such a degree that interest in external matters was, in some cases, minimal.

Some of the conclusions reached by Rusalem and Cohen concerning rehabilitation potential have important implications for rehabilitation programing, including:

1. Both physical and emotional factors lock the homebound person into his unsatisfactory social and vocational situation.

2. Much homeboundedness can be reversed or even eliminated through providing adequate rehabilitation services.

3. Because homebound persons have such pervasive and complex life problems, rehabilitation programs devised for them should be intensive, comprehensive, and of long duration.

4. Specialized rehabilitation programs are needed for specific subgroups of homebound persons, including residents of long-term care institutions, the blind, the mentally retarded, graduates of high school home instruction, and people who fail to meet competency criteria established by state rehabilitation agencies.

5. Despite very severe limitations, most of these homebound persons made constructive use of the diagnostic services offered to them, revealing, in their readiness to undergo such procedures, a determination to change their life conditions even though earlier attempts to do so had met with rebuffs and disappointments.

Though the literature about rehabilitation potential of the homebound is fragmentary, it is consistent. Whenever organized rehabilitation programs have been designed expressly for this group, these programs have included a diagnostic phase that invariably has revealed substantial rehabilitation potential. These data suggest that the paucity of suitable programs for homebound clients results from factors other than the severity of the disability since, despite their great limitations, most homebound clients retain significant capacities.

Home Care

Even as older rehabilitation services for homebound persons developed at a moderate pace during the 1960's, the provision of health services to homebound persons in their own residences flourished. Home care has taken its place in the health delivery system of the United States as a peer of traditional clinical medicine and nursing, group practice, and prepaid medical plans. The growth of this field is revealed by the fact that Edwards (14) was able to fill page after page of a bibliographical work with references dating from 1960 to 1967 concerning such aspects of home care as coordinated home services, homemaking, home health aides, meals-on-wheels, and home dental care.

The values of home care are so obvious as to be almost self-evident. However, the recent literature has stressed two benefits: 1) home care results in better utilization of other health facilities by those who really need them; in this instance, it is noted that home care services shorten or eliminate hospital stays, thus freeing precious bed-space for more critical uses (2, 26), and 2) the quality of total medical care is improved by the addition of a home care component (Nisbet and coworkers (40) among many others). Not only do professional health and welfare workers recognize the values of home care but patients themselves see the logic and worth of such services almost as readily. Thus, in Cleveland, only 9 percent of hospital patients who were offered this service declined it (1). Furthermore, home care is adaptable to a variety of environments, including urban (5, 49) and rural areas (30, 42).

In accordance with the common belief that comprehensive and coordinated programs are superior to partialistic ones (44, 60), efforts have been made by individual disciplines to spell out their roles on the home care front. For example, one guideline for assigning nurses to individual cases was suggested by Holliday (22) in a study that revealed that practical nurses in health care favored work with elderly chronically ill patients while registered nurses preferred to serve chronically ill children. Other home care components that have been examined in detail include occupational therapy (32), medicine (31), and dietetics and nutrition (9).

The dramatic growth of home care and its components is suggested by statistics presented by Ryder and others (48), which indicated that the number of home health agencies in the United States increased from 1,356 in 1965–1966 to 2,184 in early 1969.

Much of this growth was attributed to the influence of Medicare. A total of 53.5 percent of these agencies offered one service in addition to nursing; 26.6 percent offered two additional services; 9.5 percent provided three additional services; and 10.4 percent provided four or more additional services. The proportion of agencies providing the various additional services was: physical therapy, 72.7 percent; home health aide service, 48.2 percent; speech therapy, 22.1 percent; medical social service, 20.0 percent; nutrition guidance, 18.2 percent; and occupational therapy, 16.3 percent. These findings suggest that the coordinated multidisciplinary ideal of providing homebound persons with all varieties of help they need is not yet realized in most communities in this country.

The success of home care programs depends heavily upon the participation of physicians in the service. In one study in Eastern Pennsylvania, Mather and Hobaugh (31) found that 48 out of 83 local physicians interviewed had used the home care program. Ninety percent of these physicians indicated that they were ready to use it again if the need arose in their practice. These "high-use" physicians were characterized as practitioners who had broad professional interests. However, it should be noted that 75 percent of the 35 nonusers reported that they would refer patients to the service when the need arose. Although physicians are using the service increasingly, it is still not clear whether most of them use home care to the extent that their patients really need it.

Other trends in home care reported in the literature are:

1. Greater success in reaching minority and disadvantaged group members (6).

2. A move toward individualized planning of combinations of home care components rather than the imposition of "standard" programs on patients (24).

3. A tendency to create specialized programs for defined disability groups such as arthritics and the aging (8, 56).

4. A far more extensive use of trained health care aides (7, 20, 21, 25, 38, 55).

5. A growing interest in research with suggestions that the following areas require further investigation: the values and limitations of various delivery systems in the home health care field, criteria for the selection of patients, a classification system for patients' needs, and cost studies (27).

This brief sampling of the extensive recent literature on home health care programs indicates that this is one of the most vigorous and dynamic aspects of the rehabilitation of the homebound. The phenomenal growth of the 1960's may well be matched by developments in the 1970's with special reference to areas into which home health care is only now penetrating. These include:

1. Conversion of a growing number of existing programs into comprehensive and coordinated multidisciplinary efforts.

2. Incorporation of psychosocial services into more programs.

3. Integration of home health care with vocational rehabilitation, a practice that is, indeed, rare at this date.

4. Reorientation of present service delivery systems to lessen the influence of physicians who for unwarranted reasons delay or avoid referring suitable patients for home care services.

As this writer sees it, the challenge to home care is to substitute rehabilitation for mere maintenance in many instances. Perhaps this redirection of effort can be hastened by changing the name of the field to home rehabilitation and incorporating within its boundaries a broader range of disciplines. Current studies suggest that psychosocial and vocational problems loom large in the life of the homebound person. Fragmentation of service into home health care and home rehabilitation does not seem to fulfill the total care objective. The time is probably right for the behavioral scientists to penetrate the home care field and for home care workers to become increasingly sensitive to, and capable of coping with, psychosocial problems in their caseloads.

HOMEMAKING

Homemaking services often facilitate the rehabilitation of homebound persons, enabling them to improve the home ecology in which they live and freeing them from home tasks incompatible with their capacities. In general, homemaking services have shown a dramatic growth in the United States. The National Council for Homemaker Services (35) reported an increase of 150 percent in the number of homemaker programs in the United States during the period 1963 to 1967. The dimensions of the movement are suggested by the fact that a 1967 directory reported more than 800 different agencies participating in homemaker service (35). The degree of need for homemaking may be noted from the findings of a study conducted in Contra Costa, Calif. (25), which indicated that 63.9 percent of a sample of medical assistance welfare clients required some form of domestic service as their primary need with the remainder requiring home health aide service.

From the point of view of special education, strong evidence has been presented that supports the value of homemaking service delivered to families of retarded children under the age of 5 years (3, 36, 43). The observed effects include strengthening of family ties, improvement of attitudes toward the retarded child, and wider family use of community resources.

Although few instances have been reported of coordinated efforts among home care, homemaking, special education, and rehabilitation programs, these are still the exception rather than the rule. In all too many instances, homemaking services are being used exclusively as a form of crisis intervention or family maintenance plan. It is now well established that homemaker services have important roles to play in this domain. However, much less is known about their potential for contributing to individual and family rehabilitation. Needed are well-evaluated demonstrations that test the contributions homemaker services can make to total rehabilitation and the types of clients and home environments in which they achieve their foremost success.

SPECIAL SERVICES

A sparse literature belies the degree of activity that has been under way on behalf of homebound persons in several crucial fields. Thus, quietly and methodically, the advocates of the elimination of architectural barriers have extended their influence to such a degree that many new public and private buildings now are designed with particular reference to their accessibility to the severely disabled. Concurrently, a number of colleges and universities and other public institutions have taken pains to eliminate existing barriers so that their doors can open wider to the homebound.

Less has been accomplished relative to the reduction of barriers in private apartments and homes in which homebound persons reside. Unless private funds become available for modifying these local environments, the homebound person is left with two choices: 1) to move to another, less encumbered environment, a procedure that may be difficult in some areas due to housing shortages, or 2) to make the best of the current nonfunction setting, a choice that mitigates against rehabilitation. The challenge for the 1970's will be to find ways of providing suitable residential settings for the homebound that will facilitate movement toward independence.

Although evaluative reports have not yet emerged, one promising recent development is the creation of special group environments for the homebound. Such environments avoid the pitfalls of regimented institutionalization and yet provide employment opportunities, recreation, supportive medical and home care, mental health, counseling, and educational opportunities either on premises or nearby. Philosophically, such projects are discomforting to rehabilitation workers who react against so-called segregation of the disabled. However, the care and feeding of professional philosophies may be less relevant in this situation than the degree to which these special rehabilitation ecologies promote the rehabilitation and happiness of severely disabled persons. It seems logical that, when an institution or an undesirable home situation is the alternative, the special residence environment may have much to recommend it. Final judgment, however, will have to await dispassionate evaluations of the values and limitations of this approach. As yet, the literature offers virtually no clues as to the specific benefits and drawbacks of such residences.

The lack of adequate transportation probably constitutes the single most important barrier to rehabilitation among the homebound. Throughout the United States, state and local groups are grappling with this excruciatingly difficult problem, but their progress is slow, indeed. The very paucity of literature on the subject tends to confirm the generalization that advances in this area are coming at a slow pace. Whenever a breakthrough occurs in rehabilitation, it is accompanied by a rising tide of publications dealing with it. This certainly is not yet the case with transportation. However, if current interest levels are maintained, if sufficient funds are made available, and if electronic and other technical innovations are plugged into the problem, the rate of progress may be accelerated. Current interest seems to be focusing upon the use of new types of vehicles, coordinated community-wide transportation systems, and the development of service "satellites" that bring the program closer to the homebound person. In time, reports of experiments in these and other transportation areas may herald a revolution in service to the homebound. Currently, unfortunately, the dominant feeling in relation to transportation is realistic frustration.

If a breakthrough has occurred in this field in recent years, it is in the use of trained nonprofessional aides to bring services to homebound persons. Although a number of agencies are currently experimenting with similar programs, the PATH (Personal Aides to the Homebound Program) of the Federation of the Handicapped is probably the leading prototype of the genre. Devised by Milton Cohen and Herbert Rusalem, it has been supported well beyond the initial demonstration phase by the New York City Human Resources Administration and the U.S. Office of Economic Opportunity (15).

The essential feature of the Program is the training and employment of aged persons to visit homebound persons in their homes, performing rehabilitation aide functions such as motivating them toward rehabilitation, establishing semiprofessional relationships that give the homebound person security during the early phases of rehabilitation, coordinating neighborhood resources, providing a liaison with the world outside the home, referring the homebound client to the professional team when rehabilitation readiness has been achieved, and assisting the homebound person to explore and develop his capacities prior to entering a formal rehabilitation process. Between January 1, 1966, and June 30, 1969, 173 aides (compensated at well above the minimum wage for their services) assisted more than 1,000 homebound persons to come closer to a rehabilitation threshold.

Less rehabilitative in nature is a program of volunteer friendly visiting developed by the New Jersey State Department of Health (13). This experience indicated that such a program can be conducted on a county basis but data are not yet available that indicate the impact of the program upon the client. The emphasis of this program is suggested by the terminology used in the title of Duffy's article: "Volunteer Friendly Visitors Bring Sunshine to Shut-ins."

In the concentration of recent years upon bringing medical services to homebound persons, there has been some neglect of dental problems within this group. However, progress is being made. Reporting on an experience in Cuyahoga (Cleveland) County, Ohio, Waldman and Stein (59) described procedures for delivering den-

tal services to severely disabled persons in private residences, nursing homes, and outpatient clinics. As they see it, the key is coordination of community resources, including dentists, dental students, and auxiliary students. The whole spectrum of dental services to the homebound and chronically ill was reviewed by the Workshop on Community Action to Promote the Oral Health of the Chronically Ill, Handicapped, and Aged conducted at the University of Michigan (57). This Workshop confirmed the feasibility of offering dental services to homebound persons and suggested that a variety of local models could be used depending upon community resources and conditions.

One of the central concerns of the homebound person who lives alone is that of communicating with the outside world in emergencies. The American solution to the problem has been twofold: 1) arranging for a person in the community to call periodically at the residence of the homebound person, and 2) to have a central facility or a designated person telephone the homebound once or twice a day. These procedures give a degree of security to the homebound although they are by no means infallible. In areas where the telephone is less ubiquitous or where it is financially unfeasible, other devices may be useful. Some of these approaches have been tried with success in Great Britain (37), including window cards, lights, bells, and buzzers. It is recommended that those who serve the homebound should draw upon a large repertoire of "warning" devices so that individual needs and local conditions can be taken into account in selecting the protective scheme that is most functional in a particular situation.

The delivery of religious services to homebound persons has received scant attention in the literature. It has been taken for granted that the local clergyman will visit the homebound person regularly and that radio and television services as well as religious reading matter will be available to him. Yet, the spiritual needs of homebound persons may require additional provisions. In one attempt to satisfy this need, the United Methodist Church (17) conducted a conference at Duke University in 1965 at which a program for the homebound, especially the aged, was developed. An essential aspect of the program concerned special resources, including books, magazines, and films that can be used with homebound persons as well as techniques for delivering the spiritual service to them. Other faiths we hope will recognize their obligations to the homebound in the future and devise innovative means for reaching them.

The special services noted above are not peripheral. On the contrary, such services as transportation, the removal of architectural barriers, and nonprofessional rehabilitation aides can make a vast difference in the lives of homebound persons, contributing to the total process of converting them into community participants. Other services such as dentistry can play key roles in health maintenance. Still others, like religion and warning aids, can be instrumental in sustaining the homebound person in the community rather than in an institution. Although progress is being made in all of these domains, there is little evidence of a well-mounted attack on the problems to which they address themselves. One of the recommendations of this paper will concern a means for launching a coordinated offensive against the physical restraints, lack of transportation, and inaccessibility of these and other services.

EDUCATION

Traditionally, home instruction has been the behavioral science area in which the greatest progress in service to the homebound has occurred. The recent past is no exception. On the local level, increased selectivity in assignment of children to home instruction, the development of differentiated programs for homebound emotionally and behaviorally impaired children, the modification of school and transportation facilities reducing the need for home instruction for some physically limited children, and the wider use of electronic devices have all contributed to the maturation of this field. Updating an earlier study by Simches and Cicenia (50), Best reported on current state administrative practices relating to the homebound in 47 states (4). This study concluded that telephone teaching was receiving increasing recognition and that home instruction services for the socially and emotionally handicapped were still in a state of flux, with questions being raised about their applicability to children who do not have severe physical limitations.

Conventional home instruction programs have been reported in a wide variety of communities (18, 33, 41, 53). These program descriptions suggest a one-to-one teacher-student relationship in a home environment to be highly flexible in that it can be adapted to a variety of community and family situations without losing its effectiveness. Furthermore, they reflect the unique quality of the relationship between the homebound student and his teacher and suggest that this, indeed, may be a central factor in determining the success of home instruction programs despite the relatively small number of hours devoted to actual teaching. Finally, these program descriptions indicate that home instruction is equally useful when applied to children who have short-term disabilities, those who will remain on home instruction for more extended periods, and those for whom it will be terminal experience.

The special nature of the home instruction transaction among students, teachers, educational systems, and parents is sharply delineated by Connor (10) in her definitive volume on the homebound and hospitalized child. It is apparent from Connor's work that the home teacher cannot be merely a retread. On the contrary, the home teacher should be a person eminently qualified by personality to work on a one-to-one basis with severely limited children in the restricted home environment, capable of using imagination and creativity to devise substitutes for classroom experiences. In a similar vein, Wolinsky (61) suggested that the role and preparation of home teachers should be re-examined with a view to reconstructing the system on a broadened educational base. This re-examination should be conducted in such areas as teacher preparation patterns, the degree of educationally relevant exclusion that has occurred in the child's life, and current certification and licensing practices for home instruction teachers. Included in Wolinsky's concern for the quality of teaching in home instruction is her recommendation that consideration should be given to the nature of continuing education for such teachers.

The field of home instruction is turning increasingly toward a fuller use of available electronic equipment. Although educational tape recordings hold promise (62), the emphasis seems to be moving in the direction of home-to-school and conference telephone hook-ups. While some growth in the home-to-school telephone system is reported in the literature, the costs of such a system seem to deter its rapid acceptance for homebound children in some communities. On the other hand, two of the largest educational systems in the United States—Los Angeles and New York City—have ventured into two-way conference telephone hook-ups with apparently gratifying results. New York City (unpublished report of a Title VI Project) has been extending the scope of its program year after year and, now, after a successful experience in the teaching of foreign languages and science (as well as the other traditional subjects) through conference telephone, is moving into group guidance.

Los Angeles developed the prototype large-city conference telephone system, which has long since passed out of the experimental stage into full-scale operation on a routine basis. Curnow (12) noted that during the 1964–1965 school year 338 homebound pupils were taught by 24 teleclass teachers (16 at the secondary and 8 at the elementary level). Nineteen of these pupils participated in teleclass for the entire school year. The growth of this program and its widening application to homebound children in Los Angeles confirms its special value in providing a group educational experience to children at all educational levels. However, it should be noted that the use of electronic devices such as teleclass, home-to-school telephone, and tape recordings do not eliminate the need for a one-to-one teacher-student relationship. Educators agree that these devices supplement but do not replace the live teacher. For example, in using two-way communication systems in the instruction of homebound students, North Dakota provides for a minimum of two hours of live instruction per week (52). Even more hours of live instruction are required in New York City plus participation in School of the Air radio programing and TV assignments.

Formal evaluations of home instruction programs are still rare. Lolis (28) reported on findings derived from a study of children in New York City who received the combined home teacher-School of the Air-Teleclass Program. Students in the combined program did not attain superior intellectual functioning, reading or arithmetic achievement, speech performance, or teachers' marks as compared to home instruction students who received home teaching and School of the Air service, but not Teleclass. However, the Teleclass group did attain superior levels of functioning in the areas of social interest, feelings of self-worth, and motivation. Apparently, the major measured impact of the Teleclass component was in the social rather than the academic area. Replications of this study are needed to ascertain if the failure of Teleclass to generate superior academic functioning is generalized or limited to this specific sample and educational situation.

Rusalem (unpublished), working out of the Teachers College, Columbia University Research and Demonstration Center for the Education of Handicapped Children, followed a group of 116 long-term high school home instruction graduates and found that the majority of them entered employment, college, or rehabilitation training outside the home subsequent to graduation. The only exceptions to this finding were the "emotionally disabled" males who really were behavior problems who had been excluded from school and assigned to home instruction because other educational alternatives were not available. In these instances, home instruction was not necessarily the most appropriate educational arrangement. This group did not fit into employment and gave little evidence of readiness to assume an adult role in the community.

Rusalem also reported that high school home instruction graduates who go on to college do as well as other students in their peer group. A subgroup of severely physically limited and emotionally and behaviorally disabled students remained unengaged in adult activities (college, training, and employment) subsequent to graduation. Existing community services did not seem effective in rehabilitating this subgroup.

There appears to be a trend in some communities to offer multidisciplinary services to home instruction students in conjunction with the home teaching they receive. The New York City Board of Education, in coopera tion with Federation of the Handicapped and the New York State Office of Vocational Rehabilitation, has for more than a decade provided group mental health and prevocational services on an out-of-school basis to homebound children who have multiple and complex life adjustment problems. Periodic evaluations of this program indicate that the supportive services provided contribute to academic progress and facilitate post-school adjustment to college and employment. Curfman and Arnold (11) described a Denver program in which a social worker and an occupational therapist served severely mentally retarded children and their families. This program has been instrumental in preparing parents and children for entry into appropriate training programs and

has made it possible for these children to develop essential skills while still in the home.

By all accounts home instruction for the homebound child is alive and well. Today, most homebound children in the United States are participating in an educational process. This may be contrasted with the current status of homebound adults, few of whom are participating in rehabilitation programs. The foregoing should not be interpreted to suggest that home instruction is without problems. On the contrary, limited funds, perseveration in outmoded administrative arrangements, the survival of unsophisticated teaching technics, the use of arbitrary and unreasonable procedures to exclude some children from class instruction as well as from home instruction, the failure to use electronic devices more fully, and the lack of research in this area all contribute to a situation that calls for additional concerted action by educators, parents, and rehabilitation workers.

Perhaps the most important challenge of all is to find means of getting more children off home instruction at an earlier date. Initially, some of these children should never have been placed on the home instruction rolls. Then, too many have not had the intensive habilitation services they need to prepare them for the earliest return possible to the classroom. Finally, the prejudices of educators have kept some youngsters out of the classroom when simple school adjustments and improved transportation would have facilitated re-entry into group learning. Virtually all agree that rehabilitation workers should join the education team during a homebound student's high school years, providing him with vocational counseling, prevocational and vocational training, and job experiences in accordance with his needs. The instances in which this occurs to a meaningful degree are still all too few.

REHABILITATION

Prior to 1967, with the exception of a few bright enclaves of involvement with homebound clients, rehabilitation agencies concerned themselves primarily with apparently more visible and compelling disability groups. From a rehabilitation viewpoint, services for the homebound were almost as invisible as homebound people, themselves. Although the situation in 1971 still leaves much to be desired, the changes nevertheless are dramatic:

1. A growing number of public and voluntary rehabilitation agencies are offering differentiated programs for the rehabilitation of homebound persons.

2. There is evidence of a mounting national commitment to the homebound group.

3. More grant awards for innovative projects in the area of the homebound were made in the 1967–1970 period than in the previous 25 years.

4. A dissemination conference on the homebound conducted by Federation of the Handicapped at Greyston in 1969 considered itself fortunate to attract 30 participants. In 1971 the National Conference on the Rehabilitation of Homebound Persons sched-

uled for Arden House in February, 1971, received twice as many applications for admission as it had openings. Its participant roster included some of the most distinguished rehabilitation leaders in America.

5. New and creative designs were developed in a variety of rehabilitation areas to facilitate the rehabilitation of homebound persons. Several states implemented these designs without the benefit of federally initiated grant funds.

6. A subtle change in attitude occurred in relation to the rehabilitation of the homebound. From avoidance and even annoyance, rehabilitation workers began to view the problem with greater hope and expectation.

The causes for these changes within a brief five-year period are imbedded in the oral rather than the written history of the period. Few of these phenomena have been examined at length in the literature and, consequently, observation rather than documentation supports the conclusion that the following forces were the mainsprings of this metamorphosis:

1. The Social and Rehabilitation Service and the Rehabilitation Services Administration lent incalculable support and leadership to those who spurred the drive for improved and extended services for the homebound. This support was manifested in encouragement, guidance, catalytic actions, grants, and priorities. Very much less would have been accomplished during the period under review without this national effort.

2. An expanding list of public and voluntary agencies resisted the ten-

dency to develop programs in more "popular" disability areas and launched viable services for the homebound. This movement was sparked by rehabilitation administrators whose sense of humanity and justice overshadowed expediency and conservatism.

3. The Programmatic Research Project on the Rehabilitation of the Homebound sponsored by Federation of the Handicapped with a grant from the Social and Rehabilitation Service (SRS) initiated or participated in many of the activities that resulted in change for the homebound people of the United States. Although Programmatic Research Studies and Demonstrations may prove ultimately to be the Project's most important contribution to the field, at present its value has been primarily in focusing interest upon the homebound and persuading lay and professional people alike that homebound persons have rehabilitation potential that can be developed without the necessity of engineering monumental modifications in current service patterns.

4. Along with the flow of convention addresses and publications emanating from the Programmatic Research Project and its associates, sponsored conferences are having an important impact upon the rehabilitation of the homebound. In addition to the previously mentioned Rehabilitation Services Administration-sponsored National Conference on the Homebound, the Programmatic Research Project is planning five Social and Rehabilitation Service-funded Regional Conferences on the Rehabilitation of Homebound

Persons in the Northeast, the Southeast, the Midwest, the Southwest, and the West. Literally hundreds of rehabilitation professionals and lay persons will be reached during 1971 with the message that it is feasible to rehabilitate our homebound people within the present federal-state-voluntary agency program in the United States.

5. Homebound persons, themselves, have been stimulators of programs on their behalf. Whenever services are established for these highly deprived and limited people, their readiness to use the services and the degree of benefit they derive from them are almost always a source of wonder and gratification to those who serve them. Given proper means of disseminating the information, homebound rehabilitation clients could conceivably serve as the best advertisement for expanded services in this area.

Although much of what has been discussed thus far in the rehabilitation section of this paper is anecdotal and experimental in nature, the fact is that an important body of literature has developed during the last five years that also reflects the growth of this field. An important aspect of this literature concerns descriptions of successful rehabilitation programs for homebound persons. Traxler (54) described a statewide vocational rehabilitation program conducted by the Easter Seal Society for Crippled Children and Adults of Iowa that featured client selection, evaluation, training, and follow-up. This important project demonstrated that:

1. Homebound persons with multiple disabilities can live, work, and learn

with each other in a group situation.
2. More than 80 percent of the homebound clients served learned one or
more skills that enabled them to produce salable products.
3. The most successful skill areas
taught in this project were woodwork-
ing, sand painting, sewing, weaving,
and ceramics. The least successful were
candles, graphics, jewelry, and doll
repair. The lack of success experienced
in the latter was due partially to sales
problems.

This project fulfilled its objectives
to such a degree that it has now
become an ongoing service of the
Easter Seal agency in Iowa.

One of the studies undertaken by
the Programmatic Research Project on
the Rehabilitation of the Homebound
(15) concerned the experimental use
of a variety of interventions with a
sample of severely limited homebound
persons who had been unable to benefit from a relatively rich community
program developed for their group by
public and voluntary rehabilitation
agencies. Rehabilitation interventions
were accepted by 53 (94.7%) of the 56
homebound persons to whom service
was offered. The Project team was
unable to suggest interventions for 3
(5.1%) of 59 persons originally considered for rehabilitation.

In all, 67 different major interventions were provided to the 53 people
who were offered and consequently
accepted service. The distribution of
these interventions was:

Entry into a comprehensive voca-
    tional rehabilitation program
    conducted cooperatively by
    Federation of the Handicapped

and the New York State Office
    of Vocational Rehabilitation 34
Entry into industrial and elec-
    tronics homework   4
Entry into a mental health pro-
    gram   8
Participation in a recreational ser-
    vice   11
Health, Welfare, and Counseling
    Interventions arranged by the
    Project with other community
    agencies   8
Other interventions, including the
    acquisition of a specially equip-
    ped automobile.

At the time of survey, 60.8 percent of this homebound caseload were
in employment or in a vocational
rehabilitation program leading thereto,
5.3 percent were awaiting initiation of
vocational rehabilitation service, 3.8
percent were participating in a post-
secondary school educational program,
7.5 percent were in an interrupted
status due to health and personal
problems, and 22.6 percent had not
yet experienced a change in their
homebound life status.

On the basis of this experience
with homebound persons who had not
been able to fit into existing community programs, the Project team concluded:
1. Even the most difficult "rejected"
homebound component of the total
homebound population in a community has rehabilitation potential that
warrants service intervention.
2. Such interventions tend to be used
constructively by homebound clients
in pursuit of reasonable rehabilitation
goals.
3. At least half of those served in a
special rehabilitation program for the
homebound may be expected to en-

gage in some level of remunerative employment. Subsequent follow-ups may give cause for elevating this tentative percentage.

4. Fewer than one-fourth of such clients may be expected to experience no substantial change in their life status as a homebound person in conjunction with participation in a suitable rehabilitation program.

As Rusalem has indicated in addresses before the National Rehabilitation Association, the American Personnel and Guidance Association, and other groups, these outcomes suggest that it is feasible and economical to offer comprehensive rehabilitation services to homebound persons who have not been able to establish even partial independence in response to other health, social, and vocational programs in the community.

In 1969 when the Programmatic Research Project on the Rehabilitation of Homebound Persons was less than midway in its five-year term, it followed the Social and Rehabilitation Service mandate to apply its findings at the earliest possible date and, on the basis of its intervention experience, it recommended strengthened programs on a service level. Thus, in cooperation with the New York State Office of Vocational Rehabilitation, Federation of the Handicapped implemented Project recommendations and established Higher Horizons for the Homebound, an ongoing service program that now routinely accepts and works with severely limited and blind homebound people who cannot obtain comparable assistance elsewhere in the community. Higher Horizons is only one

of six continuing programs for the homebound maintained by Federation of the Handicapped. These six are:

1. Programmatic Research
2. Higher Horizons for the Homebound
3. Homebound Employment Service, offering a variety of industrial and white-collar homework opportunities, all provided under agency direction and supervision.
4. The High School Homebound Program, conducted in cooperation with the New York State Office of Vocational Rehabilitation and the New York City Board of Education, which provides prevocational and mental health services for high school students who are on home instruction.
5. Personal Aides to the Homebound (PATH), a program that trains and employs older persons to serve as rehabilitation aides for homebound clients.
6. The Homebound Recreation Program, which offers nonvocational leisure-time activities for homebound persons.

Although the rehabilitation literature does not chronicle them in any detail, a number of other agencies offer appropriate and, often, noteworthy services for the homebound. For example, the Wisconsin State Division of Vocational Rehabilitation maintains one of the most extensive craft training and employment programs in the United States. Representatives of many of these programs met for the first time in Harriman, New York, at the National Conference on the Rehabilitation of the Homebound in February, 1971. Brief reports of their programs appear in the Conference Proceedings. It is obvious from these presentations that a variety of organizations have found economically and socially feasible means of rehabilitating homebound persons. Therefore, it must be concluded that communities that fail to provide assistance to the homebound do so for reasons other than lack of suitable models.

The Programmatic Research Project on the Rehabilitation of the Homebound has made special efforts to study this phenomenon. After discovering that communities with comparable demographic and social characteristics varied in their provisions for homebound persons, Rusalem (46) concluded that the powerlessness of homebound persons in a power-sensitive rehabilitation establishment accounted for some of the neglect accorded to the homebound. In doing so, he identified seven sources of powerlessness that characterize the homebound group:

1. The Power of Patrons—The homebound have not achieved identification with a distinguished family or a powerful and well-known person as some other disability groups have.

2. The Power of Advocates—Few key rehabilitation leaders have adopted the cause of the homebound as their special mission.

3. The Power of Organization—Homebound persons have no organization of their own to represent them in transactions with other groups in society.

4. The Power of the "Squeaky Wheel"—Homebound persons make very little trouble. They conduct no demonstrations, engage in no shouting matches, and make few demands upon the nondisabled. In a society which responds to crises, the relatively placid homebound group has access to few levers for precipitating community action on their behalf.

5. The Power of Reward—Although rehabilitating homebound persons can be difficult and can require extraordinary skill and creativity, few incentives are available to encourage rehabilitation workers to serve this group.

6. The Power of Popularity—Disability entities sometimes achieve the spotlight in American rehabilitation, resulting in enhanced services for them, at least for some period of time. Unlike many other disability groups, the homebound have not yet achieved such popularity.

7. The Power of Visibility—Some disabled groups maintain day-to-day contact with the general public. In the course of this contact their evident disabilities arouse emotional reactions that become translated into action on their behalf. The homebound, however, are out of sight and out of mind, so that their anxiety-producing potential is relatively low. It is easy to overlook or forget them.

Rusalem described several means used by the Programmatic Research Project to augment the power of homebound persons in certain communities, including the enlistment of local "heroes" to serve as advocates of the homebound, the provision of status and rewards to those serving the homebound, and the strengthening of support services that give a community security in its initial efforts to rehabilitate homebound persons. In view of the fact that a spontaneous augmentation of interest in the homebound is not to be expected, Rusalem urged a judicious application of increased power. Using current minority group social action as a model, he advocated a power orientation that will pressure community leaders and groups to serve this group more effectively.

A highly promising development in the rehabilitation of homebound persons is the emergence of the first signs of a research interest in this field outside of the Programmatic Research Project. Thus, Gersten (19) reported on a Denver, Colorado, project that offered rehabilitation services to chronically ill and physically disabled persons under two conditions: 1) in a hospital outpatient center and 2) in the disabled person's home. No differences were found in degree of improvement in the two settings but both the patients and the professionals preferred the clinic setting. Insofar as such variables as treatment outcome, duration, and cost are concerned, rehabilitation of disabled persons in their homes, whenever this becomes necessary, can be accomplished with adequate effectiveness.

In another trail-blazing study, McKenna, Wilson, and Frumkin (29) studied the response of homebound persons to a variety of work tasks offered under the auspices of The Associated Health Industries of Akron, Ohio. Focusing upon those with arthritis and multiple sclerosis, the authors found that the members of their sample preferred such home industry tasks as sorting and stamping and expressed a dislike for such tasks as addressing, sewing, assembling, and telephone soliciting. Neutral attitudes were expressed toward television monitoring, packaging, collating, sealing, and tagging. Generally, preference was related positively to the ability to do a particular job. The investigators concluded that homeworkers' preferences should be taken into account in making job assignments and that certain jobs should be avoided in service to the homebound, including those that require writing or good manual or finger dexterity.

Although several innovative projects are still in progress, the tentative data concerning the following seem especially promising:

1. Federation of the Handicapped, George Washington University, and Abilities, Inc., are exploring homework possibilities in such industries as banking, insurance, and communications. A number of new employment opportunities have already been developed in each of these fields.

2. New ideas are emerging concerning residences for homebound persons. Federation of the Handicapped is experimenting with apartments for homebound persons in regular high-rise residences close to rehabilitation facilities, and other agencies are assessing the values and limitations of special residences for the homebound. The initial tentative results of these experiments seem favorable.

3. The mental health component in the homebound experience is receiving wider recognition. For example, Federation of the Handicapped has found group psychiatric treatment to

be an essential adjunct to other rehabilitation services for this group.

4. Institutions are beginning to think about restructuring their organizations to provide a greater rehabilitation thrust to their programs. In many cases, this new rehabilitation emphasis features the development of sheltered work opportunities and greater self-determination on the part of residents.

5. Initial consideration is being given to possible applications of recently developed electronic devices to the problems of homebound persons, including closed circuit television, conference telephone, and, as is the case so often in Australia, short-wave radio.

The above suggests that a quiet revolution is occurring in the rehabilitation of homebound persons. Not only does this revolution manifest itself in relation to expanded programs, but new approaches and creative service patterns are emerging. At present, the homebound are still far behind other disability groups in terms of having access to needed rehabilitation services but, for the first time, the gap seems to be narrowing.

SUMMARY

Services to homebound persons have grown in number and effectiveness during the period 1967–1970, especially in the following areas:

1. Home care has undergone a dramatic growth but still is not well enough integrated with other rehabilitation services.

2. Homemaking is being increasingly recognized as an essential service for homebound persons but it, too, still clings to a medical rather than a total rehabilitation model.

3. Much remains to be accomplished for homebound persons in the special services areas such as dentistry, architectural barriers, and religion. However, transportation continues to loom as the central problem area in service to the homebound and, regrettably, it must be reported that progress in this area is painfully slow.

4. The education of homebound children is holding its own or improving slightly. The brightest sign on the horizon is the increased use of electronic aids. The biggest problem, however, is that of making the schools more accessible to physically, emotionally, and intellectually limited children so that as few as possible will need to be served in the home.

5. A ferment seems to be developing in the rehabilitation of the homebound, which, at this early stage, is more evident by movement than by accomplishment. However, this ferment is expected to result increasingly in real accomplishments in providing comprehensive rehabilitation services to homebound people. Important evidences of this can be noted in the number of agencies serving the homebound, the growing body of research, the strong interest in the field expressed by the Social and Rehabilitation Service, the Rehabilitation Servives Administration, and state and voluntary rehabilitation agencies, and the innovative approaches to the life problems of homebound people now being tested.

6. A firm foundation for future development in this field was laid during the period 1960–1970. The decade of

the 70's should prove to be the turning point in the rehabilitation of homebound persons. Perhaps, by 1980, the homebound will have achieved rehabilitation parity with other disability groups in the United States.

RECOMMENDATIONS

So much remains to be done in relation to the homebound that the catalog of reasonable recommendations would cover many pages. Five of these are presented below for discussion and consideration:

1. The U.S. Department of Transportation should coordinate a systematic attack on the problems of transportation for homebound persons. Top priority should be given to the establishment of viable demonstrations of community-wide transportation networks that afford every homebound person who can do so the opportunity to leave his home regularly to participate in vocational, health, and social activities.

2. The U.S. Department of Housing and Urban Development should enlarge its scope to take action relative to a broadened concept of architectural barriers. This concept is that no one using public housing should be restricted by location, unsuitable features, or environmental incongruity from gaining access to all that the community has to offer. Housing and Urban Development funds should support only those housing units that conform to accepted standards for elimination of architectural barriers and that give preference to homebound tenants and home owners. Fur-

thermore, HUD funds should be made available to rehabilitation agencies to construct residence facilities near rehabilitation centers and sheltered workshops that will enable certain homebound persons to lead a richer life and to become self-sustaining.

3. The Social and Rehabilitation Service, the Rehabilitation Services Administration, and the state rehabilitation agencies should establish certain incentives for agencies that undertake to serve the homebound. These incentives could be in the form of higher fees for service or special grants.

4. A Social and Rehabilitation Service grant should be awarded to a suitable group to experiment with means for overcoming community apathy to the homebound. Such experiments should be based upon current knowledge of social psychology concerning means of converting community apathy into constructive social action.

5. Through legislative mandate, the Congress of the United States should create one or more Centers for the Rehabilitation of Homebound Persons that could become fulcrums for research, training, and service to the homebound. Until such centers come into being, the Social and Rehabilitation Service should encourage regional groups to develop projects in this area, using the Programmatic Research Project on the Rehabilitation of the Homebound as a coordinating and stimulating mechanism.

LIST OF REFERENCES AND BIBLIOGRAPHY

1. Adams, Mary, Downs, Thomas, and Deuble, Hazel M. Nursing Referral

Outcome for Post-Hospitalized Chronically Ill Patients. Am. J. Public Health. Jan., 1968. 58:1: 101–106.

2. Ancker, Mary T. Hospital's Home Care Program Widened Service, Created New Beds. Hospitals. Oct. 1, 1966. 40:19:74, 77, 80–84.

3. Arnold, Irene L., and Goodman, Lawrence. Homemaker Services to Families with Young Retarded Children. Children. July–Aug., 1966. 13: 4:149–152.

4. Best, Gary A. State Provisions for Home Instruction. Exceptional Children. Sept., 1967. 34:1:33–36.

5. Blumenkrantz, Lucille, and Spencer, F. J. Patients with Chronic Disease in Richmond's Home Care Program. Public Health Reports. Jan., 1968. 83:1:75–80.

6. California State Department of Public Health. Bureau of Adult Health and Chronic Diseases. The Home Nursing Scene in California Just Prior to Medicare. Berkeley, Calif.: The Bureau, 1969.

7. Carey, Ione. Training and Use of Home Health Aides. Am. J. Nursing. Aug., 1966. 66:8:1771–1774.

8. Cohen, B. Stanley, and others. Home Care Program in the Management of Rheumatoid Arthritis. J. Chronic Diseases. June, 1966. 19:6: 631–636.

9. Committee on Dietary Services for the Chronically Ill and Aging, Community Nutrition Section, American Dietetic Association. Opportunities in Home Health Services: Guidelines for Dieticians and Nutritionists. J. Am. Dietetic Assn. May, 1968. 52:5: 381–386.

10. Connor, Frances P. Education of Homebound or Hospitalized Children. New York: Teachers College Press, 1964.

11. Curfman, Hope G., and Arnold, Carol B. A Homebound Therapy Program for Severely Retarded Children. Children. Mar.–Apr., 1967. 14: 2:63–68.

12. Curnow, B. K. C. Tele-classes in Los Angeles Schools. Calif. Educ. Jan., 1966. 3:3–7.

13. Duffy, Adriane V. Volunteer Friendly Visitors Bring Sunshine to Shut-ins. N.J. Public Health News, N.J. State Department of Health. Nov., 1966. 47:11:252–254, 262.

14. Edwards, Mabel I., ed. Selected References on Home Care Services for the Chronically Ill and Aged. Iowa City, Univ. of Iowa Inst. of Gerontology, 1967.

15. Federation of the Handicapped, New York. The PATH Program Reports. Unpublished.

16. Forés, Sally E. Home Care Program for the Chronically Ill and the Aged of the West Regional District, Mayaguez, Puerto Rico. J. Am. Med. Women's Assn. July, 1966. 21:7: 567–570.

17. General Board of Education, United Methodist Church. The Church's Ministry to the Homebound. Nashville, The Board, 1968.

18. George, A. M. Teaching the Home-Bound Child. Virginia J. Educ. Feb., 1967. 60:21+.

19. Gersten, Jerome W., and others. Comparison of Home and Clinic Rehabilitation for Chronically Ill and Physically Disabled Persons. Arch. Phys. Med. and Rehab. Nov., 1968. 49:11:615–642.

20. Goeppinger, Jean. Why a Home Health Aide? Am. J. Nursing. July, 1968. 68:7:1513–1516.

21. Grant, Murray. Health Aides Add New Dimension to Home Care Program. Hospitals. Dec. 1, 1966. 40: 23:63–67.

22. Holliday, Jane. Public Health Nursing for the Sick at Home: A Descriptive Study Conducted by Visiting Nurse Service of New York. New York, The Serv., 1967.

23. Hoyt, W. Hadley. A Study of the Need for Comprehensive Home Care in Adair County, Missouri. J. Am. Osteopathic Assn. Apr., 1967. 66:8: 831–835.

24. Indiana State Board of Health. [Visiting Nurse Service and the Services Provided a Stroke Patient.] Bul., Indiana State Board of Health. 1968. 70:5:2–13.

25. Lemon, Genelle M., and Welches, Lois. Survey of Welfare Clients to Determine Need for Home Health Aides. Public Health Reports. Aug., 1967. 82:8:729–734.

26. Lenzer, Anthony. Home Care: The Patient's Point of View. Hospitals. Nov. 1, 1966. 40:21:64, 67, 70, 74, 77.

27. Lenzer, Anthony, and Donabedian, Avedis. Needed . . . Research in Home Care. Nursing Outlook. Oct., 1967. 15:10:42–45.

28. Lolis, K. Evaluation of a Method of School-to-Home Telephone Instruction of Physically Handicapped Homebound Adolescents. New York: Board of Education, 1968.

29. McKenna, Nancy A. M., Wilson, Milton E., Jr., and Frumkin, R. M. Attitudes of Homebound Patients with Arthritis and Multiple Sclerosis Toward 11 Home Industry Employment Opportunities Perceptual and Motor Skills. Dec., 1967. 25:3:776.

30. Mary Joan, Sister. Hospital Coordinated Home Health Agency Operates Effectively in a Rural Area. Hospital Progress. May, 1967. 48:5: 70–72, 74, 76, 78.

31. Mather, William G., and Hobaugh, Robert J. Attitudes of Physicians Toward a Hospital-Based Home Care Program. Hospitals. Apr. 16, 1968. 42:8:88, 92.

32. Mendoza, Norma. The Role of an Occupational Therapist in a Home Setting. Am. J. Occupational Ther. Mar.–Apr., 1969. 23:2:141–144.

33. Mulford, Carolyn. Denver's Home Teaching Program. NEA J. Jan., 1967. 56:1:14–16.

34. Nash, David T. Home Care for the Chronically Institutionalized. Geriatrics. Feb., 1966. 21:2:215–220.

35. National Council for Homemaker Services. Directory of Homemaker-Home Health Aide Services in the United States and Canada, 1966–67. New York: The Council, 1967.

36. National Council for Homemaker Services. Homemaker-Home Health Aide Services for Families with a Mentally Retarded Member. New York: The Council, 1966.

37. National Council of Social Service (Great Britain). Emergency Call Schemes for the Housebound. London: The Council, 1964.

38. National League for Nursing. Home Health Aide Services. Nursing Outlook. Nov., 1968. 16:11:60.

39. Neumann, Alfred, and Young, Marjorie A. C. Evaluation of Homemaker Service Programs in Massachusetts. Am. J. Public Health, Jan., 1967. 57:1:128–136.

40. Nisbet, N. H., Mackenzie, M. S., and Hamilton, M. C. Follow-ups of Elderly Discharged Patients. Lancet. June 11, 1966. 7450:1314–1315.

41. Patterson, L. Helping the Homebound. Grade Teacher. Mar., 1967. 84:94+.

42. Ramos, Lorraine. Steps in the Development of the Appanoose County Homemaker's Health Service. Adding Life to Years, Inst. of Gerontology, Univ. of Iowa. July, 1966. 13:7:5–8 (Suppl. 7).

43. Retarded Infants Service. The Value of Homemaker Service in the Family with the Retarded Child Under Five; Final Report, Child Welfare Research Project, by Association for Homemaker Service and. . . . New York: Retarded Infants Serv., 1965.

44. Roth, Mitchell E., Ehinger, Robert F., and Mosher, William E. The Value of Coordinated and Comprehensive Home Care. Am. J. Public Health. Oct., 1967. 57:10: 1841–1847.

45. Rusalem, Herbert. Penetrating the Narrowing Circle: A Review of the Literature Concerning the Vocational Rehabilitation of Homebound Persons. Rehab. Lit. July, 1967. 28:7:202–217.

46. Rusalem, Herbert. Powerless in a Power-Sensitive Rehabilitation Establishment: A Theory of Homebound Neglect. J. Rehab. May–June, 1970. 36:3:19–21.

47. Rusalem, Herbert, Baxt, Roland, and Barshop, Irving. The Vocational Rehabilitation of Neighborhood-Bound Older Disabled Persons: A Program Guide. New York: Federation Employment and Guidance Serv., 1967.

48. Ryder, Claire F., Stitt, Pauline G., and Elkin, William F. Home Health Services–Past, Present, Future. Am. J. Public Health. Sept., 1969. 59:9: 1720–1729.

49. Scher, Elanor, and Topkins, Dobi. The Home Care Team Gives Individualized Service. Hosp. Management. Aug., 1966. 102:2:36–40.

50. Simches, Raphael F., and Cicenia, Erbert F. Home Teaching Provisions at the State Level. Exceptional Children. Sept., 1958. 25:1:11–15.

51. Shworles, Thomas R. Homebound Disabled People Perform Modern Business Tasks. Rehab. Record. Nov.–Dec., 1970. 11:6:28–31.

52. Smaltz, Janet M. Guides to Special Education in North Dakota: VII, Individual Instruction Program for Children Who Are Homebound or Hospitalized (Including Supplementary Instruction). Bismark, N.D.: North Dakota State Dept. of Public Instruction, 1967.

53. Times Education Supplement. Helping the Housebound. Aug. 18, 1867. 2726:285.

54. Traxler, H. W. Final Report of a Demonstration Project to Determine the Effectiveness of Training Severely Handicapped Housebound Persons in a Group Setting. Des Moines, Iowa: Easter Seal Society for Crippled Children and Adults in Iowa, 1969.

55. United States Public Health Service. Health Auxiliary Training: Instructor's Guide. Washington, D.C.: The Service, 1966.

56. United States Public Health Service. Portraits in Community Health: The Dexter Manse Story: Health Services in Housing for the Elderly. Washington, D.C.: The Service, 1966.

57. University of Michigan. School of Public Health. Proceedings of the Workshop on Community Action to Promote the Oral Health of the Chronically Ill, Handicapped, and the Aged (June 15–19, 1965); Kenneth A. Easlick, ed. Ann Arbor, Mich.: The School, 1965.

58. Vulpe, S. Home Programming by Occupational Therapy; An Approach to the Habilitation and Rehabilitation of Atypical Development in Children. Canad. J. Occupational Ther. Winter, 1968. 35:4:129–139, 145.

59. Waldman, H. Barry, and Stein, Murray. Dental Care for the Shut-in Patient: A Workable Solution. Am. J. Public Health. Nov., 1966. 56:11: 1921–1926.

60. Wisconsin State Department of Health and Social Services. Division of Health. Serving the Patient in His Home Under Medicare; Proceedings of a Workshop . . . April 4, 5, and 6, 1967. Madison, Wis.: The Dept., (1968).

61. Wolinsky, Gloria. A Special Education Problem–Home Instruction: Status, Issues, and Recommendations. Exceptional Children. May, 1970. 36:9:673–674.

62. Youngkin, R. S. Taped Togetherness. Texas Outlook. Jan., 1968. 52:34–35.

Section 13

ARCHITECTURAL BARRIERS

50 Barriers to Normality for the Handicapped Adult in the United States

Leslie D. Park

In a brilliant paper presented to an international conference in the fall of 1973, Gunnar Dybwad, professor of human development at Brandeis University in Massachusetts, gave us some perceptive definitions of what we commonly call "normalization." Dr. Dybwad says, "Normal on our earth is trouble and strife, trial and tribulation, and the handicapped person has a right to be exposed to it. Normalization thus includes the dignity of risk." He further states, "The origin of the effort to introduce the concept of normalization was the realization that a specific strategy had to be developed to counteract the process of denormalization which over the past 75 years has made such deep inroads into society's dealing with handicapped individuals."

In other words, normalization is a rational attempt to deal with the very conditions that have tended to deepen and reinforce prejudice and tended to set the severely handicapped apart from the rest of society.

From these remarks we can see that the elements of normalization involve:

1) Righting the wrongs of the past.

2) Bringing the handicapped back into the mainstream of society.

3) Developing the "normal" as a risk process that involves the elimination of the "sanitized life" and substituting for it the possibility of failure as well as the possibility of greater rewards.

All that I believe about life, man, and man's relationship to God tells me that life is or ought to be, "an adventure and a novelty." It is this aspect of life that speaks of vigor, vitality, and the satisfactions we all seek. This is "normal" in the brightest sense.

BARRIERS TO NORMALITY

I would like to set forth what I believe are the barriers in the United States that prevent the normalization process for handicapped adults. I mention adults because I believe that the adolescent is really at the beginning stages of adult life and the same problems and barriers persist throughout life.

This article is a slightly edited version of a presentation made to the Ninth Annual Seminar of the International Cerebral Palsy Society, held at the University College, Oxford, England, Apr. 18, 1974.

Reprinted from Rehabilitation Literature, 1975, 36(4): 108–111.

Barrier No. 1: A Confused Value System by a Confused Government Makes Normalization for the Handicapped Virtually Impossible

It is a fact that the United States is a country built around the philosophy of "rugged individualism." We have had physical frontiers in the United States for many years and they are only now beginning to disappear. One who travels in the American West knows that there are literally thousands and thousands of square miles of unsettled land that still beckon to the adventurous homesteader. Nevertheless, this is no longer the challenge it was 100 years ago, and people increasingly live in cities and urban settlements and the idea of "rugged individualism" has long since succumbed to more popular and realistic concepts. In spite of this, we have a social system in the United States that has still not caught up with the change from the principle of rugged individualism to *social interdependence*. This may be best illustrated by the fact that the United States is perhaps the only technically advanced country in the world that does not have a health system for its citizens, lags seriously in penal reform, and has only in the past few years developed a "right to education law" for the handicapped. At the present time we offer to our handicapped citizens social security and pension payments that are below the subsistence level.

To a very large degree, riches and ability to make money are still the standards of success in the United States. When we speak of making handicapped people "contributing members of society" we almost always mean *financially* contributing members. Our country still finds it much easier for the "rich" handicapped person to "make it" than the "poor" one. Although this is true for most industrialized countries, it is *more true* in the United States. This may be illustrated by the following facts:

1) *Achievement* by the handicapped is almost always totally related to having a job or working.

2) The United States has the most widely advertised "Hire the Handicapped Week" in the world. It is a nationally recognized time for paying attention to "hiring."

A young handicapped girl I know, an accomplished painter, recently had an art show. Although the show was highly successful and her artistic talent won wide acclaim, most people did not feel that the girl was really much of an artist until she had evidence of having sold some of her paintings. The value of her work became suddenly more acceptable when the product of her hands became a salable item. This attitude is widespread in the United States at this time. It makes it virtually impossible for handicapped people to achieve any measure of satisfaction or success in activities that do not produce financial rewards.

In a recent presentation made to one of our legislative bodies, we had occasion to illustrate that, if one were to draw a line down the middle of the page and label one side of that line "no work" and the other side "work," he would find that on the "no work" side vast expenditures were being made by the government for the care of handicapped people in institutions and in all types of community services. The great economic investment government has in the handicapped lies on the "no work" side. Bringing people out of institutions for the retarded and into more effective community-based program reduces by thousands of dollars the expenditures of government for the care of such persons. (In 1974, the annual cost of caring for one retarded child in a New York institution was $20,000.)

On the "work side" of the line, the person who holds a job is almost always holding a limited job. The taxes he pays are quite small (less than $1,200) in relationship to the saving that can be realized by the government on the "no work" side of the line. Only in recent years has this concept become evident to the Congress of the United States and only now are we beginning to develop legislation for programs that will assist handicapped people to live in the community and carry on effective adult activities without "work for pay."

Probably no event in the social history of our country is as revealing as the recently completed "War on Poverty." You will recall that this was a national program announced by former President Lyndon Johnson. It had all of the trappings of a Normandy Beach Invasion, including massive expenditures, "crash" programs looking for quick results, and the use of the poor themselves to oversee their own programs of progress. The wreckage of this disastrous war is all over the landscape! Not only was the program highly *unsuccessful,* it also was extremely wasteful and created a bitterness on the part of the taxpayers that will make it very difficult to bring about other needed social reforms. In many ways there is a built-in American impatience with chronic "here and now" problems and with slow procedures. We are generous givers to acute international calamity. Let there be an earthquake in Nicaragua, a famine in North Africa, floods in China, and there will be an outpouring of American dollars. But the problems of the handicapped are constantly with us and so escape our notice!

In a further confusion about value systems I must mention the changing role of the family. When you speak of "the family," one pictures a mother and a father (usually a white mother and a white father) and two or three healthy children. This is becoming the atypical family in many communities of America today. We have the common portrait of interracial marriages, mothers of illegitimate children choosing to raise children without a father, changes in the law that are now under consideration to have lesbian women and homosexual men raise adopted children, and a variety of patterns that change altogether the usual pattern of what constitutes the family.

In the very successful family conferences conducted by United Cerebral Palsy of New York City, we bring together family units with handicapped children for week-long counseling and recreation programs. Only very rarely do we see "intact" families appearing at these conferences. It is quite usual for us to see a mother with two or three children, an older retarded daughter, a grandmother, or a nearby neighbor coming to the comference as a "family" unit. This confusion about the social order and national value systems is perhaps the greatest barrier to providing answers to the complex problems of the handicapped in the United States.

Barrier No. 2: The Mobility Dilemma

Much has been written concerning the development of normal patterns for the adolescent child and how these relate to the handicapped child. One of the themes heard over and over again is the natural desire and healthy tendency for the adolescent to break away from usual family ties and to develop a sense of independence. Almost always this means an ability to get away from the family physically. In the United States, now made up of hundreds of suburbs, this inevitably means the ability to drive a car and get away from the home via the automobile.

One of the first cerebral palsied people I ever knew was a boy who lived in Chicago. He would get around the neighborhood by using a coaster wagon such as children use. He was able to push with one leg and steer the wagon with one hand. He almost always had a box of pencils, shoelaces, and chewing gum that he sold to people in the neighborhood. His sole system of mobility was his wagon.

I have had experience in conducting community studies in 32 different communities, both large and small. In each of these communities we discovered that transportation was a primary problem for the handicapped. In most instances, if an effective transportation system could have been developed, the number of people served by community resources would have doubled.

We must say, then, that the problem of transportation and mobility is a barrier to normality in the United States, as it is in many other countries of the world.

Barrier No. 3: The Lack of Entry System for Adolescents in the World of Work

From the time an adolescent completes his school years until the time he is old enough to establish a home and represent himself as a reasonably stable member of the community, there is a period of great confusion. This applies to handicapped as well as nonhandicapped young people. There is *no* system of preparation and entry into the world of work except by the most haphazard and discriminatory practices. This is evident by the fact that many trade unions discriminate openly against the training and employment of black workers and minority groups. It can be seen in the high cost of education in the United States, which still makes college a possibility only for the well-to-do, the intellectually gifted, or the exceptional athlete. It is further compounded by the fact that there is an increasing disenchantment with college education as a proper vehicle into the world of useful and satisfying work.

This problem manifests itself by

the confusion that presently exists concerning what to do in the training of *older* handicapped children, such as the mentally retarded and the cerebral palsied. Inevitably, in the school systems in the United States, you will find a very early effort to get older handicapped children, such as the mentally retarded and the cerebral palsied, into "vocational programs." The assumption is, of course, that because these children are handicapped they should know what they want to do in the world of work at a much earlier age.

I have a very serious concern about the limitations of the sheltered workshop concept. It has never made much sense to me. I do not see the logic of gathering a group of handicapped people and putting them *all* into *a* place where they sit down at benches and do *handwork,* when at the very outset we know these people have a serious limitation in their hand function! Sheltered workshop work around the world is surprisingly similar. We may also see that the subcontract, industrial type of work carried on in the average sheltered workshop goes contrary to work trends in the world.

At the present time, areas of work that are growing at an unprecedented rate are sales and service. Little or nothing is being done to develop sales and service occupations for seriously handicapped people. We still try to make the workshop the main avenue of vocational service. Wide experimentation is needed in the next decade to develop alternatives to this pattern of work for seriously handicapped people.

Alternatives in the work system are likewise needed with such things as apprenticeships and a restoration of apprenticeship training. New patterns are needed, such as the Australian plan of mixing handicapped and nonhandicapped people in an entire industry (so successfully carried on in Centre-Industries in Sydney). White collar and service occupations geared to handicapped people and sales programs providing meaningful income to disabled people are needed. I have rarely been in a major city in the world without seeing a cerebral palsied person working at a news-stand, cigar counter, or candy store in the metropolitan area.

A further item related to this barrier has to do with training that still exists for many nonexistent jobs. We still see handicapped people trained in chaircaning and the making of potholders! I don't mean to demean these activities, but they are illustrative of the fact that there simply is not a realistic vocational objective for much of the work training carried on for the handicapped in the world.

Barrier No. 4: Lack of Implemented Technology, Bioengineering

Let me make a bold statement at the very beginning of this discussion, "I have never met a handicapped person who could not have been functionally improved by applied technology."

The rehabilitation movement has *not* embraced bioengineering as a part of the term activity in the same way it has embraced physiotherapy, speech therapy, and medical services. Today, there exists "off-the-shelf technology" with many useful devices for feeding, transporting, and assisting the handicapped to live more effective lives. We are very remiss as a rehabilitation community in not building these technological advances into our day-to-day rehabilitation programs. It is a serious flaw in our activities.

In the United States, technology has "spun off" many useful technological advances that we must capture if we are to serve the handicapped population effectively. We are only now attempting to do this but I fear we have not mobilized to do it effectively.

SOME ANSWERS TO THE BARRIERS

Let me now move to what I think are some promising ways to remove the barriers I have discussed.

The Value System

It would certainly be presumptuous to suggest that one single organization could tell its government how to get its values in order. Nevertheless, I think this is a time in history when voluntary agencies need to play a very specific role. I see our role in this decade as one of "model-building." Nothing affects government as much as seeing real, living working models of programs that can change situations. *Now* is the time for us to be building programs that work, programs that are cost-effective, programs that call us into accountability, programs that are

effectively housed in appropriate buildings. *We must take to ourselves the establishment of clear rehabilitation goals (this is very rarely done), develop the strategies to meet these goals, and develop the tools to evaluate our results.*

If we develop one or two working models of what can be done with handicapped people by the effective use of all that we know, we will demonstrate to our government *how* it can be done best. The day is rapidly coming when governments will awaken to the fact that rehabilitation is not only the humanitarian thing to do, but the *economical* thing to do. Models are needed to do the job effectively. Before government spends millions, we as nongovernmental groups must spend hundreds to learn how it can best be done.

Religion as a Value in Rehabilitation

One of the astonishing things about the times in which we live is how confused our value system really is. Today it is no longer taboo to talk about or show films of the most explicit sexual acts between adults. (They do not even have to be man and woman!) Nevertheless, it is absolutely taboo to talk about religion or man's relationship to God as essential to successful living (and certainly not as an objective of rehabilitation)! I completely reject the idea of eliminating religion from what must be suggested to the handicapped as an important contribution to their lives. I do not suggest that a formal program of religious training be added to rehabilitation services; however, I do not think we should ignore religion as a primary motivating factor in the lives of many people in this world. I am not necessarily talking about organized religion through traditional church groups but what I am talking about is a basic relationship of *man to God* (as opposed to man's relationship to man).

Philosophical Clarity

To a very large degree we are confused in the rehabilitation movement about what we really are. There are those who suggest that we are practicing a science and therefore must adhere to rather strict scientific rules. If you pull arm A, you can expect reaction B. Others say that rehabilitation is simply an art and the real skill is in the knowledge and techniques of the artist. I submit to you that what we are doing is both an art *and* a science. We must not be confused about what is scientific and what is artistic in our efforts.

I do not anticipate that machines will ever be able to do the work in which we are all engaged, in special education, psychological counseling, vocational training, medical management, and so on. At the same time I am not prepared to say that the most effective type of human rehabilitation can be carried on *without* the application of scientific principles in what we know about learning, medicine, and human behavior. *In short, what I am saying is that we must know much more about our craft.*

At the present time in our work in New York we have accepted the philosophy of "simulating the norm" as a pattern for effective work with the cerebral palsied. If it is normal for a child to go to school until the age of 18, we try to simulate that norm. If it is normal for an adult to marry and establish a home and have a family, we help people simulate this norm. This is a very reasonable objective, and yet it is an extremely difficult one.

Handicapped Hold Key to Attitudes in the Next Generation

I would like to suggest to the handicapped themselves that they have a tremendous role to play. It is perhaps a role that is not fully realized by the organized disabled groups around the world. I believe *this* generation of handicapped people is making it possible for the next generation to live better or worse by how they conduct themselves. The embittered, cranky, poorly kept, and untidy handicapped person is unquestionably making it more difficult for the next generation of disabled people to be accepted.

Growth in Those Who Help

Perhaps one of the great achievements of rehabilitation in our time will *not* be in what we actually do with and for disabled people but rather *what we are doing for ourselves and for the non-handicapped world.*

Edwin Markham put the whole issue in the most effective language when he gave us these words:

We are all fools until we see that in the human plan, Nothing is worth the making, unless it makes the man. Why build these cities glorious if man unbuilded goes? In vain we build the world unless the builder also grows.

As builders of the rehabilitation world of the future we have a responsibility to grow ourselves if we are ever to remove the barriers to normality that we presently face.

51 A Living Environment for the Physically Disabled

The world in which we live has been designed to accommodate people who have little or no physical limitations. Yet, everyone can identify several people who have a limited functional capacity because of a medical limitation. These medical problems range from the aging and metabolic disabilities to those preventing ambulation.

There is a great need to provide services that will assist the physically impaired to live and function as independently as possible. A brief look at some of the current statistics will provide a picture of the need.

At any given time, in the United States, 30 million people are suffering from a temporary or a permanent physical handicap. Continued population growth and the large increase in the number of older persons could raise this total to more than 40 million by 1985. Every day, 1,000 Americans pass their 65th birthday and enter the period when strokes, arthritis, and other crippling impairments are most likely to occur.

Traffic accident figures mount every day. It is estimated that within the next 10 years growing numbers of traffic accident victims will become permanently disabled. Our technological advances linked with more leisure time have led to increased diving, skiing, ski mobile, and other "recreational" accidents.

World War II left 2,000 living paraplegics, of whom 1,700 are alive today. Vietnam, with its land mines and booby traps, resulted in proportionally more crippling wounds. Medical advances enable more men to live. Therefore, the number of war veterans who must use wheelchairs is also increasing.

One out of 10 persons has some disability that prevents him from using buildings and facilities designed for only the physically fit. There are no statistics on how many disabled people are not working or living productive lives because of inadequate housing and transportation.

Rehabilitation, as a concept, has been geared to treatment, not to living. Too long have the practitioners in rehabilitation looked away from the living environment within which the disabled function. Housing can serve as a pivotal base on which can be developed a living environment for all people, some of whom are disabled.

ADAPTED AND SPECIALIZED HOUSING

Housing is not a simplistic problem. It involves a myriad of concerns with many tied to the very complex American economic system. Isolating any one factor as more important is diffi-

Reprinted from Rehabilitation Literature, 1973, 34(4): 98–103.

cult, and there are many paradoxes. Housing is governed by state law, federal law, local law, safety regulations, union regulations, and money. Housing needs to be "sold," "rented," or "leased." Except for public housing, it must "make money."

The following definitions of terms I will use will be helpful.

Adapted Housing: Homes or apartments incorporating special features such as: wide doorways; kitchens with adjustable counter tops, wall ovens, counter-mounted burners; a bathroom with a modified shower stall and commode. (This list is not inclusive.)

Specialized Housing: Special types of living arrangements, such as congregate living, halfway houses, and the village type of development for single-disability groups.

Accessible Housing: Minimal adaptations, such as a ramped entryway.

Some known factors that apply to housing are listed below.

Housing should be designed for all the people, some of whom are disabled.

The life of a house or an apartment is considered to be 40 years (for mortgage purposes).

Housing is a basic problem in the rehabilitation of the disabled.

Technology is available to eliminate housing problems for the disabled.

Communities can marshal their forces to meet housing as a problem.

Builders and developers need to be made aware of the adaptations needed by the physically disabled, the cost of the adaptations, and the marketability of adapted apartments.

Sufficient data have not been gathered in reference to the needs of the disabled and the location of the disabled.

There should be a choice of types of housing available to meet individual needs.

Change in the way housing is perceived is necessary. It will require a consortium of planners, builders, developers, consumers, and other specialists to work together. By tradition, we are concerned with feeding the hungry, providing living facilities for the homeless, and supplying education for the masses. We have agreed on the necessity for adequate medical care, the alleviation of substandard housing, and the provision of services matched to the needs of the people.

Change and challenge go hand in hand because innovative approaches will be required and the consortium will need imagination.

A community approach is needed since a resident is the "purchaser" and "user" of community services, which may include transportation, education, social services, recreation, medical services, shopping facilities, and religious institutions.

Currently, there is a tremendous impetus to construct apartments for the elderly, for the handicapped, for those with special handicaps, and for special interest groups.

Federal law stipulates that, in projects for the elderly funded with federal monies, 10 percent of the units must be adapted for the handicapped. Individual states have responded in various ways to this law in state-aided housing. In Massachusetts, 5 percent of such units must be adapted for the handicapped, and housing authorities are encouraged to adapt more.

Housing finance agencies are also a supplier of money to builders and developers. Currently, in most states, there is no legal requirement for adaptation of the living units that they fund. The law in each state needs to be examined to insure that the handicapped are not overlooked. Again in Massachusetts, legislation is pending to amend the housing finance regulations to stipulate that all housing whose construction is funded by the agency be accessible to the disabled and that 10 percent of all apartments be adapted.

Three apartment buildings specifically designed for the physically disabled are, in order of their construction, Center Park in Seattle, Wash.; Highland Heights in Fall River, Mass.; and New Horizons Manor in Fargo, N.D. These buildings have been constructed with Housing and Urban Development (HUD) monies and are operated by the respective local housing authorities. Variations of these buildings are being considered in numerous parts of the country with great variance in the services to be offered.

The philosophical concern of deinstitutionalizing the elderly and disabled has led to some new types of housing. The newest is the "village concept." The village, also called an "adult community," provides a complete living environment for a single disability group. Most frequently, the group is comprised of mentally retarded adults. The living environment provides everything the adult needs,

including sheltered workshop employment and, in some cases, employment in a nearby community.

Two villages for the physically handicapped in Ohio and Michigan are being discussed.

KEY ISSUES IN HOUSING

Earlier, it was indicated that housing is a pivotal base around which a living environment is developed. The key issues in housing are largely based on forces impinging upon the living environment. It must be remembered that, philosophically and practically, ideas are changing in relationship to dealing with the solution to human problems. The rights of individuals are being protected. The words *advocate* and *advocacy* are becoming an integral part of modern vernacular, as is *consumerism.*

Integration Versus Segregation

Should the disabled be in an apartment complex for the nondisabled or should they be segregated in apartment complexes (ghetto concept)? If an apartment complex built for the disabled accommodates families, it will contain a significant number of nonhandicapped people. In this way, there is built-in integration.

Theoretically a mix of elderly and handicapped can be in low-income housing by virtue of federal legislation. The question then has to be asked regarding the legitimacy of this "mix." Handicapped persons are eligible for these units if they are over 21 years of age. However, since many handicapped are in the over-fifty age bracket and could live in these units, the younger persons may not be considered for these housing units.

What, then, happens to young, handicapped adults who come out of school prepared to work but poorly trained in independent living? In most instances, they probably cannot find accessible housing. What of adults whose injuries stem from automobile collisions, war, skiing mishaps, or diving accidents? Do they want to be integrated into the community, live in housing for the elderly, or be segregated in apartments for the handicapped?

Look around at what is happening. Society verbalizes "integration" but often lives "segregation." Laws are being promulgated that will greatly influence the attitudes of young adults and people with acquired disabilities. Exemplifying this are the impending laws in special education.

The Education Commission of the States, headquartered in Denver, is advocating that children with special needs be integrated into regular classrooms. This may mean the demise of the "orthopedic room." This integration will require that the physically disabled child learn to compete earlier in a normal environment. Needed adaptations will be prescribed for him at an earlier age. His self-concept will be affected, for he will know at an earlier age how he can function in society.

Can we ask the physically disabled who have been integrated to then segregate themselves by living in segregated housing? In housing for the elderly? It must be remembered that what is built today is considered to last for 40 years. Can the model law in special education[1] be used as a viable model for housing?

Labeling

Labeling of people by disease entity or diagnostic category has been a practice in rehabilitation, as rehabilitation has emulated the field of medicine.

Architectural adaptations in housing, while not labeled for specific diagnostic categories, have traditionally been labeled for wheelchair users. This causes a complicated problem in adapted housing, because managers of buildings cannot hold vacant adapted apartments until persons in wheelchairs need them. (This also amplifies the need to design for all persons.) Conceptually, this causes another problem, since the ambulant disabled also need architectural adaptations.

Across the country, various advocates are encouraging the end to "labeling" children and adults. A paradox arises, since in order to take advantage of some provisions for the disabled, a "label" is needed to establish eligibility. An example of this is the specialized clinic in a medical center.

How, then, can we define people with special needs? Three definitions

---

[1] Model Special Education Law, Education Commission of the States, 300 Lincoln Tower Bldg., 1860 Lincoln St., Denver, Colo. 80203.

currently being used by the Social Security Administration, HUD, and Vocational Rehabilitation are broad and do not include diagnostic labels but relate to the capacity of the individual.

These definitions are:

Section 223—Social Security Act
"A disabled person is unable to engage in any substantial gainful activity by reason of any medically determinable physical or mental impairment which can be expected to result in death or has lasted or can be expected to last for a continuous period of not less than twelve months."

Housing and Urban Development
"A handicapped person is one who has a physical impairment which:
a. is expected to be of long, continued, and indefinite duration;
b. substantially impedes his ability to live independently; and
c. is of such a nature that such ability can be improved by more suitable housing conditions."

Vocational Rehabilitation
"A handicapped person is someone with one or a combination of physical, mental, educational, age, income, environmental or skill disqualifications. The disqualifications act to impair an individual's ability to perform his major life activity."

If "labeling" is eliminated, what can be the criteria for a living environment based on individual need? An evaluation of the individual's functional capacity is one approach. This approach would relate to the definitions used federally and it also would relate to the model as developed by the model education law mentioned earlier.

In evaluating the functional capacity of the physically disabled, several characteristics of physical impairments need to be considered.

First of all, a permanent but fixed defect has a significantly less limiting effect on the functional capacity of the individual as he acquires skill in compensating for the handicap. An example of this would be an amputee with an artificial leg. As he gains experience in walking with the limb, his functional capacity increases.

Secondly, progressive impairments may allow the functional capacity of the individual to plateau for an extended period of time, but as the condition progresses it will be increasingly hampered. Illustrations would be metabolic diseases such as diabetes, where no immediate problem exists but the health and efficiency of an individual may decrease as the condition worsens, or, multiple sclerosis in persons who may have maintained a certain level of functional capacity for some time but who, as the condition progresses, will lose capacity while becoming more uncoordinated.

Since the functional capacity of the individual is not static but may progress or regress, the housing manager must adapt housing policies to meet these needs. It is obvious that one cannot anticipate moving residents around for short periods of time. However, a knowledgable tenant selection committee, utilizing a functional capacity scale, will be able to judiciously place the resident in appropriate housing, keeping the long-range problems of the physically impaired in mind.

Getting the
Consumer to the Proper Housing

Many consumers are knowledgable about adapted and accessible housing, but, although there are no statistics available, it is doubtful that the majority are aware that their environment could be changed to make their lifestyle more convenient and comfortable.

Rehabilitation workers need to assume the broader responsibility of educating consumers to the concepts of a living environment. The follow-up of a client should include attention to proper housing. Adaptations in the client's home should be considered or the client told about adapted or accessible housing. (This could be part of an ongoing information, referral, and follow-up program.)

The development of the private housing market will require working with realtors, builders, and developers to make them aware of the needs of the disabled. A tenant selection procedure is followed with all applicants for public housing.

A three-year Study of Independent Living is being conducted at Highland Heights in Fall River. One part of the study concerns the tenant selection procedure in a building constructed for the elderly and handicapped. The procedure being used is very sophisticated, with social workers conducting interviews. Following an interview, the social worker rates the applicant on a scale from 1 to 5. The rating "1" is given an applicant who does not need adapted housing and "5" denotes an applicant who cannot live independently and may require nursing home care. The "3" and "4" ratings are of applicants most in need of adapted housing.

New Horizons Manor in Fargo uses the standard application admission form along with a medical questionnaire filled out by the physician. This form includes a functional evaluation. The tenants for the building are selected by a tenant selection committee composed of two physicians, a nurse, an occupational therapist, and the receptionist at New Horizons Manor (a member of the Red River Valley Handicapped Club).

Architectural Adaptations

In modern parlance, the question of "maxi" or "mini" architectural adaptations arises.

One school of thought advocates very few adaptations—no more than are absolutely necessary to the well-being of the handicapped person. The rationale behind this philosophy is that the handicapped need to adjust to the environment in which they live, for, if they can function in a normal environment, they will be able to participate in normal activities. In other words, they will have conquered their environment.

Another philosophy would provide a maximally adapted environment. The proponents of this philosophy have been working to produce an environment in which everyone can function.

If maximum adaptations are made in the kitchen, including easy accessibility to cupboards, stove, counter top, sink, and refrigerator, anyone could function. However, the disabled person accustomed to and dependent on these would not be able to function in a kitchen that was not adapted. Theoretically, this would limit the person in choice of housing. However, if the person always had made extra effort and managed to function in a regular kitchen, a wider range of housing could be pursued.

Community Services

The question of how community services can reach the consumer is complicated, with many facets. For the purposes of this article, only problems relating to services within housing complexes will be considered. The assumption is made that the handicapped living in private homes either can obtain home services or can be taken to outpatient services and health centers.

Medical, social, recreational, transportation, shopping, religious, and meals-on-wheels services should be offered, with the community the major factor in their provision. Out of the community should come leadership, financing, broad understanding, support, and the climate with which services can be carried out successfully.

An apartment complex can be made into a medical institution by supplying too many of the services for the residents and leaving them with little or no motivation to leave their apartments. A very delicate balance exists between the desire to provide service and the desire to create an atmosphere for maximum independence. It is very difficult to decide how much service is enough and how much is too much.

The commitment of agencies and agency boards to provide additional services or to expand services to include housing complexes is extremely important. Agencies need to be brought into the initial planning of housing facilities for the physically disabled, and it is the responsibility of the sponsor of the projected facility to make an active inventory of community services. About two to two-and-a-half years elapse from the time buildings are conceived and plans are drawn to the time of full occupancy. During this time, in our fast-moving society, communities will change and, we hope, community services improve. The lead-in time for developing services for apartment complexes such as we have today should start at least six months prior to the initial ground-breaking. This would enable a coordinated group of community agencies to work together and function as a planning and implementing group.

REHABILITATION—
TRAINING FOR LIVING

Rehabilitation needs to turn to training the disabled for living so that each person can develop to his or her fullest potential. This becomes increasingly important as we continue to turn away from the nuclear family. The disabled young adult wants to live as independently as possible, including having his or her own apartment. In doing so, each has to be able to cope with everyday life such as shopping and getting to community activities. The ultimate objective may be a job either in sheltered employment or in the community.

At this point in time, one of the paradoxes we have in housing relates to our provision of adapted housing in low-income facilities. If rehabilitation trains a disabled person to be independent and ultimately trains him for remunerative employment, he may become ineligible for adaptive housing in a low-income facility by virtue of earning more than the income allowable for the facility. Subsequently, such persons have to move out of the building, oftentimes into homes or apartments not suited to their needs.

The gaps in housing, as a service, become evident. Various solutions are needed. Specialized units such as have been considered in Washington, Massachusetts, and North Dakota comprise one way of providing housing. Other alternatives are town houses (with the first floor adapted); adapted leased-housing programs for families, standard apartment units in which the first-floor apartments have been adapted; and standard homes with adaptations.

WHAT CAN BE DONE?

Various issues, questions, and problems have been raised. To date, there has been activity in low-income hous-ing because it has been "fundable." The construction of single family and multifamily housing is a major product of two interrelated forces: the nature of the economy and the government's fiscal and monetary policies. Dollars for housing have competed in the marketplace with money for government spending in other areas.

Legislation needs to be upgraded, particularly in the funding of moderate-income housing.

Rehabilitation needs to be upgraded and expanded.

Whatever can be suggested will need manpower and cooperation—among agencies, communities, volunteers, and consumers.

An example of what one Easter Seal Society is doing might be helpful. The Easter Seal Society of Massachusetts has a Task Force on Housing, which is chaired by a board member. The Task Force includes consumers, an architect, an investor, a banker, a builder, and two representatives from local housing authorities.

In February of 1971, the Society sponsored a half-day Seminar on Housing. The Seminar pulled together representatives from a variety of public and private agencies. One of the recommendations coming out of the Seminar favored organizing a statewide council on specialized housing.

A similar recommendation was the result of a study done by the Massachusetts Association of Paraplegics, Massachusetts Council of Organizations for the Handicapped, and the Massachusetts Rehabilitation Commission.

The Easter Seal Society Housing

Task Force formed the statewide council, which functions with a chairman elected by the council. The Easter Seal Society sits on the council but in no way dominates the council.

The five regional Easter Seal offices have regional housing task forces. Currently, these task forces are surveying 12 communities in Massachusetts to identify the handicapped and their needs, surveying communities for accessible housing, contacting realtors and interesting them in housing for the handicapped, meeting and lecturing to local boards of realtors, and surveying available resources in the 12 communities.

Volunteers, consumers, and staff are blending their talents to solve problems of the disabled. In the process of interviewing the disabled, referrals to appropriate agencies are made when this is indicated.

Currently, on a state basis, the Easter Seal Task Force on Specialized Housing has been working with builders and developers. Within a short time, a seminar will be held for the builders and developers to acquaint them with the housing needs of the handicapped. Hard data will be available for regions on the market for adapted housing.

Information relating to the cost of adaptations will also be available. For the past year, five architects have been working together to isolate costs for adaptations.

Most of the housing for the handicapped has been constructed with public money from the Housing Finance Agency. In order to make an impact so that housing becomes adaptable for all

people, it may be necessary to change regulations. Regulations concerning funding, land use, site selection, and architectural design would need to be changed. Since changing these regulations may take some Congressional action, some national organization should assume this as a responsibility.

Similar action is necessary on a state level. Armed with some good information, the individual reader can be effective in bringing about the change necessary on the state level. Contacts can be made with local Congressmen to familiarize them with the issues involved in housing as well as architectural barriers.

These efforts will become a partnership between local and state affiliates and a national organization.

CONCLUSION

In looking at the issues of housing, we are uniquely challenged. We do not know the criteria for independence. Each housing facility, on the basis of its plan, will need to determine its criteria before beginning the tenant selection process.

We know little of the life-style of the disabled. One who has an acquired handicap has experienced a profound change in his life. Historically, the picture painted of the handicapped is that of a loser. The responsibility for housing extends beyond providing a roof; it involves helping a person get into social balance. A human being acts, feels, and performs in accordance with what he imagines to be true about himself and his environment.

Building on this fact, we can provide living facilities that will be supportive according to the needs of the individual, eliminate barriers to maximize the independence of the resident, and provide the necessary training to maximize the disabled's ability to contribute to society. If we can do this, with the assistance of the consumers, it will be rehabilitation in its full meaning and concept.

BIBLIOGRAPHY

Donahue, Wilma, ed. Housing the Aging. Ann Arbor, Mich.: Univ. of Michigan Press, 1954.

Engberg, Engenie; Jensen, Lars Fjord; and Lange, Carl. Rehabilitation and Care of the Handicapped. Copenhagen, Den.: Ministries of Labour and Social Affairs, 1967. Available from Society and Home for Cripples, 34, Esplanaden, Copenhagen K, Denmark.

George Schermer Associates. More Than Shelter; Social Needs in Low- and Moderate-Income Housing. Prepared for the National Commission on Urban Problems. (Research Report No. 8) Washington, D.C.: U.S. Govt. Print. Office, 1968.

Goldsmith, Selwyn. Designing for the Disabled. ed. 2. New York: McGraw-Hill, 1968.

Lowman, Edward W., and Klinger, Judith Lannefeld. Aids to Independent Living: Self-help for the Handicapped. New York: McGraw-Hill, 1969.

Musson, Noverre, and Heusinkveld, Helen. Buildings for the Elderly. New York: Reinhold, 1963.

Nugent, Timothy J. A Challenge—New Concepts in Living, p. 1—11, in: Proceedings of the National Institute on Making Buildings and Facilities Accessible to and Usable by the Physically Handicapped, November 21—24, 1965. Chicago: National Society for Crippled Children and Adults, 1966.

Parker, W. Russell. Multi-Unit Retirement Housing for Rural Areas: A Guide to Design Considerations for Architects, Engineers, and Builders. (Agriculture Information Bul. No. 297) Washington, D.C.: U.S. Govt. Print. Office, 1965.

Pastalan, Leon A., and Moyer, L. Noel. Vistula Manor Demonstration Housing for the Physically Disabled. Final Report; prepared for the Toledo Metropolitan Housing Authority. Toledo, Ohio: Toledo Research Foundation, University of Toledo, 1969.

Selwyn, Donald. Independence for the Severely Handicapped Through Systems Engineering. Prepared for the U.S. President's Committee on Employment of the Handicapped. Pompton Lakes, N.J.: The Author, 1966.

Taggart, Robert, III. Low-Income Housing: A Critique of Federal Aid. Baltimore, Md.: Johns Hopkins Press, 1971.

U.S. Department of Housing and Urban Development. Housing for the Physically Impaired; A Guide for Planning and Design. Washington, D.C.: U.S. Govt. Print. Office, 1968.

52 Adaptive Housing for the Severely Physically Handicapped

David D. Stock and
Jean A. Cole

The lack of suitable housing has been a major impediment to integrating persons with severe physical disabilities into the community. Frequently, the only housing alternatives available are residence in chronic care institutions or dependent living with families, both of which often preclude participation in education, employment, and leisure activities in the mainstream of society. Current efforts to deal with the housing problem are reviewed. One adaptive housing model, the Cooperative Living project, sponsored by the Texas Institute of Rehabilitation and Research in Houston, is described.

Rehabilitation personnel have been concerned for years about the large number of physically disabled persons who quickly begin lives of isolation and dependency after discharge from rehabilitation programs. This occurs even though individuals may possess good educational and vocational potential and have been equipped with skills and devices for self-help. If the rehabilitation goal of active, productive living is to be achieved, the severely physically handicapped person must be integrated into the community and must simultaneously be offered opportunities for education, job training, placement, and continuing medical care. Yet the goals of independent and productive living are achieved by only a small number of catastrophically injured persons because there are serious limitations in the availability of necessary living arrangements and supportive services such as attendant care and transportation, key elements in successful integration.

The consequences of limited resources are all too clearly demonstrated by the lives of countless young disabled persons who are confined to nursing homes or isolated in home settings where there are no opportunities for participation in the mainstream of society. Until special housing arrangements are available, catastrophically injured persons with vocational potential who have physical care support needs and unique living requirements will not be allowed to become vocationally productive. This problem will continually thwart the efforts of vocational rehabilitation

This work was supported in part by the Regional Research and Training Center Grant RT-4 from the Social and Rehabilitation Service, Department of Health, Education and Welfare, and by a Research and Demonstration Grant 14-P-55487/6-01 from the Social and Rehabilitation Service, DHEW.

counselors to provide job training and placement and to maintain the severely physically handicapped in appropriate competitive employment settings.

It is important to recognize at the outset that disabled persons differ greatly in their level of physical functioning, in their personality traits, and in their predisability life styles. Their housing needs are consequently diverse. Many disabled persons are able to become entirely independent in residential structures designed for wheelchair accessibility. Yet, others have functional limitations so severe that physical assistance in day-to-day activities is necessary. The physical assistance needed by persons who are medically stable should be clearly distinguished from nursing care that is provided in institutional settings.

In this article, we will briefly review current efforts to meet the residential needs of the physically disabled population in general. We will then narrow the focus to deal specifically with what is defined here as adaptive housing. Adaptive housing refers to special living arrangements that provide an ensemble of services (attendant care, food, transportation) to physically impaired persons who cannot live effectively in traditional housing environments and who, at the same time, no longer require an institutional health care setting. Adaptive housing is intended to aid those persons who, by congenital deformity, trauma, or progression of disease, have significant limitation in performing activities which necessitates daily living assistance in transferring from bed to wheelchair, eating, dressing, and other personal needs.

Following the general review of existing efforts to meet the housing needs of the disabled, we will describe the adaptive housing project, Cooperative Living, sponsored by the Texas Institute for Rehabilitation and Research in Houston. During its three years of operation, the project's 39 severely disabled residents have demonstrated that persons with very limited physical functioning can lead active and productive lives if appropriate services and opportunities are available and affordable.

CURRENTLY EXISTING HOUSING PROGRAMS

The most comprehensive programs to provide adaptive housing for the disabled are the Fokus system of apartment clusters with attendant assistance in Sweden (Brattgard, 1971), the Het Dorp village for the disabled in the Netherlands (Het Dorp, no date), and the Stiftung Rehabilitation vocational training complex in Germany (Stiftung Rehabilitation, no date).

In the United States, efforts have been largely limited to providing wheelchair-accessible residential structures. Several accessible highrise apartment buildings have been constructed with HUD funds, including Highland Heights in Fall River, Massachusetts (Fishman, 1971), New Horizons Manor in Fargo, North Dakota (Lavine, 1974), and Center Park Apartments in Seattle, Washington (Fishman, 1971). Massachusetts has the most active state government in the development of wheelchair-accessible housing. It has passed pilot legislation requiring that 5 percent of the units in newly constructed apartment projects must be wheelchair accessible. Massachusetts also has an active Department of Community Affairs that has initiated the construction of a number of accessible residences (Massachusetts Association of Paraplegics, 1970).

Various organizations in other parts of the country have urged private owners to make accessible apartments available and have established clearinghouses for information on such apartments. These organizations include Independent Living for the Handicapped in New York City (Lavine, 1974), the Eastern Paralyzed Veterans Program in New York (Lavine, 1974), and the Center for Independent Living in Berkeley (Fay, 1974).

The wheelchair-accessible residences listed above have made it possible for many disabled persons to live without assistance. Yet, a well-designed physical structure is of very little use to many severely handicapped persons if supportive services are not available. The number of adaptive housing projects that include such services is limited. In addition to a physical structure, adaptive housing programs must also provide an organizational system for structuring services and coordination of sources of financial support to make these services affordable.

In 1972, the Department of Health, Education and Welfare funded a pilot Research and Demonstration project at the Texas Institute for Rehabilitation and Research in Houston to investigate the feasibility and consequences of a cooperative self-support housing system based on shared services and shared costs. In addition to the original project, three apartment clusters with supportive services are now in operation in Houston.

Several universities have developed programs to coordinate supportive services that enable handicapped students to live independently. Among the most active are programs at the University of Illinois at Champaign-Urbana, the Center for Independent Living at the University of California-Berkeley, and a new project at Boston University (Fay, 1974). In university programs, attendant care is often structured on a one-to-one basis with each disabled student having a single attendant in contrast to the model of shared services used in the Houston projects.

There have also been a number of efforts by private organizations to develop adaptive housing projects. These are perhaps best exemplified by the Creative Living program in Columbus, Ohio. A number of planned projects of this type have failed to materialize, but those that are in existence are reviewed in the *Rehabilitation Gazette* (Laurie, 1973). More detailed summaries of currently existing housing programs for the severely disabled are described by Fishman (1971), Fenton (1972), Fay (1974), and Melia (1974).

Efforts in this country have only begun to meet the housing needs of the disabled population, particularly for those persons who require attendant assistance and transportation in addition to an accessible physical structure. The funding of such programs is often problematic. In spite of this fact, some important progress has been made. It has been demonstrated by experience that persons with severe physical disabilities can live safely and comfortably outside of chronic care institutions. Evidence suggests that health problems in such housing are no more numerous than in institutions, and medical complications may, in fact, be fewer. The cost of adaptive housing is usually considerably less than long-term institutionalization. Alternate means for structuring services and for providing financial support have been developed, and models of successful programs do exist. Perhaps most important, the consequences of providing needed services and opportunities for education, work, and leisure activities have been demonstrated in terms of vocational productivity and personal fulfillment.

EVOLUTION OF A MODEL

A review of the literature indicates that adaptive housing as a concept has been slow to evolve. This is due in part to the absence of proven models of service as well as the many funding constraints imposed by agencies. Historically, most agencies have been unaccustomed to providing services on a shared basis, which is the key to adaptive housing programming.

The first model of adaptive housing in the United States to use the concept of shared services was developed at the Texas Institute for Rehabilitation and Research. Personnel at the Institute had continually experienced limited success in dealing with the needs of severely handicapped persons who had vocational potential but who also had physical care needs and living requirements that did not allow them to become vocationally and educationally productive. Since special living arrangements with supportive services were not available in the community at reasonable or affordable costs, severely handicapped persons were being relegated to living arrangements in nursing homes and home situations that could not support or foster their vocational goals.

After reviewing a large population of severely handicapped persons for whom vocational placement had been declared unfeasible—even after they had been given maximum services to prepare them for employment—a new housing venture was initiated. A cooperative self-support model of services was developed in January 1972 to assist this segment of the handicapped population. The model combined architectural arrangements, shared attendant service and transportation, vocational training experiences, and counseling services.

The evolution of this adaptive housing model has carried with it a calculated process of development. According to Fishman (1971), adaptive housing cannot be an updated version of a chronic disease institution, nor can it be thought of as an extended care facility. It must take on new dimensions that depend in part on physical design. But the major goal must be to create new life style options for the severely physically handicapped. This requires a commitment on the part of those who develop the program to provide a functional environment that does not have overtones of excessive control, paternalism, or traditionalism and, most important, is not built on a medical model.

To devise a model that would embody more positive features, interviews were held with severely handicapped persons who were living in long-term facilities and in home situations that could not support their vocational aspirations. Interviews indicated two major problems with the current nursing home or extended care method of meeting the needs of the young handicapped. First, the facilities are planned, programmed, and managed to provide an environment for the elderly whose needs differ greatly from the needs of young disabled persons. Second, nursing services are staffed to provide more extensive care than is required for the handicapped person whose condition has stabilized. In essence, too much care in an institutional environment at a higher cost than is necessary or desired becomes the generally available option.

Those persons who resided in home situations also expressed several predominant limitations. The family of a severely handicapped person is faced with a responsibility for physical care that frequently takes precedence over the provision of vocational and educational support. Often the family does not have sufficient economic resources to offer financial support, transportation, or good preventive health services. The handicapped person may become entangled in predisability attitude patterns or else may develop patterns after onset that reflect the family's frustrations.

A planning committee of handi-capped persons and the project director began work in 1971 to create a model using the interview results. The primary consideration was to develop organizational policies that allowed maximum independence and flexibility for each resident in an informal and unstructured atmosphere. Many characteristics of an institutional environment such as regimented schedules, monitoring of behavior, restriction of visitors, and limitation of the freedom of residents to come and go were purposely avoided. The plans made by this group were implemented in January 1972 when the program opened with its first residents.

Cooperative Living is housed in a modern, dormitory-style structure owned by the sponsoring Institute and located near downtown Houston. It has a maximum capacity of 18 residents. Meals are available if the residents choose to eat at the project. Nonprofessional attendant assistance is provided 24 hours a day, with heavy staffing during hours of peak activity and minimal staffing at other times. Attendants are trained by the residents themselves. As the project opened, the group of residents devised a transportation system in which a driver was hired to take persons to school or work in vans owned by various residents who were reimbursed for the use of their vehicles. Now the project has its own van. Services are scheduled using a system of sign-up sheets which allows each resident to plan his or her own activities and also permits attendants and drivers to budget their time.

Initially, there was a single project manager, a quadriplegic resident who assumed the responsibility of operating the program as a full-time job. Now it is governed by a Resident Management Council made up of three elected representatives who are paid to share the tasks of supervising attendants, hiring and firing staff, choosing new residents, and keeping financial records.

Financial support for the project is provided in part by the HEW grant and by the sponsoring Institute. Individual residents are assisted by rent subsidies from the Houston Housing Authority, by maintenance support from the Texas Rehabilitation Commission, and by payments from the federal Supplemental Security Income and Social Security Disability programs. Coordinating these multiple sources of support was a major task in the development of the project, and the ultimate goal was to make the system financially self-sustaining.

BENEFITS OF COOPERATIVE LIVING

Several criteria are used as a basis for selecting residents in the Cooperative Living project. First, potential residents must be persons who are impeded by the inaccessibility of needed health care services, psychosocial services, vocational counseling, peer relationships, education, or recreation in their present living situation so that maximum physical, personal, or vocational potentials are not achieved. Second, residents must have a permanent disability which is thought to be so severe that they require assistance with

functional activities of daily living such as dressing, toileting, eating, and mobility. Finally, they must have a desire to pursue a goal of education, vocational training, or employment and have the ability to profit physically, emotionally, socially, or vocationally from an improved environment in which a constellation of services is available in a planned and coordinated manner.

Since its inception, the Cooperative Living program has served 39 persons who range in age from 19 to 30 years. This group has been drawn from rural and urban home settings throughout the southwestern United States as well as from nursing homes in the greater Houston area. Most of the residents have been spinal cord injured quadriplegics with C-4 to C-7 cord lesions. Table 1 shows the effectiveness of the adaptive housing concept in terms of the activities of residents before and after they entered the project.

Almost all residents have initiated new educational and vocational activities during their stay in the project. Peer support and role modeling are primary factors in providing both the motivation and the know-how for initiating new activities, particularly for the 19 persons who were inactive before entering the project. Educational and vocational achievements of others often become challenges.

The consequences of the program can perhaps best be illustrated by the 20 residents who have benefited from their experience at Cooperative Living and have now moved into houses in the community or into one of the

Table 1. Activities of residents before and after entering project ($N = 39$)

	Inactive	Education	Vocational assessment & training	Part-time employment	Full-time employment
Before	19	20	0	0	0
After[a]	2	28	6	13	10

[a]The total number of persons in this row exceeds the number who have lived in the project because many residents have progressed from education or vocatiional training to employment during their stay.

other two adaptive housing projects developed in apartment settings by former residents of Cooperative Living. Ten persons have been able to initiate full-time employment as a result of living in the project. Nine are still working full-time, and one has had to adopt a part-time schedule because of recurring skin breakdowns due to prolonged sitting time. The mean period of employment for persons working full-time is 19.8 months.

The transition quality of adaptive housing is also important as a process in which greater economic productivity and independence can be attained in gradual steps starting with entry-level employment earnings. Table 2 compares the costs for basic

needs and services using typical costs in the Houston area.

The Cooperative Living project of adaptive housing is the most economical way to provide basic services with a high level of continuity. The total cost ($530) is often affordable by a handicapped person securing his or her first job. As earnings increase, the individual is able to consider an apartment arrangement with shared services for $650 a month or an apartment or house with a private attendant which is more costly. Thus, with greater job stability and higher earnings, the handicapped person is able to examine alternative life style options. Probably none of these options would have been available if the individual had not been

Table 2. Living costs in various residential environments (in dollars/month)

Item	Nursing home	Cooperative living project	Shared apartment with shared services	Apartment with private attendant
Rent	↑	110	150	170
Meals	513	60	120	120
Attendant assistance	↓	190	200	320
Transportation	100	40	50	100
Personal needs	130	130	130	130
Total costs	743	530	650	840

able to initiate independent living in a system of adaptive housing with shared services.

Achieving a satisfying level of living and productivity is often an overwhelmingly difficult goal if viewed as a single step by a disabled person. A transitional process can make this long-term goal feasible for a large number of individuals.

REFERENCES

Brattgard, S. O. Fokus: A way of life for living. Goteborg, Sweden: Fokus Society, 1971.

Fay, F. Housing alternatives for individuals with spinal cord injury. Unpublished manuscript, 1974. (Available from Urban Institute, 2100 M Street, N.W., Washington, D.C.)

Fenton, J. Residential needs of severely physically handicapped nonretarded young children and young adults in New York state. Rehabilitation Monograph 46. New York: New York University Medical Center, Institute of Rehabilitation Medicine, 1972.

Fishman, P. Adaptive housing for the handicapped. Boston: Tufts-New England Medical Center, 1971.

Het Dorp Foundation. Het Dorp: A unique experiment in humanity. Arnhem, Holland: Author, no date.

Laurie, G. Housing and home services for the disabled in the U.S. Rehabilitation Gazette, 1973, 16, 38–45.

Lavine, E. M. (Ed.) Proceedings of the National Conference on Housing and the Handicapped. U.S. Department of Health, Education and Welfare, Rehabilitation Services Administration, Division of Developmental Disabilities, Grant No. 56-P-71097/3-01. Bethesda, Md.: Health and Education Resources, Inc., 9650 Rockville Pike, 1974.

Massachusetts Association of Paraplegics, Inc. Housing needs of the handicapped. Bedford, Mass.: Author, 1970.

Melia, R. P. Special services in housing for handicapped persons. Unpublished manuscript, 1974. (Available from DHEW, Rehabilitation Services Administration, Washington, D.C.)

Stiftung Rehabilitation. Stiftung rehabilitation: Auftrag und aufgaben. Heidelberg, Germany: Author, no date.

Section 14

CIVIL RIGHTS

53 Civil Rights and Employment of the Severely Handicapped

Patricia J. Thoben

Forty-four million disabled Americans comprise a large minority group that has joined the civil rights movement to address the social, economic, and political injustices affecting their human rights. Architectural, transportation, and attitudinal barriers place handicapped individuals at a disadvantage in obtaining adequate education, equal housing, recreational opportunities, or employment commensurate with their abilities. Recent legislation requires federal agencies and private employers under federal contracts to take affirmative action in hiring, placing, and advancing handicapped individuals in employment. Legislation has extended employment rights; however, obstacles still exist that prevent handicapped individuals from achieving equal employment. Handicapped persons must accept responsibility for their own destiny and continue to speak up against those forces that would prevent them from receiving equal treatment in our society.

The civil rights movement of the past decade established a climate of active concern for the social, economic, and political issues affecting the human rights of many Americans. Within this climate, handicapped citizens have raised their voices in an effort to awaken America's collective consciousness to the needs and concerns of the physically and mentally handicapped. The disabled are a large minority group but most people would not expect them to take such dramatic action. Civil rights concepts are equated with racial minorities. For another group of citizens outside the boundaries of the equal rights movement to join the fight has presented a challenge not only to civil rights advocates but to every individual who does not understand the needs and problems of the disabled.

Discrimination because of disability has been an uncomfortable concept to accept and a difficult one for many to understand. Yet the emotional reaction to a visibly impaired physique is no different from the reaction to color, nationality, or sex; the same inequities exist, only the dimensions of the problem are more encompassing.

The motivation for the civil rights movement for the handicapped is the violations of the human rights of an estimated 44 million disabled citizens. Equal educational opportunities do not exist for them due to discriminatory admission policies and architectural barriers. Once handicapped persons acquire an education, work opportunities are difficult to find at best. Many of the disabled are unable

---

to obtain jobs related to their abilities and seldom receive pay commensurate with that received by the nondisabled. Qualifications are ignored because of disabilities unrelated to job performance.

Public transportation is not accessible and airlines serving the public establish practices that literally deprive disabled citizens of their constitutional right to move about freely within the country (*U.S. v. Guest* 1966). Architectural barriers and discrimination by landlords often exclude the disabled from public or private housing areas. Many cannot use public streets because of high curbs; they are denied access to a theater or restaurant because the presence of a wheelchair or crutches supposedly constitutes a fire hazard; they are denied employment because the office is too small for a wheelchair; they are denied the right to test drive a car before purchasing it because of the need to use a hand-control; they are denied protection from the economic exploitation reflected in the high prices of drugs and special equipment.

In the spring of 1972, several organizations of the disabled assembled to demonstrate their grievances publicly. Approximately 100 severely disabled individuals marched 6 miles from the Washington Hilton Hotel to the steps of the U.S. Capitol. The 100 marchers were enthusiastic and strongly determined in their demands for equality. When one sees a young man severely disabled with cerebral palsy push his wheelchair backwards for 6 miles uphill without assistance using only his feet, a young woman on crutches who could not stop to rest

for fear she wouldn't be able to continue, another man whose body is totally paralyzed except for some slight finger movement manage his electric wheelchair—is there any doubt about the urgency of their cause (Thoben, 1972)?

This public expression of strong convictions concerning human rights was met with mixed reactions. Many felt that the marchers were radicals, exhibitionists, and troublemakers frustrated by their disabilities. Perhaps—but not really. They were radical, yes, because they dared to expose publicly their concerns about and frustrations with disability and society's reactions toward it. Exhibitionists, yes, exhibiting real sensitivity and concern for human dignity. Troublemakers, yes, if that term is used to mean individuals who care enough to make waves in a depersonalized society. One can only guess about the attitudes of the people on the street or observing from windows in government and business offices along the way, but the meaningful silence was deafening (Thoben, 1972). This public demonstration was only a beginning; there are still many challenges ahead if the handicapped are to achieve equal treatment in society.

Although civil rights legislation for the disabled would be the most uniform and far-reaching solution, it may be long in coming if it comes at all. Meanwhile, there are many areas to be addressed and employment is one of the most significant in terms of defining an individual's self-worth, social acceptance, and equal opportunity in our society. Although the federal government has played an active and important role in employment of the handicapped for many years and although as early as 1948 Public Law 617 was enacted to amend the Civil Service Act so ". . . that no person shall be discriminated against in any case because of any physical impairment. . . ," substantial barriers to employment still exist. It is extremely difficult for employers to deal with the emotional issues of physical impairment on the one hand and the economic issues of productivity, employee compensation costs, insurance rates, and facility modification on the other.

The Rehabilitation Act of 1973 (Public Law 93-112) as amended (Public Law 93-516) could have far-reaching effects in bringing about some equilibrium to the employment world of the severely disabled. Sections 501–504 of this Act are directed to employment opportunity. Section 501 provides for an Interagency Committee on Handicapped Employees. The purpose of this committee is to provide a focus for federal and other employment of handicapped individuals and to review, in cooperation with the Civil Service Commission, the adequacy of hiring, placement, and advancement of handicapped individuals in the federal service. This committee is cochaired by the Secretary of the Department of Health, Education and Welfare and the Chairman of the Civil Service Commission. Work groups have been established to (a) address issues and formulate recommendations to reduce attitudinal, transportation, and architectural barriers to employment of handicapped individuals and disabled veterans; (b) develop standards for evaluation of agency Affirmative Action Programs; (c) provide guidance to agencies in restructuring jobs and inform them of job accommodation techniques; (d) develop an informational system for the collection of data on federal employment of handicapped individuals; and (e) review existing federal employment practices and procedures in order to facilitate the employment of handicapped individuals.

Section 501 further requires that all agencies, departments, and instrumentalities in the executive branch of the federal government (including the U.S. Postal Service and the Postal Rate Commission) submit annual affirmative action program plans to the U.S. Civil Service Commission. The Commission reviews, evaluates, and monitors the implementation of these plans and submits an annual report to Congress on the results of this program.

Architectural and transportation barriers are a major obstacle to the mobility of the handicapped, affecting all phases of life. Lack of accessibility to the work place and to public transportation is the problem many qualified handicapped individuals face in their attempts to achieve their employment goals. The Architectural and Transportation Barriers Compliance Board, established by Section 502 and administratively housed within the Department of Health, Education and Welfare, will have a significant impact on employment of the handicapped.

The Board will be comprised of cabinet-ranking officials of the Departments of Health, Education and Welfare, Transportation, Housing and Urban Development, Labor, and Interior;

the General Services Administration; the Postal Service; and the Veterans Administration. Public hearings will be held and investigations conducted in order that the Board may carry out its major functions: (a) ensuring compliance with the Architectural Barriers Act of 1968 (Public Law 90-480, as amended Public Law 91-205); (b) investigating alternate approaches to architectural, transportation, and attitudinal barriers confronting the handicapped; (c) examining the efforts being made by federal, state, and local governments and other public agencies to eliminate barriers; (d) promoting the use of the International Accessibility Symbol in all facilities accorded to Public Law 90-480; and (e) making recommendations to the President and Congress for legislation or administrative direction necessary to eliminate barriers.

The Department of Labor has issued regulations to implement Section 503 of the Act, which provides that ". . . any contract in excess of $2500 entered into by any Federal department or agency for procurement of personal property and nonpersonal services (including construction) for the United States shall contain a provision requiring that, in employing persons to carry out such contract, the party contracting with the United States shall take affirmative action to employ and advance in employment qualified handicapped individuals. . . ."

The regulations to carry out this provision require that (a) all nonexempt contracts and subcontracts that provide for performance in less than 90 days and exceed $2,500 include a nondiscrimination provision

and affirmative action clause in the contract; (b) all nonexempt contracts and subcontracts that provide for performance in 90 days or more and do not exceed $500,000 include a nondiscrimination provision and affirmative action clause in the contract and establish an affirmative action program in order to comply; and (c) all contracts and subcontracts that provide for performance in 90 days or more and exceed $500,000 include a nondiscrimination provision and an affirmative action clause. Further, an affirmative action program must be developed and submitted to the Employment Standards Administration of the Department of Labor 90 days after a contract award is made. Also included in the regulations are procedures for handicapped individuals to file discrimination complaints and a number of suggested affirmative action steps for contractors. Affirmative action under this program requires that qualified handicapped individuals be actively recruited, considered, and employed and that all qualified handicapped employees not be discriminated against for promotions, training, transfers, and other job opportunities. Individuals may not be discriminated against on the basis of their handicaps.

Further nondiscrimination provisions are included under Section 504 of the Act. It encompasses all programs and activities receiving federal financial assistance and will involve qualified handicapped individuals who participate or benefit from these programs. The Office of Civil Rights of the Department of Health, Education and Welfare will issue regulations and guidelines to implement this section.

Section 403 of Public Law 93-508, the Vietnam Era Veteran's Readjustment Assistance Act of 1974, adds a new thrust to the federal efforts on behalf of the disabled veteran. All departments, agencies, and instrumentalities of the executive branch of the government are required to include disabled veterans in affirmative action program plans.

These laws have extended the employment rights of the disabled. However, the enactment of federal legislation is not the end of the struggle. It is only a part of the process. The disabled still face many obstacles in achieving equal employment opportunities at the state and local levels. The handicapped must accept the major responsibility in the process, the responsibility of their own destiny, of realizing their hopes of participating in a society in which all are equal to live, work, and move about freely. Let us hope that society will also accept its responsibility by not retreating with guilt through apathy but by participating with understanding and concern for equality for all its members.

REFERENCES

Architectural Barriers Act of 1968 (Public Law 90-480), 90th Congress, 2nd Session, S-222, August 12, 1968.

Amendments to Architectural Barriers Act of 1968 (Public Law 91-205), 91st Congress, 2nd Session, HR 14464, March 5, 1970.

Public Law 617, 80th Congress, 2nd Session, HR 4236, June 10, 1948.

Public Law 93-508, 93rd Congress, 2nd Session, HR 12628, December 3, 1974.

Rehabilitation Act of 1973 (Public Law 93-112), 93rd Congress, 2nd Session, HR 8070, September 26, 1973.

Amendments to Rehabilitation Act of 1973 (Public Law 93-516), 93rd Congress, 2nd Session, HR 17503, December 7, 1974.

Thoben, P. J. Disabled people march for civil rights. Rehabilitation Record, 1972, 13(5), 24–26.

U.S. Department of Health, Education and Welfare. Chronic conditions and limitations of activity and mobility. National Health Survey Series 10, No. 61. Washington, D.C.: DHEW, 1971.

United States v. Guest, 383 U.S. 745,757.

U.S. Health Services and Mental Health Administration. Department of Health, Education and Welfare. Use of special aids. National Health Survey Series 10, No. 78, Public Health Service Pub. No. (HSM) 73-1504). Washington, D.C.: DHEW, 1973.

U.S. Social Security Administration. Department of Health, Education and Welfare. Social security survey of the disabled: 1966. Report No. D. Washington, D.C.: DHEW, 1970.

54 A Bill of Rights for the Disabled (Editorial)

Arthur S. Abramson and
Bernard Kutner

Whereas, the disabled in the United States, constituting a large minority with a commonality of need and a unity of purpose, seek only to obtain for themselves what all Americans believe to be their birthright—life, liberty and the pursuit of happiness; and

Whereas, impediments and roadblocks of every nature are to be found at every hand, effectively preventing the fulfillment of life's promise for a large proportion of the disabled; and

Whereas, the American people, largely through lack of knowledge and misinformation, have not as yet recognized the disabled as fellow human beings with a handicap to which all should make some accommodation, and who deserve equal opportunity as citizens; and

Whereas, the Congress of the United States and the legislatures of the various states, counties and municipalities have not as yet, by legal means, made it possible for the disabled person to attain equal access to those benefits of life enjoyed by the able-bodied, be it resolved:

Health—1.

That all disabled persons be afforded the opportunity for full and comprehensive diagnostic, therapeutic, rehabilitative and fol-low-up services in the nation's hospitals, clinics and rehabilitation centers without regard to race, religion, economic status, ethnic origin, sex, age or social condition.

Health—2.

That all disabled persons requiring same be given and trained to use such orthotic, prosthetic or adaptive devices that will enable them to become more mobile and to live more comfortably.

Education—3.

That all disabled persons be given every opportunity for formal education to the level of which they are capable and to the degree to which they aspire.

Employment—4.

That all disabled persons, to the extent necessary, have the opportunity to receive special training commensurate with residual abilities in those aspects of life in which they are handicapped, so that they may achieve the potential for entry into the labor market in competitive employment.

Employment—5.

That all employable disabled persons, like other minorities, be covered by equal opportunity legisla-

Reprinted from the Archives of Physical Medicine and Rehabilitation, 1972, 53(3): 99–100.

tion so that equal productivity, potential and actual, receives equal consideration in terms of jobs, promotions, salaries, workloads and fringe benefits.

Employment—6.

That those disabled persons who because of the severity of their handicaps are deemed unable to enter the normal labor market, be given the opportunity for special training and placement in limited work situations including sheltered workshops, home-base employment and other protected job situations.

Employment—7.

That a nationwide network of tax-supported sheltered workshops be created to offer limited work opportunities for all those severely disabled persons unable to enter the competitive labor market.

Housing—8.

That nationwide and local programs of special housing for the disabled be established to permit them an opportunity to live in dignity and reasonable comfort.

Architectural Barriers—9.

That federal, state and local legislatures pass laws requiring the elimination of architectural barriers to buildings, recreational, cultural and social facilities and public places. Such legislation should include architectural standards for all new construction.

Architectural Barriers—10.

That federal, state and local legislation be passed establishing stan-

dards and a reasonable time for modification of existing sidewalks, buildings and structures for the comfortable use of the handicapped.

Transportation—11.

That every community, county or other legally constituted authority establish programs and standards for the creation of special transportation for the disabled including modification of existing mass transportation systems and the development of new specially designed demand-schedule transportation facilities.

Income Maintenance—12.

That every disabled person who because of the nature of his handicap is unable to be self-supporting, be given a guaranteed minimum income not below established federal standards adequate to live in reasonable comfort and in dignity.

Institutional Care—13.

That federal, state and local laws be enacted for the benefit of the disabled confined to any form of institution, setting minimum standards of housing, conveniences, comfort, staff and services.

Civil Rights—14.

That civil rights legislation, national and local, be amended to include disability as one of the categories against which discrimination is unlawful.

Training—15.

That federal and state tax-supported programs of training be established to prepare professional and non-professional personnel for work with the handicapped in the fields of health, education, recreation and welfare.

Research—16. That federal legislation be enacted expanding existing and developing new programs of research and demonstration, by grant and contract, in both basic and applied fields, dealing with the problems of disabling conditions and the disabled.

Be it further resolved that these rights, being urgent and critical to the well being of the disabled population of the United States, be given the high priority they justly deserve in the hearts, minds and programs of our nation's leaders.

Index